THE UNIVERSITY OF CHICAGO
ORIENTAL INSTITUTE PUBLICATIONS

Edited by

JAMES HENRY BREASTED

THE UNIVERSITY OF CHICAGO
ORIENTAL INSTITUTE PUBLICATIONS
VOLUME III

THE EDWIN SMITH SURGICAL PAPYRUS

PUBLISHED IN FACSIMILE AND HIEROGLYPHIC TRANSLITERATION WITH TRANSLATION AND COMMENTARY IN TWO VOLUMES

BY
JAMES HENRY BREASTED

VOLUME ONE
HIEROGLYPHIC TRANSLITERATION
TRANSLATION AND COMMENTARY

WITH EIGHT PLATES

THE UNIVERSITY OF CHICAGO PRESS
CHICAGO, ILLINOIS
1930

PRINTED IN GREAT BRITAIN AT THE UNIVERSITY PRESS, OXFORD
BY JOHN JOHNSON, PRINTER TO THE UNIVERSITY

TO THE MEMORY OF

WILLIAM HARVEY

DISCOVERER OF THE CIRCULATION OF THE BLOOD

AT THE THREE HUNDREDTH ANNIVERSARY OF HIS GREAT DISCOVERY THIS PUBLICATION OF THE EARLIEST KNOWN SURGICAL TREATISE

IS

DEDICATED

TABLE OF CONTENTS

LIST OF PLATES

FOREWORD

The science of surgery has made such revolutionary progress during the last two generations that there might seem to be a greater gulf between the surgeons of the American Civil War and those of the present than there ever was between the surgery of the ancient world and that of the American Civil War. Nevertheless, the fundamental transformation in the field of surgery, as in medicine, resulting from the earliest recognition of natural causes as distinguished from demoniacal possession, occurred in ancient times. A superstitious view of the universe, involving belief in demoniacal possession, especially among the ignorant, has persisted into modern times, as illustrated in the Salem witchcraft, or even in the case of an educated man like Increase Mather, once president of Harvard University (see *infra*, p. 15). It is strikingly illustrated in the conditions among which Mormonism arose only a century ago in western Pennsylvania and New York State. It is obvious, therefore, that the transition from superstition to a scientific point of view cannot be placed at a fixed date.

In this document, therefore, we have disclosed to us for the first time the human mind peering into the mysteries of the human body, and recognizing conditions and processes there as due to intelligible physical causes. The facts in each given case of injury are observed, listed, and marshaled before the mind of the observer, who then makes rational conclusions based on the observed facts. Here then we find the first scientific observer known to us, and in this papyrus we have the earliest known scientific document.

While the copy of the document which has come down to us dates from the Seventeenth Century B.C., the original author's first manuscript was produced at least a thousand years earlier, and was written some time in the Pyramid Age (about 3000 to 2500 B.C.). As preserved to us in a copy made when the Surgical Treatise was a thousand years old or more, a copy in which both beginning and end have been lost, the manuscript nowhere discloses the name of the unknown author. We may be permitted the conjecture, and it is *pure conjecture*, that a surgical treatise of such importance, appearing in the Pyramid Age, may possibly have been written by the earliest known physician, Imhotep, the great architect-physician who flourished in the Thirtieth Century B.C. In that case the original treatise would have been written over thirteen hundred years before our copy of the Seventeenth Century B.C. was made.

We should mention in this connection the recent discovery of an Old Kingdom palace physician's tombstone at Gizeh by H. Junker.[1] This court physician, who bore the name of Iry, lived and died some eight hundred years before the surviving copy of our treatise was made, in an age when our unknown surgeon's autograph manuscript may possibly have been still in existence. Iry was not only the Pharaoh's palace

[1] See H. Junker, "Die Stele des Hofarztes Irj," *Zeitschr. für aegyptische Sprache*, 63 (1927), pp. 53–70.

physician, but he was also chief of the medical corps in which the court physicians were organized. He was furthermore an important specialist, for he served also as "palace eye-physician," and "palace stomach-bowel-physician," literally "palace physician of the belly," in which capacity he bore the titles: "one understanding the internal fluids," and "guardian of the anus," showing that he was particularly versed in internal medicine, and that he specialized in diseases of the digestive organs. This specialization in the Old Kingdom is further illustrated by the existence of the "palace dentist," who might at the same time serve as "chief palace physician." The reader will find an example of the remarkable work of the dental surgeon as far back as the Fourth Dynasty (about 2900–2750 B.C.) in the extraordinary mandible showing the alveolar process pierced to drain an abscess under the first molar (Pl. I, Fig. 1). These facts demonstrate the existence of a body of medical knowledge in the Old Kingdom already so large and detailed as to require specialization.

Very few visible and unmistakable evidences of the surgeon's work, like this Fourth Dynasty dental operation, however, have thus far been found in the large number of Egyptian bodies recovered from the ancient cemeteries. Since this volume went to press the Metropolitan Museum has published in photographs an extraordinary series of wounds found in the bodies of a group of sixty Eleventh Dynasty soldiers, slain in battle a generation or two before 2000 B.C., and buried together in one tomb discovered by the Metropolitan Museum Expedition at Thebes.[1] A series of five of these interesting examples of injuries inflicted in ancient oriental warfare will be found on Plates VII and VIII (Figs. 14–18) at the end of this volume.[2] They arrived too late to be mentioned in the text of the present volume or included in the references, but besides two extraordinary arrow wounds (Plate VIII) they display especially injuries to the skull fully described by our ancient surgeon in his discussion of head wounds. These wounds convincingly justify the editor's surmise, in print before the photographs were available, that our surgeon had followed an army in time of war (*infra*, p. 11).

Another interesting, although much later, wound in the skull was discovered at Thebes last season by the Oriental Institute Expedition of the University of Chicago. This skull, belonging to Harsiese, High Priest of Amon at Thebes in the reign of Osorkon II (Ninth Century B.C.), reveals for the first time the fact that the great man was assassinated; for he had received a mace wound in the forehead (Plate VII, Fig. 13), which perforated the skull. Dr. D. E. Derry, who has kindly examined the wound, concludes that it did not cause immediate death, but that some absorption of the bone around the wound took place during an interval before the High Priest's

[1] See H. E. Winlock, The Egyptian Expedition, *Bulletin of the Metropolitan Museum of Art*, New York, Section II, Feb. 1928, pp. 11–17.

[2] The author is greatly indebted to Mr. A. M. Lythgoe and the Trustees of the Metropolitan Museum for kind permission to publish these photographs.

death. Unfortunately the wound discloses no indications of any operation by the surgeon before death ensued.

Of all these cases, only the first (Plate I, Fig. 1) discloses clear evidence of the surgeon's operation. This one, however, is the earliest in the series, and, as already stated, it demonstrates that surgery had already reached an advanced stage in the Old Kingdom. A very interesting mention of medical treatises in an Old Kingdom inscription, which demonstrates the existence of books on medical science in the age between 3000 and 2500 B.C., will be found in the present editor's *Ancient Records* (I, §§ 242–246).[1] There is therefore no inherent impossibility in the above conjecture that our surgical treatise may have been the work of the great physician Imhotep.

That our Surgical Treatise was a book already ancient in the Seventeenth Century B.C., when our copy was made, is further shown by the fact that the terms it employed were no longer clear to the ancient Egyptian reader of that remote day; for after circulating presumably for some centuries, it was supplied with a commentary, which in our ancient copy has already been incorporated into the text. This commentary is to us a priceless revelation of the meaning of many words and terms which would otherwise have remained hopelessly unintelligible, coming down to us as they have done, from an age when surgery was first creating its technical terms some five thousand years ago. The study of these terms is a fascinating revelation of the human mind struggling with the first stages of science-building, when even the terms it needed did not yet exist, but had to be created, and we watch the process of their creation actually going on. Here we see the word "brain" occurring for the first time in human speech, as far as it is known to us; and in discussing injuries affecting the brain, we note the surgeon's effort to delimit his terms as he selects for specialization a series of common and current words to designate three degrees of injury to the skull indicated in modern surgery by the terms "fracture," "compound fracture," and "compound comminuted fracture," all of which the ancient commentator carefully explains. Like the modern scientist, he clarifies his terms by comparison of the things they designate with more familiar objects: the convolutions of the brain he likens to the corrugations on metallic slag, and the fork at the head of the ramus in the human mandible he describes as like the claw of a two-toed bird; a puncture of the cranium is like a hole broken in the side of a pottery jar, and a segment of the skull is given the name of a turtle's shell. Here are the earliest known anatomical, physiological, and pathological descriptions. The observation of effects on the lower limbs of injuries to the skull and brain, noted by the ancient surgeon with constant reference to *that side of the head which has been injured,* shows an astonishingly early discernment of localization of function in the brain—an observation which has been more fully developed by modern surgeons only within the present generation.

[1] See also *Quarterly Bulletin,* New York Historical Society, Vol. VI, No. 1 (April, 1922), p. 1.

While this early surgeon undoubtedly gained much of his knowledge from injuries incurred in civil life, it is highly probable, as already stated above, that he had followed an army and had therefore treated wounds received in battle. It is in treating such injuries that he makes the earliest known references to adhesive tape and surgical stitching. At the same time injuries were obviously not the sole source of the surgeon's knowledge. He practiced also dissection. He knew of a cardiac system and was surprisingly near recognition of the circulation of the blood, for he was already aware that the heart was the center and the pumping force of a system of distributing vessels. He was already conscious of the importance of the pulse, and had probably already begun to count the pulse, a practice heretofore first found among the Greek physicians of the Third Century B.C. in Alexandria. He had begun an acquaintance with a muscular system, but he knew little more of the nerves than the recognition of brain and spine as the important centers of nervous control. He had, for example, made the remarkable observation that a dislocation of the cervical vertebrae was accompanied by a seminal emission. His discussion of the digestive system, if the treatise contained one, is unhappily not included in the preserved portion of our document. In view of the titles of the court physician Iry, noted above as a specialist in diseases of the digestive organs, it is probable that our treatise did contain a discussion of the surgery of the digestive system, if not also of the respiratory organs.

Such a loss fills us with the keenest regret. The present editor has endeavored to indicate in the Introduction (pp. 9–18) the significance of such a mind as that of the author of our Surgical Treatise in the history of human development, and to that Introduction the reader must turn for fuller discussion. The scribe of over 3,500 years ago, to whom we owe our present manuscript, could have had little consciousness of the momentous decision he, or possibly some one for him, was making when he pushed aside the ancient Surgical Treatise, then already a thousand years old, while his own copy was still incomplete. He had copied at least eighteen columns of the venerable treatise and had reached the bottom of a column when, pausing in the middle of a line, in the middle of a sentence, in the middle of a word, he raised his pen, and ceased writing. After a pause, of which we cannot divine the cause, but during which his well-filled reed pen nearly dried, he again applied it to the papyrus. He made two more very faint strokes with the almost exhausted pen, which he thereupon dipped deep into his ink pot. After heavily retracing the two pale strokes, but so carelessly that the original faint lines are still visible, he laid down his pen and pushed aside forever the great Surgical Treatise he had been copying, leaving $15\frac{1}{2}$ inches (39 cm.) bare and unwritten at the end of his roll.

When I reached this blank space in my first study of the document, I felt as if I had been peering through a newly revealed window, opening upon the once impenetrable gloom enveloping man's earliest endeavors to understand the world he lived in. It was as if I had watched a hand slowly raising the curtain that covered this window, and then suddenly that hand had refused to lift the curtain further. That provincial scribe sitting over his roll, three thousand five hundred years ago, little dreamed that every word he added would one day be hungrily pondered as the sole surviving copy of the ancient treatise he was transcribing. He had reproduced at least eighteen columns of the older original—something over four hundred lines.

Beginning at the top of the head, and proceeding systematically downward, the treatise had marched on through carefully arranged discussions forming a series of forty-eight cases. He had been none too careful in his copying, and he made many errors. In two places he inserted on the margin unintentional omissions and indicated their proper position in the text by a cross, the earliest known asterisk in the history of books. He had industriously shifted from his black ink to his red, and had liberally distributed his rubrics. He was much more interested in these matters than in the content of the extraordinary treatise he was copying. He found his work somewhat trying, for it contained unfamiliar terms, and unaccustomed signs like the human mandible, which caused him difficulty and sometimes resulted in awkward, uncertain characters. He had finished the cases on the thorax and had begun the first case on the spinal column when he stopped. One can imagine him yawning, rising indifferently and going home to his dinner, quite unconcerned, and altogether unaware of the fact that he was leaving the future civilized world entirely without any knowledge of his great ancestor's cases on the surgery of the internal organs, which in all likelihood followed immediately on that of the spine.

When our scribe returned to his task, he left blank the unwritten space following his unfinished copy of the Surgical Treatise and turned it face down. Upon the unoccupied back he began copying totally different material which he or his master had meantime brought forth. On resuming his copying he left another blank space of 15½ inches (39 cm.) at the beginning of the back, and hence the new material copied on the back was separated from the Surgical Treatise not only by being placed on the other side of the papyrus, but also by 31 inches (78 cm.) of unwritten space. This was a wise separation, for the new material was merely a hodge-podge of the customary magical recipes, drawn from the traditional folk medicine inherited from the superstition of a remote past. A later hand added some recipes for a youthful complexion, including especially one for " Transforming an Old Man into a Youth."

Of the subsequent history of our document after it went forth from the hands of the professional copyist we know nothing. For discussion of its character and function, whether it was a physician's handbook, a medical professor's lecture outlines, or in its present form a medical student's notebook, the reader must be referred to the Introduction (*infra*, pp. 72–73).

Its more recent history is well known; for it was acquired by Mr. Edwin Smith nearly two generations ago at Luxor during the American Civil War. It is of no little interest to Americans to know that its discovery goes back to the earliest days of Oriental science in the United States, and indeed to the first generation of Egyptology anywhere.

Edwin Smith, after whom the papyrus is named, was born in Connecticut in 1822, the year that witnessed the first decipherment of Egyptian hieroglyphic by Champollion. Smith was one of the earliest students of Egyptian in any country. He studied hieroglyphic in London and Paris when the science was only a quarter of a century old, and was probably the first American to learn scientifically the little then known about the Egyptian language. He then removed to Egypt and by 1858 was living in Luxor, where he remained for nearly twenty years. He acquired the papyrus, now bearing his name, at Luxor in 1862.[1]

Smith knew enough Egyptian to recognize its character as a medical treatise, and must have devoted much time to its study, but he never made any effort to publish it, although he showed it to several European scholars who visited him at Luxor. Their vague references to it in their published notes in the early '70's (see *infra*, pp. 22–24) gave no hint of its extraordinary character and importance. Thereupon it seems to have been totally forgotten by the scientific world.

When we consider that the first university teaching of Egyptian in America began in 1895, and that it was not until after this that the first professorship in Egyptology was established in an American university, we can easily understand that Edwin Smith's studies received little encouragement from his own country. The publication of such a document, moreover, would have required a considerable subvention. On the death of Edwin Smith, therefore, the papyrus was still unpublished, and it was thereupon presented to the New York Historical Society by his daughter in 1906.

When in 1920 I was requested by the New York Historical Society to translate and publish the papyrus, I was at first inclined to refuse, in view of heavy administrative responsibility for the affairs of the Oriental Institute. Imagine my surprise, however, when I saw the splendid folio columns of this magnificent papyrus manuscript! And when I had examined its content even summarily, I was unable to refuse. In palliation for the delay that has since ensued,[2] I can only plead long absences from America in the Near East, and other responsibilities on behalf of the Institute.

[1] Further information regarding Edwin Smith will be found *infra*, pp. 20–24. See also the literature cited there, especially Dr. Caroline Ransom Williams, "The Place of the New York Historical Society in the growth of American Interest in Egyptology," in *New York Historical Society Quarterly Bulletin*, Vol. IV, No. 1 (April, 1920), pp. 16–17; and the present editor's notes, *ibid.*, Vol. VI, No. 1 (April, 1922), pp. 6–9.

[2] Based on a brief initial examination of the document, the editor published a preliminary account of it in the spring of 1922. See "The Edwin Smith Papyrus," *New York Historical Society Quarterly Bulletin*, Vol. VI, No. 1 (April, 1922), pp. 1–31. This was followed by a fuller and more technical preliminary report for Egyptologists. See "The Edwin Smith Papyrus: Some Preliminary

Moreover, the interpretation of the papyrus has required much study of the medical papyri as a class, and such an effort has made the editor painfully aware of the lack of any modern comprehensive treatment of the ancient Egyptian medical documents. Especially troublesome has been the fact that no one has ever attempted an inclusive treatment of the technical terms with which these medical papyri are filled. There is no comprehensive glossary of the highly specialized words employed by the ancient Egyptian in pathology, physiology, anatomy, surgery, etc. It is of course needless to say that the present editor possesses no competence in these fields of medical science. After interpreting the document as best I could with my limited knowledge of the human body, I handed the manuscript to my medical colleague, Dr. Arno B. Luckhardt, who very kindly undertook the burdensome task of looking it through and appending his suggestions. I have acknowledged these notes in their proper places, but I wish to express here my sincere appreciation of Dr. Luckhardt's valuable assistance.

The editor would also acknowledge the co-operation of several other colleagues. To my old friends Alan H. Gardiner and Kurt Sethe, I am indebted for valuable suggestions on several difficult passages. In 1922, with the consent of the New York Historical Society, I handed to the editors of the Berlin *Wörterbuch der aegyptischen Sprache* photographs of the Edwin Smith Papyrus, so that the light which it throws on Egyptian knowledge of the human body might be incorporated into the *Wörterbuch.* I handed my transliteration of the text to Professor Grapow, one of the editors of the *Wörterbuch,* and he was kind enough to make several suggestions. At the same time the editors generously permitted me to make full use of the *Wörterbuch* files, which were then available in alphabetic arrangement as far as the end of 𓋴. To all of these colleagues I am very grateful, and additional acknowledgements will be found in the text of the commentary.

The heavy task of verifying all references, and checking statistics, has been carried out by Dr. Edith Williams Ware, Research Associate in the Oriental Institute. She has been of constant assistance also in the reading of proofs throughout the work. To her likewise I am indebted for the compilation of the Egyptian glossary, as well as the indices.

Dr. Caroline Ransom Williams, who first called my attention to this remarkable papyrus, was kind enough to compare my set of large-scale photographs with the original, and to add detailed red ink indications of the extent of the rubrics, thus making the photographs a sufficient record which enabled me to dispense with the original during most of the work on the text.

Observations," by James Henry Breasted, in *Recueil d'Études Égyptologiques dédiées à la Mémoire de Jean-François Champollion.* Paris 1922, pp. 385–429. The observations reported, and the views expressed in these two introductory discussions, based as they were on a brief preliminary study of the papyrus, have naturally undergone some modification in the present final publication.

To the New York Historical Society, who are the fortunate possessors of the Edwin Smith Papyrus, I wish to express my appreciation of their invitation to interpret and publish this extraordinary document. At the same time I would also thank their Executive Committee for permission to include these volumes in our Oriental Institute Publications.

The cost of such a publication is very heavy, and these arrangements have been made possible by the action of the General Education Board in voting a subvention for carrying on the publication program of the Oriental Institute. For this generous support the Institute is deeply indebted to the members of the General Education Board.

The content of the Surgical Treatise is obviously of interest and importance to many outside of the ranks of professional orientalists, especially to medical men and historians of science. For this reason I hope that my colleagues in Egyptology will recognize the necessity of some concessions obviously superfluous to us, but indispensable to the outside reader. It is for such readers that practically all words cited in the commentary have been followed by a transliteration in Italic letters; and for such readers also it has seemed indispensable to add a few hints regarding the nature of Egyptian writing, in order to make the commentary more intelligible. To these "Explanatory Notes" the professional orientalist will of course pay no attention, but orientalists should read the introduction in Volume II before proceeding to the study of the papyrus and the perusal of Volume I.

The manuscript of this work was already being put into type when Dr. Alan H. Gardiner's invaluable *Egyptian Grammar* appeared. I regret, therefore, that the commentary does not contain references to this important treatise beyond what it was possible to insert in the proof. Examples from this papyrus found in Dr. Gardiner's Grammar were not drawn from these volumes, but from photographs very gladly loaned to Dr. Gardiner in advance of the present publication of the papyrus.

Finally, it is a pleasant duty to express here my sense of obligation to the University Printer and his associates of the Oxford University Press for their constant and invaluable co-operation in the production of these typographically difficult volumes, and to Emery Walker, Ltd., for their admirable series of plates in Volume II.

CHICAGO HOUSE, THE COLOSSI,
LUXOR, UPPER EGYPT.
February, 1929.

JAMES HENRY BREASTED.

GENERAL EXPLANATORY NOTES

FOR PHYSICIANS AND OTHER NON-EGYPTOLOGICAL READERS

Readers who are not professional orientalists will find much in this book which is unintelligible to the non-Egyptologist. This is unavoidable. The editor of such an ancient document must bring to bear upon it all the available evidence necessary to justify his interpretation,—a task especially complicated and laborious in the case of a treatise like this, containing as it does a body of ancient technical terms which were growing up in the infancy of a new science. Many of these words, like the term for "brain," are totally new and unknown, or are old words with entirely unfamiliar technical meanings. They have required much discussion. The editor hopes that this discussion has not entirely submerged or made unintelligible to medical readers the interpretation of the document as a whole.

The question may be raised why it was not possible to publish by itself a translation of this document for medical readers, without burdening it with all this technical apparatus of interpretation. A consecutive translation of the papyrus will indeed be found at the end of the commentary in this volume; but the editor strongly advises medical readers not to try to read and understand it without first having read the General Introduction (*infra*, pp. 1–29) and the Special Introduction (pp. 33–73), omitting the conclusion (pp. 73 below, to 77). The long lists in the Special Introduction are inserted only for convenience of reference and therefore need not be carefully studied until later.

In using the commentary and the discussions of Egyptian words, the medical reader will find some questions arising regarding the writing and language with which we are dealing in this document. Egyptian writing was originally purely pictographic, each picture signifying the thing it depicted or suggested. These pictures, which we call *hieroglyphs*, were never relinquished by the Egyptians, who retained them, for all monumental records inscribed on stone, long after they had become phonetic signs, and throughout the independent history of Egypt. Strictly interpreted, the word "inscription" as applied to an Egyptian record always indicates one written in hieroglyphic. These hieroglyphic pictures were, however, slow and difficult to make. The effort to make them rapidly with pen and ink on papyrus paper for the daily affairs of business and government, resulted in a more rapid, cursive form of the signs,—a hand which we call *hieratic*. This more rapid manuscript hand is, in origin and character, exactly parallel with our own handwriting, which arose in the same way from our carefully made uncials (capital letters). The efforts of our European ancestors to write rapidly on papyrus or parchment the letters which we still print, gave rise to our own handwriting. The origin of hand-written letters in the older forms which we still preserve as capitals, may in some cases still be observed. For example, our letter " b " as we write it with the pen still contains the upper loop of its ancestor, the capital B ; but the lower loop is imperfect because the hand of the writer, running rapidly onward to the next letter without lifting the pen, did not stop to return to the vertical line and complete the lower loop.

Long before 3000 B.C. the Egyptian scribes were keeping the records of business, government, and society in their rapid hieratic handwriting on papyrus, and vast quantities of manuscript documents were produced. Very few of them have survived.

Our surgical treatise, and the other material on the Edwin Smith Papyrus, were likewise written in hieratic, which will be found reproduced in facsimile in Volume II (Plates I to XXII). At the present day, if we were editing the manuscript diary of some important ancestor, we would prepare for purposes of convenient study a *typewritten* copy, that is a copy in the letters out of which the handwriting used in the diary originally developed. Similarly it is found practical and convenient to transliterate an Egyptian hieratic writing into the hieroglyphic pictures from which the hieratic signs originally developed, and which are thus seen to be roughly parallel with the letters we still print. This hieroglyphic " transliteration," as it is called, will also be found in Volume II (Plates I A to XXII A). Each column of hieroglyphic (on the right) faces the corresponding column of hieratic (on the left). The two columns correspond line for line, and also in the arrangement of the signs within the line. All detailed correspondences may therefore be easily followed sign for sign, although this arrangement of the signs is not characteristic of hieroglyphic. The words printed in red in the hieroglyphic transliteration (Plates I A to XXII A) are those originally written in red ink in the papyrus, where such rubrics are easily recognizable on the facsimile plates by their lighter colour, all the rest being in black ink.

It should be noted that like the hieratic original, the hieroglyphic version is written from right to left, and the beginning of the lines is at the right. Hieratic was always so written, but hieroglyphic, though prevailingly written from right to left, might be written either way. For convenience in type-setting, hieroglyphic print reads from left to right and does so in the text of the commentary.

For convenience of reference, the entire text of the papyrus is printed in hieroglyphic in Volume I, with all rubrics indicated by underscoring ; the surgical treatise is divided into cases, and these again subdivided into convenient, short sections, each followed by translation and commentary. In this commentary, the Egyptian words cited and explained are always transliterated into our own alphabet as far as possible. The reader will observe that these transliterations are made up exclusively of consonants, because Egyptian writing was a system of consonantal signs and possessed no signs for the vowels. To indicate these unfamiliar consonants, it is customary to employ (in all but two cases) our own consonants, with distinguishing marks attached.

In this way are indicated the consonants for which our alphabet possesses no letters. These consonants were not all identical with ours. Otherwise all the English letters used in transliteration indicate sounds approximating their sounds in English.

The other signs and modified letters are the following nine:

ʾ A sound closely akin to the Hebrew א (Alef), a smooth breathing for which we have no letter in our alphabet. It is like the initial breathing represented by the unpronounced *h* in our "humble".

ʿ A guttural sound entirely foreign to English, and for which of course we have no sign. It corresponds to the Semitic consonant *ʿayin*.

ḥ An emphatic or explosive *h*.

ḫ A deep guttural like German *ch* in "Dach" or "Bach".

ẖ A deep *h* which early interchanged easily with *š*; and was therefore perhaps like German *ch* in "*ich*".

š Pronounced *sh*.

ḳ A deep palatal *k*.

ṯ Like *tsh*, or *th*.

ḏ Originally *dj*, but becoming an emphatic *s* approaching *z*.

In pronouncing the unvocalized forms of the transliterated words, it is customary to insert arbitrarily as many e's as may be necessary to pronounce the word. Thus for Egyptian *mt*, "canal, vessel", etc., we say "*met*"; for *ḥsb*, "a break, fracture", we say "*ḥeseb*"; for *mrḥ·t*, "grease", we say "*merḥet*". For the two difficult sounds: ʾ (a breathing) and ʿ (the guttural *ʿayin*), we usually use merely a vowel *a*, e.g., *ʿr*, "penetrate," is commonly called "*ar*," and *pʾḳ·t*, "shell," is pronounced "*paḳet*," with Italian *a*. We know that the above vocalizations do not remotely resemble the actual pronunciations used by the ancient Egyptians themselves; but they are approximately correct as to the consonants, and the arbitrary vowels serve to make Egyptian words pronounceable. It is unscientific to *write* such vowels however, for a scientific transliteration must include only the sounds indicated by the signs in the original text.

While individual Egyptian words have regularly been transliterated in the commentary, considerations of space have deterred the editor from including transliterations of entire passages or sentences quoted in Egyptian in the commentary; but they have always been accompanied by translations, in which the significant words are followed by transliteration in parenthesis.

The following additional arbitrary typographical signs employed in the translation should be noted:

⌜ ⌝, or half-brackets, enclosing a word or words, indicate that everything so enclosed is of uncertain translation. Thus the words "⌜shown exhaustion⌝"

(p. 199) are a rendering of two Egyptian words of which the meaning is not entirely certain.

[ ] indicate that words so enclosed are restored by the present editor, and though not found in the original, are regarded by the editor as a probably correct restoration. When only part of a word is so enclosed, it means that the word is mutilated, but partially preserved ; thus " [like cou]nting " (p. 104) means that the latter part of the second word is visible in the original.

[⌜ ⌝], a combination of brackets and half-brackets, indicates a restoration regarded by the editor as uncertain. Thus "[⌜like counting⌝] " (p. 104) means that these two words are not found in the original and are regarded by the editor as an uncertain restoration.

- - -, three or more short dashes mean the loss of words, whose possible but not certain number is indicated by the number of dashes. See examples on p. 104. When enclosed in half-brackets, such dashes indicate fragmentary or uncertain words.

( ), whenever employed in the translation, indicate that a word or words so enclosed are editorial interpretations, not the restoration of a loss in the original text.

In the hieroglyphic text the following should be noted :

————, employed as underscoring in the hieroglyphic text in Volume One, indicates that words so underscored are written in red ink in the original manuscript. In Volume Two, these rubrics will be found actually printed in red in the hieroglyphic text on Plates I A to XXII A.

In the hieratic text (Volume Two, Plates I to XXII), the rubrics, although not in red, are distinguishable by being slightly lighter in color than the text in black.

GENERAL INTRODUCTION

It has long been a matter of common knowledge that for many centuries before the rise of Greek medicine, there was a considerable medical literature in the Ancient Near East. The recognized social and legal position attained by medicine and surgery in Western Asia before 2000 B.C. was revealed by the presence of a legally established tariff for the services of both the physician and the surgeon in the Code of Hammurapi (Twenty-first Century B.C.) when that extraordinary monument was discovered a generation ago. These legal regulations of medical and surgical practice toward the end of the Third Millennium B.C. would indicate that medicine in ancient Babylon was already centuries old at that time, and that the beginning of medical knowledge must reach back well toward 3000 B.C. The important social and official standing of the physician in Assyria is also reflected to us in the Seventh Century B.C. in the surviving cuneiform letters of the Assyrian Empire, which had inherited, seemingly without much change, the medical lore of earlier Babylon. In these letters we find Arad-Nanai, a famous medical man and royal court physician of Esarhaddon, the son of Sennacherib, advising the king regarding an uncertain ailment, perhaps rheumatism, and admonishing him besides washings to employ enchantments. On another occasion Arad-Nanai felicitates the royal patient on his recovery from toothache. He also sends the king several reports on the health of the monarch's younger brother, a young prince in feeble health. Very interesting communications in the form of letters report to the king the sickness of his mother. Arad-Nanai and one of his medical colleagues, however, succeeded in restoring the queen-mother to health, so that she survived her royal son. Her daughter-in-law, however, the queen-wife, was less fortunate, and the physicians were unable to save her. Such letters, of which there is a considerable series, make quite evident a recognized medical profession and a body of medical knowledge in the Assyrian Empire.

Unfortunately the actual tablets on which was recorded the medical literature of ancient Babylonia and which obviously must have existed in Hammurapi's day have practically all perished, and the treatises which have survived to us are copies made in the Assyrian Empire, chiefly the Seventh Century B.C. These copies, furthermore, are themselves in a very incomplete and fragmentary state. We may derive from them, however, an impression of the range and character of medical treatises in Western Asia for probably some 2,000 years before the Christian Era.[1] They cover a considerable series of ailments arranged roughly according to the part of the body chiefly affected. The leading treatises deal with ailments of the head, including

[1] For the best account of this literature see B. Meissner, *Babylonien und Assyrien*, Vol. II, Heidelberg, 1925 (in Kulturgeschichtliche Bibliothek, edited by W. Foy).

mental troubles, infections, baldness, and affections of the eyes, ears, and temples; ailments of the respiratory and digestive organs, and of the muscles and ligaments, as well as of particular parts of the feet; affections of the anus, including a good description of haemorrhoids. It is possible that these and some related treatises were combined in a general work on therapeutics but this is uncertain. There were, besides, specialized tractates on pregnancy, child-birth, obstetrics, and diseases of the genital organs. The *materia medica* employed in treatment of these ailments included a long list of animal, vegetable, and mineral substances, most of which it is still impossible to identify. A frequent method of use, after especial preparation, was by direct application, that is "laying" the remedy on the affected part, or binding it on; but the commonest method of administering was internally through the mouth, and occasionally by the insertion of a suppository into the anus.

There is slight indication that the physician discovered anything of the real nature of the ailment or, except in the more obvious cases, the function of the organs affected. Among the long list of available remedies, a few, like oil for stiff limbs, or milk for stomach troubles, may have been beneficial, but most of the remedies employed were entirely valueless, as is shown by the indifference with which the physician moved through a long list of medicines, shifting from one to another *for the same disease.*

We see then that these fragmentary treatises surviving from ancient Babylonia and Assyria reveal a wide range of observation of disease and an extensive list of herbs and minerals in the physician's *materia medica.* There is, however, no systematic knowledge or discussion of the human body, nor any rational consideration of disease. The causes of disease and the operation of remedies, as conceived by the physician, are so interfused with belief in supernatural forces, that a rational understanding of the organs and functions of the human body, sick or well, or of the operation of remedies when applied, was impossible. It is evident that primitive folk medicine, with all its superstitions, completely dominated the medical teaching of the ancient Babylonians, just as such superstitions also suffused their general outlook on the natural world, with the possible exception of the latest developments in Babylonian astronomy, which contributed much to the rise of astronomy in Greece.

Ancient Babylonian knowledge of anatomy, physiology, and pathology was therefore limited, and under these circumstances the contributions of Babylonian medicine to later medical science are not likely to have been important. Our own knowledge of Babylonian attainments, however, is unhappily limited by the fact that *not a single Babylonian treatise on surgery has descended to us.* We cannot doubt the existence of such treatises in early Babylonia in view of the legally recognized and regulated position of the surgeon in Babylonian society in the Twenty-first Century B.C. already mentioned. One of the most important discoveries of future excavation, to which we may look hopefully forward, may sometime restore to the world one of the lost ancient Babylonian treatises on surgery. It is not impossible that such a discovery may prove to be as unexpected a revelation as that of the Edwin Smith Surgical Papyrus.

As we turn from the Assyro-Babylonian world to Egypt we enter both an earlier and a higher civilization, and at the same time a cultural *milieu* which interfused with that of the mainland and the islands forming the south-east extension of Europe. The situation was one of intimate interpenetration between the Nile valley and nearest Europe. Obvious geographical considerations demonstrate the truth of these statements, and if any confirmation were needed it is amply furnished by the history of civilization in the Eastern Mediterranean. In the history of medical science in particular, it is no accident that the leading patron god of medicine in early classical Europe—he who was called Asclepios by the Greeks and Aesculapius by the Romans—was originally an historical personage, an ancient Egyptian wise man and physician called Imhotep by the Egyptians, grand vizier, chief architect, and royal medical advisor of the Pharaoh in the Thirtieth Century B.C., the earliest known physician in history.[1]

In harmony with the high position of this venerable Egyptian physician of five thousand years ago the historical documents of Egypt reveal to us the existence of medical treatises early in the Third Millennium B.C. in the age which we call the Old Kingdom (roughly 3000 to 2500 B.C.).

In the middle of the Twenty-eighth Century before Christ the Pharaoh Neferirkere was one day inspecting a new building in course of construction under the superintendence of the chief architect Weshptah. The king and his court were all admiring the work and the Pharaoh was turning with words of praise to his faithful minister, when he suddenly noticed that Weshptah was unable to hear the words of royal favor. The king's exclamation alarmed the courtiers. The stricken minister was quickly carried to the court and the priests and the chief physicians were hurriedly summoned. "His majesty had brought for him a case of writings. . . . They said to his majesty that he was unconscious." Such are the words of the ancient inscription in which the incident is recorded. The king, smitten with sorrow as the news of his favorite's death reaches him, can only retire to his chamber in prayer and order sumptuous arrangements for the great man's interment. The mortuary inscription of Weshptah which thus narrates his death incidentally furnishes us, therefore, the earliest historical reference to medical literature. There is conclusive evidence that in the Edwin Smith Papyrus we have a later copy of one of the medical documents already in existence

[1] See K. Sethe, *Imhotep, der Asklepios der Aegypter: ein vergötterter Mensch aus der Zeit des Königs Doser. Untersuchungen zur Geschichte und Altertumskunde Aegyptens.* Hinrichs, Leipsic, 1902, Vol. II. For an interesting popular account of this earliest-known physician see J. B. Hurry, M.A., M.D., *Imhotep, the Vizier and Physician of King Zoser.* Oxford, 1926. On his place in history see the present author's *History of Egypt*, pp. 112–114.

in the Old Kingdom, and it is not impossible that it lay with the others in the "case of writings" brought in by the Pharaoh's command in an endeavour to save a court favorite's life in the Twenty-eighth Century B.C.

Our knowledge of the character of these Egyptian medical treatises has heretofore been based chiefly on few papyri: the famous Papyrus Ebers at the University of Leipzig; the Berlin Medical Papyrus in the State Museum at Berlin (No. 3038); the London Medical Papyrus (British Museum No. 10059), and the Papyrus Hearst, now at the University of California.[1]

Besides the above longer documents only a few fragments of three other Egyptian medical documents have survived. These are perhaps as old as about 2000 B.C. They include the scanty remains of a treatise on diseases of women, and fragments of a veterinary manual treating diseases of cattle, both of which have been published by Griffith,[2] and finally 29 lines of recipes for diseases of women and children, but still unpublished.[3] They will be edited later by Dr. Alan H. Gardiner.

It will be seen that all three of these earlier, incomplete documents are special treatises, while the four large, post-Middle Kingdom papyri listed above are each a compilation of a whole series of special treatises. These compilations were probably all put together in the interval between the Middle Kingdom and the Empire, that is in the period from the early Eighteenth to the early Sixteenth Century B.C.

In one important particular all of these medical rolls, early or late, are alike, in that they all consist of *recipes*. They were lists of prescriptions, compiled for use by the practicing physician, or possibly in one case for the instruction of medical students. For the most part the diseases are not described, but each receives the vaguest designation, as an introduction to the recipe. In Papyrus Hearst we find *one* diagnosis, and in the Berlin Papyrus (No. 3038) *two*; in the London Papyrus none. Among these recipe-papyri only the Papyrus Ebers shows any attention to a record of the examination and diagnosis of the case, and this almost exclusively in the concluding section of the document. Papyrus Ebers records in all forty-seven diagnoses.

A careful study of these treatises has still to be made, but it is quite clear that they treat disease as entirely due to demoniacal intrusions. They make constant use of

[1] The sizes and dates of these ancient treatises are as follows:

Document.	*Columns.*	*Lines.*	*Recipes.*	*Date.*
Papyrus Ebers	110	2,289	877	Early Sixteenth Cent. B.C.
Papyrus Hearst	16 (and fragments)	273 (and fragments)	260	Sixteenth Cent. B.C.
Berlin Papyrus	24	279	204	Sixteenth Cent. B.C.
London Papyrus	19 (very fragmentary)	253	63	Eleventh Cent. B.C.

The dates given are those of the manuscripts. The materials themselves are obviously older.

[2] F. Ll. Griffith, *The Kahun Papyri*, London, 1898, pls. VI–VIII and pp. 5–14.

[3] I am indebted to Dr. Gardiner for permission to make a copy of these recipes.

spells and incantations combined with the remedies and are evidently the product of a medical practice still dominated by primitive folk medicine. These recipe-compiling physicians were magicians contending with a demon-infested world. Their whole outlook on the world, like their conception of disease, was that of spiritistic superstition, incapable of discerning the causes of disease as arising in a rationally conceived world. They occupy the same point of view which we have found in Babylonian medicine.

This attitude of the physician's mind toward disease is essentially the theological outlook on nature which characterized the early Orient as a whole, and was never discarded by ancient man until the rise of Greek thought. It is illustrated very clearly by the conventional account of the divine origin of their medical documents commonly found stated somewhere in these early treatises. Thus the Berlin Medical Papyrus already mentioned above says that the roll was "found in ancient writings in a chest containing documents under the feet of Anubis in Letopolis in the time of the majesty of King Usephais, deceased; after his death it was brought to the majesty of King Sened, deceased, because of its excellence. . . . It was the scribe of sacred writing, the chief of the excellent physicians, Neterhotep, [⌜who made⌝] the book." [1]

Similarly the London Medical Papyrus states: "This book was found in the night, having fallen into the court of the temple in ⌜Khemmis⌝, as secret knowledge of this goddess, by the hand of the lector of this temple. Lo, this land was in darkness, and the moon shone on every side of this book. It was brought as a marvel to the majesty of King Khufu." [2]

In the Papyrus Ebers a recipe for "soothing the itch" is stated to have been "found during an inspection in the house of Wennofer" (Osiris) (Papyrus Ebers, column 75, lines 12–13); and the discussion of twenty-two canals of the body is said to have been "among things found in writing under the feet of Anubis in Sekhem. It was brought to King Usephais, deceased." (Papyrus Ebers, column 103, lines 1–2). Such mythical origins not only attributed these documents to the gods, and gave them a vast antiquity which added to their sacredness, but also placed medical lore outside of human observation, as something of supernatural origin. As we shall now proceed to illustrate, our new surgical papyrus must be placed in a different class.

The Edwin Smith Papyrus comprises twenty-one and a half columns of writing, of which seventeen columns (377 lines) are on the front (*recto*) and four and a half columns (92 lines) are on the back (*verso*). Owing to narrowing of the column width, resulting in shortening of the lines, the writing on the back amounts in volume to less than one-seventh of the entire document. This material on the *verso* consists exclusively of recipes and incantations, identical in character with those of the other

[1] Berlin Medical Papyrus 3038, column 15, lines 1 ff.

[2] London Medical Papyrus, column 8, lines 8–13.

Egyptian medical documents, the recipe-papyri which we have just discussed. The first three and a half columns (65 lines) on the *verso* contain chiefly incantations against pestilence, and the remainder, about a column (27 lines), in a different hand, is devoted almost entirely to a long recipe for restoring youth to an old man. These incantations and recipes on the back are a later addition having no relation with the front, which is indeed separated from all connection with the back by a considerable blank space following the end of the writing on the front. A full discussion of the recipe material on the back will be found introducing Part II, The Incantations and Recipes.

The seventeen columns (377 lines) on the *recto*, that is, about six-sevenths of the document, are part of a treatise which is fundamentally different from any of the surviving medical documents of the ancient Orient thus far discovered. These differences are the following:

1. The seventeen columns on the *recto* comprise part of a *surgical* treatise, the first thus far discovered in the ancient Orient, whether in Egypt or Asia. It is therefore the oldest known surgical treatise.
2. This surgical treatise consists exclusively of *cases*, not recipes.
3. The treatise is systematically organized in an arrangement of cases, which begin with injuries of the head and proceed downward through the body, like a modern treatise on anatomy.
4. The treatment of these injuries is rational and chiefly surgical; there is resort to magic in only one case out of the forty-eight cases preserved.
5. Each case is classified by one of three different verdicts: (1) favorable, (2) uncertain, or (3) unfavorable. The third verdict, expressed in the words, "an ailment not to be treated," is found in no other Egyptian medical treatise.
6. This unfavorable verdict occurring fourteen times in the Edwin Smith Papyrus marks a group of cases (besides one more case) which the surgeon cannot cure and which he is led to discuss by his scientific interest in the phenomena disclosed by his examination.

It will be seen that the above six points mark off this surgical treatise as disclosing a point of view distinct from that which characterizes the other medical documents of the Ancient East. A detailed discussion of its content will be found (pp. 33 ff.) introducing the translation and commentary.

The forty-eight cases preserved in this treatise begin at the top of the head and proceed downward to the thorax and spine, where the document unfortunately breaks off. In each of these cases we see the surgeon first making his examination of the patient and determining the character of the injury: whether the wound affects only the soft tissue or whether it has also reached the bone, or even penetrated the bone to important internal organs; what are the physiological effects, etc. The method of the examination sounds rational and modern. The information the surgeon desires may be elicited by questioning the patient or directing him to attempt certain movements or postures ; further it may be obtained by the surgeon's own observations, ocular, olfactory, or tactile. The last frequently include probing with the fingers (palpation) or manipulation with the hand, and what is most important and significant, observation of the action of the heart by means of the pulse, 2,500 years before the pulse appears in Greek medical treatises. It is significant also to observe that the surgeon's purely mechanical treatment of an injury is, in the majority of cases, included in the *examination*, and not in the discussion of the treatment with medicaments. We have here evidently an ancient distinction between surgery and medicine (see p. 42).

On the basis of the examination the surgeon then pronounces his diagnosis, the earliest such conclusions that have survived. The development of a full diagnosis is a relatively recent matter. Even in European medicine it was customary to describe only the *conspicuous* symptoms in a diagnosis until the advances made by Sydenham in the Seventeenth Century.[1] In view of the fact that the elaborate diagnosis of the present day was so recently preceded by a simple description of the more noticeable symptoms, we may not expect the surgeon of nearly five thousand years ago to have gone very far in this direction. The most important thing for the ancient surgeon was the effect of the examination on his immediate course of action toward the patient. Hence he makes a diagnosis which always includes one of the three verdicts to which we have already referred, and this is the surgeon's declaration that he (1) can treat and cure ; (2) can treat and try to cure ; (3) cannot treat, the case being practically hopeless. Three diagnoses consist of this final hopeless verdict and nothing more ; but in forty-nine diagnoses in our treatise the three verdicts are preceded by other observations on the case. In thirty-six of these forty-nine diagnoses the other observations are nothing more than a repetition of the title of the case, or of observations already made in the examination ; but in the remaining thirteen, the diagnosis adds one or more *conclusions based on the facts determined in the examination.* These are the earliest surviving examples of observation and conclusion, the oldest known evidences of an inductive process in the history of the human mind.

In taking up the treatment which the ancient surgeon applied, it is important to notice that in sixteen instances out of fifty-eight examinations he attempted no treatment. These untreated cases form a unique body of discussions to which we shall have occasion to return (p. 52). There are forty-two examples of treatments out of the forty-five injuries discussed. We find that in three instances the treatment is

[1] See Knud Faber, *Nosography in Modern Internal Medicine*, Hoeber, New York, 1923.

exclusively mechanical or surgical, while in twenty purely surgical treatment was combined with external use of medicaments, and in the remaining nineteen the external applications were employed alone.

The mechanical appliances or processes employed by our ancient surgeon, as revealed by the new treatise, were not numerous, but some of them appear for the first time in the history of medicine. He makes frequent use of absorbent lint, and in injuries to the nose or outer ear he employs plugs, swabs, or tampons of linen. Among bandages, it is interesting to find that one variety was manufactured for the surgeons by the most skillful bandagist of antiquity, the Egyptian embalmer. For drawing together a gaping wound the surgeon might employ strips of adhesive plaster, which was already known. More serious wounds, however, were closed by surgical stitching which here appears for the first time in the history of surgery although it is known to have been used much later in sewing up the abdominal incision made for the evisceration of a mummy [1] in the Twenty-first Dynasty (Eleventh Century B. C.).

Splints of three different types were already in use. In a case of tetanus the surgeon makes it possible to administer liquid food by holding the mouth open with a " brace of wood padded with linen." A second type of splint said to be " of linen " may possibly be a wooden splint wound with linen such as was found by Dr. G. Elliot Smith on two Egyptian bodies of the Old Kingdom (3000–2500 B. C.). They may also be composed of layers of linen impregnated with glue and plaster and moulded while soft to conform to the limb. This material, now called " cartonnage," and often found shaped to the limbs of the mummy, is well known in mummy cases. It is essentially identical with the modern surgical cast employed for the support of fractured limbs. It has never been found still attached to a broken limb, for it should be remembered that such an appliance would be buried with the deceased only in case the sufferer died of his injuries, and the embalmer left the splints in place. This would be unlikely and indeed, as Elliot Smith has observed, only two ancient bodies still wearing splints have ever been found in Egypt. This surgical use of the embalmer's cartonnage becomes the more probable when we recall the fact revealed by our treatise that the surgeon drew his supplies of a certain type of bandage from the embalmer. A third type of splint was a stiff roll of linen, used apparently where a softer splint was needed, as in the case of a fractured nasal bone. The Egyptian surgeon's treatment of fractures was effective. Out of over a hundred ancient bodies showing healed fractures, only one was observed to show any signs of suppuration by Dr. Elliot Smith (see *infra*, p. 56). When a compound comminuted fracture of the skull made it necessary, the patient was held upright by supports of sun-dried brick or *adobe*, presumably moulded to fit his figure on each side under his arms.

Of instruments the treatise mentions only the " fire-drill," employed when hot for

[1] G. Elliot Smith and W. R. Dawson, *Egyptian Mummies*, London, 1924, Fig. 36, facing p. 96.

cauterization. A mandible of the Fourth Dynasty (2900–2750 B.C.) disclosing a drill hole in the mental foramen for the purpose of draining an abscess under a molar tooth (see Pl. I, Fig. 1) makes it evident that specialized surgical instruments of metal, presumably bronze, already existed in the age which produced our surgical treatise, but they are taken for granted by the ancient author. It is noticeable, furthermore, how often, in his directions to the practitioner, the probing of the wound is to be done with the fingers. An instrument is never designated for this purpose. Unfortunately no systematic study of the surviving Egyptian surgical instruments has ever been made (see p. 53), although the museums of Europe and America contain a large number.

The injuries which the ancient surgeon is instructed to treat are fully discussed in the special introduction to the treatise (pp. 43–45) ; but we may note here that his therapeutic was primitive and simple, showing that surgery was far in advance of medicine. After purely surgical measures the surgeon's favorite remedy for an injury was " fresh meat " applied on the first day only. It was bound on and was usually followed by an application of lint saturated with ointment composed of grease and honey, also bound on. In the nineteen cases in which no specific surgical treatment is prescribed we find the surgeon instructed to employ only medicaments externally applied, and likewise usually bound on. In symptoms of tetanus following serious injury to the skull, the treatise suggests only hot applications to the constricted ligaments of the mandible. Among his *materia medica* it is interesting to find a decoction of willow (*salix*), essentially salicin, employed as a disinfectant; an ammoniacal application for allaying inflammation; and for astringent purposes a solution containing salts of copper and sodium.

Apart from purely surgical procedure, the treatise repeatedly instructs the practitioner to let nature do the work, an attitude which reminds us of Hippocratic medicine. In critical cases the surgeon is admonished to adopt a waiting attitude, and uses a formula " until thou knowest that he has reached a decisive point," recognizing that the course of the case will not be settled until a point is reached which discloses progress or the reverse. This point reminds us strongly of the Hippocratic " crisis " (κρίσις).

There is good evidence that this surgical treatise, as thus far discussed, was written in the Old Kingdom (3000–2500 B.C.) and presumably, as we shall see, in the early part of that remote age. The manuscript nowhere hints at the name or station of the author. We are free to wonder whether the author of this earliest known investigation of human anatomy and physiology could have been identical with our oldest-known physician, the venerable Imhotep already mentioned above, who lived in the Thirtieth Century B.C. However that may have been, it will probably have circulated as a book on surgery when the Great Pyramid of Gizeh was being built. There may be a hint of its title heading a quotation in the Papyrus Ebers ; for we find there an isolated passage on the heart which is said to be quoted from another ancient medical book entitled " Secret Book of the Physician." Now this passage on the heart, quoted in Papyrus Ebers, is also found in the Edwin Smith Papyrus, and has every appearance of being original there. If so, then Papyrus Ebers is quoting from the Edwin Smith Papyrus and the title of the source quoted is the ancient title of the Edwin Smith Papyrus (see commentary, p. 108). It is not improbable, therefore, that our surgical treatise was known to its ancient users as the " Secret Book of the Physician."

It is evident from his treatise that our ancient surgeon, whoever he may have been, was a man of observant and discerning mind, with a wide outlook upon the life of his time. The terms which he uses, to be sure, may have been already current in the surgical jargon of his age, but to the present editor they convey the impression of a man actually involved in the process of building up a terminology in a field of observation not yet possessing a fund of current terms. He seems to be doing for the first time in any field of science what has since happened in one area of scientific observation after another. He draws his descriptive terms from nature, from the mechanical arts, from architecture, and from many sides of daily experience. He has observed the crucibles of the copper foundry and he compares the convolutions of the brain to the corrugations on metallic slag. In describing the articulation of the human mandible, he likens the fork at the head of the ramus to the claw of a two-toed bird clasping the temporal bone. He applies the name of a certain water worm to fibrous strings of coagulated blood ; the region of the frontal sinus is " the secret chamber," as of a sanctuary ; the bridge of the nose is for him " the column of the nose ; " a puncture of the cranium is like a broken hole in a pottery jar. These terms were, as we shall see, not always familiar to later readers and had to be explained—a fact suggesting that they originated with our author.

After circulating for some generations, more probably for several centuries, it was found that the book was antiquated in its terms. Not a few words and expressions were evidently no longer wholly intelligible. In the latter part of the Old Kingdom, probably not later than 2500 B.C., some " modern " surgeon, as unknown to us as the original author, equipped the document with a commentary in the form of brief definitions and explanations, which we term glosses, appended to each case. For example when the original treatise directed the practitioner to " moor him (the patient) at his mooring stakes," the commentator knows that this curious idiom is no longer intelligible and appends the explanation, " It means put him on his accustomed diet and do not administer to him any medicine." Thus he carefully explains all the terms describing the various injuries, or designating the condition of the patient or his symptoms. Similarly, the commentator added many descriptions of anatomical terms and other designations drawn from nature or the arts : the corrugations, the water worm, the " column of the nose," the " secret chamber," etc. In a total of sixty-nine such brief discussions, forming a little dictionary of early Egyptian medical terms, this unknown ancient commentator has given us invaluable revelations of his knowledge of anatomy, physiology, pathology, surgery, and therapeutics; while at the same time he has made clear many terms in the original treatise which would not have been intelligible to us without his little dictionary.

This surgical treatise, as it has come down to us, is therefore a composite made up of the original author's text and the ancient commentary.[1] It is an original source of absorbing interest as a unique document in the early history of civilization. Socially considered it is an outgrowth of the earliest great age of civilization, the age that saw the first civilized society of some millions of souls organized into a homogeneous nation. It was only in such a situation that oriental medicine could develop and in any aspect approximate the character of a science. We learn this fact when we take up the study of the cemeteries where the Egyptian communities buried their dead. A single campaign of excavation which exhumed between 5,000 and 6,000 bodies, disclosed one person with a fractured bone among every thirty-two people, that is over three such injuries among every hundred persons. A broken neck is stated by our treatise to have been caused by a fall on the head—evidently from some elevation. Among the mechanics and workmen employed on the vast buildings of Egypt, such as the Great Pyramid of Gizeh, there must have been many such accidents. We can easily understand why there are thirty-three cases of injured bones among the forty-eight cases in our treatise; many, perhaps most, of these injuries were received while the injured man was following the peaceful routine of civil life. No one can read this treatise, however, without concluding that some of the wounds in the skull, e. g., the "perforations" found in the skull, the temporal bone, the zygoma, and the sternum—not to mention the gashes in the soft tissue of the nose, lip, chin, outer ear, neck, and shoulder—were spear and sword wounds received in war (compare Pl. I, Figs. 3 and 4). Some of the experience and knowledge of the human body, which the ancient author discloses, was therefore doubtless gained on the battlefield. In harmony with this observation it should be noted that the patient is always a man. There is other knowledge of organs and tissues which would indicate that our ancient surgeon practiced dissection of the human body. In this earliest known investigation of anatomy and physiology the surgeon gained knowledge which could not have been acquired in the mere process of embalming.

We see that in the above situation the surgeon was daily called upon to deal with human ills which were the obvious result of observable physical causes, having no connection with the maligant demons of disease. For our treatise shows us the surgeon examining case after case of organs and tissues injured by intelligible physical agencies

[1] We shall refer to these two parts as "author's text" or merely "text", and "ancient commentary" or "glosses." In order not to confuse the latter with the present author's *modern* commentary the ancient commentary will usually be called "the glosses."

forming a realm of familiar forces, quite uninvaded by magical powers. In this realm the ancient surgeon was able to gather a considerable body of fact regarding human anatomy, physiology, and pathology—the earliest known recorded group of rational observations in natural science. Indeed these two men, the surgeon who was the original author of the treatise, and his later successor, who wrote the glosses forming the ancient commentary, both living in the first half of the third thousand years B.C., were the earliest known natural scientists. In the long course of human development they are the first men whom we can see confronting a great body of observable phenomena, which they collected and stated, sometimes out of interest in the rescue of the patient, sometimes out of pure interest in scientific truth, as inductive conclusions which they drew from observed fact.

If now we endeavor to summarize the knowledge of the human body discernible in this ancient treatise, we discover that the inevitable and even childish limitations to be expected in an age so remote are found side by side with observations and discernment penetrating in directions which we could hardly have anticipated. For the first time in recorded human speech, our treatise contains the word "brain," which is unknown in any other language in this age, or in any other treatise of the Third Millennium B.C. The earliest discussions of the brain have hitherto been found in Greek medical documents probably over two thousand years later than our Egyptian treatise, which describes the external appearance of the brain as like the corrugations arising in metallic slag—an apt description of the convolutions of the brain. In a case of compound comminuted fracture of the skull, he discusses the rupture of the sack containing the brain, an obvious reference to the meningeal membranes. The seat of consciousness and intelligence was from the earliest times regarded by the Egyptians as both the heart and the bowels or abdomen. Our surgeon, however, has observed the fact that injuries to the brain affect other parts of the body, especially in his experience the lower limbs. He notes the drag or shuffle of one foot, presumably the partial paralysis, resulting from a cranial wound, and the ancient commentator carefully explains the meaning of the obsolete word used for "shuffle." In this connection the surgeon has already made the extraordinary observation that the effects on the extremities shift from side to side according to the side of the head which has received the injury. This is a recognition of the localization of function in the brain, although the ancient surgeon was apparently misled by a case of *contre-coup* regarding the side of the lower limbs affected. Here then is discovery of the fact that the brain is the source of control of the movements of the body. As another center of nervous control, our surgeon had also recognized the spinal column, and he had observed the interesting fact that after a dislocation of the neck the injured man suffered an erection and a seminal emission, a phenomenon which has been observed in modern times in men executed by hanging. These two centers of nervous control, the brain and the spinal column, are not correlated in our treatise. The means of that control in a system of ramifying nerves is not mentioned and was evidently unknown, for the observation and demonstration of the distinction between *nerves* and *vessels* was apparently the work of Erasistratos at Alexandria in the Third Century B.C., while the connection between the brain, the spinal cord, and the nervous system was first clearly demonstrated by Herophilos, also in the Third Century B.C.

While our surgeon had made only preliminary observations which might eventually contribute toward the recognition of a nervous system, he had, on the other hand, already unmistakably recognized the heart as the center of a system of distributing vessels. The importance of observing the action of the heart in determining the condition of a patient, appears here for the first time in medical history. The passage containing these observations unfortunately falls in the only broken and fragmentary column in our document, resulting in some uncertainty on the following important point. In spite of the imperfect condition of the text of this passage, there is much probability that the surgeon *counts* the strokes of the pulse, and it is doubtless a significant fact that the first physician who is known to have counted the pulse, Herophilos of Alexandria (born 300 B.C.), lived in Egypt. It will probably also not have been wholly an accident that this was done in the land which produced the earliest known time-pieces, for Herophilos used an Egyptian water-clock for timing his count of the pulse. Herophilos is well known to have been an investigator of much independence, and he was the one Greek physician who so nearly approached the discovery of the circulation of the blood that there are historians of medicine who believe that he actually achieved this discovery. Before his time Greek medicine had been long misled by the dogma that a force resident in the *arteries* caused the pulse. Our treatise, however, already knows that the pulse is due to the force and action of the *heart*. Herophilos was the first *Greek* physician to recognize this fact. That he should have lived in Egypt, where the cardiac system disclosing the *heart* as the central force had already been known for perhaps 2,500 years, is hardly likely to have been a pure coincidence. It should be made quite clear, however, that our treatise, while it shows knowledge that the action of the heart affects and supplies all extremities and all parts of the body with blood, does not indicate a recognition of the *circulation* of the blood.

The treatise discloses acquaintance, furthermore, with a system of muscles, tendons, and ligaments. For example, it discusses in some detail the muscles of the human mandible and their anchorage on the temporal bone. The Egyptian word for tendon, however, in our treatise, is the same as that for "blood-vessel," and we recall the fact already mentioned above, that the distinction between *nerves* and *vessels* was not demonstrated until the Third Century B.C., when it was made clear by Erasistratos. It is likely, therefore, that the three systems of nerves, muscles, and vessels, were not yet clearly disengaged by our surgeon.

If the treatise had anything to say on the digestive system, the discussion has been lost owing to the fact that our ancient copy in the Edwin Smith Papyrus stops in its progress downward at the thorax and upper part of the spinal column. Whatever our surgeon has to say regarding any parts below these limits is suggested by symptoms, such as those affecting the legs or the genital organ, induced by injuries of the brain or a cervical vertebra, that is, injuries in the upper regions under discussion. It is noticeable also that even in this upper region our ancient surgeon does not carry his observations of detail far toward the interior. He discerns the " corrugations " on the exterior of the brain, he discovers the meningeal sack containing it and knows when it is ruptured; he probes with his fingers to the interior and discovers cardiac pulsations, or as he says the " fluttering and throbbing like that on the crown of an infant's head before it has grown together; " but he goes no further toward the interior of the head. We find him doing some investigation of the ear, but he gives no attention to the eye, and we recall that the first detailed description of the eye, and especially the connection of the optic nerve with the brain, was given by Herophilos in his *ἀνατομικά*.

Similarly, in the discussion of the shoulders and thorax, our treatise, as far as preserved, does not carry its observations to the interior, with the exception of a remark, doubtless intended as a caution, calling attention to the presence of two vessels beneath the thorax, one leading to the lungs, and the other to the heart. This restriction of recorded observations to external matters or conditions not far below the surface, is obviously due to the fact that the treatise is a discussion of injuries, and so largely injuries rupturing or otherwise affecting external tissue. It is not a systematic treatise on the human body.

The most significant characteristic of the treatise is the ancient surgeon's attitude in studying these injuries. He evidently is filled with desire to heal his patient whenever he concludes there is any possibility of doing so; but he does not stop there.

One of the most important observations in appraising this surgical treatise is the fact that out of 58 examinations the surgeon recommends treatment in 42 instances, leaving 16 without treatment. This latter group evinces the surgeon's interest in the human body quite apart from any thought of healing or treating it, and reminds us of the Hippocratic treatises on epidemics in which, among 42 case-records, 25 were fatal cases. This group of 16 injuries described but not treated in our surgical treatise is without parallel in Egyptian medical literature, as we have already noticed above.

These discussions demonstrate the surgeon's scientific interest in the human body as a field of observation, and disclose him to us as the earliest scientific mind which we can discern in the surviving records of the past.

The current view, that in all cases Egyptian medical practice invariably employed magic devices, a view in which I formerly also shared, is quite evidently wrong. There was, indeed, surviving from primitive times a large body of traditional practices in medical treatment wholly or chiefly magical which never disappeared. Such practices, universally and implicitly followed by the common people, forming what we may call "demoniacal medicine," always had its devotees, the descendants of the old "medicine men," with their rolls of ancient hocus-pocus, like the medical papyrus of the British Museum, or the "Charms for Mother and Child" in the other well-known roll at Berlin. Such primitive superstition dies hard. It lasted far down into the history of our own land. Increase Mather, President of Harvard University, in his treatise on *Remarkable Providences,* insists that the smell of herbs alarms the Devil and that medicine expels him. Such beliefs have probably even now not wholly disappeared from among us. We cannot wonder that this was the almost universal point of view in the early world with which we are dealing.

The author of our treatise was one of a group of men who will likewise inevitably have been children of their time. We cannot conceive that they ever ceased to believe in the power of magic; but they had learned that in surgery and medicine they were confronted by a great body of observable phenomena, which they systematically and scientifically collected, sometimes out of interest in the salvation of the patient, sometimes out of pure interest in the scientific truth. The class of men thus revealed to us are the earliest natural scientists of whom we know anything, who, confronting a world of objective phenomena, made and organized their observations and based inductive conclusions upon bodies of observed fact.

The current conclusion regarding the mind of the ancient Egyptian, a conclusion in which I have myself heretofore shared, has been that he was interested in scientific principles, if at all, solely because of the unavoidable necessity of applying them in practical life—that if he discussed the superficial content of a many-sided geometrical figure or the cubical content of a hemisphere it was because he was obliged to measure fields for taxation purposes and to compute the content of granaries. In the field of Egyptian mathematics Professor Karpinski of the University of Michigan has long insisted that the surviving mathematical papyri clearly demonstrate the Egyptians' scientific interest in pure mathematics for its own sake. I have now no doubt that Professor Karpinski is right, for the evidence of interest in pure science, as such, is perfectly conclusive in the Edwin Smith Surgical Papyrus.

Astronomy and medicine are the oldest sciences. Both arose, as we have seen, in remote ages, still clouded by the darkest superstition, and in the closest association with magic, religion, and theology, of which it may be said both astronomy and medicine at first really formed a part. The complete dissociation of medicine from magic and religion was the achievement of the Greeks. It was not an achievement which they completed at one stroke, but a slow transition, a gradual process. The Hippocratic School, in spite of notable ability in observation, and a spirit admirably rational in the main, did not succeed in wholly divesting themselves of superstition. Even the vision of the intellectual colossus, Aristotle, was now and then obscured by the mists of ancient superstition, and at the present day, one may still be surprised by the lurking superstitions which persist and survive in out-of-the-way corners of some modern mind, otherwise thoroughly emancipated and scientific in attitude and outlook.

In the history of Greek medicine there is still far too much obscurity to permit a rapid survey such as might serve to furnish the connection between Greek medical science and the earlier knowledge of medicine which arose and was in general use in the ancient Near East at least 2,500 years before the age of Hippocrates. Nor is a brief introduction like this the place for such a comprehensive presentation.

Nevertheless we may here call attention to a few salient facts observable in any consideration of the possible relation between early Greek medicine and that of Egypt. In the first place we have already noticed that the greatest of the Greek medical investigators, at the climax of Greek achievement in medical science in the Third Century B.C., lived in Egypt, as so many of the intellectual men of Greece had for centuries before that time traveled and studied in Egypt. The effect of this intimate contact is visible at many points in Greek life and science, which cannot even be summarized here. The contribution of Babylonian astronomy to the early development of astronomy among the Greeks was not generally recognized until even the names of the Babylonian astronomical observers, whose data were used by the Greeks, were recently identified in the Babylonian astronomical records on surviving cuneiform tablets, like the Greek Kidenas, Babylonian *Kidinnu* of the Fourth Century B. C., or Greek Naburianos, Babylonian *Nabu-rîmannu* of the Fifth Century B. C.[1]

In our surgical treatise the practitioner is instructed how to treat a dislocated mandible. He is directed just how to place his hands, in reducing the dislocation. The instructions are as follows :

> " Thou shouldst put thy thumbs upon the ends of the rami of the mandible in the inside of his mouth, and thy two claws (=two groups of four fingers) under his chin and thou shouldst cause them to fall back so that they rest in their places."

Now it happens that the Greek physician, Apollonios, who lived at Kitium in Cyprus in the First Century B. C., wrote an illustrated commentary on the Hippocratic treatise *περὶ ἄρθρων* " concerning the joints." This commentary has survived in a late manuscript copy of the Ninth Century of our era, which is now preserved at Florence as Codex Laurentius LXXIV.[2]

An examination of the illustration of Hippocratic practice in the case of a dislocated mandible shows us (Pl. VI) the patient seated, with head firmly held by an attendant

[1] See Meissner, *Babylonien und Assyrien*, Vol. II, p. 416.

[2] See H. Schöne, *Apollonius von Kitium : Illustrierter Kommentar zu der Hippokrateischen Schrift* ΠΕΡΙ ΑΡΘΡΩΝ, Leipsic, 1896.

while the surgeon, thrusting his thumbs into the patient's mouth, his fingers remaining outside and beneath, grasps the mandible to restore it to its place. The text [1] also refers to the position of the surgeon's hands: χρὴ γὰρ τὸν μὲν κατέχειν τὴν κεφαλήν, τὸν δὲ περιλαβόντα τὴν κάτω γνάθον καὶ ἔσωθεν καὶ ἔξωθεν τοῖς δακτύλοις κατὰ τὸ γένειον κ.τ.λ. These directions, prescribing that the surgeon's fingers shall be placed both inside and outside, show much agreement with the above cited direction in the Edwin Smith Papyrus. When clarified by the illustration (Pl. VI) and by the fact that the Greek δάκτυλος, though commonly meaning "finger," was also applied to the thumb, the Hippocratic method of reducing a dislocated mandible is seen to be identical with that prescribed in the Edwin Smith Papyrus.

This identity of the Greek surgeon's practice in the third century B.C. with that of our Egyptian surgeon of some 2,500 years earlier, establishes the existence of a certain amount of old Egyptian influence on Greek medicine. Our treatise, or some other old Egyptian book of surgery, containing our surgeon's directions for reducing a dislocated mandible, must have been known to the early Hippocratic practitioners. In view of this fact, we see more probability in the recognition of the Egyptian influences, suggested above, as having had some effect on the great Greek medical investigators, Herophilos and Erasistratos, residing as they did in Egypt where such influences were obviously possible.

The lapse of time between our latest Egyptian medical document and the rise of Greek medical science at Alexandria was one of many centuries. But we have interesting evidence of the continuance, during this interval, of Egyptian medical teaching in the Sixth Century B.C. under the patronage of Darius I of Persia, the greatest and most enlightened administrator of the early world before the rise of the Romans. Darius introduced into his administration the Egyptian calendar, restored the ancient Egyptian "Suez canal," built a great Mediterranean fleet for commerce with Persia, and although his people had been an illiterate and semi-barbarous group of peasant and shepherd tribes only a generation before his reign, his statesmanlike ability to discern the value of much which he could adopt from the civilization of the conquered was perhaps his greatest quality. Among his foreign functionaries in Persia was one Uzahor-resenet, an Egyptian ecclesiastic, who was High Priest of the goddess Neith at her temple in the Delta city of Sais. A statue of this priestly aristocrat, now in the Vatican at Rome, carries inscriptions giving some autobiographical details of great importance in the history of medicine. Uzahor-resenet says:

"His Majesty King Darius commanded me to come to Egypt, while His Majesty was in Elam as Great King of every country and Chief Prince of Egypt, in order to establish the Hall of the House of Life,[2] the house . . . after their decay. The barbarians brought

[1] Schöne, *ibid.*, p. 13.

[2] The term "House of Life" was an old one applied to archive chambers, libraries, and the like. It probably refers here to such a place, rather than to a hospital; and the following break in the inscription probably contained the more specific name of the school.

me from country to country, and conducted me to Egypt as the King had commanded."

" I did as His Majesty had commanded me. I equipped them (the two houses above) with all their students from among sons of men of consequence, no sons of the poor were among them. I placed them under the hand of every wise man . . . for all their work."

" His Majesty commanded to give them every good thing in order that they might do all their work. I equipped them with all their needs, with all their instruments which were in the writings, according to what was in them (the houses) aforetime."

" His Majesty did this because he knew the value of this art, in order to save the life of every one having sickness, and in order to establish the names of all the gods, their temples and their revenues, that their feasts might be celebrated forever." [1]

In this remarkable inscription we find the earliest known mention of a medical school as a royal foundation. It is important to note that this Egyptian medical school at Sais was not being founded for the first time, but was being *restored* as the surviving old writings in Uzahor-resenet's hands showed him it had been " aforetime." We note with interest that the medical students of the Sixth Century B.C. in Egypt were selected from families of good social station, and that as the last lines show, these young physicians were evidently also priests in the temple of the goddess. Indeed the High Priest himself, Uzahor-resenet, bore the title, " Chief Physician." Among the branches of instruction the reference to " instruments " shows us that surgery was included.

Among these highly civilized cities of the Nile Delta, the first large cities the Greeks had ever seen, the Macedonian kings of Egypt set up their enlightened scientific foundations at Alexandria. We see now that in medicine at least Darius had anticipated them. The important point to note is the fact that the support of old Egyptian medical instruction was continued by the Persians after their conquest of Egypt (525 B.C.). When, two centuries later, the Alexandrian physicians began to enjoy the princely support of the Ptolemies, they found themselves among the surviving native Egyptian medical schools and medical libraries of the Delta, where such contacts and influences as we have suggested could hardly have been escaped.

The Edwin Smith Papyrus has revealed to us an ancient Egyptian *surgeon* in contrast with the physician, as a man with the ability to observe, to draw conclusions from his observations, and thus, within the limitations of his age, to maintain a scientific attitude of mind. Such men will not have been numerous. The ancient commentator is disclosed as another man of the same type, living probably some centuries later. Our treatise and the commentary demonstrate the fact that such men produced discussions of the human body which represent the beginning of scientific effort to investigate and understand its innumerable problems and mysteries. The literature which these men created, representing the earliest known chapter in science, has perished, and there is small likelihood that we shall ever see any more of it.

[1] See H. Schaefer, *Zeitschrift für Aegyptische Sprache*, XXXVII (1899), pp. 72–74. Schaefer was the first scholar to recognize the real meaning of this inscription.

The ancient history of our document as a whole illustrates the hazards which beset such records and their meager prospects of survival. It is now without doubt thousands of years since the complete disappearance or destruction of the original copy of this surgical treatise, as penned by the hand of the nameless author himself, probably nearly 5000 years ago. In the same way, the copy to which the ancient commentator appended his explanations, long ago perished. At least one copy of treatise and commentary together, however, survived the fall of the Old Kingdom (3000–2500 B. C.) and, as transmitted, probably through successive copies, survived the fall of the Middle Kingdom (early Eighteenth Century B. C.) and the advent of the Hyksos. The surviving copy of the great mathematical papyrus made under a Hyksos king has revealed the fact that literary and learned activity still continued under these foreign rulers of Egypt whom we call the Hyksos. It was at this time, in the late Seventeenth Century B. C., when upper Egypt was striving to throw off the foreign yoke of the Hyksos, that a Theban scribe sat down to copy our ancient treatise on surgery. In *content* the book was then probably over a thousand years old. It was as if a man sat down to-day to copy a manuscript written in the reign of Charlemagne. It was full of old words, and archaic turns of speech, though some of its antique spelling had been modernized. The scribe was master of a stately and beautiful book hand, but he was totally ignorant of medicine and when confronted with some highly specialized picture-sign, like that of the human mandible, he completely lost his ready command of his usual graceful and running forms, and awkwardly smeared together a blotted and angular picture. He was excessively inaccurate, but occasionally noticed and corrected his errors—in one case placing an omitted word in the margin and calling attention to it by a cross, the earliest known asterisk in the history of book-making. He may have been an employe on the staff of some ancient copyist's office. In any case when he had copied the old treatise on surgery from the beginning (the human head) down to the thorax and the spine he stopped in the middle of a case, in the middle of a line, in the middle of a sentence, and leaving the end of the long roll bare of all writing for some space, he turned it over and copied on the unwritten back a series of incantations against pestilence, to which he added three recipes, one for female troubles and two for improving the complexion. It is possible that the first purchaser, some local Theban practitioner who saw the unfinished treatise on surgery, ordered the scribe to stop and to copy for him this unsavory magical hodge-podge on the back.

Eventually this unknown owner probably handed on the roll to some later worthy in the same craft. The last owner was much attracted by a roll containing a recipe for " transforming an old man into a youth," and he, or some scribe for him, took pains to copy this at the end of the older material collected by his predecessors, adding a totally unrelated remedy for some ailment of the anus. Meantime much handling and daily use of the document had frayed the beginning of the roll and at least one column of the fine old Book of Surgery containing the title of the book (with perhaps the name of the author) and the beginning of the first case dropped off in tatters. When at last the village quack himself fell sick and found his art unable to exorcise the demons of disease, his surviving relatives doubtless carried him up and laid him away in a rock tomb in the great Theban cemetery. Luckily for us, they seem to have laid his roll in his coffin with him; for it is hardly likely to have survived in any other conceivable place. There in his tomb it reposed in perfect safety throughout a vast sweep of human history for some three and a half millenniums, from the migrations of the Hebrew patriarchs and the prehistoric wanderings of the Greek barbarians to the American Civil War. The modern descendants of the old Egyptian quack, searching the tombs for salable plunder, probably found the roll beside the body of their Theban ancestor and saw in it prospects of gain. Unfortunately, however, as we shall see, our information on this point is not conclusive. The modern vandals stripped off the tatters of papyrus still hanging on the outside, to make it look more " ship-shape." After selling this roll to Mr. Edwin Smith in January 1862, they patched up another out of indiscriminate rubbish and gave it the appearance of a papyrus roll by wrapping it and gluing in place the tattered fragments which they had stripped off the genuine roll. Two months after the first sale they put this dummy roll also on the market and sold it, likewise to Mr. Smith. Detecting the fraud, Mr. Smith recognized and rescued the new fragments of the precious medical book, thus recovering for science the extraordinary, even though fragmentary, discussion of the heart and its system of canals, to which we have already referred.

The above discussion may serve to inform the non-Egyptological reader regarding the place of our new document in the history of science; but some further details in the modern history of the document must be added, besides a fuller account of its physical characteristics, the writing and age of the roll.

1. *History of the Edwin Smith Surgical Papyrus*

Mr. Edwin Smith, after whom the papyrus is named, went to Egypt about the year 1858. He was at that time thirty-six years of age and had studied Egyptian in both London and Paris before proceeding to Egypt. Although as far as I know he never published anything, it is quite evident from his papers in New York that he had become very fully grounded in the new science, which was then only a generation old. His knowledge of hieratic is praised by the sagacious Goodwin, who says, with reference to the date of the calendar on the verso of the Ebers Papyrus: " The numeral attached to the name of the king is neither 3 nor 30—both of which numbers have been suggested—but 9. It is due to Mr. Smith, *whose acquaintance with hieratic texts is very extensive* [italics mine], to mention that he pointed this out to me as long ago as 1864, when he communicated to me a copy of the endorsement upon his papyrus." [1] It is evident from these remarks of Goodwin that Edwin Smith was the first scholar to read correctly the date in this famous calendar.

Among Mr. Smith's meager papers handed to me by the New York Historical Society I find a manuscript containing a remarkable attempt by Mr. Smith at a complete translation of the papyrus which now bears his name. When we recall how scanty was the knowledge of hieratic in the sixties of the last century, when this effort at a translation was written out, not to mention also the very limited knowledge of the Egyptian language itself available at so early a stage of Egyptian studies, it is extraordinary how much of the document Mr. Smith has understood. It should be mentioned here also that of the eight fragments of the papyrus which, as we shall see, Mr. Smith rescued, he was able to place three with exactness and two more at least in their approximate connection. Even as early as 1854 he "was able to read correctly a name hitherto undeciphered on a wooden stamp in" [2] the Abbot Collection. In spite of the fact that he published nothing it is evident that he was one of the pioneers of Egyptian science. By a curious coincidence the year of his birth—1822—was likewise the memorable year in which Champollion deciphered and read Egyptian hieroglyphic. It was very fitting, therefore, that some mention of this little-known scholar and of the papyrus which bears his name should have found a place in a volume which was intended to commemorate the centenary of Champollion's great achievement.[3]

During his residence in Luxor, from 1858 to 1876, Mr. Smith met a number of the leading Egyptologists of the time and likewise many of the distinguished English travelers who so frequently visited the Nile in those days. Dr. Caroline R. Williams has noticed in a letter written by Lady Duff Gordon in October 1864 a reference to him as "an American Egyptologist at Luxor, a friend of mine," for whom Lady Gordon was securing books to be sent out by her husband.[4] Birch refers to him as having descended with the British Vice-Consul into a tomb shaft ninety feet deep to bring up "thirty mummies and their coffins" for the entertainment of the Prince of Wales during his visit to Egypt in 1868.[5] In the documents still surviving Mr. Smith's habitual intercourse with eminent scholars and distinguished visitors in Egypt, as well as his scientific knowledge, are quite evident. The reasons for mention of these matters will also be evident as we proceed.

In January 1862, during his stay at Thebes, Mr. Smith purchased the document which is the subject of this book. The fragments of page one, which he put together, are accompanied by a memorandum in his own handwriting which reads as follows:

[1] *Zeitschrift für Aegyptische Sprache*, Sept.-Oct. 1873, p. 107.

[2] Dr. Caroline Ransom Williams, "The Place of The New York Historical Society in the Growth of American Interest in Egyptology," in *The New York Historical Society Quarterly Bulletin*, April, 1920, p. 16.

[3] See *Recueil Champollion*, Paris, 1922, pp. 385–429.

[4] *Ibid.*, p. 16.

[5] *Ibid.*, pp. 16–17.

"These fragments were recovered from a factitious papyrus made up of the fragments from 3 others March 17, 1862, nearly 2 months after the original purchase, Jan. 20, both from Mustapha Aga, and the fragments A and C were saturated with glue which was removed by maceration and carefully scraping the glue away which had been used to seal the factitious papyrus composed of these fragments." After his death in 1906 Mr. Smith's daughter, Miss Leonora Smith, presented the document to the New York Historical Society, to whose courtesy I owe the permission to publish the great papyrus.

The problem of the provenience of the Edwin Smith Papyrus unfortunately involves us in some reference to the unjust reflections upon the character of Mr. Smith contained in Ebers' introduction to his papyrus, and also makes it necessary to take up at this point the connection between Papyrus Ebers and the Edwin Smith Papyrus. I trust that the mention of the following facts will be understood only as an unavoidable fulfillment of duty in defending the reputation of Mr. Edwin Smith, and in no sense as a reflection or an attack upon the memory of the gracious and kindly Ebers. It is obvious, however, that Ebers was misled in allowing to escape his pen the reflections on Mr. Smith which we find in his accounts of his purchase of Papyrus Ebers. He states:

"Er empfing meinen Namen gemäss dem Herkommen, dass wichtige Papyrosrollen nach denjenigen Gelehrten oder Freunden der Wissenschaft benannt werden, die sie auf eigene Gefahr in Aegypten erwerben. Daher die Bezeichnung Papyros Salt, Pap. Anastasi, Pap. d'Orbiney, Pap. Harris, etc." [1]

As far as my knowledge of the early history of Egyptology goes the papyri which Ebers mentions were not given these designations by the original first purchasers themselves but by *others*, especially by scholars who later, designating them by the names of their first European possessors, found it convenient to identify them in this way. I do not know of another example in the whole range of Egyptological studies in which a scholar has deliberately named an important papyrus after himself. In this connection one may refer to the example of the high-minded Lepsius in naming the Papyrus Westcar after the English lady who presented it to him. The evident eagerness of Ebers to attach his name to the magnificent papyrus he had acquired, betrayed him into unmistakable resentment toward Mr. Edwin Smith, whose name had already become connected with the document. The source of this resentment is thus obvious. As far back as December 1870 Lepsius had published some remarks entitled: Einige Bemerkungen ueber denselben Papyrus Smith,[2] and by "Papyrus Smith" he designated the great papyrus which with pardonable pride its later purchaser wished should bear the name of Ebers. Evidently without knowledge of Ebers' purchase Goodwin as late as the summer of 1873 calls the document "the Smith Papyrus."[3] It is quite evident that the great roll which we now know as Papyrus

[1] See Georg Ebers, *Papyros Ebers*, Leipzig, 1875, p. 2.

[2] *Zeitschrift für Aegyptische Sprache*, Dec. 1870, pp. 167 ff.

[3] *Ibid.*, Sept.–Oct. 1873, pp. 107–109.

Ebers had already begun to be known in the early seventies as Papyrus Smith. When, therefore, in the spring of 1873 Ebers handed Lepsius a manuscript account of the new and splendid hieratic manuscript which he had so recently acquired, it was very necessary that the name of Edwin Smith be completely dissociated from it. The document which had been discussed by the editor of the *Zeitschrift* in December 1870 under the title " Papyrus Smith " was now announced by Ebers in an article entitled " Papyrus Ebers," which appeared in the same *Zeitschrift* in May–June, 1873—too late, unfortunately, to prevent Goodwin's reference to it as " the Smith Papyrus " in the summer or autumn of the same year.

We are now in a position to understand why the otherwise always amiable Ebers permitted himself to accuse Mr. Edwin Smith of having endeavoured to masquerade as the owner of the great papyrus—an ownership which Ebers then emphatically denies. And yet Ebers himself characterizes these reflections on Mr. Smith as merely a " suspicion " (Vermuthung).[1]

As far back as 1864 Edwin Smith had already communicated to Goodwin the now famous calendar from the verso of Papyrus Ebers and at that time, as we have shown above, Smith was the first scholar to read the year date " 9 " correctly. The first mention of the later Papyrus Ebers in scientific literature seems to have been in connection with a hieroglyphic transliteration of the calendar published by Brugsch in the summer of 1870 (*Zeitschrift für Aegyptische Sprache,* July–Aug. 1870, pp. 108–111). Brugsch says that it was from the " Rückseite eines Papyrus " and that he had secured it from the papers of an Egyptological friend in Egypt during the winter of 1869–70. This friend was Eisenlohr who then sent in the hieratic text to Lepsius, intimating that he had not given Brugsch permission to publish it. Lepsius published Eisenlohr's note in December 1870 (*Zeitschrift für Aegyptische Sprache,* pp. 165–167). Eisenlohr states that in February 1870 he visited Edwin Smith in Luxor and that Smith showed him his collection, including " Zwei von ihm erworbene Papyrusrollen medicinischen Inhaltes, von welchen die eine über 100, die andere 19 Blätter enthält." In Eisenlohr's above article Lepsius substituted his own more accurate tracing (which he had received from Naville) in place of Eisenlohr's facsimile. Naville had been allowed by Smith to make this tracing in the autumn of 1868 with permission to publish, a permission later granted orally by Smith to Lepsius in person in Luxor.

Dr. Haigh next published a " note on the Calendar in Mr. Smith's Papyrus " (*Zeitschrift,* May–June, 1871, pp. 72–73) which adds nothing to the above facts, and Goodwin also wrote " Notes on the Calendar in Mr. Smith's Papyrus " (*Zeitschrift,* Sept.–Oct. 1873, pp. 107–109). He refers to the document (Papyrus Ebers) as " the medical papyrus in the possession of Mr. Edwin Smith of Luxor."

The outstanding facts discernible after a careful study of these earlier notices show

[1] *Ibid.*, 1873, p. 42, foot-note.

clearly that at one time both the Papyrus Ebers and the Edwin Smith Papyrus were in the physical possession of Mr. Edwin Smith, and they were seen in his possession by Eisenlohr, who refers to them both in unmistakable terms. I have seen no evidence in the contemporary documents that Mr. Edwin Smith anywhere stated that he was the owner of Papyrus Ebers, except in the accounts given by Professor Ebers, who, as we have already seen, had very personal reasons for his conclusions. Under these circumstances we can quite understand how Ebers might easily fall into the error which led him to the unwarrantable reflections on Mr. Edwin Smith. Mr. Smith, however, did own a large and important medical papyrus, next to the Papyrus Ebers then and now the largest ancient Egyptian medical document in existence. The casual use of the words " von ihm erworbene Papyrusrollen " by Eisenlohr are very easily understood by any one who has purchased antiquities on the Nile and who may have obvious reasons for desiring that the native owners of a valuable monument should not become too well known to Europeans who might become competitive bidders.[1]

It would be quite comprehensible if Mr. Smith had made no reference whatever to the ownership of the Papyrus Ebers, but the mere fact of its being in his physical possession at the time might easily create the impression that he owned it, and as he did own the smaller of the two papyri which he showed Eisenlohr it was always true after January 1862 that he owned a large and important medical papyrus. Any statements anywhere in the literature that he was the owner of a medical papyrus may, therefore, be quite true and need not be interpreted as false statements referring to the Papyrus Ebers.[2]

[1] It is possible that the earliest reference to Papyrus Ebers in print was in a sales catalogue of antiquities which I have never seen, but which is reported to have appeared in 1869 : " In 1869 there appeared in a catalogue of antiquities an advertisement of a large medical papyrus in the possession of Edwin Smith, an American farmer of Luxor near Thebes. This papyrus was said to be in excellent preservation and dated about the middle of the sixteenth century before Christ. The advertisement contained a reproduction of the calendar which was on the back of the papyrus. This calendar aroused an unusual interest among Egyptologists. The first mention of this papyrus in the Egyptian literature was by Birch of London. He was making some notes on the appearance of the name Cheops in the London Papyrus, and incidentally mentioned the existence of the medical papyri of Berlin and Turin and the advertised papyrus of Edwin Smith." (Bayard Holmes and P. Gad Kitterman, *Medicine in Ancient Egypt*, Cincinnati, The Lancet-Clinic Press, 1914, p. 14.) The authors just quoted seem to be under a misapprehension as to the reference by Birch to an " advertised papyrus of Edwin Smith." Birch's article appeared in the *Zeitschrift*, May–June, 1871, and he does indeed refer there to a medical papyrus " in possession of Mr. Edwin Smith of Thebes " but he makes no reference to an "advertised papyrus." Nor is this reference of Birch the first mention of this papyrus in Egyptian literature. The calendar had been published by Brugsch a year earlier, as we have seen. The curious reference to the learned Edwin Smith as " an American farmer " is, as we have seen, decidedly misleading and is so recognized in a letter, included by the authors (*ibid.*, p. 17), from an American tourist who learned nothing regarding Mr. Smith except some vague reminiscences by a person whom he calls the " German Consul at Luxor . . . a Copt," who was, of course, Moharb Todrous.

[2] I have not overlooked Professor Ebers' very specific statement as to his " Vermuthung: "

The fact that the Papyrus Ebers was so early connected with the Edwin Smith Papyrus might be of some value in discussing the problem of the source and date of the latter document. There is, unfortunately, nothing in Mr. Edwin Smith's papers regarding the reports of the natives from whom he purchased his papyrus, nor any conclusions of his own as to its origin. Ebers says that the native from whom he secured the Papyrus Ebers affirmed that it had been found in a tomb in the Assassîf, between the legs of a mummy. The discoverer, however, was at the time of Eber's purchase already dead and it was not possible to identify the tomb. Ebers likewise refers to the possibility that his papyrus belonged to the considerable group purchased by the British Consul Harris in 1857, a group reported to have been found in a "grotte," a rough shaft in the rocks some twenty feet deep by Deir el-Medineh. As to the date when the Papyrus Ebers was discovered, Ebers says it was found " vor nunmehr vierzehn Jahren." He does not date the introduction containing this remark, however, and therefore he does not indicate clearly the *terminus ad quem* from which we should reckon backward his fourteen years. If he means fourteen years before the date of the publication of his papyrus (1875), the discovery would have been made in 1861. This would bring the date fairly close to January 1862, when Edwin Smith purchased the papyrus now bearing his name. This fact does not make it certain, however, that the Edwin Smith Papyrus was found together with the Papyrus Ebers. In view of the fact that the ancient houses and other buildings of Thebes have thus far yielded so few papyri, there nevertheless is every probability that the Edwin Smith Papyrus was found in a tomb, and in my preliminary account of the document in the Bulletin of the New York Historical Society I have suggested this origin of the document. If it was indeed found together with the Papyrus Ebers, the native story communicated to Ebers might be regarded as external evidence, however unsatisfactory, that the Edwin Smith Papyrus originally came out of a tomb.

2. *Physical Condition, Writing and Date of the Manuscript*

As at present unrolled and mounted between glass the Edwin Smith Papyrus has a length of about 4·68 meters (about 15 ft. 3½ in.). At least a column of writing has been lost at the beginning, so that it originally had a minimum length of five meters (about 16 ft. 4 in.). The roll has a height of 32½ to 33 centimeters (about 13 in.), corresponding to the usual full-height roll of the period from the Middle Kingdom through the Hyksos Age to the early Empire. It is put together out of twelve sheets of the usual size, about 40 cm. (about 15¾ in.) wide, the first now surviving being

" Ich darf diese Vermuthung kühnlich aussprechen, da Mr. Smith meinem verehrten Collegen und Freund Prof. Eisenlohr und mir selbst erzählte, neben dem grossen einen kleinen medicinischen Papyrus zu besitzen." (*Zeitschrift.*, May–June, 1873, p. 42, foot-note.) Ebers, of course, translates "besitzen" from some English word used by Smith, which may have been nothing more than the innocent word "have," while the word " own," if used by Smith, may have applied exclusively to the smaller papyrus.

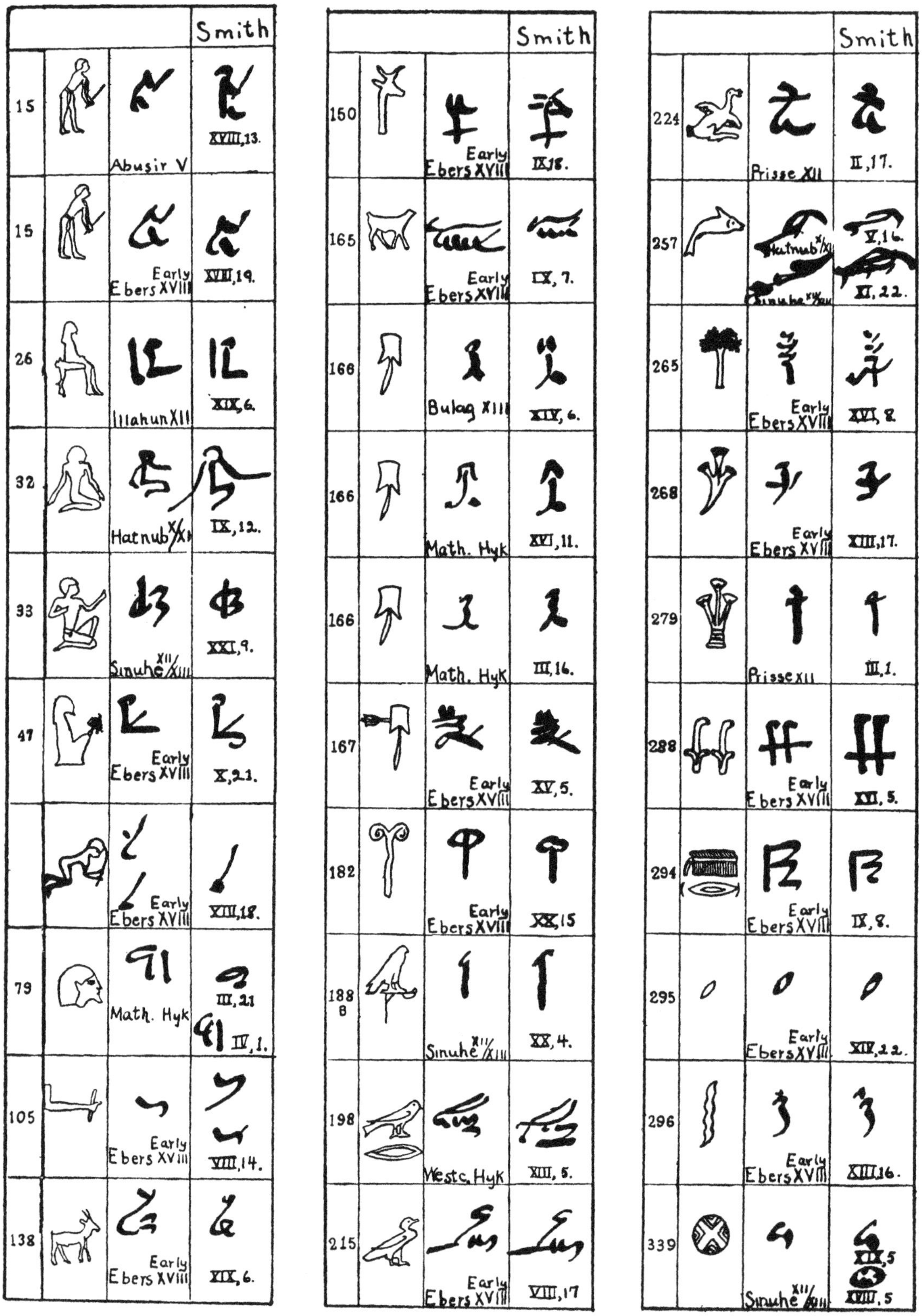

COMPARATIVE TABLE OF PALAEOGRAPHIC FORMS

First column hieroglyphic forms; second column hieratic forms from other papyri for comparison; third column hieratic forms from the Edwin Smith Papyrus.

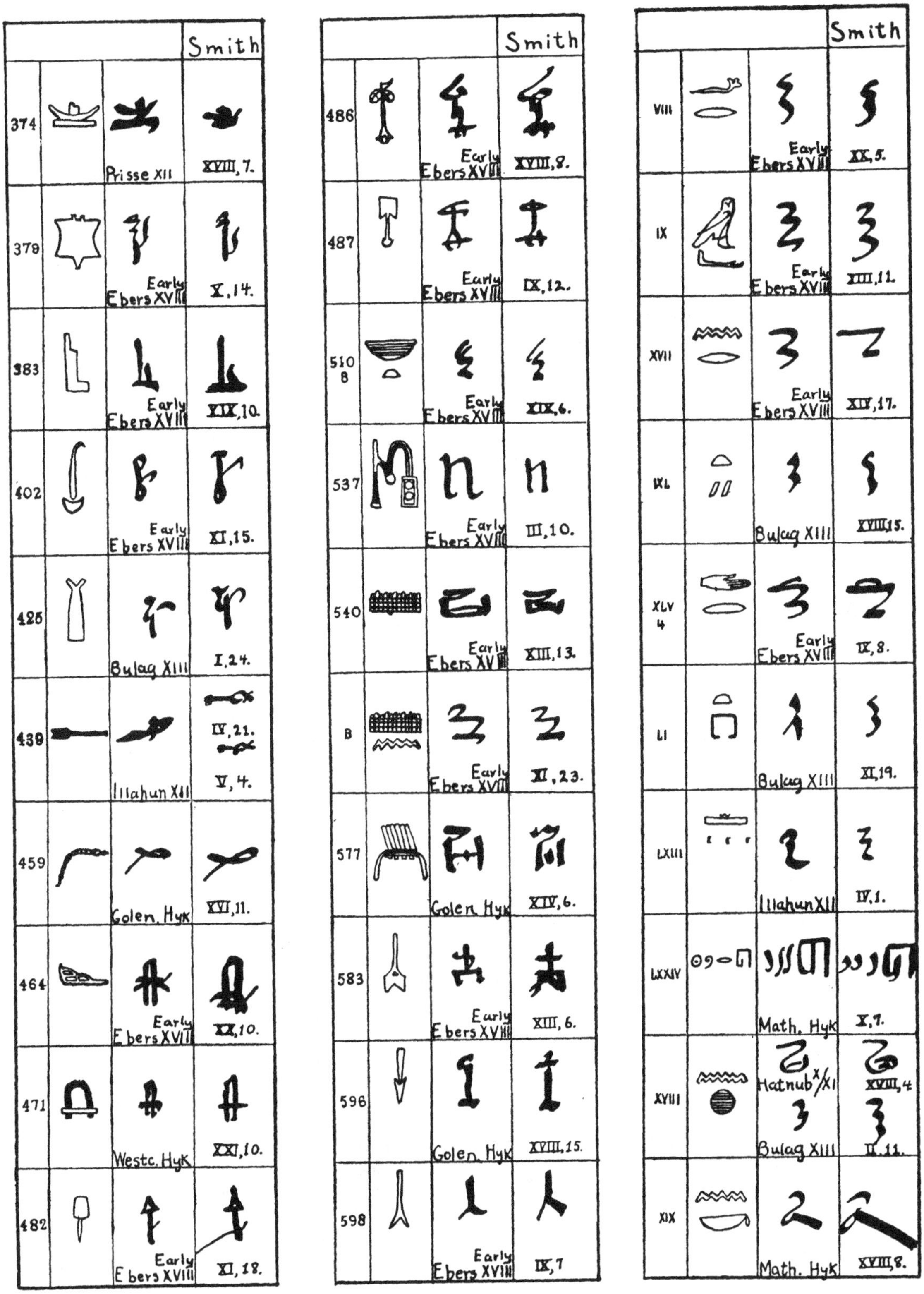

COMPARATIVE TABLE OF PALAEOGRAPHIC FORMS

First column hieroglyphic forms; second column hieratic forms from other papyri for comparison; third column hieratic forms from the Edwin Smith Papyrus.

unfortunately fragmentary. The eleven joints are admirably done, and in its craftsmanship the roll is an excellent piece of work. It now bears seventeen columns of writing on the recto and five on the verso, all in horizontal lines. The columns are about 28 to 29 cm. (about 11 in. to 11½ in.) in height and they vary in width from 18 to 27 cm. (about 7 in. to 10½ in.). The number of lines in a column varies also, from 18 to 26 (in the fragmentary first column). The recto contains 377 lines, and the verso 92. The entire front, 17 columns, and the first 3½ columns of the verso (XVIII—XXI 1–8) are the work of one hand.[1] The concluding section (column XXI 9–21 and all of XXII 1–14: making 27 lines) is by a totally different and possibly somewhat later hand.

The first question which confronts us is the date of the document, and in taking up first the palaeographic data I shall draw examples only from columns I—XXI 1–8 (omitting the concluding section, XXI 9–21 and XXII). The general resemblance of our scribe's hand to that of Papyri Ebers and Westcar is noticeable at the first glance. This superficially probable, general date is confirmed at once by observing that 𓂝 is written both 𓂝 and 𓂝, a confusion characteristic of Middle Kingdom and Hyksos documents, which, however, disappears after Amenhotep IV.[2] Similarly the ear (𓄔) is used in our document with one stroke at the base both as a determinative and for *ydn*, whereas in the Nineteenth Dynasty the form for *ydn* has two strokes and the form for the determinative has but one.[3] An examination of the accompanying comparative tables[4] suggests that the Edwin Smith Papyrus is not far removed in date from Papyrus Ebers. Nevertheless our document uses a group of forms distinctly older than those of Ebers. Thus Nos. 26 and 32 carry us back to the Middle Kingdom before we find complete parallels. No. 79 occurs very frequently in our document, and the usual form (given second in the table) is that of the Hyksos Age (Mathematical Papyrus). The same is true of two forms of No. 166, and a third form of the same sign is that of the Thirteenth Dynasty. No. 279, without the oblique cross stroke below, is a Middle Kingdom form. The same is true, though less decisively, of No. 374. For a parallel to LI we must go back to the Thirteenth Dynasty, and LXIII likewise is a Middle Kingdom form, while LXXIV is of Hyksos age.[5]

[1] In the Bulletin article (pp. 11–12) above referred to I have attributed the three and a half columns of the verso (XVIII—XXI 1–8) to a different hand from that of the recto. Further examination indicates that Recto I—XVII and Verso XVIII–XXI 1–8 are by the same hand.

[2] See Moeller, *Zeitschrift*, Vol. 56, p. 40.

[3] *Ibid.*

[4] The first and second columns are drawn from Moeller's invaluable tables (*Palaeographie* I). I have also retained his numbers for convenience of reference; but note correction of 49 B. The examples in column 3 are traced from photographs not always on the same scale and here reduced in size (pp. 26–27).

[5] It should be mentioned in this connection that among the papyrus fragments in the Edwin Smith collection as handed to the New York Historical Society by Miss Leonora Smith, there was a small fragment bearing but a word or two from each of six lines. Among these the fifth line contains the name of Thutmose I. Unfortunately this fragment cannot be joined up with our document and is clearly in a different hand. It may serve, however, further to confirm the period of the early Empire as the one to which the papyri of this collection are to be closely related.

These Hyksos and Middle Kingdom forms might at first lead one to consider a late Middle Kingdom or early Hyksos date for the document; but the large number of signs identical with those of Ebers and Westcar are not in favor of such a date. It cannot be doubted that our manuscript was written between the close of the Twelfth Dynasty and the age of Papyrus Ebers. It shows some close resemblances to the Mathematical Papyrus but I would be reluctant to decide whether it belongs before or after the Mathematical Papyrus. It seems certainly to belong in the Hyksos Age. How much weight in terms of time we should give to the early forms might possibly be decided by a more adequate comparison with all the closely related manuscripts. It would seem that the early forms, not found in Westcar or Ebers, could hardly have been lost in less than a generation. We may conclude therefore that the Edwin Smith Papyrus is not less than a generation older than the Papyrus Ebers, with the possibility of a still earlier date by no means excluded. Whether we must push it back of the latter part of the Seventeenth Century B.C. is a question then for further study. It is quite evident that in content the document is older, as we shall see.

Our scribe, as already stated above, was master of a beautiful book hand (not excluding some cursive forms), but shows evidence of the fact that he was not himself a medical man. Schaefer [1] has called attention to corrected errors of omission in Papyrus Ebers. The scribe of the Smith Papyrus has likewise made and sometimes, but not always, corrected similar errors of omission. He was guilty of a surprisingly large number of omissions, which he failed to notice. More often his mistakes require cancellation or change. In almost all cases he has detected these errors and has made his corrections in red ink over black, and in black ink over red. See Case 35 below. Similar corrections, though not so frequently, are found in Papyrus Ebers (e.g. 60,10 and 70,3).

The scribe of the Edwin Smith Papyrus employs very plentiful rubrics, so plentiful indeed that his discussion of a case may conclude with a remark in red, obliging the scribe to begin the next case in black in order to secure his desired contrast.

In taking up the translation and detailed discussion the reader should note that the materials fall into the following parts:

PART I

THE SURGICAL TREATISE (THE RECTO):

1. Special Introduction.
2. Translation and Commentary.

PART II

THE INCANTATIONS AND RECIPES (THE VERSO):

1. Special Introduction.
2. Translation and Commentary.

[1] *Zeitschrift*, Vol. 31, 61–62 and 117.

PART I

THE SURGICAL TREATISE

(THE RECTO)

THE SURGICAL TREATISE

SPECIAL INTRODUCTION

I. *Content and Character of the Treatise*

THE seventeen columns (377 lines), all that is preserved of this ancient treatise, occupying the front of the Edwin Smith Papyrus, contain forty-eight cases, all injuries, or induced by injuries (with two possible exceptions). The discussion begins with the head and skull, proceeding thence downward by way of the nose, face and ears, to the neck, clavicle, humerus, thorax, shoulders and spinal column, where the text is discontinued, leaving the document incomplete. Without any external indication of the arrangement of the text, the content of the treatise is nevertheless carefully disposed in groups of cases, each group being concerned with a certain region.

These groups are as follows:

A. Head (27 cases, the first incomplete):
   - Skull, overlying soft tissue and brain, Cases 1–10.
   - Nose, Cases 11–14.
   - Maxillary region, Cases 15–17.
   - Temporal region, Cases 18–22.
   - Ears, mandible, lips and chin, Cases 23–27.

B. Throat and Neck (Cervical Vertebrae), Cases 28–33.

C. Clavicle, Cases 34–35.

D. Humerus, Cases 36–38.

E. Sternum, Overlying Soft Tissue, and True Ribs, Cases 39–46.

F. Shoulders, Case 47.

G. Spinal Column, Case 48 (incomplete).

There is every probability that the complete treatise continued the discussion to the lower parts of the body and concluded with the feet.

The complete list of cases by groups is as follows:

A. Head

Case 1. A Wound in the Head, Penetrating to the Bone (incomplete).
,, 2. A Gaping Wound in the Head, Penetrating to the Bone.
,, 3. A Gaping Wound in the Head, Penetrating to the Bone and Perforating the Skull.
,, 4. A Gaping Wound in the Head, Penetrating to the Bone and Splitting the Skull.
,, 5. A Gaping Wound in the Head with Compound Comminuted Fracture of the Skull.

B. Throat and Neck

C. Clavicle

D. Humerus

Case 36. Fracture of the Humerus.
,, 37. Fracture of the Humerus with Rupture of Overlying Soft Tissue.
,, 38. Split in the Humerus.

E. Sternum, Overlying Soft Tissue, and True Ribs

Case 39. Tumors or Ulcers in the Breast Perhaps Resulting from Injury.
,, 40. Wound in the Breast.
,, 41. Infected or Possibly Necrotic Wound in the Breast.
,, 42. Sprain of the Sterno-Costal Articulations.
,, 43. Dislocation of the Sterno-Costal Articulations.
,, 44. Fractured Ribs.
,, 45. Bulging Tumors on the Breast.
,, 46. Abscess with Prominent Head on the Breast.

F. Shoulders

Case 47. Gaping Wound in the Shoulder.

G. Spinal Column

Case 48. Sprain in a Spinal Vertebra (incomplete).

As stated above, the arrangement of these groups with reference to each other clearly discloses the ancient surgeon's organization of his discussion, beginning with the head and proceeding downward presumably to the lower limbs and feet. *References* to such an order of treatment are discernible in Papyrus Ebers, where we find on the first page (I 4–5) that the ailments to be treated are " in this my head, in this my neck, in these my shoulders, in this my flesh, in these my members." This list is referred to again in the same page (I 7), but it has here fallen into confusion. In the actual arrangement of his materials the compiler of the Papyrus Ebers followed no plan or order of treatment, and it is difficult to imagine worse confusion than we find in the magical hodge-podge of *recipes* (not cases) making up the Papyrus Ebers. The other medical papyri display the same lack of any principle of arrangement. They are simply miscellaneous lists of *recipes*. In the organization of its materials, therefore, Papyrus Edwin Smith is unique. It is interesting to notice that this arrangement and order of discussion from the head downward has survived into modern times. Many modern surveys of human anatomy still follow this order of treatment, e. g., W. Spalteholz, *Handatlas der Anatomie des Menschen* (Leipzig, 1913).

It is observable also, that *within each of the above groups* there is likewise a definite principle of arrangement. In general the surgeon obviously intends to arrange his materials so as to pass from trifling to more serious or fatal cases. We see that he begins, in his treatment of each region, with slight superficial injuries involving only the overlying soft tissues, and then proceeds gradually to more serious injuries affecting the underlying bone. Thus in the first section in the treatise, the section dealing with the head (A), the first case in the ancient book is a superficial scalp wound, followed by a more gaping cut (Case 2). Both these wounds, while penetrating to the bone, leave it uninjured. The next case, however (Case 3), begins a series of deeper wounds affecting the skull, which suffers a " perforation " (Case 3), a " split " (Case 4), a compound comminuted fracture (Case 5), the same with rupture of the meningeal membranes (Case 6), and these are followed by similar, usually fatal, injuries of the skull (Cases 7–9). As the discussion passes by way of the frontal bone and the nose, to the maxillary and zygomatic regions, we again find first a flesh wound in the side of the nose (Case 14), then injuries of the bone, passing from " perforation " (Case 15) to a " split " (Case 16), and concluding with a compound comminuted fracture (Case 17). Then five cases concerning the temple (Cases 18–22) proceed from an injury of the soft tissue (Cases 18–19) through progressively more serious injuries of the temporal bone (Cases 20–22). This arrangement is especially apparent in the group of cases concerning the throat and neck (B), in which the surgeon again passes from injuries of the soft tissue to a " sprain " in the cervical vertebrae (Case 30), a " dislocation " (Case 31), a " displacement " (Case 32), and concludes with an obviously fatal case of a crushed cervical vertebra (Case 33). The large group (E) of eight cases in the region of the breast (Cases 39–46) quite clearly displays a similar arrangement ; but it has appended two cases on tumors and abscesses on the breast (Cases 45–46), perhaps having no connection with injuries and presumably for this reason thrown to the end of the section.

The discussion of *each case within itself* likewise discloses a systematic order of materials and topics—an arrangement which, with the exception of some elaboration in six cases, is always strictly followed. It is as follows :

1. Title.
2. Examination.
3. Diagnosis.
4. Treatment (unless a fatal case, considered untreatable).
5. Glosses (a little dictionary of obscure terms, if any, employed in the discussion of the case).

The elaboration of the above scheme, found in six cases (7, 8, 28, 34, 37, and 47), is due to the interesting fact that the surgeon's records disclosed an alternative group, or even more than one alternative group of symptoms, requiring in each case a different treatment, or demonstrating the certainty of a fatal outcome and hence followed by no suggestions for treatment. Thus in Case 8, a compound comminuted fracture of the skull, although there is little or no prospect of recovery, we first find all the above subdivisions of the discussion, including treatment, followed by a description of a second or alternative group of symptoms, which are regarded by the surgeon as certainly indicating a fatal issue of the case, and therefore not to be treated. (See same arrangement in Cases 34 and 37). More elaborate is Case 7, the longest case in our treatise, a gaping wound in the skull with perforation of the sutures. This case is first discussed in accordance with the above scheme. An alternative group of unfavorable symptoms is then enumerated, with indication that the patient cannot recover and hence suggesting no treatment. A second alternative set of symptoms (the third set in the discussion of the case) is then recounted by the surgeon, who seems to imply the possibility of recovery and therefore suggests a treatment. More elaborate, though not so long, is Case 47, in which the surgeon's record of experience shows him that he may normally expect a favorable development in two stages, each requiring its own special treatment. An alternative second stage, however, may be unfavorable and require a modification in treatment (the third in the discussion), followed by a favorable final (third) stage, with simple treatment (the fourth in the discussion).

The modern term available does not in every case correspond completely or perfectly with the ancient Egyptian idea, and the designations of the above subdivisions involve some accommodation—in one case, as we shall see, more than we should wish. It will be necessary, therefore, to discuss these subdivisions before the reader can understand their application in the present work.

1. *The Title*

The *title* consists of the word 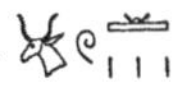 *šsꜣ·w*, "Instructions," followed by the identifying designation of the injury, together with indication of the region or organ affected, and sometimes with additional details. Thus the title of Case 4 reads :

" Instructions concerning a gaping wound in his head, penetrating to the bone, (and) splitting his skull."

In Case 6 the title is even fuller :

" Instructions concerning a gaping wound in his head, penetrating to the bone, smashing his skull, (and) rending open the brain of his skull."

These titles often lack specific indications of the exact region which would be found in a modern designation of such an injury. More specific in this particular is the title of Case 9 :

" Instructions concerning a wound in his forehead, smashing the shell of his skull."

Or Case 10 :

" Instructions concerning a wound in the top of his eyebrow."

In general it may be said that these titles are more accurate and specific in defining the *nature* of the injury than in indicating its exact position, although the latter indications are sometimes very precise and specific. Usually the title indicates roughly the position of the injury, leaving more accurate specification to the discussion; e. g. Case 31, a dislocation of a cervical vertebra does not indicate in the title which one is meant, but later discusses certain symptoms accompanying the dislocation of the *middle* one.

2. *The Examination*

The *examination* is conceived as spoken by some one addressing a second person, who is regularly designated by a pronoun in the second person singular. The form of the examination therefore is that of a teacher instructing a pupil that he shall do so and so. This fact raises the question whether this medical roll is not simply an instruction book. The indications are that the treatise has grown up as the product of an effort to record the instructions of a master in the very words which he used in the process of instruction, even including the person and number of the verbs addressed to the pupil. The same question applies to the relatively brief portions of the other ancient Egyptian medical rolls, which disclose the same form.

Logically the examination is a long protasis, of which the diagnosis forms the apodosis; in other words, the examination is the first part of a long conditional sentence comprising a recital of the symptoms which it is assumed the surgeon has observed that the patient displays, and which form the basis of the resulting conclusions expressed in the diagnosis. The examination therefore regularly begins thus: 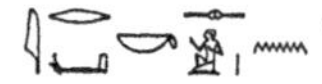 "If thou examinest a man having . . . " (see commentary in Case 1, I 3). This formula is always followed by the name of the injury or ailment already placed at the head of the discussion in the title of the case. It is probable that these words designating the injury or ailment and following the introductory formula of the examination were drawn from the examination for the purpose of serving as a title at the head of the discussion. The source of the title was, therefore, probably the examination.

The usual form and characteristics of the examination are most clearly observable in the following frequently recurring clauses:

" If thou examinest a man having, etc. . . .,
thou shouldst place thy hand upon him,"
or
" thou shouldst probe his wound,"
or
" thou shouldst inspect his wound,"
or
" thou shouldst examine his wound."
" Shouldst thou find . . . "

These assumed conditions then are followed by the conclusions of the diagnosis, introduced by the words, " Thou shouldst say concerning him : '. . .' " (see discussion of diagnosis below, pp. 45 ff.).

In six different cases (7, 8, 28, 34, 37 and 47) the surgeon's information or experience in each case have acquainted him with one or more alternative groups of symptoms. These may be drawn from (*a*) two cases of the same injury, which nevertheless exhibited different symptoms ; or (*b*) they may refer to two or more successive stages of the same case. Thus in Case 34, illustrating (*a*), the dislocation of the two clavicles is examined and described, and the surgeon is instructed to reduce the dislocated bones to their places. The treatise then adds :

 (XI 21).

" If, however, thou shouldst find his two collar-bones having a rupture (of the tissue) over it, etc." This second examination is then followed by a second diagnosis, originally indicating that a fatal outcome is to be expected,[1] and hence no treatment is prescribed. In the parallel case (37) the surgeon introduces the second examination with the same words (XII 19). That a second examination introduced in this way really discusses a *second case* is demonstrated by the fact that the two cases of a fractured humerus (Case 36 and 37) correspond exactly to two cases of a dislocated clavicle discussed as a first and second examination in Case 34.

In Case 8 illustrating (*b*) the second examination probably discloses merely a further or second stage of the same case. It is introduced by the words,  meaning, " Now as soon as thou findest that smash " (compound comminuted fracture, IV 10), in which we miss the adversative particle  *śwt*, "however," often indicating an alternative development of the case, e. g., the second examination in Case 28 (X 2).

In one case (7) we find after the first examination, a second and a third disclosing *two* alternative groups of symptoms. Both are introduced by  meaning : " If on the one hand thou findest that man . . . ; if on the other hand thou findest that man . . . " See the discussion in the introduction to Case 7. The second examination (III 8 ff.) is followed by a diagnosis with the unfavorable verdict 3, after which, as usual, no treatment is suggested ; the third (III 13) leads to no diagnosis, but is followed at once by a treatment, suggesting possible recovery.

In Case 47 the first examination is even followed by *four more*, a second, third, fourth, and fifth. The second examination simply records the progress of the case toward recovery. Hence it begins  (XVII 3), " If thou findest that wound," that is without any adversative particle, " however." On the other

[1] Verdict 1, actually in the text, is an evident error of the ancient scribe for verdict 3. See Case 34, commentary on XI 22.

hand the third examination begins with the same words, but including the adversative particle, " however " (XVII 6), and proceeds with unfavorable symptoms indicating an alternative second stage, feverish and critical and hence followed by a diagnosis concluding with the uncertain verdict 2, " An ailment with which I will contend." The surgeon's experience has taught him to expect either of two different developments following the stage just mentioned, and he therefore records a fourth and fifth examination. The first of these two final alternatives (the fourth examination) begins :

" If on the one hand thou shouldst find that man continuing to have fever " (XVII 12). The treatment which follows puts the man on normal diet without any medicine. The second of the two final alternatives, that is the fifth examination, begins :

" If on the other hand his fever abates " (XVII 13–14). It is followed by no diagnosis but merges into suggestions for very simple treatment until the patient recovers.

Very often the text of the examination does not disclose the *method* by which the surgeon makes a given observation, that is, the method is frequently taken for granted. The following methods of observation, however, are either expressly stipulated in the text, or are clearly implied.

(*a*) Answers elicited from the patient by questions which the surgeon addresses to him. Regarding a man with a wound in the temple the surgeon says, " If thou ask of him concerning his malady " (Case 20). Again of another man with a wound in the same region it is stated, " It is painful when he hears speech " (or noise, Case 21), an observation perhaps gained by questioning the sufferer.

(*b*) Ocular observations. In a case of a perforated temporal bone the surgeon is charged, " Thou shouldst inspect his wound " (Case 19); the word rendered " inspect " is the common verb " to see." Compare with this the injunction, " Thou shouldst examine his wound " (Case 26), which without doubt implies more than visual observation. In a case of serious injury to the skull the surgeon observes facial distortion : " both his eye-brows are drawn, while his face is as if he wept " (Case 7, III 11–12). The color of the patient's face, or of a wound or swelling, is frequently mentioned as a datum observed, e. g., ruddiness of the face (Case 7, III 10) ; paleness of the face (Case 7, IV 4). In order to aid visual observation in Case 22 we find the following directions regarding an ear affected by an injury in the temple, " Cleanse (the ear) for him with a swab of linen until thou seest its fragments (of bone)." In order to aid him in his observations the surgeon may also watch the effect or lack of effect when he addresses a remark to the patient. Thus in Case 22, a compound comminuted fracture of the temporal bone, the surgeon in this way demonstrates the patient's speechlessness. In the case of an injury in the same region the surgeon discovers that sound is painful to the patient's ear (Case 21), perhaps by watching some expression of pain on the patient's face, although it is possible that the patient actually answers the surgeon's remark; see p. 40, (*a*).

(*c*) Olfactory observations. In a case of perforated sutures of the skull we find that the surgeon observes that "the odor of the chest (crown) of his head is like the urine of sheep" (Case 7, III 11).

(*d*) Tactile observations. Besides directions to probe, the surgeon is very often charged, "Thou shouldst lay thy hand upon it" (the wound, Case 47). Again such an application of the hand is often assumed, when a given condition is recorded as observable "when thy hand touches him" (Case 39); "when thou pressest . . . with thy fingers" (Case 40); "if thou puttest thy hand upon his breast upon these tumors, (and) thou findest them very cool, there being no fever therein when thy hand touches him, . . . and they are bulging to thy hand" (Case 45). Very often conditions are recorded as observable "under thy fingers" (Case 4, II 4; Case 6, II 21; Case 8, IV 11, etc., etc.). Among such observations it is important to notice that the pulsations of the human heart are observed: "if . . . any physician put his hands (or) his fingers [upon the head, upon the back of the] head, upon the two hands, upon the pulse, upon the two feet" (Case 1, I 6–7). It is possible that this application of the hand or fingers is for the purpose of enabling the surgeon to count the pulse. See commentary on Case I, pp. 105–114. In the case of a dislocated mandible the surgeon is particularly instructed just how to place his fingers and his thumbs in order to force the bone back into its place (Case 25), and we shall see that he was inclined to include this kind of manipulation *in the examination* rather than in the treatment.

(*e*) Movements of parts of his body by the patient as directed by the surgeon. In a serious injury of the skull the surgeon is instructed thus, "Thou shouldst cause him (the patient) to lift his face" (Case 7, III 3). In examining injuries to the skull and the cervical vertebrae, "he (the surgeon) says to him (the patient): 'Look at thy two shoulders;' should his doing so be painful (even though) his neck turns around (only) a little, etc., etc." (Case 19). Similarly in treating a sprain in the cervical vertebrae we find the surgeon charged thus, "Thou shouldst say to him: 'Look at thy two shoulders and thy breast;' when he does so the seeing possible to him is painful" (Case 30). Again in a displacement of a cervical vertebra the same direction by the surgeon to the patient is followed by the observation, "He is unable to turn his face that he may look at his breast and his two shoulders" (Case 32). One of the most interesting of these tests by the surgeon is in the last case in the treatise, a sprain in the spinal vertebrae. The surgeon is directed as follows, "Thou shouldst say to him: 'Extend now thy two legs (and) contract them both (again).' When he extends them both, he contracts them both immediately because of the pain, etc." (Case 48).

We find that our ancient Egyptian practitioner was inclined to include some things in the examination which the modern surgeon would obviously classify with the treatment. It is quite natural that the cleansing of the ear to secure unobstructed observation should be included in the examination (Case 22). On the other hand we do not at first understand why our surgeon should include in the examination the process of stitching a gaping flesh wound in six cases out of the seven in which this mechanical process is prescribed (Cases 10, 14, 23, 26, 28, and 47). Similarly the application of adhesive plaster to draw together a wound is placed by our treatise in the examination (Case 47, XVII 3–4). We have already noted that the manipulation of a dislocated mandible to force it back into its proper place is included in the examination (Case 25). Over against these examples, however, it should be observed that a replacement of dislocated clavicles (Case 34), the setting of a fractured clavicle (Case 35), and the setting of a dislocated humerus (Case 36) are all three included in the treatment. Nevertheless it must be regarded as significant that eight out of eleven surgical operations are classified by our treatise with the *examination* rather than with the *treatment.* These facts suggest at least that what our ancient practitioner regarded as constituting a proper *treatment* must include the use or application of medicaments and recipes, the characteristic agencies of the physician, while the operations of the surgeon, so often consisting exclusively of mechanical processes, were not real treatment. He therefore placed the operation in the great majority of cases in the examination, and reserved for his treatment the use or application of alleviatory and curative medicaments, the *recipes* which so abound in all the other medical documents of ancient Egypt, and are so few and unimportant in our surgical treatise. There is here an intimation of a sharp distinction between the *surgeon* on the one hand and the *physician* on the other.

This distinction is illustrated by Case 9, the only case in our treatise, in which the method is obviously that of the recipe-vending physician as distinguished from the operating surgeon. The injury is a compound comminuted fracture of the frontal bone. There is no examination at all, properly speaking, and the place of the examination has been filled up by the words: "If thou examinest a man having a wound in his forehead, smashing the shell of his head." The introductory formula of the examination is retained, but no observations of any kind are recorded, and even the name of the injury is confusingly altered by the substitituon of the word "head" for the word "skull" employed in the title. Immediately following the above alleged examination is an absurd recipe for external application accompanied by a magical charm to be repeated over it when it is applied. It is obviously not an accident that the only typical case of the recipe-hawking physician in our treatise should contain no other examination properly speaking than an inaccurately worded repetition of the title. When we contrast this case and especially its lack of any observations in the examination with the surgeon's careful observation whether a wound in the skull is on the same side as the paralysis in the lower limbs (Case 8, IV 7), we cannot doubt that a case from one of the *recipe papyri* has found its way into our *surgical treatise.*

Disregarding Case 9, we have in our treatise a series of fifty-seven examinations, almost exclusively of injuries of the human body forming a group of observations furnishing us with the earliest known nucleus of fact regarding the anatomy, physiology, and pathology of the human body. Crude and elementary as they are, the method by which they were collected was scientific, and these observations, together with the diagnoses and the explanatory commentary in the ancient glosses, form the oldest body of science now extant.

Our treatise, then, is a series of discussions of *injuries,* not of diseases. In Case 39, which discusses certain tumors or ulcers on the breast, we find that these may have arisen from an injury ; and the only other instances of possible disease are two cases of tumors or boils on the breast (Cases 45 and 46). The remaining forty-five cases are all injuries. They range from slight flesh wounds to the gravest injuries to the bony structure of the body—injuries from which the patient cannot possibly recover. Many of these are such injuries as might have been incurred in the ordinary round of daily civil life ; others were evidently the result of murderous attack, presumably in battle. It is highly probably, if not certain, that our treatise is in part a record of surgical experience in war. The word " wound " occurs no less than 142 times in the forty-eight cases preserved. The reader should consult the commentary on the word " wound " in Case 1 (pp. 81–84).

Omitting Cases 39, 45, and 46, a general list of the injuries described in the remaining fifty-five examinations, arranged progressively from the less to the more serious, is as follows :

Twelve Flesh Wounds :

Scalp wound	Case	1
Gaping scalp wound	,,	2
Gaping wound in the eye-brow . . .	,,	10
Wound in the nostril	,,	14
Wound in the temple	,,	18
Perforation of the temple	,,	19
Slit in the outer ear	,,	23
Wound piercing the upper lip . . .	,,	26
Gaping wound in the chin	,,	27
Wound in the throat piercing to the gullet . .	,,	28 (two examinations)
Gaping wound in the shoulder . . .	,,	47 (five examinations)
Infected wound in the breast . . .	,,	41

Thirty-three Injuries to the Bones and Articulations :

Sprain of a cervical vertebra	Case	30	
,, ,, the sterno-costal articulations	,,	42	
,, ,, a spinal vertebra	,,	48	
Displacement of a cervical vertebra	,,	32	
Dislocation of the mandible	,,	25	
,, ,, a cervical vertebra	,,	31	
,, ,, both clavicles	,,	34	(two examinations)
,, ,, the ribs	,,	43	
Perforation of the skull	,,	3	
,, ,, sutures of the skull	,,	7	(three examinations)
,, of bones of the maxillary-zygomatic region	,,	15	
,, ,, the temporal bone	,,	20	
,, ,, a cervical vertebra	,,	29	
,, ,, the sternum	,,	40	
Split in the skull	,,	4	
,, ,, maxilla	,,	16	
,, ,, temporal bone	,,	21	
,, ,, humerus	,,	38	
Fracture of the nose	,,	11	
,, ,, nasal bone	,,	12	
,, ,, mandible	,,	24	
,, ,, both clavicles	,,	35	
,, ,, humerus	,,	36	
,, ,, ,, with rupture of overlying soft tissue	,,	37	(two examinations)
,, ,, ribs	,,	44	
Compound comminuted fracture of the skull	,,	5	
Compound comminuted fracture of the skull with rupture of meningeal membranes	,,	6	
Compound comminuted fracture of the skull displaying no external contusion	,,	8	(two examinations)
Compound comminuted fracture of the frontal bone	,,	9	
,, ,, ,, ,, nasal bone	,,	13	
,, ,, ,, ,, temporal bone	,,	22	
Impacted fracture of a cervical vertebra	,,	33	
Compound comminuted fracture of the maxilla	,,	17	

Full discussion of the above injuries and ailments will be found in the commentary accompanying the various cases. The range of these cases from the skull downward to the thorax and spinal vertebrae but not further downward is of course due to the loss of the continuation of the manuscript, which stops at the first case concerning the spinal vertebrae. This is the more regrettable in view of the fact that the inclusion of injuries of the brain (especially Case 6) would suggest that we might have expected in the lost portion the consideration of injuries of the internal organs, like the heart, lungs, stomach, etc.

The most noticeable gap in the type of injury treated is the lack of simple and less serious fracture of the skull. Simple fracture of a bone like the clavicle or the humerus is duly included (Cases 35 and 36), but in discussing injuries of the head the surgeon passes from scalp wounds directly to a perforation or split of the calvaria, and thence directly to compound comminuted fractures of the skull, including rupture of the meningeal membranes. It is possible that his use of the word "split" may have been loose enough to include the simple fracture. The reader should consult the commentary on Case 4.

Besides the injuries listed above, there is of course a considerable list of accompanying symptoms, local affections, and various pathological consequences noticed by the ancient surgeon in discussing the successive cases. For these the reader is referred to the text of the commentary on each case. It is needless to say that the present editor does not possess the competence to put together a comprehensive discussion on the pathological knowledge displayed in this ancient treatise. It is highly desirable that this should be done. Probably the most important fact disclosed by our treatise is the surgeon's discovery of the brain as the seat of nervous control of the body, and his knowledge of the fact that such control in the brain was localized.

3. *The Diagnosis*

The diagnosis is always introduced by the words: 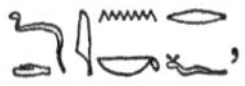, "Thou shouldst say concerning him" (the patient), addressed to the student or young surgeon by some unknown speaker, presumably the unknown lecturer, or author of the treatise. As we have found to be the case in the examination, the form of the diagnosis likewise is that of the instruction of a master addressed to a pupil. The concluding statement of the diagnosis, however, consists of an utterance very often in the *first* person, being a statement placed in the mouth of the student or young surgeon by the instructor. What the young practitioner or student is thus charged to say, therefore, consists of two parts: *first*, "One having . . . (followed by the description of the ailment); and *second*, a concluding statement by the young surgeon himself in the first person, expressing his coming course of action toward the case. The diagnosis thus has the following form:

"Thou shouldst say concerning him" (the patient):

a. "'One having . . .'" (followed by the description of the ailment).

b. "'An ailment which I will treat'."

The second part (*b*) of the above diagnosis is always one of three different statements, varying according to the degree of seriousness disclosed by the symptoms in the case. These three statements are as follows :

1. " An ailment which I will treat."
2. " An ailment with which I will contend."
3. " An ailment not to be treated."

It will be seen then, that on the basis of an examination, our treatise classifies all cases under three categories, as : 1. Certainly successfully treatable ; 2. possibly curable ; and 3. untreatable. These three verdicts are not prognoses ; they are not so much statements regarding the *cases*, as they are each the surgeon's *declaration of his own future course of procedure*. Each verdict is simply a practical statement of the course the surgeon proposes to follow toward a case disclosed by the examination to be such and such.

The question might be raised as to whether the verdict belongs to the diagnosis or to the treatment, for it follows the former and precedes the latter, and might be considered as belonging to either. In two cases we have the verdict connected by a preposition directly with the treatment. In Case 39 the surgeon says, " An ailment which I will treat with the fire-drill ; " and in Case 46 he says, " An ailment which I will treat with cold applications." The same connection is found four times in Papyrus Ebers, when the surgeon four times says, " An ailment which I will treat with the lancet " (e.g. Pap. Ebers 106, 20). It is probable that these six occurrences of an inseparable connection between verdict and treatment are simply illustrations of the naturally close relation between the two in the mind of the Egyptian. Grammatically we cannot doubt that the verdict is part of the diagnosis ; for being always expressed in the first person it is obviously a part of the utterance of the surgeon following the injunction, " Thou shouldst say," as already demonstrated in the above discussion. In the cases where the verdict constitutes the entire diagnosis, the words " Thou shouldst say concerning him " have not been prefixed. There are only three such cases in the treatise. Of these, two (6 and 8, second diagnosis) have verdict 3, and in the third (the second diagnosis of Case 34) it is obvious that verdict 1 is an error of the ancient scribe for verdict 3. Disregarding the purely alleviatory measures in Case 6, we find that no treatment follows any of these three verdicts, and we might here understand that verdict 3 more or less fills the entire blank left by the lack of diagnosis or treatment.

Logically the diagnosis as a whole is a conclusion based on conditions established by the examination and stated there. The diagnosis is grammatically an apodosis, of which the examination is the protasis. On this point the above discussion of the examination should be compared. In the forty-eight cases discussed in our treatise there are fifty-two of these verdicts. Five cases contain two verdicts, according as the surgeon's findings vary (Cases 7, 8, 34, 37, and 47). As we have already noticed in discussing the examination (pp. 42–43), Case 9 contains no such verdict. The lack of this characteristic, together with the fact that the case contains no diagnosis of any kind, relegates this case to the class of magical recipes drawn from the recipe papyri employed by the recipe-vending physicians. Its presence does not alter the unique character of our treatise, as an assemblage of over fifty groups of symptoms, each group the result of an examination and followed by the surgeon's verdict in every case. It should be noted that the word *unique* employed in the preceding statement is applied with exactness. None of the other surviving medical papyri of ancient Egypt contains such a body of case discussions, each one thus assigned to one of three different classes. Indeed verdict No. 3, "an ailment not to be treated," is unknown in any of the other Egyptian medical papyri, and is therefore one of the important evidences of the unique character of the Edwin Smith Surgical Papyrus (see commentary, Case 5, II 15). Verdict No. 2, "an ailment which I will contend with," is found twice in Papyrus Ebers (105, 12, and 105, 19–20), but is unknown otherwise outside of the Edwin Smith Papyrus (see commentary, Case 4, II 6). As might be expected, verdict No. 1 is better known. It is found twice in the Berlin Medical Papyrus (No. 3038, Nos. 154 and 161), once in the Hearst Papyrus (No. 174; 12, 2) and sixteen times in Papyrus Ebers, fourteen of which are in the concluding group of suppurating sores at the end of the papyrus (see commentary herein on Case 1, I 2). In referring to these verdicts or statements by the surgeon, it will be found convenient to designate them by the numbers already given them above, and call them verdict 1, verdict 2 or verdict 3, as the case may require.

The most important among them, as we have already seen, is verdict 3. Although unknown in any of the other ancient Egyptian medical papyri, it occurs, as already stated above, no less than fourteen times in Papyrus Edwin Smith. In one of these cases (Case 17), this verdict has been inserted by evident error of the scribe. Of the remaining thirteen all but three are left without any suggestion of treatment, and in the three exceptions the treatise suggests only slight alleviatory measures not expected to cure. The inclusion of these thirteen hopeless cases (about one fourth of the material in the treatise as preserved to us) is a remarkable evidence of the surgeon's scientific interest in recording and discussing the observable facts in a group of cases for which he could suggest no treatment. The papyri which contain nothing else but recipes, that is *treatments*, have of course found no place for such discussions, and this fact emphasizes the significance of our papyrus as consisting of a group of observed *cases*, quite irrespective of the possibility of treatment, which in the majority of the cases that he declines to treat is not even mentioned.

Parallel with the systematic use of these three verdicts is a similar series of temporal clauses bearing more directly on the condition of the patient, although not so regularly employed, and placed at the end of the *treatment*. These read :

A. " Until he recovers."

B. " Until the period of his injury passes by."

C. " Until thou knowest that he has reached a decisive point."

Of these clauses A is commonly used with verdict 1, B is found with all three verdicts, while C properly belongs to doubtful cases with verdict 2. See commentary on these three clauses in Case 1 (I 3), Case 3 (I 23) and Case 4, Gloss C. They do not add any precision to the verdict itself, except possibly in the case of A, which intimates certain recovery.

To an understanding of the real significance of the ancient surgeon's diagnosis, it is essential to observe that in the verdict, *b*, at the end of the diagnosis, we have a statement invariably present, and fairly precise in its practical indications for the surgeon. Indeed, as we have already noted, in three cases (6, 8, and 34), *the verdict constitutes the entire diagnosis*. This is the more intelligible, when we note that in the first two cases (6 and 8) it is verdict 3 which thus serves as the entire diagnosis. In Case 34 likewise there can be no doubt that verdict 3 also served as the entire diagnosis, although the notoriously inaccurate scribe has written verdict 1 (see commentary on Case 34, second diagnosis, XI 22).[1] The verdict, therefore, which might sometimes stand alone as a sufficient diagnosis, might very naturally be accompanied, if at all, by only a very brief additional description of the case in *a*. The following statistics are instructive :

A. Diagnosis consists of *b*, that is, a verdict only . . . . . 3 cases
B. Diagnosis consists of *a* and *b*, thus :
  1. *a*, a verbatim repetition of the title only, + *b* . . . . . 20 ,,
  2. *a*, an abbreviated repetition of the examination, + *b* . . . 15 ,,
  3. *a*, including conclusions based on observations stated in the examination, + *b* . . . . 12 ,,

It will be seen that the only indispensable part of the diagnosis is *b*, the verdict. We observe also that the verdict may be preceded either, *first*, by a mere mention of the name of the case, or *second*, by a repetition of some of the observations stated in the examination, or *third* and finally, by a statement of conclusions based on the observations brought out by the examination.[2] This third group, consisting of thirteen

[1] The lack of any diagnosis in Case 9 has been discussed above, p. 47. It is due to the fact that Case 9 is not a case discussion, as are all the other 47 cases in our treatise, but simply a *recipe*. In view of this fact the lack of a verdict has no significance.

[2] The above statistics are, by cases, as follows :

1. *a* is verbatim repetition of title only in Cases 2, 10, 11, 12, 13, 15, 16, 18, 25, 30, 32, 34, 35, 36, 38, 42, 43, 45 (title even abbreviated in diagnosis), 46, 48 ; total 20 cases.

diagnoses containing *conclusions* drawn directly from observations recorded in the examination, forms perhaps the most important body of materials in the whole treatise; for they constitute the earliest existent evidences of an inductive process in the history of the human mind, in so far as the surviving documents have revealed it to us. It is interesting to note that such conclusions have been made in about one fourth of the cases preserved to us in this document. It will be worth while, therefore, to enumerate these twelve cases, and examine briefly the conclusions made in the diagnoses.

In the first case in the treatise, although its fragmentary condition requires much restoration, a superficial wound in the head is found by the surgeon in the examination to be a rupture of the overlying soft tissue, " not having a gash ; " and in the diagnosis he concludes that " his wound does not have two lips."

In Case 7, a wound in the head, penetrating the skull, the surgeon's examination discloses that " it is painful for him to open his mouth " (III 3). Thereupon the surgeon states among other things in the diagnosis : " the cord of his mandible is contracted," perhaps indicating that the patient is suffering from tetanus. Otherwise the diagnosis is a repetition of the examination. On the basis of alternative symptoms (III 8–12) the surgeon formulates a second diagnosis (III 12–13), but the only new conclusion unfortunately contains an unintelligible term (𓏏𓇋𓄿[hieroglyph] *ty'*). See commentary.

Case 8 contains the most important diagnosis in the treatise. The examination has disclosed an unusual case : a compound comminuted fracture of the skull without any visible external injury. As phrased in the examination the injury is " a smash in his skull under the skin of his head, there being no wound at all upon it." This is explained in a gloss as meaning, " a smash of the shell of his skull, the flesh of his head being uninjured " (IV 12–13). It is obvious that the lack of any externally visible trace of the injury might easily mislead the practitioner to conclude that the patient's condition of partial paralysis of the lower limbs on the same side as the injury, and distortion of the eye likewise on the same side as the injury, might be due to *disease*. The ancient author was so keenly aware of the real nature of the facts in the case and the character of the conclusion to be set forth in the diagnosis, that he forgot entirely his otherwise invariable formula for introducing the diagnosis (" Thou shouldst say concerning him," etc.), and began the warning diagnosis at once with the admonishing words : " Thou shouldst account him one whom something entering from the outside has smitten " (IV 7–8). This immediate insistence on the external cause, as contrasted with some internal disease, is further interestingly explained in a gloss which states, " As for ' One whom something entering from the outside has smitten,' . . . it means one whom something entering from the outside presses, on

2. *a* is abbreviated repetition of examination in Cases 3, 4, 5, 14, 21, 23, 26, 27, 28, 33, 37 (twice), 40, 41, 44, 47 ; total 15 cases.

3. *a* includes conclusions based on observations stated in the examination in Cases 1, 7 (twice), 8, 17, 19, 20, 22, 24, 29, 31, 39, 47 ; total 12 cases.

the side of him having this injury " (Gloss C, IV 15–16). The attention given to the side of the head which has received the injury, in connection with a specific reference to the side of the body nervously affected, is in itself evidence that in this case the ancient surgeon was already beginning observations on the localization of functions in the brain. We have here the earliest known observations on the connection between the brain and the nervous system, disclosing to us man for the first time dimly aware of the mysteries of his own body and its intelligent control. It was interest in this problem which led our ancient surgeon to make these observations ; for he concludes his diagnosis with verdict 3, and can suggest only attention to the sufferer's comfort, without hope of his recovery. The entire extraordinary diagnosis is due to the surgeon's scientific interest in the case. Detailed discussion of this case will be found in the commentary on Case 8 below.

In Case 17, a compound comminuted fracture of the maxilla, the surgeon notes in the examination : "it is painful when he opens his mouth because of it" (the injury). The brief diagnosis is made up chiefly of repetition of the statements in the examination, but adds, "he is speechless." The inclusion of this observation in the diagnosis, rather than in the examination, suggests that the surgeon has made the conclusion that the patient is speechless from the observation that it is painful for him to open his mouth. In Case 13 (VI 6), the observation, " he is speechless," is included in the examination, where it would seem more properly to belong. The grammatical construction of examination as a group of observed conditions, and of diagnosis as a group of conclusions based on the observed conditions, is obvious, but the line drawn by the surgeon between observation and conclusion was not always a sharp one, as this example shows.

In this respect the next case (19) is much clearer. The patient has suffered a perforation of the temple, possibly affecting the bone. In the examination we find the following : " Thou shouldst inspect his wound, saying to him, ' Look at thy two shoulders.' Should his doing so be painful, (even though) his neck turns around (only) a little for him," etc., etc. Thereupon the diagnosis states : " He suffers with stiffness in his neck ; " but otherwise contains only a repetition of the title.

In the next case, a wound in the temple perforating the bone (Case 20), the examination is one of the most interesting, and certainly the most picturesque in the whole treatise. The diagnosis, as in Case 19, affirms stiffness in the neck, although the examination does not refer to the matter at all, as in Case 19. Speechlessness, however, affirmed in the diagnosis, is carefully based on the facts of the examination, as we see by rendering the statements concerned, just as they stand in examination and diagnosis: "If thou examinest a man having a wound in his temple, . . . ; if thou ask of him concerning his malady and he speak not to thee ; . . . ; thou shouldst say concerning him, ' One having a wound in his temple, . . . (and) he is speechless '."

In Case 22, a compound comminuted fracture of the temporal bone, we find in the examination, " if thou callest to him (and) he is speechless and cannot speak." Here the examination has included both the observation and the conclusion ; and in stating the conclusion as the diagnosis does (" he is speechless," VIII 13), it simply repeats the logical process already anticipated by the conclusion stated in the examination. The diagnosis concludes that there is a discharge of blood from the nostrils, based on observations in the examination ; but its statement that the patient suffers with stiffness of the neck is not drawn from any observation in the examination.

The discussion of the fractured mandible in Case 24 does not exhibit a very clear logical connection between examination and diagnosis, and suggests that the surgeon in pronouncing such a diagnosis, was often drawing on experience tacitly assumed, and nowhere expressed. We find in this diagnosis two statements which are really new observations: "the wound over it (the fracture) being broken open, . . . (and) he has fever from it." The examination does not contain any basis for these statements.

Case 29, a gaping wound in a cervical vertebra, furnishes a good illustration of close connection between diagnosis and examination. The latter states, " he is unable to look at his two shoulders and his breast," corresponding to which the diagnosis concludes : " he suffers with stiffness in his neck." Otherwise the diagnosis is repetition of the examination.

In Case 31, a dislocation of a cervical vertebra, the examination discloses among other interesting evidences of paralysis, the fact that " urine drops from his member without his knowing it." The diagnosis then concludes " his urine dribbles." In an explanatory gloss (X 21–22) we are told that this statement " his urine dribbles," means " that urine drops from his phallus, and cannot hold back for him," indicating the paralysis of the controlling nerves concerned.

Case 39 concerning obscure ulcers or tumors on the breast, perhaps resulting from some injury, is a difficult case to understand. The examination discloses that " swellings have spread with pus over his breast," and the diagnosis concludes that the patient has tumors on his breast which " produce ⸢cists⸣ of pus."

Finally in Case 47, a gaping wound in the shoulder, the mention of fever (XVII 11) is probably rather a new observation than a conclusion based on observations in the examination.

4. *The Treatment*

In discussing the foregoing list of fifty-eight examinations, the ancient surgeon does not always decide to treat. It is an important fact in properly appraising our treatise, that out of fifty-eight examinations the surgeon omits all suggestion of treatment in sixteen. These sixteen instances are an extraordinary evidence of the surgeon's interest in the pathological conditions exhibited, as mere knowledge of the human body and its workings. They form a unique group in Egyptian medicine ; for the other medical papyri known to us, made up as they are exclusively of *recipes*, by their very nature constitute a series of *treatments,* whereas as we have stated, these sixteen instances in Papyrus Edwin Smith consist of a body of *observations* which lead the surgeon to the conclusion that no treatment is to be undertaken.

Twelve of these sixteen instances have the unfavorable verdict 3 appended, and of these twelve, ten are followed by no suggested action of any kind; while of the remaining two, one suggests a sitting posture for the patient (Case 8, I), and the other (Case 5) warns against binding and prescribes a normal diet without any medicine. Three of the sixteen have the uncertain verdict 2, for one of which (Case 21) the surgeon can suggest only normal diet; for another (Case 45) he explicitly states, "There is no treatment," while he makes no suggestion for Case 47, II 1. Finally one of the sixteen (Case 47, II 2), an unfavorable alternative development of the case, receives no verdict at all, and suggests no treatment beyond the caution against binding, and the admonition to normal diet without the use of any medicine.

List of cases omitting treatment, either by explicit instructions or by omission of all reference to any treatment:

Case 45. Bulging tumors on the breast;	Verdict 2; statement: "There is no treatment."
Case 47, II 1. Gaping flesh wound in shoulder with inflammation and discharge;	Verdict 2; all reference to treatment omitted.
Case 47, II 2. Gaping flesh wound in shoulder and persistent fever;	No verdict; binding forbidden; normal diet, without medicine.
Case 31. Dislocation of a cervical vertebra;	Verdict 3; all reference to treatment omitted.
Case 34, II. Dislocation of both clavicles with rupture of overlying soft tissue;	Verdict 3[1]; ,, ,, ,, ,, ,,
Case 7, II. Perforation of sutures of the skull; symptoms of tetanus;	Verdict 3; ,, ,, ,, ,, ,,
Case 21. Split in the temporal bone;	Verdict 2; normal diet, no medicine.
Case 24. Fracture of the mandible;	Verdict 3; all reference to treatment omitted.
Case 37, II. Fracture of the humerus; rupture of overlying soft tissue;	Verdict 3; ,, ,, ,, ,, ,,
Case 44. Fractured ribs, overlying flesh wound, ribs broken through (probably compound fracture);	Verdict 3; ,, ,, ,, ,, ,,
Case 5. Compound comminuted fracture of the skull;	Verdict 3; binding forbidden, normal diet, without medicine.
Case 8, I. Compound comminuted fracture of the skull, no visible external contusion;	Verdict 3; sitting posture till crisis.
Case 8, II. Same, with less favorable conditions;	Verdict 3; all reference to treatment omitted.
Case 13. Compound comminuted fracture of the nasal bone;	Verdict 3; ,, ,, ,, ,, ,,
Case 22. Compound comminuted fracture of the temporal bone;	Verdict 3; ,, ,, ,, ,, ,,
Case 33. Impacted fracture of a cervical vertebra;	Verdict 3; ,, ,, ,, ,, ,,

It will be seen that in this group of almost exclusively very serious cases, if the surgeon has any hope of recovery at all, he depends on nature to do its healing work.

[1] Verdict 1 by error.

He may take precautions, like the sitting posture in Case 8, I, but the recovery is the work of nature, not of any remedies the surgeon can offer. This is the doctrine which is later so prominent in Hippocratic medicine.

Out of forty-five injuries in our treatise, there are forty-two instances in which treatment is prescribed at some stage. This treatment may be:

(*a*) Exclusively mechanical or surgical (3 cases).

(*b*) A combination of purely surgical treatment with external use of medicaments (20 cases).

(*c*) Exclusive use of medicaments externally applied (19 cases).

(*a*) *Exclusively mechanical or surgical treatment*

The mechanical appliances and processes upon which our surgeon relied do not form a long list, but they are of interest in view of the fact that some of them appear in our document for the first time in the literature of surgery. It is a remarkable fact that actual physical survivals of evidence of surgical procedure in ancient Egypt, as recovered by modern investigation, have been unexpectedly scanty. A systematic study of the large number of hard bronze implements now preserved in our museums would undoubtedly disclose a certain number which are demonstrably surgical instruments. The writer has himself noticed small knives which had every appearance of being scalpels and lancets; but no thoroughgoing and exhaustive examination of all such surviving implements by a surgeon or an archeologist familiar with ancient surgical appliances has ever been made. We are still awaiting a final monograph on this subject.[1]

It has been stated that "there is a complete absence of evidence, in all bodies [ancient burials] hitherto examined, of surgical procedure apart from splints."[2] It is indeed true that the only additional evidence of surgical procedure disclosed by the ancient bodies, besides Dr. G. Elliot Smith's discovery of splints, is Dr. Hooton's observation of the boring of a Fourth Dynasty mandible for the purpose of draining an abscess under a tooth.[3] While very little evidence of the surgical processes employed has survived in the ancient bodies, it is to be remarked, however, that the success of Egyptian surgery in setting broken bones is very fully demonstrated in the large number of well-joined fractures found in the ancient skeletons. Unfortunately these do not reveal the method employed by the operator. Under these circumstances the written evidence to be drawn from our papyrus is the more interesting.

List of surgical processes and devices in Pap. Edwin Smith:

Lint, made from a vegetable tissue, and frequently applied both as a vehicle for

[1] Historians of medicine have taken casual notice of such instruments, and Egyptian surgical instruments of bronze have been collected by Prof. Meyer-Steineg. See Meyer-Steineg and Sudhoff, *Geschichte der Medicin*, Jena, 2d ed., 1922, p. 29, abb. 16.

[2] G. Elliot Smith and Warren R. Dawson, *Egyptian Mummies*, London, 1924, p. 161.

[3] See *Harvard African Studies*, I, Dr. E. A. Hooton, "Oral Surgery in Egypt during the Old Empire," Pl. I. See also *infra*, Pl. I, Fig. 1.

the medicaments externally used, and as an absorbent of blood, secretions, etc. It was called *ftt*; see full commentary in Case 1 (I 3).

Plugs or *swabs of linen* usually in pairs, inserted into the nostrils in cases of injury to the nose, both for the purpose of cleansing, and when saturated with a medicament, for the purpose of applying the latter. They are called " *ššm·wy* of linen." See full commentary in Case 7 (III 18), Case 11 (V 11), and Case 14 (VI 9–11).

Bandages, made of linen and manufactured for surgical use by the embalmers, at least in the case of a particular bandage known as " covering for physicians' use " (Case 9, IV 21). The commonest Egyptian word for " bandage " is *ššd*, although this word occurs in only three cases in our document (Case 2, I 16, Case 9, V 5 and Case 10, V 9 ; see commentary, V 5), for the probable reason that the discussion, in its instructions to the surgeon, regularly employs the verb, that is *wt*, " to bind " (see Case 1, I 2) or *wdy*, "to apply" (see Case 11, V 11–12). Medicaments applied externally were almost always bandaged on. The art of mummification developed surprising skill in bandaging.

Adhesive plaster, made of bands or strips of linen, always in pairs, especially applied transversely across gaping flesh wounds, or as the ancient surgeon himself said, " to the two lips of the gaping wound, in order to cause that one join to the other " (Case 10, V 9). Such plaster was called "two *ʾ-wy* of linen." (See commentary in Case 2, I 15 and Case 10, V 9). See also following paragraph.

Surgical stitching, for the first time in the history of ancient surgery, as far as known to us. In a list of six " gaping wounds," all of them flesh wounds, the surgeon is in each case charged, as for example in Case 10, a gaping wound over the eye-brow, " Thou shouldst draw together for him his gash with stitching." The new word designating the noun " stitching " or the verb " to stitch " is *ydr*. See commentary on Case 10, V 6. At stages in these cases the surgeon used also his adhesive plaster. Whether the surgeon is applying plaster, or using stitching, the result of the process is in both cases designated by the verb *nḏry*, "to draw together."

Cauterization, also for the first time in ancient medical literature as early as this. It occurs in only one treatment, in a case of unidentified tumors or ulcers on the breast. The verb is *šʾm*, " to burn," and the instrument employed was the fire-stick or fire-drill used by the Egyptians for kindling fire. See commentary in Case 39, XIII 6 and 7.

Splints or *braces* of three different kinds were known to the practice of the surgeons, as described in the Papyrus Edwin Smith :

(1) A "brace of wood padded with linen," for insertion in the mouth of a patient suffering with constriction of ligaments controlling the mandible (tetanus ?), in order to hold the mouth open and permit feeding with liquid food. It is called " *mḏʾ·t* of wood." See commentary in Case 7 (III 14). There is no reference to this device in connection with fractures.

(2) A kind of splint said to be "of linen" is applied in two different fractures of the humerus (Cases 36 and 37) and one of the clavicle (Case 35). In view of the ancient wooden splints, carefully wound or even padded with linen, as found by Dr. Elliot Smith, this Egyptian term  "*sš* of linen" may designate possibly a wooden splint wound with linen, the modifier, "of linen" being loosely used. See commentary on Case 7 (III 18). On the other hand it is conceivable that a "*sš* of linen" may be a strip of stiff "cartonnage" moulded to the broken limb, and much resembling the modern surgical cast in its physical make-up. See commentary on Case 7 (III 18) and Case 12 (V 18).

(3) A stiff roll of linen, made by rolling a strip of linen into a more or less solid and rigid post. It was used especially where a *soft* splint or support was needed, as applied to a broken nose (Cases 11 and 12) or a dislocated clavicle (Case 34). See commentary on Case 11 (V 13). They were called 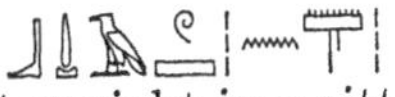 literally "posts of linen."

Supports for maintaining a patient upright in a sitting posture, especially in cases of injury to the skull producing a condition which makes motion dangerous and forbids lying down. These supports are always in pairs and are made of sun-dried brick, or *adobe,* probably moulded to fit the figure of the patient, on each side under his arms. They were called 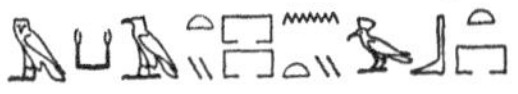 "two supports of *adobe.*" See commentary on Case 4 (II 7).

Additions to this list of surgical devices might be made from Papyrus Ebers.

List of cases prescribing exclusively mechanical or surgical treatment:

Case 39. Tumors or ulcers on the breast perhaps arising from an injury;	Verdict 1. Cauterization; "wound treatment."
Case 48. Sprain in spinal vertebra;	Verdict 1. Patient placed prostrate on his back. N.B.: End of document leaves treatment incomplete.
Case 7, III. Perforation of sutures of skull; symptoms of tetanus; final more favorable stage;	No verdict. Linen-padded, wooden brace to hold mouth open in order to feed liquid food; sitting posture supported on *adobe* props.

(*b*) *Combination of surgical treatment with external use of medicaments*

In twenty cases we find a combination of purely surgical treatment with the external application of medicaments. The simplest flesh wounds are drawn together by adhesive plaster in strips, as in Case 2, a scalp wound, and Case 27, a flesh wound in the chin. If the flesh wound is deeper or forms a yawning gash, and in one case even though the bone beneath is injured, the surgeon resorts to stitching, which we find in a list of seven cases (Cases 3, 10, 14, 23, 26, 28, and 47). Full discussion of stitching will be found in Case 10 (V 6). In some cases both stitching and adhesive plaster were employed in succession on the same wound.

Passing from flesh wounds to injuries to the bones we find the reduction of dislocations carefully described, e. g., dislocated clavicle (Case 34). The reduction of a dislocated mandible (Case 25) is described in terms showing that the position of the surgeon's hands was identical with that depicted in the illustration of the same operation in the commentary on Hippocrates by Apollonius of Kitium in the first century B.C. (see Pl. VI). The treatise describes also the reduction of a number of broken bones. We find among others directions for setting a fracture of the clavicle (Case 35), and two different fractures of the humerus (Cases 36 and 37). When the injured humerus is accompanied by a serious rupture of the overlying soft tissue the injury is regarded as fatal. With each of these fractures two of the splints called  "*sš* of linen" were applied, as the Egyptian said "one of the two on the inside of his arm (humerus), the other of the two on the underside of his arm" (XII 13). This is in contrast with the two cases of fracture (femur and forearm) which Elliot Smith found still wrapped in the surgeon's splints. In the case of each fracture the splints were *three* in number. The modern usage in native village practice is with two splints, just as prescribed in our papyrus.[1]

The effectiveness of the Egyptian surgeon's methods in the use of such splints is demonstrated by Elliot Smith's report on more than a hundred examples of fracture of the forearm. He found among these only one example of ununited fracture of the ulna, and, as he further says, "in spite of the fact that a certain proportion of the cases of fracture (always due to direct violence) must have been compound, only one of my series (of more than 100 examples) shows any signs of suppuration having occurred."[2] In view of the frequency of fracture of the forearm as found still visible in ancient Egyptian bodies, it is remarkable that our treatise leaves the arm, after discussing two cases of fracture of the humerus, without any reference to fracture of the forearm. A broken nose, or a fractured nasal bone, or a dislocated clavicle, must be supported in place by softer splints, stiff rolls of linen, called 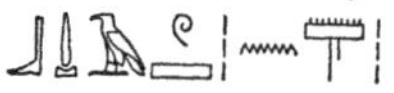 "posts of linen." See Cases 11 and 12 and Case 34.

The surgeon was evidently at a loss regarding the immediate mechanical manipulation of a serious fracture of the skull. He recognized the importance of quiet, as we have seen above (p. 55), combined with a sitting posture maintained by *adobe* piers supporting the patient upright, with normal diet but with no binding of the injury and no medicine (see Case 4). After initial probing, however, it would seem that no direct manipulation of the wound was attempted. Neither do the surviving bodies show any indications that the process of trepanning was practised by ancient Egyptian surgeons.

It is an interesting fact that in our ancient treatise there is a sharp distinction between such mechanical and surgical manipulations as we have been discussing and the treatment with medicaments. In nearly all these cases of injury the surgeon is

[1] Dr. G. Elliot Smith, *The British Medical Journal*, 1908, V. 1, p. 734. [2] *Ibid.*, p. 733.

charged to probe the wound, a process carried out with the fingers in most instances, that is, palpation. It is natural that the directions to probe should be included in the examination, to which the probing would contribute essential information ; but we would not expect that a process like the reduction of a dislocation or the stitching of a flesh wound should be included in the text of the examination. Nevertheless such is often the case in Papyrus Edwin Smith. The directions for the reduction of the dislocated mandible in Case 25 are all *included in the examination*. Of our seven examples of surgical stitching, six include the directions to do so in the examination. The distinction between surgical and medical practice here suggested has been discussed above (p. 42).

In the therapeutic which the surgeon combined with the above purely surgical procedures, he was still in an archaic stage, suggesting that surgery was far in advance of medicine. In nearly all the cases which our surgeon regarded as at all treatable, he followed up his surgery with the application of medicaments. These were for the most part very primitive in character. His favorite remedy was " fresh meat " regularly applied to a wound on the first day, but no longer, and usually followed by a daily application of lint saturated with an ointment of grease and honey. In cases of great soreness of the tissues, as after the reduction of a dislocated mandible, he applied a mixture of honey and an unknown mineral called *imru* (*ymrw*). All of these medicaments were regularly bound on. We shall later see that some of his *materia medica* were useful agents.

List of cases combining surgery with external use of medicaments :

Flesh Wounds (*except the last, Case* 3)

Case 2. Flesh wound in the scalp ;	Drawn together with adhesive plaster; fresh meat bound on, first day ; then honey-ointment on lint, bound on.
Case 27. Flesh wound in the chin ;	Drawn together with adhesive plaster ; fresh meat bound on, first day ; then honey-ointment on lint, bound on.
Case 10. Flesh wound in eye-brow ;	Drawn together with stitching ; fresh meat bound on, first day ; followed by adhesive plaster ; honey-ointment.
Case 14. Flesh wound in one side of nose ;	Drawn together with stitching ; cleansed with two swabs of linen ; fresh meat bound on, first day ; honey-ointment on lint, bound on.
Case 23. Slit in outer ear ;	Drawn together with stitching ; stiff rolls of linen as supports behind ear ; honey-ointment on lint, bound on.
Case 26. Flesh wound in upper lip ;	Drawn together with stitching ; fresh meat bound on, first day ; honey-ointment.
Case 28. I. Wound in the throat penetrating to the gullet ;	Drawn together with stitching ; fresh meat bound on, first day ; honey-ointment on lint, bound on ; 28 II, dry lint ; normal diet, no medicine.

Case 47, I 1. Gaping flesh wound in the shoulder;	Drawn together with stitching; fresh meat bound on, first day.
Case 47, I 2. Same, second stage;	Adhesive plaster; honey-ointment on lint, bound on.
Case 47, II 3. Same; fever and inflammation abate;	Honey-ointment on lint, bound on.
Case 3. Perforation of the skull;	Drawn together with stitching; fresh meat applied without binding, first day; normal diet, no medicine; honey-ointment on lint, bound on.

Bone injuries

Case 34, I. Dislocation of both clavicles;	Reduction of dislocated bones; application of stiff linen rolls as splints; honey-ointment.
Case 25. Dislocated mandible;	Reduction of dislocated bone; *imru* and honey bound on.
Case 35. Fracture of both clavicles;	Reduction of fractured bones; application of *sš*-splints; *imru* bound on; afterward honey every day.
Case 36. Fracture of humerus;	Reduction of fractured bone; application of *sš*-splints; *imru* bound on; afterward honey every day.
Case 37, I. Fracture of humerus, with rupture of overlying soft tissue;	Reduction omitted; application of *sš*-splints; *imru* bound on; afterward honey-ointment on lint every day.
Case 11. Broken nose;	Cleansing nostrils with two swabs of linen; insertion of two swabs of greased linen to reduce swelling; application of two stiff rolls of linen as splints; honey-ointment on lint, bound on.
Case 12. Fracture of nasal bone;	Reduction of fracture; cleansing nostrils with two swabs of linen; insertion of two plugs of greased linen; application of stiff rolls of linen as splints; honey-ointment on lint, bound on.
Case 4. Split in the skull;	Warning against binding; sitting posture supported on two *adobe* piers; normal diet, no medicine; grease applied to head, neck, and shoulders.

(c) *Exclusive use of medicaments externally applied*

In nineteen instances we find our surgeon suggests no treatment other than the external application of medicaments. This is not surprising in the treatment of a group of flesh wounds, like a scalp wound (Case 1), a wound in the temple (Case 18), or a perforation in the temple (Case 19), an infected wound in the breast (Case 41), or finally an abscess in the breast (Case 46). It is likewise to be expected in sprains, as of a cervical vertebra (Case 30), or the sterno-costal articulations (Case 42); or even of a perforation of the bone, e.g., in the region of the maxilla and zygoma (Case 15), the temporal bone (Case 20), a cervical vertebra (Case 29), or the sternum (Case 40). Perhaps it is a recognition of the surgeon's helplessness that in a case of perforation of the sutures of the skull, with symptoms of tetanus (Case 7), the only suggestion he makes is a hot application to the mandible to relieve the constricted ligaments, followed by his inevitable honey-ointment on lint. Even a displacement of a cervical vertebra (Case 32) receives an application of fresh meat on the first day, followed by *imru* and honey, while the patient is carefully kept in a sitting posture.

A dislocation of the ribs (Case 43), omitting the fresh meat, is otherwise treated in the same way. We find the fresh meat again, applied as usual for the first day only, to a split in the maxilla (Case 16), with caution to keep the patient in a sitting position, while continuing treatment with honey-ointment on lint. The same injury in the humerus (Case 38) receives only the frequent *imru* followed by daily application of honey.

Modern skull surgery has been so marvellously developed in the last few years that we are not surprised to find our surgeon of three and a half millenniums ago offering the unfavorable verdict 3 in a case of compound comminuted fracture of the skull with rupture of the meningeal membranes. He could suggest no more than an alleviative application of grease, while cautioning against bandaging or adhesive plaster. The same type of injury in the maxilla (Case 17) receives the unfavorable verdict 3 by scribal error, whereas the surgeon has some hope of recovery and prescribes the same treatment as for Case 16 above. Finally Case 9, a compound comminuted fracture of the frontal bone, prescribes a treatment which is unique in our treatise. From some old *recipe papyrus,* like all the others preserved to us in Egyptian medicine, the surgeon has culled the only magical treatment in our book of surgery and external medicine. It is a well-known fact that, even in the mind of a modern man otherwise rational and scientific, there may be found lurking surprising manifestations of superstition. Undoubtedly our surgeon never more than partially escaped the current superstitions of his age, even those which ran counter to his general attitude toward his craft or, as here in the treatment of Case 9, to the rational views which he usually held regarding each individual case.

While the general content of his *materia medica* would not commend itself to modern surgery, it may be noted with interest that in the case of an infected or necrotic wound in the breast (Case 41), he prescribes the earliest known external application of salicin, in the form of a decoction of willow (*salix*) leaves, experience having probably taught his ancestors centuries earlier the antiseptic effect of its use. In the same case another application for allaying the inflammation contains dung and is probably ammoniacal. His astringent application in this case, after he has reduced the inflammation, is a solution containing copper and sodium salts.

List of cases prescribing exclusive use of medicaments externally applied :

Case 1. Flesh wound in the scalp ;	Fresh meat bound on, first day only ; honey-ointment on lint, bound on daily.
Case 18. Flesh wound in the temple ;	Fresh meat bound on, first day only ; honey-ointment daily.

Case 19. Perforation in the temple ;	Normal diet with no medicine ; honey-ointment on lint, bound on daily.
Case 41. Infected wound in the breast ;	Cooling application : decoction containing willow leaves ; astringent application : solution containing copper and sodium salts ; poultices of unidentified herbs.
Case 46. Prominent abscess in the breast ;	Two cooling applications, the second containing " mason's mortar ; " decoction for allaying inflammation : sycamore leaves, acacia leaves, and " ox dung ; " astringent applications : solution containing copper and sodium salts ; poultices of herbs.
Case 30. Sprain in cervical vertebrae ;	Fresh meat, bound on, first day only ; *imru* and honey daily.
Case 42. Sprain in sterno-costal articulations ;	*Imru* bound on ; afterward honey daily.
Case 15. Perforation of bone in region of maxilla and zygoma ;	*Imru* bound on ; honey-ointment daily.
Case 20. Perforation of temporal bone ;	Sitting posture ; constricted muscles of head softened with grease ; uncertain fluid (milk ?) in both ears.
Case 29. Wound in cervical vertebra ;	Fresh meat, bound on, first day only ; normal diet, no medicine.
Case 40. Perforation of the sternum ;	Fresh meat, bound on, first day only; honey-ointment on lint, bound on daily.
Case 7, I. Perforation of sutures of the scalp with symptoms of tetanus ;	Verdict 2 ; hot applications to ligaments of mandible ; honey-ointment on lint, bound on.
Case 32. Displacement of cervical vertebra ;	Fresh meat, bound on, first day only ; ointment applied to head (sic !) ; *imru* bound on injury ; afterward honey daily ; patient must maintain sitting posture.
Case 43. Dislocation of the ribs ;	*Imru*, bound on ; afterward honey daily.
Case 16. Split in the maxilla ;	Fresh meat, bound on, first day only ; patient must maintain sitting posture ; honey-ointment on lint, bound on daily.
Case 38. Split in the humerus ;	*Imru* bound on ; afterward honey daily.
Case 6. Compound comminuted fracture of the skull with rupture of meningeal membranes ;	Verdict 3 ; application of ointment ; caution against binding ; caution against application of plaster.
Case 17. Compound comminuted fracture of the maxilla ;	Verdict 3 ; fresh meat, bound on, first day only ; patient must maintain sitting posture ; honey-ointment on lint, bound on daily.
Case 9. Compound comminuted fracture of frontal bone ;	Magical treatment ; see commentary and translation.

This surgeon's general word for treatment is 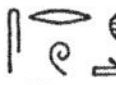 *śrwḫ*, the original meaning of which is uncertain. See commentary in Case 1 (I 3). It is applied to all kinds of treatment, so that the surgeon may be charged, " Treat (*śrwḫ*) according to these directions " (e.g., Case 41, XIV 7). Nevertheless, as used in our treatise *śrwḫ* designates the external application of medicaments in at least twenty-six cases, and possibly more, out of thirty-three. In four cases it designates the maintenance of the patient in a sitting posture, expressed in the words, " His treatment (*śrwḫ*) is sitting " (Case 4,

II 7; Case 7, III 15; Case 8, IV 9; Case 16, VI 20). There was a special course of treatment for wounds (perhaps also including sores) evidently already long current, or at least well known, called *śrwḫ wbnw*, "wound treatment," which is twice mentioned in our document (Case 39, XIII 7–8, see commentary; and Case 46, XVI 7). Unfortunately we know nothing about this treatment. It was perhaps contained in a surgical treatise already in circulation in our surgeon's day and probably already old, which bore the title, "Treatise on What Pertains to a Wound" (see commentary on Case 5, II 17).

5. *The Glosses Forming the Ancient Commentary*

The sixty-nine glosses in our treatise form the most valuable body of materials which it has brought to us. They constitute a little dictionary of terms distributed through the treatise, which was already so old in the Twenty-sixth Century B.C. that it contained numerous terms no longer current and requiring explanation. At the end of any case containing such terms, or discussing any matters which needed explanation, a commentator has added his definitions and explanatory comments. His identity is as totally unknown to us as that of the author of the treatise himself. He cannot have been the scribe who copied our papyrus. This worthy was far too careless, and betrays his ignorance of medical science far too obviously to have been able to produce such a remarkable little medical dictionary. It is evident then that this commentary was added at some date not merely earlier than our surviving copy, but earlier even than the Middle Kingdom, and doubtless toward the end of the Old Kingdom (see discussion, pp. 9–11).

In twenty-nine out of our forty-eight cases, it was found necessary to add one or more of these explanatory glosses, making altogether a total of sixty-nine. The only other ancient Egyptian medical papyrus containing this kind of commentary is the Papyrus Ebers, which has twenty-six glosses.[1] Unfortunately they are broken up into groups by irrelevant matter which has been intruded by error of some scribe or editor. None follows the case or prescription which it is supposed to explain, and the entire body of glosses in Papyrus Ebers has thus been separated from the treatise to which it belonged, an accident which has seriously limited their value.

In form each gloss is invariably introduced by *yr*, "as for" or "with regard to," followed by a verbatim quotation of the word or phrase to be explained. The term to be discussed or explained in the gloss is thus clearly brought before the reader. The definition follows, usually marked by the copulative *pw*, "it is," i.e., "it means." The whole gloss then has the following form:

(*yr*)..............(quoted words to be explained),
(*pw*)..............(explanatory proposition).

[1] They were first noted by Schaefer in 1892. See *Zeitschrift für Aegyptische Sprache*, Vol. 30 (1892), pp. 107–109.

The *pw* is of course postpositive, as usual, and does not stand at the head of the explanatory proposition or phrase, but after the first word or two. The form of the gloss in English is then :

As for : "............." (quoted words to be explained),
it means.............(explanatory proposition or phrase).

Occasionally we find the definition introduced by  "he (meaning the author of the treatise) is speaking of" (four times, Cases 30, Gloss A ; 31, Gloss A ; 32, Gloss A ; and 33, Gloss A). Twice we have the definition introduced by  " it says" (Case 1, Glosses B and C). In five glosses there is no introduction of the definition at all (Cases 6, Gloss A ; 11, Gloss B ; 31, Gloss B ; 40, Gloss A ; and 41, Gloss E).

In these glosses the commentator's chief purpose was first to ensure that the *terms designating and describing the injury* should be understood. Accordingly in the first eight cases concerning injuries of the skull, we find the following matters selected first for explanation in the glosses :

Case 1, C. " Penetrating to the [bone of his skull, (but) not having a gash]."
,, 2, A. " A [gaping wound in his head, penetrating to the bone]."
,, 3, A. " [Perforating his skull]."
,, 4, A. " Splitting his skull."
,, 5, A. " Smashing his skull" (compound comminuted fracture).
,, 6, A. " Smashing his skull, (and) rending open the brain of his skull" (rupture of meningeal membranes).
,, 7, A. " Perforating the sutures of [his skull]."
,, 8, A. " A smash in his skull under the skin of his head, there being no wound at all upon it."

It will be noticed that the first gloss (designated A) under each case, except the *first* case, regularly discusses and explains the nature of the injury. In the first case some preliminary explanations have naturally been placed first ; but after Case 1, throughout the treatise this explanation of the nature of the injury appears as the first gloss in every important case.[1]

These explanations of the nature of the injury deal chiefly with its physical and mechanical character. They make clear to the ancient medical student what he should understand by a "perforation," a "split," or a "smash" of the skull. Following the discussion of a  *thm*, that is, a "perforation" of the skull, the commentator explains that it means "a contracted smash, through his incurring a break like a puncture of a (pottery) jar" (Case 3, Gloss A). Explaining 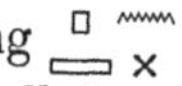 *pšn*, a "split" of the skull, the commentator says, "it means separating shell from shell of his skull, while fragments remain sticking in the flesh of his head and do not come away" (Case

[1] See Cases, 12, 14, 18, 22, 26, 30, 31, 32, 33, 34, 39, 41, 42, 43, 45, and 46.

4, Gloss A). Finally the commentator explains *śd*, as meaning, " a smash of his skull (such that) bones, getting into that smash, sink into the interior of his skull. The ' Treatise on What Pertains to His Wounds ' states : ' It means a smash of his skull into numerous fragments, which sink into the interior of his skull ' " (Case 5, Gloss A). The commentator draws upon another treatise on wounds for a description, making it clear that the injury is a compound comminuted fracture of the skull. Similarly we find an injury of the neck called a *wnẖ* of the neck, regarding which the commentator says, " He is speaking of a separation of one vertebra of his neck from another, the flesh which is over it being uninjured ; as one says, ' It is *wnẖ*,' concerning things which had been joined together, when one has been severed from another " (Case 31, Gloss A).

These examples may serve to illustrate this type of explanation added by the commentator. Having thus explained the physical character of the injury, the commentator also devotes much attention to the symptoms and the condition of the patient, explaining all terms which he regards as needing some definition. For example, he discusses the ancient word describing the shuffling motion of one foot in walking, presumably an evidence of partial paralysis resulting from an injury to the brain (Case 8, Gloss B), and in the same case he endeavors to explain the convulsive motions of the hands and arms, which he intends to be distinguished from similar symptoms accompanying some disease. One of the most interesting glosses in the treatise is a discussion of the observation that a dislocation of the neck is accompanied by an erection and seminal emission (Case 31, Gloss B). An ancient word for " speechless," designating a symptom accompanying a compound comminuted fracture of the temporal bone, calls for explanation (Case 22, Gloss C). Along with these evidences of paralysis resulting from injuries to the head and neck we find a whole series of discussions explaining other symptoms, like stiffness of the neck (Case 3, Gloss C ; Case 7, Gloss E), clammy countenance (Case 7, Gloss D), odor of the skull wound (Case 7, G), facial distortion (Case 7, I), paleness (Case 7, J) and others. In the treatment of these dangerous head wounds, and likewise in the case of a fracture of the humerus with a wound over it (Case 37), the surgeon is charged to adopt a waiting policy, " until thou knowest that he has reached something." This obscure clause is explained in Gloss C (Case 4) as meaning " until thou knowest whether he will die or he will live." This seems very much like an early recognition of the Hippocratic κρίσις (" crisis "). The cases in which it appears will be found listed in the commentary on Case 4, Gloss C.

The *external* source of the causes which induce all these symptoms is a matter regarded by the commentator as a very important fact, which must be fully recognized. A crushed cervical vertebra is discussed in the gloss (B, Case 33) and explained again as due to a fall on the head, although the text had already stated this fact. In a case where a dangerous compound comminuted fracture of the skull has occurred without leaving any externally visible contusion the commentator has repeated and further explained the statement of the text that the patient must be regarded as " one whom something entering from the outside has smitten " (Case 8, Gloss C). This term " something entering from the outside " must also be further explained, and the commentator takes it up in another gloss (D, Case 8), one of the most interesting explanations in our treatise. Here he warns his reader that " something entering from the outside " is " not the intrusion of something which his (the patient's) flesh engenders," that is, the patient's condition is not due to disease, which is strikingly recognized here as " something which his flesh engenders." On the contrary " something entering from the outside " means " the breath of an outside god or death," that is, the external casualty, the accident from the outside, the *force majeure,* which was to the Egyptian as to later men an impenetrable mystery, and which in the Papyrus Ebers is deified like a *Fortuna* or a *Τύχη* (see commentary on Case 8, Gloss D).

In the course of these sixty-nine short paragraphs of explanation a good deal of light is thrown upon the Egyptian surgeon's knowledge of anatomy and physiology. The first gloss in the treatise, which is also the longest in the entire series (Case 1, Gloss A), deals with the meaning of " thou examinest a man." It takes up the pulse in some detail, in a discussion which is the more remarkable in view of the fact that we find no mention of the pulse in early Greek medicine until the observations of Democritus regarding it. The earliest reference to it in Greek medical documents seems to have been in a treatise entitled *περὶ τροφῆς*, " On Nutrition." It has been stated that Hippocratic medicine knew nothing of the pulse ;[1] but the Hippocratic school certainly recognized tactile observations in examining a patient, and regarded touch as a means of testing the pulse.[2] In our treatise it is not improbable that the method of employing the touch in observing the pulse was that of counting the strokes, a method the more remarkable if really employed over twelve centuries before Hippocrates.

In observing the pulse our surgeon knows that he is examining the operation of the heart, and he states that the observation of the pulse is undertaken " in order to know the action of the heart." He also affirms that there is a canal leading from the heart to every member of the body. He enumerates the extremities and other points where the pulsations of the heart are discernible and adds that its " pulsation is in every vessel of every member." It is clear, therefore, that he has recognized the existence of a cardiac system, with which he is dealing, no matter what region may be affected by the injury he is treating. He takes up this fact in connection with the very first case under discussion, a wound in the head, as a matter of the first importance for the surgeon. As he advances to injuries of the skull penetrating the brain, he finds

[1] W. H. S. Jones, *Hippocrates,* V. 1, p. xx, foot-note.

[2] See Meyer-Steineg and Sudhoff, *Geschichte der Medicin,* 2d ed., p. 60.

within the brain itself the action of the heart evinced in what he calls "something throbbing and fluttering under thy fingers, like the weak place of an infant's crown before it becomes whole" (Case 6, II 20–21). His recognition of a cardiac system therefore is clearly demonstrated; we cannot affirm that he recognized the circulatory character of that system. In any case, however, he was so near a discernment of the circulation of the blood, that it will be necessary to re-examine the evidence regarding a possible knowledge of the circulation of the blood by the Alexandrian physicians after 300 B.C.

This extraordinary account of the cardiac system introduced to explain the nature of a surgical examination is quoted in the Papyrus Ebers (99, 1–5), where it is preceded by the title, "Beginning of the Secret Book of the Physician." It would seem, therefore, that Papyrus Ebers drew the material from an ancient book of that name. If Papyrus Ebers drew this discussion from our treatise, which is therefore cited by its title, we have at the head of this citation in Papyrus Ebers the title of our treatise, as we shall see in the commentary on Case 1 (Gloss A).

The human brain appears for the first time in medical literature in the text and the glosses of our treatise. Our surgeon knows that the folds of the brain lie in convolutions, which he says are "like those corrugations which form on molten copper." He takes up this comparison in a gloss (Case 6, Gloss B), and explains that the reference is to the floating slag forming on molten copper, which the copper-smith rejects before he pours the metal into the mould. Any one who has observed the convolutions into which metallic slag forms itself will recognize the aptness of the ancient surgeon's comparison. In another gloss (A) appended to the same case, the commentator explains, that "rending open the brain," accompanying a compound comminuted fracture of the skull, is a reference to "the membrane (or skin) enveloping his brain," which is rent, "so that it breaks open his fluid in the interior of his head." This is the earliest known reference to the meningeal membranes.

The earliest observations showing that the brain is a center of nervous control are likewise contained in the text and glosses which we are now discussing. The surgeon has noticed that injuries to the skull and brain result in disturbing the normal control of various parts of the body, even as far away as the feet. As the result of a perforation of the sutures of the skull (Case 7) he records extreme facial distortion, which the commentator has explained in Gloss I. In the same case he also notes constriction of the ligaments of the neck, and the commentator discusses this matter in Gloss E. Similar effects in the temporal muscle controlling the mandible are likewise observed, and in two interesting glosses (Case 7, Glosses B and C) the commentator explains the anatomy and pathology involved. The most remarkable observation of this kind is made in connection with a case of compound comminuted fracture of the skull which however displays no visible external contusion (Case 8). The surgeon makes the following note: "His eye is askew because of it, on the side of him having that injury which is in his skull; he walks shuffling with his sole, on the side of him having that injury which is in his skull." The repetition of the words "that injury which is in his skull" suggests that the surgeon is calling attention to the fact of the effects of an injury in a situation which may be distant from the place of the observed effect. Much more remarkable is the repetition of the detail, "on the side of him having that injury which is in his skull," showing that the surgeon was already aware of the importance of the relationship between the side of the brain which has suffered the injury and the side of the body which is affected by the brain injury. The fact that he distinctly specifies in both cases on which side the affected eye and foot are with reference to the injured side of the brain is highly significant, and indicates that he has already discerned the localization of control in the brain. All this raises the question whether the absence of any visible external contusion may not have been due to the fact that the actual fracture itself was a *contre-coup*, throwing the paralysis of the foot over to the same side which had received the blow. In this case we must suppose that the surgeon's term "injury" refers to the blow causing the *contre-coup*. The commentator takes up this paralysis of one foot for discussion (Case 8, Gloss B), but unfortunately goes no further than an explanation of the evidently archaic word used for "shuffle."

There is no effort on the part of the commentator to correlate these evidences of a nervous system centering in the brain, with similar effects arising from injuries of the vertebrae. We find him adding two very interesting discussions of an *emissio seminis* and inability to control the flow of urine, both due to a dislocation of a cervical vertebra (Case 31, Glosses B and C); but he does not discuss the speechlessness ensuing when a cervical vertebra has been crushed (Case 33, examination). In the diagnosis of this case and also that of Case 31 (dislocated neck), the surgeon makes the interesting observation that both arms and both legs are paralysed. In both cases the commentator adds an excellent explanation of the mechanical processes which have caused the fracture and the crushing of the cervical vertebra, but he leaves without remark the observation of the paralysed limbs.

It will be seen then that our surgeon and the commentator had already observed a series of effects arising in other parts of the body as a result of injuries to the brain and the spine. They were furthermore already aware of the shift of these effects from one side to the other, according as the injury to the brain was on one side or the other, and in so doing had probably been misled by the *contre-coup*. These observations, however, had not been correlated into a system, nor connected with a complex of ramifying nerves. Indeed our document, as far as preserved, discloses no word for nerves, and there is no indication in any of the Egyptian documents that such a designation existed at this remote stage of scientific knowledge of the human body. As we shall see in the following paragraphs our Egyptian surgeon was still in a very early stage of observation concerning such filaments and cord-like connections as the nerves, and when he found them as disclosed by dissection, he was probably not aware of their function. The clear correlation of brain and spine with the nervous system was first achieved by Herophilos at Alexandria in the Third Century B.C.

While the ancient commentator was unaware of nerve filaments, he was acquainted with the character and function of the muscles and ligaments, and was interested in them. Case 7, a perforation of the sutures of the skull, records the surgeon's observation of a constriction of the " cord of his mandible ; " also that " the ligaments of his neck are tense." The commentator appends three discussions of these observations, two to explain the meaning of the ancient word for " contracted," " constricted " or " tense " (Glosses B and E), and one to define the " cord of his mandible " (Gloss C). In explaining the constriction of the " cord of his mandible," the commentator says that it refers to " a stiffening on the part of the ligaments at the end of his ramus, which are fastened to his temporal bone " (Gloss B). It is not likely that he had already built up a complete catalogue of the muscles of the body, but the above examples suffice to show that he had studied them in dissection and in the treatment of wounds, and not merely casually as revealed in the course of embalming. It is noticeable, however, that the surgeon says nothing of the muscles of the arms and shoulders, although he was aware of their effects as he directs the practitioner how to reduce a fractured humerus or clavicle, by prying on a fulcrum against the pull of these muscles (Cases 35 and 36).

Before leaving the subject of the commentator's discussion of the soft tissues of the body, especially the cardiac system, the nerves and the muscles, it should be noted that our surgeon and the commentator likewise, both use the same word for canal or vessel, and muscle or ligament. This word *mt* is employed throughout the commentator's long discussion of the cardiac system as the word for " canal " or " vessel " (Case 1, Gloss A). Again where the surgeon has used *w*ʾ*·t*, an old word for " cord " to designate the temporal muscle, the commentator explains it as meaning the *mt·w* (plural), " ligaments " fastened to the temporal bone. It is certain therefore that the same word served both for " vessel " and for " ligament " or " sinew." Under these circumstances it would not be surprising if the Egyptian had included also the nerves among these cord-like connections. The Egyptian surgeon knew quite well that the vessels or canals of the cardiac system were hollow and conveyed blood, but he nevertheless applied to them the word *mt*, which must have been a general term for any cord-like connection, which in external form might not be so unlike a sinew or a nerve. In this use of a common designation for sinew and canal, and perhaps also nerve, we doubtless have one of the reasons why the three groups of such connections, namely nerves, blood-vessels, and muscles were not clearly grouped as three separate systems.

On the other hand the bony framework of the body must have been early familiar to the Egyptian, in a climate where skeletons last so long. Even among the Greeks, that is, in a climate less favorable to such preservation of the bones, the physicians knew far more of the bones than of the soft tissues. The commentator's above discussion of the temporal muscle and the mandible connects very interestingly with his explanations and descriptions of the anatomy of the mandible and the temporal bone. In discussing a compound comminuted fracture of the temporal bone the surgeon naturally is involved in a reference to " the end of his ramus " (condyle and coronoid process). For ramus he uses a term derived from the name of a bird. The commentator fears that this perhaps already ancient name is no longer familiar to the reader, and he therefore adds a remark explaining " the end of his ramus " by saying that " it means the end of his mandible. The ramus (*ʾmʿ·t*),—it is in his temporal bone just as the claw of an *ʾamʿe*-bird (*ʾmʿ*) grasps an object " (Case 22, Gloss A). The fork at the summit of the ramus is thus compared to the claw of a two-toed bird, which grasps a thing as the bifurcating tip of the ramus engages with the temporal bone.

These anatomical explanations of the commentator thus make use of a variety of objects from the world of nature or of the arts to suggest the shape or the function of the parts to be described, just as modern science employs similar figures. We have already seen how the surgeon likens the convolutions of the brain to slag formations floating on molten metal, and the commentator's discussion of the comparison. In the same way, we have the dome of the skull designated as " the chest of his head," and the commentator thinks it wise to add an explanation here, saying " it means the middle of his crown, next to his brain. The likening of it is to a chest " (Case 7, Gloss H), a very common article of furniture in an Egyptian household. Similarly, an architectural term is applied by the surgeon to the nose ; he deals in Case 11 with a " break in the column of his nose." The commentator adds what is for us a confused and difficult explanation of the exact limits of the portion of the nose included under this term (Case 11, Gloss A). In Case 40 it is doubtless the appearance of the sternum, with its bristling lines of ribs, which has suggested that the manubrium be called by the name of an animal like a porcupine or hedgehog, having vigorous hair or spines. This term likewise leads the commentator to add an explanation indicating what animal has suggested the designation (Case 40, Gloss A).

In one case the commentator warns the reader against accepting such a descriptive term too literally. In discussing a fracture of the nasal bone, the surgeon is instructed to cleanse both nostrils " until every worm of blood which coagulates in the inside of his two nostrils comes forth." The commentator adds a gloss to this case explaining that only a *comparison* is involved in the passage, which he says designates merely " the clotting of blood in the inside of his two nostrils, likened to a worm (*ʿnʿr·t*), which subsists in the water." The word " worm " was obviously employed by the original writer of the treatise to designate the fibrous, stringy formations in coagulated blood (Case 12, Gloss C).

The interest of the commentator in the text he is explaining is both scientific and pedagogic. With the gloss just discussed we have probably passed from the scientific to the pedagogic. The same motive has led to the insertion of not a few of the commentator's explanations, especially where the text contains an ancient word no longer commonly current. Indeed he was so concerned lest the ancient word for " ruddy " should not be understood, that he has inserted his explanation of the word in no less than three different cases (Cases 7, Gloss F; 41, Gloss C; and 46, Gloss C). We find him explaining the presumably old or unusual words for " shuffling " (Case 8, Gloss B), " blood-shot " (Case 19, Gloss A), " piercing through " (Case 26, Gloss A), " dribbles " (Case 31, Gloss C), or the word  *bkn*, a no longer current word for " urine " of a sheep (Case 7, Gloss G). In one case it is an extraordinary and picturesque idiom or figure of speech which the commentator explains to us, and which seems to have been as enigmatic to the reader of the Third Millennium B.C. as it is to us. We find the surgeon given the curious instructions " Moor him (the patient) at his mooring stakes," or " Put him at his mooring stakes " in nine different cases. At the first occurrence of this remarkable injunction (Case 3, I 22–23), the commentator has added an explanation (Gloss D), which reads, " It means putting him on his customary diet, without administering to him a prescription."

We are often at a loss to know exactly what kind of an appliance is intended when the text of the case prescribes the use of some surgical device, and we are usually not enlightened as to the character of the device or the manner of its use. We must suppose that such information was a matter of common knowledge among surgeons. Of adhesive plaster the commentator has thought it advisable to add an explanation (Case 2, Gloss B); but by the time he reached Case 10 he had forgotten this fact and he therefore inserted the same explanation again (Case 10, Gloss A). In explaining a certain kind of bandage he also gives us the interesting information already mentioned above, that it was prepared by the embalmers (Case 9, Gloss A).

The full value of this ancient body of commentary can be understood only by reading it in connection with the text of the treatise which it is intended to explain. Preliminary to such a reading, it will be found useful to study the following complete list of the passages which the commentator has selected for explanatory discussion.

List of terms and expressions explained in the glosses in Papyrus Edwin Smith:

Case 1. A. " Thou examinest a man." The explanation contains a possible reference to counting the pulse and also an account of the cardiac system.
B. " While his wound does not have [two lips]."
C. " Penetrating to the [bone of his skull, (but) not having a gash]." Compare Case 18, A.

Case 2. A. " A [gaping] wound [in his head penetrating to the bone]."

Case 2. B. " Two strips of linen," meaning adhesive tape or plaster.
C. " Not having a split, a perforation, (or) [a smash]."
Case 3. A. " [Perforating his skull]."
B. " Unable to look at his shoulders and his bre[ast]."
C. " Suffering with stiffness in his neck."
D. " Moor (him) at his mooring stakes : " an ancient idiom for " putting him on his customary diet, without administering to him a prescription."
Case 4. A. " Splitting his skull."
B. " The swelling which is over it protrudes."
C. " Thou knowest he has reached a decisive point : " the crisis.
Case 5. A. " Smashing his skull," explaining a compound comminuted fracture.
Case 6. A. " Smashing his skull, (and) rending open the brain of his skull," explaining a rupture of the meningeal membranes.
B. " Those corrugations which form on molten copper," used as illustrating the external appearance of the convolutions of the brain.
Case 7. A. " Perforating the sutures of [his skull]," explaining " sutures " as " what is between shell and shell of his skull."
B. " The cord of his mandible is contracted," explaining probable symptoms of tetanus, and the anatomy of the mandible and its ligaments.
C. " The cord of his mandible."
D. " His countenance clammy with sweat."
E. " The ligaments of his neck are tense."
F. " His face is ruddy."
G. " The odor of the chest of his head is like the *bkn* of sheep," *bkn* being an ancient word for urine.
H. " The chest of his head," this being an ancient term for the dome of the skull.
I. " His mouth is bound, (and) both his eye-brows are drawn, while his face is as if he wept : " facial distortion accompanying an injury of the skull.
J. " He has become pale and has already ⌜shown exhaustion⌝."
Case 8. A. " A smash in his skull under the skin of his head, there being no wound at all upon it : " a compound comminuted fracture of the skull without visible external contusion.
B. " He walks shuffling with his sole : " partial paralysis of one foot resulting from an injury to the brain.
C. " One whom something entering from outside has smitten," emphasized because of lack of external contusion.
D. " Something entering from outside," outside destiny, the will of Providence, " not the intrusion of anything which his flesh engenders."
E. " One who does not release the head of his shoulder-fork and who does not fall with his nails in the palm of his hand : " obscure convulsive action like symptoms accompanying injury to the brain.
Case 9. A. " Covering for physicians' use," explained as a bandage prepared by the embalmers.
Case 10. A. " Two strips of linen," repeating the explanation already given in Case 2, Gloss B.
Case 11. A. " The column of his nose," explained as the soft outer nose, including the septum.
B. " His two nostrils."
Case 12. A. " A break in the chamber of his nose."
B. " His nose is bent, his face disfigured."
C. " Every worm of blood which coagulates in the inside of his two nostrils."
Case 13. No glosses.
Case 14. A. " A wound in his nostril, piercing through."
Cases 15–17. No glosses.
Case 18. A. " A wound not having a gash, while it penetrates to the bone ; " compare Case 1, C.
B. " His *gmꜣ*," explained as meaning his temple, and therefore evidently some old designation no longer current at the date of the insertion of this explanation.

Case 19. A. " His two eyes are blood-shot," the term for " blood-shot " being some old and unfamiliar term.

Cases 20–21. No glosses.

Case 22. A. " The end of his ramus," the term for " ramus " being an ancient word derived from the name of a two-toed bird, whose forked claw suggested the fork at the head of the ramus.

B. " Thou seest its fragments in the interior of his ear," the term for " fragments " being an archaic word designating the fragments of bone visible in the inside of the ear after a compound comminuted fracture of the temporal bone.

C. " He is speechless : " a symptom accompanying the compound comminuted fracture of the temporal bone, but designated by an uncommon word.

Cases 23–25. No glosses.

Case 26. A. " A wound in his lip piercing through to the inside of his mouth," the term " piercing through " being some old word requiring elucidation.

Cases 27–29. No glosses.

Case 30. A. " A sprain : " evidently an archaic word explained as meaning " a rending of two members, (although) it (=each) is (still) in its place."

Case 31. A. " A dislocation in a vertebra of his neck," explained in the following words : " He is speaking of a separation of one vertebra of his neck from another, the flesh which is over it being uninjured ; as one says, ' It is *wnḥ* ' (dislocated), concerning things which had been joined together, when one has been severed from another."

B. " It is an *emissio seminis* which befalls his phallus : " a result of a broken neck.

C. " While his urine dribbles," the ancient word for " dribbles " requiring explanation.

Case 32. A. " A displacement in a vertebra of his neck."

Case 33. A. " A crushed vertebra in his neck."

B. " His falling head downward has caused one vertebra to crush into the next."

Case 34. A. " A dislocation in his two collar bones," with an interesting description of the anatomy in this region.

Cases 35–38. No glosses.

Case 39. A. " Tumors with prominent head in his breast."

Case 40. A. " The manubrium of his sternum," named from a spiny animal like a porcupine.

Case 41. A. " A diseased wound in his breast, inflamed : " a wound sluggish in healing, persistently remaining open, explained by quoting an ancient work called, " Treatise on what Pertains to a Wound."

B. " A whirl of inflammation in his wound."

C. " Its two lips are ruddy," explaining the archaic term for ruddy which had been already explained in Case 7, Gloss F.

D. " His flesh cannot receive a bandage."

E. " While heat continually issues from the mouth of his wound at thy touch," explaining an archaic word for " issue " employed in the discussion.

Case 42. A. " Ribs of his breast," explaining the presumably archaic term for ribs.

Case 43. A. " A dislocation in the ribs of his breast," explained as meaning " a displacement of the heads of the ribs of his sternum, which are articulated in his sternum."

B. " He suffers with swellings in his two sides."

C. " His two sides."

Case 44. No glosses.

Case 45. A. " Bulging tumors on his breast."

Case 46. A. " An abscess with prominent head on his breast."

B. " Clamminess of their surface."

C. " There is no ruddiness upon it," explaining the meaning of the term for ruddiness again, after having explained the same term twice above, Case 7, Gloss F, and Case 41, Gloss C.

Case 47. No glosses.

Case 48. Glosses, if any, are lost.

II. *Function and Age of the Treatise*

In studying the surviving treatises of the Hippocratic school of medicine one is struck by the fact that the physician of that school was far more interested in the human body when it was sick than when it was well. His knowledge of anatomy and physiology, therefore, as based on a study of the *normal* human body, was not extensive or systematic. Hippocratic study of the human body when *ailing*, furthermore, was evidently more often inspired by a desire for knowledge than by the hope of curing the patient. Thus among the forty-two case-histories recorded in the Hippocratic treatises on Epidemics I and III,[1] twenty-five, that is considerably more than half, end in death, and this group of case-histories may fairly be regarded as a body of evidence collected by the methods of scientific investigation, rather than the casual observations incident to the physician's daily practice. It may be for modern medical men to decide whether this evidence might possess any value in a subsequent effort to heal or cure ; but such a conclusion would seem to be very doubtful.

In the same way the author of our surgical treatise was obviously interested in the human body and the phenomena it exhibited, even though he could do nothing for the patient. That the knowledge of the human organism which the ancient Egyptian surgeons gained by this attitude of mind was laid down in systematic treatises, we can hardly doubt. These treatises, if they really existed, have unhappily been lost.

It should therefore be clearly borne in mind when examining our treatise, that while the observations on the structure and functions of the human organs here recorded are not purely casual, nevertheless our treatise is not a systematic discussion of the human body. In the systematic organization of the materials, beginning with the head and proceeding downward, we note, however, that it has some outward resemblance to an organized treatise on anatomy and physiology. It is nevertheless a group of discussions of *injuries*, and not of organs and parts of the body.

We see then that the treatise may have served one or more of a number of different functions. There were evidently at least three classes of surgical documents in ancient Egypt. *First,* handbooks used by surgeons in their daily practice, just as the physicians must have used the recipes collected in the Papyrus Ebers ; again, *second,* it is obvious that there were outlines from which Egyptian surgeons, in those medical schools which preceded the one founded by Darius, lectured to their students ; for we cannot suppose that the great mass of details discussed in the Edwin Smith Papyrus was a matter of oral transmission. It was doubtless in the use of such lecture outlines that the lecturer's comments on already ancient discussions, formulas and directions would gradually accumulate. These explanations of all matters needing elucidation would appear as the glosses which form the commentary in our treatise.

[1] W. H. S. Jones, *Hippocrates*, London, 1923, V. 1, p. 144.

Finally, *third,* there must have been records of the instruction received by students of medicine and surgery : lecture note-books and clinical note-books such as modern students produce. Was our treatise any one of these three ?

In view of the magical recipes on the back of our papyrus, the probabilities are that its owner was a practicing physician, and that our treatise was a reference book from his medical library. Even so, however, our treatise may likewise have partaken of the nature both of the lecturer's outline and the student's note-book ; for the student will have roughly reproduced the form and content of his instructor's lecture notes and may afterward have continued to employ his note-book as a reference hand-book.

In this connection it is well to emphasize the memorandum character of our treatise, which is very noticeable. Repeatedly a whole paragraph is merely suggested by an introductory phrase or two, or merely a few catch words. Important surgical processes are indicated by a short phrase. The surgeon is charged to apply this or that method or process, without the slightest explanation of the details or the method of procedure. Devices designated by a single word are in no way described, and terms which are not explained are tacitly assumed to be understood. All these things may have been matters which received full and sufficient oral explanation not included in the present text of the treatise. As a whole therefore, the treatise is very much in the nature of notes, whether those of lecturer or student. One is reminded of the condition in which some of the treatises attributed to Aristotle have come down to us.

These notes originally took form and were recorded, whether by lecturer or student, at a very early date. Both in vocabulary and grammar the language repeatedly exhibits the characteristics of Old Kingdom speech, that is of the period between 3000 and 2500 B.C. The following is not a complete list of these evidences, but it contains the more noticeable examples of these early words or forms. It is important in this connection to note whether these archaisms are found in the original discussion (called " text " below), or in the ancient glosses forming the commentary, which we have discussed above (pp. 61–71).

List of archaisms in the language of the surgical treatise :

I. Text :

1. Grammar :

   a. The ancient third person *dual* of the pseudo-participle, *pḫd-wy* (Case 34, XI 18).

   b. The archaic and very rare *dual* of the feminine genitive particle *nty* (Case 4, II 7 ; Case 7, III 15 ; and Case 25, IX 4).

   c. The ancient third person dual, *śny,* " of them both " (Case 14, VI 8 ; Case 36, XII 13 *bis*) ; compare also the incorrect (Case 35, XII 7).

d. The archaic construction in which we must probably recognize the pseudoparticiple *preceding* a nominal subject. See the discussion in Case 4, II 4.

e. The particle *ny*, " for it " or the like, in verdict 3 : . See the commentary on Case 5, II 15. This form, first noticed by Gardiner, is regarded by him as already " moribund " in the Old Kingdom (*Proceedings of the Society of Biblical Archaeology*, 40 (1918), p. 7).

f. The uniformly archaic writing of the noun *ẖnw*, " inside " or " interior," without the determinative of the house, regularly appearing in the Middle Kingdom and later. It occurs in our treatise twenty-two times (see glossary), of which nine occurrences are in the text and thirteen are in the ancient commentary (see below).

g. The archaic use of *ḏr*, meaning " when " or " as soon as " (Case 4, II 6, consult commentary).

h. Use of *my* with the phonetic value *mr* in *ymrw* (Case 15, VI 17).

i. Omission of the preposition *m* : before *ydr*, surgical " stitching " (Case 26, IX 8) ; before *by·t* " honey " (often, e. g., Case 32, XI 6 ; Case 35, XII 8, etc.) ; before *mrḥ·t*, " grease," *passim* (e.g., Case 15, VI 17). The last case has been thought to be due to mergence of the preposition *m* with the following initial *m* of the word. In view of the other cases this is unlikely. Another explanation may be the memorandum character of the treatise, involving intentional abbreviation.

2. Dictionary :

a. The word *pšn*, " split," found elsewhere only in the Pyramid Texts and the Middle Kingdom Book of the Dead.

b. The archaic word *nẖbẖb*, " break through," occurring elsewhere only in the Pyramid Texts (three times) and once at Abydos (see commentary on Case 13, VI 4–5). Besides the five occurrences in our papyrus it is not found in the Egyptian medical documents.

c. The obsolete word *wʾ·t*, " cord," explained in Gloss C, Case 7, III 18.

d. The obsolete word *yšw*, " protrude," found only in the Pyramid Texts and its oldest derivatives.

e. The archaic word *ʿr-ty*, " mandible," explained by the ancient commentary as equivalent to the current word *wgw·t*, " jaw " (Case 7, Gloss C, III 18 ; compare III 7 and Gloss B, III 16–17).

f. The archaic word *ḥtr*, " contracted," explained in Gloss B, Case 7, III 16–18.

II. Glosses Forming the Ancient Commentary:

1. Grammar:

   a. The archaic writing *ḥ'ty*, "heart," for the classic, in Gloss A (Case 1, I 9).

   b. The writing *ẖnw*, "inside" or "interior," without the determinative. Out of twenty-two examples, thirteen are found in the ancient commentary (see above).

   c. The archaic interchange of *ẖ* and *ś* in *nẖ*, "fluid," Gloss A (Case 6, II 24–25), and elsewhere in our treatise always written with, *ś* (five times, see glossary).

   d. Indiscriminate use of and. See discussion, Case 1, I 10, Gloss B.

   e. Archaic writing for *ymytw*, "between" in Gloss A (Case 7, III 16).

2. Dictionary:

   A number of the archaic words listed above as found in the text occur also in the ancient commentary; but as quotations from the text they cannot be called original to the glosses.

While the ancient commentary does not disclose as many archaic words as the text of the discussions, nevertheless it is obvious that the glosses contain conclusive evidence of their Old Kingdom origin. The alphabetic writing of *ḥ'ty*, "heart," and the exchange of *ẖ* and *ś*; besides thirteen out of twenty-two examples of the archaic writing of *ẖnw*, "interior" without a determinative, all in the glosses, are very significant. It is hardly to be doubted, therefore, that the commentary is older than the Middle Kingdom.

If an explanatory commentary on the text of the treatise was already necessary before the end of the Old Kingdom, the treatise itself must be dated to the early part of the Old Kingdom, and may therefore be an example of the medical learning which made Imhotep, the earliest known physician, already famous in the Thirtieth Century B.C. In that case our treatise would be some five thousand years old.

III. *The Lost Beginning of the Treatise and the Reconstruction of Column I from the Fragments*

When the papyrus was placed in the present editor's hands, it consisted of twenty-one complete columns and was accompanied by a group of seventeen fragments, pasted mostly at random on a sheet of manila paper. The paper bore interesting notes in ink in the hand-writing of Mr. Edwin Smith. The most important of these notes reads:

"These fragments were recovered from a factitious papyrus made up of the fragments from 3 others March 17, 1862, nearly 2 months after the original purchase, Jan. 20, both from Mustapha Aga, and the fragments A and C [our A and B] were saturated with glue which was removed by maceration and carefully scraping the glue away which had been used to seal the factitious papyrus composed of these fragments."

It is obvious at the first glance that these fragments were written by the same scribe who made our copy of the Surgical Treatise. When the native discoverer or owner sold the main roll of the document to Mr. Smith on January 20th, 1862, he had lying at home outer fragments of it, which he had removed, perhaps with the intention of producing the impression that the document proffered for sale to Smith was complete and perfect. A cursory examination would have disclosed to Mr. Smith the presence of the lower right hand corner of a column (our fragment E) preceding Column II, and doubtless did betray to him the fact that a column preceding Column II was lost.

Mustapha Aga on returning home took the fragments of the roll which he had removed and pasted them around a dummy roll, as the modern natives very often do. He waited two months and then took this dummy roll, looking very attractive on the outside, to Mr. Smith, who forthwith purchased it, well knowing as the event disclosed, the real character of his new roll. The methods of papyrus salvage as it is now so skillfully practiced by such deft preparators as Ibscher, were of course entirely unknown two generations ago; and Mr. Smith deserves great credit for rescuing these fragments as successfully as he has done.

Moreover Mr. Smith was not content with merely disengaging the fragments from the bogus roll. He examined them with care, and recognizing that they were a part of the papyrus which he had bought from Mustapha Aga two months previously, he endeavored to put them together. I find the date " Dec. 10, 63 " written beside some of the smaller fragments, showing that some twenty-one months after the purchase of the fragments he was still engaged in trying to put them together. His efforts were crowned with several successes. He recognized that fragments A and B (see Vol. II, Plate I A) belong together, with B at the right, and an interval between them. He discerned that C and D belong on the right edge of B and he had roughly added to the right edge of B the readings from C and D. He had probably concluded that F was from the lower half of the column and had continued the numbering of the lines to include F (14–26). He knew also that G and I belong on the right edge of F, as his memoranda show. That was as far as he had gone, but his progress shows him a keen and penetrating student of the document.

The reader will find on Plate I A (Vol. II) the materials enabling him to follow the process of reconstruction. The connection between fragments A and B is demonstrated not only by the duplicate passage in Papyrus Ebers (see Case 1, Gloss A, pp. 106 f.), but also by recurrences of the same passage from Pap. Smith, like l. 3 or l. 12. The most difficult connection to establish was that between the group of fragments ABCD forming the upper half of the column and the group FGHI forming part of the lower half of the column. The connection is demonstrated in two ways. First by the sequence of the content: the group ABCD ends with a diagnosis (ll. 13–14) and the group FGHI begins with a verdict and a treatment. This is the correct order of content of the cases throughout the treatise. Secondly the joint between A and F, which is just at the level of l. 13, can be reconstructed, notwithstanding the fact that only a few traces of l. 13 have survived along the upper edge of fragment F. It is possible to read along the lower edge of A the words . On the left of the fragment A still preserves the upper part of the , the small loop at the upper end of the heavy oblique stroke, which will be found intruding into l. 14 on fragment F. The short above it on A will be found illustrated in *gm* in l. 25 of the same column. Again, in the word the rent between A and F passes directly along the second , so that the lower edge of the horizontal stroke forming the hieratic *n* is visible in the original along the upper edge of F. We thus have two signs here part of each of which is visible on both A and F.

The fragments therefore belonged to a single column of which we have approximately the upper right and left, and the lower left-hand quarters. The greatest loss is the lower right-hand quarter and a vertical strip along the right edge of the page extending from top to bottom, some of which can be restored as on Plate I A (Vol. II), from the surviving parallels.

The question now arises: where did this fragmentary column belong? Did it immediately precede the columns of the main roll, beginning with our Column II? These questions are easily answered. Fragment E, now inserted on Plate I A (Vol. II), was still part of the main roll at the right of the foot of Column II when the papyrus was handed to the present editor. It contains the ends of eight lines, and a study of these shows that they are the ends of ll. 19–26 of our reconstructed column, which is thus linked up with our main roll as Column I.

Of the seventeen fragments the reconstruction of Column I now disposes of all the large ones and the most important of the small ones, or a total of nine. This leaves eight very small pieces which have not been placed. The writing has faded considerably, from the rough handling by the natives and the maceration to free them from the glue used in patching up the dummy roll. These pieces have been assembled on Plate I and lettered from K to R inclusive. They are so small and the ink so pale that I have not been able to place them in the text of Column I.

Column I contains parts of three cases, of which the first is evidently the first case in the treatise. Its beginning occupied the last few lines of the preceding column. Unless the introduction preceding the cases was very long, the remainder of the lost column, that is nearly all of it, would have furnished sufficient space for the introduction. In that case we have lost only one column at the beginning of the treatise, preceding our present Column I.

TRANSLATION AND COMMENTARY

CASE ONE

Bottom lines of lost column—I 12

A WOUND IN THE HEAD PENETRATING TO THE BONE

The beginning of this case is lost at the bottom of the last column preceding Column I. Only a portion of the last twelve lines of the case is preserved at the top of the fragmentary Column I. At the bottom of the preceding lost column the beginning of Case 1 must have occupied at least nearly two lines, each about 28 cm. long, for the restored text measured in hieratic of the proper scale is about 56 cm. long (see Vol. II, 1b). It is highly probable that no other case preceded our Case 1, as we shall see. This observation shows us that the preceding portion of the lost column, probably over twenty lines, was not devoted to the discussion of cases.

From the twelve lines of Case 1 which are preserved at the top of Column I, it is quite evident that this case was arranged and organized as to subject matter in the same way as all the others which follow. We must expect, therefore, that the diagnosis will have been substantially a repetition of the examination, and that the title, with which the case was introduced, consisted of the first part of observations recorded in the examination. It is quite possible therefore to restore a large part of the beginning of Case 1, now lost at the bottom of the lost column. There is unavoidable uncertainty as to the length of the title, as it is impossible to establish with precision *how much* of the examination was employed as title. The preserved portion, at the top of Column I, begins in the diagnosis, in the middle of a word, after which nearly two-thirds of the diagnosis is preserved. Combining the information disclosed by the glosses with our knowledge of the stereotyped form of the diagnosis as found in other cases, it is possible to restore the entire diagnosis with the exception of a lacuna of three or four words. From the diagnosis thus restored, it is possible to work back in the same way through the examination to the title, as already indicated.

Title

Bottom of lost column

Translation

[Instructions concerning a wound in his head, penetrating to the bone of his skull.]

Commentary

Of the forty-seven other cases preserved in Papyrus Smith, every one begins with a title anticipating the examination, and employing its introductory words. It cannot be doubted that like the remaining forty-seven, Case 1 also began with a title of the same form.

šśꜣw, "instructions, indications." This word is preserved as the first word of the title in 46 out of the 48 cases in our treatise, and it was obviously present also in Case 3 (as shown by the preserved portion of the title, I 18), giving us 47 cases introduced by it, out of 48. We cannot doubt that it also introduced Case 1. The word is written with the transferred sign, because of the word *šśꜣw* "antelope," e.g., Davies, *Deir el-Gebrawi*, I, pl. XI; *Ptahhetep*, II, pl. XIX; Mariette, *Mastabas*, D. 15, &c. It is construed with a following noun, either in the direct or indirect genitive. In the earlier documents we find the *direct genitive* exclusively; e. g., throughout Pap. Smith, and the M.K. Kahun Medical Papyrus, 1, 15; 2, 18; 1, 23; 1, 27; *et passim*. Pap. Ebers also uses the direct genitive quite commonly (100, 15 with suffix pronoun; 109, 2; 109, 18; 103, 19; etc.); but it at the same time employs the *indirect genitive* (109, 11; 36, 4; 106, 13; 107, 5; 108, 17; etc.), as does also the late Berlin Medical Papyrus 3038 (14, 3; 14, 6; 12, 12, three times in all). *Šśꜣw* does not occur in Pap. Hearst.

Outside of the medical treatises the meaning of the word is fairly clear. Thus in a Hymn to Thoth the worshiper says:

"Come to me, (O Thoth), that thou mayest make regulations for me, and that thou mayest make me instructed in thy office" (Pap. Anast. V, 9, 3). In the self-laudatory phrases of oriental scribes and officials the term is frequently used to describe the experienced or well-informed man.

In the medical literature the exact shade of meaning has still to be determined. It is used in four of the medical treatises: Papyrus Ebers, Kahun Papyrus, Papyrus Smith, and Berlin Medical Papyrus, to designate the entire discussion of the case. It is not employed as a title of mere recipes, though it approaches this usage in the Kahun Papyrus; for this reason it does not appear at all in the exclusively magical documents like Papyrus Hearst or the London Medical Papyrus, and is used only three times in the Berlin Papyrus (3038). The chief question is whether the word designates the *objective indications* observable in a given case, or the *instructions* based on these.

A significant case in Pap. Ebers in the discussion of the heart might indicate the former. The physician is discussing the meaning of a term indicating a symptom of the heart and says: "It means the non-pulsating of the heart, or that the vessels of the heart are silent (not pulsating),  there being no indications of them (the 'vessels') under thy two hands" (Ebers 100, 14–15). It is highly probable that *šś'w* here means the "indications" observable in the objective situation, that is, that the physician laying his hands upon the vessels of the heart is unable to discern any pulsations. It is conceivable also that we should render *šś'w* here "instructions," understanding the statement to mean that the physician will find at hand ("under thy two hands") no available instructions compiled from past experience; but I am strongly inclined to the opinion that the former interpretation is the correct one. The word may therefore originally have meant the observable "indications," and as the records of such indications accumulated and were accompanied also by the instructions to be followed by the practitioner, *šś'w* still continued to appear in the title and thus came to cover both the "*observations*" of the surgeon and the "*directions*" he was expected to follow. In such cases as those in the Kahun Papyrus it is difficult to find any other rendering for the word than "instructions," and this is the rendering I have employed in the translation of Papyrus Smith. The word is used in the plural throughout our treatise, and is three times accompanied by the plural demonstrative , "these" (XIV 7–8; XV 16; XVII 6). In these three cases the physician is admonished to treat the patient  "according to these instructions," and this passage favors the rendering "instructions" rather than "indications."

While the restoration of the initial word "Instructions" in the title of Case 1 is obviously correct, justification for the insertion of the next phrase is not so obvious at first. Its correctness is demonstrable on the basis of an examination of the group of cases in which it occurs, and especially of a comparison of this group with a later analogous group. Reference to the index of titles (p. 33) makes it evident at once that following upon Case 1 is a group of six cases each called "a wound in his head." A similar group of five cases in the temporal region begins with Case 18. The first of these five cases is designated merely as "a wound in his temple," and the subsequent discussion shows that it is not a serious wound. The remaining four cases, however, are much more serious, involving injury to the temporal bone beneath the fleshy tissue which limited the injury in the first case. Examining again Cases 2 to 7 we find that the last five involve injuries to the skull, while Case 2 preceding them is a wound of the exterior overlying soft tissue, not involving injury to the bone. It is evident then that Cases 2 to 7 form a group arranged like the group of Cases 18–22, with the flesh wound placed first and injuries to the underlying bone following after. If now we turn to the preserved text of Case 1 we find that it begins (I 1) with the words " his head," followed shortly by the words " his wound." The character of " his wound " is also explained in Gloss B (I 9–10), and we learn that it has no gash. We must conclude therefore that this group of seven cases of wounds in the head was introduced by *two* so-called flesh wounds (Cases 1 and 2), after which the surgeon continues with injuries to the skull (*calvaria*). As we are explicitly told that the wound had no gash, the word " wound " in the title of Case 1 must be followed immediately by the words " in his head " (see I 1), just as in Case 18 we have : " a wound in his temple." The "gash-wounds" or "gaping wounds" are then discussed in Cases 2–7.

The character of the wound is then further discussed, but it is impossible to understand this discussion without further investigation of the use of the word " wound " in our treatise.

[hieroglyphs] *wbnw*, " wound," is one of the commonest, if not the most common surgical term in our treatise. It occurs 142 times. It is either written in full as above, or with the determinative [hieroglyphs] ; but it is often abbreviated to a varying extent, thus: [hieroglyphs] (once only, VIII 18), [hieroglyphs], [hieroglyphs], [hieroglyphs] ; or this : [hieroglyphs], [hieroglyphs], [hieroglyphs], [hieroglyphs], or even [hieroglyphs] (twice only, X 3 ; XII 17). The plural strokes are rare and never appear with the full phonetic writing. The *gradual* appearance of the abbreviated writings is interesting and is an illustration of the fact that Case 1 is too near the beginning of the document to have been preceded by many cases. Throughout the first three cases (eight times preserved, several lost) the scribe carefully employs the full phonetic writing, [hieroglyphs], but at the very beginning of Case 4 he drops into an easy abbreviation, [hieroglyphs] (II 2), although he at once returns to the full writing (twice). With occasional reversions of this kind, he nevertheless reaches [hieroglyphs] at the bottom of the fourth column (IV 21). Indeed, after a full writing in II 18 and III 2 (Case 7), we find prevailingly [hieroglyphs] throughout the remainder of the treatise. It is reasonable to conclude that this *gradual* resort to abbreviated writing on the part of the scribe took place near the beginning of the document.

Wbnw designates the commonest form of injury treated in the document, as its frequent occurrence demonstrates. It stands as the first word of the title in the nineteen cases in which the injury is so designated in the diagnosis. These cases are as follows : 1 (probable, though title is lost), 2, 3, 4, 5, 6, 7, 9, 10, 14, 18, 20, 23, 26, 27, 28, 29, 40, and 47. Although the word has long been known and rendered " wound," the nature and character of the injury it might designate has not heretofore been precisely determined, and it is the new material from Papyrus Smith which now makes this possible. The word usually designates any injury to fleshy tissue, which may be severed or gashed as with a knife or sword blade, or ruptured as with the blow of a blunt weapon like a club, or rent as with the crushing action of some heavy object, or laid open by any agency which might destroy the skin ; but more rarely it may also indicate an injury to the bone.

A. *Injuries of the Soft Tissue*

A *wbnw* is often described or indicated as obviously in the fleshy tissue, e. g., Pap. Smith several times refers to " its (the *wbnw*'s) flesh" (XVII 1 and 5). In Pap. Ebers there is a small group of " Recipes for healing a *wbnw* inflicted on the flesh " (Ebers 70, 1). An interesting case in Pap. Smith deals with a fracture of the skull incurred without injury to the overlying external tissue (Case 8). The surgeon states that "there is no wound upon it (the *wbnw*) . . . the flesh of his head being uninjured" (IV 13). The clear implication is that the *wbnw* would be in the " flesh " of the head. There are frequent references in Pap. Smith to an injury to the bone (fracture, split, perforation, etc.), having " a *wbnw* over it" (VII 15 ; IX 1 ; XII 15 ; XII 16–17 ; etc.). Such a *wbnw* must necessarily be in the fleshy tissue. The same is true of a *wbnw* in the chin (Case 27), the bone beneath which is " uninjured " (IX 14, 15).

Papyrus Smith furnishes numerous important indications of the character of a *wbnw* in the soft tissue overlying a bone, for in practically every case of *wbnw* in our treatise, it is said to penetrate to the bone, or if there is no underlying bone, then to the underlying organ. For the sake of completeness all important data from the other Egyptian medical documents are also adduced in the following collection of materials.

1. Penetration. The *wbnw* treated in Pap. Smith, as we have already noted, is usually described as  (also)  "penetrating to the bone" (II 3 ; II 12 ; II 18 : etc.). Of a *wbnw* where there is no immediately underlying bone, we have a similar description (Case 28) : 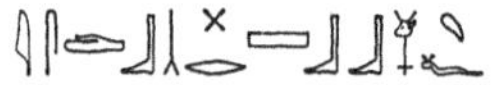 " piercing through to his gullet" (IX 19). The reference is to a wound in the throat.

2. Gash produced by a sword, knife or battle axe. In an ironical catalogue of the miseries of a military officer we find it stated that " his head is split with a wound (*wbn*) " (Pap. Anast. IV, 9, 7 = Anast. III, 5, 8). This is a type of wound often discussed in Pap. Smith and called  or " *wbnw* of a gash," meaning " a gaping wound." It occurs thirty-one times in our treatise (II 2 ; II 11 ; III 2; etc.). Such a wound may be called indifferently a *wbnw*, or a " gash ; " compare the two following parallel passages :

Case 14  (VI 8–9).

Case 47  (XVI 20).

The same variant, that is *kf·t*, " gash " for *wbnw* will be found by comparing IX 8 (Case 26) with V 6 (Case 10). See the commentary on *kf·t* in Case 1 (examination, pp. 90 ff). The character of this type of wound is very clearly indicated in several cases, especially Case 10, in discussing which the surgeon is instructed to apply a certain type of bandage " to the two lips of the gash-wound, in order to cause one to join to the other " (V 9). The " two lips " of such a wound are referred to in Pap. Smith a number of times, e. g.: I 1 ; VI 8 ; VI 13 ; VIII 21 ; etc. Similarly the " gash " and the " two lips " are introduced to describe a wound of different character of which it is said :

" It (the *wbnw*) has no gash . . . and his *wbnw* has not two lips " (VII 12–13). The character of a " gash-wound " is also indicated in the directions to the surgeon to " bring together his gash with stitching " (XVI 20). Such a wound may also be described as having a " mouth " (IX 20 ; XVII 9) ; but this term is not decisive for it is also employed of wounds which are not called " gash-wounds " (IV 20 ; VII 24–VIII 1 ; or especially Case 41, which employs it five times !). The "mouth" of a wound is also referred to in Pap. Ebers (70, 5 and 71, 15), and in Pap. Hearst (XII 11) there is mention of a " wound (*wbnw*) having an open mouth."

3. Perforation produced by a pointed weapon like an arrow or spear. Such wounds are not clearly and precisely defined in our treatise. The word  *thm* indicating the verb " to perforate " or the noun " perforation " is usually applied to injuries to the *bone,* as in Cases 3 (see commentary, I 18), 7, 15, etc. The verb  *šdb* " to penetrate " or " perforate " is, however, employed to indicate that a perforating wound in the fleshy tissue has penetrated through the lip to the interior of the mouth (Case 26), or through the nose to the interior of the nostril (Case 14). See the discussion of these two cases.

4. A contusion or a less clearly defined rupture of the tissue, produced by a blunt weapon like a club. This is the type of wound referred to in the familiar apostrophe to a drunkard : 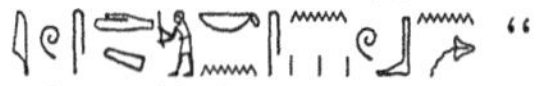 " (People flee from thee, for) thou inflictest wounds (*wbn*) on them " (Pap. Anast. IV, 11, 12). Such wounds are described in Pap. Smith as having no gash and therefore lacking two lips (Case 18, VII 12–13, cited above under 2).

5. Laceration and rupture of the soft tissue caused by the crushing action of a heavy object which lays open the flesh. Papyrus Ebers refers to a " wound (*wbnw*) of crushing " (Ebers 110, 4), and it may be that Case 18, just classified under 4, should be placed here. The only direct reference to crushing in Pap. Smith is a case of a crushed cervical vertebra (Case 33).

6. Burns. There is no reference to burns in Pap. Smith, but Pap. Ebers contains a recipe for a " burn-*wbnw* " (Ebers 68, 17–18), that is a " burn-wound," and it contains other recipes for burns not designated as " wounds," e. g., 68, 20 ff.

B. *Injuries of the Bones*

Wbnw is not commonly applied to injuries of the bones. In Case 29, however, Pap. Smith clearly defines a " gaping wound in the vertebra of his neck " (X 3 ff.). More often the terms for injuries in the bones are not general like " wound," but specific, like 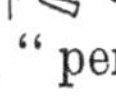 *šd* " smash " (compound comminuted fracture), 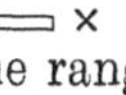 *pšn,* " split," *thm,* " perforation," or *sḥm,* " crushing," etc. The range of our sur-

geon's knowledge and mention of wounds must include a study of such words, which will be found in the index. Nor do these wholly exhaust the available materials, for the surgeon deals with wounds of the brain (Cases 6 and 8); and the reference to canals leading to the lungs (XII 2) would indicate that if our treatise were preserved to the end, we would find injuries to the internal organs.

The observed symptoms of various types of *wbnw* and the surgeon's medicinal or surgical treatment will be discussed in the commentary on the cases themselves.

C. *Sores*

Somewhat less common is the use of *wbnw* to designate a sore, the origin of which may not have been a wound; e.g., even in our treatise, written to discuss injuries, *wbnw* appears in Case 39 (XIII 9) with the probable meaning "sore." Confer the Greek ἕλκος which means both "wound" and "sore."

m tp·f, "in his head." Regarding the correctness of restoring these words after "wound," there cannot be any doubt, as we have the injury called "a wound in his head" in the diagnosis (I 1). The word for "head" demands some discussion, partly grammatical, but chiefly anatomical. The scribe has used the word-sign, and it is well known that in such cases we are often unable to determine which of the two common Egyptian words for head we should read, *tp* or *ḏ'ḏ'*.

Taking up first the word *tp*, it should be noted that it never occurs written with phonetic complement in Pap. Smith. In my judgment we cannot be certain therefore that the reading *tp* is correct, although the employment of *tp* for the "head" as a whole is in accordance with Egyptian usage. In view of the possibility that we should read *tp* here, we must examine the anatomical meaning of the word as determined by usage. The word originally meant the "tip, top," or "head" of a thing. This meaning is very old. As far back as the Pyramid Texts we find "the tips of the two wings" (Pyr. 2043b, 1122b pl.); "the tip[s] of their (female) breasts" (Pyr. 1282a); or in an example very appropriate to our inquiry, "the *nbś*-tree inclines its head (*tp*) to thee" (Pyr. 808a). It is also used as far back as the Pyramid Texts for the *human* head as a whole, e.g., "He has given to thee thy head" (*tp*), said to the deceased king (Pyr. 639b); or "Thy head (*tp*) is fastened on" (Pyr. 1262a, cf. 682e). References to the detached head of the deceased with the word written phonetically *tp* continue down into Greek times. Cf. de Morgan, *Ombos*, I, 39, 36, *bis*, and often at Ombos; likewise in Naville, *Mythe d'Horus*, XV. The severed head of Osiris at Dendera (Mariette, *Dendérah*, IV, 37, 66) is called *tp ntr*. The best anatomical evidence that *tp* means the whole head is perhaps the phrase "the seven openings of the head" (read *tp* as shown by the Demotic, Bilingual Pap. Rhind, I, 3, 3). The "seven openings" are of course the ears, nostrils, eyes and mouth,— a good indication of the anatomical meaning of *tp*, viz., the whole head.

As we turn to the use of *tp* in the medical documents however, we meet with a difficulty; for they do not contain a single example of *tp* (*caput*) with a phonetic writing ensuring the reading *tp*. Examples of anatomical usage of *tp* are common in Pap. Smith, with the original meaning, " tip, top, head " of some other organ or part of the body. The list is as follows:

 " tips of his toes " (IV 14–15).

 " tip of his shoulder-fork " (IV 17).

 " top of his eye-brow " (V 6).

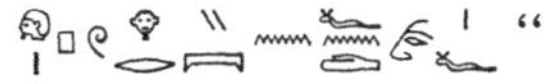 " It is the upper tip of his nose " (V 14).

 " the tip[s] of his two clavicles " (XI 18).

 "it means the displacement of the tips of his *ḫ'b*-bone " (XI 22–23).

 " the tips of them (clavicles) are fastened in the upper bone of his breast " (XI 23).

 " *tp-šḳr* in his sternum " (XIII 3).

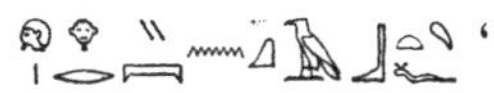 " The uppermost tip of his sternum " (XIII 17).

 . . . . .  " the ribs of his sternum . . . and their heads [are red] " (XIV 23–XV 1).

 " the heads of the ribs of his sternum are displaced " (XV 4).

 " *šḥr tp-šḳr* in his sternum " (XVI 12–13).

Tp is not phonetically written in any of these cases, but the reading *tp* cannot be doubted in view of the meaning of the word and the context in the above examples. The fact that these unquestionable examples of *tp* are all invariably written  is perhaps a fair reason for regarding this writing  where it means " head (*caput*) " as likewise intended for *tp*, and although this conclusion is not certain, the reading *tp* has been adopted herein for all such writings, of which there are forty-seven occurrences in our treatise.

The other word for " head,"  *ḏ'ḏ'*, occurs only three times written out phonetically in our text (IV 13; IV 20; XI 16). This word likewise indicates the head as a whole. In Pap. Ebers it is used of the head of a fish (Ebers 52, 22), of an ass (*ibid.*, 25, 15; cf. 91, 10; 88, 15); and Pap. Westcar (8, 21–22) employs it of the head of a goose cut off by the magician. The severed head of an ox written 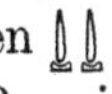 appears in a tomb relief at Leyden (Leemanns, *Mon. fun.*, pl. XXIV; cf. also Pap. judic. de Turin, 3, 2 and Pap. Boulaq, 11, obverse). Similarly it is used of the human head in the Book of the Dead (Naville, 18, 31 Aa); also for the severed head of Osiris (*ibid.*, 93, 5 Ca).

In Pap. Anastasi (III 5, 8) the well-known example:  "His head is split with a wound," is a good illustration of our group of head wounds, as well as a demonstration that it was customary to use *ḏ'ḏ'* in such connections. A demonstration that *ḏ'ḏ'* designates anatomically the whole head is to be found in the phrase: 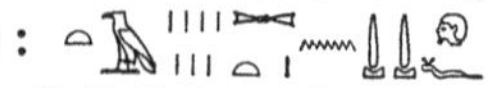 "the seven openings of his head" (*ḏ'ḏ'*) (Pap. Leyden, 345, verso 5, 5–6, from text prepared for Berlin *Wörterbuch* by Gardiner). This example demonstrates that the anatomical meaning of *ḏ'ḏ'* is essentially the same as that of *tp* which, as we have seen above, likewise contains seven openings. When used of the human head in the medical papyri and phonetically written out so as to be unmistakable, the occurrences of the word *ḏ'ḏ'* are not numerous, e. g., Ebers 66. 11; 86, 15; 90, 18; 109, 10 (probably); Kahun Med. Pap. 2, 26; Pap. Hearst, II, 1. In the vast majority of cases in the medical papyri the word "head" is written , which we may of course read either *tp* or *ḏ'ḏ'*, e.g., Ebers 1, 4.

An important variant in Pap. Smith illustrates the loose use of *ḏ'ḏ'* as "skull." In discussing an injury of the forehead in Case 9, the surgeon twice refers to the injury as follows:

 "fracture of the shell of his skull" (IV 19).

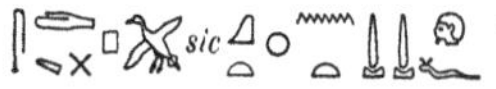 "fracture of the shell of his head" (IV 19–20).

It may be therefore that *ḏ'ḏ'* is more closely related to or connected with "skull" than *tp*. In this connection the following list of phrases is important:

A fracture of the skull is under  "the skin of his " (IV 12–13).

Fragments (of bone) are embedded in 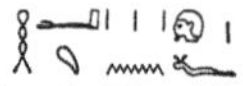 "the flesh of his " (II 9).

"The odor of the crown (literally "chest") of his " (III 21).

"As for (the following statement of the text) 'His countenance is wet with sweat,' it means his  is a little moist" (III 18–19).

Whether we are to read *tp* or *ḏ'ḏ'* in the above list of passages it is evident that  means more than the calvaria.

The word  *ḏnn·t*, which we have rendered "skull" above should be carefully examined in this connection. In the first place it should be noted that the serious injuries of the skull, like "fracture" (II 11), "perforation" (I 19), and "splitting" (II 5), are all said to be in the *ḏnn·t*. In describing different kinds of fracture of the *ḏnn·t*, the surgeon mentions "bones that have got into this fracture and sunk deep into the interior of his *ḏnn·t*" (II 16). Again a fracture is described as "large and opening into the interior of his *ḏnn·t*" (II 24). Of a fracture in the forehead, the surgeon says, "the shell of his *ḏnn·t* is fractured" (IV 19). In our own Case 1 the surgeon mentions the "bone of his *ḏnn·t*" (I 11). Under these circumstances we cannot doubt that the surgeon's technical use of the word identifies it with the calvaria. In the other medical papyri the word occurs only in Pap. Ebers and Pap. Hearst, which do not employ it of the human body, except possibly Ebers 90, 16–17, where *ḏnn·t* is significantly parallel with " bones." Otherwise Ebers and Hearst employ *ḏnn·t* only for the head of a fish as a medicinal ingredient of a prescription (Ebers 47, 12 ; 47, 14–15 ; 88, 8 ; Hearst, VI, 4). Outside of the medical papyri the word does not occur in the entire range of the older documents and is not found until Greek times, e.g., Dümichen, *Geogr. Inschr.* III, 43 (Dendera) ; Piehl, *Inscr.* II, 68, 3 and 63, 4 = Rochem. I, 576, 5 (Edfu). The indications are that our document has taken a term current, though not of *common* use, and has adopted it as the technical anatomical term for skull.

The justification for the restoration *ʿr n ḳś* " penetrating to the bone " is the fact that the ancient commentary (Gloss C, I 10–12) contains an explanation of this phrase. The reason for the insertion of the phrase just at this point is its occurrence after " his head " in all the other cases of this group, 1 to 7, except Case 5, where its omission in the title is doubtless an oversight, for it is inserted in the examination (II 12).

ʿr, " to extend, penetrate." It appears twice in our document in the archaic form *yʿ* (XIII 13 ; XIII 15) ; otherwise it is written with the greatest regularity (twenty-nine times), and always without . There is no trace or indication of a third weak radical, as sometimes in the M.K., even where reduplication would be required by the form in case the root were III-inf. To the total of thirty-one passages in which it occurs, we can add some others with certainty by restoration of Case 1, which must have contained several more occurrences. It was probably used at least 35 times in Papyrus Smith.

Its first occurrence in our treatise was in Case 1, for as already noted the commentary on this case contains an explanation of it (Gloss C), which is unfortunately very fragmentary. Before we undertake to discuss it, we should examine a cognate gloss in Case 18 (Gloss A, VII 12) in which we find the following parallelism :

Phrase to be explained : = " *ʿr* to the bone."

Explanation : = " arriving at the bone."

It is obvious then that our word *ʿr* means " to reach, to arrive " or with the following preposition " to reach as far as," " to arrive at," for the explanation can only be understood as meaning : " to arrive at," " to reach as far as " the bone.

We are now in a position to study the fragmentary gloss, explaining our word and its context in Case 1 (Gloss C, I 10–12). Accepting the restorations of the broken text which will be further justified in the commentary (p. 117), the gloss may be rendered : " As for (the quoted words) : '*ʿr* to the bone of his skull, (but) not having a gash,'—it means (literally, 'it says'), there is a gaping of the flesh, although ⌜—⌝ . . . (loss of several words) . . . ⌜—⌝ over the bone of his skull, without gaping of one (lip) from the other, being narrow, not wide." The general sense of this fragmentary comment is evidently that the exterior orifice of the wound, while gaping slightly, is not large nor gaping like a gash with two lips; but that in depth it penetrates through the flesh to the bone.

The simplest meaning of *ʿr* as an anatomical term is to be found in its use to define the extent of a region or organ. In Papyrus Smith we find the following examples of this kind:

1. "The two sides of his nose" 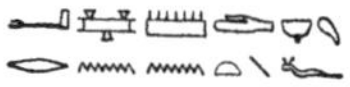 "extending (*ʿr*) to his maxillary" (V 15).

2. "The chamber of his nose is the middle of his nose as far as the back" (or "end"), 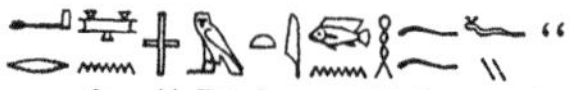 "extending (*ʿr*) to the region between his two eyebrows" (V 21).

3. "It is a dislocation of the vertebra of his neck," 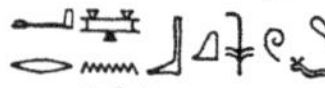, "extending (*ʿr*) to his backbone, which causes him to be unconscious of his arms and his legs" (X 15–16).

4. "In the upper bone of his breast," 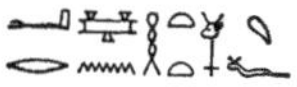 "extending (*ʿr*) to his throat" (XI 23).

The examples of the anatomical use of the verb 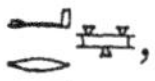, *ʿr* certainly do not confirm its usually accepted meaning "to ascend." Gardiner has made the same observation regarding its meaning in other connections (*Notes on ..... Sinuhe*, pp. 12–13). It is obvious that the verb must mean "to pass on" in the first place, and then "to reach," "to pass by," or "pass through," or "pass beyond." For example, in the Book of the Dead the deceased says:  "I reach it (dung) not with my two hands" (BD ed. Budge, 189, from Nu 19, 13; six duplicates all with same text). It is this meaning "reach," "penetrate to," which has led our surgeon to employ it to indicate the passage of a wound rupturing the fleshy tissue, through that tissue to the bone beneath. He employs it especially to describe deep wounds, both "gaping wounds" (*wbnw n kf·t*) and others with a smaller and more irregular orifice, described as "having no gash" (*nn kf·t* or *n wnt kf·t*), in all twenty-seven times. In all of these examples, *ʿr*, which in such cases we may render "penetrate," is followed by a preposition and the word "bone," thus: 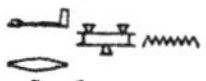 (twenty-three times), or 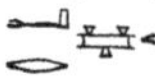 (four times, twice with archaic writing ).[1]

It is significant that this anatomical and surgical use of  with the meaning "extend" (anatomical), or "penetrate" (surgical) is *unknown outside of our treatise.* It is evident that our Egyptian surgeon or his ancestors had built up a list of words with specialized medical or surgical meanings not occurring in other literature. As we shall see, it is largely if not exclusively these terms which have gained a technical

[1] The Berlin *Woerterbuch* has only six examples with the preposition , and only four with . Our material in Papyrus Smith shows that is the normal preposition. The phrase 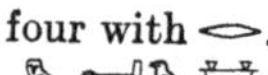, which Gardiner in his commentary on Sinuhe has shown to mean "in the vicinity of" or similar, is of course related to the verb *ʿr*.

or professional meaning, to which the ancient reader of the roll found it necessary to append an explanatory commentary.

The inclusion of the phrase "of his skull" in the title may be open to question. That it occurred in the examination and diagnosis cannot be doubted, for reasons fully indicated in the discussion below. The commentary on *ḏnn·t* will be found above.

EXAMINATION

Bottom of lost column to I 1

 (from Case 18, VII 8–9) ; or

 Case 2, I 13 ; cf. Case 7, III 9–10).

[a] This position of the beginning of I 1 is almost certain. See Vol. II, Pl. I B, l. 1.

Translation

[If thou examinest a man having a wound in his head, penetrating to the bone of his skull, (but) not having a gash, thou shouldst palpate his wound (or, thou shouldst lay thy hand upon it) ; shouldst thou find his skull uninjured, not having a perforation, a split or a smash in it,] (conclusion in diagnosis).

Commentary

The restoration as a whole is drawn from Case 18, but also with the use of Case 7 and Case 2. In some minor points the restoration is uncertain, but in the main it represents without doubt the general content of the examination as it was originally written in the lost column. The following parallel between the group to which Case 1 belongs and the analogous group of injuries to the temporal region in Cases 18 to 22 will demonstrate the correctness of basing the restoration on Case 18.

Cases 1 & 2. Superficial wound ; bone uninjured.	Case 18. Superficial wound ; bone uninjured.
Case 3. Skull perforated.	Cases 19 & 20. Temporal bone perforated.
Case 4. Skull split.	Case 21. Temporal bone split.
Case 5. Skull fractured.	Case 22. Temporal bone fractured.

An examination of the content of Case 1 as revealed in the partially preserved diagnosis, and also in the glosses which quote from the discussion of the case, as we shall see in discussing the diagnosis itself, demonstrates that Case 1 was closely parallel in content and arrangement with Case 18. This is also true of Case 1 as compared with Case 2, which was also a wound exposing but not injuring the calvaria, and Case 2 furnishes a number of valuable hints for the recovery of the text of Case 1. All these details will be noticed in the following commentary.

In the description of the wound there are two chief observations: it penetrates to the bone; and there is no gash (*kf·t*). In the diagnosis the observation regarding the lack of a *kf·t* comes first, and penetration to the bone second, as shown by the preserved text (I 2). In Gloss C however, in the quotation of the words to be explained, the penetration to the bone comes first and the lack of a *kf·t* is second. Gloss C therefore did not quote from the diagnosis, and consequently must be quoting from the examination. The examination therefore must have contained a statement having the penetration of the bone mentioned first and the lack of a *kf·t* second. A variation in arrangement as between examination and diagnosis is sometimes observable in other cases of our treatise. The restoration of the two observations regarding the wound in the examination is therefore drawn from the quotation in Gloss C (I 10–11, p. 116).

In the opening words of the examination the word "examine" itself is an important technical term, which will be found discussed in the commentary on Gloss A (I 3–9, pp. 104–6), a long explanation of the meaning of the term by the ancient practitioner himself.

 *kf·t*, noun, "gash, cut." There was no inherited word-sign for the word and it is therefore always written out phonetically, with a knife as the determinative. It is hardly likely that this knife once served as the word-sign. The existence of no word-sign may suggest that this exclusively surgical word did not find written form until after the picture stage of writing had been left behind.

This surgical word is found only in Pap. Smith and the fact that it occurs there no less than thirty-six times enables us to establish its meaning with certainty. The ancient commentator found it necessary to explain the term *wbnw n kf·t*, "gash-wound" (Case 2, Gloss A, I 15–16), but the entire explanation is lost in the lacuna at the beginning of l. 16, only its last words "his wound" being preserved. The knife-determinative gives us a preliminary indication of the meaning, which is amply corroborated by the use of the word. In Case 18 we have a wound in the temple which is said to have no *kf·t*, and the ancient commentator explains in a gloss (VII 13) that this means "his wound has not two lips." "Two lips" are obviously the chief characteristic of a gash. Concerning this wound of similar character Case 1 says in Gloss B: "There is no gaping (*kf·t*) of one (lip) from the other" (I 10; again in l. 11).

Complete parallelism between " two lips " and *kf·t* is clear in the following two examples (XVI 18–20 and VI 8–9) :

1. 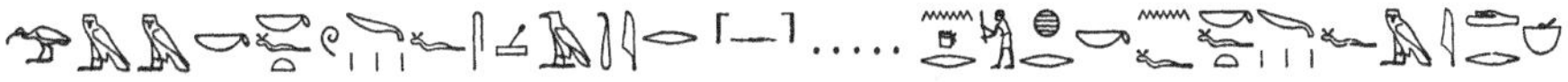

2. 

1. " Shouldst thou find its *kf·t* separated from ⌜—⌝ . . . thou shouldst draw together for him his *kf·t* with stitching " (Case 47 ; XVI 18–20).

2. " Shouldst thou find the two lips of that wound separated from each other, thou shouldst draw together for him that wound with stitching " (Case 14 ; VI 8–9).

In the second part of the above parallelism, it is important to note that " his *kf·t* " (plur.) is parallel with " that wound " in the other text. In other words, the term " his *kf·t* " (plur.) is simply a variant for " that wound." The same parallelism of " his *kf·t* " (plur.) and " his wound " occurs again in Case 26 (IX 8) and Case 10 (V 6). See commentary on Case 10 (treatment). Further examination shows that what is here designated both by *kf·t* (plur.) and " wound " is the injury to the soft tissue. The use of *kf·t* in the plural in the first example above (XVI 19–20) is found also in V 6; XVII 4 (*bis*). That the plural is meant is clearly shown by the use of the plural demonstrative in XVII 4. This usage throws light on the origin of the word. It is obvious that in the cases where this plural occurs, as shown by the above parallelism with " his wound," only *one* gash is being discussed ; but such a gash is shown by the discussion to be gaping, thus exposing *two* faces of gashed tissue, and it is these which the surgeon is to draw together. Such gashed tissue is *laid bare*, and reminds us at once of the well-known verb 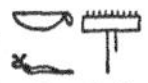 *kfy*, " to lay bare," of which our word must be a regular feminine infinitive. It is highly probable that the term was consciously devised by the surgeon to describe this particular kind of injury, in view of the facts that the word is found nowhere else outside of our surgical treatise, and that it needed an explanatory comment (Gloss A) in order to be understood.

Kf·t is used especially to add greater precision to the more general word *wbnw*, " wound " (see p. 82), being appended as a genitive after *wbnw*. As we say " a thing of beauty," so the Egyptian might say " wound of a gash," meaning a " gashed wound." This phrase,  *wbnw n kf·t* occurs thirty-one times (five restored from context in Cases 2 and 3) in our treatise, and in all cases designates a deep and dangerous wound. Although the table on p. 92 does not contain all the available data for describing each case and the symptoms developed, the depth and serious nature of the wound will be evident.

Out of the eleven cases the *wbnw n kf·t* (" gash-wound ") penetrates to the bone in nine, while of the two remaining, it penetrates the throat to the gullet in one, and the other (Case 47) is shown by the context to be a yawning wound. In six out of the eleven cases there is serious injury to the bone beneath the " gash-wound ; " and it is evident that the whole injury has been produced by a violent blow with a weapon like a sword or battle axe (Cases 4, 5, 6) or a spear (Cases 3, 7, 29). Obviously such wounds are those of battle, and we must conclude that the surgeon had gained knowledge of such injuries while following the Egyptian armies and treating the wounded on the field—a fact of substantial historical importance, for the author of this treatise on wounds is the earliest known surgeon in history to possess such experience. His employment in such work denotes a high degree of civilization and of humanitarian sentiment.

Case.	*Injury to bone if any.*	*Depth of flesh wound.*	*Reference.*
2	Head : skull uninjured	" penetrating to the bone "	I 12 ; I 12–13 ; I 14 ; I 15
3	,, ,, perforated (*thm*)	,, ,, ,, ,, ,,	I 18 ; I 19 ; I 21
4	,, ,, split (*pšn*)	,, ,, ,, ,, ,,	II 2 ; II 3 ; II 5.
5	,, ,, fractured (*šd*)	,, ,, ,, ,, ,,	II 11 ; II 12 ; II 14.
6	,, ,, fractured (*šd*) brain ruptured	,, ,, ,, ,, ,,	II 18 ; II 18–19.
7	Head : *tp'w* of skull perforated	,, ,, ,, ,, ,,	III 2 ; III 5 ; III 12.
10	,, eyebrow ; no injury to bone	,, ,, ,, ,, ,,	V 9.
27	,, chin ; no injury to bone	,, ,, ,, ,, ,,	IX 13 ; IX 13–14 ; IX 15.
28	Throat	" perforating to gullet "	IX 18–19.
29	Neck : " vertebra of his neck "	" penetrating to the bone "	X 3 ; X 4.
47	Shoulder	gaping wound	XVI 16 ; XVI 17 ; XVII 1 ; XVII 10.

It will be obvious that the absence of *kf·t* was an important negative observation in the description of the wound in our case as also in Case 18.

As the wound penetrates to the bone it is the duty of the surgeon to investigate the injury and determine whether it not only " extends to " but also *includes* the bone. This investigation is designated by the word  *ḏʿr*, " to seek, search, search out, investigate, probe, palpate." The word has long been known outside of the medical papyri, where it is common ; but its surgical use has never been determined clearly, for it occurs outside of Pap. Smith only in Pap. Ebers, and there only three times. One of these passages is of importance for determining the surgical meaning of the word. It reads :  " If thy finger palpates and it is like *ḫpʿ* under thy fingers, . . . " (Ebers 106, 18–19). The surgeon is investigating a lanced boil or cyst, and the verb *ḏʿr* indicates his subsequent palpation with the finger. This is quite in accord with the usage in Pap. Smith, where the word occurs ten times besides the restored passage in our Case 1. The significant passages are as follows :

" Thou shouldst palpate (*ḏʿr*) his wound, and if thou findest something disturbing therein under thy fingers " (Case 4, II 3–4).

" Thou shouldst palpate (*ḏʿr*) his wound, and if thou findest that smash (fracture) which is in his skull deep and sunken under thy fingers " (Case 5, II 12–13).

" Thou shouldst palpate (*ḏʿr*) his wound and if thou findest that smash (fracture) which is in his skull . . . and something therein throbbing and fluttering under thy fingers " (Case 6, II 19–21).

" Thou shouldst palpate his wound and if thou findest the temporal (bone) uninjured " (Case 18, VII 8–9 ; cf. Case 27, IX 14–15).

Besides the explicit statement that the surgeon palpates with his fingers, it is interesting to note that it would only be in this way that he could feel the pulsations in the brain. There is no reference in the surgery of our treatise to probing with an instrument. Another evidence that such investigation is done with the fingers is found in the fact that Case 2 and Case 7 display a variant but parallel text at this point, which reads : " Thou shouldst lay thy hand upon it " (see text of examination above). It should be noted also that our word " palpate " (*ḏʿr*), as found in Case 10 (V 6), is twice represented by the variant " examine " in Case 26 (IX 7) and Case 29 (X 5). See commentary on *ḫ'y*, " examine " in Case 1 (I 3). This would suggest that " *ḏʿr* " may sometimes also connote the idea of making a more general examination. In this connection it is important to observe that in Case 8 (IV 5–6) the surgeon is directed to " palpate " (*ḏʿr*) a serious fracture of the skull, when the overlying soft tissue is uninjured. See commentary on Case 8, examination, IV 5–6.

gmm·k, "Shouldst thou find, etc.," is restored as in Case 18. Case 2 has a slightly different text at this point.

The list of three injuries to the bone : *thm*, *pšn*, and *śd* (" perforation," " split," and "smash" ("fracture")) are restored here in the order in which they are taken up in Cases 3, 4, and 5 respectively ; but Case 18 gives the list at this point in a different order, viz., *pšn*, *thm*, *śd* (VII 9 ; likewise Case 2, I 17), although the cases following Case 18 take up the injuries in the order *thm*, *pšn*, *śd*.

Diagnosis

I 1–2

[a] The amount of space lost here at the beginning of l. 2 may be seen by comparing the certain restorations at the beginnings of the lines of this column on Pl. I B and C.

[a] Part of this sign is preserved at the beginning of the lacuna ; see commentary.

Translation

[Thou shouldst say regarding him : " One having a woun]d in his head, while his wound does [not] have two lips, - - -, nor a gash, although [it penetrates to the bone of] his head. An ailment which I will treat."

Commentary

That Column I begins with the diagnosis is shown by the fact that the verdict is in l. 2, and in all cases it is preceded by the diagnosis which makes the verdict possible. It will not have differed in form from the other cases in the same group and throughout the document. The beginning of the preserved text of Column I must be compared with an analogous case to justify the restorations suggested. As we have already noted Case 1 is the first of a group of cases chiefly concerned with grave injuries to the skull. In the same way Case 18 is the first of a group of cases dealing chiefly with injuries of the temporal bone. See comparative table in examination, p. 89. Case 1 and Case 18 deal with flesh wounds over the bone, and they are parallel or analogous both in position, each in its respective group, as well as in the character of the content of the discussion. Like Case 1, Case 18 states that the wound has no gash, and a gloss explains this statement as meaning that the wound does not have two lips (VII 13). Placing the two statements together :

 "while his wound has [not] two lips" (I 1, from Case 1) ;

 " and his wound has not two lips " (VII 13, from Case 18),

we cannot doubt that the lacuna in Case 1 contained a negative, although it is difficult to determine the exact word which will fit the fragmentary signs still visible on the upper edge of the papyrus at this point. In view of the certainty that some negative filled the lacuna in Case 1 at this point, it is remarkable to find the verb  *mn* preceding *špt·wy* in the repetition of this passage quoted for purposes of explanation by the ancient editor in Gloss B (I 9–10). This difficulty will be found discussed in the commentary on Gloss B (pp. 114–116).

Continuing the discussion of the restoration before taking up the commentary, it is regrettable that the short lacuna at the beginning of l. 2 resists all efforts to determine its former content. The only source for material is Case 18 and nothing drawn thence seems to fit the sense, though it would be easy to fit the space. The restoration in the last bracket is certain. In the first place the edge of the papyrus at the beginning of the lacuna has preserved the right end of the cross stroke of . Turning now to Case 18 (VII 12) we find after *n wn·t kf·t*, the words *yst św ʿr n ḳś*. This makes the correctness of our restoration quite certain.

 *špt·wy*, " two lips." This term is used eleven times in the Pap. Smith to designate the two edges of a gaping gash-wound. This usage is peculiar to our treatise, for it is not found in any of the other medical papyri. Pap. Ebers employs it once for the " two lips of the vulva " (95, 22, correcting determinative), which is a similar comparison; but otherwise it is used only for the shores of a body of water.

The concluding statement of the diagnosis is the most important proposition it contains. For lack of a modern equivalent, we call it the " *verdict*." The reader is referred to the discussion in the introduction (pp. 46–48). As we have noticed in the introduction, the verdict is the conclusion of the diagnosis, both together forming an apodosis of which the examination is the protasis. It is quite certain that the principal proposition of the apodosis is the statement " Thou shouldst say," at the head of the diagnosis, and the verdict is simply a second direct object of the verb " Thou shouldst say."

 *mr* " hurt, injury, pain, ailment, disease." This word, used both as verb and noun, evidently applied either to artificial and accidental injury, or to natural suffering and disease. An old example of its use in connection with an artificial case is found in the Fifth Dynasty tomb of  at Sakkara in a scene of manicure and pedicure treatment in which the patient says to the man operating on his foot:  " Do not let it hurt " (*mr*) (from my own copy). Its use in our treatise is exclusively confined to artificial injuries.

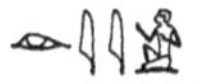 *yry·y*, " which I will treat " (literally " make ") is grammatically a fine example of the new " prospective relative " form, of the existence of which Gunn has recently given a brilliant demonstration in his *Studies in Egyptian Syntax*. See p. 3, example No. (3) for the form . Strong and unquestionable evidence as additional proof of the correctness of his recognition and identification of the new form might have been adduced from Papyrus Ebers, where it occurs sixteen times in this form of the physician's verdict.

Of the three forms of the verdict this one which we call verdict 1 is found outside of our papyrus a total of nineteen times: twice in the Berlin Medical Papyrus (3038, Nos. 154 and 161); once in the Hearst Papyrus (No. 174, 12, 2) and sixteen times in Papyrus Ebers (fourteen times in the concluding group of suppurating sores and the like, Nos. 857–860, 863–872, and twice elsewhere, Nos. 200 and 617). Among the fourteen occurrences at the end of Papyrus Ebers are four in which this verdict receives the addition , thus: 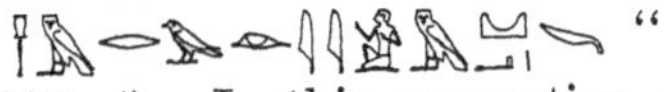 " An ailment (*mr*) which I will treat with the lancet " (105, 4). In this connection one might conclude that *yr* means " operate," but it is used so often in cases where no operation is involved that one can hardly doubt the rendering " treat." In Pap. Smith this verdict occurs thirty times, and in twenty-nine of these treatment is prescribed. The case lacking treatment is the second group of symptoms in Case 34, where it is quite evident that the scribe has inserted verdict 1 when he really intended verdict 3, a verdict indicating treatment is useless. Compare his similar error in Case 35 (see list of titles). In these thirty occurrences of verdict 1 the result of the treatment is given in twenty-five and in all of these twenty-five it is continued " until he recovers " (*r nḏm-f*). Of the five cases in which no result (like *r nḏm-f*) is given, one is due to the loss of the conclusion (Case 48), one to the error of the scribe already noted (Case 34) ; and in only three is there really no statement of the result, which, as we have seen, where given at all is uniformly favorable. It is evident that verdict 1 suggests a favorable outcome of a case easy to treat, although it is not evident that *r nḏm-f* always indicates complete recovery.

TREATMENT

I 2–3

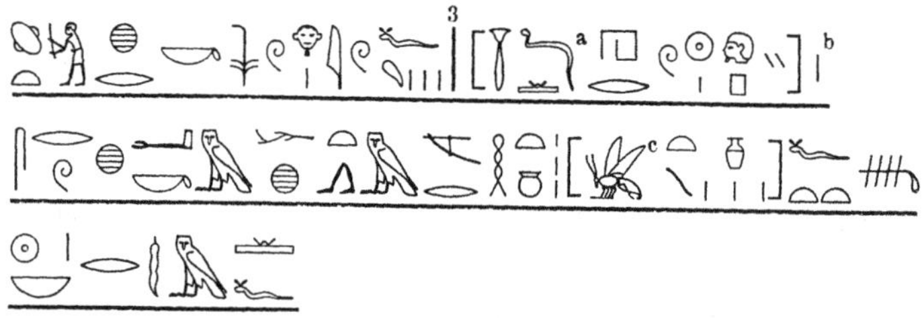

[a] Written out fully as in XIII 16 ; the restoration then exactly fills the gap. Otherwise it is taken from Case 18.

[b] Remains of a single sign in red ; the scribe has employed the red for the entire text of the treatment.

[c] Restored as in Case 18.

Translation

Thou shouldst bind it with [fresh] meat [the first day] (and) treat afterward with grease, [honey] (and) lint every day until he recovers.

Commentary

 *wt*, "to bind, to bandage." The Egyptian idiom seems to us curiously perverted. It literally means " Thou shouldst bind it (the wound) upon fresh meat." Any one who has visited a modern museum and seen a really good example of the Egyptian embalmer's bandaging knows that he was a master in the art of applying and arranging bandages (see Pl. III, Figs. 6–7). The same skill was available for the benefit of a wounded patient. We therefore find bandaging occupying an important and effective place in Egyptian surgery and medicine. Bandages were applied for two purposes : for covering and keeping effectively in place the medicaments prescribed ; or for mechanically retaining in position and protecting while healing the ruptured

tissue or the broken bone of the injury. The first is a matter chiefly of medicine, the second is purely a matter of surgery. We shall postpone the discussion of the second until later (Case 7, Gloss C, III 18; Case 11, treatment, V 13), as we are concerned here solely with the first.

The medicaments applied by being bound on are either simple remedies like the fresh meat above, or a combination of two ingredients, especially grease and honey applied with lint as above; or a more elaborate prescription of as many as five ingredients to be triturated together and bound on (Cases 41 and 46). There are in our treatise thirty-three instances in which medicaments are externally applied in this way. They are the following:

Fresh meat: Cases 1, 2 (restored), 3 (restored), 10, 14, 16, 17, 18, 26, 27, 28, 29, 30, 32, 40, and 47.

Grease, honey, and lint: Cases 7 and 14. These are the cases with our verb *wt* "to bind"; but all the instances employing *śrwḫ* "treat" with grease, honey, and sometimes lint, as shown in Case 1 (pp. 100–102), should also be added here. There are nineteen of these instances, see *śrwḫ*, below, p. 100.

With *ymrw*: Cases 15, 32, 35, 36, 37, 38, 42, 43.

With *ymrw* and honey: Case 25.

With a triturated prescription of several ingredients up to five: Cases 41 (three prescriptions), and 46 (four prescriptions).

We will take up the discussion of these medicaments as we meet them in the course of translating the document.

 *ywf w’ḏ*, "fresh meat." In all of the sixteen cases in which meat is employed in this way as an external medicament, it is carefully specified in fifteen (omitting Case 2) that "*fresh* meat" shall be used, and that it shall be applied for the first day only. It was a preparatory remedy, anticipating the application of other medicaments. In only one case (Case 29) do we find "fresh meat" as the only medicament employed. As a "folk remedy" it has survived down to the present day, although modern scientific therapeusis would regard it with a smile. It has been suggested that its use was purely magical. This suggestion is at once refuted by an examination of the table below, showing that in the most dangerous cases where the assistance of supernatural forces would be most needed, like Cases 4 and 5, it was not employed.

Cases in which "fresh meat" is bandaged on a wound the first day

Case 1. Flesh wound on head over calvaria, penetrating to bone (verdict 1, treatment "till he recovers").
,, 2. Flesh wound on head over calvaria, penetrating to bone (same).
,, 3. Wound on the head, puncturing the calvaria (same).
,, 10. Flesh wound in top of eyebrow, penetrating to bone (same).

Case 14. Flesh wound in nose (verdict 1, treatment "till he recovers").
„ 16. "Split" (*pšn*) in maxilla (verdict 1, treatment "till he recovers").
„ 17. "Fracture" (*śd*) in maxilla (verdict 3 by error, treatment "till he recovers").
„ 18. Flesh wound in temple (verdict 1, treatment "till he recovers").
„ 26. Flesh wound in upper lip (verdict 1, treatment "till he recovers").
„ 27. Flesh wound in chin (verdict 1, treatment "till he recovers").
„ 28. Flesh wound in throat (verdict 2, treatment "till he recovers").
„ 29. Wound in cervical vertebra (verdict 2, result doubtful).
„ 30. Sprain in cervical vertebra (verdict 1, treatment "till he recovers").
„ 32. Displacement in cervical vertebra (verdict 1, treatment "till he recovers").
„ 40. Wound in sternum (verdict 1, treatment "till he recovers").
„ 47. Wound in shoulder (verdict 1, treatment "till he recovers").

Out of the sixteen cases thirteen receive the favorable verdict 1, and there should be fourteen including Case 17, q. v. In fifteen cases the verdict is followed by treatment "*until he recovers.*" This would indicate that the surgeon employs the application of fresh meat almost exclusively in simple and less dangerous cases, in which recovery is regarded as practically certain. It is significant that after having recommended its use in two head wounds which penetrate to the calvaria without injury to the bone (Cases 1 and 2), he also advises its employment when the calvaria itself has suffered a perforation (Case 3), but not in the case of a more serious injury like a split (Case 4), or a fracture (Case 5). On the other hand a split or a fracture of the maxilla is not serious in our surgeon's opinion, and may wisely receive the application of fresh meat.

In all but one (Case 29) of the sixteen cases employing the application of fresh meat, it is introductory to further remedies. In seven cases (1, 2, 18, 26, 27, 28, and 40) it is followed at once after the first day by an application of grease and honey sometimes bandaged on with lint. In two cases (16 and 17) there is intervening treatment for reducing the swelling before the application of the grease, honey, and lint. In one case (14) there is special attention to the bandages holding together the wound in the nose, before the grease, honey, and lint are to be bandaged on. This is also true of Case 10, a wound in the eyebrow, of Case 47, a gaping wound in the shoulder, and of Case 32, the only dangerous wound of the fifteen—a displacement of one of the cervical vertebrae. In this case the final bandaging is with the problematical *ymrw*, which we find combined with honey for the bandaging immediately after the fresh meat in one case (30).

In the other medical documents the use of an external application of "fresh meat the first day" is not common. It occurs twice in Pap. Ebers, once for crocodile bite

(64, 13) and again for human bite (64, 9). For the crocodile bite it is also employed in Pap. Hearst (XVI 5) and likewise for the bite of a swine (XVI 6), but is limited to these two cases. Pap. Ebers employs other kinds of meat in poultices and ointments, especially for softening stiffness of the limbs (83, 9, where the meat is called " living flesh ") or limbering the groin, etc. (77, 7; 80, 19; 81, 1; 82, 19, all employing "ox flesh;" and 76, 20 employing "fat meat"; cf. also Pap. Hearst VIII 16, and XV 5).[1] It is quite characteristic of the gross superstitions of the Ebers papyrus that it should advocate the use even of decayed meat for application to an open wound (70, 12–14); but this has nothing to do with the use of fresh meat. As an ingredient in prescriptions for *internal* use Pap. Ebers employs " fat meat " a number of times (50, 21; 51, 10; 51, 14; 55, 1; 38, 1; 38, 21; likewise Pap. Hearst III 12) and once even " decayed meat " (55, 11). The London Medical Papyrus and the Berlin Medical Papyrus 3038 do not employ "fresh meat," but the Berlin Papyrus once advocates the use of "living flesh " internally (13, 8–9); compare also " meat of living ox " (Ebers 23, 2).

 *ṡrwḫ*, " to treat," " treatment." Usually with , but again with in II 7; the abbreviation occurs twice (VI 17 and XV 16), once (XIV 7), and once (VIII 21). This word was long read *ṡtwḫ*, and is found in this form in all the existent glossaries. In his transliteration of Pap. Hearst Wreszinski was the first to be able to employ the correct reading, which had been communicated to him by Dévaud. The real reading *ṡrwḫ* has, however, long been available in hieroglyphic texts, e.g., Harhotep 337 (old 463); cf. 350 and 306–307 (old 476 and 432–433). Gardiner calls my attention to its existence in Book of the Two Ways 11, 2 and 6 (Schack-Schackenburg, *Das Buch von den Zwei Wegen*, p. 32). An interesting example is found also in Newberry, *Rekhmara*, pl. VII, ll. 22–23:  " I fostered my office " (as collated by Gardiner).

In meaning the word is a general term for " foster " or " cherish," and then in a medical sense to "care for," or to "treat." It is employed in the medical papyri with the widest and most inclusive meanings. In Pap. Hearst it is used only eleven times, six of them for the treatment of diseased fingers or toes (Hearst XI 17; cf. Ebers 78, 16; Hearst XII 3, cf. Ebers 78, 12–14; Hearst XII 7–8, cf. Ebers 78, 10 and 18–19; Hearst XII 13; XIII 2, cf. Ebers 78, 10–12; Hearst XIII 4, cf. Ebers 78, 18). The remaining five uses are for the lungs (Hearst IV 8, cf. Ebers 6, 17–18; 11, 19), blood (Hearst I 7), urinary affections (IV 12), the " left side " (II 12) and an uncertain ailment (V 4). The four occurrences of the word in the Berlin Medical Papyrus are instructive; among them are two treatments for the heart: one external fumigation with incense, etc. (7, 5) and the other internal (10, 2), but both treatments are called *ṡrwḫ*. In Papyrus Ebers it appears forty-five times for both external and internal treatments. It may take as its object (if a verb) either the patient, the

[1] The use of " meat " without further qualification in Pap. Ebers 103, 13 is not clear.

organs to be affected, like the teeth (89, 12–13), or the bowels and anus (30, 18); or the ailment itself (a wound, 107, 1) or the agent of the ailment (worms, 22, 16). In the London papyrus it does not occur at all.

This highly promiscuous application of the term in the other medical documents is confirmed by its use in Papyrus Smith. As a surgical treatise Pap. Smith employs the term chiefly to designate external applications. It is used as in our passage above nineteen times for the application of grease, honey, and sometimes lint, six times for application of honey alone, and once for *ymrw* and honey, a total of twenty-six times with the meaning treatment by external applications bandaged on. Again the treatment is to be "according to these directions," whatever they may be (Cases 41 and 45). In two cases the surgeon is to "treat with a wound treatment" (Cases 39 and 46, as in Ebers 107, 1). The troublesome (sometimes without *pw*) "his treatment is sitting," which occurs four times (Cases 4, 7, 8, 16), will be taken up in the discussion of these cases.

The omission of the object of *šrwḫ* as in our passage is common.

mrḥ·t, by·t, ftt, "grease, [honey], lint." The kind of *mrḥ·t* "grease" intended, when the word is left without any further indication or qualification, is unknown. It was made from the fat of various *animals.* For example, in Pap. Hearst an ointment for making hair grow was made of gazelle fat, serpent grease, crocodile grease, and hippopotamus grease (X 6–7). Even this relatively small collection of recipes in Pap. Hearst contains, beside the above, four more kinds of animal grease: ox, *ʿpnn·t* reptile, cat and fish grease. In Pap. Ebers, where it occurs as an external remedy scores of times, we find the grease of the above-mentioned animals and a number of others. Goose grease is very frequent (e.g., 11, 13 *et passim*), and the most grotesque animal grease is that of the hippo's foot (67, 6). An ointment found in the tomb of Tutenkhamon yielded on analysis "90 per cent. of neutral animal fat and 10 per cent. of some sort of resin or balsam," of course of vegetable origin.[1] The surviving recipes likewise show that in making *mrḥ·t, plants* were also employed, e.g., castor beans (Ebers 27, 11), and (76, 11–12), evidently the oil of the castor bean (so Loret), and called *mrḥ·t* . In such cases *mrḥ·t* might properly be rendered "oil," as doubtless also occasionally elsewhere; but the occurrence of *mrḥ·t šw(·t)* "dry *mrḥ·t,*" would indicate the meaning grease very clearly (Ebers 33, 14; 96, 14). Other sorts used medicinally are "new grease" (Ebers 73, 15); "grease two days old" (Ebers 82, 7); "pure grease" (Ebers 26, 4); "white grease" (Ebers 26, 12; also Hearst); "fuller's grease" (Ebers 85, 4–5); and "foreign *mrḥ·t* (perhaps "oil," Ebers 22, 8). "Head grease" (Ebers 35, 10) is obscure in

[1] Paper by A. Chaston Chapman and Dr. A. Plenderleith read at ninety-fourth meeting of British Association for Advancement of Science, Oxford, 1926. See *New York Times,* Aug. 6, 1926, p. 4, col. 6.

meaning. *Mrḥ·t* as the designation of a fragrant toilet pomade is widely mentioned outside of the medical papyri and constantly appears in tomb paintings and reliefs, for it was a universal luxury of the toilet. Much additional information regarding it might be added from such sources. See the useful essay by Chassinat on *mrḥ·t* (*Recueil Champollion*, pp. 447–465).

The combination of *mrḥ·t*, " grease " with honey (*by·t*), was evidently a recognized standard mixture. The proportions are given in a prescription for ear trouble in Ebers 91, 7. In Pap. Ebers in a case of internal ear trouble we find the instructions : 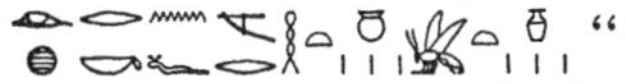 " Thou shouldst prepare for it grease and honey " (Ebers 92, 1–2) " applied in its interior with lint " and bandaged on. The combination was a kind of honey ointment. In Pap. Smith we find *mrḥ·t* used alone only six times, whereas the honey ointment (written simply " grease-honey ") is employed twenty-two times. Besides this, *mrḥ·t* appears twice as the vehicle in an ointment prescription (IV 20 ; XVI 11).

In our treatise honey *alone* is applied externally to a wound in six cases. If bandaged on, it might have been protected from the swarms of flies which otherwise would have settled on it. More often, as noted in the preceding paragraph, honey is employed in an ointment, by mixing it with *mrḥ·t*, or " grease." In two cases in Pap. Smith honey is mixed with the problematical *ymrw* mineral for external application (IX 6 ; X 11).

Of the twenty-two cases in which honey ointment is employed in Pap. Smith, its application is effected by means of absorbent lint in seventeen. This lint was called  *ftt*, a masculine noun in which the final *t* is not the feminine ending. It was some kind of vegetable tissue obtained from a plant called  *dby·t*. Three times in cases where  is prescribed in Pap. Ebers it is said to be 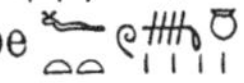 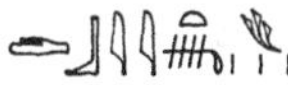 *ftt·w nw dby·t* (Ebers 70, 4) or  *ftt n dby·t* (Ebers 70, 17 ; see variant in 73, 15–16). The plant *dby·t* has not yet been identified with certainty. In these three passages in Pap. Ebers *ftt* is laid over an injury and bandaged on. It occurs in four more cases in Pap. Ebers (seven in all), and these are very instructive as to the character of *ftt*. In a recipe for preventing conception *ftt* is impregnated with the medicaments and inserted into the vulva (93, 8). Similarly it is dipped into an ointment and inserted into the anus (Ebers 32, 2), and likewise into the ear (Ebers 91, 7 and 92, 2). Medicated *ftt*-lint was thus employed both for external application and for insertion into the orifices of the body. Its preparation was understood as a matter of course, as shown by one of the ear cases just cited :

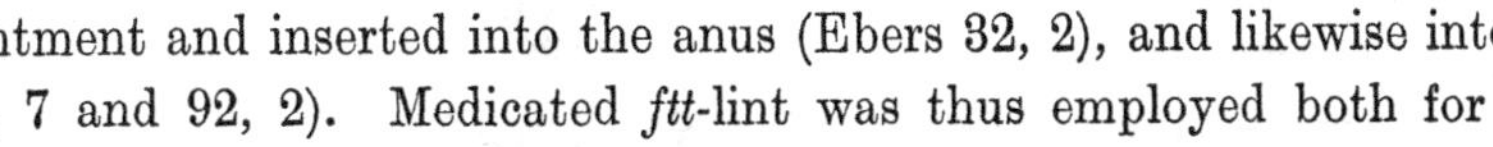

" Thou shouldst prepare for him lint (*ftt*), grease (*mrḥ·t*) ⅔ and honey ⅓, applied to it frequently " (Ebers 91, 7–8). In our treatise lint is used with honey ointment in seventeen instances out of a total of eighteen. In the one case (X 2) in which it is employed alone "dry *ftt*" is prescribed to be applied to a wound in the throat in the secondary stages of healing, and seemingly when the bandages had been removed because of fever (Case 28).

 *r nḏm-f*, "until he recovers." This phrase, which is common in the medical papyri, has been of somewhat vague meaning heretofore. Its force is rendered more definite by the use of it in Pap. Smith. It is never used with the untreatable or hopeless cases, and its appearance in Case 17, seemingly after verdict 3, the hopeless verdict, is an error. As shown in the commentary on that case verdict 3 is either an error for verdict 1, or the insertion of *r nḏm-f* is an error. With the doubtful verdict 2, designating cases of uncertain outcome, the result "until he recovers" occurs once (Case 28) in a total of eight cases. On the other hand we find it inserted after the treatment in twenty-five out of thirty instances receiving verdict 1, the favorable verdict (see p. 46). Of the five cases with verdict 1 not inserting "until he recovers," the conclusion, where it should appear, is lost in one (Case 48); the verdict itself is an error in one (Case 34, XI 22); and the conclusion "until he recovers" is therefore really lacking in only three. It is certain then that this often repeated result should be rendered by "until he recovers," "until he is well," or the like, with perhaps some uncertainty as to the unqualified completeness of the recovery from a scientific point of view.

GLOSS A

I 3–9

Explaining: "Thou examinest a man"

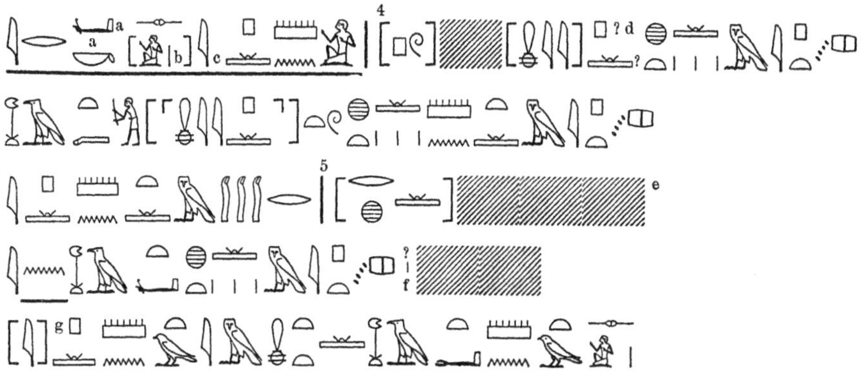

[a] The right-hand ends of these two signs make their restoration certain.

[b] The restoration is based upon the certainty of the *s* and the preceding context.

[c] Part of the sign is preserved.

[d] The traces fit the restoration fairly well, but are hardly sufficient to make it certain.

[e] Fragments of three uncertain signs are visible.

[f] Remains of a vertical sign.

[g] The left-hand half of the sign is preserved; one expects something under it, see Vol. II, p. x, col. 2.

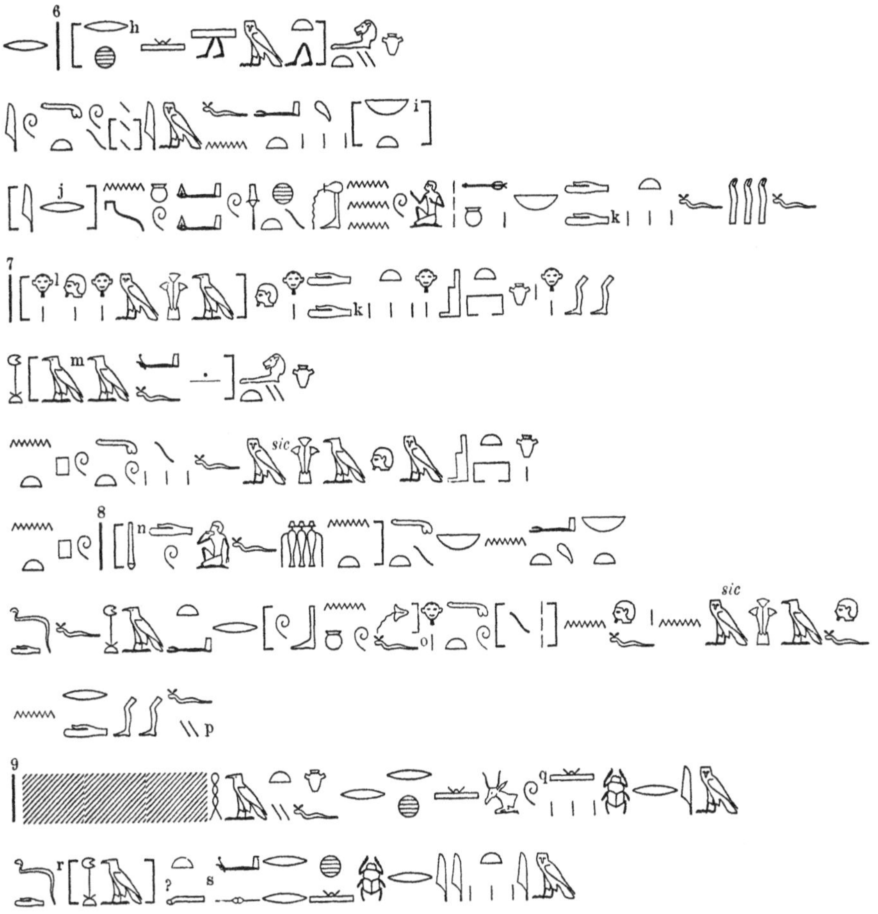

h Restored from Ebers 99, 1.

i Restored from Ebers 99, 4.

j Restored from Ebers 99, 2.

k This sign in l. 6 might be read *r*, giving us *dr·t*; but in l. 7 it is clearly a hand.

l Restored from Ebers 99, 3.

m Restored from Ebers 99, 4.

n Restored from Ebers 99, 5. Left end of a short horizontal sign, which is certainly *n* is visible. The length of these lacunae at the beginnings of all the lines in Gloss A may be seen on Pl. I B, Vol. II, especially by examination of the certain restorations bridging the gaps.

o This *f* is certain, although almost entirely gone, for the tail may be seen in l. 9 just at the left of the middle lacuna of Column I.

p In all probability there is nothing lost at the end of this line.

q The word is fragmentary, but the restoration is certain, although not at first evident owing to the distortion caused by the mounting of the papyrus on paper. See full discussion of this reading in the Introduction, Vol. II, p. x.

r The right-hand half of these two signs is preserved.

s In this group of four signs: , there is some displacement owing to distortion on the edge of the papyrus fragment. For the writing with , see l. 4 (p. 102) and Pl. I, Vol. II.

Translation

As for: "Thou examinest a man," [it means] counting any one - - [⌜like cou]nting⌝ things with a bushel. (For) examining (*ḫ*ꜣ*·t*, literally "measuring") is [⌜like⌝] one's [⌜counting⌝] a certain quantity with a bushel, (or) counting something with the fingers, in order to [know] - - -. It is measuring (*ḫ*ꜣ*·t*) things with a bushel which - - - one in whom an ailment is [cou]nted, like measuring (*ḫ*ꜣ*·t*) the ailment of a man; [in order to know the action] of the heart. There are canals (or vessels, *mt*) in it (the heart) to [every] member. Now if the priests of Sekhmet or any physician[a] put his hands[b] (or) his fingers [upon the head, upon the back of the] head, upon the two hands, upon the pulse, upon the two feet, [he] measures (*ḫ*ꜣ*y*) [to] the heart, because its vessels are in[c] the back of the head and in the pulse; and because its [pulsation is in] every vessel of every member. He says "measure" (*ḫ*ꜣ*·t*) regarding his [⌜wound⌝] because of the vessels (*mt·w*) to his head and to the back of his head and to his two feet - - - - his heart in order to recognize the indications which have arisen therein; meaning [⌜to meas]ure it⌝ in order to know what is befalling therein.

[a] Pap. Ebers has a third investigator here, a *s*ꜣ, or "priest of a phyle;" see variant text, p. 106.
[b] Literally "two hands."
[c] The preposition *m* is omitted by an error common before another *m*.

Commentary

The words to be explained in Gloss A, , form the first clause of the examination, which is itself always introduced by . It might be at first supposed therefore that our paragraph beginning is an *examination*. Its position, however, at the end of a case, that is, following upon the *treatment*, shows conclusively that we are here dealing with a gloss, introduced as usual by the particle *yr* and followed by the quoted words to be explained: *ḫ*ꜣ*y-k s*, "thou examinest a man." With regard to the restoration of "man," it should be noted that the preceding word "thou examinest" is certain. It is followed by the horizontal *s* at the top of the line, leaving room below for the determinative and stroke as usual in forty-six cases in our papyrus. Granted that the particle *yr* must be followed by a quotation from the preceding text of the case as reconstructed from other cases, it is obvious that the quotation must read .

The reading of as *ḫ*ꜣ*y* is not new. It was known from Ebers 36, 4–5: as compared with 38, 17: . In Pap. Smith the abbreviation is used in all forty-eight cases (Cases 1 and 3 restored) in the introductory formula of the examination: *yr ḫ*ꜣ*y-k*; but it occurs in other connections in Pap. Smith written out: (IX 7) and (XVII 6).

The meaning "examine" or "investigate" drawn from the frequent use of the word in Pap. Ebers, is now confirmed by the variant *ḏʿr*, found in Pap. Smith in the following two passages, which immediately precede the parallel passages exhibited in the commentary on Case 10, treatment (V 7–8):

Case 26  (IX 7).

Case 10  (V 6).

From this parallelism it is evident that *ḫʾy* must be very similar in meaning to *ḏʿr*, "to seek, search, search out, investigate, probe." See commentary on this word in Case 1 (examination, p. 92). Compare also *ḫʾy* in Case 29 (X 4–5) in parallelism with *ḏʿr* in Case 4 (II 3).

The word may be related to the well-known verb 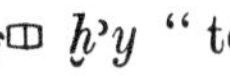 *ḫʾy* "to measure,"[1] used of grain or of the superficial area of land, or of weighing. Our treatise conceives that the physician or surgeon "counts" or "measures" the symptoms observable in a patient and as it were appraises his condition. It is with these parallels that this explanatory gloss deals, when it states "'thou examinest' means counting any one - - -, [⌜like cou]nting⌝ things with a bushel." In the next comparison the short lacuna after  (middle of l. 4) perhaps requires a little more than the word  *yp* to fill it up, but it is obvious that he is here explaining *ḫʾ·t* as like or identical with "measuring (or counting) a certain quantity with a bushel, (or) counting something with the fingers." It is barely possible that the three uncertain signs at the end of the lacuna at the beginning of l. 5 are part of the word  *ḥʾty* "heart," for the long narrow Fragment C bearing these traces is distorted (see Vol. II, Pl. I A). It matches badly with the lines on Fragment B. It might also be moved to the right a trifle, for there is a slight loss of a narrow vertical splinter of papyrus between Fragment C and Fragment B. Making these changes it is perhaps *possible* to reconstruct the word "heart," although the determinative (see l. 6 directly under it) would be lacking. To reconstruct here then  "in order to know the action (lit. 'going') of the heart," is too hazardous; but there can be no doubt about the correctness of the restoration of the same phrase (from Ebers 99, 1) at the beginning of l. 6.

When we note that the discussion in the next few lines (ll. 6–8) pictures the physician as placing his hands or fingers at various points along the body of the patient and discerning the pulsations of the heart from one extremity to the other, the question inevitably arises whether he is not discussing the counting of the pulse in making these references to  *yp*, "counting." If so it is the earliest such reference in the history of medicine, for the counting of the pulse was unknown to early Greek medicine and is not mentioned until Democritus and the Hippocratic treatises. It first occurs in the treatise περὶ τροφῆς about 400 B.C. It would be of especial interest as occurring

[1] In discussing the meaning of *ḫʾy* the possibility of some connection with 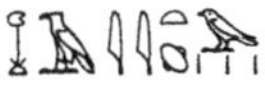 *ḫʾy·t* or *ḫy·t* "disease" may be disregarded as remote.

at this remote age, not only in the history of physiology, but also in the history of the development of instruments for time measurement; for it would be impossible to count the pulse without an instrument finely enough developed to measure *small* intervals of time. The Egyptian water clocks or shadow clocks now known to us would have been rather ill suited for use in accurate counting of pulse beats. The physician would have needed a portable time measurer. Such an instrument was carried by Thutmose III on his first campaign in Palestine in the Fifteenth Century B.C.; and an actual example of such a portable shadow clock was found in Palestine at the excavation of Gezer. It bears the name of the Pharaoh Merneptah (Thirteenth Century B.C.).[1] The earliest known counting of the pulse with a time measurer was done by the distinguished Herophilos of Alexandria in the Third Century B.C.

On this whole point of counting the pulse the fragmentary condition of the text unfortunately leaves us in some uncertainty. Beginning with "one in whom, etc." it is perhaps possible that we should divide the text differently and render thus: "Counting an ailment is like examining (*ḫ’·t*, lit. 'measuring') the ailment of a man, in order to know the action of the heart." Observing that the counting is done with the fingers (l. 4) and that this counting is done "in order to know the action of the heart," the conclusion that counting of the pulse is what is meant is very plausible.

It is in explanation of the term *ḫ’·t*, "examine," literally "measure," that all this obscure discussion of counting is introduced. Evidently the author of our treatise considered that the origin of the term "measure" = "examine" was to be found in an *enumeration* of some kind. In usage *ḫ’y* (infinitive *ḫ’·t*) may take as its object either the ailment, the diseased organ, or the patient, the last being much the most common. It would seem that the last is the only object which really suits the explanation, although our surgeon uses the word "ailment" itself as the object of both *yp* "count" and *ḫ’·t* "measure."

The correctness of the restorations based on the duplicate passage in Pap. Ebers will be more evident if the two texts are placed parallel for comparison. The passage paralleled in Pap. Ebers (99, 1–5) extends from the beginning of l. 6 into l. 8.

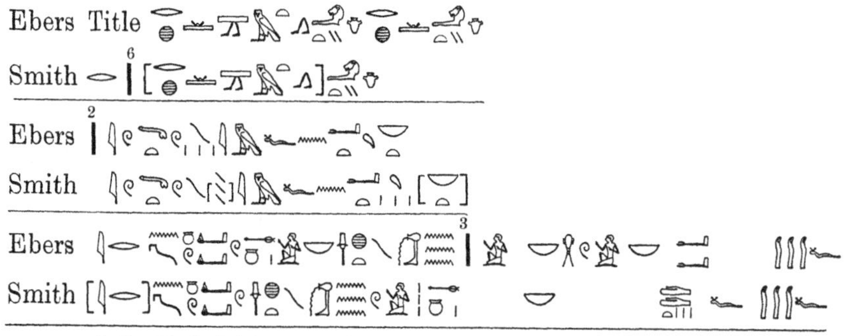

[1] See E. J. Pilcher in *Palestine Exploration Fund*, LV (1923), pp. 85–88.

Ebers [hieroglyphs]

Smith [hieroglyphs]

Ebers [hieroglyphs]

Smith [hieroglyphs]

Ebers [hieroglyphs]

Smith [hieroglyphs]

Ebers [hieroglyphs]

Smith [hieroglyphs]

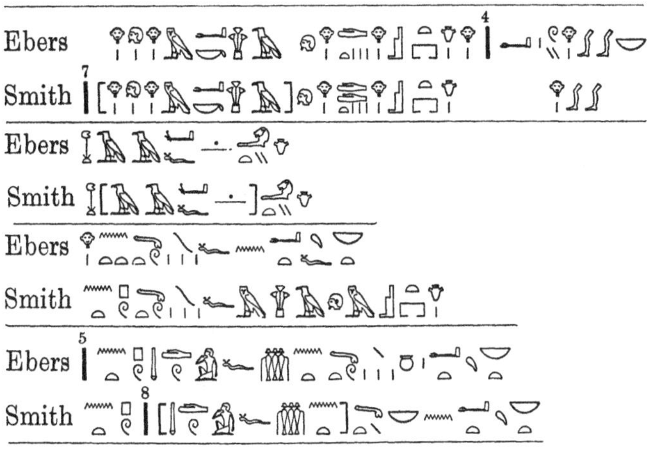

At the beginning of the parallel the question might be raised whether the [hieroglyph] of Smith, l. 6, should correspond to the first or to the second [hieroglyph] in the text of Ebers. The question is easily settled. An examination of Pl. I A (Vol. II) shows that the lacuna at the beginning of l. 6 has the same length as the words: [hieroglyphs] restored at the head of l. 13. The length of this phrase in the original proportions of our column will be found by measuring it in l. 18. This length carried over with the dividers to our lacuna shows we have a liberal amount of room for the restoration of [hieroglyphs], but not for the restoration of [hieroglyphs]. The lacuna in the middle of l. 6 cuts off the right end of the group [hieroglyph]. At the end of the lacuna beginning l. 8 the end of [hieroglyph] from the word [hieroglyph] is well preserved.

This extraordinary discussion of the action of the heart is preceded in Papyrus Ebers by the title: [hieroglyphs], " Beginning of the Secret Book of the Physician." The papers of the scribe who was copying Papyrus Ebers, however, were in such confusion that his excerpt on the action of the heart is cut in two by intrusive matter made up of glosses incorrectly introduced in the middle of the excerpt.[1] Must we conclude that this treatise has perished? How far we have in the material following this title in Pap. Ebers a trustworthy excerpt from it is a doubtful question, and in view of demonstrably intrusive matter now appearing embedded in it, we may seriously question whether it represents an unalloyed citation. It is significant that the Ebers text is paralleled by Pap. Smith only from the beginning of the " Secret Book," to the point where the latter leaves the heart and begins a catalogue of the vessels or canals of the heart. It is highly probable that this catalogue is from another source. It displays much less sane and intelligent command of the scanty knowledge regarding the heart and its system than the preceding general statements about it. We have indeed in the section placed in parallel lines from the

[1] See Schaefer, *Zeitschrift*, 30 (1892), pp. 107–108.

two papyri above (Ebers 99, 1–5 = Smith I 5–8), a little summary of the cardiac system as known to the ancient physician. In Pap. Ebers this summary is obviously a citation and its source is indicated. In Pap. Smith, however, there is no indication that it is a citation. Indeed its beginning in Pap. Smith (I 5–6) appears as the completion of what would otherwise be an incomplete sentence, a fact which goes far to show that the whole summary of the cardiac system is an integral part of the text in Pap. Smith. If in Pap. Ebers it is quoted from Pap. Smith, then the title given in Ebers is the title of our treatise. If this conclusion is correct, and I do not regard it as wholly certain, the title of our book of surgery was: "The Secret Book of the Physician." Quotation by Pap. Ebers directly from *our copy* of Pap. Smith is of course impossible, in view of the difference in text. The scribe of Pap. Smith was not an accurate copyist, and his text, at three points slightly less full than that of Ebers, doubtless contains omissions; or the transmitted text used by the scribe of Pap. Smith was less full than that employed by the scribe of Pap. Ebers.

In any appraisal of this summary of the cardiac system two important questions arise: has this ancient surgeon discerned the circulation of the blood? and whatever its meaning, why has this little account of the heart and its connections been inserted in this place? Taking up the first question, Dr. Luckhardt remarks that our surgeon "must have noted that the apex beat and the pulsation of the peripheral arteries were roughly synchronous and therefore that the rate, volume, and regularity of the latter were roughly an index of the state of functional activity of the former." It is then obvious that the ancient surgeon has discerned that the action and influence of the heart are carried to all parts of the body by means of canals or vessels. From the enumeration of these canals in Pap. Ebers it is also clear that he conceived these vessels as supplying the organs they reached, some of them with blood, some with water, some with air. With regard to the air we have the remarkable statement of the physician: "As for the air that enters at the nose it enters to the heart and lungs, and they convey to the whole body" (Ebers 99, 12–13). He had thus recognized that the heart was the center of a system which conveyed needed supplies from the heart to all parts of the body. There is no intimation that these supplies came back to the heart again, much less that they went through a process of oxygenation before being again discharged into the system. Oxygenation involves a knowledge of chemistry and of chemical elements which the world of science did not attain until thousands of years after our Egyptian physician was dead. It would carry us much too far afield to discuss the difficult question of whether the Hellenistic physicians of Alexandria had gained a knowledge of the circulation of the blood. There are scholars who think they did, and certainly our old Egyptian physicians of the Seventeenth Century B.C., nearly fifteen hundred years before the highest development of Hellenistic science, had already summarized a knowledge of the cardiac system in a form very likely to suggest the circulation of the blood. They brought investigation to the point where it would be obliged to meet the question of what happened to the blood and water carried by the heart to all parts of the body. Under these circumstances it would seem not at all unlikely that this question would be dealt with by the Alexandrians, and the mere fact of the circulation of the blood (leaving out the process of oxygenation) is not a phenomenon so difficult of discernment that we must conclude it was beyond the means of observation available by Alexandrian scientists.

We may take up now the second question, that of the physician's reason for introducing this brief summary of the cardiac system in discussing the word *ḥ'·t,* " measure, examine," incident to an injury in the head. It is clear from the remarks which follow the discussion of the heart, that the physician regards the connection between the injury or the injured region and the heart as of great importance. The injury has an effect upon the heart, which he calls "the indications which have arisen therein," or " what is befalling therein " (l. 9), meaning in the heart. It is clear that he means the heart is a gauge by means of which the patient's condition may be appraised. This he recognizes, no matter where the injury may be located. When we consider that all that the ancient physician could examine in the heart was the rate and power of its pulsations, the probability that he counted the pulse is considerably increased. One cannot but admire the physician's intelligence, which in an age of such limited knowledge of the human body, discerned the vital importance of the heart's action and endeavored to determine its condition as a gauge for establishing that of the patient.

In this connection we have no means of determining the extent of the Egyptian physician's knowledge of the heart itself. Popular custom and belief, already ancient in our ancient medical man's time, made the heart the seat of emotions and intelligence. Philosophical theologians regarded it as the shrine of the god, whose very voice was heard there.[1] Over against these notions, and probably divesting himself of them to no small extent, our physician endeavors to determine the anatomical and physiological character of the heart. The fuller form of the text in Pap. Ebers gives as the subject of the brief summary of the cardiac system this title : " Knowing the action of the heart and knowing the heart." Here is a clear distinction between anatomy (" the heart ") and physiology (" the *action* of the heart "). There is no reference to inherited popular notions regarding the heart. The physician merely states his observations regarding it, its connections, and its action discernible at the remotest points in those connections.

Several terms in the discussion of the cardiac system require some commentary. The first of these is  *mt,* " canal, vessel, ligament, muscle." The plural is 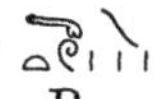 *mt·w.* The meaning " canal, vessel " has long been recognized from its use in Pap.

[1] See the present writer's essay in *Zeitschrift,* 39 (1901), pp. 45–50.

Ebers. The meaning "ligament, muscle," however, seems to have remained unnoticed.[1] This meaning is perfectly clear from a number of passages in Pap. Smith, especially the gloss in Case 7 (III 18), where *mt* is used to explain the word "cord." See the discussion in the commentary on Case 7.

As canals or vessels of the cardiac system it is important to know to what organs and parts of the body the *mt·w* lead. The following list makes no attempt at organization.

List of organs or parts of the body to which the "mt·w" lead:

Heart: their connection with the heart is shown by our Gloss A, now under discussion and the corresponding passage in Pap. Ebers. The latter also states (103, 2–3) that these canals are twelve in number, an error of the scribe for *twenty-two*, as Schaefer has shown.[2] See also Ebers 100, 18; 100, 21–101, 1; and especially 100, 19–20 which states, "It is the heart which causes them to enter into his canals (*mt·w*)."

Two to the *šrtyw* of the two maxillae: Ebers 103, 3 (emended after Berlin 3038, 15, 6).

Two to the loins: Ebers 103, 6.

Two to the neck: Omitted in Ebers 103, 8 (see Schaefer, *loc. cit.*).

Two to the arms: Ebers 103, 11.

Two to the back of the head: Ebers 103, 13–14.

Two to the forehead: Ebers 103, 14.

Two to the eyes: Ebers 103, 14.

Two to the eyebrows: Ebers 103, 14–15.

Two to the nostrils: Ebers 103, 15.

Two to the right ear: Ebers 103, 15.

Two to the left ear: Ebers 103, 16.

This completes the list of twenty-two.

Another list of fifty follows immediately upon the summary of the cardiac system in Pap. Ebers. They are the following:

Four to the two nostrils (Ebers 99, 5–6).

Four to the two temples (? *gmḥ·ty*): Ebers 99, 6–7.

Four to the crown (read *pšn* ?) of the head: Ebers 99, 10.

Four to the two ears: Ebers 100, 2.

Two to the right shoulder: Ebers 100, 2.[3]

Two to the left shoulder: Ebers 100, 2–3.[3]

[1] Stern has used the word "*junctura*" to define *mt* (*s. v.* in Glossary of Pap. Ebers); but does not indicate any such function of *mt*.

[2] See Schaefer, *Zeitschrift*, 30 (1892), pp. 35–37.

[3] Schaefer (*Zeitschrift*, 30, pp. 35–37) makes a total of forty-six *mt·w* by omitting these four which are introduced by a different formula in connection with the four leading to the two ears; but I see no good reason for such omission.

Three to the right arm : Ebers 100, 5.
Three to the left arm : Ebers 100, 5. These six lead also to the fingers.
Three to the right leg : Ebers 100, 6.
Three to the left leg : Ebers 100, 6. These six lead also to the bottom of the sole.
Two to the two testicles : Ebers 100, 7.
Two to the *pḥd·w* (kidneys ?) : Ebers 100, 7–8. One to each of a pair.
Four to the liver : Ebers 100, 8.
Four to the lungs and spleen : Ebers 100, 10.
Two to the bladder : Ebers 100, 11.
Four to the anus : Ebers 100, 11–12, cf. 100, 13.

Not in connection with any list, Pap. Smith mentions two *mt·w* which are under the thorax and lead to the lungs (XII 1–2), and Ebers and some other documents make casual references to the *mt·w* as being in the groin (*m'š·t,* Ebers 79, 19) ; toes (Ebers 81, 2 ; 81, 5 ; Hearst VIII 15) ; lower legs or calves (*yns·t,* Pap. Berlin 3038, 10, 10–11) ; feet (Ebers 103, 18 ; Berlin 3038, 16, 5) ; " every member " (Ebers 81, 14 ; 99, 2; 99, 4 ; Hearst XV 10; Ebers 108, 13; Hearst XV 12). In the Metternich Stela (l. 170) they are called the " *mt·w* of the flesh."

When we recall that the *mt·w* of the above lists are possibly not always canals, but that some of them may be ligaments or nerves, the effort to identify them severally and one by one with the various blood-vessels of modern science must proceed with discretion. In so far as they are avenues conceived as conveying substances, the latter are said to be : blood (Ebers 61, 3) ;  *nšw·t* (Ebers 99, 5–6) ; water (Ebers 99, 19) ; air (Ebers 100, 9–10 ; and very clearly implied in 99, 12–13) ; and semen (Ebers 100, 7). Popularly they seem to have been regarded as vital to health and essentially contributing to it, so that a friend might be greeted with a wish for the health of his *mt·w*, and such a wish was not infrequently placed on his tombstone.[1] This popular notion is supported by the views of the physician. He regards the *mt·w* as " taking up " (*šsp*) the remedies or the disease. There were recipes supposed to accelerate the process of absorption by the *mt·w* of the remedies administered (Ebers 80, 15–81, 1) and the *mt·w* of an affected region are said to have " taken up " the disease (Ebers 103, 6–7 ; cf. also Hearst VIII 12). In a document relying so largely on magic as does Pap. Ebers, the *mt·w* are made to disgorge disease by magic (Ebers

[1] On the wooden statue at Turin No. 176 we find  " may his *mt·w* flourish " (*Recueil de trav.*, 2, p. 175 ; the same, Amon Ritual, Berlin, P 3055, 12, 10 ; and tomb of Vizier Peser, Sethe's copy 11, 23) and quite commonly. A similar good wish is  " may (his) *mt·w* be comfortable " (Tomb of Paheri 9 in Taylor, *Paheri*, pl. XVI ; Tomb of Nebamon, Bouriant, *Recueil de trav.* 9, p. 96). Less common is 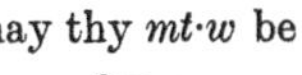 " may thy *mt·w* be sound " (Tomb of Vizier Peser, Sethe's copy 11, 50). In Ptolemaic times we find once  " may (his) *mt·w* be excellent " (Edfu, Rochem. I 192).

108, 14). They are addressed by the magician in the Metternich Stela (l. 170). It is in accordance with magical notions that an ailment is conceived as an " enemy of the *mt* " (Ebers 109, 17).

Based on saner pathological conceptions, however, there are diseases of the *mt·w* themselves as observed by the physician. It is obvious that some of these ailments are those of the muscles and ligaments, as when they are said to be " stiff " (Ebers 85, 12 ; Hearst VIII 11), and probably also when they are said to " tremble " (Ebers 91, 6). Unfortunately it is impossible to determine with any degree of certainty what the designations of the various diseases of the *mt·w* mean, or how they should be rendered in the modern terminology of scientific pathology. We find the following ailments of the *mt·w* in the medical papyri :

nhp (Ebers 84, 14 ; Hearst VIII 3 ; or Ebers 80, 18).

ṯḥn (Pap. Anast. IV 13, 6).

nrw (Pap. Berlin 3038, 18, 7).

ʿ·t (Ebers 106, 20 ; 108, 3 ; 108, 6 ; 108, 9 ; 108, 11–12).

wšʿ (Ebers 82, 21 = Hearst VIII 17).

šf·t (Ebers 109, 14 ; 109, 11 ; 106, 17–18).

šḳr (Ebers 109, 14).

šp·t (Ebers 84, 19).

šf·wt (Hearst VIII 13). " Swellings " of some kind.

św·t (Ebers 82, 16 = Hearst VIII 14). The recipe is for the " softening of the *św·t* of the *mt*."

The physician acquainted with a list of troubles like this, affecting the *mt·w*, of course had treatments for these ailments. We find the following :

" giving life to the *mt·w* " (Ebers 81, 17 = Hearst VIII 5 and IX 1).

" making vigorous the *mt·w* " (Ebers 81, 17 = Hearst VIII 5).

" making firm the *mt·w* " (Ebers 79, 5 ; 70, 18 ; 84, 21).

" making comfortable the *mt·w* " (Ebers 108, 2; 81, 20; 79, 5; 81, 10, 14 = Hearst XV 6 ; VIII 1 ; VIII 4 ; VIII 6 ; Berlin 3038, 4, 12).

" cooling the *mt·w* " (Ebers 85, 10 = Hearst VIII 18; XVI 3 ; VII 16 ; XVI 13).

" softening the *mt·w* " (Ebers 85, 3–4 ; 81, 7 ; 82, 10–11 ; 82, 22 ; Hearst VII 14).

" quieting the *mt·w* " (Ebers 85, 2 = Hearst VIII 7).

" anointing the *mt·w* " (Hearst VIII 14).

Some of these remedies, like the one for " softening the *mt·w* " doubtless refer to affections of the muscles or ligaments, and have nothing to do with the circulatory system.

It will now be clear to the reader that the observations of the Egyptian physician regarding the heart and its " canals " (*mt·w*) had disclosed to him that the heart was the center and active force in a system which conveyed the effects of both disease and remedy to all parts of the body. It is on the basis of this knowledge that our surgeon introduces a discussion of the cardiac system and the importance of examining the heart and pulse in treating a wound in the head.

ś·t-yb (or *yś·t-yb*), " pulse." Gardiner has remarked that the word (*ś·t*) "when prefixed to words meaning some member of the body, . . . expresses the activity of that member " (*Proc. Soc. Bib. Arch.,* 35 (1912), p. 261). This statement cannot be improved upon ; the " *ś·t* of the heart " means the activity of the heart, and in this case that activity as it is locally manifested at the pulse. Otherwise the more inclusive term for the pulsation of the heart as a general and continuous activity, and not any local manifestation of it, is *mdw,* literally " to speak."

ḫnt, commonly "before." On the meaning "in," see Sethe, *Zeitschrift,* 44 (1907), Tafel II, l. 12 and p. 32, n. 13.

mḥ' must be regarded as a scribal error for *mkḥ',* in spite of the fact that our copyist has written it twice in two successive lines. The omission of *m* before this word is like the frequent omission of *m* before *mrḥ·t* (p. 74).

[⸢*wbnw*⸣]-*f.* The restoration is a guess based upon the preservation of the *f.* It fits the requirements very well, but is not entirely certain.

yḫ·wt ḫpr ym "indications having arisen therein" with the *perfect* participle, seems to be explained by *ḫpr·y·t ym,* " what is befalling therein," with the *imperfect* participle. The physician recognizes that the effects observable in the heart are a continuing process. It should be observed that the technical medical use of *ḫpr* " to happen " very often includes an unfavorable implication like that of our word " befall." The other technical meaning of *ḫpr* is " arise, originate." Besides the two cases in our Gloss A, the verb *ḫpr* occurs fourteen times in Pap. Smith. A typical example is :

"every wound that befalls in his breast" (XIII 9). See also VII 12–13 ; X 16=X 19–20 ; XIII 17 ; XIV 7 ; XIV 21 ; and further discussion in Case 30 (X 10). A similar usage of *ḫpr* occurs in Pap. Ebers, e. g., 106, 5.

The question may arise whether *ym* may not be rendered "to it," the heart, as in the Coptic ϣⲱⲡⲉ ⲙ̄ⲙⲟ- "happen to" (Zoega, p. 304). If so our phrases would mean " the things that have befallen it " (the heart), and " what is befalling it." It is not likely that the implied pronoun after *ym* could refer to anything else than the heart which is the last noun mentioned in the preceding context. To happen in an unfavorable sense is expressed in the Pyramid Texts by *ḫpr r* (Pyr. 1654 c), and it occurs in the Middle Kingdom with *mꜥ*, e.g., Shipwreck, l. 22; and see also Case 30 (X 10).

On the translation of the final phrase see note s, p. 103.

GLOSS B

I 9–10

Explaining: " While his wound does not have two lips."

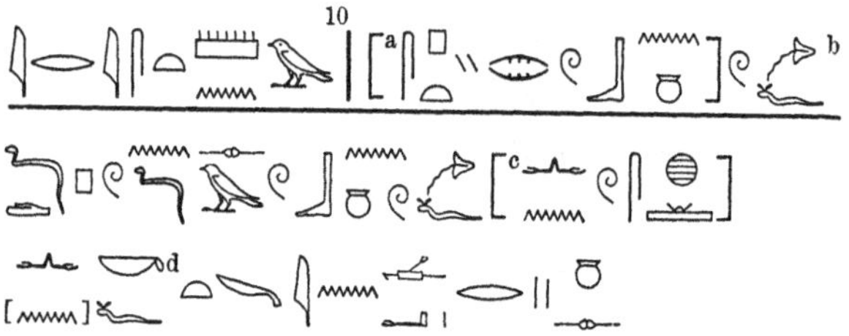

[a] On the amount of space available see Vol. II, Pl. I B. The restoration is certain; see discussion, p. 115.

[b] This sign  is placed low in the line as in l. 12, Vol. II, Pl. I B.

[c] The space is sufficient for this restoration, as will be seen by measuring the same phrase (*nn wšḫ*) in l. 12. Cf. Vol. II, Pl. I B.

[d] The word is fragmentary, but parts of each sign are preserved and the reading is certain.

Translation

As for: " While his [wou]nd does not have [two lips]," it means his wound is narrow, [not wide]; without gaping of one (lip) from the other.

Commentary

The chief difficulty in this passage is the word 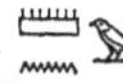 *mn*, " be ailing, sick," where we expect a negative. This difficulty cannot be discussed until the restoration at the head of line 10 is made certain. The restoration of the words " his wound " is shown to be indubitably correct by the survival of the last three signs of the group *wbnw-f*, discernible in red on the original. The preceding group, *špt·wy* " two lips," is demonstrated to have been present in the quoted statement by the phrase  *šn-nw-s*, "its (fem.) second" = "the other." The use of the numeral "second" proves that a pair was mentioned in the lacuna. If it be argued that the feminine pronoun *s* shows that this pair could not have been *špt·wy* " lips," which is not feminine, it may be replied that *špt* is nevertheless treated unmistakably as a feminine noun in Case 10 (V 9), which tells us of bandages "applied to the two lips of a gash-wound" 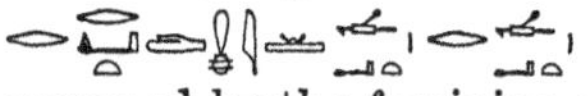 " in order to make one join to the other." Here *špt* is twice resumed by the feminine substantive adjective *wꜥ·t*, written with the feminine ending.

Furthermore Gloss B introduces for explanation a quotation beginning with *yśt.* In our case there are only *two* occurrences of this word, both in the diagnosis. Now the clause introduced by the second occurrence of *yśt* is explained in Gloss C, leaving only the first *yśt* clause as the one explained in Gloss B. On this basis alone we are entitled to restore in Gloss B the quoted words *śpt·wy wbnw-f.* Unfortunately there is in the diagnosis a small lacuna preceding the word *śpt·wy* ; but it is obvious that this lacuna contained the negative (see the discussion of the diagnosis, p. 94). We may now place the two texts parallel : the phraseology of the diagnosis and the quotation from it in the gloss :

Text of diagnosis :

Text of Gloss B :

Where the gloss has *mn* the diagnosis has a negative. That the gloss is in error is obvious. The error may have arisen from oral dictation at some stage in the transmission of the text, the scribe hearing *mn* for *nn* ; or he may have heard the wrong *mn*, and while *mn* was read to him he wrote *mn* "be sick"; although we must admit that this would be an early occurrence of the New Egyptian negative. In any case our statement, quoted from the diagnosis, must mean " while his wound does not have two lips," just as it does in the diagnosis itself. It may be remarked here that a comparison of the quotations in the glosses with the texts from which they quote discloses quite commonly gross carelessness and inaccuracy of the scribe. Whether these are due to the copyist of Pap. Smith, or to some earlier scribe, is not always to be determined, although our copyist is obviously very careless.

This gloss should be compared with Case 18, Gloss A.

ḏd pw, literally " it says," is perhaps a fuller form of the simple *pw*, which we found in Gloss A, and which is by far the more frequent. *Ḏd pw* is found in six passages besides Gloss B (I 11; II 11; III 1; X 20; XIII 11; XIV 11, perhaps *ḏd-tw*).

nn wśḫ, " not wide." In view of the *nḏs nn wśḫ* of Gloss C (I 12), this restoration is highly probable, though perhaps not entirely certain. The space available is probably sufficient, though not quite as long as that occupied by the same words in l. 12. On the use of the negative *nn* as a conjunction see Gunn, *Syntax*, pp. 162–163. In such cases it should be called an adversative conjunction. Gunn also discusses its use with adjectival predicates as here (*ibid.*, Chap. XXVII). The phrase *nḏs . . . nn wśḫ* is curiously reminiscent of the well-known description of the highway in the Peasant (R. 45).

n [⌜*n*⌝] *kf·t.* There is probably room for the insertion of the *n*, as in *nn kf·t* in l. 11 in the next gloss. The use of alone would be another evidence of the antiquity of our text; for as Gunn has observed (*Syntax*, p. 195) the indiscriminate use of *n* and *nn* is old and continued no later than the early Middle Kingdom. He has an excellent discussion of the infinitive negatived by *nn* (*Syntax*, pp. 155–159) and has organized all the cases of this infinitive with following modifiers. No case of the negatived infinitive with following logical subject introduced by  seems to have come under his notice. There is another case in the next line (l. 11) of our text; but otherwise it does not occur again in Pap. Smith, and I do not recall having met it elsewhere.

 *wʿ r śn-nw-s*, "one from the other." The text is inconsistent: it should read either *wʿ r śn-nw-f*, or *wʿ·t r śn-nw-s*. In the example above quoted (V 9) *wʿ·t* (fem.) referring to "lip" appears twice. The phrase makes clear the meaning of *kf·t*, which has been discussed fully above (pp. 90–92).

Gloss C

I 10–12

Explaining: "Penetrating to the bone of his skull but not having a gash."

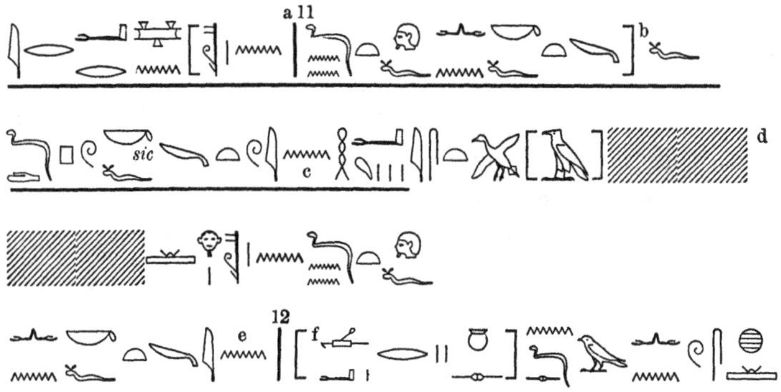

[a] The line division may have been before the *n*, but certainly not after *ḏnn·t*.

[b] An unmistakable part of the possessive *f* is preserved. The tail of it is visible on the original crossing the *d* of *ḏd*; see Vol. II, p. x, col. 2. The remnant of another sign is doubtless the handle of the knife.

[c] The sign is unusually short for *n* and also rather thick; but the right end of *n* preserved at left end of l. 11 is equally thick. The probabilities are in favor of *n*.

[d] The lacuna in the middle of the column begins to be wider at this point; see Vol. II, Pl. I.

[e] Only half of the sign is preserved, but the reading is certain in view of the duplicate passage in Gloss B.

[f] The restoration repeats the text of Gloss B without correcting the inconsistency in gender.

Translation

As for: "Penetrating to [the bone of his skull, (but) not having a gash]," it means that there is a gaping of the flesh, although ⌜-⌝ - - - - ⌜-⌝ over the bone of his skull, without gaping [of one (lip) from the other], being narrow, not wide.

Commentary

As we have already noticed in discussing the examination itself, this gloss is an explanation of words quoted from the examination. Unfortunately the quotation is not perfectly preserved. Regarding the restoration of the loss at the end of l. 10 and beginning of l. 11, there can be no question, except the minor one: whether we should restore the negative *nn*, or *n wn·t*. There is practically no difference in the meaning of these two negatives in such a construction (see Gunn, *Syntax*, p. 166, IX), and there is only room for *nn*. With reference to the order of the two observations: " penetrating to the bone, &c." and " not having a gash," the fragments at the end of the lacuna at the head of l. 11 prove that the last of the lost words was not *ḏnn·t-f*; but some other word with the possessive *f* written at the top of the line. This is only possible when hieratic *f* is begun somewhat high along the back of some sloping sign, that is in this case . The *ḏd pw* immediately following this *f* shows that the suffix " his " was the last sign in the quotation, and the quotation could end only in *ḏnn·t-f* " his skull," or *kf·t-f* " its gash." As it is not *ḏnn·t-f* it must be *kf·t-f*.

In the explanation after the introductory *ḏd pw* the scribe inadvertently omitted (following *kf*) and inserted it afterward. The possible reading *pw* would seem to require the infinitive *kf·t*, while *yn* permits a preceding passive. I am unable to suggest any probable rendering as far as *ḥr ḳs*. This is the only passage in our treatise in which " bone " is preceded by the preposition *ḥr*. The remainder of the explanation is unfortunately practically a repetition of Gloss B. Gloss B deals with the *lateral* dimensions of the wound, while we should expect Gloss C to discuss the *depth* of the wound. The structure of the explanation therefore probably was: first a statement of the depth of the wound (in the obscure first half of the gloss preceding *ḥr ḳś*) penetrating to the bone, followed in the second half by a natural reference to the fact of the narrow lateral extension of the wound, meaning that this lateral limitation is a fact notwithstanding its depth; hence the repetition from Gloss B. See discussion of Gloss C above in commentary on *ꜥr* " penetrate " (p. 87), and compare Case 18, Gloss A.

Regarding the three glosses on this case together, it is obvious that they furnish explanations of terms an understanding of which is a prerequisite to the comprehension of such cases as those discussed in our treatise. The term " examine," explained in the first gloss, is employed in all the cases in this document, without reference to the nature of the case. It is quite evident that such a term would be explained early in such a treatise as Pap. Smith. It is so unlikely that it would be explained in connection with any other case than the first, that we must regard its occurrence among the glosses of our first preserved case as satisfactory evidence that it was in real fact originally the first case in Pap. Smith.

On , *ḥꜥ·w* (plural) meaning " flesh," see Montet, *Sphinx*, 13, pp. 1 ff., and Gardiner, *Sinuhe*, p. 111.

CASE TWO

I 12–18

A GAPING WOUND IN THE HEAD PENETRATING TO THE BONE

Case 2 differs from Case 1 only in the addition of the word " gaping." In Case 1 the soft tissue overlying the bone has been ruptured as by some blunt weapon, leaving an ill-defined and constricted orifice; in Case 2 on the other hand there is a well-defined gash such as may be produced by a knife or a sword, with a resulting yawning or gaping of the orifice.

Title

I 12

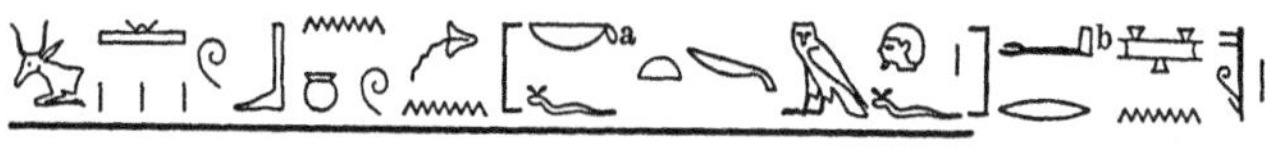

[a] The word *kf·t* itself, curiously enough, falls in a lacuna wherever it occurs in Case 2; but the genitive *n* following *wbnw* both in the title and Gloss A make the restoration certain, cf. I 18.

[b] The left ends of the arm and the *r* are preserved.

Translation

Instructions concerning a [gaping] wound [in his head], penetrating to the bone.

Commentary

All the terms needing explanation will be found discussed in the commentary on Case 1. It is noticeable that after the word " bone " the further defining words " of his skull " are here omitted, probably because they have been used in Case 1, which is regarded as making clear what bone is meant.

Examination

I 12–14

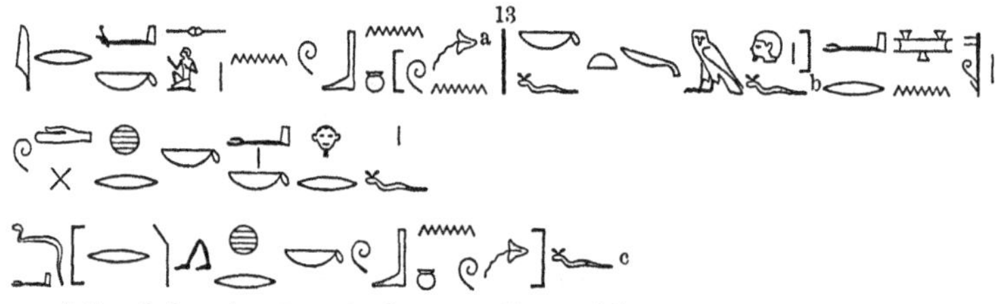

[a] Traces of the determinative of *wbnw* are discernible.

[b] The tail of the *f* is preserved. The text is a repetition of the title, making the restoration quite certain.

[c] The traces on left edge of fragment B might be the head and one foot (thrust forward) of the *gm*-bird (following *wd-ḥr-k ʿ-k ḥr-f* here as in III 10, q. v.); these same traces also fit , a restoration which I rejected for reasons given on p. 119; but Dévaud again urges the correctness of this restoration, and the at the end (tail crossing l. 14 above *tp-f* on fragment F) is a strong argument for restoring as above in accordance with IX 14 (q. v. p. 310), which is also followed by *yr gmy-k* as here in I 13.

[d] For these words compare IX 14 in the same context. In our text the head of the *gm*-bird is a little thicker and shorter than normal, but the *m* is perfect. The *k* crosses the tear between fragment A and fragment F, but the top of its loop is visible on fragment A and its heavy oblique stroke is well preserved on fragment F. This is part of the proof that these two fragments belong together.

[e] This restoration is based on IX 14. The place of the line division is not quite certain, but the *w* was certainly in l. 13, for remains of it are visible above the tail of the *f*, just as in VII 9 in the same context. In IX 15 *wḏ*ꜣ is the first word of the line and is therefore separated from the preceding *f* which is in l. 14.

[f] The *nt* preceding *thm* makes this restoration certain.

Translation

If thou examinest a man having a [gaping] wound [in] his [head], penetrating to the bone, thou shouldst lay thy hand upon it (and) [thou shouldst] pal[pate hi]s [wound]. If thou findest his skull [uninjured not hav]ing a perforation in it, (conclusion in diagnosis).

Commentary

The examination repeats the title as usual. It might be concluded that the laying of the hand on the wound means purely external examination, as opposed to "palpation" (*ḏꜥr*). Such is indeed the case in III 9–10 (Case 7), but the distinction is not everywhere maintained.

The restoration *ḏꜥr-ḫr-k wbnw-f* (l. 14) urged by Dévaud is doubtless correct; see note [c], p. 118. There is nevertheless, besides the context in III 10, a grammatical argument in favor of *gmm-k*, etc., as a continuation of the condition. In twenty-eight out of our forty-eight cases in Pap. Smith it is used as the continuation of the examination. In the majority of the cases in which it appears it follows immediately upon *yr ḫꜣy-k* "if thou examinest" (twenty-one times);[1] but it occurs also immediately after *ḏꜥr-ḫr-k*, "thou shouldst palpate" (seven times: Cases 3, as restored, 4, 5, 6, 8, 18, 47), or *wd-ḫr-k* (sometimes *wd-yn-k*) *ꜥ-k*, "thou shouldst lay thy hand" (four times: Cases 2, 7, 24, and 47). In only one case (27) do we find  *yr gmy-k*, "if thou findest" continuing the examination after *ḏꜥr*. Pap. Smith evidently throws light on the normal function of *gmm-k* as contrasted with *yr gmy-k*. When our treatise desires to start afresh with a new condition observed, it does so with *yr gmy-k*, as we observe immediately following the lacuna in the above examination.

The lacuna at the end of l. 13 and beginning of l. 14 may be restored with certainty on the basis of the analogous text in Case 27 (IX 14–15). Allowing for a margin of uncertainty in the length of l. 13, we may conclude with much probability that the

[1] In Cases 12, 14, 15, 16, 21, 25, 31, 33 *bis*, 34, 35, 36, 37, 38, 39 *bis*, 43, 44, 45 *bis*, 46.

restoration completely fills the lacuna. The word rendered "uninjured" is more literally "sound," that is, it is not a word indicating injury, to which a privative syllable is prefixed to indicate freedom from injury. Hence our surgeon adds a negative statement that a certain kind of injury to the skull is *not* present. He states that the skull is sound and re-enforces this statement by also denying the opposite. The injury declared to be not present, *thm* ("perforation"), is found in the next case, and will be discussed there. We learn from Gloss C that the scribe has been guilty of an omission here. He should have included besides a "perforation" also a "split" and a "fracture." See Gloss C. As in Case 18 (VII 9), in order to make clear that there is no injury to the bone, our surgeon should have stated that the entire list of bone injuries known to him was not present.

DIAGNOSIS

I 14

[a] The readings and restorations are based chiefly on the obvious fact that the observable fragments and traces of signs show clearly that we have at this point the text of the diagnosis. The beginning falls just at the lower edge of fragment B, and above this lower edge only the upper parts of signs are preserved, like the head of the serpent, the top of *y*, and the upper part of *k* under a short *n*. As the edge wanders we are able to see the end of *r* in *rf*; and just beyond it (at the left) the upper end of the *ẖr*-sign. Beyond *ẖr* the gap is complete.

[b] The words in this bracket are restored from the usual form of the diagnosis as regularly found throughout the treatise, and the designation of the case as above in the title.

[c] The end of the knife handle is visible in front of *m*.

[d] The tail of the in *kf·t* is visible in l. 15 just over the determinative of *ftt*. It is possible that this belongs to *ftt* in l. 15, but the tail seems too high and not at the right angle for joining with the *f* in *ftt*.

Translation

Thou shouldst say regarding [him]: "One hav[ing a gaping wou]nd in his head. An ailment which I will treat."

Commentary

As noted in the introduction (pp. 48 ff.), the diagnosis often contains little more than the title, as if it were simply a catch-word memorandum. For the practical purposes of the surgeon the essential thing in such a diagnosis is the verdict at the end. See the fuller discussion in Case 1 (I 1–2). As usual this favorable verdict is followed by treatment and recovery, showing that the injury is not a serious one.

TREATMENT

I 14–15

[a] Part of this *ḥ* is preserved and recognizable.

[b] The place of the line division is not exactly determinable. At the bottom edge of fragment B traces of the last signs visible on this fragment may be the tops of three signs at the end of the above bracket or possibly at the beginning of the next bracket. The restoration in the two following brackets is fully discussed in the commentary. On the amount of space see the discussion of column I in volume II.

[c] With *m* omitted as commonly before *mrḥ·t*.

Translation

[Thou] shouldst bind [fresh meat upon it the first day; thou shouldst apply for him two strips of linen, and treat afterward with grease, honey, (and) lin]t every day until he recovers.

Commentary

Almost the entire treatment is lost in the large lacuna extending from a point toward the end of l. 14 to beyond the middle of l. 15. Nothing has survived but a few signs at the beginning and a few at the end. The beginning is marked by *wt* and the end by, the determinative of lint. The treatment therefore begins with the usual binding with fresh meat and concludes with the customary application of "grease, honey, and lint every day." But Gloss B shows that two *ʾwy*-strips were also applied, as we might expect in the case of a gaping wound. This application of the two strips must have been mentioned in the lost middle portion of the treatment. The treatment therefore consisted of three items:

(1) Binding with fresh meat.
(2) Application of the two *ʾwy*-strips.
(3) Application of grease, honey, and lint every day.

The *ʾwy*-strips are used in only five cases (2, 6, 10, 27, and 47). An examination of the other four reveals the fact that in one of them (Case 27) we find the same three items of treatment, although in a different order, the *ʾwy*-strips being first and the fresh meat application second. The limitation of the fresh meat application to the first day however is a fair justification for questioning this order in Case 27; and it should be noted that in Case 10 (which omits the lint), the order is as in Case 2, with the fresh meat application the first and the *'wy*-strips following (V 7–8). We are therefore safe in restoring from Case 27 (IX 16–17) with slight modification, chiefly in two particulars. We must insert the binding with fresh meat first to connect with the opening signs preserved in Case 2 (*wt*) ; and we must insert in the text furnished by Case 27 the words " of linen," which our Gloss B demonstrates were in the text of the treatment. The available space will barely contain the long restoration, and it helps in this direction to omit the *św* after *srwḫ-k*, as in VII 19, to omit *ḥr kf·t yptf* after *'wy* as in V 8, and to use the short writing of *mrḥ·t*.

'wy, " two strips." It is unfortunate that we do not better understand these surgical appliances. The word is unknown outside of our treatise and we are therefore confined to the data obtainable from Pap. Smith for an understanding of the term. It was not clear to the readers of the original treatise and fortunately for us the ancient Egyptian commentator has added a gloss explaining it. Almost all of the gloss is lost in the text of our case, but by a happy chance the commentator forgot that he had once explained *'wy* in Case 2, and he explained it again in Case 10 (V 9), evidently in the identical words used in Case 2 (Gloss B, I 16–17). The explanation reads : " 'The two *'wy*-strips of linen', it means two bands of linen, which one applies upon the two lips of the gaping wound in order to cause that one (lip) join to the other." Similarly in Case 10 we find the same function of the two *'wy*-strips in the directions to the surgeon: " Thou shouldst draw together (the wound) for him with two *'wy*-strips " (V 8). The injury is a wound in the eyebrow. In treating a gaping wound in the shoulder (Case 47) the surgeon is directed " Thou shouldst draw together for him its gash with two *'wy*-strips of linen over that gash " (XVII 3–4). With regard to the method of applying we find in Case 6 this significant hint. The patient has a frightful wound in the skull which has laid bare the brain, and the directions charge the surgeon : " Thou shalt not bind it (the wound) ; thou shalt not apply two *'wy*-strips upon it " (II 23). It is clear from the above cases that the *'wy*-strips are not ordinary bandages. They are always " applied," literally " laid on " (*wd*), and their effect is to " draw together " the gaping wound. The words " lay on " certainly could not be applied to *thread* employed in *stitching* together the wound. Thread and stitching being excluded the only other alternative is obviously strips of linen plaster, a kind of adhesive tape, of which two pieces are " applied " transversely across the gaping wound. It is noticeable that the word is always used in the dual, " two *'wy*-strips." The word is curiously written. In Case 10 we find *'wy* (twice, V 8 and 9), Case 6 *'ywy* (II 23), Case 47 also *'ywy* (XVII 4), and Case 27 *'yrwy* (IX 16). The root is *'r* or *'yr*, which weakened by " *mouillirung* " of the final *r*. Cf. the peculiar writings of words ending in *'r*, e. g., , , , , or even perhaps . Our

word is perhaps the source of the cord which is so commonly written after the consonants ʾr thus . The incorrect writing in our passage is due to the preceding particle *yr*, the two words producing a combination very like the writing in Case 27 :

The discussion of the final treatment with grease, honey, and lint will also be found in the commentary on Case 1.

GLOSS A

I 15–16.

Explaining : A gaping wound in his head, penetrating to the bone.

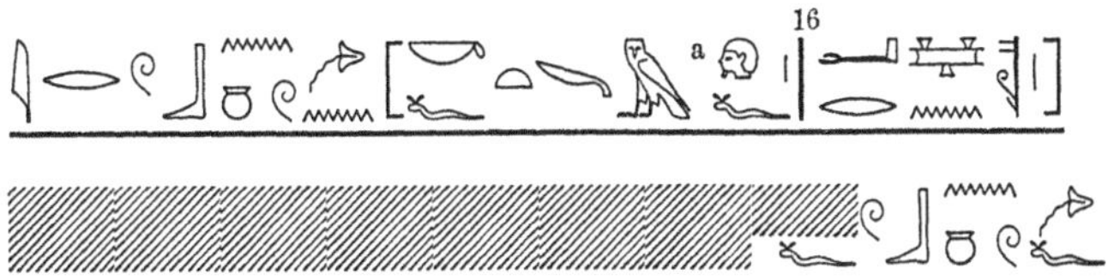

[a] The words immediately following *wbnw n* are quite certain from the parallel passages. The exact place of the line division is uncertain. It would be possible to restore further into the following lacuna, but the amount or extent of the quotation is uncertain.

Translation

As for: "A [gaping] wound [in his head penetrating to the bone," it means] - - - - - - - - his wound.

Commentary

The entire explanation of a "gaping wound" is lost. Its nature is, however, recoverable from the observations regarding a wound which is not gaping, or as the Egyptian puts it "has no *kf·t*" (gash). See the commentary on *kf·t* in Case 1 (pp. 90 ff.).

GLOSS B

I 16–17

Explaining : Two strips of linen

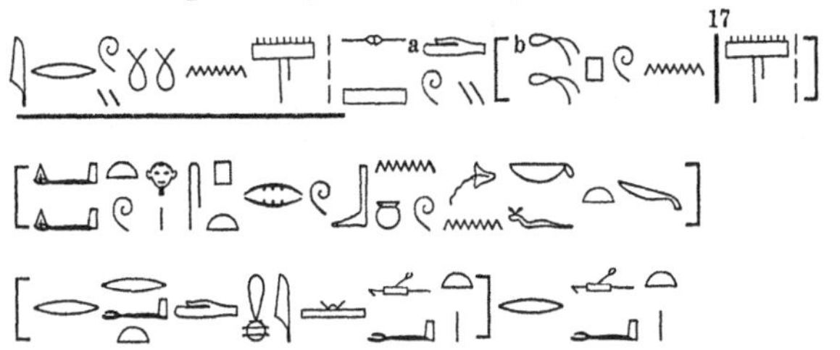

[a] Only the right end of this *d* is visible, but the duplicate from Case 10 makes the reading certain.

[b] The text of this restoration is drawn from the duplicate gloss in Case 10, V 9.

Translation

As for: " Two strips of linen," [it means] two bands [of linen which one applies upon the two lips of the gaping wound in order to cause that one join] to the other.

Commentary

Fortunately for us the ancient commentator forgot that he had supplied this explanation in Case 2, and inserted it again in Case 10 (V 9), where it begins with *śśd·wy* and ends with *r wʿ·t,* as in Case 2, showing that both glosses undoubtedly read alike. The curious use of the feminine *wʿ·t* " one " as a substantive resuming *śpt* " lip," which is not feminine, will be found discussed in Case 1 in the commentary on the lips of a wound (pp. 114 f.).

dmy " join," with the preposition *r*, literally means " to stick to." In surgical use it is applied e. g. to the " sticking " of a fragment of bone to a swab of linen (VIII 16). In our gloss it is evidently used for " heal," and might have been so rendered.

The explanation does not make clear by what physical arrangements the lips of the wound are brought together, and therefore does not indicate unequivocally the nature of the *ʾwy,* " the two strips." See the discussion in the commentary on the treatment above (p. 122), where it has been made practically certain that the strips are employed as plaster or adhesive tape.

GLOSS C

I 17–18

Explaining: Not having a split, a perforation or a smash in it.

[a] Restored from VII 9.

Translation

As for: "Not having a split, a perforation, (or) [a smash in it," it means] - - - -.

Commentary

The three injuries here enumerated constitute the list recognized by our surgeon as injuries of the bone. Undoubtedly the text of the examination (I 14) should likewise have contained all three. The ancient commentator may have quoted from memory without noticing the omission, or the omission was in the older original from which our scribe copied, or he copied carelessly and skipped two words. It is regrettable that the description of these three injuries, or the indication of what we are to understand by the statement that they were not present, is lost. Fortunately they occur frequently in the following cases, where full discussion of them will be found. On *pšn*, " split," see Case 1 and Case 4 (II 2); on *tḥm*, " perforation," consult Case 1 under " wound," and Case 3 (I 18, pp. 125–126); and on *šd*, " smash " (= compound comminuted fracture) see Case 1 under " wound," and Case 5 (II 11).

CASE THREE

I 18–II 2

A GAPING WOUND IN THE HEAD PENETRATING TO THE BONE AND PERFORATING THE SKULL

With Case 3 our treatise passes from the consideration of superficial wounds involving only the soft tissue overlying the skull, to a series of wounds which involve very serious injuries to the calvaria itself, as well as the internal organs of the head. This series forms a group of seven cases (Case 3 to Case 9), which are perhaps the most interesting in the whole treatise. They contain the first references to the brain now accessible in the whole range of earliest oriental science, including extraordinary descriptions of its appearance and even observations indicating some discernment of the localization of functions in the brain.

TITLE

I 18

[a] This determinative and the preceding *nw* sign make the restoration of *wbnw* obvious. The first word *šsꜣw* is restored from the customary form of the title, as I 12, *et passim*.

[b] Only the foot is visible.

[c] The tail of the *f* is preserved crossing l. 19 at the extreme end. *Ḏnn·t* is certain from the examination (l. 19).

Translation

[Instructions concerning] a gaping [wo]und in his head, penetrating to the bone (and) perforating his [skull].

Commentary

The title indicates that the injury is more than superficial and involves the skull. The injury affecting the bone is designated by the word 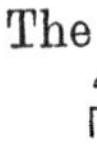 *tḥm*, " perforate." Several times we find the word written  with a circle as determinative to indicate more clearly the meaning of the term (VIII 3; XIII 13, 15). It is written out fully with all three consonants throughout the calvaria cases, but in the late cases it may be abbreviated, e.g., 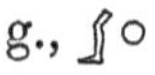 (Case 15, maxilla, VI 14), or even  (Case 20, VII 22).

Outside of the medical literature it was a not uncommon word meaning "to pass over, pass through, penetrate, pierce, perforate." It is employed, in accordance with the use of the legs as determinative, to express the idea of traversing a country. Hence it is applied to the journey of the dead in the next world: "Thou passest through (*thm*) the earth" (Berlin Pap. 3044, l. 20). Similarly the rebellious enemies of the Pharaoh lament in their defeat: 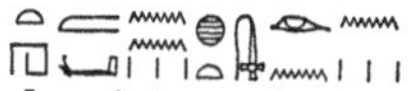 "The fire which we have made penetrates (*thm*) to us" (Semneh Stela of Amenhotep III, Brit. Mus. 138, l. 12). It is this meaning "to pass over, through," which accounts for the determinative of the leg. Illustrative of the meaning "perforate," even outside of the medical documents is the application of the word to the horn of a bull. Thus Ramses III is compared to a bull "standing in the arena, . . . his horns pointed, ready to pierce (*thm*) his adversary with his head" (Medinet Habu, Rougé, *Inscr. hier.*, 145, l. 57). Approaching its medical meaning is its significance in charms against diseases, as in those for mother and child, in which the mother says to the demon: "Fall not on his mouth, beware of being concealed; fall not on his teeth, beware of penetrating (*thm*)" (*Mutter und Kind*, Berlin Pap. 3027 E III, 10).

Our knowledge of the surgical use of the term is drawn exclusively from Pap. Smith, where it is applied to wounds in the calvaria (Cases 3 and 7), maxilla (Case 15), temporal region (Cases 19 and 20), cervical vertebra (Case 29), and ribs (Case 40). It was defined and explained in Gloss A appended to our present case, but unfortunately the text is fragmentary. One item of the explanation has however survived: "a contracted smash, through his incurring a break like a puncture of a (pottery) jar." The surgeon is here comparing the calvaria to a bulbous jar, in which a blow with some sharp instrument has punctured a hole. Such an injury may be seen in the forehead of King Sekenenre (Pl. II, Fig. 5), who lived in the time when our medical treatise was copied and in use. Such a wound may of course be very serious. In Case 7 the symptoms it causes are very grave and the patient's condition regarded as hopeless, as it was in the case of King Sekenenre. On the other hand the surgeon does not hesitate to pronounce a verdict of successful treatment, as in our Case 3, or in a perforation (*thm*) of the maxilla (Case 15), a perforation of the temporal region (Case 19), or of a rib (Case 40). A perforation of the temporal bone however (Case 20) may be hopeless; and a perforation of a cervical vertebra very doubtful (Case 29). It is obvious that a *thm* is customarily a perforation of the *bone*, but in Case 19 (q. v.) there may be doubt about it. Such a wound is one chiefly occurring in battle, and doubtless produced by a spear thrust; though now and again it may have occurred in civil life.

Examination

I 19–20

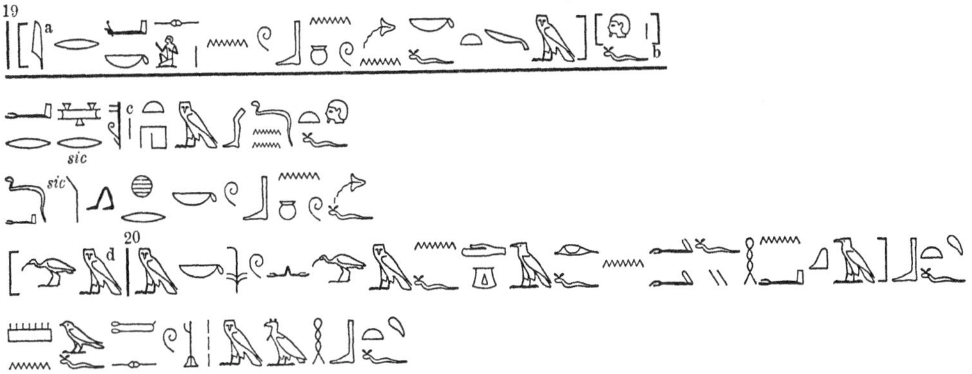

a Restored from II 3 and the usual beginning of the examination; also from the title above.

b The tail of the *f* is visible in l. 20 under the following *r*.

c Only traces of this stroke.

d The left end of the head of the owl is preserved at the right-hand edge of fragment E, l. 19, and just below it, and further to the left, as it should be, is the final stroke of the owl. By measuring the length of *gm* as found in l. 25, it will be seen that this *m* in l. 19 is the first *m* in *gmm·k*; the second *m* therefore being the first sign of l. 20. The other material in this bracket is drawn from I 25 and II 4–5. On the question of space available, see commentary.

Translation

[If thou examinest a man having a gaping wound in] his [head], penetrating to the bone, (and) perforating his skull; thou shouldst palpate his wound; [shouldst thou find him unable to look at his two shoulders] and his [br]east, (and) suffering with stiffness in his neck, (conclusion in diagnosis).

Commentary

Down to the end of l. 19 the terms needing explanation will be found fully discussed in the preceding commentary on Cases 1 and 2.

With regard to the restoration at the beginning of l. 19, there can be no question regarding its correctness; for it is obvious that l. 18 contained the title of a new case. The words "thou shouldst palpate, etc." (l. 19) show that the examination began in l. 19, and began without any doubt with the usual words as restored above. Compare also the above notes on the restoration of l. 19. Regarding the next bracket, which begins at the end of l. 19 and includes l. 20 as far as the right edge of fragment G (where the text is preserved again), we should note that this bracket begins after the injunction, "thou shouldst palpate his wound." This charge to the surgeon occurs ten times in our document; in nine of these passages the following context is preserved, and it begins in six of them with *gmm-k*, and in one with *yr gmy-k*, "if thou findest," which is the same thing. In seven out of nine passages then, the direction, "thou shouldst palpate, etc." is followed by "shouldst thou find," or its equivalent, "if thou findest," thus furnishing a satisfactory basis for the restoration *gmm-k* adopted above. There is hardly room for the restoration *yr gmy-k*, "if thou findest," as appears in Case 27 (IX 14), after "thou shouldst palpate, etc.;" but this would not alter the meaning of the restoration. There is uncertainty regarding the use of the pronoun *św*, "him;" but there is just enough space for it in l. 20. There can be no doubt about the restoration of the text after *gmm-k św*. The data are these: 1. Gloss B (l. 25) shows that the discussion of the case contained the words "unable to look at his two shoulders and his breast;" 2. At the end of the lacuna in l. 20 we find the signs , which are obviously the last four signs of the words *ḳ'b·t-f*, "his breast." By a curious coincidence the passage in l. 25 breaks off at the end of the line at exactly the same place in the word at which the passage preserved in l. 20 begins. By measuring the length of the preserved passage in l. 25 from to (the first two signs of *ḳ'b·t*, "breast"), we find by placing this measurement at the right end of l. 20 (before) that there is just room for it, when we have prefixed to it the signs , continuing the *gm* at the end of l. 19, in the words , *gmm-k św*. We may therefore regard the restoration of l. 20 as certain.

One further question, however, arises in view of our restoration of the treatment (I 21–23). This restoration mentions the fact of the stitching of the wound as already done, just as in Cases 10 and 26. Indeed all six cases which employ stitching in our treatise, place the injunction to stitch in the examination, and then refer to it again (if at all) in the treatment. We should therefore expect instructions to stitch in our examination; but it is quite clear that there is no room for such instructions in the second large lacuna above.

n gmy-n-f, "he is not able," literally "he does not find." This interesting idiom occurs in six cases in our treatise, each time with context indicating physical inability to turn or drop the head (Cases 3, 4, 5, 7, 29, and 32). Grammatically this so-called gnomic use of the *n*-form in the negative is of course common, but I do not recall a case in which it is employed attributively after a pronoun, following the verb "find." This is clearly a construction parallel with the pseudo-participle after "find," in the well-known example, "He found a man standing on the dyke" (literally "a man, he was standing"). So in our treatise the surgeon is addressed, "shouldst thou find him, being unable" (literally "he is not able"). Gunn has discussed the negative *n*-form (*Syntax*, Chap. XII), but he too seems not to have met this construction elsewhere in the available documents. *Gmy* and a negative, with the meaning "be unable," seems to be construed in our passage with a finite verb following it, literally meaning "that he should look," and really a substantive clause functioning as the direct object of "find." It is not impossible, however, that we should regard the form (*dgꜣ-f*) after "find" as an infinitive, literally meaning "his looking."

It is assumed in this examination that the physician will make this observation of the patient's inability to twist or drop his head without prescribing any means for aiding such observation. In three other cases, however, the physician is charged to say to the patient: "Look at thy two shoulders" (Case 19, VII 16), or "Look at thy two shoulders and thy breast" (Case 30, X 9), or "Look at thy breast" (*šnb·t*, Case 32, XI 2), and then to observe whether the effort causes pain or difficulty.

. The usage of this common verb *mn*, meaning "to be sick," "to suffer," has not yet been precisely determined in the medical papyri. While it may be intransitively used, e. g., "you are not sick" (Eloquent Peasant 317) and Metternich Stela 68; Louvre Stela, C 26, l. 18; it is nevertheless commonly and strongly transitive. In the Old Kingdom indeed it takes the neutral object "thing, something," even when it is used to mean "be sick," or "be ailing." Thus a man making his will says of himself: "who was not (yet) sick," , literally "who was not ailing (with) anything" (Gizeh, Tomb of Nekure, Lepsius, *Denkmaeler*, II. 15: cf. also in *Urk*. I, 152). It is evident then that this verb means "to suffer with" or "to be ailing with," without the interposition of a preposition, as we say, "He suffered a stroke of paralysis." Until recently it was understood that such transitive use of the verb is always followed by the name of the ailment, e.g., Ebers 32, 21; 49, 7; 39, 21, etc. Such was the understanding of the character of the object given in the Erman-Grapow *Handwörterbuch*, p. 64. The word *mn* is, however, constantly used in the Papyrus Ebers with some ailing *member of the body* immediately following as a direct object, e.g., "if he is ailing in his groin" (Ebers 103, 6). This usage, already noted by Stern in his vocabulary, is now in the *Wörterbuch* (see p. 66). We have then three uses of *mn* "to be sick:" (1) intransitive; (2) transitive followed by the name of the disease as a direct object; (3) transitive followed by the name of the diseased part or member of the body as direct object. These facts are of importance in the interpretation of the words immediately following *mn* in our passage.

ṯsw, "stiffness, rigidity." The word occurs seventeen times in our treatise, eight times written out fully as here, and nine times abbreviated either to (II 4; III 4; IV 9, 12; VII 18; VIII 4, 13) or to (III 13; X 7). In all seventeen occurrences it is immediately followed by the words "in his neck." At first glance, therefore, it might easily be confused with the word *ṯs*, "vertebra," which occurs thirty-two times in our document, and is twenty-five times followed by the genitive phrase "of his neck," thus, e.g., in X 3, 4, etc.: "vertebra of his neck." In every case, however, "vertebra" is written with the single sign , followed by the stroke, and is modified by the following indirect genitive; whereas our word  is followed by the adverbial phrase "in the neck." This distinction, combined with the consistently different writing, clearly distinguishes the two words.

Ten cases exhibiting "ṯsw" in the neck

Case.	*Injury.*	*Reference.*
3	Cut in head with perforation of skull	I 20, 21; I 26–II 1.
4	,, ,, ,, ,, split in skull	II 4, 6.
5	,, ,, ,, ,, fracture of skull	II 13–14, 15.
6	,, ,, ,, ,, brain envelope broken open	II 22.
7	,, ,, ,, ,, perforation of sutures of skull; various symptoms incl. constriction of "ligament of his mandible;" mouth cannot be opened	III 4, 6, 13.
8	Fracture of skull without visible injury to overlying external tissue .	IV 9, 12.
19	Perforation of temporal bone (presumably); neighboring eye inflamed .	VII 18.
20	Wound in temple with perforation of temporal bone . . .	VIII 4.
22	Fracture in temporal bone	VIII 13–14.
29	Cut in cervical vertebra and perforation of this vertebra . .	X 7.

The meaning of our *ṯsw* is superficially clear. In Case 3 the statement that the sufferer has a *ṯsw* in his neck immediately *follows* the observation that he is unable to "look at his shoulders or his breast," meaning that he is unable to lower his head either obliquely (toward the shoulders) or vertically (toward the breast). In Case 4, however, the statement that the patient suffers with a *ṯsw* in his neck is followed by what is essentially a *clause of result* stating that he is unable to "look at his shoulders or his breast" (II 4–5). It is obvious that *ṯsw* must indicate some kind of inability to operate the muscles and articulations of the neck. This conclusion is rendered certain by the explanation of the symptom "he suffers with a *ṯsw* in his neck" in Gloss C (I 26–II 1), which states, "it is a lifting up (*ṯs·t*), (resulting) from his having incurred this injury which has shifted (lit., "wandered") into his neck, so that his neck (also) suffers with it." Our *ṯsw* is therefore a noun derived from the verb *ṯsy* "to lift up," which is regularly employed of lifting or raising a member of the body, especially in a middle voice, when the member lifts itself or rises (X 21). *Ṯsw* is therefore a permanent or stationary uplift or elevation in the neck, which cannot be bent downward. Obviously, as a rendering, the word "stiffness" is pathologically very vague and unprecise. Nevertheless, Dr. Luckhardt states: "The physical findings of inability to look at shoulders and breast and particularly the stiffness of the neck are quite characteristic of a meningitis or meningeal involvement. The stiffness of the neck really makes it difficult and painful for the patient to look at the shoulders or bend the head enough to look at the chest: . . . I think the rendering 'stiffness' ('rigidity') is very good. It is so used daily in medical practice to-day. It is due to reflex spasm of the musculature of the neck." It is to be noted that *ṯsw* in the neck in every case accompanies an injury in the head. Of the ten cases in which it forms one of the symptoms, six are injuries of the skull approaching or penetrating the brain. Of the other four cases three are injuries to the temporal bone, and the last is a cut in one of the cervical vertebrae itself. The pathologist can best grasp the nature of the evidence by an examination of the preceding conspectus of the ten cases exhibiting *ṯsw* in the neck, but it should be noted that he will find in the text of the cases themselves additional important symptoms accompanying *ṯsw*, which are too bulky to be incorporated in the previous brief summary.

This effect of the injury in the head on another region differentiates this case from the two preceding, which were superficial wounds leaving the bone uninjured.

DIAGNOSIS

I 20–21

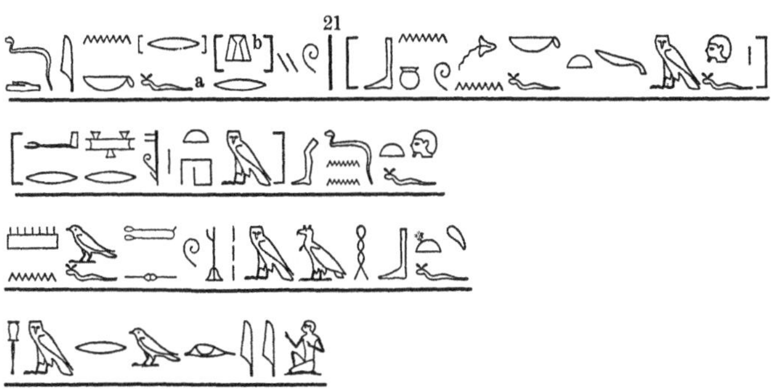

[a] Traces of the *f* are visible, especially the head on fragment F. See Vol. II, Pl. I.

[b] A fragment of this sign is visible. The other restorations in the diagnosis are obvious, being mostly drawn from the title (I 18) and the examination (I 19).

Translation

Thou shouldst say [regarding] him : " One having [a gaping wound in his head, penetrating to the bone, (and) per]forating his skull, while he suffers with stiffness in his neck. An ailment which I will treat."

Commentary

This is the first diagnosis recording symptoms or conditions elsewhere than in the wound itself. See the discussion in the introduction (pp. 45–51). On the verdict forming the conclusion see Case 1 (I 1–2). The surgeon now turns to the treatment, which is the first in our treatise to make use of a surgical suture. It is unfortunate that this important reference falls in a lacuna ; but the restoration including it (l. 22) is based on conclusive grounds.

TREATMENT

I 21–23

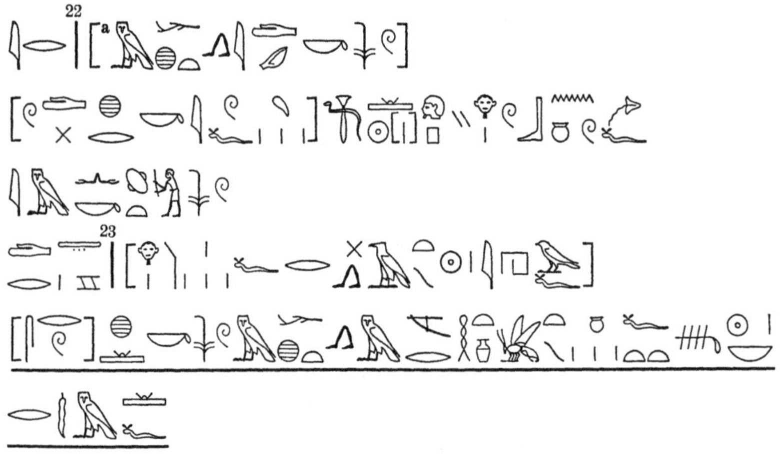

[a] On this restoration and all the following restorations in the treatment, see the following commentary and also Vol. II, Pl. I B and C.

Translation

Now [after thou hast stitched it, thou shouldst lay] fresh [meat] upon his wound the first day. Thou shouldst not bind it. Moor (him) [at his mooring stakes until the period of his injury passes by]. Thou shouldst [tre]at it afterward with grease, honey, and lint every day, until he recovers.

Commentary

The restoration of this broken text at first presented some difficulty. The large lacuna in l. 23 is easily filled by comparison with the parallel text in II 7 and in XVII 12–13; but the long gap in l. 22 is not so easily restored. Luckily the first word of the treatment is preserved at the end of l. 21. Now there are only two more cases in our treatise in which the treatment begins with 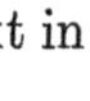 *yr* and continues with an apodosis concluding with application of fresh meat, which we find immediately after the lacuna in l. 22 above. These are Cases 10 (V 7) and 26 (IX 9–10). An examination of these two cases shows that in both of them the treatment begins with *yr* and the following context concludes with the words *ywf w'ḏ hrw tpy*, "fresh meat the first day." We can hardly doubt therefore that our text should be restored in conformity with Cases 10 and 26; at least this should be done with the context immediately following *yr*. The text in Case 26 is as follows:

" Now after thou hast stitched it thou shouldst bind it with fresh meat the first day. Thou shouldst treat it afterward [with] grease and honey every day until he recovers."

The treatment in Case 10 even more closely resembles that in our Case 3, because it likewise inserts an additional precaution between the application of the fresh meat and the final treatment with grease and honey, see Case 10 (V 7–8).

Our treatment in Case 3 displays two noticeable differences as compared with Cases 10 and 26. Case 3 has the words *ḥr wbnw-f*, " upon his wound," immediately following the words " fresh meat the first day." Furthermore Case 3 carefully enjoins the surgeon, " Thou shalt not bind it ; " whereas Cases 10 and 26 charge him to bind the wound with fresh meat, or as the Egyptian text literally rendered expresses it, " thou shouldst bind it upon fresh meat the first day," in which the object of the binding is the wound, and the meat is an indirect object. In Case 3, however, the preserved text with the phrase " upon his wound " (l. 22) shows that the wound was the *indirect* object, and that consequently meat must have been the *direct* object. The verb of which it was the direct object is lost, but this lost verb was obviously not the verb " bind," because not only does the prohibition to bind forbid, but also the words " upon his wound," a phrase never used with the verb " bind." The lost verb was therefore probably *wdy*, " lay," as restored above.

With regard to the fitness of introducing stitching into the above restoration, it should be noted that Case 3 is one exactly furnishing the conditions in which our surgeon elsewhere prescribes stitching. An examination of the list of such cases in which our treatise prescribes stitching (see Case 10, commentary on V 6) reveals the fact that they are six in number, and that in all of them we are dealing in each case with a wound in a thin stratum of soft tissue, just as in Case 3. We are therefore dealing with a wound in Case 3, such as the surgeon would stitch. When therefore we find that not only the characteristics of the wound, but likewise the preserved context on both sides of the lacuna (l. 22) are identical with the parallels in Cases 10 and 26, we may conclude that the evidence is fairly conclusive in favor of the restoration above inserted.

ydr, " stitch," see commentary in Case 10 (V 6).

wdy, " lay," used of medicaments in the directions, appears three times in our document (Case 41 twice ; and Case 46) with the preposition *r*, " to," and commonly in Pap. Ebers. With the preposition *ḥr*, " upon," as above in our text of Case 3, it is used twice in Pap. Smith, both times with plaster or adhesive tape as the object (Case 6, II 23; Case 27, IX 16). See full commentary on this word in Case 11 (V 11).

"Thou shouldst not bind it." This prohibition is found five times in our treatise. In Case 47 (XVII 12–13) this seems to be due to the appearance of feverishness in the wound. Again the seriousness of the rupture of tissue in Cases 4 (II 6–7) and 5 (II 15), perhaps causing the surgeon to apprehend displacement of the bone or soft tissue, may have been the reason for the injunction not to bind. The same is true in Case 6 (II 23), in which the surgeon is charged neither to bind nor to apply plaster or adhesive tape. The case is one of a compound comminuted fracture. Just why the surgeon should avoid binding on the fresh meat in Case 3 is not clear, but the prohibition is followed by the same context in all the other three cases.

The extraordinary injunction, "Moor (him) at his mooring stakes," is fortunately explained in Gloss D as meaning: "putting him on his customary diet without administering to him a prescription" (II 1–2). It is evidently an archaic idiom, not clear even to the usual ancient reader of this treatise, as the presence of the explanatory gloss shows. The idiom is amusingly suggestive of our western cowboy term "grub-stake." We are aided in its analysis by the variant: , "Put him at his mooring stakes," which occurs in three instances (V 12, though lacking *św*; VII 18, and VIII 9). See commentary on *wdy* in Case 11 (V 11–12). Of the ten instances in which the idiom is found, the other seven employ the form *wdy r tꜣ*, three times written *d r tꜣ* (I 22; X 8; XVII 13), three times written (II 7; II 15; X 3), and once written (II 1).

The scribe has in all cases where this idiom is found abbreviated the writing of "stakes" to (eight times) or (once, X 8). The sign is quite different from his writing of finger.[1] He always makes *mny·t*, "stake," thus , once three times repeated for the plural as we have seen (X 8); whereas his writing of "finger" (II 13; VIII 10; IX 3, etc.) or plural (I 4; I 6; II 4, and usually) always turns the tips toward the left, that is, away from the beginning of the line, as we commonly find them also in Middle Kingdom hieroglyphic, e.g., Tomb of Hepzefi, Siut). It is clear therefore that we are to read here an abbreviated writing of the word *mny·t*, "mooring stake."[2]

The regimen indicated by the injunction "Moor him at his mooring stakes" is followed by three different results:

(1) "until he recovers" (once, Case 28, X 3).

[1] The distinction was, I think, first noted by Gardiner.

[2] Dr. Grapow makes the interesting suggestion that the passage in Shipwreck 53–54, literally: "I put on the ground on account of the abundance in my hands," may be explained from our above idiom. The lack of the phrase, "at his (my) mooring stakes," however, seems to destroy the parallelism with the idiom of Pap. Smith.

(2) 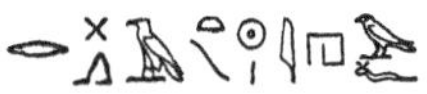 "until the period of his injury passes by" (six times, Cases 3 (restored), 4, 5, 19, 29, 47).

(3)  "until thou knowest that he has reached a decisive point" (literally, "he is arriving at something," once, VIII 9).

As we have learned from the discussion in Case 1, (1) is very common in *favorable* cases. (2) is used in *favorable, doubtful,* and *hopeless* cases; see discussion in following paragraph. (3) means a point just past the crisis, when the physician knows whether the patient will "live or die." See Case 4, Gloss C, II 10–11.

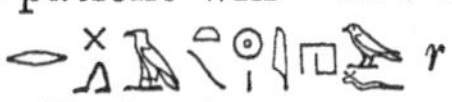 *r św'y '·t yh-f,* "until the period of his injury passes by." This time limitation never occurs except after the curious idiom, "moor him at his mooring stakes." The word  *'·t* usually means a point of time, an instant; but is also used for longer periods. Here it is obvious that it must designate a lapse of time long enough to permit a resumption of normal diet continuing at least for a number of meals, and probably longer. The interpretation of the clause depends largely upon the meaning of  *yh-f,* "his injury, ailing, pain," or the like. Does the word mean the concrete, specific wound or injury; or does it mean pain, suffering in general? Its medical or pathological use is very limited. It is found in the medical documents only *three times* outside of Pap. Smith, and all these occurrences are in Pap. Ebers. In each of these three passages (37, 15; 38, 15; 38, 16) the word is used to designate a stomach trouble,[1] that is, the ailment specifically and not pain or suffering in general. In Pap. Smith the word occurs twelve times. Five of these are in the clause *r św'y '·t yh-f,* and therefore do not aid us. Of the remaining seven cases, three designate the specific wound or injury under discussion, e.g., 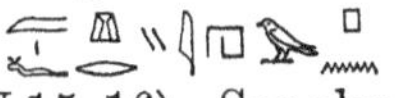 "the side of him having this injury" (viz., a fracture of the skull IV 15–16). See also IV 16 and XVI 13, which are not quite so certain. In four passages our word designates the source of symptoms, e.g., "his neck is tense and stiff because of his injury" (*yh,* III 20); see also III 17–18 and XIII 10–11, but especially Gloss C (II 1). The evidence therefore favors understanding the word *yh* in our clause, *r św'y '·t yh-f,* as the specific injury. The phrase "period of his injury" would then mean the period during which his injury continues, that is, until it can be said to have healed and thus "passes by." This interpretation is favored by the fact that in Case 28 the instructions "Moor him at his mooring stakes" are followed by the words "until he recovers" (X 3). The fact that in one case the word *yh* receives the determinative of a typhonic animal (XVII 13) does not aid us in a scientific determination of the pathological meaning of the word, though it discloses the current superstitions of the age, in which our scribe and our treatise of course both share.

[1] The other, older form of the word, *'h,* also occurs three times in Pap. Ebers: once in a magical formula (57, 21) and again designating internal troubles (37, 16; 106, 14). These throw no light on the specific meaning of the word.

GLOSS A

I 24–25

Explaining: " Perforating his skull "

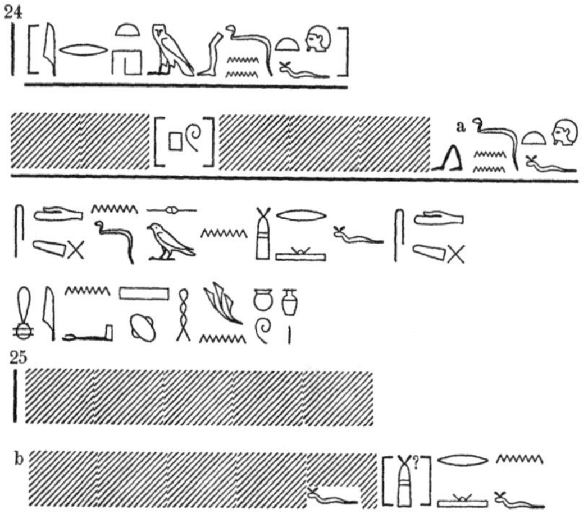

[a] The original shows clearly a pair of legs; hence we cannot read *thm*, as the following *d̲nn·t* would suggest. There are no traces of a sign over the legs.

[b] The loss is some three-fifths of a line, the longest lacuna in this broken column. The tail of  at the end of the lacuna is visible in l. 26. See Vol. II, Pl. I and I B.

Translation

[As for: " Perforating his skull," it means] - - - - his skull, a contracted smash, through his incurring a break like a puncture of a (pottery) jar, - - - - - - - - - which he incurred."

Commentary

The other three glosses appended to this case explain all the symptoms and conditions following *thm*, and we must conclude therefore that the first gloss contained an explanation of this injury. The explanation itself makes this conclusion quite certain; hence the restoration. The beginning of the explanation is unfortunately entirely lost and there is no source from which to recover it. It proceeds with a loose application of the word " smash " (*śd*), otherwise our surgeon's technical term for a compound comminuted fracture (see Case 5). It is clear that it is applied here in a loose and popular sense, in keeping with the character of the illustration, drawn as it is from the incidents of every-day life. The rendering of *nd̲s* " small," as " contracted," is justified by the surgeon's use of this word as the opposite of *wśḫ*, " wide," e. g., in the head wound of Case 1. Compare Fig. 13, Pl. VII, *infra*.

 *ʿpr-f*, " his incurring " is evidently a surgical use of the word *ʿpr*, " to acquire, gain," e. g.,  " Thou gainest thy happiness " (Letter from Ana, in Griffith, *Papyri from Kahun*, pl. 29).

nᶜš, "puncture." This noun is unknown anywhere else. Whether it is to be connected with the word *nᶜš*, "strong," or "terrible," is not clear. *Nᶜš* does not aid us in the explanation therefore; on the contrary it is the obvious meaning of *thm*, which leads to the translation of *nᶜš* as "puncture."

[ ] *ᶜpr-n-f*, "which he incurred." This restoration, while uncertain, is very probable. We cannot restore *ḫpr n-f*, as in II 21 and IV 11, for *ḫpr* never has a determinative in our document, and seldom does elsewhere.

GLOSS B

I 25–26

Explaining: "Unable to look at his two shoulders and his breast"

[a] Only the left-hand portions of these two signs are visible; they make the restoration of the preceding bracket quite certain. It is the preservation of fragment H which makes the gloss intelligible. See Vol. II, Pl. I and I B.

Translation

As for: "Unable to look at his two shoulders and [his] bre[ast," it means it is not easy for him to look at] his two shoulders (and) it is not easy for him to look at his breast.

Commentary

The restoration of the first part of l. 26 as above can hardly be doubted. The completion of the word *ḳ'b·t-f* is obvious, and the preservation of "his two shoulders," plainly parallel with "his breast" (2nd time), makes equally obvious the completion of the parallel statement preceding "his two shoulders" from the statement preceding "his breast." It is clear also that we must insert the usual *pw* in the restored parallel statement, although it is not present in the second. The silence of the explanation regarding the cause of the difficulty is doubtless due to the writer's knowledge of the coming explanation of the stiffness in the neck, which is to be inserted in the next gloss. The explanation indicates not impossibility, but difficulty and probably pain, caused by the effort to turn the face vertically or obliquely downward.

It is to be noted that Fragment H (Pl. I, l. 26) must be moved slightly to the right (as on Pl. I B) to make room for , as first observed by Dévaud.

GLOSS C

I 26–II 1

Explaining : " Suffering with stiffness in his neck "

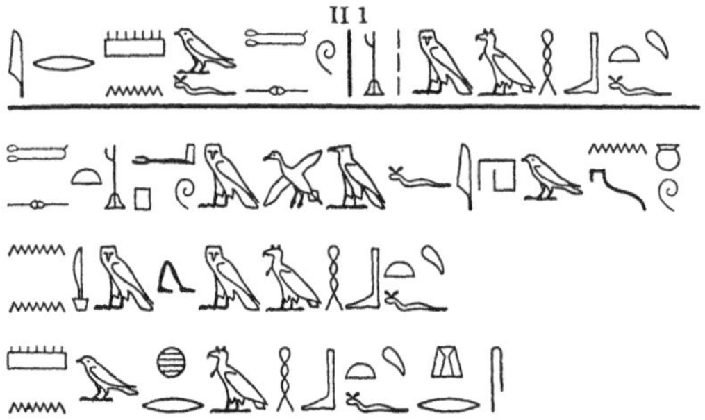

Translation

As for : " Suffering with stiffness in his neck," it means a lifting up (resulting) from his having incurred this injury, which has shifted into his neck, so that his neck (also) suffers with it.

Commentary

The general meaning of the gloss has already been discussed in the commentary on the examination (l. 20).

p'w-f, " his having incurred " is an interpretation perhaps subject to question. The auxiliary *p'w,* " to have done," is commonly followed by an infinitive ; *yh,* however, is known only as a noun. There may be some doubt whether *p'w yh* may mean " to have incurred an injury." Nevertheless the context is strongly in favor of this meaning ; for it is impossible to accept the form *p'w-f* as the possessive demonstrative " his." There are two objections : the form is not normal ; and the entire treatise contains no other example of the possessive demonstrative, for the document is not written in the Middle Kingdom *koiné.* However, even if it were accepted as the possessive demonstrative, the sense would not be essentially altered. We could render : " (resulting) from this his injury," accepting the really redundant second demonstrative as re-enforcing the first.

nnm. This reading, correcting the old reading *tnm* first noticed by Dévaud (*Maximes de Ptahhotep*, p. 28), is corroborated by our text, which has pretty clearly *nn* rather than *tn.* The word means " to go astray," " to turn aside " and the like, as of a traveler who has missed the road and gone astray (Sinuhe, B 96 ; Pyr. 1695 c). Its use by the surgeon in this connection is interesting, suggesting that as the injury is in the head, any results of it found elsewhere must have gone astray or wandered !

GLOSS D

II 1–2

Explaining: "Moor (him) at his mooring stakes"

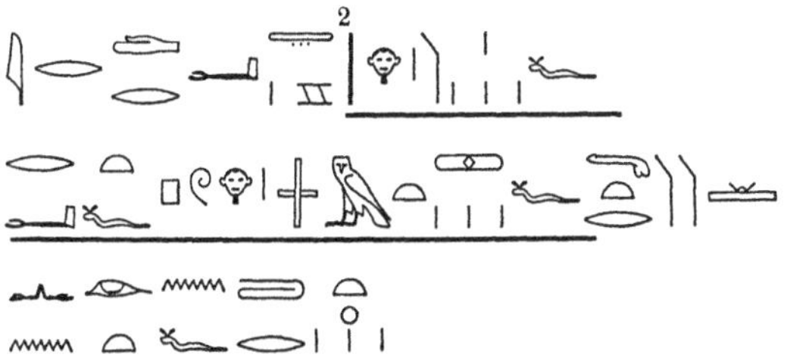

Translation

As for: "Moor (him) at his mooring stakes," it means putting him on his customary diet, without administering to him a prescription.

Commentary

The meaning of this valuable gloss in general has been already discussed in the commentary on the treatment (ll. 22–23).

mtr, "customary." This meaning of the word long awaited notice in the dictionaries; but there can be no question as to its correctness. From its use in the historical inscriptions this meaning was established twenty years ago.[1]

There might be some discussion as to the more exact meaning of the last phrase in the explanation, "without administering to him a prescription." The word rendered "administering" literally means "making," and the word "make" has in Egyptian a very wide range of meanings, such that it is possible the surgeon may mean "prepare." *Pḫr·t,* like its English equivalent "prescription," means both the actual medicine or the written recipe. Hence our final phrase may mean, either "without administering to him any medicine;" "without writing for him any recipe;" or "without preparing for him any medicine."

CASE FOUR

II 2–11

A GAPING WOUND IN THE HEAD PENETRATING TO THE BONE AND SPLITTING THE SKULL

This case is far more serious than those which preceded it. It illustrates the organization of materials in the treatise in groups of cases beginning with the simpler and easier injuries and passing then to more complicated and dangerous cases.

[1] See Breasted, *Ancient Records,* Vol. III, p. 168, note b.

TITLE

II 2

Translation

Instructions concerning a gaping wound in his head, penetrating to the bone, (and) splitting his skull.

Commentary

The terms employed in this title have all been explained in the commentary on the preceding cases except the word 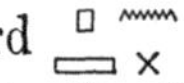 *pšn*, "splitting." It is an archaic word found outside of Pap. Smith only in the Pyramid Texts and the Middle Kingdom Coffin Texts. In the Pyramids it is found only in 305 a, 679 b, and 1963 b. One of these passages is valuable for its graphic indication of the meaning of the word, having as the determinative 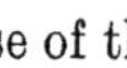, an axe actually splitting a billet of wood (Pyr. 305 a). Valuable for our surgical use of the word is the phrase , "who splits your heads, ye gods" (Pyr. 1963 b). In chapter 17 of the Book of the Dead the word is applied to the splitting of the *yšd·t* tree; cf. Harhotep 208 (old 103), and, referring to same incident, Book of the Dead, ed. Naville, 125, final address, l. 14.

Pšn is used in four different cases in Pap. Smith as the technical surgical term for designating an injury to the bone, and is not found elsewhere in the ancient medical documents of Egypt. These four injuries are in the skull (Case 4), the maxilla (Case 16), the temple (Case 21), and the arm (Case 38). It occurs as one of three different bone injuries: *pšn*, "split;" *thm*, "perforation;" and *šd*, "fracture," the presence of which may be denied to indicate that the bone under a flesh wound is uninjured, e.g., Case 2, or Case 18. *Pšn* is a kind of wound which would be produced especially by the long-headed Egyptian battle axe (see Fig. 2), which may have an edge as long as 16½ inches, a type of battle axe especially common in the Middle Kingdom. A sword might produce a similar wound in the skull, but the sword was little used in Egyptian warfare in the age preceding our document, though the Egyptian armies would probably have met some type of it in Asia. A wound in the skull to which the term *pšn* would have been applied is shown in Fig. 3, which illustrates the difference between a "split" (*pšn*) and a "fracture" (*šd*). The weight of the blow has fractured the skull at both ends of the *pšn*, which is the actual cut produced by the edge of the weapon. There are no traces of healing and it is evident that the injury produced death before any healing had occurred. A similar injury, seemingly involving only a *pšn*, is found in Fig. 4, a case with which the surgeon's art was able to deal; the wound healed and the patient recovered. Our treatise regards such an injury as serious and critical when it is in the skull (Cases 4, and 21); but when it is in the maxillary region (Case 16) or in the arm (Case 38), it is not considered serious. It is explained in Gloss A of Case 4 as meaning the "separation of one shell from another shell of his skull, while fragments (evidently of bone) remain sticking in the flesh of his head and do not come away" (II 9). See the commentary on Gloss A.

EXAMINATION

II 3–5

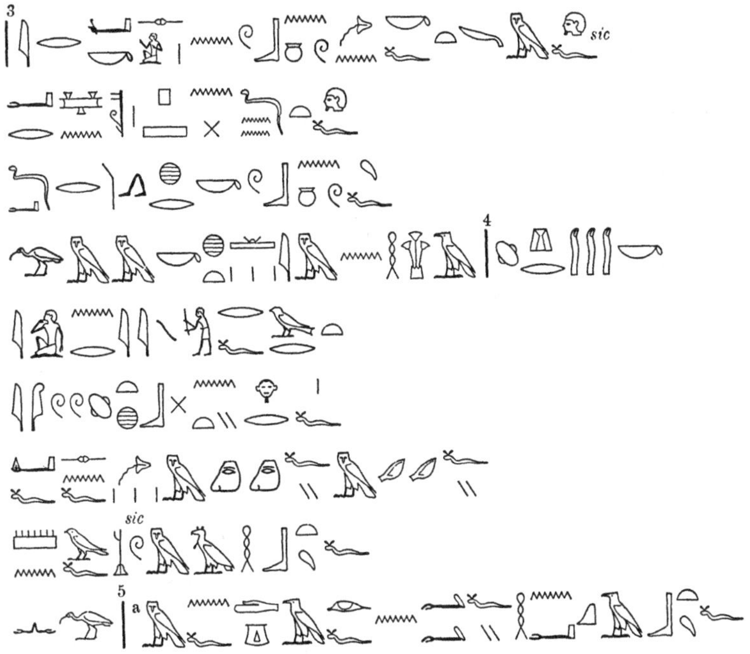

[a] This *m* is the first sign in l. 5 and is almost lost in the break between columns I and II; but the remains make the reading certain.

Translation

If thou examinest a man having a gaping wound in his head, penetrating to the bone, (and) splitting his skull, thou shouldst palpate his wound. Shouldst thou find something disturbing therein under thy fingers, (and) he shudders exceedingly, while the swelling which is over it protrudes, he discharges blood from both his nostrils (and) from both his ears, he suffers with stiffness in his neck, so that he is unable to look at his two shoulders and his breast, (conclusion in diagnosis).

Commentary

All terms preceding the results of the palpation have been discussed in the commentary preceding Case 4.

yẖ·t, "thing," as used in Pap. Smith, appears in a range of usages which require discussion. We find it used as follows:

1. Without a modifier, to designate some *material object*, e.g., to "measure something" in a bushel (I 5); to seize "something" (of a bird's claw, VIII 15); a "thing" is clammy (III 19), etc.

2. Without any qualitative modifier, and indicating something often *immaterial*, neutral or unfavorable:

a. Neutral, as in the frequent expression "until thou knowest whether he (the patient) is arriving at anything," meaning whether he is arriving at anything decisive, either favorable or unfavorable (II 8, 10, 23; III 8, 15; IV 9; VIII 9; XII 18–19).

b. Unfavorable, as in the statement that the skin overlying a fracture of the skull is uninjured, thus: "If thou examinest a man having a smash of (var. "in") his skull under the skin of his head, while there is nothing at all upon it" (the skin, Case 8, IV 5), in which "nothing at all" ()[1] clearly means an injury. Another example will be found in VIII 18–19.

3. With a following modifier, especially the following:

a. An adjective, in cases where "thing" designates something purely material, e.g., *yẖ·t šm*, "something hot" (III 7); *yẖ·t gnn*, "something soft" (VI 14; IX 13); .... *yẖ·t šfw*, "something swollen" (XIII 10; XVI 13), although this last example may possibly belong under 3 *c* or 3 *d* below.

There are indications that in some such cases the two words merge together, if not in pronunciation, at least in meaning, and serve as an abstract noun, e.g., *yẖ·t dšr* (XIII 11), "redness," literally "red things," in which "things" seems to serve like an abstract prefix or termination such as *-schaft* or *-keit* in German. This is a usage which is known in literary Egyptian, e.g., "Happy he who tells what he has tasted (experienced), when the evil is passed" (Shipwreck 124), a passage in which "evil" is expressed, *yẖ·t mr*, "evil thing" (or "things").

b. An adverb, especially *ym*, "therein," e.g., Pap. Ebers 108, 19. This *ym* is not infrequently followed by a noun in the genitive, as in our text above, *yẖ·t ym nḥ'* "something therein disturbing" (II 3–4); or it may be that we must classify this modifier as a participle, as in the following cases.

c. A participle, e.g., *yẖ·t ḳ'b*, "something folded" (XII 5); *yẖ·t pry·t* (XIV 16). A participle also sometimes follows the adverb *ym* of 3 *b*, e.g., *yẖ·t ym nhdhd np'p'*, "something throbbing and fluttering therein" (II 20).

[1] The modifier *nb·t* is not to be classed as *qualitative* within my meaning in the above discussion, and hence I have placed the example among those without qualitative modifiers above.

d. A noun, e.g., *yḫ·t nʿbꜣ* (XVI 1 with det. supplied from XVI 14), "something of clamminess," probably meaning "some clamminess." We should perhaps compare with this usage the use of "thing" with the meaning "portion," as in the archaic words for the morning and evening meal in the Pyramid Texts: *yḫ·t nhpw,* lit. "morning thing" and *yḫ·t wḫꜣ*, lit. "evening thing" (Pyr. 978 d, e). It is quite clear that in such examples as these two *yḫ·t* designates a *material* thing, and its use with a following modifier may originally have arisen in cases of this kind. It is equally clear, however, that in some of these phrases "thing" or "something" does *not* designate a material object. We may compare our English "something" or "somewhat," employed to indicate a "measure of" or a "certain amount of." This usage is closely allied to the Egyptian use of "thing" to mean "manner" or "fashion," as in the well-known example in the Piankhi Stela "in the manner (lit. 'thing') of women" (l. 63). Our papyrus has a related case in the passage *my yḫ·t rm-f,* "as if he were weeping" (III 12; IV 2), literally "like the manner ('thing') that he were weeping." Gunn has called my attention to its occurrence also in the still unpublished tomb autobiography of Gemnikai: *m yḫ·t mrr·t ny-św·t,* "in the manner (lit. 'thing') which the king desired." These various usages and shades of meaning of *yḫ·t* must be remembered in interpreting the passage above (II 3–4).

The lack of agreement in gender between *yḫ·t* and its following modifier is of course a well-known peculiarity. *Yḫ·t* is in most of the above cases obviously not plural, and it is possibly singular in all.

nḥꜣ, "disturbing," the modifier of *yḫ·t,* "thing," is a difficult word. Although it is not uncommon it is applied with highly varied meanings. It is used of a "terrible" face, of an "unfavorable" wind, of "dangerous" water, of a "terrifying" voice; it is applied to fire, and it appears parallel with, or in addition to *sḫm,* "mighty." In Egyptian medicine it is known in only four passages besides the one we are discussing: one more in our papyrus (III 1) and three in Pap. Ebers. Of these four the one in Pap. Smith is the most instructive: "something foreign (or 'disturbing') upon it like ⌜wrinkles⌝ (*py·w*)." We do not know with certainty what these *py·w* are, but the context shows that the wrinkling surface of slag floating on molten metal is meant, and this makes the rendering of *nḥꜣ* as "foreign," "disturbing," or "rough" very probable. Such a meaning would also suit Pap. Ebers 108, 18, a passage in which a cist or swelling or abscess is found to be *nḥꜣ*. In the other two passages in Pap. Ebers the determinative of *nḥꜣ* is (Ebers 39, 9–10; 39, 12) and the context does not fit the meaning "rough," nor suggest clearly any other meaning. It may indeed be that this *nḥꜣ* with is a different word.

ꜥnry, "he shudders" is not clear until it is compared with the five other passages in which it occurs in our papyrus. These disclose the following five variants:

III 3;

VIII 1;

X 5 (in red corrected in over in black);

XIII 14;

XIV 18.

These variants disclose this curiously written word as a form of the verb *nry,* "to be terrified," "to shudder," or the like. The prosthetic is once written , of which the has been inserted in red ink by the scribe as a correction over an which is in black. This is an interesting suggestion of the weak pronunciation of in Hyksos times, and also of as ʾε.

The word is usually construed with the preposition *n,* introducing the cause of the fright, but is *sometimes* employed, e.g., "Offered to thee is the Horus-eye at which () the gods are terrified" (Abydos Ritual, Mariette, tabl. 19, according to Amon). See also Lacau, *Textes relig.* XVII = *Recueil de Trav.* 27, p. 56. The which immediately follows *ʾnry* in all six passages of our papyrus, however, is evidently not an example of introducing the cause. The phrase is either the customary emphatic, or more probably its predecessor, in which is still felt to refer back to the subject and has not yet become impersonal. It is probably much like the German "*ihn*" in "*es schaudert ihn,*" an impersonal reflexive not common in English. Our form, in which the ending appears as either *y* or *w,* is probably a participle. It is noticeable that in all six passages containing our word, it follows the surgeon's palpation or manipulation of the wound, except one (XIV 18). In all cases it is followed not only by , but this is also always followed by *wr·t,* "exceedingly." Our word, therefore, evidently indicates the patient's shrinking or shuddering as a result of the surgeon's palpation. But in the case of XIV 18 it may refer to a shuddering or trembling caused by disease rather than by a wound (see Case 42).

yšw-w, "protrudes" occurs eleven times in Pap. Smith, with the following variants:

II 10;

II 13; IV 6; V 10;

V 17; VI 19;

VI 15;

psd. ptcp., VIII 6; XV 21;

psd. ptcp., XII 22.

It would seem from these examples that the root is *yšw*. Neither the verb *yšš*, nor the noun *yšw* is known in the medical papyri elsewhere; but comparing the noun  [1] *yšw*, "spittle" (Pyr. 246 a, 850 a), with the verb 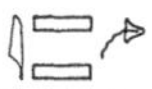 [1] *yšš*, "to spit," it is probable that our verb *yšw* is a cognate of *yšš*, "to spit," and might mean "to spit," "to ooze," "to discharge," "to excrete," meanings which would fit very well all the above passages in which *yšw* occurs. Besides these etymological and semantic evidences, we have also to consider the evidences offered by Gloss B (II 10) which contains the following interesting explanation of our passage: "As for: 'the swelling (*tḫb*) which is over it protrudes,' it means that the swelling which is over this split is large, rising upward." From this explanation we must conclude that *yšw·w* means "protrude" or "project," a meaning closely allied to the root significance of *yšš*, if we understand its fundamental meaning to be something like "exude." An exuding substance of semi-fluid consistency might be said to protrude or project. The same might doubtless be said of the bulging tissue which covers the injury. In our treatise, however, *yšw* is used exclusively with *tḫb* as subject, and if *tḫb* means "swelling," as the following commentary indicates, then it is evident that *yšw* must mean "project," "protrude."

This rare word *yšw* is further evidence of the early date of the material in the Edwin Smith Papyrus; for both verb and noun, unknown as we have said to the other medical documents of Egypt, occur elsewhere only in the oldest literature. The appearance of *yšw* certainly supports the conclusion that our surgical treatise was composed in an age far older than Hyksos times. The same is probably true of the grammatical form of the word. In six of the eleven passages employing *yšw* (IV 6; VI 15, 19; VIII 6; XII 22; XV 21) the subject *tḫb* precedes the verb, which is in the pseudo-participle with the ending  or  written out. The remaining five passages, of which ours is one, place the verb first, but everywhere give it the ending  (four times) or  (once). It is true that the pseudo-participle when *preceding* a nominal subject does not customarily take any ending, and is therefore indistinguishable from a *sḏm-f* form (see Sethe, *Verbum* II, § 3, 1); but the question arises, nevertheless, whether *yšw·w* (and *yšw·y*) in these five passages where it precedes the subject, is not a pseudo-participle. If so, we have in this form an additional indication of the great age of our document; for the sentence with the pseudo-participle preceding a nominal subject has survived only in the oldest texts (see Erman, *Zeitschrift*, 27 (1889), 73–76 and Sethe, *op. cit.*).

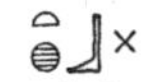 *tḫb*, "swelling" occurs fourteen times in our treatise: once written with the determinative × as here, twice with 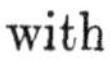, five times with 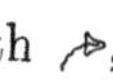, and six times with . It is evidently some cognate form of the well-known word 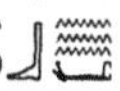 *tḫb*, "to moisten,"

[1] These highly specialized determinatives from the Pyramid Texts are not available in type. The first one is three spewing mouths, the second one is a face with mouth spewing.

L

" to water," " to irrigate," e.g., of the effect of the Nile inundation in the great Amarna Sun hymn. In the medical literature the verb *ṯḫb* is used of moistening the ingredients of a recipe for mixing, e.g., with oil (Pap. Ebers 13, 17–18), or with honey (*ibid.*, 69, 22; Hearst I 2; I 3), or with honey as a real vehicle (Berlin Papyrus 3038, 4, 48).

In all fourteen examples in Pap. Smith, however, *ṯḫb* is used as a noun exclusively, and the verb employed with it is either *yšw*, "exude," "protrude;" or it is *šṯʾ*, "be drawn off." The wound is in all cases an injury to the *bone*, which may or may not involve an injury to the overlying soft tissue. It is used in the description of the following eleven kinds of injury:

Case.	*Injury.*	*Remark about " ṯḫb."*	*Passage.*
4	split in skull	*ṯḫb* exudes or protrudes (*yšw*)	II 4, 10.
5	smash in skull	*ṯḫb* exudes or protrudes (*yšw*)	II 13.
8	smash in skull, but skin over smash unbroken (Gloss, IV 13)	*ṯḫb* exudes or protrudes (*yšw*) " on the outside of that smash."	IV 6.
11	break in bridge of nose	*ṯḫb* exudes or protrudes (*yšw*); treatment: small plugs of linen soaked in ointment inserted into nostrils, " until his *ṯḫb* is drawn off " (or " reduced ")	V 10, 12.
12	break in inaccessible portion of nose	*ṯḫb* exudes or protrudes (*yšw*)	V 17.
15	perforation in maxillary	*ṯḫb* exudes or protrudes (*yšw*), obscure detail added	VI 15.
16	split in maxillary	" thou findest *ṯḫb* protruding and red on the outside of that split "; treatment " until *ṯḫb* is drawn off " (or " reduced ")	VI 18–19, 20–21.
17	smash in maxillary	treatment " until *ṯḫb* is drawn off " (or " reduced ")	VII 6.
21	split in temporal bone	*ṯḫb* protrudes (*yšw*) " on outside of that split "	VIII 6.
38	split in arm	*ṯḫb* protrudes (*yšw*) " on outside of that split "	XII 22.
46	uncertain injury in the breast	" thou findest *ṯḫb* very large, protruding on his breast, oily, like fluid under thy hand "	XV 21–XVI 1.

In addition to the above data it should be noted that the *ṯḫb* is, in four cases out of the eleven, stated to be " on it " or " over it," namely the injury. In view of the treatment for " drawing off " the *ṯḫb*, one might conclude that *ṯḫb* is a fluid, like pus; but it is conceivable that " draw off " or " draw out " may refer to the act of reducing a swelling, as we say " to draw out the swelling," although the same verb, *šṯʾ*, is used a number of times in Papyrus Ebers for drawing off pus. The problem of the meaning of *ṯḫb* is evidently to be settled chiefly on the basis of the other data exhibited in the above table. Five of the eleven cases (4, 5, 11, 12, 15) simply refer to the *ṯḫb* as "protruding or exuding" (*yšw*), while four more of them (8, 16, 21, 38) add the phrase

" on the outside of that smash " (once, or " split," thrice). The first of these four (8) is a compound comminuted fracture of the skull, the external tissue covering which displays no injury. In this case it is a physical impossibility that the *ṯḫb* should be a fluid exuding on the outside of an external wound. We might be led to conclude that *ṯḫb* is therefore necessarily the bulge or swelling of the tissue covering the fracture; but it is nevertheless conceivable that *ṯḫb* is here *under* the covering tissue, but " outside " of the fracture, and therefore might be a substance exuding or protruding from the fracture. Another of these four cases (16) states that the " *ṯḫb* protruding . . . on the outside of this split " is red. The wound is a " split in the maxillary," and the modern surgeon may be able to determine whether the redness of the *ṯḫb* in this case is of value in identifying it. Finally in Case 46, that of a breast injury of uncertain character, the *ṯḫb* is said to be " very large (possibly " very plentiful "), protruding (or " exuding," *yšw*) on his breast, oily, like fluid under thy hand." These last hints come very near giving us a decision as between " fluid " and " swelling " for the meaning of *ṯḫb*. The phrase " very large " may mean " very plentiful " in poetry, e.g., the description of Syria in the Tale of Sinuhe (B 82), but in a prosaic description like Case 46 the meaning " very large " is almost certain. Accepting this rendering, we must conclude that the *ṯḫb* is a swelling, the bulge of the tissue over an injured bone. In Case 46 the content of this swelling is largely fluid, and under the surgeon's hand is yielding and "oily, like fluid." This conclusion is confirmed by Gloss B in II 10, which uses *šfw·t*, a common word for " swelling " in the medical papyri, as the explanation of *ṯḫb*. In Ebers (110, 3–4) we find " any swelling of a wound," precisely the kind of swelling discussed in our gloss (II 10), and the word for swelling is *šfw·t*. It would seem that *ṯḫb* was an *ancient* word for " swelling," which, like our " gathering," arose from the thought of the collected fluid within the swelling, and at the time when our treatise was written *ṯḫb* was already sufficiently uncommon or unfamiliar to need explanation by the more familiar word *šfw·t*, the only word employed in Papyrus Ebers and the other Egyptian medical documents.

šr·ty-fy, " both his nostrils." The reading *šr·t*, " nostril " and not *fnd*, " nose," is obvious from the occurrence of the word in the dual, which would be senseless with the word " nose." Moreover, when the discharge of blood is from one nostril only, we find the word regularly written *šr·t*. See VI 5; VII 3; VII 4; VIII 7; VIII 8. It is hardly likely that in such cases we are to read the unusual word *mšd·t*, "nostril" (which will be found discussed in Case 11, commentary on Gloss A), a word so unfamiliar that when used in Case 11, we find Gloss B appended as a necessary explanation of the term (V 15). The anatomical meaning of *šr·t*, which includes more than the mere orifice of the *nares*, will be found explained in the introduction of Case 13. See also the commentary on VI 3.

 *mśḏr·wy-fy*, " both his ears." In the case of this dual noun we find the same question arising as in the preceding phrase, " both his nostrils." The word is nowhere written phonetically and we are at first uncertain whether to read *ꜥnḫ·wy* or *mśḏr·wy*. It should be remembered however that *ꜥnḫ*, " ear " occurs *only in the dual*; whereas the word is commonly employed in our document in the singular in the same phrase, e.g., VI 5; VII 5; VII 14; VIII 7; etc. It is clear then that we must read *mśḏr*. It obviously designates the orifice of the ear in this case. For fuller discussion see Case 23.

The commentary on the concluding symptoms of the examination will be found in the preceding cases.

Diagnosis

II 5–6

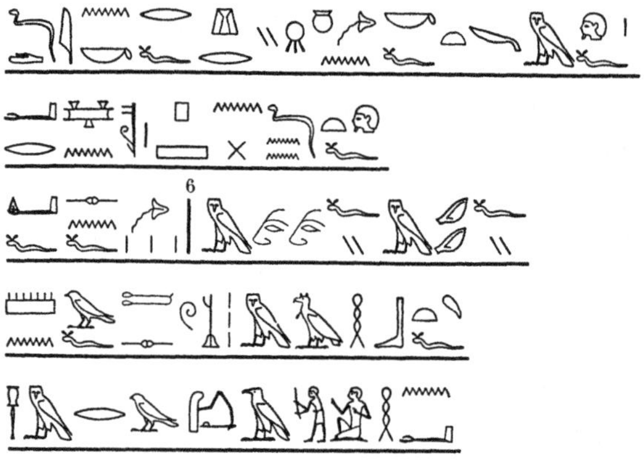

Translation

Thou shouldst say regarding him: " One having a gaping wound in his head, penetrating to the bone, (and) splitting his skull; while he discharges blood from both his nostrils (and) from both his ears, (and) he suffers with stiffness in his neck. An ailment with which I will contend."

Commentary

The terms used in this diagnosis have all been discussed in the preceding commentary, except the physician's final conclusion, " An ailment with which I will contend," which we call verdict 2. It will be found discussed in the introduction (pp. 46–48); but the following facts about it should also be noted here. It indicates a case too critical for prediction of the outcome. It is not found in any of the medical papyri except Smith and Ebers, and in Ebers it occurs only twice (105, 12 and 105, 19–20). Some light on the meaning of  *ꜥḥꜣ*, "contend" may be gained from the following passage in Ebers:  " You should contend with him with *šsm·w*-prescriptions" (Ebers 41, 15–16). This verdict might suggest demoniacal disease, with which the physician is obliged to "contend." This interpretation is, however, obviously incorrect. In the Edwin Smith Papyrus it is repeatedly the verdict in cases of wounds and injuries which have no possible connection with demoniacal causes. Such is our Case 4, a deep and dangerous cut penetrating through the calvaria. Gloss C is quite specific in its statement of the condition of the case denoted by this verdict; it says: "(until) thou knowest whether he will die or he will live; for he has 'an ailment with which I will contend'" (II 11). Verdict 2 occurs in eight cases in Pap. Smith, as follows:

Case 4. Gaping wound, penetrating to the bone, splitting skull.
,, 7. Gaping wound, penetrating to the bone, perforating sutures of skull.
,, 21. Split in temporal bone.
,, 28. Gaping wound in throat.
,, 29. Gaping wound in cervical vertebra.
,, 37. Break in the arm, with wound over it.
,, 45. Bulging tumors on breast.
,, 47. (XVII 11) Gaping wound in the shoulder.

Of these eight cases the surgeon expects a favorable outcome in only one (Case 28), although another may show a fortunate turn (Case 47, fifth examination, XVII 13–14). All the remaining six cases are distinctly doubtful, and are accompanied by clauses indicating what the surgeon is to do until the critical issue between life and death is determined.

TREATMENT

II 6–8

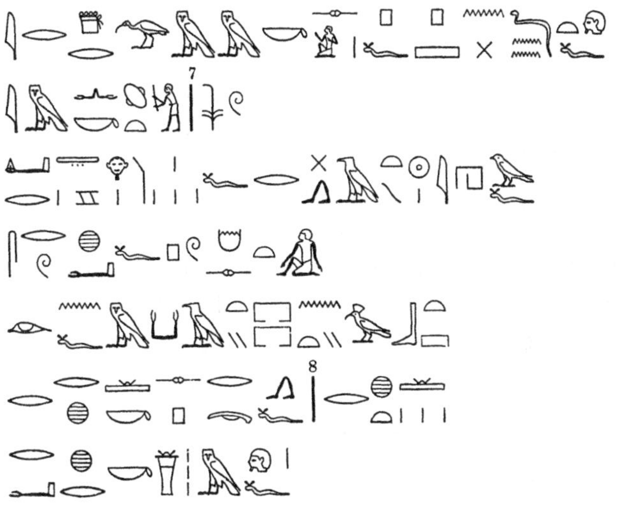

Translation

Now when thou findest that the skull of that man is split, thou shouldst not bind him, (but) moor (him) at his mooring stakes until the period of his injury passes by. His treatment is sitting. Make for him two supports of brick, until thou knowest he has reached a decisive point. Thou shouldst apply grease to his head, (and) soften his neck therewith and both his shoulders. Thou shouldst do likewise for every man whom thou findest having a split skull.

Commentary

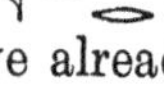 *yr ḏr.* In view of the fact that the surgeon's examination and diagnosis have already declared the presence of the "split" (*pšn*), it is clear that this clause refers back to the previous establishment of this fact. *Yr ḏr* must therefore mean "now as soon as," or "now when," introducing the observation already made. Compare Case 8 (IV 10) and Case 20 (VIII 4). It is decidedly an archaic use of the particle *ḏr.*

All terms following *yr ḏr* down to *yh-f,* "his injury" will be found discussed in the commentary on the preceding cases.

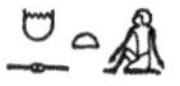 *ḥms·t,* "sitting." This word is to be understood as *comprising* the treatment. It does not mean that while being treated the patient is to occupy a sitting posture; it means that the treatment itself consists in the quiet and repose of sitting, at the same time tacitly showing that the condition of the patient is regarded by the surgeon as precluding a lying posture. The importance of the sitting position is further indicated by the special mechanical contrivance prescribed for enabling the patient to maintain it.[1] The same is true in Case 7, in which "sitting" is also prescribed. This treatment is found in seven cases in our treatise, all of them injuries of the head: 4, 7, 8, 16, 17, 20, and 32. In four of these (4, 7, 8, and 20) little or nothing in addition to "sitting" is prescribed; in the remaining three the familiar "fresh meat" or "grease, honey, and lint" appear. The significant fact seems to be that all the cases employing "sitting" as treatment are injuries of the head.

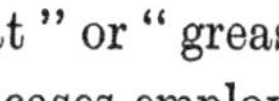 *mk᾽·ty,* "two supports." This word is clearly 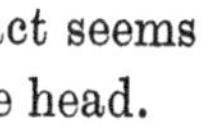 *mk·t,* "place, resting place, proper place," etc., as is shown by the fact that the word is written 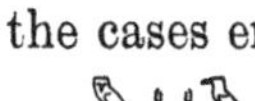 *mk·ty* in Case 7 (III 15). It is more commonly written with the determina-

[1] Gardiner has suggested to me in conversation that "sit" may be used here in the sense of "defer" or similar like *ḥmsw* in Sinuhe B 59. The suggestion is interesting, but would raise the difficulty of explaining the purpose of the supports which clearly indicate literal sitting.

tive of the book roll, but occurs twice elsewhere with ▭ : Book of the Dead 180, 25 ; and Stela of the Banishment, l. 21. The Pyramids write it, but it occurs in the Solar Litany and the Book of the Gates written or. Outside of the medical papyri the word means especially the proper place, or resting place for a thing, particularly for parts of the body, e. g., Pyr. 286 d, 396 d ; especially the heart, e. g., Stela of the Banishment, l. 21 ; Lepsius, *Denkmaeler*, Text I, p. 8 ; *Culte d'Atonou*, pp. 39, 68 ; and quite commonly. The gods and the dead are in their *mkꜣ·t* (Book of the Gates, 6th hour, below ; also 8th hour ; sometimes with the determinative).

The medical or surgical use of the word is confined entirely to Papyrus Smith, where it is used to designate a " pair of supports " (dual), designed especially to maintain in an upright sitting posture a patient having a serious wound in the skull, which makes motion dangerous and forbids lying down. Its use is confined to two cases of such injury (Case 4 and 7), in one of which (Case 7) the patient is said to be " placed between two supports (*mk·ty*) of brick " (II 7). How these were made is not indicated, but the word employed means sun-dried brick. It may be recalled that a woman in child-birth among the common people sat on two bricks (see Spiegelberg, *Recueil de Trav.*, XXVI, p. 47); and the bed in houses of the poor might be a mere bench of *adobe*. It may be of interest to note at this point that our Spanish-American word "*adobe*" is the same word here employed in our medical text of 3,500 years ago or more (see Wiesmann, *Zeitschrift*, 52 (1914), p. 130). The probability is that the clay was moulded to fit the patient's figure, and that our word *ḏb·t*, "*adobe*," is used rather for the whole mass than for a structure made of individual bricks.

The entire treatment of the patient consists in his resting quietly, sustained by the two supports until the crisis is past. Thereupon the physician may attempt alleviation by softening applications on the head, neck and shoulders. The frequent conclusion of the treatment " until he recovers " is here conspicuously lacking. In its place appears an injunction to treat all patients with a split skull in the same way.

The interesting grammar of the first and last sentences of the treatment is quite in order. In both cases *pšn* is a passive, presumably a participial form :

> " thou findest that man, his skull being split ; " and
> " every man whom thou findest, his skull being split."

It is interesting to observe that in the first case *pšn* is attached to the noun (" that man "), while in the second case the relative form *gmm-k* functions as the substantive to which *pšn* is attached.

The above interesting case contains a series of new and important terms, difficult to understand. They were not clear without explanation, even to the ancient Egyptian reader ; hence the commentator has added three glosses explaining : A, " Splitting his skull ; " B, " The swelling which is over it protrudes ; " and C, " (Until) thou knowest he has reached a decisive point."

GLOSS A

II 8–9

Explaining: Splitting his skull

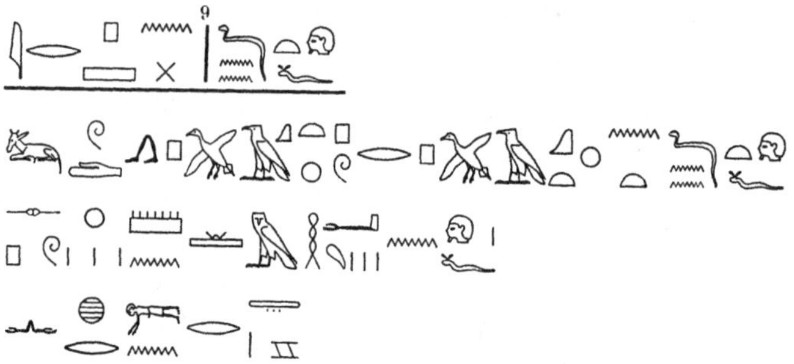

Translation

As for: "Splitting his skull," it means separating shell from shell of his skull, while fragments remain sticking in the flesh of his head, and do not come away.

Commentary

It is important to determine at once the literal meaning of *p'ḳ·t n·t ḏnn·t-f*, "shell of his skull." *P'ḳ·t* originally means a "sherd." We find it a number of times in Pap. Ebers as "Sherd (*p'ḳy·t*) of a new pot" (Ebers 61, 18; 78, 17; 94, 12); similarly Hearst XI 17; XIII 2; Pap. Westcar 6, 10. As an anatomical term it is applied to the shell of a turtle a number of times in Pap. Ebers (e. g., 67, 5–6; 86, 12–13, etc.), which even writes the turtle quite clearly in the determinative (e. g., 71, 15). As a term of the human anatomy *p'ḳ·t* is found only in Pap. Smith, where it occurs in four cases (4, 7, 8, and 9), all injuries of the skull. In all these cases it designates the *squamae*, the shell-like segments of the skull. In our Case 4, the region of the skull is not defined; the same is true of Cases 7 and 8. In Case 9, however, the region is the frontal bone, which is fractured. The case is called "a wound in his forehead," "smashing the shell (*p'ḳ·t*) of his skull" (IV 19). This passage shows us that *p'ḳ·t* may designate the *os frontale*, and if so is likely to have been limited by the sutures. Not only is this conclusion the correct one, but we even find the word probably meaning sutures in Case 7, where Gloss A defines the [ ], *tp'·w nw ḏnn·t-f*, as "that which is between shell and shell of [his skull]." See the discussion of Case 7, Gloss A. The question might arise whether in our phrase, "separating shell from shell of his skull," the ancient surgeon might not be referring to the separation of the outer table from the inner table of the same segment of the skull, as for example of the *os frontale*. There seems to be no way to decide this question from the statements contained in our Case 4. In Case 7, however, "that which is between shell and shell of his skull" is defined as *dḥr*, "hide" or "skin," obviously meaning the cartilaginous suture, and not designating the spongy bone between the outer and inner tables of the skull.

sp·w, "fragments." This meaning is not found in the dictionaries but is quite evident from the inscriptions outside of the surgical use of the word. In the Annals of Thutmose III we find "Fragments (*sp·w*) of wood (and) much firewood" (Sethe, *Urk.*, IV, 670, l. 106). Again in the Turin Papyri: "fragments (*sp·w*) of firewood" ed. Pleyte and Rossi, VI, 4. With reference to food, "my fragments" would make even better sense than "my remainder" in the Book of the Dead (ed. Budge, 189, from Nu 19, 6). The same is true in the Pyramid Texts (Pyr. 1674 d; 551 e; cf. Book of the Dead, Chap. 52, 5). The surgical meaning "fragments" is quite obvious in our passage in Gloss A, but is even clearer in Case 5, where it is stated that his skull is in "numerous fragments (*sp·w*) which sink into the interior of his skull" (II 17).

The following discussion will show that the "fragments" referred to in our gloss have been detached by the violence of the blow which inflicted the wound, and can be nothing else but bone.

mn m, "stick fast in," "be fixed in" is a phrase which the surgeon draws from the common use of it to describe a foreign or intrusive body sticking in flesh. One recalls at once the familiar words in the Tale of Sinuhe: "My arrow stuck fast in his neck" (Sinuhe, B 138–139). Similarly in the autobiography of Ahmose of El Kab: ("His majesty discharged) his first arrow, which stuck fast in the body of that foe" (Sethe, *Urk.*, IV, 8, l. 33). The same is said of a spear in the hippo's legs (Naville, *Mythe d'Horus*, Pl. VI) or of a battle axe in the head of the foe (Abu Simbel, Ptah Stela, l. 22). The Berlin *Wörterbuch* has nineteen examples of weapons "sticking fast in" (*mn m*): the crown, the head, the ribs, the *ḏr·w*, the loins (*mn·t*), buttocks, legs (*ynś·t*), belly, neck, nose, and *thnw*. Besides our example in Gloss A, Pap. Smith has one more example of a foreign substance or body which remains sticking fast in a wound. Case 23 mentions an instance of surgical stitching which "remains sticking in (*mn m*) the two lips of his wound" (VIII 20–21). Parallel with this use of *mn m* describing a foreign substance "sticking in" tissue where it does not belong is its use elsewhere to indicate the natural articulation and attachment of parts belonging to each other anatomically and functioning together. Of this use of the words *mn m* there are three very interesting cases in Pap. Smith.

(1) "Ligaments at the end of his ramus, which are attached to (*mn m*) his temporal bone" (III 17).

(2) "The heads of them (clavicles) are attached to (*mn m*) the upper bone of his sternum" (XI 23).

(3) .... "the tips .... of the ribs of his sternum, which were attached (*mn m*) to his sternum" (XV 4).

Case 23 (VIII 18–19) is difficult to place in the above classification.

The fragments which have been broken away by the blow and remain "sticking fast" are said to be "in the flesh of his head." This last term means the tissue exterior to the calvaria as is shown by Case 8, a fracture of the skull inflicted without injury to the external tissue of the head, which is called "the flesh of his head" (IV 13) in the commentary explaining "the skin of his head."

n ḫr-n r t', "(and) do not come away," literally "do not fall to the earth." The same idiom is found also in Pap. Smith of spittle hanging at the lips of an unconscious man (III 4), where it might possibly be taken literally, but more likely means simply "does not come away." In Pap. Ebers a finger nail that is coming off is said to be "falling to the earth" (Ebers 78, 18). Similarly in the Shipwreck (l. 53) the hero says of the superfluous food which he found on the island: "I threw (some) away" (literally "to the ground," *r t'*). This use of *r t'* "to the earth" meaning "away," "off," may be connected with the use of the same phrase as meaning "completely." See Ebers 91, 12; *Mutter und Kind*, 1, 3; 5, 7 (see also *ibid.* 3, 4, where the variant *r ẖrw* is instructive). In our papyrus this use of *r t'* is found three times (Case 4 as above, Case 7, III 4; and Case 47, XVII 14). This last example is significant for the verb is *śty*, "scatter, disappear" or the like, which entirely precludes any local meaning in *r t'*, and shows conclusively that it means "entirely." In Case 41 we find the variant *ḥr t'* instead of *r t'*.

GLOSS B

II 10

Explaining: The swelling which is over it protrudes

10
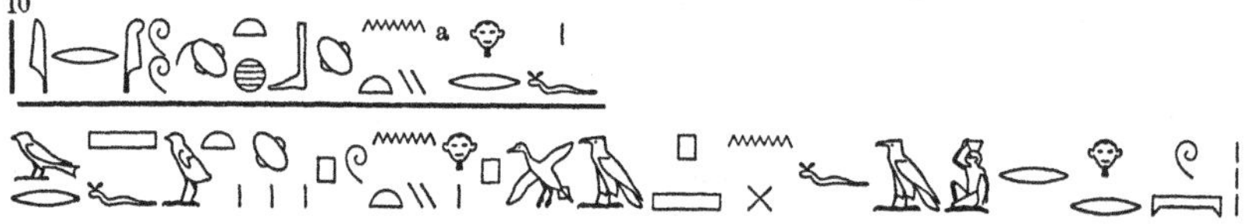

a, written very small, is a later correction inserted above.

Translation

As for: "The swelling (*tḫb*) which is over it protrudes," it means that the swelling (*šfw·t*) which is over this split is large, rising upward.

Commentary

This gloss has been fully discussed in the commentary on *yšw·w* and *tḫb* in the examination above. It should be noticed that the explanation employs a different word for "swelling" (*šfw·t*) from that (*tḫb*) found in the quotation to be explained.

GLOSS C

II 10–11

Explaining: (Until) thou knowest he has reached a decisive point

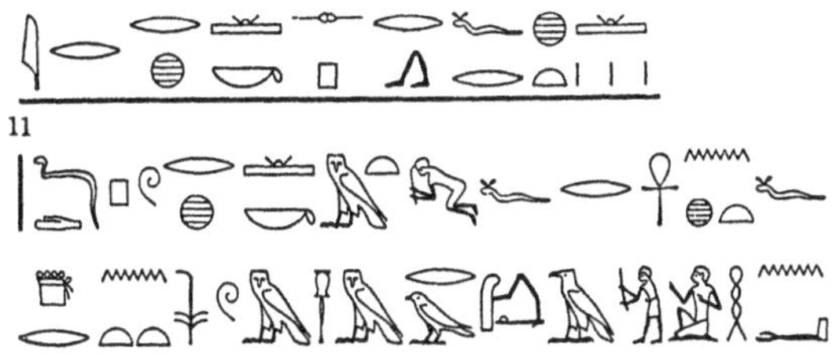

Translation

As for: " (Until) thou knowest he has reached a decisive point," it means (until) thou knowest whether he will die or he will live; for he is (a case of) " an ailment with which I will contend."

Commentary

In our translation the clause " until he has reached a decisive point " is far clearer than in the Egyptian, for we have translated it on the basis of the ancient commentator's explanation. Literally rendered the clause runs: " until thou knowest that he has reached something," to which our rendering above adds the idea " decisive." Gloss C shows that all cases receiving the comment, which it explains, are doubtful cases. It is employed in the following six cases:

Case 4. Gaping wound in his head . . . splitting his skull.
,, 6. Gaping wound in his head . . . smashing his skull.
,, 7. Gaping wound in his head . . . perforating the sutures of his skull.
,, 8. Compound comminuted fracture of the skull, without injury to external tissue.
,, 21. Split in his temporal bone.
,, 37. Break in the arm, with external wound.

It is possible that the climate of Egypt with its frequent cases of blood poisoning or infection, whenever an external wound is present, may account for the doubtful character of a case of a broken arm (Case 37).

 is undoubtedly the correct reading. The  is joined in ligature with  in a cursive form, but it is quite unmistakable (see Vol. II, Pl. II, l. 11). This reading makes a good form; see Gardiner, *Grammar*, § 407.

CASE FIVE

II 11–17

A GAPING WOUND IN THE HEAD WITH COMPOUND COMMINUTED FRACTURE OF THE SKULL

Just as Case 4 involved a more serious wound than the preceding cases, so Case 5 discusses an injury more dangerous than Case 4. The fracture is such that fragments of bone have been driven deep into the interior of the skull. The surgeon is unable to suggest any treatment, and evidently anticipates a fatal issue of the case.

TITLE

II 11

Translation

Instructions concerning a gaping wound in his head, smashing his skull.

Commentary

All the terms in this title have been discussed in the preceding commentary on Cases 1 to 4, except the important word "smashing" which remains to be discussed here.

šd, "smashing." This common word appears frequently in Egyptian as the verb for "to smash," "break." In the Pyramid Texts its word sign, a pottery jar with a hole smashed in it (Pyr. 491 a), and again a pair of crossed sticks either breaking each other or the two parts of a broken stick, suggest its meaning very graphically. The crossed sticks long survived as the graphic determinative of the word, as regularly in our document. It is used of smashing or breaking the most varied objects, a board, a pen-case, sealed bolts, a clay seal, or of breaching a city wall. Important for our treatise are especially the determinative of the broken pot ( ), and the use of the word for breaking an egg-shell (Pyr. 1969 c; Amarna Sun-Hymn, Davies, *Amarna*, Vol. VI, pl. XXVII). Outside of the medical papyri the word appears for breaking a head, e.g., "Thy head is broken (*šd*) with that knife" (Book of Apophis, Brit. Mus. Pap. 10188, 30, 1). Similarly it appears to express the breaking of bones in general in the name of a weapon called: "Bone-breaker" (*Zeitschrift*, 18 (1880), 94–95, transliteration as emended for Berlin *Wörterbuch*). A mortuary demon hailing from Heracleopolis also bore the name "Bone-breaker" (Book of the Dead, ed. Naville, 125, 9).

Surgically the word may designate either (1) a fracture of a bone, (2) a rupture of a membrane or of fleshy tissue, or (3) the opening of cists and the like by the external application of medicaments causing the swelling to break and discharge pus.

(1) Fracture of the bone. The known cases are all in Pap. Smith. It is used of fracture of the skull in all twenty-three times, of which twenty-one are in the four following cases: 5, 6, 8, and 9; of the nose (Case 13); of the maxilla (Case 17); of the temporal bone (Cases 18 and 22).

(2) Rupture of a membrane or of fleshy tissue. In Pap. Smith, Case 6, there is an interesting use of the word to indicate a rupture of the meninges of the brain (II 24–25). Again it is used of the rupture of fleshy tissue overlying a fracture of the bone: in the mandible (Case 24); in the clavicle (Case 34); in the arm (Case 37); and in the ribs attached to the sternum (Case 44).

(3) Opening of cists and the like by external applications. In Pap. Ebers such applications are called 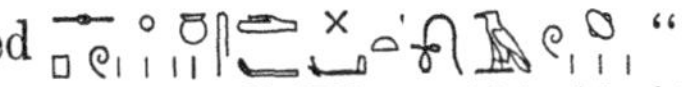 "medicines for rupturing (*šd*) swellings (and drawing out the pus)" (Ebers 104, 10–11; similarly 105, 5; cf. also Ebers 23, 2; 24, 10; 30, 3; Hearst II 14; II 10; Pap. Berlin 3038, 5, 2; 5, 6; 5, 7; 5, 8; 5, 9; 12, 10; 13, 7; 13, 11–14, 1; 18, 8).

The only gloss appended to our case explains the simple term *šd ḏnn·t-f*, "smashing his skull," as meaning a fracture so extensive and serious that broken pieces of bone have gotten into the break and have penetrated deep into the interior of the skull (Gloss A, II 16–17). Our ancient commentator quotes some old authority as affirming that a *šd* of the skull means that it is broken into many fragments (II 17). This definition of a *šd* of the skull is useful in aiding us to distinguish between a "split" (*pšn*) and a *šd*. It is quite evident that what we would call a fracture of the skull might be called by the ancient Egyptian surgeon a "split;" while the injury which he calls a *šd*, literally a "fracture," is what modern surgery would term a "compound comminuted fracture." In other words the Egyptian surgeon has given the common word "smash" a specialized and technical meaning, "compound comminuted fracture." It may be noted as without doubt more than an accident, that in our treatise *šd* is not applied to any injuries of the bones except those of the head. As we shall see, when he wished to indicate a simple "break" or "fracture" elsewhere, as of the *arm*, he uses a different word, viz.,  *ḥsb*, "fracture." (See Cases 11, 12, 24, 35, 36, 37, 42, and 44). But as *šd* could be used as a verb meaning "to produce compound comminuted fracture," and we have no such single verb in English, the translation of *šd* as a verb would involve an *interpretation* of the term rather than a translation. Under these circumstances the best rendering for the verb is evidently the original meaning "to smash," which gives us also the noun "smash," employed above for "compound comminuted fracture." The appropriation of this common word as a technical term in surgery did not preclude its older loose or popular application. We find the surgeon in one case calling a "perforation" or "puncture" (*thm*) of the skull a *šd*, or "smash" (Case 3, Gloss A, I 24). Grammatically considered *šd* is probably a participle in our title, parallel with *pšn*, "splitting" (in the title of Case 4), and can then only be interpreted "producing compound comminuted fracture."

EXAMINATION

II 12–14

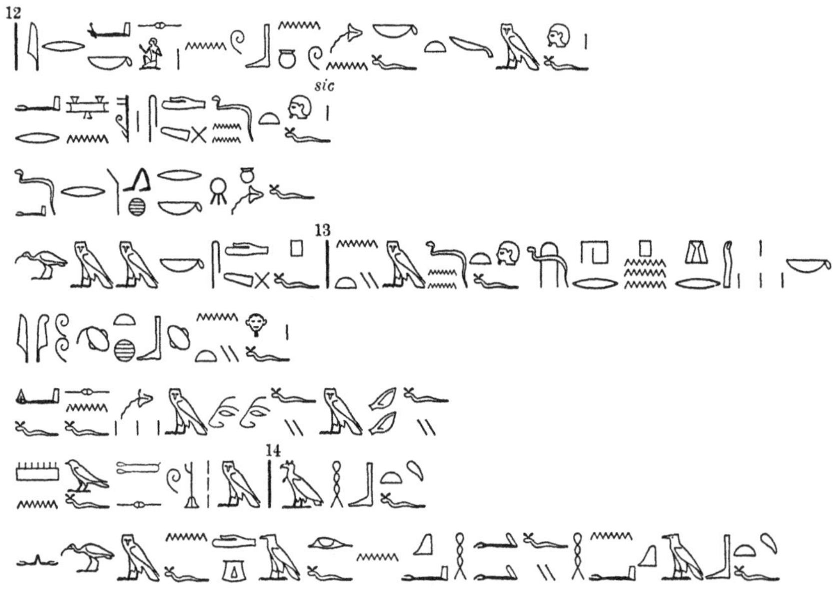

Translation

If thou examinest a man having a gaping wound in his head, penetrating to the bone, (and) smashing his skull; thou shouldst palpate his wound. Shouldst thou find that smash which is in his skull deep (and) sunken under thy fingers, while the swelling which is over it protrudes, he discharges blood from both his nostrils (and) both his ears, (and) he suffers with stiffness in his neck, so that he is unable to look at his two shoulders and his breast, (conclusion in diagnosis).

Commentary

All the terms employed above have been already discussed in the preceding commentary except the following two:

 *mḏ*, "deep," an abbreviated writing as if the scribe was commonly employing the word. This is, however, the sole occurrence of it in our document. A more accurate transliteration into hieroglyphic will be found in Pl. II A, l. 13 (Vol. II).

 hrp, "sunken" occurs only in this case and in Case 32, where it is explained by comparison with the sinking of a man's foot into plowed ground (XI 8), a graphic and clear indication of its meaning. It is used twice also in a medical sense in Pap. Ebers: once of the sinking of the heart from its proper position (Ebers 101, 14–15, emend *dḫr* to  *dḥ*, " sink "); and again of a swelling which sinks under the fingers (Ebers 110, 5).

DIAGNOSIS

II 14–15

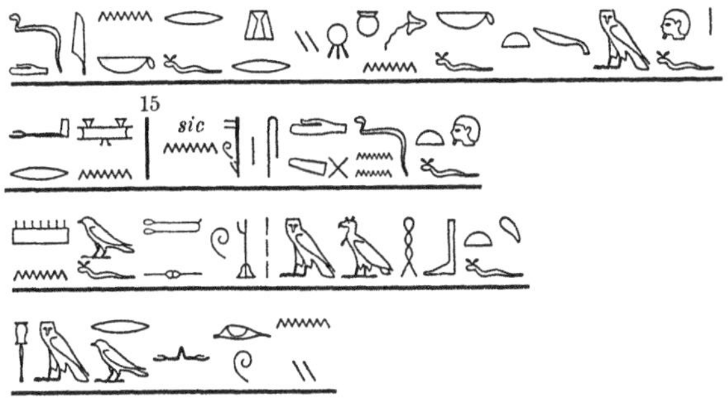

Translation

Thou shouldst say regarding him: " One having a gaping wound in his head, penetrating to the bone, (and) smashing his skull, while he suffers with stiffness in his neck. An ailment not to be treated."

Commentary

In this diagnosis, which contains only repetitions of the examination, the most important part is the conclusion, " An ailment not to be treated," which is new. We call it verdict 3, and a discussion of its significance in this treatise will be found in the introduction (pp. 46–48). This remarkable verdict is not found in any of the other medical documents of Egypt, although it occurs no less than fourteen times in Papyrus Smith. One of these cases (17) has received this verdict by an evident error of the scribe, as the commentary on Case 17 shows. We have left, therefore, thirteen instances to which verdict 3 is correctly applied. Of these thirteen, ten contain no therapeutic suggestions whatever; the remaining three commend certain precautionary and alleviatory measures not intended to cure. Hence the outcome is referred to in only two cases (6 and 8 a), in both of which it is indicated as entirely uncertain, by the use of the above discussed clause, " until thou knowest he has reached a decisive point " (see commentary on Case 4, Gloss C)—a clause which indicates that either life or death may follow. In these two cases the possibility that the patient may live is suggested; in all the other (eleven) cases containing this verdict there is no suggestion that the patient can survive. It may be said, therefore, that, with rare exceptions verdict 3 indicates a hopeless case.

The cases containing verdict 3 are the following:

Case 5. Compound comminuted fracture of the skull.
 ,, 6. Compound comminuted fracture of the skull with rupture of meningeal membranes.
 ,, 7. Perforation of sutures of the skull.
 ,, 8a. Compound comminuted fracture of the skull without visible external injury.
 ,, 8b. Same with rupture of meningeal membranes.
 ,, 13. Compound comminuted fracture of the bones of the nasal region.
 ,, 17. Compound comminuted fracture of the maxilla (verdict 3 scribal error).
 ,, 20. Perforation of the temporal bone.
 ,, 22. Compound comminuted fracture of the temporal bone.
 ,, 24. Fracture of the mandible.
 ,, 31. Dislocation of cervical vertebra.
 ,, 33. Crushing of cervical vertebra.
 ,, 37. Fracture of the arm with overlying wound.
 ,, 44. Fracture of the "ribs of the sternum."

Regarding these cases Dr. Luckhardt remarks: "Such cases were certainly hopeless in those days, and most of them would be nearly so now." In view of the fact that the surgeon discusses nine of these thirteen cases without recommending any treatment, and that in four instances (Cases 5, 6, 8a, and 20) conditions seem to him to permit only slight alleviatory measures, we can conclude that the inclusion of such a large number of hopeless cases (about one fourth of the material in the treatise as preserved to us) is due solely to scientific interest of the surgeon in the observed facts—an interest which would not permit him to exclude his observations, in spite of the fact that most of these cases were incurable and hopeless. Indeed at the time of the successive examinations of these cases it must often have been evident to the surgeon at once that he could do nothing for the sufferer; yet he nevertheless continued making and recording his observations in the same form as for the more hopeful cases which he could treat. There is here an interest in truth and in science for its own sake, quite unprecedented and not observable elsewhere in any of the ancient documents of Egypt whatever the character of their content.

Grammatically considered the words  offer some uncertainty.  *ny* is without doubt the form  discussed and first noticed by Gardiner (*Proc. Soc. Bib. Arch.*, 40 (1918), pp. 5–7). He concludes that it may "best be translated 'through which' in a relative clause," and thinks that the word "will in itself mean something like 'thereby' or, if the expression be allowed, 'therethrough.'" These observations, based on only four Old Kingdom cases, are undoubtedly on the right track. There is an additional example of this curious *ny* in the Misanthrope (l. 104), where we find unfaithful friends described as , "friends of to-day, not to be loved." As in the Arabic the passive of even an intransitive verb may be used to indicate that the action denoted by the verb does not take place, so here, if we understand *mr* as a passive participle, we may gain a relative clause literally meaning "for whom (or "through whom") the act of loving does not occur." There can be no doubt that our *n yrw ny* is parallel with the *n mr(w) ny* of the Misanthrope. The use of *ny* in our surgical treatise would indicate that we must add to the meaning "through which," suggested by Gardiner, also the meaning "for which" or "for whom." As Gardiner has noticed, in all four of his examples *ny* is preceded by a nominal form of the verb. We may therefore look for such a form here, and possibly regard *yrw* as a passive participle. In view of the fact that all four of his examples were from Old Kingdom texts, Gardiner regarded the form *ny* as "probably moribund even at the time of the Old Kingdom." This observation is undoubtedly correct, and we have in our verdict *mr n yrw ny* a current expression surviving from a very remote stage of Egyptian medical practice.

With regard to the increasing seriousness of the cases successively taken up by our treatise, the following glimpse of the successive verdicts will indicate it clearly:

Cases 1, 2, and 3, verdict 1.
Case 4, verdict 2.
Cases 5 and 6, verdict 3.

TREATMENT

II 15–16

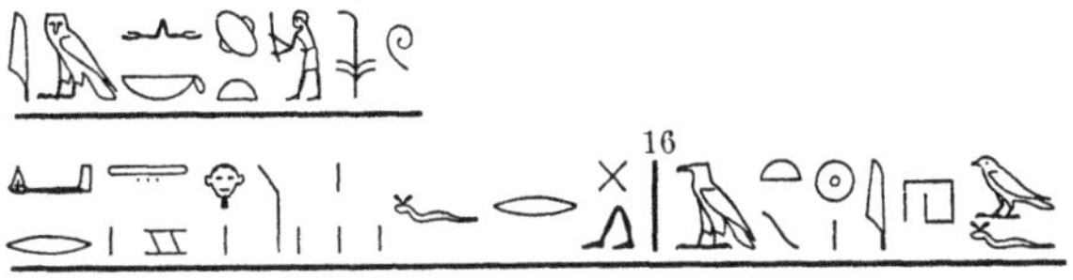

Translation

Thou shalt not bind him, (but) moor (him) at his mooring stakes, until the period of his injury passes by.

Commentary

The case is so serious that the surgeon can prescribe nothing, and makes no remark suggesting his conclusions regarding the outcome. The gravity of the patient's situation is indicated in the following interesting gloss (A), which describes how the fragments of the shattered skull have sunk into the interior of the brain. The quotation of an old and authoritative surgical treatise by title is of importance in the early history of medicine. Full commentary on the curious idiom, "moor him etc.," will be found in the discussion of the treatment in Case 3.

GLOSS A

II 16–17

Explaining: Smashing his skull.

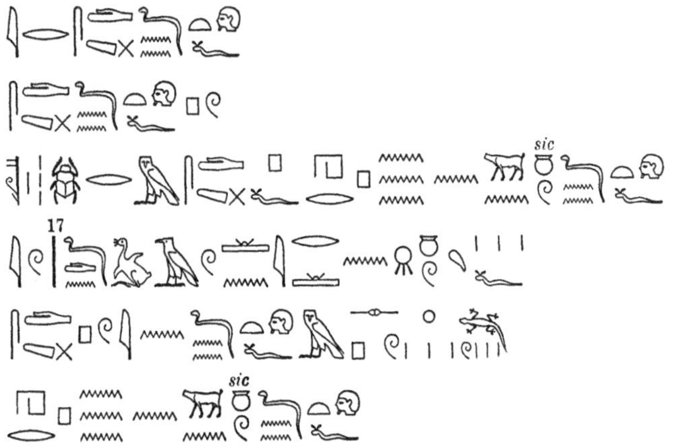

Translation

As for: "Smashing his skull," it means a smash of his skull (such that) bones, getting into that smash, sink into the interior of his skull. The "Treatise on What Pertains to His Wounds" states: "It means a smash of his skull into numerous fragments, which sink into the interior of his skull."

Commentary

šd, "smash." See commentary on the title of this case.

ḫnw, "inside, interior," occurs twelve times in our document, and is always written without the later common determinative. This is another evidence of the very early origin of our treatise. Compounded with *m*, "in," we also find *ḫnw* twelve times more in the *recto*, and in only two of these is it written with. In these two (Case 35, XII 7 and Case 36, XII 13) there is undoubtedly some difference in meaning implied by.

ṯ'w, perhaps meaning "book, roll, treatise, regulation" or the like, is a rare word. In the well-known passage in the Installation of the Vizier: "Lo, it is a saying which was in the regulation of Memphis (=the Memphite ceremonial, *ṯ'w*), as uttered by the king, etc." (*Urk.* IV, 1089, l. 12), Sethe has suggested that *ṯ'w* must be some long-accepted roll containing the ancient ceremonial installation as practiced at Memphis (Sethe, *Einsetzung*, pp. 14–15). Similarly the statues in crypt 3 at Dendera are made "according to the book (*ṯ'w*) of the sacred glyphs" (Mariette, *Dendérah*, III 30a; Duemichen, *Resultate*, 37; *Kalenderinschriften*, pl. 60, c). Here *ṯ'y n mdw nṯr* must be an ancient " book of hieroglyphs " containing the forms of the gods as traditionally established. Otherwise the word *ṯ'w* is unknown outside of our treatise, in which it occurs three times :

(1) As above in Gloss A.

(2) 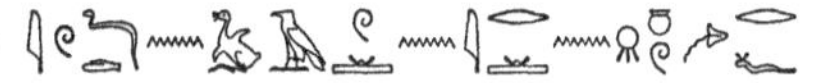 " The ' Treatise (*ṯ'w*) on What Pertains to a Wound ' says concerning it " (Case 41, XIV 10).

(3) 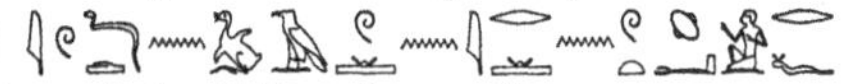 " The ' Treatise on What Pertains to the Embalmer ' (or " Bandager ") says concerning it " (Case 19, VII 20–21).

In view of the three passages in our papyrus it is highly probable that the word means a book or treatise. In that case we find the author of our papyrus quoting from two other treatises, which very interestingly suggest the existence of a literature of medical science now totally lost to us. It should be noted that in our Gloss A the possessive *f*, " his," at the end of the title (" his Wounds ") is very likely to be an error of the scribe for *r-f* " concerning it," as in the other two occurrences of the same title just quoted above. " His wound " is such a common group in our text that the mistake would be a very easy one.

yry, probably meaning " what pertains to." The word is certainly to be read *yr*, not *yt*. An examination of all three passages in which it occurs will leave no doubt of the correct reading. It is each time followed by the determinative of the book-roll, done with care and fullness, not in an abbreviated cursive form. In view of the great age of our treatise we should consider whether the book roll in this group may not be an Old Kingdom writing of the word *mḏ'·t*, " letter," or " document," giving us possibly the title *yry mḏ'·t*, " keeper of letters," or " keeper of documents." This title may be written , that is without the determinative of the man. See treatment of the word by Gunn, *Annales du Service*, XXV, pp. 251–252. The title is not, however, written with the , as in our text. Moreover the acceptance of this official title in our ancient book title would make nonsense. It is true that when it means " what pertains to," our word *yry* is customarily in the feminine *yry·t* ; but masculine formations of this kind are not unknown. Compare *ymy·w*, " interior," literally " the things (masculine) that are in " (Case 12, V 18, and again Case 22, VIII 11). It is doubtless a word of literary origin, being much like the *de* and *περί* of Latin and Greek essay titles.

yn is several times employed in our treatise to introduce the subject after an infinitive as so commonly elsewhere in Egyptian writings, but with modifications in sense, due to the unusual surgical and physiological connections, to which we are unaccustomed. For example :

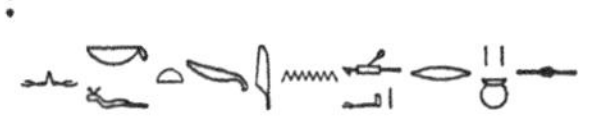

" without a gaping of (*yn*) one (lip of a wound) away from the other (lip)" (I 10).

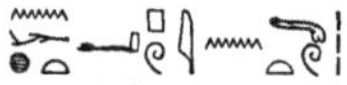

" It means a stiffening of (*yn*) the ligaments " (III 17).

" It means a smashing of (*yn*) his skull into many fragments " (II 17).

" A rending apart of (*yn*) two members " (X 12). See also I 11.

In the last two of these examples the word introduced by *yn* is obviously the so-called " logical " object, whose place after *yn* is doubtless due to the lack of voice characterizing the Egyptian infinitive, as it does likewise the Semitic infinitive. The last two examples would be more intelligible to us if the noun had followed the infinitive at once as an objective genitive.

CASE SIX

II 17–III 1

A GAPING WOUND IN THE HEAD WITH COMPOUND COMMINUTED FRACTURE OF THE SKULL AND RUPTURE OF THE MENINGEAL MEMBRANES

Of the five wounds of the head thus far taken up by the surgeon, this one is far the most serious. It is in content also the most important we have met, revealing the fact that the surgeons of this remote Egyptian age were acquainted with the appearance and a number of important characteristics of the brain, which is mentioned in this case for the first time in any ancient document. Its reference to the meningeal membranes is also the earliest mention of this envelope of the brain. Unfortunately it is not possible to determine the exact meaning of all the terms employed, although the general sense of each section of the case is in the main intelligible.

TITLE

II 17–18

Translation

Instructions concerning a gaping wound in his head, penetrating to the bone, smashing his skull, (and) rending open the brain of his skull.

Commentary

The last clause contains important new terms involving the internal anatomy of the head, which will be found discussed in the following commentary on the examination.

EXAMINATION

II 18–22

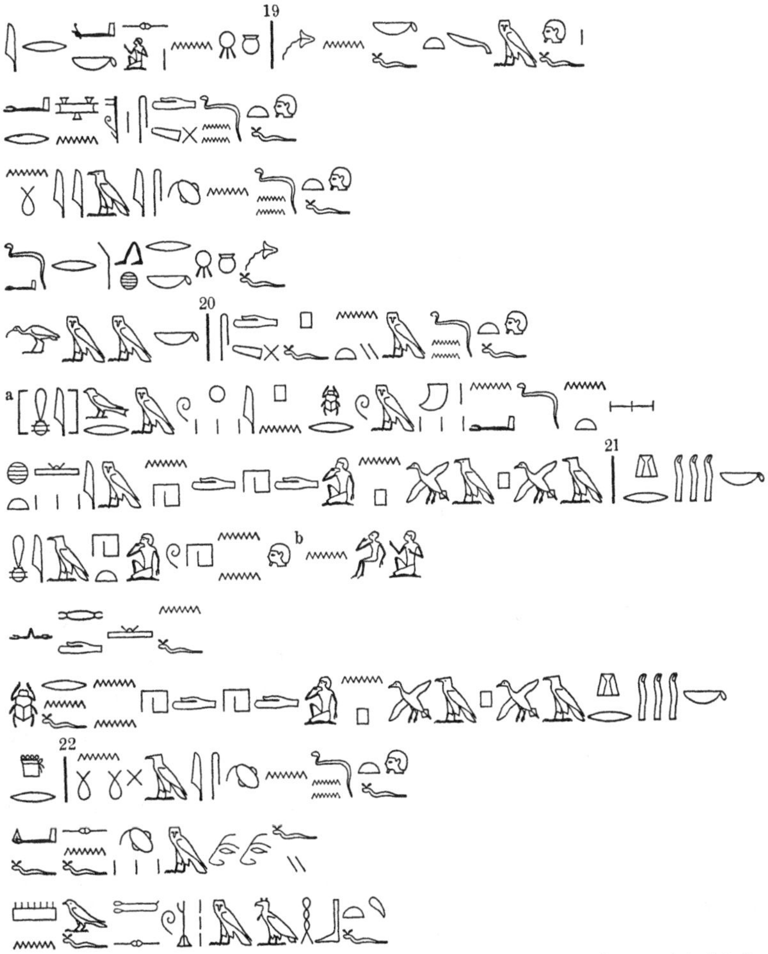

[a] Inserted from the duplicate text (IV 10), which shows that the scribe has omitted it here.
[b] Compare IV 11.

Translation

If thou examinest a man having a gaping wound in his head, penetrating to the bone, smashing his skull, (and) rending open the brain of his skull, thou shouldst palpate his wound. Shouldst thou find that smash which is in his skull [like] those corrugations which form in molten copper, (and) something therein throbbing (and) fluttering under thy fingers, like the weak place of an infant's crown before it becomes whole—when it has happened there is no throbbing (and) fluttering under thy fingers until the brain of his (the patient's) skull is rent open—(and) he discharges blood from both his nostrils, (and) he suffers with stiffness in his neck, (conclusion in diagnosis).

Commentary

ng'y, " rending open," is a word of well-established meaning, although the writing here employed is not the usual one. The reading is rendered certain by the gloss (II 23) which furnishes the following parallelism :

Text of examination : 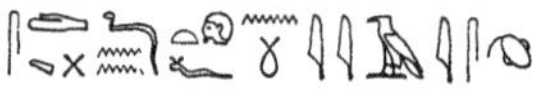

Text of gloss : „ „ „ 

The has gone over into as so often when it is final, for the root of the word is undoubtedly *ng'* originally, and we have here the common word *ng'*, " to open, break open " and the like. It is written in our treatise in three different forms : (1) ; (2) ; (3) (same in Ebers 40, 14). The change of to seems to have produced a verb IIIae Inf., making a feminine infinitive. Cf. *ng·t*, X 12 ; and *ng·t* " break," in a dam (Eloquent Peasant, 277) ; similarly, Ebers 39, 7. The medical and surgical use of the word is confined to our treatise and Pap. Ebers, where it is once employed to indicate an opening or discharge in a case too obscure to assist us (Ebers 39, 7). It is again used for a similar internal trouble in Ebers 40, 14. The meaning in Pap. Smith is quite obvious, and may be based on the usual significance of the word outside of the medical documents.

'yś, " brain," is a word of extraordinary interest, being the earliest reference to the brain anywhere in human records. In the known documents of ancient Egypt it occurs only eight times, seven of which are in Pap. Smith. The eighth case is in Pap. Ebers (65, 13–14), which commends " the *'yś* of many *wḥ'*-fish " as a recipe for preventing gray hair, when rubbed on the head. Preceding this delectable remedy in the same document is a decoction of the horns of a *black* ox, made into an ointment for the head, and likewise constituting a perfect preventive of gray hair. We may conclude therefore that the *wḥ'*-fish was a *black* fish, whose head gear, like that of a black ox, might furnish a powerful protector of black hair on the human head. This sole occurrence of the word *'yś* in Pap. Ebers did not, however, suggest to anyone that the word meant " brain " and it remained for many years a unique occurrence of an enigmatic word, or was understood as viscera—a common ingredient of recipes in ancient medicine. Indeed it may designate organic substances of a viscous or semifluid consistency like marrow; for in five out of the seven occurrences of the word in Pap. Smith it is followed by the phrase " of his skull," as if to render the word *'yś* more

specific. "Marrow of the skull" would thus be the earliest designation of brain. It occurs twice, however, in our treatise, without this modifying phrase (II 24 and IV 1).

There can be no doubt about the meaning "brain." It is a substance or an organ disclosed and "rent open" (II 18; II 19) beneath a compound comminuted fracture of the skull. When the surgeon probes with the fingers he feels "a throbbing and a fluttering, . . . like the weak place of an infant's crown before it becomes whole" (II 20–21). In a gloss explaining the exposure of the *ʾyś*, we are informed that "the fracture is large, opening to the interior of his skull, (to) the membrane enveloping the *ʾyś*, so that it breaks open his fluid in the interior of his head" (II 24–25). Perhaps the most convincing item of the surgeon's description is his comparison of the convolutions of the *ʾyś* with the rippling surface of metallic slag (II 20). No one can doubt that he means the convolutions of the brain. The word occurs in our treatise only in Cases 6, 7, and 8.

wrm·w, "corrugations," belongs to that interesting class of words drawn by our surgeon from the range of common observation, and employed as a descriptive term intended to render outward and physical form and shape more clear and vivid than would otherwise be possible. This is a method still employed in description by modern science. Our word has various applications. In architecture its feminine form means the crenellations along the top of a battlemented wall; e. g., Sethe, *Urk.* IV, 389; see also Mariette, *Abydos*, I, 52, 17. In the Pyramid Texts it is used of the ribs of a booth: (Pyr. 2100b), which of course produce a rippling along the top of the roof. This meaning was already known to Brugsch, *Wörterbuch*, II, pp. 335–336. See discussion of the word by Sethe, *Gött. Totenbuchstudien*, in *Zeitschrift*, 57 (1922), p. 32, commentary on III 22.

The gloss which explains this term (Gloss B, II 25–III 1) makes it quite clear that it is employed to describe the convolutions of the brain, which are compared to the rippled surface of metallic slag forming on the top of molten metal. It is a term drawn from the craft of the coppersmith, and graphically suggests the external appearance of the convolutions of the brain.

The passage fortunately occurs twice and the duplicate (IV 10) contains the preposition *my* before *wrm·w*, which in Case 6 has been omitted by error of the scribe. The *śd* itself is said to be "like those corrugations" found on the surface of molten metal, meaning doubtless that the convolutions of the brain are exposed at the bottom of the *śd*, or within it.

ʿdn·t, with the determinative, is unfortunately an unknown word, occurring, so far as I know, in no other document known to us. The Berlin *Wörterbuch* files contain no other examples. The Sign Papyrus gives *ʿdn* as the value of, which must equal or having the related value *ʿnd*. The Middle Kingdom Coffins contain *ʿdn·t*, seemingly an armlet or collar (Cairo, 28024; in

Lacau, *Sarcophages*, Vol. 1, p. 58, and especially Lepsius, *Denkmaeler*, II 147b). The determinative is probably an armlet or bracelet, but might possibly be confused with a melting pot or crucible in the coppersmith's workshop. I have therefore conjectured "crucible copper" meaning "molten copper" as the rendering of . It is defined in Gloss B as "metal which the coppersmith pours off before it is ⌈forced⌉ into the ⌈mould⌉, because of something foreign upon it like ⌈wrinkles.⌉" In spite of the three uncertain words in this passage, it is evident that "*⌈ḏn·t*-metal" is something that gathers on the surface of molten copper. It has "corrugations," meaning the wrinkles and folds which are characteristic of the appearance of slag, and whatever the exact and specific meaning of *⌈ḏn·t*, it must in some way characterize the metal as molten.

The *n* before *⌈ḏn·t* is so high above its group that it was probably corrected in by the scribe. At first sight it looks like the negative *n* , owing to the fact that in the line above it comes down into it. The lower end of this vertical stroke has been cut off by the detachment of a surface fibre of the papyrus, producing the appearance of the dot over the horizontal stroke of . It is however the genitive , as in IV 10, where it is quite clear.

yḫ·t ym nhdhd should be compared with *yḫ·t ym nḫ'* of II 3–4, on which see commentary s.v., Case 4, II 3–4.

nhdhd np'p', "throbbing (and) fluttering." Although these two interesting words are peculiar to our treatise, and are found nowhere else, the root meanings, the formation and the context combine to make them fairly clear to us. Both verbs are of course the familiar formation displaying biconsonantal reduplication with a prefixed *n*. As in the Semitic grammar the reduplication commonly indicates intensity and repetition. In Egyptian the formation is especially common with verbs of motion. *Np'p'* is the easier of the two words. It is of course built up on the root *p'*, "to fly," and *np'p'* obviously means "to flutter," describing the sensation experienced by the fingers of the surgeon as he lays them on or even *into* the exposed brain which "flutters" with the pulsations received from the heart—pulsations which Gloss A describes as identical with those discernible on "the weak place of an infant's crown before it becomes whole" (II 21). *Nhdhd* is built up on the root *hd* as in *hd*, "to thrust" and the like, which is used for example of a bull, thrusting with his head. In the mastaba reliefs it appears over two bulls fighting. There seems to have been a verb formed from *hd* by prefixing *n*, which is used of a bull in the Pyramid Texts (397a) and similarly in the name of a bull (Pyr. 1767b, cf. also London Med. Pap. 13, 3).[1] The reduplicated form *nhdhd* of course

[1] This *nhd* seems to have no connection with *nhd* of our treatise (III 14), which appears as a variant of *'ht*, "weakness, feebleness, faintness" and the like. This is doubtless the *nhd* of Berlin Pap. 3038, 10, 1; or London Med. Pap. 13, 3 and 13, 4–5; or of Pap. Ebers 100, 21.

signifies "to thrust repeatedly," and may be rendered by "throb." The use of the determinative of speech is in accordance with the usage of the medical papyri in terming the pulsation of the heart its "speaking" (*mdw*).

ʾht, "weak place." This word is peculiar to our treatise, and is not found in any other known Egyptian document. Whether the final *t* is the feminine ending or the third radical is uncertain. With regard to its use and meaning we note that it is used as a variant of *nhd*; for in Case 7 the text of the examination has *nhd* (III 14), while the quotation of the same passage in the gloss has (IV 4). In the same way our text in Case 6 has *ʾht* (II 21), while the corresponding passage in the duplicate text (Case 8) has *hd*, which is doubtless an error for *nhd*. Evidently *ʾht* and *nhd* are synonyms. In the explanation (Case 7, Gloss J, IV 4) it is pretty evident that *ʾht* must mean something like "weakness, feebleness, exhaustion." This leads us to compare our word with *ʾhd*, "to be weak, feeble" or the like in VII 21–22, q.v. If this comparison indicates actual root relationship, the *t* in our word may be a weakening from *d*. On the basis of the meaning "weakness" for *ʾht*, the rendering "weak place" for the fontanel of an infant would seem satisfactory.

whnn, "crown of the head." This rare word is known only in a recipe for the head in Papyrus Ebers and Hearst (Ebers 86, 17, 18 and 21 = Hearst II, 2 and 4). These passages in Ebers and Hearst do not identify the portion of the head designated by the word. It occurs only twice in Pap. Smith, both times to designate the region of the fontanel of an infant's head, thus identifying with precision the portion of the head included in the meaning of the word. In the Ebers and Hearst papyri the determinative of *whnn* is always (5 times); whereas in Pap. Smith it is once (II 21), and the other time (IV 11) it is quite different from that used for *tp*, *ḏʾḏʾ*, or *ḏnn·t*, and may possibly be read, a chest. Indeed our word *whnn* is likely to be connected with the term *hn*, "chest," actually applied to the head several times in our treatise (e.g. III 11, 21 and IV 1).

n ʿd-n-f (*ʿnd-n-f*), "before it becomes whole," more literally rendered, means "it has not (yet) become whole." There is no temporal adverb "yet" in Egyptian, and it must regularly be understood from the context (see my note in *Untersuchungen*, II, Heft 2, p. 11, ed. Sethe). There is here what Gunn calls "an implicit restriction of the time-field" (*Syntax*, p. 111), although he does not cite this particular construction in which has the force of "not yet."

The duplicate of our passage exhibits the interesting variant: (for) "before it is knit together" (IV 11), where the verb *ṯs*, "to knot, to join together," appears instead of, "to be whole." It is possible in II 21 to transliterate ; but the and the lack of a cross stroke distinguishing from in hieratic forbid transliterating for in II 21. Grammatically the form (in IV 11) may be pass. in *tw*, or *śḏm·t-f* with negative = "not yet." See p. 208.

ḫpr-n-f. The connection and rendering of the following context is exceedingly difficult. The rendering "When it has happened," referring back to the completion by the fontanel of the process of becoming whole, is perfectly good syntax, and the interpretation of *n* as the negative *n* is justified in our very passage in the duplicate text which employs for in the temporal clause, *n ṯs·t-f*, "before it is knit together." We must also consider *nhdhd* and *np'p'* as impersonal *śḏm-f* forms; if they were nominal or substantive in character, the form of the negative would be *nn*; although Gunn notes the use of *n* for *nn* in such sentences as late as the Nineteenth Dynasty (*Syntax*, p. 195, 3). "As soon as" or "when" is the usual meaning of *ḏr* in Pap. Smith. It occurs eight times, and in seven of these it means "as soon as" or "when" (*ḏr* alone three times: II 21; IV 11; XIII 9: *yr ḏr* four times: II 6; III 7; IV 10; VIII 4); but this "when" evidently has the force of "until" when it is preceded by a negative (II 21; IV 11).

The meaning seems to be that "when it has happened," that is when the fontanel has become whole, the throbbing and fluttering it displayed are no longer visible until the skull is broken open. The ancient anatomist is calling attention to the fact that the pulsations once visible in the fontanel, though they are no longer visible when it grows over, are nevertheless still going on under the calvaria, and are disclosed when it is ruptured.

DIAGNOSIS

II 22

Translation

[Thou shouldst say]: "An ailment not to be treated."

Commentary

Full commentary will be found in Case 5, which contains the same verdict (II 15), and in the introduction (pp. 46–48).

The significance of the fact that the surgeon has entirely omitted any further diagnosis than this unfavorable verdict, declaring the case untreatable, is, of course, that for the practicing surgeon such a verdict serves alone as his diagnosis. It classifies the case as belonging among those for which the surgeon can suggest no remedy, no treatment; and such a classification is in itself a sufficient diagnosis. The long description and list of observations in the examination, however, show that the brief diagnosis by no means ends the surgeon's interest in the case. Neither does this fatal verdict necessarily end the surgeon's concern for the patient, nor his effort to alleviate the injured man's sufferings. It is here followed by alleviatory measures.

TREATMENT

II 22–23

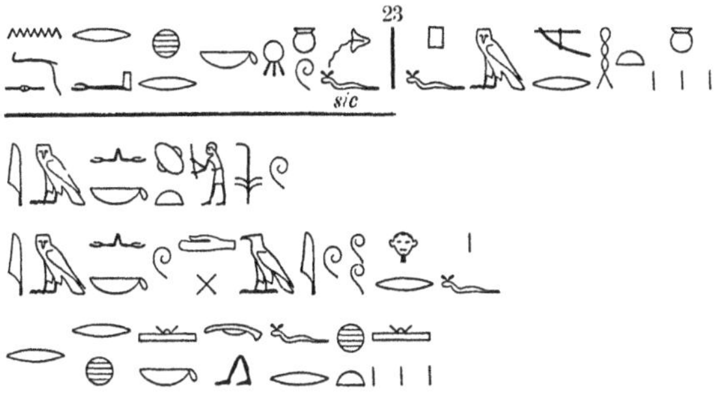

Translation

Thou shouldst anoint that wound with grease. Thou shalt not bind it; thou shalt not apply two strips upon it: until thou knowest that he has reached a decisive point.

Commentary

 *nsr*, rendered above "anoint," is a word entirely unknown elsewhere. The rendering "anoint" is a guess based on the context.

The other terms employed in the treatment have been discussed in the commentary on Cases 1 to 5. It is evident that the treatment suggested is purely alleviatory. The injury is so serious that neither bandage nor strip (adhesive tape) shall be applied to it, and the surgeon is simply to await the issue of a serious or hopeless case.

GLOSS A

II 23–25

Explaining: Smashing his skull (and) rending open the brain of his skull.

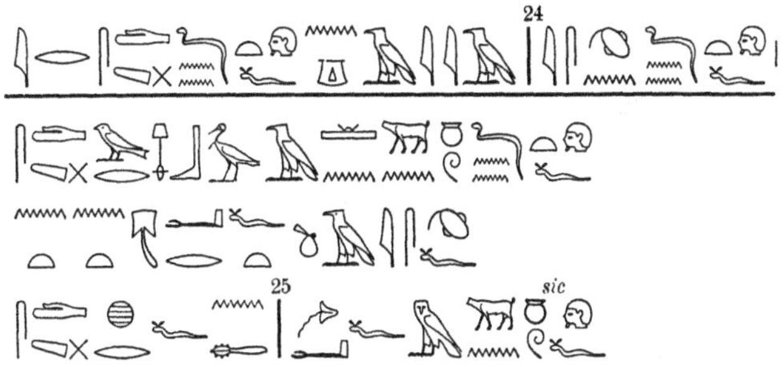

Translation

As for: "Smashing his skull, (and) rending open the brain of his skull," (it means) the smash is large, opening to the interior of his skull, (to) the membrane enveloping his brain, so that it breaks open his fluid in the interior of his head.

Commentary

This extraordinary gloss discloses the fact that our ancient Egyptian surgeon had already discovered the meningeal membranes of the brain. Two difficult words in the explanation need more precise definition.

ntn·t, "membrane." The determinative is somewhat different in form from the usual hieratic sign for a skin: but it is different from (*bnr*, see Moeller, *Palaeogr.* I, 297 Illahun) and also from (*rd*, *ibid.*, I, 298, Prisse). Hence there seems to be no other possible transcription than the skin. When we reflect that *ntn·t* is followed by the words "enveloping his brain," there can be little doubt that *ntn·t* should be rendered "skin" or "membrane." Outside of our treatise the word is found only once, in a list of parts of the body with the sternum (*ḳ'b·t*) and the breast (*mnd*) and followed by "belly" and "navel" (*Mutter und Kind*, 4, 5). It is not likely that it has any connection with the *ntnt*, "filth" or similar. On the determinative see (*Annales du Service* V, 234–235). Cf. also Blackman, *Zeitschrift*, 47 (1910), 118 and Gardiner on Participial Formations in *Rev. Ég.* 2 sér., 2, pt. 1–2, p. 52. The *t* after *ʿrf·t* would indicate that *ntn·t* is a feminine noun from a root *ntn*.

nẖ, "fluid" is evidently the same as *nẖ* (Pyr. 1965a) and (Pyr. 686b). The determinative of the latter example is the human mouth spitting or drooling. Very important in this connection is the form "water" (Pyr. 25c). Compare also the noun (Pyr. 1965a). Elsewhere this word occurs five times in our papyrus (XIII 19; XIV 15, where *m* is an error for *w*; XIV 16; XVII 9; X 20), written with *š* instead of *ẖ*, the interchange so often observable in the Pyramid Texts, and another evidence of the great age of our treatise. It is explained in a gloss (XIV 15–16; consult commentary) as meaning to "issue, stream forth, flow out." As a noun it means "exudation," "fluid," and the like. The noun is found designating some fluid secretion (in *Mutter und Kind*, 1, 2: 3, 1 *et passim*) which is adjured to "run out" (1, 2–3 or 3, 4). Cf. Oefele, *Zeitschrift*, 39 (1901), pp. 149 ff. The reference in our passage is possibly to the soft or viscous consistency of the brain itself. Dr. Luckhardt remarks that this description "most certainly refers to the cerebrospinal fluid by which the brain is surrounded." "his head" is abbreviated to the determinative. It is impossible to determine whether the surgeon means "head" (*tp* or *ḏ'ḏ'*) or "skull" (*ḏnn·t*).

* The uncertain word-sign, possibly , with *pds·t-f*, does not throw any light on the meaning. Grammatically the verb is a *śḏm·t-f* form with preceding negative, meaning "not yet," "before." I have rendered it as a passive although Gardiner notes lack of "certain examples with pronominal subject" (*Grammar*, 404). Our pronoun may indeed refer to the smith and we might render "before he ⌈forces⌉ (it) into, etc.," but this leaves us without an object.

GLOSS B

II 25–III 1

Explaining: Those corrugations which form in molten copper.

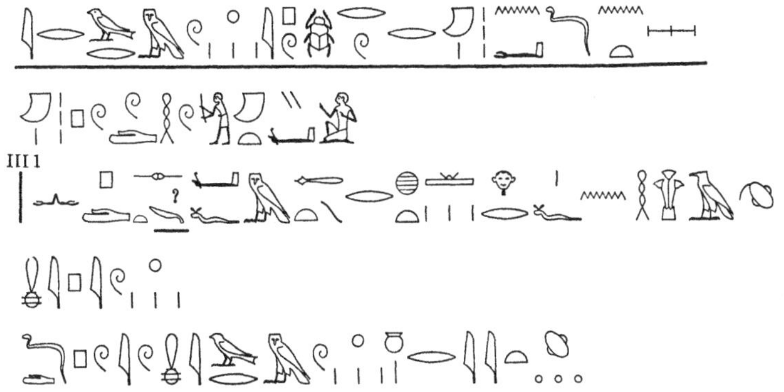

Translation

As for: "Those corrugations which form on molten copper:" it means copper which the coppersmith pours off (rejects) before it is ⌜forced⌝ into the ⌜mould⌝, because of something foreign upon it like ⌜wrinkles⌝. It is said: "It is like ripples of pus."

Commentary

This explanation makes it quite certain that the surgeon is comparing the convolutions of the brain to the slag which gathers on molten copper. He employs some of the terms of the coppersmith's craft, which, however clear they may have been to medical students on the Nile 3,500 years ago, are far from clear to us. When we recall that the technical terms employed in his autobiography by Benvenuto Cellini to describe the successive steps of pouring the cast of a statue are very difficult to understand, although written in a language of which we know more than we shall ever know of Egyptian, it is to be expected that a comparison drawn from the ancient coppersmith's processes will not be wholly clear to a modern reader. The first difficult word is  *pds·t-f*. The only verb *pds* now known is the one occurring five times in our treatise and written  e.g., V 10. It means "to stamp, trample, knock in, smash in" and the like, and applies exclusively to injuries to the face, especially the nose in Cases 11 and 12. It might conceivably designate here the act of "forcing" the molten metal into the mould. See foot-note, preceding page.*

 r, "on" is a significant preposition in this connection. It is to be compared with the use of the same preposition with members of the body, like "at (*r*) the nose," or "at (*r*) the throat," meaning "near" or "upon," that is on the surface, as of a piece of jewelry. The word here suggests the idea of something on the ***surface*** of the copper, before it is poured off.

An examination of the gloss as a whole discloses two processes (1) the pouring (*wdḥ*); (2) the act of *pds*, which is done with or into an *ʿꜣ·t*. This last is probably an *ʿꜣ·t*, that is a "stone vessel," meaning a stone mould. It is well known that the copperfounder's moulds in ancient Egypt were commonly of stone, as they were likewise in early Europe. *Pds m ʿꜣ·t* is therefore likely to be the term for "pouring into," or "forcing into the mould." This would designate the final process with the clean metal, from which the floating impurities have been separated. This act of "forcing into the mould" is thrust into our text as a parenthesis, between the "pouring off" (*wdḥ*), that is the rejection, of the slag, and the words indicating the reasons for rejecting it (*r yḫ·t ḥr-f nḥꜣ*). These two stages of the process may be made clear in the rendering thus: "It means copper

(1) which the coppersmith pours off (rejects) . . . because of something foreign upon it;

(2) before it is forced into the mould."

The rendering of the preposition *r* should be more literally "against" in the sense of "to avoid."

Dr. Grapow has suggested another rendering of interest, which connects *r yḫ·t* with *n pds·t-f m ʿꜣ·t*, thus: "before it stiffens in the mould to (become) something (a cast), its surface (*ḥr-f*) is rough like *py·w*." The existence of the inseparable phrase *yḫ·t ym nḥꜣ*, however, indicates conclusively that we have a similar phrase here, thus:

 (III 1)

 (II 3–4)

The parallelism of the two phrases cannot be doubted, and it is therefore inadmissible to separate *ḥr-f* from the preceding *yḫ·t*.

py·w, which has been rendered "wrinkles" above, is a word otherwise unknown, unless it be connected with the feminine (Ebers 39, 9), employed in very obscure context, of no value in determining the precise meaning.

or *ry·t* (or *ty·t*?) "pus." In our passage (III 1) the more probable reading is decidedly *ry·t*, but the word does not occur in hieroglyphic, and it has always been read *ty·t* in Pap. Ebers. The word occurs five times in our papyrus, and with one exception (XIII 12), one can hardly doubt the reading with *r* (see III 1; XIII 4; XIII 6; XIII 11). A careful examination of the writing of the word in Pap. Ebers leaves little if any doubt that we should *always* read *r*. Compare the form of the first letter in Ebers 105, 9, with the *r* in *rꜣ-pw* in the very next line (Ebers 105, 10). Very decisive in favor of *r* are the following: Ebers 104, 10; 104, 11; 104, 14; 104, 15; 104, 16; 105, 12; 105, 19; 107, 9; 107, 10; 107, 16. We shall therefore read the word *ry·t*. The reference must be to pus drying in ripples about a suppurating wound or open sore.

CASE SEVEN

III 2–IV 4

A GAPING WOUND IN THE HEAD PENETRATING TO THE BONE AND PERFORATING THE SUTURES

This interesting case is the longest in our treatise. The surgeon had met it a number of times and had found that, following upon the conditions disclosed by the first examination, the case might further develop along two different lines, one favorable, the other unfavorable. The discussion of the case therefore contains two examinations following the first, that is, three in all. In construction the discussion is consequently more complicated than any case we have yet met. The three examinations are marked off and introduced as follows:

First Examination

The usual formula omitted by error of the ancient scribe.

. . . . (III 2), " If thou examinest a man having, etc.

Second Examination

 (III 8), " If then, thou findest that man, etc."

Third Examination

 (III 13), " If however, thou findest that man, etc."

This arrangement shows us that , usually meaning " If however," is employed as a correlative to introduce both the alternative groups of symptoms. The same will be found at the end of Case 47. It is obvious that the two clauses: *Yr ŝwt* . . . *Yr ŝwt* . . . must mean: " If on the one hand . . . ; if on the other hand . . ." The correlative relationship of these two clauses is probably sufficiently well indicated by the above rendering: " If then . . . ; if however, . . . "

The arrangement of the discussion is as follows:

I

Title (III 2).
First Examination (III 2–5).
First Diagnosis (III 5–6) with verdict 2.
First Treatment (III 7–8).

II

Second Examination (III 8–12).
Second Diagnosis with verdict 3 (III 12–13).
No Treatment.

III

Third Examination (III 13–14).
No Diagnosis.
Third Treatment (III 14–15).

All three of these stages of the case exhibit symptoms which would suggest tetanus. Dr. Simon Flexner informs me, however, that if the tetanus infection had reached the brain, there was no possibility of recovery. In I, however, our surgeon regards the conditions as indicating possible recovery; but his efforts to alleviate the patient's suffering and to relieve the tensely drawn ligaments of the mandible by hot applications, while the wound in the skull receives no attention, would not essentially affect the patient's condition. In II the case takes an unfavorable turn, the patient is feverish, flushed or livid, and the only diagnosis offered by the surgeon is verdict 3, followed by no suggestion of treatment. It is evident that if the symptoms set forth in II follow upon the first examination, a fatal issue is inevitable. In III, however, the surgeon finds the patient pale, as contrasted with the flushed or livid face in II, and although exhaustion is noticeable, there is evident hope. The surgeon adds no diagnosis or verdict after the third examination, but he proceeds at once with an effort to feed the patient with liquid food, introduced through his clenched teeth by means of a wooden device; while the sufferer is to be maintained in an upright position upon two supports of sun-dried brick until the doubtful outcome is decided. No attempt is made to touch the wound.

The long discussion of the case is followed by no less than ten important glosses, defining and explaining the various terms employed in the text. They take up what seem to be the sutures, which are well defined (Gloss A); the rigidity of the ligaments of the mandible (Gloss B); these ligaments themselves (Gloss C); the patient's perspiring face (Gloss D); the tense ligaments of the neck (Gloss E); the color terms applied to the patient's face (Gloss F); the odor of the wounded crown (Gloss G); the definition of "crown," literally "chest of the head" (Gloss H); description of the distorted features (Gloss I); and the exhaustion of the patient (Gloss J).

Perhaps the most interesting item in this case is the description of the sutures, which seem to appear here for the first time in the history of science.

TITLE

III 2

Translation

Instructions concerning a gaping wound in his head, penetrating to the bone, (and) perforating the sutures of his skull.

Commentary

The title introduces a new term, the "sutures" (*tp*ᵓ·*w*), which will be found explained in the commentary on Gloss A, pp. 185 f. All the other terms have been explained in the discussion of the preceding cases.

EXAMINATION

III 2–5

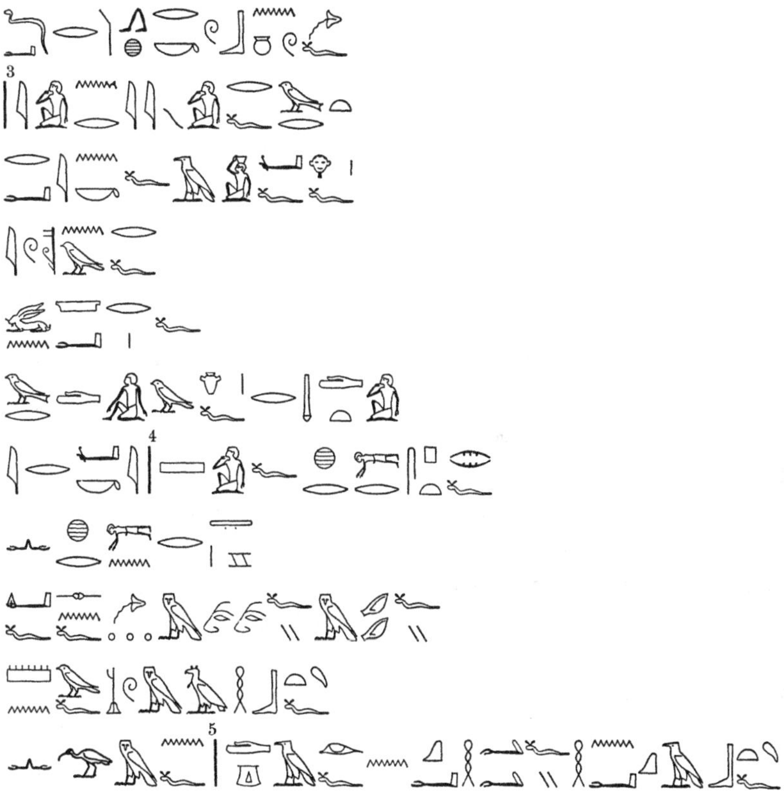

Translation

[If thou examinest a man having a gaping wound in his head, penetrating to the bone, (and) perforating the sutures of his skull], thou shouldst palpate his wound, (although) he shudders exceedingly. Thou shouldst cause him to lift his face; if it is painful for him to open his mouth, (and) his heart beats feebly; if thou observe his spittle hanging at his two lips and not falling off, while he discharges blood from both his nostrils (and) from both his ears ; he suffers with stiffness in his neck, (and) is unable to look at his two shoulders and his breast, (conclusion in diagnosis).

Commentary

The surgeon's purpose in having the patient lift his face is probably to disclose the stiffness in the neck, although this is not immediately mentioned. In view of the hanging spittle it may be that we should separate *wn r'-f* from the preceding and connect it with the following context thus: "his mouth being open, etc." Such a rendering, however, would seem to require *r'-f wn*, with the verb in the pseudo-participle.

"His heart beats feebly" is an interpretation of the literal meaning: "His heart is weary to speak," or perhaps "too weary to speak." The use of the verb *md·t*, "to speak," as a designation of the "beating" of the heart has been noted already in Case 1. In view of the preceding reference to difficulty in opening the mouth, we should perhaps render literally: "his heart (= "his spirit" or "his mind") is too weary to speak," or "for speech."

yš, "spittle," has been discussed in the examination of Case 4 in connection with the word *yšw*. The scribe has written the suffix *f* so far forward that it seems at first sight to be in front of the determinative, giving us a word *yšf*. In the writing of *f*, however, the scribes are accustomed to use a good deal of latitude in placing the letter, and the context shows clearly that we have here *yš*, "spittle," and the suffix. It is followed by the verb "fall," but in view of the phrase "at his two lips," which immediately follows "fall," accompanied by the statement that the spittle does *not* fall, we must render here "hangs," that is "falling" but not completely. It may be that we should render *r t'* literally here "to the ground," as this rendering quite fits the preceding context; but *r t'* is often an idiom for "completely," of which I have intended to bring out the force by the adverb "off." It is quite clear that the surgeon means, as indeed he literally says: "falling at his two lips, but not falling completely."

All other terms will be found discussed in the preceding commentary on Cases 1 to 6.

The scribe, or possibly the surgeon himself, has omitted the usual introduction of the examination, which we have placed in brackets and prefixed to the translation above. In view of the fact that the text of the examination, which we have now gone through, does not mention the perforation of the sutures of the skull, the most important feature of the injury, it is obvious that it must have been mentioned in the omitted introduction. The omission in this case was the more easy in view of the fact that the words omitted would have been a repetition of the title for the most part.

FIRST DIAGNOSIS

III 5–6

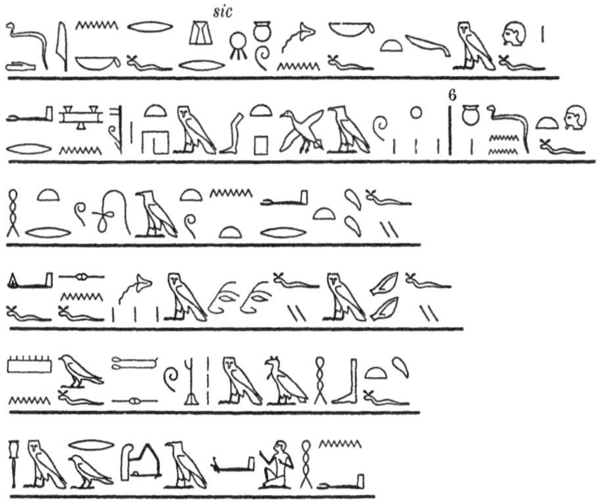

Translation

Thou shouldst say regarding him: "One having a gaping wound in his head, penetrating to the bone, (and) perforating the sutures of his skull; the cord of his mandible is contracted; he discharges blood from both his nostrils (and) from both his ears, while he suffers with stiffness in his neck. An ailment with which I will contend."

Commentary

The injury is shown to involve the anatomy and pathology of the sutures and the mandible. The terms employed in these connections are explained by the ancient surgeon in the glosses (A and B) and will be found fully discussed there. The surgeon's statement, "the cord of his mandible is contracted," is based upon the observation in the examination that the patient suffered pain when he opened his mouth, and possibly indicates the presence of tetanus. This is a good example of induction. See the introduction (pp. 49 ff.), and also the commentary on this verdict in Case 4 (II 6).

FIRST TREATMENT

III 7–8

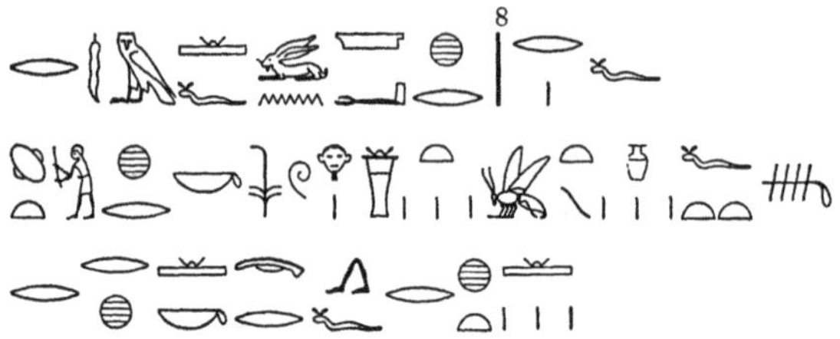

Translation

Now as soon as thou findest that the cord of that man's mandible, his jaw, is contracted, thou shouldst have made for him something hot, until he is comfortable, so that his mouth opens. Thou shouldst bind it with grease, honey, (and) lint, until thou knowest that he has reached a decisive point.

Commentary

 *yr ḏr*, "as soon as;" see above Case 4 (II 6), and below Case 20 (VIII 4).

The use of both words for " mandible " and " jaw " here would indicate that the second word (read *wgw·t*), which is a later and more common term, is an old gloss which has crept into the text. It was intended to explain the other word *ʿr·t*, which, as we shall see in Gloss C, was a very archaic term. On the use of the dual here see also Gloss C.

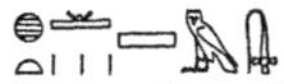 *yḫ·t šm*, " something hot " (compare commentary, Case 31, X 19), is obviously a hot application, intended to relax the rigid muscle, " until he is comfortable so that his mouth opens." After this the surgeon is to bind on a softening application as long as the case remains uncertain, or until the critical point is reached.

The anatomical terms will be found discussed in the glosses on this case, and everything else in the commentary on the preceding cases (1–6).

SECOND EXAMINATION

III 8–12

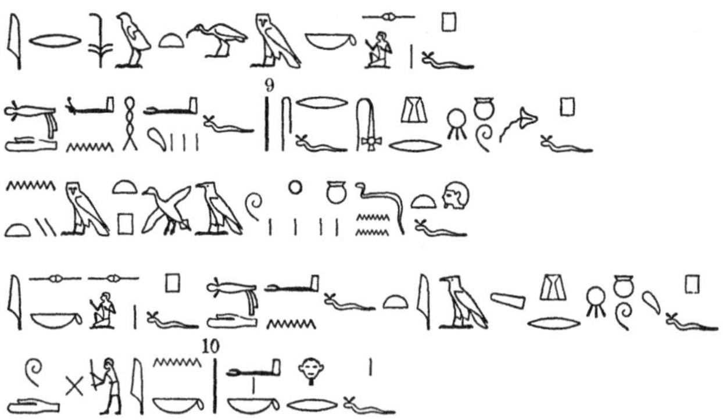

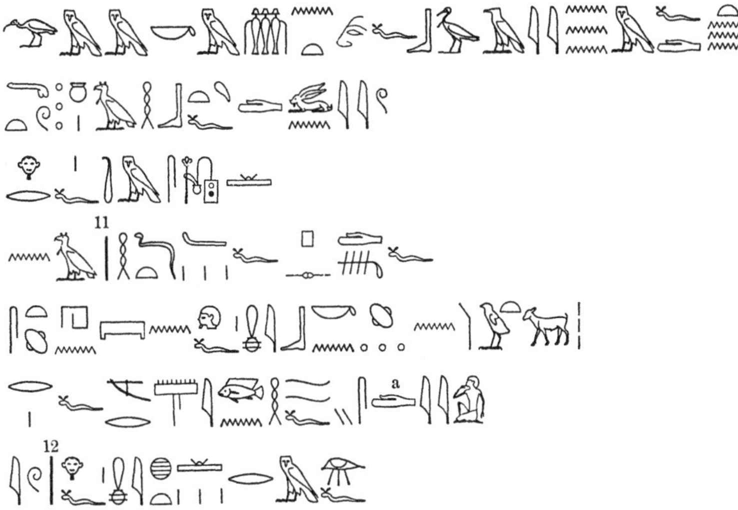

[a] This sign resembles *r* ; for similar writing of *d* see Moeller, *Palaeogr.* I, No. 115=Pap. Westcar, 6, 7. It is clearly *d* in our text, IV 2.

Translation

If, then, thou findest that the flesh of that man has developed fever from that wound which is in the sutures of his skull, while that man has developed *ty'* from that wound, thou shouldst lay thy hand upon him. Shouldst thou find his countenance is clammy with sweat, the ligaments of his neck are tense, his face is ruddy, his teeth and his back [-], the odor of the chest of his head is like the *bkn* (urine) of sheep, his mouth is bound, (and) both his eyebrows are drawn, while his face is as if he wept, (conclusion in diagnosis).

Commentary

When a further examination discloses the persistent continuance of a fever already discovered in a previous examination, the surgeon says :

" If, then, thou findest that man continuing to have fever " (Case 47, XVII 12) ; whereas the disclosure of a fever for the first time as the result of a second or later examination is expressed as above in our present case (III 8–9).

ty'. As a symptom this word is known only in our Case 7 and does not occur outside of Pap. Smith. The context is of little assistance in ascertaining its meaning, and it will remain for the pathologists to suggest a guess. The or *ty'* and *tyw* of Pap. Ebers (55, 11 ; 83, 14 ; 83, 5), which is an unknown ingredient of prescriptions, furnishes no help. This is probably the same as *ty'* in 24, 16. Cf. also *ty'·w* in Kahun Med. Pap. 3, 26 ; 1, 16, and 3, 8. Gardiner calls my attention to a passage in a magical text among the unpublished Ramesseum papyri which refers to the birth of Set and then proceeds:  "before he comes forth (from the womb) to the world, *ty'*-." Unfortunately the loss of the immediately following context leaves the meaning of *ty'* obscure. Dr. Luckhardt queries "convulsions" or "delirium."

"His face livid" ("red" or "flushed") is to be noted as a symptom differentiating the patient's condition from the second group of alternative symptoms (III 13–14) in which the patient is pale.

"His teeth and his back" are left without any observation of their condition attached, and we can only suppose that the scribe has again been guilty of an omission.

 *my yḫ·t*, "as if," is discussed in Case 4 in the commentary of the examination (II 3).

All the other terms will be found taken up in the commentary on the glosses attached to this case.

SECOND DIAGNOSIS

III 12–13

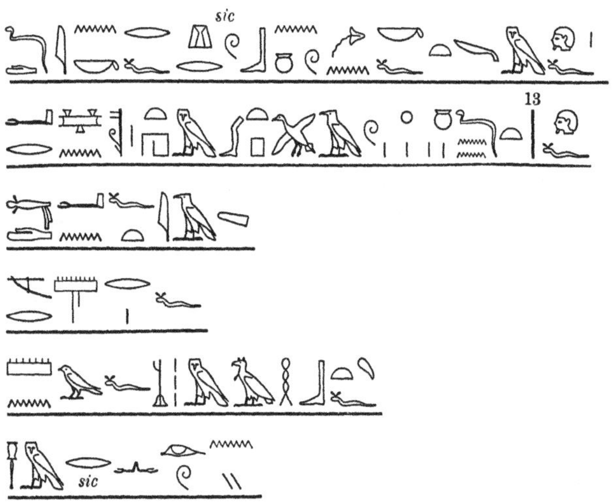

Translation

Thou shouldst say regarding him: "One having a gaping wound in his head, penetrating to the bone, perforating the sutures of his skull; he has developed *ty'*, his mouth is bound, (and) he suffers with stiffness in his neck. An ailment not to be treated."

Commentary

All of the terms employed in this diagnosis have already been discussed in the preceding commentary. It would seem that the essential item in the new diagnosis is the enigmatic *ty'* (see above, p. 49). The symptoms disclosed by this second examination are so unfavorable that the case is regarded as hopeless, and the surgeon closes his diagnosis with verdict 3. See full commentary on this verdict in Case 5 (II 14), and also the discussion in the introduction to the treatise (pp. 46–48). As a result no treatment is suggested.

THIRD EXAMINATION

III 13–14

Translation

If, however, thou findest that that man has become pale and has already ⌜shown exhaustion⌝.

Commentary

In these second alternative symptoms the patient displays paleness, as contrasted with the first alternative symptoms in which he is hot, perspiring and flushed. There is some uncertainty in the exact rendering of the second symptom "shown exhaustion," which will be found discussed in Gloss J.

Following these symptoms the surgeon records no further diagnosis or verdict, but proceeds at once to a treatment which would indicate that the second alternative symptoms are somewhat more favorable than in the preceding (second) examination.

THIRD TREATMENT

III 14–15

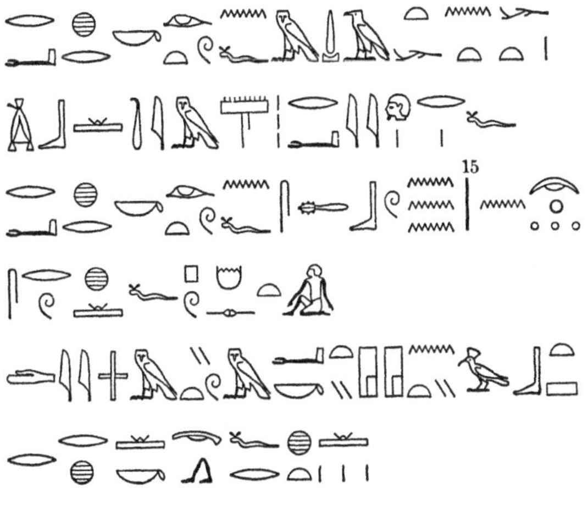

Translation

Thou shouldst have made for him a wooden brace padded with linen and put into his mouth. Thou shouldst have made for him a draught of *wꜥḥ*-fruit. His treatment is sitting, placed between two supports of brick, until thou knowest that he has reached a decisive point.

Commentary

It is unfortunate that this interesting treatment is not taken up in the numerous glosses appended to this case. The patient's mouth, it will be remembered, is "bound" and difficult to open. Here we find he is to be fed on liquid food, and without doubt for the purpose of introducing this food some kind of a wooden device is placed in his mouth. Meantime he is to be kept quiet and remain sitting, as in Case 4. A number of terms need explanation.

 *mḏꜣ·t n·t ḫt*, "a wooden brace," literally "a brace of wood." The surgeon regards this term as in itself sufficient and furnishes no explanation of its construction or method of use. We must conclude that it was sufficiently well known to need no explanation. This is, however, the sole occurrence of the word in the medical papyri, and as a result we must conjecture the exact character of the device, and the manner in which it was applied. It is possible that the word is identical with 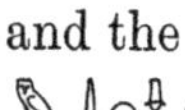 *mḏꜣ·t*, some kind of "chisel" or "graver" (Leyden, K 15, Leemans, *Mon. fun.*, pl. XXIV; Schiaparelli, *Libri dei funerali*, T. 70, lowest row, No. 2; cf. also Griffith on 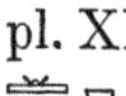 *mḏꜣ·t*, in *Proc. Soc. Bib. Arch.*, 21 (1899), p. 270). It is likely to be the same word as 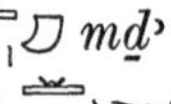 *mḏꜣ·t*, mentioned only in Book of the Dead (Budge, 153 A, from Nu 20, 30–31) as part of a fowling net, and being made of wood is doubtless one of the posts or braces which support the net. It is true that *dmḏ·t* is preferred by some as the reading of  (e.g., Sethe, in Borchardt, *Sahure*, Vol. II, p. 76). The question then arises: how was the "wooden *mḏꜣ·t*" used in our Case 7. It was padded or wrapped in linen for some purpose—doubtless to make it less hard and harsh before insertion into the mouth. Was it simply a wedge (cf. "chisel" above) or means of holding the mouth open, like the modern surgeon's pieces of cork, while the liquid food was being administered? Dr. Grapow makes the interesting suggestion that it was a *tube* intended for the introduction of food by suction on the patient's part. In Pap. Ebers a tube used for inhalation is a hollow reed, which would seem much more suitable for use in our case also. I am not sure that the preposition  *tp* should be rendered "into," as I have done. Its exact force is difficult to grasp, and much depends upon understanding it correctly.

 *sḫbw*, "draught," is a rare word, found elsewhere only in Berlin Med. Pap. 3038, 9, 4, where it designates a draught employed in reducing fever.

 *wꜥḥ* is an unknown fruit or grain, which we see piled up in the granaries or magazines of the Empire, e.g., in the tomb of Rekhmire (Newberry, *Rekhmara*,

XII). It must have been a nutritious product, as it seems to be used in our Case 7 as food rather than as medicine. Cf. Oefele, *Zeitschrift*, 39 (1901), p. 150.

The treatment " sitting, placed between two supports of brick " is found also in Case 4, although with less precision regarding the manner of use. The two supports evidently rose on each side of the patient, probably to the height of the arm-pits, where they stopped, thus supporting the patient under his arms. In this case also, as in Case 4, the treatment is quiet. The patient is to be given liquid nourishment of the lightest character, and supported in an upright position until the critical point is reached.

GLOSS A

III 15–16

Explaining: Perforating the sutures of his skull.

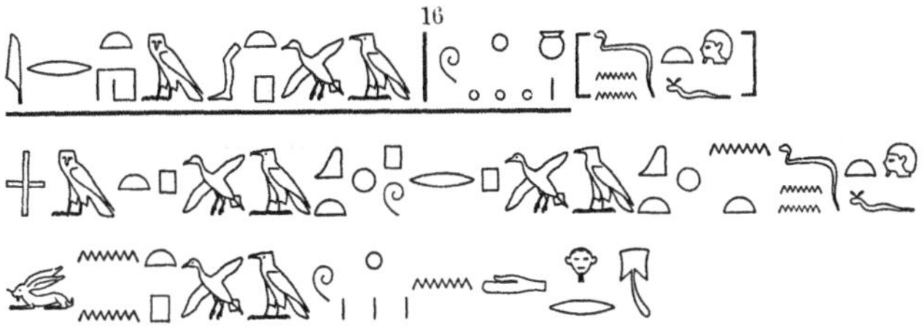

Translation

As for: " Perforating the sutures of [his skull]," it means what is between shell and shell of his skull; and that the sutures are (composed) of hide.

Commentary

This explanation probably discloses the earliest mention of the sutures in the history of anatomy. What our surgeon calls " shell " is obviously the " *squamae* " of the skull, as they are known to the modern anatomist. The original meaning of the term (*p'ḳ·t*), that is a " potsherd," or the "shell" of a turtle, will be found discussed above in the commentary on Case 4 (Gloss A, II 8–9). The  *tp'·w*, " sutures," are said to be "what is between squama and squama of his skull," a very good identification of the suture joint. In view of the separative *r* it is evident that  should be read *ymytw*, " between," obviously an archaic writing of this preposition. The force of *wnn* with *n* is somewhat vague; whether we should render " belong to " or " composed of " does not greatly modify the surgeon's obvious intention of indicating that the sutures are not of the bone so much as something between the bones in the nature of skin or hide, which is evidently the ancient surgeon's designation of cartilage. The word  *dḥr*, " skin " or " hide " seems like an excellent designation of the tough, hide-like tissue which fills the sutures before complete ossification has taken place. The term *tp'·w*, "suture," is probably itself a word with some such meaning as "cartilage." In our treatise it is found only in Case 7, where each time (six passages) it seems to designate the sutures; but it occurs also five times in Pap. Ebers, where it probably designates: (*a*) "goat's gristle" as an ingredient of prescriptions (Ebers 80, 11–12; 83, 17; 85, 9); (*b*) the tough gristly rind of the *wʿn*-tree (Ebers 82, 6 = Hearst IX, 4), and (*c*) some affection of the head, perhaps a thick, tough dandruff (Ebers 86, 15 = Hearst II 1).[1] These are probably special applications of a more general term with the meaning "cartilage" or the like. When the limiting phrase "of the skull" is added, *tpʾ·w* then designates the cephalic sutures.

The only doubt or question about the identification of the sutures in this passage lies in the interpretation of the phrase "between shell and shell of his skull." This phrase may be understood as designating the meandering seam of the suture separating one squama of the skull from another; but it might also be interpreted as referring to the spongy bone which in places lies between the outer and inner plates or tables of the skull. The objection to this latter interpretation lies in the ancient commentator's final remark, namely, "the *tpʾ·w* are composed of skin" (or hide), a statement hardly likely to be made regarding the spongy bone. We may therefore regard the identification of the *tpʾ·w* with the sutures as fairly certain.

The genitive 𓏌 *nw* "of" after *tpʾ·w* in our gloss makes it quite clear that the scribe has inadvertantly omitted *ḏnn·t*, "skull" in quoting from the diagnosis (III 5–6).

GLOSS B

III 16–18

Explaining: The cord of his mandible is contracted.

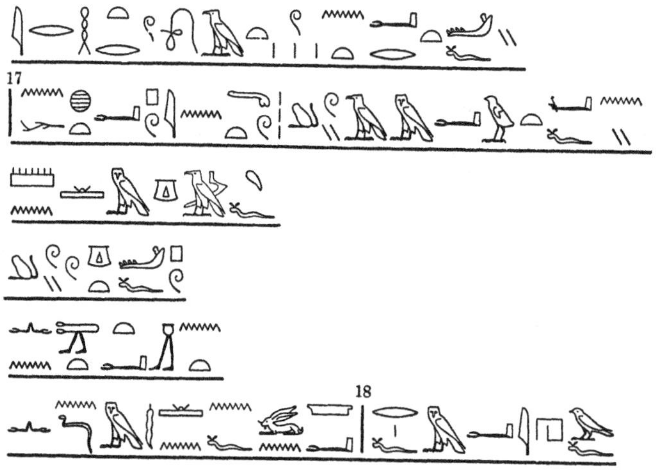

[1] There is also a feminine of the word, *tpʾ·ut*, occurring four times in Ebers (32, 20; 103, 5; 106, 1-2; and 42, 20). It is a botanical term, except possibly 42, 20.

Translation

As for: " The cord of his mandible is contracted," it means a stiffening on the part of the ligaments at the end of his ramus, which are fastened to his temporal bone, that is at the end of his jaw, without moving to and fro, so that it is not easy for him to open his mouth because of his pain.

Commentary

This remarkable discussion of the muscular articulation of mandible and temporal bone should be compared with the related account of the articulation of the same two bones in Case 22, Gloss A, and also with the ancient surgeon's indication of the situation of the temporal region in Case 18, Gloss B. The statement which our gloss is intended to explain contains only four words in the Egyptian, and of these, three are archaic: " cord " (*wꜣ·t*), " two jaws " (*ʿrʿ·ty*), and " is contracted " (*ḫtr*). The first is explained in the next gloss (C); the other two in this one (B).

ḫtr, " is contracted." The archaic noun from this root, (sic) *ḫtr·w*, " cords," is found in the Pyramid Texts referring to the cords with which a ladder is bound (Pyr. 2080 b); but the verb is exceedingly rare and unknown before Greek times when it appears as an archaic revival, e. g., " The four courtiers twist (or bind, *ḫtr*) a cord of reeds " (Mariette, *Dendérah*, IV 20 = Duemichen, *Kalenderinschriften*, pl. 104). The verb *ḫtr*, " to catch, seize, bind," etc., used of already captured birds is probably the same verb as ours, cf. Gauthier, *Inscr. dédicatoire*, 86.

ʿrʿ·ty-fy, " his mandible," is a very ancient and rare word of curious application, architectural and anatomical, much like our words " buttocks " and " buttress," both of which are covered by the single Egyptian word *ʿrʿ·ty*. In a developed form it meant one side, that is the doorpost and half of the lintel, of a doorway. See for example the writing , with half the doorway as determinative (Coptos Decree of Pepi II, Weill, *Décrets Royaux*, p. 25). The same determinative is found in the Pyramid Texts with *ʿrw·t* (Pyr. 292 d), and hence we find a right and left *ʿrw·t* (Book of the Dead 125, Budge, from Nu 24, 28–29; cf. Gardiner, *Journ. of Egypt. Arch.*, IV, 1917, p. 147). Written with the entire gateway as determinative it occurs in the Pyramid Texts (1740 b). Designating the whole gateway it was probably at first a dual, " two sides of the door." In this connection it passed over, perhaps in a derived form, to designate the council that sat in the city gate. Anatomically it appears already as early as the Pyramid Texts written to designate the " buttocks " of an ox (Pyr. 1349 a) or other animal. Similarly it is used of the buttocks of a man in the Coffin Texts with reference to the anus: " I defecate with my *ʿrʿ·t* " (B 1, l. 350 = Lacau, *Textes relig.*,

p. 72 and p. 108). In the same age it was applied to the two arms of man or woman in the Coffin Texts (*ibid.* l.c.; compare also *ibid.* p. 77, 31; p. 110, LXIII, 5; p. 78, XXVII, 31, and pp. 136 and 209). In our treatise it is employed twelve times to designate the mandible, and characteristically appears six times in the *dual.* This dual does not mean the upper and lower jaw; but refers to the *two sides* of the mandible, as is demonstrated by the passages where the scribe has written the determinative of the dual twice, both times depicting the mandible, for example in IX 4 and IX 5, thus: . In writing the dual determinative of *śpt·wy,* "two lips," however, the scribe regularly indicates both the upper and lower lip, thus: . If in the case of our word *ʿr·t* he intended to designate the upper and lower jaw, he would have indicated each in the determinative, just as in the case of the two lips. This employment of a dual to indicate the mandible because of its two branches is known as early as the Pyramid Texts, where we find (Pyr. 30 a). In our gloss *ʿr·t* is explained by the word *wgw·t,* which is the common and current word for "jaw," meaning, as the determinative shows, the mandible. *Wgw·t* "jaw" is likewise used to explain *ʿr·t* in Gloss C (III 18). As we noticed above also (III 7), the scribe has inserted the common current word *wgw·t* "jaw" as an explanation after the archaic *ʿr·t,* thus: "his two *ʿr·t,* his jaw."

yn. See commentary on Gloss A, Case 5 (II 17), pp. 163 f.

mt·w, "ligaments," is explained in the next gloss by the ancient commentator; for full discussion see commentary on Gloss A, Case 1. In our passage here it is evident that the surgeon is referring to the *musculus temporalis,* which is attached to "the end of his ramus" (coronoid process) and is "fastened to his temporal bone." It has been customary to attribute the Egyptian's knowledge of human anatomy to the familiarity of the embalmer with the bodies he was eviscerating and embalming. Here, however, we find the surgeon familiar with a muscle of the head which was never touched by the embalmer. His knowledge of it could have come only from dissection and from treatment of wounds.

pḥ·wy, "end," is commonly employed in our treatise for the end of a bone, or the limit or margin of a region or organ. The phrase "end of his ramus" occurs in three other passages, Case 22 (VIII 10, 14) and Case 25 (IX 3). See the discussion of *pḥ·wy* in the commentary on Case 12, Gloss A (V 21).

ʾmʿw·t, "ramus." See full discussion in Case 22, Gloss A (VIII 14) and compare Case 8 (IV 17).

ny. The force of this particle is not clear in this connection. See discussion in Case 5, verdict (II 15). If we render *ny* "thereby" (its usual literal meaning), we must conclude that *pḥ·wy* is here not prepositional in force, and then translate: "stiffening on the part of the ligaments, and (also of) the back (or end) of the ramus thereby."

mn m, " fastened in," has been explained in commentary on Case 4 (II 9).

gm', " temporal bone." See full discussion in Case 18 (VII 9, and 13–14).

yṯ·t yn·t, " moving to and fro," literally " taking away, (or) carrying to " has been discussed by Gardiner, *Journ. of Egypt. Arch.*, I, p. 104, note 3.

yh, " pain," has been discussed above in commentary on Case 3 (I 23). If the patient is suffering from tetanus, which has infected the brain through the wound in the skull, there is no possibility of recovery, as Dr. Simon Flexner informs me, and the verdict which follows the observation of this symptom (III 6) should have been the hopeless one (verdict 3).

GLOSS C

III 18

Explaining: The cord of his mandible.

Translation

As for: "The cord of his mandible," it means the ligaments which bind the end of his jaw, as one says, " the cord " of a thing in (or as) a splint.

Commentary

w'·t, " cord," is an archaic word of great rarity. It will be found in an example from Greek times above in the commentary on Gloss B (III 16). In our treatise it occurs only in Case 7. It is evidently a simpler form of the better known *w'w'·t*, " cord," an ancient ceremonial word occurring only in the temple foundation ceremony of " stretching the cord."

Both " mandible " and " jaw " are here written in the dual—a writing discussed above in Gloss B (III 16). There is intelligible reason for its use here, because the temporal muscles are indeed a pair, one on each side.

The colloquial phrase at the end for explaining *w'·t* does not make the matter very clear to us. It was evidently some current expression, the full force of which escapes us.

sš, " splint," is a new word, the correct understanding of which is at first not easy. In three cases it is obviously an external appliance of linen for holding in place the fractured bone. These cases are:

Case 35, broken clavicles;

Case 36, a broken arm (humerus);

Case 37, the same with a wound over it.

It should be noted that in these three cases the surgeon is charged as follows: "Thou shouldst make for him two *sš* of linen" (XII 12). This linen device is therefore something made by the surgeon himself. In all cases where the device is mentioned it is in pairs. In the use of a pair of *sš*, the surgeon is charged as follows: "Thou shouldst apply for him one of them both on the inside of his arm, (and) the other of them both on the under side of his arm." The phrase "the inside of the arm" (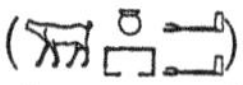) is a common one meaning "embrace" (noun). We cannot doubt that the two *sš* of linen were applied, one in the hollow of the elbow, the other on the opposite side of the arm, and that they were long enough and rigid enough to serve as splints. They are always said to be "of linen." The only ancient Egyptian splints as yet recovered were excavated by A. C. Mace in a Fifth Dynasty cemetery at Naga ed-Deir in Upper Egypt about a hundred miles north of Luxor. They have been carefully examined by Dr. G. Elliot Smith and described by him in *The British Medical Journal*, Vol. I (1908), pp. 732–734. These splints, in one case of wood, in the other of bark, were bound about with linen before being applied. On the wooden splints this bandaging is still preserved. Now the phrase "of linen" may conceivably be loosely employed in our papyrus to designate wooden splints covered with linen; just as the Egyptians spoke of things in their inscriptions as being "of gold," when only overlaid with gold. Another possibility is conceivable, namely, that these "splints of linen" were stiffened with plaster or gum, forming a cartonnage. The mortuary craftsmen were accustomed to shaping masks, pectorals, and the like to conform with the body. These craftsmen of the cemetery were moreover regularly furnishing this kind of equipment to the surgeons (see Case 9, IV 21), and in view of the fact that cartonnage was shaped to the human body when dead, it would have been an easy step to apply it to the broken limb of a living patient. Hence our "two splints of linen" may have been the earliest known casts, like those employed in modern surgery. It is noticeable that our treatise prescribes only two splints, whereas Elliot Smith found three on the forearm and four on the femur (*op. cit.*). Modern native village practice still employs only two, continuing the tradition of 3,500 years ago.

Again our word  appears in two other cases, where it would seem to designate a tampon or swab for cleansing clotted blood from the interior of the nostrils (Cases 12 and 14). The difference between this usage and the one discussed above (Case 35–37) is evident. Obviously the two are quite different devices of linen. Both are used in pairs; but the first is *made by the surgeon himself* and applied externally to serve as a splint; while the other is a swab or plug for insertion into the nostrils. We are dealing, therefore, with two different things. Moreover, it will be remembered that in Case 11 the nostrils of the injured nose are cleansed, not with  *sš·wy*, but with  *ššm (?)-wy*. Otherwise the treatment is identical with that in Cases 12 and 14. Note the following comparison:

Case 11

"Thou shouldst cleanse (it) for him [with] . Thou shouldst place two (other)  saturated with grease in the inside of his two nostrils" (V 11–12).

Case 12

"Thou shouldst clean out for him the interior of both his nostrils with  . . . Now afterward thou shouldst place  saturated with grease and put into his two nostrils" (V 18–19).

Case 14

"Thou shouldst make for him  (and) thou shouldst clean out all coagulation of the blood which has formed on the inside of his nostril" (VI 9–11).

In Case 41 (XIV 11–12) the form 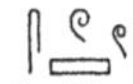 *šwš*, indicating some action of heat or fever, has no connection with our word *ššm*. The text in Case 11 raises the question whether the cleansing swab should not in all three cases be  *ššm*, which the scribe in Cases 12 and 14 has momentarily confused with the linen splint  *sš*. It is much to be doubted that there is any word *sš*, "swab," "plug," or "tampon." In conclusion then, the two linen devices under discussion seem to be: (*a*)  *sš*, usually  *sš·wy*, "two splints;" (*b*)  *ššm* (?), often  *ššm(?)-wy*, "two swabs."

Returning now to Gloss C, *sš*, if properly rendered "splint," is a perhaps better designation of the broad, flat temporal muscle than "cord." On the other hand it may be noted that our scribe seems to have trouble with the words for these linen devices. He has inserted the word  where it evidently does not belong in Case 12 quoted above, and we may raise the question whether he has not made a similar mistake here, perhaps using  *sš*, when he really meant  *ššd*, "bandage," which suits the requirements of the passage here in our gloss very much better.

The surgeon employs the phrase "end of his jaw" here as about the same in meaning as "the end of his ramus" in Gloss B (III 17).

The entire gloss is an illustration of how limited our knowledge of Egyptian is, whenever we are called upon to deal with highly specialized terms; and even when the ancient commentator has furnished us with a definition we are often unable to understand the terms he uses in explanation.

Gloss D

III 18–19

Explaining: His countenance clammy with sweat.

Translation

As for: "His countenance clammy with sweat," it means that his head is a little sweaty, as (we say), "A thing is clammy."

Commentary

is an error of the scribe in quoting (III 10), *mḫnt*, "countenance," a rare and ancient word. In referring to the color of the face in III 10, the surgeon employs the common *ḥr*. The explanation of *mḫnt* would indicate that it might mean more than merely the face.

bꜣy-w, "clammy," is again a rare word of which the only related example seems to be *b-y*, "pool" or "body of water" (Golénischeff Glossary = Pap. Hood, l. 10, in Maspero, *Études égyptiennes*, v. 2, pp. 1 ff.), which may be connected with the well-known *byꜣ*, "celestial ocean." It was a word insufficiently familiar to the Egyptian reader of 3,500 years ago, and needed explanation. Nevertheless it seems still to have been used in one current expression quoted by the ancient commentator at the end.

Gloss E

III 19–20

Explaining: The ligaments of his neck are tense.

Translation

As for: "The ligaments of his neck are tense," it means that the ligaments of his neck are stretched stiff by reason of his injury.

Commentary

 *dwn-y*, " tense " is a very common word, most often referring to the human body and its parts. It is doubtless for this reason that the surgeon purposes to indicate that in his use of the word it designates something special and abnormal and not the usual *dwn*, so commonly applied to parts of the body. Hence in the explanation he adds the word *nḫt*, " stiff," indicating an extreme stretching, like that when the word *dwn* is employed for the stringing or stretching of a bow (e. g., Pyr. 673 b). This was the more necessary in view of the fact that there was a medical use of the word indicating the " stretching " of contracted muscles to a normal condition. Pap. Ebers contains a recipe entitled : 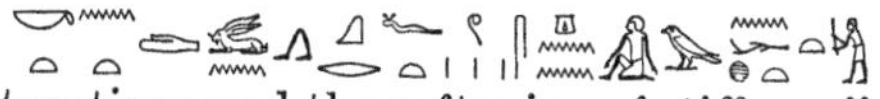 "Another (recipe) for the stretching (*dwn*) of contractions and the softening of stiffness" (85, 5–6). Dévaud also calls attention to  (*ibid.* 87, 6).

All other terms will be found discussed in the preceding commentary.

GLOSS F

III 20–21

Explaining : His face is ruddy.

Translation

As for : "His face is ruddy" (*tmś*), it means that the color of his face is red, like the color of *tmś·t*-fruit.

Commentary

The significance of this passage turns on two color designations. It is well known that ancient color names are exceedingly difficult to bring out with precision or to render with exact modern equivalents. To this day the Arabs, for example, will cover a wide range of colors with one term, and when an Arab guide tells you a hill is اخضر, you may think of it as being any color from green to black. Our treatise furnishes valuable material for defining the two colors employed in the above explanation.

 *tmś*, " ruddy " is evidently a color, prevailingly red or reddish. This is shown by a gloss in Case 46 :

" As for : ' There is no ruddiness (*tmś*) upon it ; ' it means there is no redness upon it " (XVI 15–16). This conclusion is confirmed by another important gloss in Case 41 :

" As for : ' Its two lips are ruddy (*tmś*),' it means its two lips are red like the color of the *tmś·t*-tree " (XIV 12–13). We learn also from this example that *ṯmś* is a color designation drawn from a tree of some kind, although it is impossible to identify it. There seems to be no other occurrence of the tree in the Egyptian documents unless we recognize it also in the  *ṯmś* of the Dream Stela (*Urk.* III, 68), but this passage is of no assistance in identifying the tree. Besides the three glosses above the word occurs eight times more in our treatise. It designates the colors of the following :

the human face, Case 7 (III 10 ; III 20);
a swelling, Case 16 (VI 19) ;
cists or the like on the breast, Case 39 (XIII 5) ;
the two lips of a wound, Case 41 (XIII 20 ; XIV 12–13) ;
the "heads of the ribs of the sternum" when dislocated, Case 43 (XIV 22–XV 1);
absence of *tmś*-color in a swelling on the breast, Case 46 (XVI 2).

The emphasis on red in the first two glosses quoted above suggests " ruddy " as an approximately correct rendering. Its use in Case 46, the last example cited in the above list, would indicate that *ṯmś* sometimes is neutral, meaning simply " color ; " and as we say of a pale face that it lacks color, so the Egyptian might say it had no *ṯmś*. And when we say this we mean by " color " red ; but this negative meaning of " color " will not fit our Gloss F, where some positive color designation must be implied.

Dr. Luckhardt adds the following interesting remark :

" I am inclined to the view that the color meant is the one medical men have in mind when they say that the person is ' cyanotic '. It is a mixture of a red and a blue with the blue more in evidence, particularly as the ' cyanosis ' increases in severity. The purplish discoloration in this condition is due essentially to a deficient oxygenation of the blood."

 *yrty·w* " blue." Like *tmś* this color name is derived from a plant, more specifically presumably from its fruit, as we say " orange ; " or from its flower as we

say "violet." We find it in festive garlands in the Mut Ritual (Pap. Berlin 3053, 18, 4). It is employed as an ingredient in recipes in Pap. Ebers 30, 5; Pap. Hearst IX 5; and Pap. Berlin 3038, 5, 2.

As a color designation it appears as the name of *colored linen* as follows:

In addition to green linen at Dendera (Duemichen, *Resultate,* 26, XIII).

In addition to red (*ydm*) and an uncertain color at Edfu (Rochem. I, 126).

In addition to red (*ydm*) (*ibid.*).

In addition to white and red (*ibid.*, I, 413).

In addition to red (*ibid.*, I, 289).

In addition to white, green and red in Room 18 at Dendera (Duemichen, *Resultate,* 23 = Mariette, *Dendérah,* II 1 b).

All the above are from Greek times, but it is found in earlier examples of colored linen, as follows:

In addition to green and red at Deir el-Bahri (Naville, *Temple of Deir el-Bahari,* pl. 130, with five chests). The above examples alone would by comparison indicate that *yrtyw* means "blue," notwithstanding its occurrence over *red* in the sarcophagus of Sebek-o (Berlin 45; *Mitth. Orient. Samml.* IX, p. 8).

In a relief at Dendera four calves led by Ptolemy IV are marked (green), (red), (black), and (white). In the accompanying text they are called (white), (green), (red) and (*yrtyw*). Here *yrtyw* corresponds to the well-known word for black in the preceding list, as dark blue much resembles black. The *yrtyw*-dye, according to an inscription at Dendera in Room 6, was made of *wʿn wꜣḏ*, "fresh *wʿn*," which seems to have been a needle-wood, growing in Syria (Mariette, *Dendérah,* I 72 c = Duemichen, *Tempelinschriften,* Vol. 2, pl. XIX, 8); but this may have been a blue dye called *yrtyw* with its color meaning, and therefore having no botanical significance. Gardiner concludes that *yrtyw* may mean simply "color" (*Zeitschrift,* 47 (1910), p. 162).

In the medical papyri the use of the word to designate color is found only in our treatise and in Pap. Ebers. It seems actually to designate the contents of a pus cist of some kind (Ebers 105, 11; 105, 3), and again to call such content "like *yrtyw*" (104, 7). This might refer to the cloudy bluish color of discolored pus. It is used nine times in Pap. Smith, as follows:

To describe a hue mingled with the color of a ruddy, flushed or livid face, Case 7 (III 20–21).

To describe the hue of the two lips of a wound which are "like the color (*yrtyw*) of the *tmś·t*-tree," Case 41 (XIV 13; see commentary on *tmś* above).

Yrtyw also appears in Pap. Smith in connections which would indicate that it sometimes means simply "color," e. g.: "the shell, the color being like the egg of an ostrich" (Case 9, V 1). Similarly in Case 19 (VII 20), the *yrtyw* of an inflamed eye is said to be like " *yrtyw* of the *š'š*-plant," evidently referring to the color of the fruit or flowers of some unidentified plant. Again in Case 46 Gloss B contains the following explanation :

Ignoring the obscurities in the passage, it is obvious that " their *yrtyw* " is rendered in the explanation by " their skin " or " their hue " (XVI 14–15). In such a connection *yrtyw* must mean something like " tint." It is such a shade of meaning as this which makes it possible to say : " their *yrtyw* is hot," where it must mean something like " surface " (Case 41, XIII 22).

To sum up in conclusion, *yrtyw* originally means a fruit or blossom of uncertain identity, presumably bluish in color. It then became a color designation, indicating a dark hue, verging into blue, and thus came to indicate blue linen. In some way it also gained the meaning " color, hue, tint," or even " surface." We may compare it with our use of " carnation," which may designate a flower, a color, the hue of flesh, both the color laid on by an artist in painting flesh, and in art criticism sometimes having a meaning not unlike " surface ; " although the derivation of the term " carnation " is not at all parallel with that of our Egyptian word.

pr·t, " fruit," lacks the phonetic complement ; but we meet the same difficulty if we read *rw·t*, perhaps the same as *ry·t*, " pigment," " color," which occurs in hieroglyphic (e. g. Mariette, *Abydos*, I 31 a).

GLOSS G

III 21–IV 1

Explaining : The odor of the chest of his head is like the *bkn* of sheep.

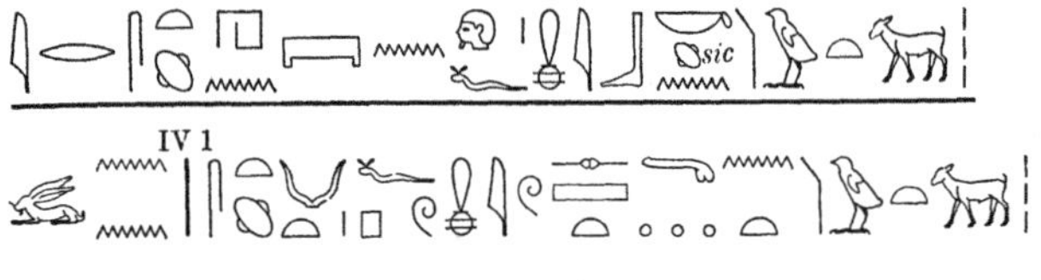

Translation

As for : " The odor of the chest of his head is like the *bkn* of sheep," it means that the odor of his crown is like the urine of sheep.

Commentary

This gloss is intended to explain the unfamiliar word *bkn*, which is unknown anywhere in Egyptian documents outside of our treatise. The genitive after *bkn* has led to the omission of the final of the word itself, as the scribe copied the excerpt from III 11. Whether a wound of the head like this one customarily exhales such an odor would be an interesting question for experienced surgeons of to-day. It may be noted that the word *ʿw·t*, rendered " sheep " above, really means " small cattle," including a number of varieties of both sheep and goats.

GLOSS H

IV 1–2

Explaining: The chest of his head.

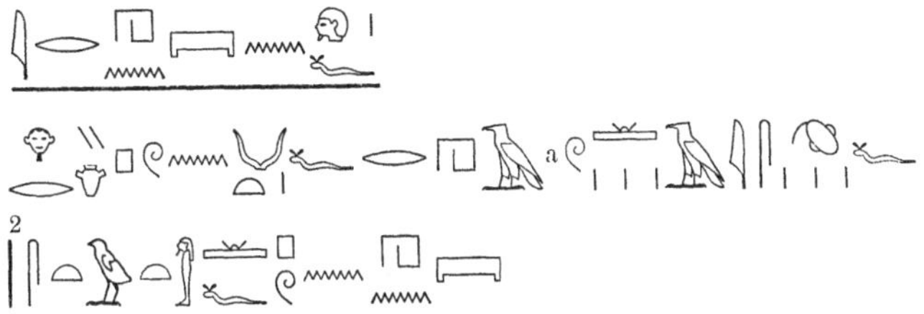

[a] In *r ḥ>w* the scribe at first wrote *r ḥw* and then corrected the error by writing over and adding .

Translation

As for: " The chest of his head," it means the middle of his crown next to his brain. The likening of it is to a chest.

Commentary

The explanation is intended to make clear the word " chest " as applied to the head. This application of the word " chest " to the dome of the skull is exactly parallel to the German " Gehirnkasten." Our own designation " chest " for the region under the thorax is a similar example of the use of the word to indicate a capacious container and protector of organs. The region of the head thus designated in our treatise is defined as the *wpw·t*, " crown," the situation of which is graphically pictured in the writing of the word with the horns of an ox.

As in the case of *whnn* (IV 11), the hieratic determinative of *hn* is different from that employed with *tp* and *ḏ>ḏ>* (" head ") or *ḏnn·t* (" skull "). This determinative is consistently given this special form in all four passages where it occurs (III 11; III 21; IV 1; IV 2). Furthermore, an examination of the above six passages shows clearly that the determinative of *hn* is quite different from that of *whnn*. The determinative of *hn* in our treatise is always (4 times) to be transliterated ; that of *whnn* is once and once probably . See p. 169.

Gloss I

IV 2–4

Explaining: His mouth is bound, both his eyebrows are drawn, while his face is as if he wept.

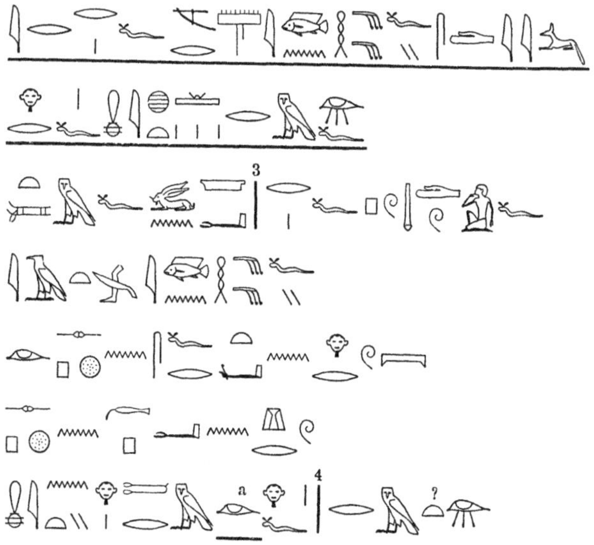

[a] This sign is inserted above the line as a subsequent correction by the scribe in red ink.

Translation

As for: "His mouth is bound, (and) both his eyebrows are drawn, while his face is as if he wept," it means that he does not open his mouth that he may speak, both his eyebrows are distorted, one drawing upward, the other drooping downward, like one who winks while his face weeps.

Commentary

 *šdy*, "distorted," or "drawn." In the list of symptoms from which this is quoted, it is written with a sign which resembles *r*. Nevertheless we must read *d*. It is written clearly *d* in our gloss, and the name of the god  (Mariette, *Mastabas*, D 19, and Palermo Stone, First dynasty, Year x + 11), also written with a jackal as in our text above, likewise shows that we must read *d*. Such a verb is unknown elsewhere, and its meaning is determined exclusively from this gloss, in which the explanation renders the significance of the word sufficiently clear.

 *my yḫ·t*, "as if," will be found discussed in the examination in Case 4, II 3.

 *y't*, "distorted." It occurs also in the form  *'t* (Ebers 108, 7). The verb originally means "to wound," or "to injure." It has also the meaning "to twist,"

or "to distort," applying especially to facial distortion. In the Book of the Dead we read that when Re addressed his followers "his mouth was distorted" (Budge, 115, from Nu 18, 5). Gardiner also calls my attention to *Zeitschrift*, 57 (1922), p. 3*, 14 for a further example of distortion of the mouth; and to the causative "*ś-y'ty*," "pervert," in Eloquent Peasant B 1, 99. A similar medical meaning is evidently to be found in our treatise, in its only other use of the word, to indicate the "diverting" of fever till it passes off (Case 47, XVII 13–14).

. . . . . . , literally "making a case of (drawing upwards), (and) a case of (drooping downwards)." Such a use of *sp* is common enough, e.g., the acts of extortion forbidden in the laws of Harmhab.

śfr·t, "drawing." The meaning has been surmised from the context. No such verb is known from any other example. Its opposite *k'p* literally means "to cover," referring to the covering of the eye by the drooping lid and eyebrow, and hence the above rendering "drooping."

trm, "to wink." The meaning of this word has been successfully cleared up by Spiegelberg (*Zeitschrift*, 54 (1918), p. 134). The act involved unpleasant implications among the Egyptians and the deceased denies in the Book of the Dead (Naville, 125, 26 Aa). Cf. also Coffin Texts (*Recueil de Trav.* 29, p. 145).

"his face weeps." For another example of this see Newberry, *Rekhmara*, pl. IV 5. The *t* is probably an error of the scribe. The form must be a pseudo-participle, 3d masculine, singular.

GLOSS J

IV 4

Explaining: He has become pale and has already shown exhaustion.

[a] This has been inserted in red ink as a subsequent correction, and a second which had been written incorrectly after *h* has been canceled with an oblique stroke of the pen.

Translation

As for: "He has become pale and has already ⌜shown exhaustion⌝," it means becoming pale, because he is (a case of) "Undertake [⌜him⌝], do not desert [⌜him⌝]," in view of the exhaustion.

Commentary

The scribe or commentator has again quoted inaccurately. At the end of the citation he has written  *ʾht,* whereas the text excerpted has  *nhd.* We may conclude that the two words are approximately synonyms. The meaning " weakness " rests on the use of the word *ʾht* to designate the " weak place," the fontanel on the crown of an infant's head (see commentary on II 21, Case 6), and from this meaning the rendering " exhaustion " is not far removed. From this rendering one may infer that *wd·t ʾht* means "to show exhaustion." The use of the infinitive following *pʾw,* " to have done " is common.

 *ś-ḥḏ·t,* " to become pale," would be an intransitive use of an otherwise transitive verb, but whatever the interpretation adopted, it is evidently left without object, and therefore intransitive in our passage. Literally rendered, *ś-ḥḏ* would mean " to cause to be white," " to make white," and an intransitive use of a causative transitive is a common phenomenon. " To become pale " is therefore a justifiable rendering. It does not occur elsewhere in the medical papyri, and I do not know of any other passage in which it has the meaning " to become pale."

 *ntt św pw,* " in that he is." The proposition " he is, etc." is apparently substantivized by the prefix of *ntt,* as commonly, and then left in an accusative case, like the accusative infinitive in Arabic, indicating cause. More commonly in such cases *ntt* is introduced by *ḥr,* or by *ḏr,* e.g., II 11.

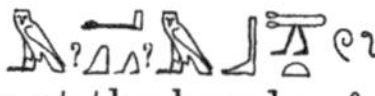 *m ʿḳm bṯw.* In all probability these words have suffered corruption at the hands of an inaccurate scribe. The original phraseology can be drawn from the four occurrences of the same passage in Pap. Ebers. We find it there in two forms: positive and negative, as follows :

Positive :

 *ʿḳ r-f m bṯw św,* " Undertake him ; do not desert him " (Ebers 40, 7 ; 41, 20–21 ; 42, 5).

Negative :

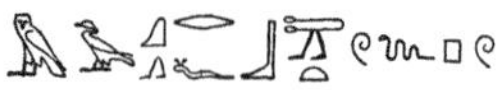 *m ʿḳ r-f bṯw pw,* " Do not undertake him ; he is an incurable " (Ebers 41, 15).

The word 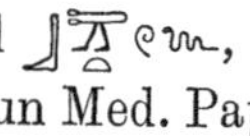, or in the Middle Kingdom  (e. g., Pap. Prisse 10, 2 ; see also Kahun Med. Pap. 2, 18 ; 1, 20), *bṯw,* literally means " one deserted," or " one to be deserted," from the verb 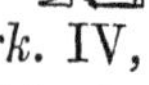 *bṯ,* " to desert, forsake." Gardiner also calls my attention to examples in *Urk.* IV, 117 and 500. From meaning " an incurable," the noun is also employed with the meaning " incurable disease " (Metternich Stela 57) and related to this use of the word is doubtless its employment as the name of a serpent in the so-called Book of Apophis (British Mus. Pap. 10188, 32, 45) and in the Turin Pap. (ed. Pleyte and Rossi, recto, 131, 6, magical text of the Empire).

In view of the above four passages from Pap. Ebers, in which ʿḳ precedes *bṯw*, it can hardly be doubted that the doubtful word preceding *bṯw* in our gloss is to be read ʿḳ. This word occurs six times in our treatise, and only twice is it written with the usual bird. In the other four cases it is each time written alphabetically thus (IV 8; IV 15; IV 16, twice). In none of these four cases does the form a ligature with the ; although in IV 16 the is very small and hastily made. Even if the reading ʿḳ be accepted, our text would still be out of order as compared with the four passages in Pap. Ebers, where ʿḳ is followed by , and *bṯw* by *św* or *pw*. Nevertheless the use of the passage in Ebers establishes it as a kind of verdict characterizing the case and the physician's attitude toward it, like one of the three verdicts in Pap. Smith. One of these verdicts in Pap. Smith is used to characterize a patient thus: "Until thou knowest whether he will die or he will live, for he is (a case of) 'an ailment with which I will contend'" (II 11). With this our passage is strikingly parallel, in spite of the lack of *ḏr* before *ntt*.

The negative *m* before *bṯw* would indicate that we have here the *positive* form of the admonition as above, that is: "Undertake him, do not desert him," and the *m* before ʿḳ is doubtless the introduction to the quotation, like the *m* before *mr* in verdict 2 (II 11) just quoted. We must also understand that a case receiving this verdict ("Undertake him, do not desert him") is a serious and doubtful case, involving "exhaustion" (*ʾḥt*). Emending the text as follows then: [ ] [ ] [ ], we may render: "For he is (a case of) 'Undertake [⌈him⌉], do not desert [⌈him⌉].'" The emendations are too extensive to make the result entirely certain.

ʾḥt, "exhaustion." See commentary on Case 6 (II 21).

CASE EIGHT

IV 5–18

COMPOUND COMMINUTED FRACTURE OF THE SKULL DISPLAYING NO VISIBLE EXTERNAL INJURY

This case like Case 7 is one of unusual interest. Notwithstanding the terrible blow which has shattered the skull like an egg-shell, there is no discernible external contusion. The present editor would not of course feel competent to express any opinion on the possibility of such a terrible fracture being produced without any visible external mark, were it not for the fact that some years ago he lost a friend and colleague whose skull was fractured in exactly this manner, though without any visible external contusion. The injury was caused by a fall on an icy side-walk. In our case a set of alternative symptoms (II) probably gives us really a second case.

The discussion is divided as follows :

I

Title (IV 5).
Examination (IV 5–7).
Diagnosis (IV 7–9), and Verdict 3 (IV 9).
Treatment, only complete rest and quiet (IV 9).

II

Second Examination (IV 10–12). (Duplicate of Examination, Case 6, II 19–22).
Second Diagnosis (Verdict 3, IV 12).
No Treatment.

III

Five Glosses (IV 12–18).

In the first set of symptoms (I) the surgeon, for the first time in the history of science, has noted the effect of the cranial injury on the lower limbs *with reference to the side of the skull which has received the injury.* In other words the ancient Egyptian surgeon has begun observations on the localization of functions in the brain. He carefully notes that both an eye that is askew and a partially paralysed leg and foot are on the *same side* as the injury in the skull. It would seem that *contre-coup* must have taken place in the case which he is reporting. He gives the unfavorable verdict 3 and prescribes only quiet.

The second set of symptoms (II) involves laying open the injury and disclosing the pulsating brain, which is described in the same terms as in Case 6 (II 19–22). Thereupon the surgeon renders verdict 3, and evidently regards the case as hopeless, for he suggests no treatment.

The five glosses (III) contain explanations of extraordinary interest. It is evident that the lack of any visible external mark of the blow creates in the mind of the surgeon the apprehension lest his readers, possibly his students, should in such a case conclude that the observable symptoms may be due to disease, or what might be termed some *internal* cause. In the diagnosis he cautions his reader to regard the patient as " one whom something entering from outside has smitten." In the glosses he carefully explains what this means, and warns his reader that he is not dealing with " the intrusion of something which his (the patient's) flesh engenders," meaning some seemingly spontaneous form of disease. In this connection the surgeon's point of view toward the whole range of casualties afflicting humanity from outside reveals a conception of an accident as due to the action of the gods, not unlike the notion of " divine Providence " still widely current in our own day. It is evident that " something entering from outside " was actually personified and deified (see Gloss D).

TITLE

IV 5

Translation

Instructions concerning a smash in his skull under the skin of his head.

Commentary

The meanings of the above terms describing this injury are taken up in Gloss A by the ancient surgeon himself. It will be recalled that what the surgeon calls a " smash " of the skull is a compound comminuted fracture, as shown by Gloss A in Case 5 (II 16–17). See also the discussion of the title of Case 5 (II 11).

EXAMINATION

IV 5–7

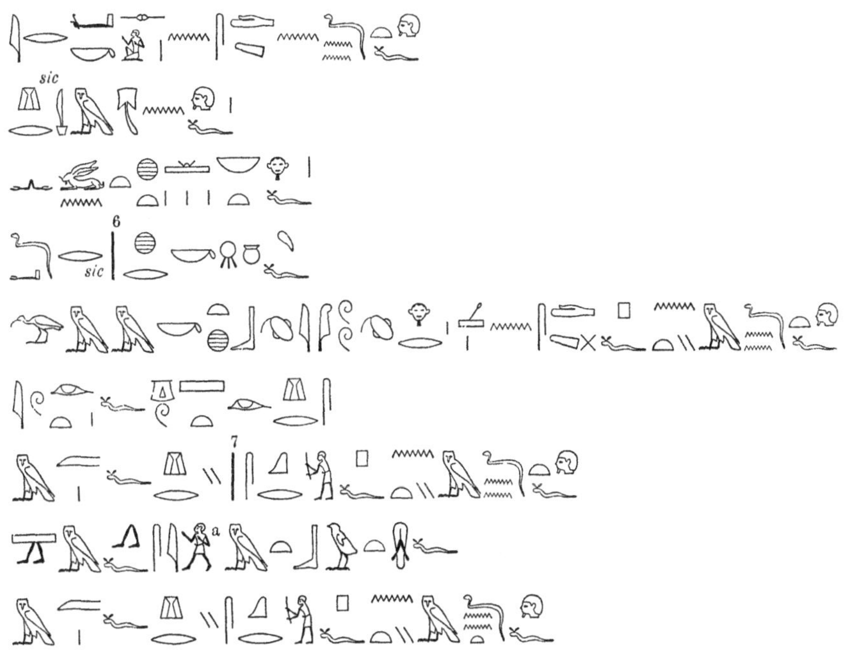

[a] For the correct form see Vol. II, Pl. IV A, l. 7.

Translation

If thou examinest a man having a smash of his skull, under the skin of his head, while there is nothing at all upon it, thou shouldst palpate his wound. Shouldst thou find that there is a swelling protruding on the outside of that smash which is in his skull, while his eye is askew because of it, on the side of him having that injury which is in his skull; (and) he walks shuffling with his sole, on the side of him having that injury which is in his skull, (conclusion in diagnosis).

Commentary

The slight variant *šd n ḏnn·t-f,* "smash *of* his skull," while the title has *m* "in" his skull, is of no significance. As shown by the title and the repetition in Gloss A (IV 12–13), the scribe has omitted , the first three signs of *ynm,* "skin."

The scribe's inability to copy an excerpt correctly is useful to us in the following:

Examination (IV 5):

Quotation in Gloss A (IV 13): .

The parallelism shows that *yẖ·t,* "thing" is equivalent to *wbnw,* "wound." See the discussion of *yẖ·t* in Case 4 (examination, II 3).

ḏʿr evidently means "palpate" here; but we know that at some stage of his investigation the surgeon cuts through the unruptured tissue covering the fracture, for it is evident in the following development of the discussion that the surgeon has access to the brain. See the discussion of *ḏʿr* "palpate" in Case 1.

Tẖb yšw-w, "swelling protruding" has been discussed in Case 4 (examination, II 4).

ḥr šꜣ, "on the outside of." This meaning is demonstrated by the use of this compound preposition as the opposite of *m ẖn,* "on the inside of," e.g., Louvre Stela C 12, l. 8. Of its surgical use we have four examples in our document (Cases 8, 16, 21, and 38), all of which modify the phrase, *tẖb yšw-w,* "swelling protruding." See also for the medical use of the preposition, Pap. Ebers 60, 10, where it means "on the outside of" (both eyes).

gwš-t(y), "askew" is evidently the rare verb *g-w-š,* "to turn aside, diverge, be askew," or as an adjective, "crooked." See Pap. Anast. IV 11, 10; de Rougé, *Inscr. hier.* 142; Papyrus of Nesikhonsu IV 22; IV 22–23; IV 23 (Maspero, *Momies royales,* pl. XXVI); Papyrus judic. de Turin, 2, 9; *Maximes d'Ani* (Pap. Boulaq 4), 9, 13; 8, 18–19. The determinative varies: (Anast. and Pap. judic.); (de Rougé); and (Nesikhonsu and Ani).

šḳr, "injury," is doubtless a derivative from the familiar verb *šḳr,* "to strike, to smite," written in the same way. It must mean "bruise," or "contusion," and this is doubtless its meaning in the two passages in which it occurs in Pap. Ebers (109, 13; 109, 14). It is not known elsewhere in the medical papyri, and occurs otherwise only in the Book of the Dead, referring to the injury to the eye of Horus, which is called a (ed. Naville, 112, 6 and 8 Aa). In Pap. Smith it occurs seven times as follows:

Case 8, as a designation of the compound comminuted fracture on the side of the skull (IV 7, thrice; IV 15) with *yh* as a variant (IV 15–16 twice).

Case 17, as a designation of a compound comminuted fracture of the maxilla (VII 3).

Case 19, as a designation of a perforation in the temporal bone (VII 17).

Case 21, as a designation of a split in the temporal bone (VIII 8).

The surgeon notes that the affected eye is on the *same* side as the injury to the skull. He also observes that the partially paralysed leg is on the *same* side as the wound in the skull. It must be, therefore, that the case which he is recording was one in which the *contre-coup* on the *opposite* side of the patient's skull resulted in paralysis on the same side as that which had received the blow.

Since writing the above I have received the following interesting remark from Dr. Luckhardt: "The interpretation of a *contre-coup* fracture is convincing. However, the paragraph dealing with it is not quite clear. Early after such an injury there may be a conjugate deviation of head and eyes to the side of lesion with a hemiplegia of the opposite side because of weakness of the muscles which turn the head and eyes to the hemiplegia side. But this does not fit this particular case. This case can be interpreted only as a *contre-coup* fracture since the hemiplegia is definitely stated to be on the side of the injury."

 *śy*, "shuffling" is probably an inaccurate writing, for the quotation in Gloss B (IV 13) has *śy-f*. See commentary on Gloss B.

DIAGNOSIS

IV 7–9

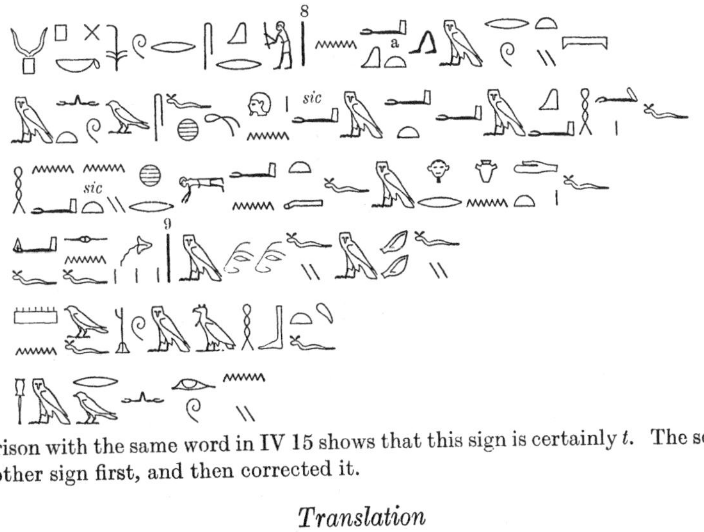

a Comparison with the same word in IV 15 shows that this sign is certainly *t*. The scribe evidently made some other sign first, and then corrected it.

Translation

Thou shouldst account him one whom something entering from outside has smitten, as one who does not release the head of his shoulder-fork, and one who does not fall with his nails in the middle of his palm; while he discharges blood from both his nostrils (and) from both his ears, (and) he suffers with stiffness in his neck. An ailment not to be treated.

Commentary

This obscure diagnosis is almost unintelligible in the second and third items. The first is fairly clear. It is intended to affirm that the symptoms observed are due to an injury arising from an *external* cause, and by implication, as explained in Gloss D, not due to the "penetration of something which his flesh engenders" (IV 17). This distinction is obviously made in view of the fact that the absence of any visible external injury might mislead the surgeon to conclude that the symptoms were due to some internal disorder arising from disease "which his flesh engenders." It can hardly be doubted that the second and third items of the diagnosis are similar indications of causes or symptoms affirmed not to be present, and evidently concerning the shoulder and hand on the side affected. Apparently the condition of the patient is similar to that resulting from some other injury or disease, producing the symptoms noted in the second and third items, and the surgeon is warned against false conclusions resulting from this similarity. These matters will be found discussed in Gloss E.

It should be noted here that items two and three of this diagnosis contain two scribal errors. The initial 𓂝 of *ʾmʿ·t* "fork," is an error for initial 𓄿, which the scribe has written correctly in Gloss E (IV 17) and elsewhere in our treatise. Again the 𓈖𓏏𓏭 of the second item should be the negative 𓂜𓏏𓏭𓄿 as likewise shown by Gloss E (IV 17).

All other items of the diagnosis have occurred before and will be found discussed above (I 20).

In spite of its obscurity this diagnosis is the most important one in our entire treatise. It discloses its unique character in the first place, in the fact that it is not in the usual form and is not introduced by the otherwise invariable formula, "Thou shouldst say concerning him, etc." It is evident that this departure from the usual form is due to the apprehension of the surgeon lest his reader should make the mistaken conclusion that the symptoms are in any way due to internal causes, rather than to the externally invisible injury, which nevertheless originated externally. In view of the hopelessness of the case, this anxiety of the surgeon to ensure a right understanding of it is a remarkable evidence of his scientific interest. Throughout the treatise he shows his understanding of the fact that the troubles he is treating are due to intelligible physical causes, not to demoniacal invasion. In the discussion of this case, however, the surgeon really makes some effort to define this distinction in scientific terms, although undoubtedly hampered in this effort by the superstitions of his age. See the discussion of this diagnosis in the Introduction, pp. 49–50.

The hopeless conclusion (verdict 3) will be found discussed in Case 5 (II 15); see also the introduction to the treatise (pp. 46–48).

TREATMENT

IV 9

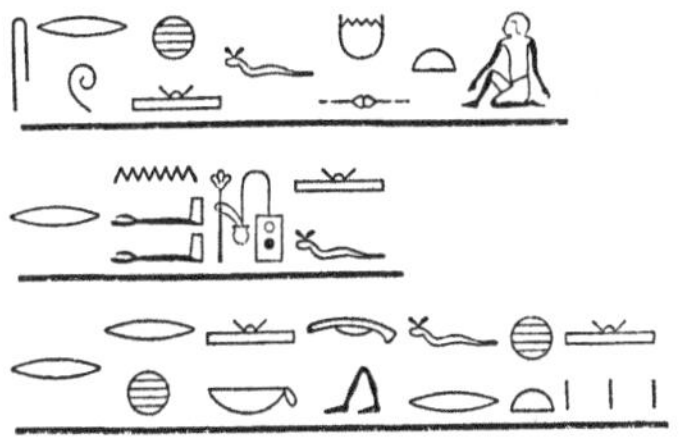

Translation

His treatment is sitting, until he ⌜gains color⌝, (and) until thou knowest he has reached the decisive point.

Commentary

The treatment in this case consists simply in keeping the patient quiet, in a restful posture. See discussion in Case 4 (II 7). The *pw* employed in this sentence in Cases 4 and 7 is omitted here.

, *nʿʿ*, occurs here for the first time in such medical connection as a symptomatic indication, presumably of the patient's facial color. The word is used of both natural and artificial coloring: of a cyst (Ebers 108, 20–109, 1); of a calf (Newberry, *Beni Hasan*, Vol. II, pl. VII); of a woman (Tale of the Herdsman, Berlin Pap. 3024, 160); wooden chariots (Annals of Thutmose III, *Urk.* IV, 690); a coffin (Berlin Pap. 10496, verso 13); clothing (often in Papyrus Harris). It seems to mean "brightly colored," or "parti-colored." It is doubtful whether the rendering "gain color" as above is correct. The ancient commentator furnishes no explanatory gloss.

SECOND EXAMINATION

IV 10–12

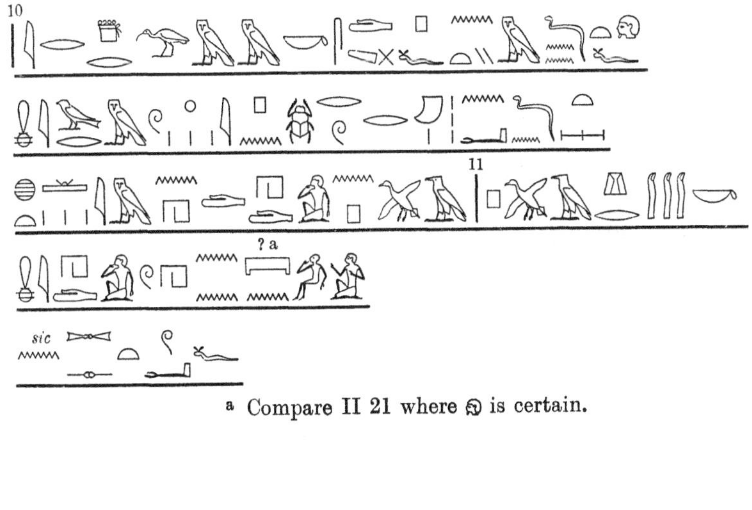

[a] Compare II 21 where is certain.

Translation

Now as soon as thou findest that smash which is in his skull like those corrugations which form on molten copper, (and) something therein throbbing and fluttering under thy fingers like the weak place of an infant's crown before it knits together—when it has happened there is no throbbing and fluttering under thy fingers, until the brain of his (the patient's) skull is rent open—(and) he discharges blood from both his nostrils and both his ears, (and) he suffers with stiffness in his neck, (conclusion in second diagnosis).

Commentary

We have here a group of symptoms which are a duplicate of the examination in Case 6 (II 19–22), and will be found fully discussed there. Some variants, etc. should be noted.

yr ḏr, "now as soon as," as in II 6 and III 7. Hence the symptoms are probably those of a second stage of the same case.

hd, "weak place," is a variant quite different from *ʾht* of Case 6. It is doubtless a scribal error for *nhd*, which will be found discussed in Case 7, Gloss J (IV 4) and Case 6 (II 21).

ṯs·t-f, "it is knit together." See variant in II 21 (p. 169). Grammatically it may be passive in *tw*, or *sḏm·t-f* with negative = "not yet."

for the more common is of course a well-known variant. See the same writing in Case 20 (VIII 4).

The observation of the pulsations in the brain, beneath a fracture which has been accompanied by no visible external injury or rupture of the soft tissue over the fracture, would of course be impossible unless the surgeon operated and laid back a flap of skin covering the fracture. It is strange that the ancient surgeon makes no mention of this procedure; but it is perhaps due to the fact that he regards the case as hopeless and suggests no treatment. The omission of all reference to any possible treatment may have resulted in the omission of any mention of the operation also; on the other hand the direction to "palpate" in the examination may have been regarded by the surgeon as a sufficiently clear indication that the fracture was to be rendered accessible.

SECOND DIAGNOSIS

IV 12

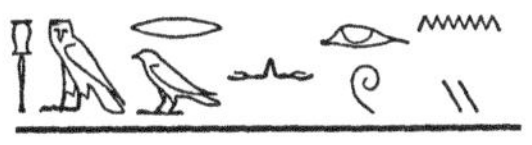

Translation

[Thou shouldst say]: " An ailment not to be treated."

Commentary

As in Case 6 the surgeon attempts no further diagnosis than the unfavorable verdict. He evidently considers that the conditions disclosed by the second examination make the case hopeless. He therefore appends the unfavorable verdict 3 and leaves the case without suggesting any treatment. Verdict 3 will be found discussed in Case 5 (II 15) and in the introduction (pp. 46–48).

GLOSS A

IV 12–13

Explaining: A smash in his skull under the skin of his head, there being no wound upon it.

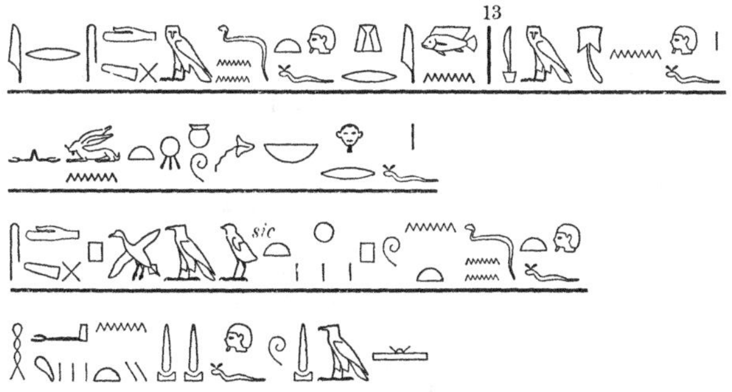

Translation

As for: " A smash in his skull under the skin of his head, there being no wound at all upon it," it means a smash of the shell of his skull, the flesh of his head being uninjured.

Commentary

The gloss has misquoted the text of the case which reads: " there being nothing at all upon it " (IV 5). This does indeed need some explanation, but when converted into " there being no wound at all upon it," the misquotation furnishes a large part of the explanation. One would like to know whether this inaccuracy in quotation was due to the scribe or to the commenting surgeon himself. It is quite conceivable that the scribe, reading " nothing at all," and knowing what it meant, thoughtlessly wrote its meaning, viz. " no wound at all." See discussion of *yḫ·t*, " thing " in Case 4 (II 3).

p'w·t is obviously a scribal error for *p'ḳ·t*, " shell." See Case 4 (II 9).

The negative statement that there is " no wound at all upon it " is followed by the positive corollary that the flesh of his head is whole. The verb in the Egyptian *wḏ'* literally means " to be whole," not as I have rendered in English, " to be uninjured ; "—that is, it does not have the force of a denial of injury (which is expressed in the preceding denial of the existence of an external wound), but an assertion of soundness.

GLOSS B

IV 13–15

Explaining : He walks shuffling with his sole.

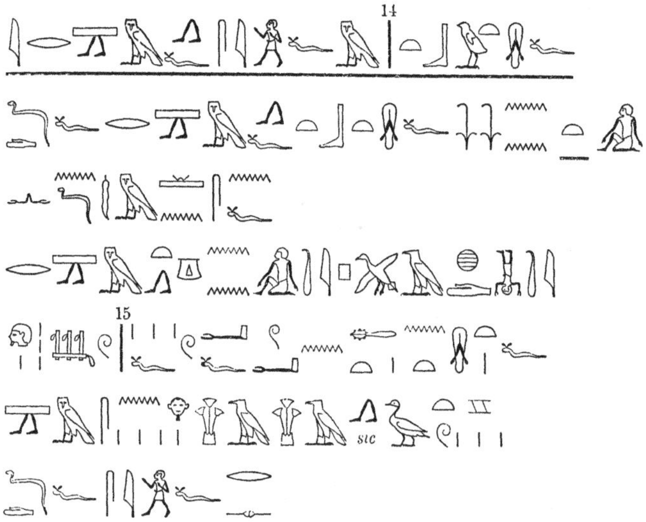

Translation

As for : " He walks shuffling with his sole," he (the surgeon) is speaking about his walking with his sole dragging, so that it is not easy for him to walk, when it (the sole) is feeble and turned over, while the tips of his toes are contracted to the ball of his sole, and they (the toes) walk fumbling the ground. He (the surgeon) says : " He shuffles," concerning it.

Commentary

šy-f. The quotation in the gloss inserts *f*, which is lacking in the text of the case (IV 7). This word is probably different from of the Nastesen stela (cf. Maspero, *Mél. d'archéol.* III, p. 126, note 5 ; suggested to me by Dévaud).

Its meaning is sufficiently clear from its use in our Case 8, which is the only case employing it in Papyrus Smith.

nny-ty, from the verb *nny*, means "to move feebly," "to drag sluggishly along" as of slack inundation water, or of uncontrolled urine dribbling sluggishly (see X 22). The was inserted by the scribe in red.

pꜣḫd-ty, "turned over," is known as early as the Pyramid Texts (685 a). Besides this gloss it occurs once more in our treatise in Case 34 to describe a dislocated clavicle (XI 18), but it is there written *pḫd*. It is evidently identical with the frequent verb *pḫd*, employed especially in the hymns of victory in the Eighteenth and Nineteenth Dynasties to describe the overthrow of the enemy. In Greek times it is twice written with an overturned ship as determinative.

tp·w, "tips," literally "heads." On the anatomical use of the word to indicate "ends" or "tips," see Case 1 (lost column, commentary on *m tp-f*, p. 85).

ẖ·t, "ball" of the foot. I can find no other example for this meaning of the word, but followed as it is by the words "of his sole" the usual meaning "belly" can hardly be understood as anything else than "ball."

ḥꜣḥꜣ, "fumble," is a rare word. It is known elsewhere in the medical papyri only in the obscure passage in Ebers in which it designates some ailment of the heart (Ebers 101, 3). Its ordinary meaning seems to be to "go astray, wander, err," related doubtless to the common verb *ḥyḥy*, "to seek." The rare examples: *ḥꜣḥꜣ* (Granite statue, Cairo Cat. 547 = *Urk.* IV, 994) and (Theban Tomb of , Tomb No. 110) refer to loss of the mummy. Cf. Davies, *Amarna*, Vol. V, pl. XXVIII. The rendering "fumble" seems to convey the idea intended by the surgeon—the action of a partially paralysed and contracted foot, shuffling along in the helpless effort to walk.

GLOSS C

IV 15–16

Explaining: One whom something entering from outside has smitten.

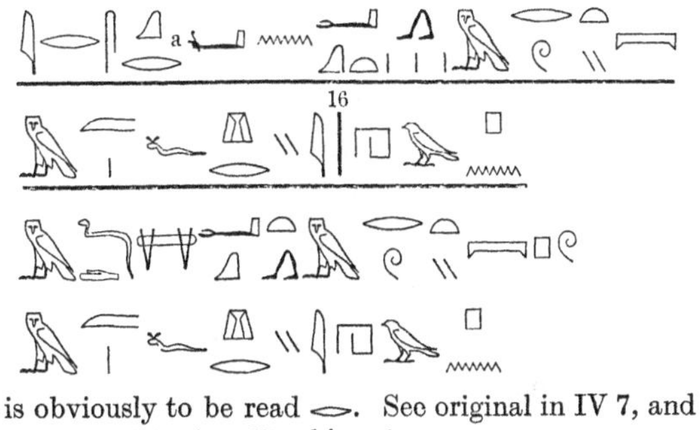

[a] This seeming is obviously to be read . See original in IV 7, and compare (IV 12) in which also appears as a straight line like hieratic .

Translation

As for: " One whom something entering from outside has smitten " on the side of him having this injury, it means one whom something entering from outside presses, on the side of him having this injury.

Commentary

The commentator has included in his quotation the words " on the side of him having this injury," but this is an error, for they do not belong in the above context (IV 7–8), but were used in the earlier discussion of the affected eye and the paralysed foot " on the side of him having that injury " (IV 6–7). There is no relevancy in their inclusion in the text to be explained in the above gloss. They present an interesting variant, the use of the word  *yh* where the original phrase has  *sḳr.*

 *mḏd,* "presses," is the important word of the explanation, and undoubtedly indicates that the chief cause of trouble from this injury is the intrusive pressure on the brain from without.

GLOSS D

IV 16–17

Explaining: Something entering from outside

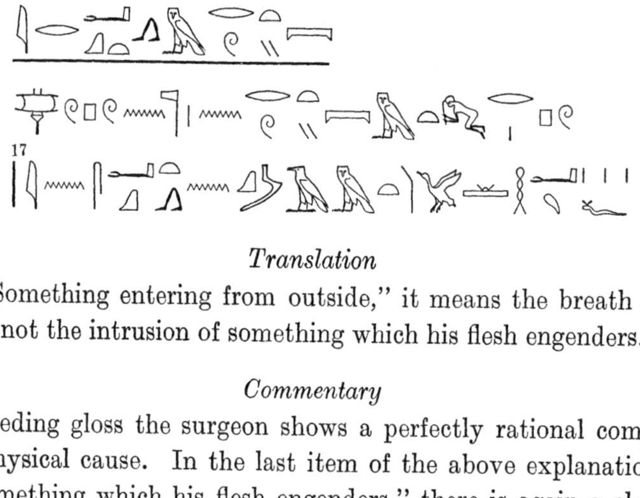

Translation

As for: " Something entering from outside," it means the breath of an outside god or death; not the intrusion of something which his flesh engenders.

Commentary

In the preceding gloss the surgeon shows a perfectly rational comprehension of an external physical cause. In the last item of the above explanation: " not the intrusion of something which his flesh engenders," there is again a clear distinction between an internal affection, " something which his flesh engenders," arising as it seems to the Egyptian surgeon from *within,* and the *external* physical cause of this injury with its resulting internal disturbances. This rational distinction is unmistakable and demonstrates the surgeon's ability to discriminate judicially in the world of objective phenomena and natural causes. But side by side with this scientific attitude of mind, we find equally unmistakable evidences of ancient superstition. In the experience of early man the power of the gods impinged hourly upon the daily life of man, and in the earliest scientific investigation of the human body the surgeon could not entirely divest himself of such primitive prepossessions. Even in the thought of a scientifically minded surgeon the accidental injury which he calls " something entering from outside " has not taken place without some relation to divine decrees. I cannot find this phrase " something entering from outside " in any of the other medical papyri, except in Papyrus Ebers, where it occurs only once, and in this unique passage it is given a very interesting and unique writing (Ebers 102, 14–15). It has heretofore been read  *ʿk·t m ḥr·t* (e.g., Wreszinski, *Der Papyrus Ebers*, p. 212); but there can be no doubt that the last word is not *ḥr·t*, but  *rwty*. The group appears twice in our gloss (Pap. Smith IV 16) and the first writing of the two is less cursive, disclosing the true reading *rwty* quite unmistakably. In Pap. Ebers therefore the phrase is to be read: . What makes this appearance of the term in Pap. Ebers of especial interest and importance is the insertion after it of the figure of a god as determinative. What god is meant is impossible to determine.[1] The important point to notice is, that for the physician of Pap. Ebers, " something entering from outside " is personified and deified. The accident from without, the external casualty, is a *Τύχη*, a Fortuna, or rather a " Fortuitas," always unfavorable. It is the surgeon's *force majeure*, always to him a mystery. A serious accident was not thinkable without the decree of the controlling deity. And so our surgeon explains " something entering from outside " as " the breath of an outside god," and possibly alternative to this is " death." The two are set up here side by side : one the stroke of the *fatal* accident ; the other a casualty from which one *may* survive, if not assured life, which would be the logical correlative of " death." Among the superstitions of the Pap. Ebers is one which has bearing here. Its author in discussing the blood-vessels says that there are four leading to the ears, two to each ear :

" The breath of life enters at the right ear ; the breath of death enters at the left ear " (Ebers 100, 3–4). The surgeon of Pap. Smith is pathologically more sound. In the first place he recognizes that the accident may be on either side, and that on either side " something entering from the outside " is either :

(1) " the breath of an outside god ; " or
(2) " death."

[1] It is impossible to recognize this divine figure, although it may be that of a buck. Moeller has included the figure in his list (I 75) ; but it is his only example, and he does not attempt to connect it with any known hieroglyphic form.

(1) corresponds to "the breath of life" in Pap. Ebers, and seems to mean possible survival for the sufferer; (2) means a fatal accident and seems not to be personified or deified. In our gloss a good deal turns on the interpretation of *rʾ-pw*, "or." Does it in Egyptian always mean that *something different* is introduced as an *alternative*, or something *identical* merely mentioned again under another name; as we may say "twenty shillings, or one pound." In this case the two terms on both sides of "or" are identical in essential meaning. If we could so interpret our gloss, "death" would be simply a synonym of "the breath of an outside god." In this case the force of *rʾ-pw* would be simply "namely," or "that is," for which the Egyptian usually employed , as is well known.

yn, "not," is a rare negative. See Gunn, *Syntax*, pp. 89–90.

ś-ˁḳ·t-n, literally rendered means "what (that which his flesh engenders) brings in."

GLOSS E

IV 17–18

Explaining: One who does not release the head of his shoulder-fork, and who does not fall with his nails in the middle of his palm

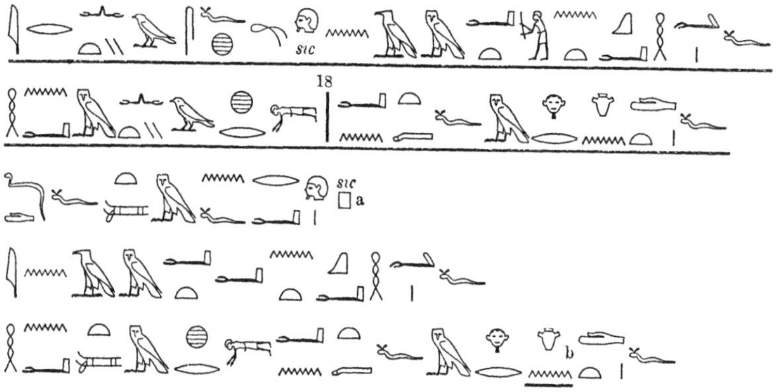

[a] The scribe has omitted the *w* of *pw*.

[b] This *n* was at first omitted by the scribe and corrected into the text in red ink above the line, after the line was complete.

Translation

As for: "One who does not release the head of his shoulder-fork, and who does not fall with his nails in the middle of his palm" it means that he says: "One to whom the head of his shoulder-fork is not given, and one who does not fall with his nails in the middle of his palm."

Commentary

This gloss, intended to explain the difficult statement of symptoms in the diagnosis (IV 7–9), hardly accomplishes its purpose for a modern reader. In the first place the last item of the explanation merely repeats the text to be explained; and the first item is too obscure to aid us. A number of errors in the original text of the diagnosis are corrected, and these corrections are useful. The word *ʾmʿ·t*, written *ʿmʿ·t* in IV 8, is correctly written here. We have here literally "the fork *of* his shoulder," that is "his shoulder-fork," while the diagnosis had less clearly "the fork *in* his shoulder" (IV 8). The diagnosis has  *nty ẖr*, "one who falls," which is here corrected to  *ywty ẖr*, "one who does not fall." In view of the explanation in the gloss which uses  *tm ẖr*, "one who does not fall," with the negative *tm*, duly spelled out, it is evident that the ancient commentator accepted the negative force as the correct one. Dr. Luckhardt's comment below indicates good internal reasons for *not* accepting the negative reading.

As already noted above in the commentary on the diagnosis, the surgeon is warned against mistaking the symptoms in Case 8 for those of a patient who exhibits some affection of the shoulder and who falls down with his fist clenched and his finger nails tight against the palm of his hand. It is important in this case to note that the word "hand" or "palm" is *not* written in the dual. He is thinking of an injury which affects only one side. The same is true of the word "shoulder." When the patient with a stiff neck is told to look at "his shoulders," the *dual* indicating *both* shoulders is regularly indicated by the scribe (see above Case 3). Here however we are dealing with a symptom discernible in *one* shoulder only, and the word is correctly written in the singular.

Turning now to the details of these similar symptoms, which however our patient of Case 8 does *not* exhibit, we may note the following points.

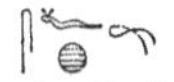 *ś-fẖ* literally means "to cause to be loose" or "to loosen," but its exact surgical significance is not determinable. It is not the usual term for "dislocate," for which our treatise employs  *wnẖ*. I have supposed it indicated a stiff joint due to contraction of the ligaments, which the patient is unable to "release" (*ś-fẖ*).

 *ʾmʿ·t n·t ḳʿḥ-f*, literally "the fork of his shoulder." The rare and interesting word *ʾmʿ·t* means a "two-toed claw" or a "fork," as is shown in Case 22, Gloss A (VIII 14–15). It is primarily applied to the fork at the top of the ramus, and must designate here some bone of the shoulder sufficiently double at the end to be called a "fork," like the claw of a two-toed bird. It may be that the two projecting processes at the top of the shoulder-blade (*scapula*) are meant; that is the *acromion* and the coracoid process, which are not unsuggestive of a bird's claw. In view of the other symptom affecting the hand, one would look for some bone of the *arm* as the one affected. It may be therefore that the top of the ulna is meant, where the *olecranon* and the coronoid process project to form, it is true, a much less pronounced fork. Here then at the shoulder would be the articulation which the patient is said to be unable

to " release," or the " head " of which, according to the gloss, " is not given " to the patient.

The other item of these symptoms consists of two observations: the patient does or does not fall prostrate and lie with clenched fist so that his finger nails " are in the middle of his palm." Two possible alternative renderings should be considered here. It is possible that "finger nails" should be construed as the subject of "fall," in which case we must render " one whose finger nails fall into the palm of his hand." This in itself would eliminate the falling of the patient. It should be noticed that the word *ʿn·t*, " finger-nail," is written in the *singular*, both in the diagnosis (IV 8) and in the gloss (IV 18 twice), so that we have it written three times, all in the singular. *ʿn·t* designates the whole " claw " of a bird, as in VIII 15, and the rendering " finger-nails," meaning as it were the whole claw of the hand, has therefore been retained as probable. On the basis of this rendering it remains for the pathologist to suggest what ailment is indicated.

Dr. Luckhardt has kindly added the following important remarks on this difficult passage:

" My interpretation of this case is as follows: The surgeon sees this patient some time after the injury. I base this statement on the stated fact that the patient ' walks shuffling with his sole.' Immediately after an injury to the brain involving the motor cortex (or internal capsule) the opposite side of the body would be paralysed (hemiplegia) and walking would be impossible. However, the hemiplegic recovers the power of walking even if, after a few months, the affected arm may at that time still remain powerless. At this time the arm is particularly affected by what is termed ' contracture.' The upper arm is adducted (at the shoulder). This the scribe characterizes as ' one who does not release the head of his shoulder-fork.' The lower arm is bent at a right or acute angle with a pronated and slightly flexed hand and with the *proximal phalanges, and particularly the terminal ones, quite flexed.* Since the upper arm is adducted and fingers flexed, such a patient would fall as ' one who does not release the head of his shoulder-fork,' and ' who falls while the nails are in the palm of his hand.' What I cannot understand is that the gloss reads ' one who does *not* fall while his nails are in the palm of his hand.' It would seem to me that one must accept the positive form as given in the beginning of this history as the correct one. The negative form in the gloss would seem to be an error of the scribe. When a normal person falls during walking he involuntarily extends the hand at the wrist and extends and abducts his fingers. He breaks the fall by extension of the upper arm (not abduction) and landing on the palm of his hand, not ' while his nails are in the middle of his palm.' "

CASE NINE

IV 19–V 5

WOUND IN THE FOREHEAD PRODUCING A COMPOUND COMMINUTED FRACTURE OF THE SKULL

The examination in this case contains only an inaccurate repetition of the title; the treatment which immediately follows this examination is a *recipe*, a grotesque product of superstition and belief in magic, accompanied indeed by a magical charm to be repeated over it in order to ensure its efficacy! It is obviously not an accident that a discussion containing a treatment of this character should at the same time not only lack an examination containing any observations, but also contain no diagnosis nor any verdict! Without these essentials of our surgeon's customary method, the case becomes merely a recipe to which have been prefixed a title and the undeveloped formula of examination introducing no observations. The entire discussion is without any doubt a characteristic product of the recipe-hawking physician (as contrasted with the surgeon). See the discussion of this case in the Introduction, pp. 42–43.

This case represents our surgeon's sole relapse into the superstition of his age, of which he has elsewhere so surprisingly divested himself. It was doubtless the resemblance of the frontal bone to a segment of the shell of an ostrich's egg, which beguiled some ancient physician into the belief that a paste made by triturating the shell of an ostrich's egg would be efficacious in healing a shattered frontal bone! Such a recipe and such a method of treatment are obviously drawn from current folk medicine universally practiced in ancient oriental lands. The recipe must have circulated in one of the recipe-papyri which have hitherto constituted our sole inheritance from ancient Egyptian medicine. We cannot but wonder whether our observant surgeon could really have allowed himself to take over into his extraordinary treatise on *cases*, a discussion which was such a typical product of the recipe-mongering physician of the time. The character of our ancient book therefore raises the question whether some later copyist is not to be held responsible for the insertion of this solitary example of a folk-loristic recipe into his otherwise surprisingly rational treatise.

TITLE

IV 19

[a] The scribe wrote 𓄣𓏤 *yb*, "heart" immediately after the word "instructions," but noticed the error and canceled the word with an oblique stroke of black ink over the red of the rubric.

Translation

Instructions concerning a wound in his forehead, smashing the shell of his skull.

Commentary

 *p'ḳ·t nt ḏnn·t-f*, "shell of his skull," is evidently here the frontal bone, the *squama frontalis*. On our surgeon's use of the word *p'ḳ·t*, see above Case 4, Gloss A.

 *šd*, "smashing," see Case 5, Gloss A.

 *ḏnn·t*, "skull," see above, Case 1, title, commentary on .

EXAMINATION

IV 19–20

Translation

If thou examinest a man having a wound in his forehead, smashing the shell of his head, (conclusion in treatment).

Commentary

This case exhibits the methods and the form of the great bulk of the materials in Papyrus Ebers. There is no real examination, and its place is taken by a mere repetition of the title. Even in this repetition the word "skull" of the title is replaced by the vague and inexact word "head" (*ḏ'ḏ'*). There is no diagnosis, nor any verdict, but after the suggestion of an examination, the discussion turns at once to a grossly superstitious and unscientific treatment.

TREATMENT

IV 20–V 4

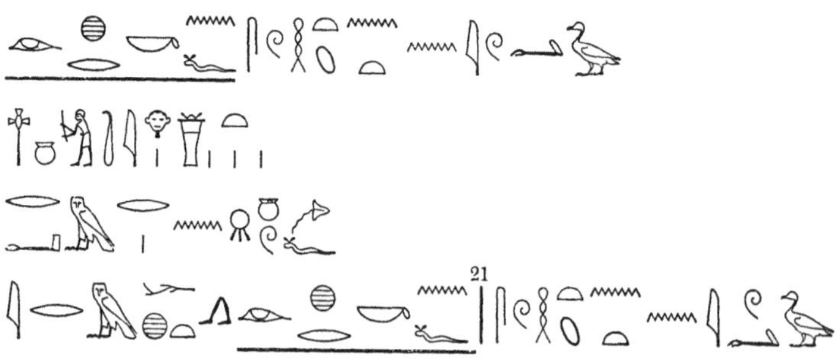

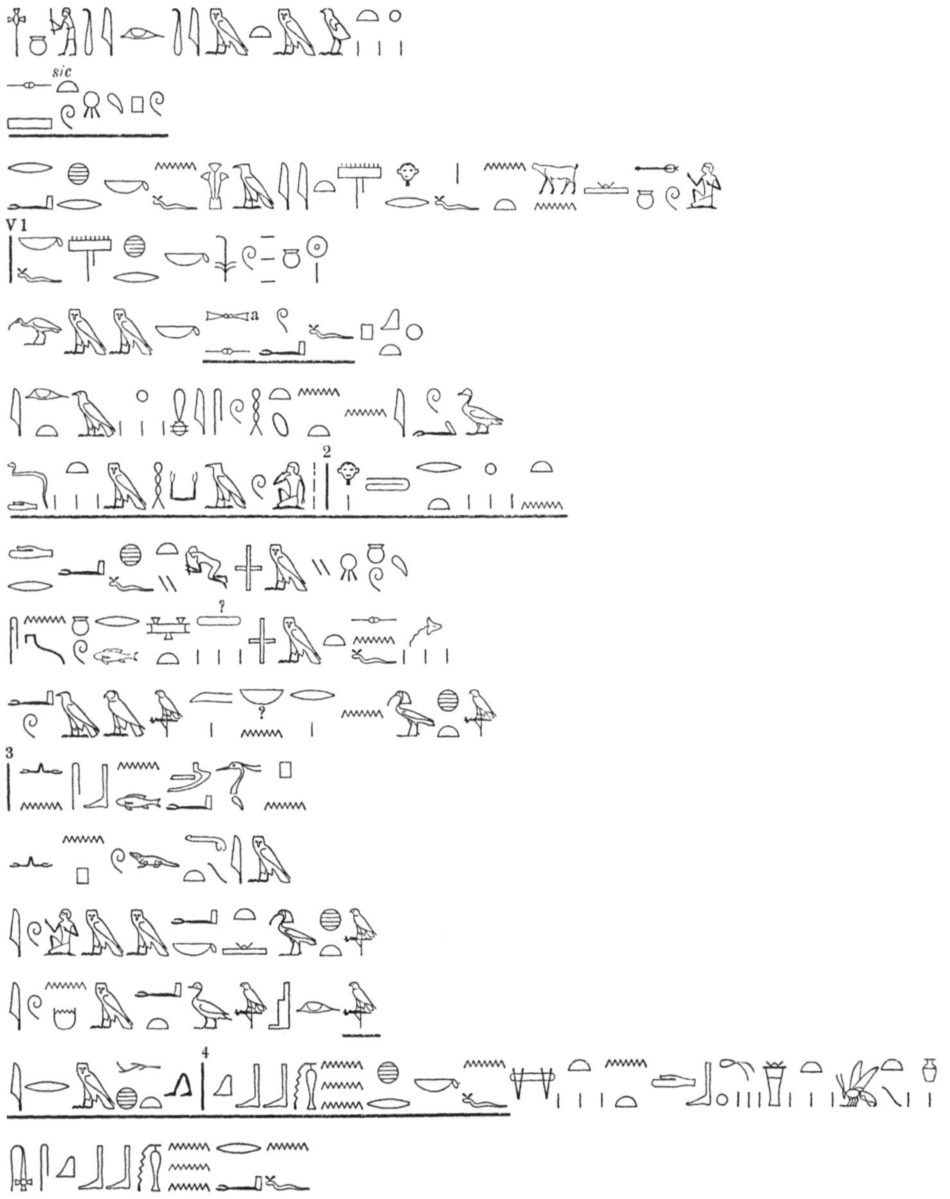

[a] This word was at first omitted by the scribe and afterward inserted in red ink above the line. Its exact position in the line was then indicated by a tiny × in red between *gmm-k* and *p'ḳ·t*.

Translation

Thou shouldst prepare for him the egg of an ostrich, triturated with grease (and) placed in the mouth of his wound. Now afterward thou shouldst prepare for him the egg of an ostrich, triturated and made into poultices for drying up that wound.

Thou shouldst apply to it for him a covering for physician's use; thou shouldst uncover it the third day, (and) find it knitting together the shell, the color being like the egg of an ostrich.

That which is to be said as a charm over this recipe:

Repelled is the enemy that is in the wound!
Cast out is the ⌜evil⌝ that is in the blood,
The adversary of Horus, ⌜on every⌝ side of the mouth of Isis.
This temple does not fall down;
There is no enemy of the vessel therein.
I am under the protection of Isis;
My rescue is the son of Osiris.

Now afterward thou shouldst cool [it] for him [with] a compress of figs, grease, and honey, cooked, cooled and applied to it.

Commentary

This treatment is a curious hodge-podge of superstitions, without a suggestion of the scientific attitude of mind which is so prominent in the ancient surgeon's discussion of the other cases. As already stated, the significance of the "egg of an ostrich" without doubt lies in its resemblance to the frontal bone. In some way the soundness of the egg-shell, not vitiated by its being triturated, is conveyed to the fractured shell of the skull. All this folk superstition is then reinforced by the recitation of a magical charm. In the customary practice of medicine the procedure of the physician was of course dictated by the current superstitions of the day, among which the mythical story of the rivalry between Horus, the good and faithful son of Isis and Osiris, and Set, the malicious and destroying enemy, played a great part. The wounds of the two heroes in their combat with each other, and the maternal solicitude of Isis in caring for the injury of her son Horus, constantly appear in the physician's charms. The same means employed so successfully by Isis in relieving Horus are frequently referred to in the spells uttered by the medical man. The patient becomes Horus; his ailment is Set, the enemy of Horus and murderer of Osiris the father of Horus. Hence in the above charm, "the enemy that is in the wound" and the "adversary of Horus" are of course Set, while the patient enjoys the "protection of Isis" and of Horus, "the son of Osiris" and Isis.

The following matters of detail require some explanation:

 *tmt·w* (or *tm·wt*), "poultices." The word occurs only in Pap. Ebers and in our treatise. In Ebers it is written with the sign  *tm*, showing that we must read *tm* and not *rm* (see Ebers 78, 14 and 15). The form of the root is a little uncertain. In Ebers it is written all four times *tmt·w*. Of the three passages in Pap. Smith

two write *tmt·w*, and one (IV 21) *tm·wt*. It may therefore be a masculine noun *tmt*, plural *tmt·w* ; or a feminine noun *tm·t*, plural *tm·wt* ; but the genitive *n* in the masculine (Ebers 91, 8 ; though it should be *nw*) favors the masculine *tmt·w*. It is not to be confused with 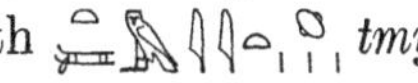 *tmy·t*, which is some sort of disease (e.g., *Mutter und Kind*, I, 4, etc.). Our word *tmt·w* has commonly been translated " boluses." If bolus is understood as a remedy administered *internally* (that is through the mouth), this rendering is clearly incorrect. The word appears only four times in Pap. Ebers. It is employed once for application to diseased toes, doubtless some rheumatoid or gouty trouble, so commonly discernible in the feet of ancient Egyptian bodies from the earliest times (Ebers 78, 14; and 78, 15). Again it is employed for a discharging ear :  " Thou shouldst make for him *tmt·w* for drying up a wound" (Ebers 91, 8–9). Here the *tmt·w* are most probably poultices. The third and last case in Pap. Ebers employs the *tmt·w* for treating pustules or sores in the anus, perhaps piles. The remedies prescribed are to be made into *tmt·w*, obviously for local application though this is not stated (Ebers 106, 2). In this case they might possibly be suppositories. In Pap. Smith *tmt·w* are employed three times, that is twice besides our Case 9. In both the other cases they are for external application : Case 41, which instructs the physician, " Thou shouldst make for him *tmt·w* " . . . . , *wt ḥr-ś*, " (and) bind upon it " (Smith XIV 6–7) ; and Case 46, which likewise directs : " Thou shouldst make for him *tmt·w* " . . .  *wdy r-ś*, " and apply to it." The *tmt·w* applications seem to have been designed especially to dry up a sore or wound, e.g., the above case in Pap. Ebers (91, 8–9) ; and again Pap. Smith Case 46 states that the physician is to prepare remedies for " drying up his wound " (XVI 9–12). This leads us to the discussion of :

. The text is certainly corrupt. The most obvious corruption is the omission of the determinative of the first word, viz., , because it was identical with the word-sign beginning the next word. The same error has occurred in XVI 9–10. Compare the following passages :

 " Thou shouldst make for him remedies for drying up the wound " (XIV 4–5).

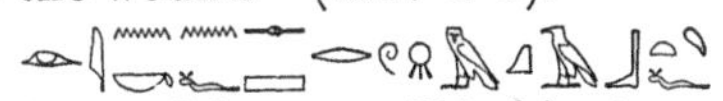 " Thou shouldst make for him [remedies for] drying up [the wound] in his sternum " (XVI 9–10). And finally

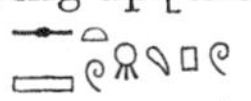 of Case 9 above (IV 21), in which we have a second stage of corruption, the passage in XVI 9–10 representing the first stage. Obviously our text of Case 9 should be emended with the aid of XIV 4–5 as follows :

meaning "*tmt·w* for drying up that wound." The writing of the corrupt text (XVI 9–10), quoted above, might suggest that we should read here 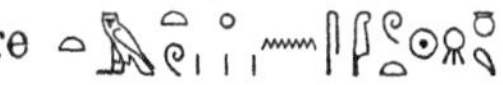

tmt·w n[w] s-šw·t wbnw, literally " poultices for causing the wound to dry up " (Ebers 91, 8–9, cf. also 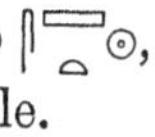, Ebers 65,15), but the emendation on the basis of Smith XIV 4–5 is more probable.

 .....  *ḥ'y·t* ..... *nt ḫn swnw,* " a covering for physician's use," is a device found in the medical papyri only in this passage. The word *ḥ'y·t,* " covering " is written exactly like the verb  *ḥ'y,* " to be naked," of which the noun is 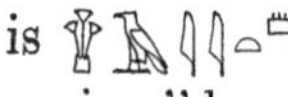 *ḥ'y·t,* " nakedness." There can be no doubt that our word means " covering " however. In the first place it is something which the surgeon is " to apply . . . to it " (the wound) ; and in the second place the wound is *thereupon,* after an interval of three days, to be " uncovered." Although no other case of its medical use is known, our word *ḥ'y·t,* " covering " is doubtless to be connected with the word  employed in the phrase *m ḥ'·wt,* which must mean something like " in secret," literally " under cover," in the Pyramid Texts (303 a).

 *ḫn,* " use." The usual word for a " hide " or a leathern " (water)-skin " is feminine,  *ḫn·t.* Nevertheless there is a masculine word  *ḫnw,* " skin." It is used of goat skins and sheep skins ; cf. Spiegelberg, *Rechnungen,* taf. XV c, d, and XIII (col. a, 5; col. b, 9, 16, and 18). This masculine is also found in Pap. Mallet I 5:  " hide (*ḫn*) made into a coat of mail " (in *Recueil de trav.,* Vol. I). The transliteration is from Gardiner's copy, and he has written " sic ! " before the determinative of *ḫn,* to call attention to the lack of the expected feminine *t.* It occurs again without *t* in the same document (I 4). A sack called  (Naville, *Festival-Hall,* pl. 19 and 24) and the word 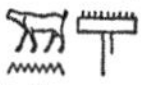 *ḫn,* " tent," are doubtless both simply the word " skin " to designate something made of it, as we say " skin " for a leathern water bottle, or " canvas " for a tent. In our passage *ḫn* is further given a special meaning by an added genitive of specification. It is some kind of material prepared especially for the use of physicians by the embalmers. The whole " covering, etc." is explained in Gloss A as a " bandage," which the embalmers furnish. The first difficulty in rendering our *ḫn* as " skin " lies in the determinative, which is, in both passages where it occurs, a papyrus roll. Sethe therefore suggests to me the possibility of connecting the word with the well-known verb  *ḫn,* " to approach, to near," making a noun " nearness, approach, association, use." Thus it is conceivable that *ḫn swnw* might mean " physician's use." Then by construing the genitive *nt* as meaning " for," a common meaning, we might render the whole " a covering for physicians' use." See commentary on Gloss A.[1]

The subject of the verb following " find " (V 1) is masculine. It may therefore

[1] Lacau has called attention to the fact that in the Middle Kingdom coffins the phrase  means " in his hand " (*Recueil de trav.* 35, 220, n. 1); that is, there is a rare word  or *ḫn,* meaning " hand ". Our word, with the determinative can hardly be identified with this rare word *ḫn,* " hand."

resume the noun "wound;" but not "covering" or "egg," both of which are feminine. The word employed here for the knitting together of the wound is the same as the surgeon used for the knitting together of the infant's fontanel in Case 8 (IV 11). Grammatically our treatise more commonly follows the verb "find" with a noun, which is then resumed by a pronoun as immediate subject of the verb following "find;" in other words Egyptian prefers to make a substantive the object of "find," rather than a proposition, such as we find here in V 1.

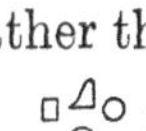

[hieroglyphs] *pḳ·t*, "shell" is of course the word *p'ḳ·t*, which we have met several times before for the "shell," meaning one of the *squamae* of the human skull. It does not here designate the "shell" of the egg, which we find called the [hieroglyphs] *ynr*, "stone" of the egg in the great Amarna Sun-hymn (Davies, *Amarna*, Vol. VI, pl. XXVII, l. 7).

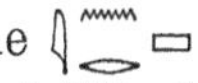

[hieroglyphs] *yrtyw*, "color," see above, Case 7: III, 20.

The charm is introduced by the usual formula often used in Pap. Ebers.

[hieroglyphs] is new and not found elsewhere. It is parallel with *dr*, "repel" and must have some similar meaning. It is possibly a causative derived from the verb [hieroglyphs] *nwr*, "to tremble" (Book of the Gates, 3rd Hour, Seti II, 12 = Ramses IV, Pl. 21).

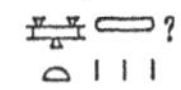

[hieroglyphs]? *w'·t* is a little uncertain in the reading. The first sign has some resemblance to the hieratic form of *wḥʿ*. The determinative is likewise questionable. The rendering is based on the Middle Kingdom word [hieroglyphs] *w'·t* in the laudatory phrase [hieroglyphs] *šwy m w'·t*, "free from *w'·t*," in which the word must mean something evil.

[hieroglyphs] *nb n*, is possibly a questionable reading. Dr. Grapow has suggested [hieroglyph], but with entirely problematical meaning.

[hieroglyphs] *'ḫ·t*, literally the "splendid one" (feminine) is an epithet for Isis.

[hieroglyphs] *śbn*, "fall down," "sink down," is common applied to serpent enemies in the Pyramid Texts, where it is written [hieroglyphs], and appears in parallelism with [hieroglyphs] *ḫr*, "to fall." As for the fish, it must be employed here because of the *śbn*-fish known only in the Misanthrope 89. The "temple" of the patient is here identified with the injured forehead, perhaps in reference to the fact that the dead sink down on one temple as they lie with head northward and facing the rising sun.

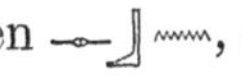

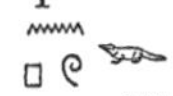

[hieroglyphs] *npw*, with crocodile determinative reminds one of the word [hieroglyphs] *dpy*, "crocodile." It is quite evident, however, that the word here means something hostile to the patient, and there is a word [hieroglyphs] *np*, which is an abusive epithet applied to Apophis (Metternich Stela 1–2, twice; and the Book of Apophis, British Mus. Pap. 10188, 29, 22, copy by Lange in Berlin *Wörterbuch*).

[hieroglyphs] *mḏ·t*, "compress" is unknown elsewhere, unless the sole occurrence of the masculine (Ebers 88, 5) is to be compared here. This is the reading of Wreszinski (p. 179) and is questionable, as he has correctly recognized. The meaning "compress" has been drawn from the root significance of the verb. The construction of *mḏ·t*, as a direct object of a seemingly intransitive form of *ḳbb*, " to be cool " indicates probably corruption of the text. One expects *š-ḳbb*, "to cool," followed by an object such as a pronoun referring to the wound, and a preposition " with " (𓅓) before *mḏ·t*.

GLOSS A

V 4–5

Explaining : A covering for physician's use.

Translation

As for : " A covering for physician's use," it is a bandage which is in the hand of the embalmer, and which he (the physician) applies to this remedy which is on this wound which is in his forehead.

Commentary

This explanation has been partially discussed above in connection with the word *ẖn*, " use." The " covering for physician's *ẖn* " is here explained as a *ššd*, " bandage." The word is well known. It is found employed to designate the bandages employed in wrapping the mummy, or as a fillet about the head ; as a New Year's gift, or accompanying a charm (possibly tied with the customary seven magical knots). All such " bandages " were without any doubt made of linen. We would therefore expect that the " covering " explained in our gloss would necessarily be made of linen ; and this is probably the strongest argument against the translation of *ẖn* as " skin." The embalmers must have required enormous quantities of linen bandages for the practice of their profession. Any one who has examined their work has been impressed with the extraordinary skill disclosed by it. It is the neatest and most elaborate bandaging ever done anywhere. The embalmers therefore became remarkably adept in the art of bandaging, and finally even practiced it as a decorative art, skilfully manipulating the final outer wrappings of the mummy into elaborate decorative designs (see Vol. I, Pl. III, Figs. 6 and 7). Their skill in producing bandages made them the inevitable source for such materials, and our gloss above furnishes us with the interesting fact that they manufactured bandages for the use of the physician. The young practitioner is here told where he can secure his bandages, just as he is to-day given the address of some manufacturer of proprietary preparations.

CASE TEN

V 5–9

A GAPING WOUND AT THE TOP OF THE EYEBROW, PENETRATING TO THE BONE

The surgeon's discussion of this case consists of a few hasty notes regarding a flesh wound over the eyebrow. The diagnosis does not state as much as the title. The treatment is, however, sound surgery, without any such relapse into superstition as we found in the preceding case, and is of unusual interest as containing the earliest known mention of surgical stitching of a wound.

Title

V 5–6

Translation

Instructions concerning a wound in the top of his eyebrow.

Commentary

m tp, " in the top." This rendering is the more probable one, but it should not be forgotten that the anatomical meaning of *tp* is frequently the " end," or " tip," of some other organ or part (see commentary on in Case 1). It may possibly be that the inner or outer end of the eyebrow is meant. It should be noted also that in the diagnosis (V 7), the text has only , " in " showing that the position of the wound, " in " or " in the top of " the eyebrow, is not very precisely maintained. We may compare : " a splitting blow upon his two eyebrows " (Pap. Anast. III, 5, 7–8), in which the preposition is " upon " (*ḥr*), and both eyebrows seem to be involved.

Examination

V 6

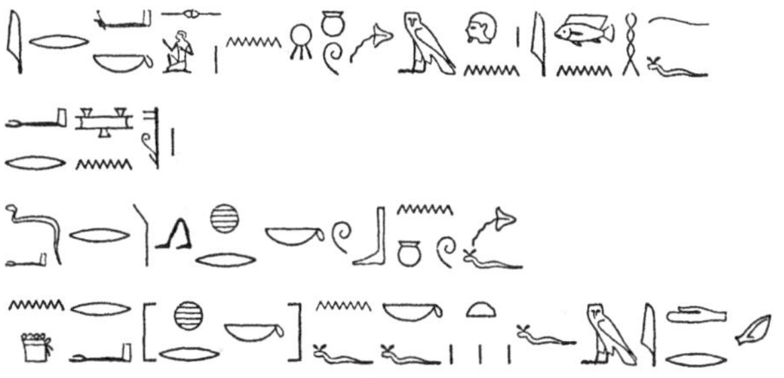

Q

Translation

If thou examinest a man having a wound in the top of his eyebrow, penetrating to the bone, thou shouldst palpate his wound, (and) draw together for him his gash with stitching.

Commentary

Important terms needing discussion will be found explained in the commentary on the preceding cases, as follows :

 *ḫ'y-k,* " thou examinest," see Case 1, pp. 104–106.

 *wbnw,* " wound," see Case 1, pp. 81–84.

 *ꜥr,* " penetrating," see Case 1, pp. 87–88.

 *ḏꜥr,* " palpate," see Case 1, pp. 92–93.

The last item, the " stitching," is new and important. It seems to be regarded as a kind of " first aid," and is included in the examination in all of the six cases in which it occurs in our treatise—that is preceding the diagnosis and the verdict. Apparently the surgeon is to lose no time in drawing together and closing up the gaping wound, whatever the treatment that is to follow may be.

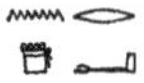 *nḏry,* " draw together." In all of the eight occurrences of this word in Pap. Smith, it is written either *nḏr-ḫr-k,* " thou shouldst draw together " (six times) or *nḏr-yn-k,* " thou shouldst draw together " (once XVII 3, written incorrectly *nḏr-n-k*), except our case above (V 6), where we should of course emend to *nḏr-ḫr-k.* The word is common and in current non-surgical usage means " to seize, grasp." It takes as its object : *inanimate objects,* like weapons, fishing or fowling net, leg of a slaughtered ox, etc.; *persons or animals*: enemies, arrested criminals, oxen, game, wild animals, serpents ; or *parts of the human body,* the hand, or the breasts in mourning. It is important for understanding our passage to notice that one of its non-surgical meanings is to " close " (a door). The six cases in which it occurs in Pap. Smith will make it quite clear that its surgical meaning is " to close up," " to draw together." Before turning to these cases it should be noted that the surgical use of the word is found elsewhere only in three cases, as follows : 1. An obscure passage probably prescribing the bringing together (*nḏry*) of the lips of the vagina (Kahun Med. Pap. 3, 19) ; 2. Description of the preparation of a lancet (Pap. Ebers 109, 6 and 7), very difficult to understand ; and 3. Description of lancing or treating a swelling of some sort (Ebers 109, 10), likewise very obscure. These materials outside of our treatise are therefore of slight value in understanding the surgical meaning of *nḏry.* See commentary on *ydr* immediately below.

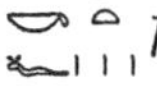 *kf·t,* " gash," has been fully discussed in Case 1, q.v., pp. 90–92. The surgeon's notes on this case are so hasty that there has been no indication heretofore that the

injury was a *wbnw n kf·t*, " gaping wound," but it is clearly so designated in the gloss at the end of the case (V 9).

 *ydr*, " stitching," is a new and difficult word. In seven different cases in our treatise the surgeon is charged to " draw together the wound " " with *ydr*," or to " *ydr* it." It is instructive to note where these wounds are, and their character :

Case 3. Gaping wound in the head, perforating skull (*ydr* in restored passage).
Case 10. Gaping flesh wound over the eyebrow.
Case 14. Gaping flesh wound in the nose, penetrating to the nostril.
Case 23. Gaping flesh wound in the *auricula* of the ear.
Case 26. Gaping flesh wound in the upper lip, penetrating into the mouth.
Case 28. Gaping flesh wound in the throat or neck, penetrating to the gullet.
Case 47. Gaping flesh wound in the shoulder.

It should be observed that six of these seven cases are *flesh* wounds. It is further noticeable that, with the possible exception of the last case (47) the wound is in a relatively thin stratum of soft tissue, through which it pierces, so that it is inconceivable that a *bandage* which would " draw together " the wound could be applied. In six cases, that is all but the last, no bandage could be applied at all, except by winding it entirely around the head or neck. The pressure exerted upon the wound by such a bandage could not possibly " draw together " the " two lips " of the wound. Such "drawing together" requires two forces pulling toward each other, that is in opposite directions, and as nearly as possible in the general plane of the surface around the severed tissue, and not at right angles with this surface, as would certainly be the case with a bandage passing entirely around the head. It is highly important to note that in Case 3 the *surgeon is charged not to bind the wound.* Unfortunately this is in a case in which *ydr* has been restored, though the correctness of the restoration of the word can hardly be doubted. The only conceivable devices for meeting the requirements and " drawing together " these wounds as described by the surgeon are either plasters or stitching. We have already seen that adhesive plaster is called 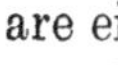 *ꜣ·wy*, or 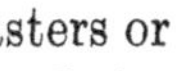 *ꜣyr·wy*, " two strips " (Case 2, commentary on treatment), which are taken up also in Gloss A (V 9) appended to the present case. There is strong *a priori* probability that we are dealing with surgical stitching in six of the cases listed above ; but the question requires close examination of the context in all six cases (omitting Case 3, because of the restoration of *ydr* and its context). The material is arranged below.

Case 10 : Gaping flesh wound over the eyebrow

a. 

" Thou shouldst draw together for him his gash with *ydr*."

b. Diagnosis.

c. Verdict 1.

d. 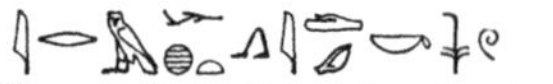

" Now after thou hast *ydr* it,

e. [Thou shouldst bind it] with fresh meat the first day." See demonstration of this restoration in commentary on V 7–8.

f. 

" If thou findest that the *ydr* of this wound is loose,

g. 

thou shouldst draw (it) together for him with the two strips (of plaster)."

h. " Thou shouldst treat it with grease and honey every day until he recovers."

Case 14 : Gaping flesh wound in the nose

a, *b*, and *c*, as in Case 10; in place of *d*, Case 14 has directions for cleansing the wound of coagulated blood ; *e*, as in Case 10.

f. 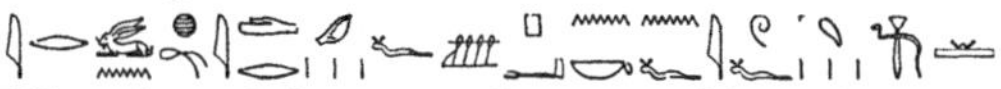

" When its *ydr* loosens, thou shouldst take off for him the fresh meat " (VI 11–12).

g. omitted.

h. " Thou shouldst bind grease, honey and lint upon it every day until he recovers."

Case 23 : Gaping flesh wound in the auricula of the ear

a. 

" Thou shouldst draw (it) together for him with *ydr* behind the interior (of the *auricula*) of his ear."

b and *c* as in Case 10.

d and *e* are omitted.

f. 

" If thou findest the *ydr* of that wound loose and sticking in the two lips of his wound (VIII 20–21).

g. 

thou shouldst make for him stiff rolls of linen and pad the back of his ear therewith " (VIII 21).

h as in Case 10, but with lint added.

Case 26 : Gaping flesh wound in the upper lip penetrating to the mouth

a, *b*, *c*, *d*, and *e*, as in Case 10.

f and *g* are omitted.

h as in Case 10.

Case 28 : Gaping flesh wound in the throat penetrating to the gullet

a and *b* as in Case 10.

c. Verdict 2.

d of Case 10 omitted.

e as in Case 10.

f and *g* of Case 10 omitted.

h as in Case 10, with lint added.

Case 47 : Gaping flesh wound in the shoulder

a, *b*, and *c* as in Case 10.

d of Case 10 is omitted.

e as in Case 10.

f. 

" If thou findest that wound open and its *ydr* loose,

g. 

thou shouldst draw together for him his gash with two strips of linen (plaster) upon that gash " (really plural, see commentary on *kf·t*, Case 1, examination).

h as in Case 10, with lint added.

Unlike any of the other cases, Case 47 at this point discusses alternative symptoms, among which the wound is found " feverish, open and its *ydr* loose " as in the first examination. No further light is thrown upon the meaning of the terms we are examining, for the surgeon is then forbidden to bind the wound ; but if the fever passes off he may treat with grease, honey and lint until recovery.

An examination of the procedure in the above six cases, in all of which the wound is first " drawn together with *ydr* " (*a*), discloses the fact that in four of them (Cases 10, 14, 23, and 47) after an interval during which a fresh meat application may have been used (*e*), the *ydr* is found " loose " (*f*), when the fresh meat (if used) has been removed (Case 14)—a condition which in two (Cases 10 and 47) of these four so found necessitates drawing together the wound again with two strips of plaster. In Case 23 on discovering the *ydr* loose, the surgeon puts supports of linen padding behind the *auricula*, that is between the *auricula* and the skull of the patient. In Case 14, however, after finding the *ydr* loose the surgeon thinks it necessary only to proceed with the customary bandaging with grease, honey and lint. In Cases 26 and 28, wounds piercing the lip and the throat respectively, the surgeon does not anticipate that the *ydr* will be found loose, and so does not prescribe any resulting precautions.

The nature of the *ydr* is unmistakably disclosed in Case 23, where the surgeon not only mentions finding the *ydr* loose, but adds that they are found " sticking in the two lips of his wound." The words for "sticking in" are 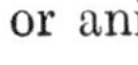 *mn m*, the customary phrase for describing weapons " sticking in " human or animal flesh, or fragments of bone "sticking in" the fleshy tissue of a wound. Consult especially the commentary on Case 4, Gloss A (II 9). In describing a foreign, intrusive substance invading organs or tissues *mn m* always means "sticking in," not "adhering to." In view of this fact there can be no doubt that *ydr* is a word for surgical "stitching" or "stitches." We have here then a surgical suture, the earliest known reference to sewing up a wound in the history of surgery.

We must next inquire what happens to this "stitching" when it is *wnḫ* "loose." This term is explained in two different glosses (Case 31, Gloss A, X 17–19; and Case 43, Gloss A, XV 3–4) q.v. In the first, where it refers to the dislocation of a cervical vertebra, it is said to designate the separation of one vertebra from another, and the commentator refers to the colloquial use of *wnḫ* to indicate the separation, or loosening from each other of two things that had formerly been joined (see Case 31, Gloss A). Applying this knowledge to *wnḫ*, used to describe the condition of a stitched gash, we find that in Case 47, when the stitching is found "loose" (*wnḫ*), the wound is "open" (*pgy*, see above summary, Case 47, *f*). We must conclude then that in the four cases of stitched wounds which the surgeon finds with the stitching "loose," he means that the wound has failed to close wholly by healing, and still gapes. In two of these cases therefore (Cases 10 and 47), the surgeon is charged to draw together the wound again with the "two strips," that is with plaster. Of the remaining two with the stitching "loose," one (Case 23) is to be aided by appropriate supports of linen pads behind the gashed *auricula* of the ear; the other receives only the usual application of grease, honey and lint, bandaged on (Case 14). Finally, in two of the cases (26 and 28) as we have already noted, the surgeon does not apprehend and does not provide for failure of the wound to heal after being stitched.

We may now return to consider further the word *ydr* itself, the meaning of which has been drawn from its *context* in our treatise. It is used thirteen times in Pap. Smith (exclusive of the restored passage in Case 3, I 22), and with the exception of an obscure passage in Pap. Ebers (109, 9), it is otherwise unknown in the medical papyri. In the thirteen passages employing it, it is eleven times a noun and twice a verb (Case 10, V 7 and Case 26, IX 10). In this passage: "Now after thou hast stitched it," it is obvious that *ydr* must be rendered "to stitch" or "to sew." Hence the noun must primarily mean "stitching, sewing, stitches, suture," rather than "thread" or "gut" or the like. Curiously enough the Egyptian word for "to stitch," "to sew," common as it must have been in every day life, is unknown to us. It is not unlikely that we have recovered it in this surgical use of *ydr*.

We find it written very erratically. As to determinative, the writings fall into two groups: *a* with and *b* with :

a. With :

(V 6); (VI 11); (V 7; IX 10); (V 8); in VI 9 the scribe seems to have written , having evidently raised his pen between and the seeming , but in view of the unmistakable spellings with , we cannot doubt that he intended to write here, just as he has intended to do in the writing of the ligatures for *dr* in the next group, where the looks exactly like (compare *ḫkr* in XIII 11–12), as it often does in a ligature with some other sign above it, as in *nr* or *ʿr* (see Moeller, *Palaeogr.* I, Anhang, I and XVII). It would seem that the *r* of *ydr* was pronounced so much like *l* and *n*, as to suggest *ydn* and the use of the ear (*ydn*) as a determinative.

b. With :

(IX 21, clearly , detached and not in ligature); (in ligature, VIII 19; IX 8; XVI 20); (in ligature, VIII 20; XVII 3; XVII 8).

DIAGNOSIS

V 7

Translation

Thou shouldst say concerning him: "[One having] a wound in his eyebrow. An ailment which I will treat."

Commentary

The omission of *ḫry*, "one having," is an obvious scribal error. The change of *m tp* "in the top," to *m*, merely "in," may be due to the haste of the surgeon himself, in making his notes.

The diagnosis is here reduced to the briefest terms, suggesting merely a few notebook catch-words, containing even less than the title, to which is added the hopeful verdict 1. See commentary on this verdict in Case 1 (I 2).

TREATMENT

V 7–8

[a] The scribe has canceled the three phonetic signs preceding  with a red stroke.

Translation

Now after thou hast stitched it, [thou shouldst bind] fresh meat upon [it] the first day. If thou findest that the stitching of this wound is loose, thou shouldst draw (it) together for him with two strips (of plaster), and thou shouldst treat it with grease and honey every day until he recovers.

Commentary

The omission of the bracketed passage in the text is an obvious haplography due to the occurrence of  *św* twice in the same line ; the scribe having copied as far as the first one jumped to the words following the second one. It is of great importance to establish the fact of this error, for otherwise we would have a sentence : *ydr-k św ḥr ywf w'ḏ*, which might be rendered : "thou hast bandaged (*ydr* !) it with fresh meat," which would seem to give us the meaning "bandage" for *ydr*—a meaning which has indeed already found its way into the dictionary from this very passage.[1] It is important to demonstrate that there is no basis for the meaning "bandage," or "to bandage." This will be evident when we have placed our passage in Case 10 in parallelism with the corresponding passage in Case 26, thus :

Case 26  (IX 8).
Case 10 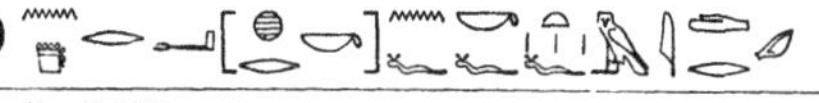 (V 6).

Case 26  followed by diagnosis and verdict (IX 8–9).
Case 10  followed by diagnosis and verdict (V 7).

Case 26  (IX 9–10).
Case 10 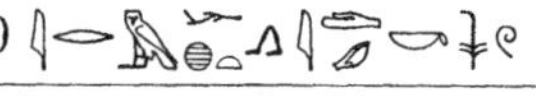 (V 7).

Case 26 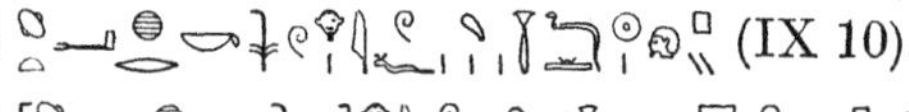 (IX 10).
Case 10  (V 7).

The continuous parallelism between these two cases, extending from the examination, through the diagnosis, verdict and treatment, makes it perfectly certain that the scribe has omitted the words , *wt-ḥr-k św*, "thou shalt bind it," after

[1] See *Wörterbuch der Aegyptischen Sprache*, p. 154.

ydr-k św, "(after) thou hast stitched it." We must therefore insert these omitted words and thus separate "thou hast stitched (*ydr-k*) it" from the following words: "with fresh meat, etc." *Ydr* has therefore no connection with binding with fresh meat in Case 10, and there is no other evidence that *ydr* has anything to do with the idea of binding or a bandage. The above demonstration should be borne in mind in reading the discussion of the meaning of *ydr* in the examination (V 6).

The application of "fresh meat" will be found discussed in Case 1 (I 2–3).

wnḫ, "loose," is discussed in preceding examination.

nḏry, "drawn together," is discussed above in V 6.

ʾ·wy (for *ʾr·wy*), "two strips," will be found discussed in Case 2 (I 14–15), and in Gloss A below.

The treatment with grease and honey is discussed in Case 1, treatment (I 3).

Gloss A

V 9

Explaining: Two strips of linen

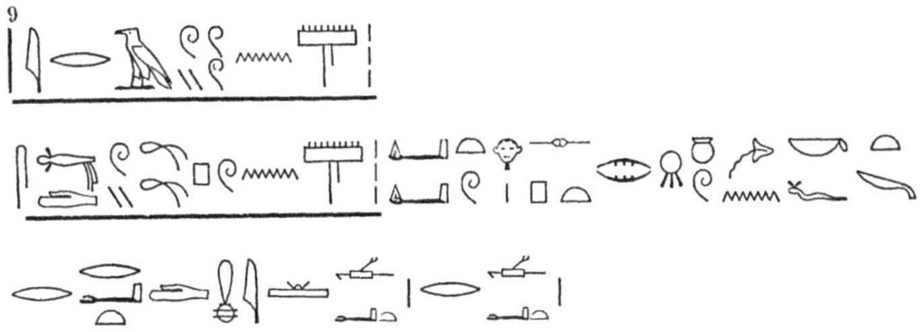

Translation

As for: "Two strips of linen," it means two bands of linen, which one applies upon the two lips of the gaping wound, in order to cause that one (lip) join to the other.

Commentary

This gloss is a repetition of Gloss B in Case 2 (I 16–17), where it will be found discussed, and the evidence adduced which shows that the "two strips" mean more than ordinary bandages, being in reality strips of adhesive tape or plaster.

The curious resumption of the masculine word *spt*, "lip" by means of the feminine substantive adjective *wʿ·t*, has already been discussed above, Gloss B, Case 1 (I 9–10).

CASE ELEVEN

V 10–15

A BROKEN NOSE

This case involves interpretation of local indications so limited in extent that it is difficult to determine with precision exactly what parts of the nose the ancient surgeon intends to define. It is highly probable that the injury is a rupture between the cartilaginous tissue, especially the *septum* and the *cartilagines laterales* on the one hand, and the nasal bone on the other. The process of setting seems to have been no more than the insertion of soft plugs or tampons, saturated with ointment, into the nostrils and the support of the nose in a normal position by binding on rolls of linen, evidently sufficiently stiff to act as splints, and called indeed " spars " or " posts " of linen.

Title

V 10

Translation

Instructions concerning a break in the column of his nose.

Commentary

The terms for the injury and the parts affected can be better explained in the discussion of the examination, q.v.

Examination

V 10–11

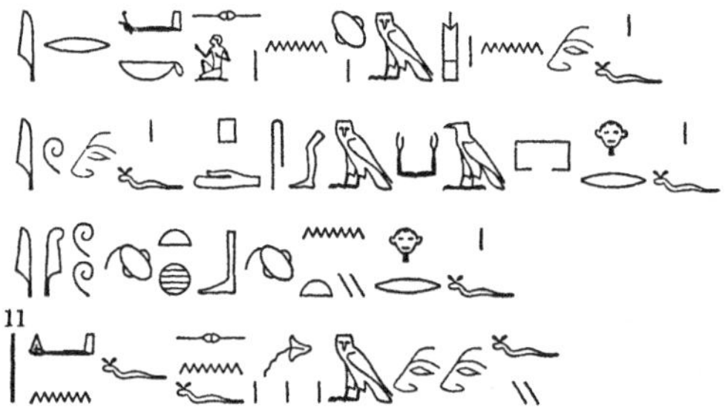

Translation

If thou examinest a man having a break in the column of his nose, his nose being disfigured, and a ⌜depression⌝ being in it, while the swelling that is on it protrudes, (and) he has discharged blood from both his nostrils, (concluded in diagnosis).

Commentary

ḥśb is a very ancient word for "break," graphically suggested by the word sign, ×, the pair of crossed sticks, just as in the case of *śd* (see Sethe, *Zahlen*, pp. 75 ff.; and Grapow, *Zeitschrift*, 49 (1911), pp. 116 ff.). It is found as early as the Pyramid Texts (e.g., 954 b; 1144 c; 2030 b). While it designated breakage of any ordinary object, it already appears in the Pyramid Texts applied to the breakage of bones: "He has broken the vertebrae of the back" (Pyr. 409 b). Also "A bone of N. is not broken" (Pyr. 1043 b). The identity of our word with this *ḥśb* is not to be doubted; for it is written out as (V 11) and (XIV 18). Should the identity of these words with our be doubted, the following demonstration is complete:

Case 42 is an injury of the "ribs of the sternum" *without* *wnḫ* or *ḥśb*.
Case 43 is the same with *wnḫ*.
Case 44 is the same with .
The equivalence between *ḥśb* of Case 42 and of Case 44 is obvious.

The surgical use of the word is unknown outside of our treatise, and the *noun*, *ḥśb*, "fracture" has not yet been found in any connection elsewhere. The surgical meaning of *ḥśb* has nowhere been defined for us in Pap. Smith, as the ancient commentator has defined the meaning of *śd*, "smash" in Gloss A, Case 5 (II 16–17). Nevertheless the definition of *śd* in the above gloss and the examples of its use enable us, by a process of elimination, to determine the character of the injury designated by *ḥśb* as the complementary term of *śd*, "smash:" *ḥśb* being used for a simple fracture, while *śd* is applied to injuries so serious that they are even compound comminuted fractures; see commentary above (Case 5, title, II 11). Another distinction is the fact that in our treatise *ḥśb* is always employed to designate an injury of the *bone*, while *śd* may also apply to a rupture of the fleshy tissue.

Ḥśb is employed in our treatise in eight different cases, a total of twenty-nine times, as follows:

Case 11. Fracture in the bridge of the nose (*os nasale*).
,, 12. ,, ,, ,, *glabella* (?), or possibly *spina frontalis* (?).
,, 24. ,, ,, ,, mandible.
,, 35. ,, ,, ,, clavicle.
,, 36. ,, ,, ,, arm (*humerus*).
,, 37. ,, ,, ,, fracture in the arm (*humerus*) with wound over it.
,, 42. Sprain (*nr·t* without *ḥśb*) in the "ribs of the sternum."
,, 44. Fracture in the "ribs of the sternum."

ywnw, "column" (of the nose). This term is explained by the treatise itself in Gloss A (V 14–15), pp. 240–242.

 *fnd*, " nose," is a common and current term which has hardly gained technical anatomical meaning. It will be found discussed in connection with Gloss A, V 14.

 *pdš*, " crushed in " is explained in Gloss B, Case 12, q.v.

 *mk' ḥr-f* is a very difficult phrase. In the first place it is impossible to determine whether *ḥr-f* is the prepositional phrase " upon it " or " in it " (the nose), or the noun " his face." In the latter case *mk'* would be some stative verb describing the condition of his face ; in the former case *mk'* would be a noun designating some injury or disfigurement of the nose, which has a " *mk'* upon it." The determinative makes the latter alternative more probable. *Mk'* is probably to be connected with *mk'·t* " support, resting place " (see above, Case 4, II 7). Considering that the bridge of the nose is crushed in and flattened, the lower fleshy and cartilaginous portions might abruptly project, suggesting a support or notch or depression. In a situation of such detail, however, guesses like this are very hazardous.

The last two items will be found discussed above, especially Case 4.

DIAGNOSIS

V 11

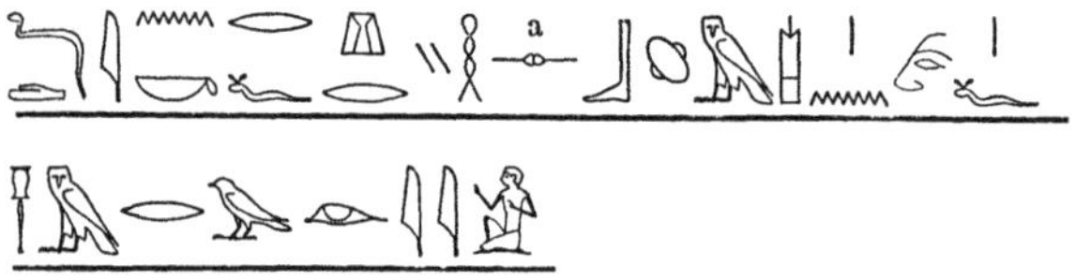

[a] The scribe at first omitted this *s* and afterward inserted it as a correction.

Translation

Thou shouldst say concerning him : " One having a break in the column of his nose. An ailment which I will treat."

Commentary

This diagnosis is again a mere memorandum—a catch-word or two actually containing only the title of the case. It produces the impression which we have often gained before, that in such places the text is a hasty record of memorandum notes. As in the preceding case its practical value lies in the concluding verdict 1 which will be found discussed in Case 1 (I 2). Such brief notes serving as a diagnosis raise the question whether the gradually developing diagnosis was not *originally* merely what we find here, that is a repetition of the title to which was appended the practical direction furnished to the surgeon by the verdict. Out of such a beginning the more fully developed and logical diagnosis, of which our treatise furnishes a number of examples, may then have gradually evolved. See also the Introduction (p. 73).

TREATMENT

V 11–14

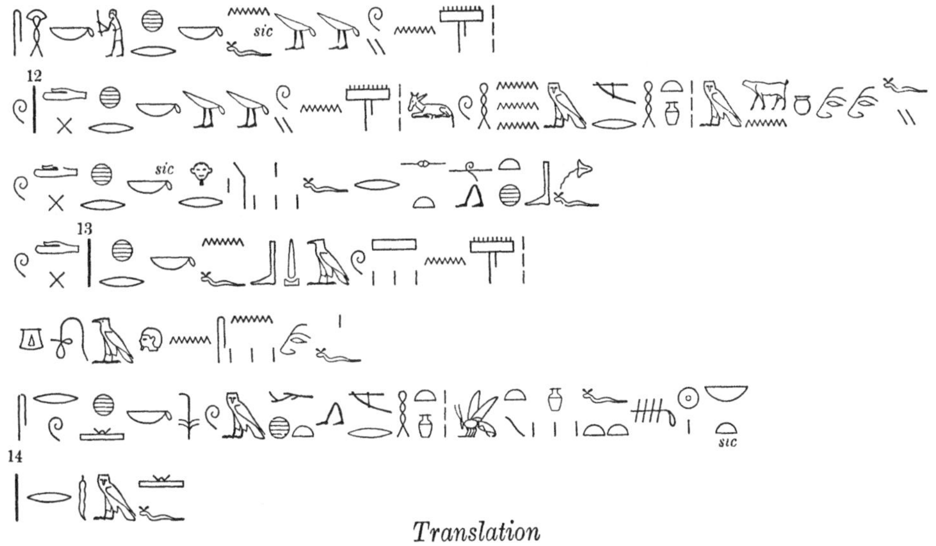

Translation

Thou shouldst cleanse (it) for him [with] two plugs of linen. Thou shouldst place two (other) plugs of linen saturated with grease in the inside of his two nostrils. Thou shouldst put [him] at his mooring stakes until the swelling is reduced (lit. drawn out). Thou shouldst apply for him stiff rolls of linen by which his nose is held fast. Thou shouldst treat him afterward [with] grease, honey (and) lint, every day until he recovers.

Commentary

 *šk*, "cleanse," a rare word, originally written with a broom as determinative. It seems in this passage at first sight to take "the two plugs" as its object, but we must recall here the frequency with which this document omits the 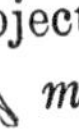 *m*, "with," even when the following instrument or remedy does not begin with *m*; e.g., "honey" (*by·t*) in XI 6; XII 8; XII 14; XIII 2; XIV 20; XV 3. In fact in every case in which treatment "with honey" is prescribed in Papyrus Smith, the "with" (*m*) is regularly omitted. The following passage:  "Cleanse for him *with* a swab of linen" (VIII 11–12), clearly shows that the normal construction of *šk* followed by "swab" is with an *m*, "with," between *šk* and "swab." In these cases *šk* is left without a direct object (cf. also VIII 16). Otherwise it takes a direct object designating the organ or region to be cleansed (V 18); or the impurity which is to be removed (VI 10). In the latter case *šk* means to "clean off," or "clean out." The only surgical occurrences of the word are the five passages above cited.

 *ššm(?)·wy n ḥbś*, "two plugs of linen." This surgical device, a tampon, occurs only in our treatise, and is never written out phonetically. Hence the reading may be a little uncertain ; but the sign in its hieratic form is quite clear and seems to be the well-known  *ššm*. It should be noted that in Case 12 (V 18) the two plugs or swabs employed in cleansing the nostril before insertion of the two tampons are called . See commentary, Case 7, Gloss C, III 18. It designates a device made of linen, and employed in every case for the cleansing of an internal passage: twice of the nostrils (Cases 11 and 12) and once of the ear (Case 22). There is no indication of its form or construction further than the genitive of material, "of linen," which follows it in four out of the five passages in which it occurs. The fact that it could be inserted into the nostrils and left there would indicate that it was probably a small and soft mass or wad. It was also employed for the application of remedies. In our case above (V 11), in which the surgeon first cleanses the nostrils with the two tampons, it is obvious that (as in Case 12) he is then to take two fresh ones which he is to saturate with fat and insert into the nostrils until the swelling is reduced.

 *wdy*, "put" is an important surgical word. It is employed in our treatise with five different meanings, or at least in five different connections :

a. With the preposition  *ḥr*, "upon," in directions to the surgeon for "placing" his hand or fingers in examination or operation, for example in the manipulation of the mandible in the treatment of a wound in the temporal bone in Case 22 (VIII 10). Its force in this connection is suggested by the fact that it is exactly parallel with  *rdy* "put" (literally "give") in the setting of a dislocated mandible in Case 25 :

Case 22 : 

"Place (*wdy*) thy thumb upon his chin" (VIII 10).

Case 25 : 

"Place (*rdy*) thy thumb(s) on the ends of the two rami" (IX 3).

The other passages containing this usage of *wdy* are: I 13 ; III 9–10 ; VI 4 ; VIII 23 ; and XVII 8–9.

b. With the meaning "apply" a bandage or remedy, with or without a preposition. In the case of a remedy, if it is external, the preposition in our treatise is  *r*, "to" (XIV 3 ; XIV 4 ; XVI 12), and once  *ḥr*, "upon" (I 22 where *wdy* is a restoration). In the case of a bandage it is of course an external matter and the preposition is  *ḥr*, "upon." If the remedy is to be absorbed by a "tampon" or "plug" of linen as in our treatment above, and inserted into a passage, *wdy* must be supplemented by a very specific preposition, like *m ẖnw* (V 12), literally "in the inside of." It is interesting to note that in the two similar Cases 11 and 12, one (Case 11) employs *m ẖnw*, " in the inside of," after *wdy*, and the other (Case 12) has *rdy m*, " put into," in place of *m ẖnw*, after *wdy*, thus :

Case 11 : 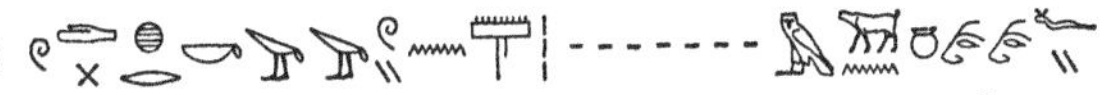

Case 12 : ,, ,, ,, 

" Thou shouldst place two plugs of linen . . . in the inside of (so Case 11, but Case 12, " put into," passive participle modifying " plugs ") his two nostrils."

Similar usage of *m ẖnw* with *wdy* will be found in Case 35 (XII 7) and Case 36 (XII 12–13).

c. To indicate the position of the patient during examination or treatment, accompanied by the words " stretched prone " (XII 4–5 ; XII 10–11 ; XVII 18–19) or " between two supports " (III 15).

d. To indicate the return of a broken or dislocated bone, which is " put (*wdy*) into its place : " of the nose (Case 12, V 18) ; dislocated jaw (Case 25, IX 5) ; dislocated scapula (Case 34, XI 19).

e. In the phrase 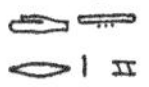 *wdy r t'*, literally " put to land," that is " moor," with the addition " at his mooring stakes," the whole already explained in Gloss D, Case 3 (II 1–2), and especially in the commentary on I 22–23, in the treatment in Case 3. In our passage (V 12) the phrase *r t'*, " to land," is omitted, as also in Cases 19 and 21. It may be noted that two of these cases furnish us the correct reading with  *św*, " him " after *wd-ḥr-k*, " thou shouldst put," which our scribe has incorrectly omitted in Case 11.

 *tḫb*, " swelling," has been treated in Case 4, commentary on II 4.

 *bḏ'·w*, " stiff rolls," is a difficult term to define with exactness. It is a rare and archaic word otherwise found only in the oldest religious texts, where it twice occurs as a "spar" of a ship (Book of the Dead, Naville, 99, 20 Aa and Lacau, *Recueil de trav.* 30, 67, No. 15a). This second passage is a Coffin Text list of parts of a ship, which are identified by the ancient text with the various members of Osiris, or some other divinity. *Bḏ'·w* is identified with the phallus of Osiris, which is so often shown in reliefs during erection. This doubtless indicates the shape of the *bḏ'·w*. We must conclude that it means a post-like roll of linen, of sufficient stiffness to hold the broken nose in its proper or normal position. It is unknown in the medical papyri elsewhere, and besides its use in our Case 11 the surgeon employs it also in Case 12 in the identical manner ; in Case 23 for supporting the slit *auricula* of the ear ; and finally in Case 34 for the support of a dislocated clavicle. It should be noted that even in hieratic the determinative is a narrow, elongated rectangle made with noticeable care. This is doubtless a side view of the roll, seen across its axis.

The word is written in the plural and is resumed by a plural pronoun in the immediately following context, notwithstanding the fact that it is construed with the genitive *n* in the singular. In case 34 the plural is followed by , and in Case 12 we have the dual (*bḏ*ꜣ*·wy*) followed by ; while in Case 23 the writing of both the noun and the genitive is again exactly as in Case 11, with in the singular. These facts raise the question whether we have in Cases 11 and 23 defectively written duals, in which case the pronoun (V 13) would be a plural resuming a dual, just as in IX 4.

*gw*ꜣ is another difficult word. It is as old as the Pyramid Texts where it occurs once in a very obscure passage (Pyr. 709 d). Its one occurrence in the Book of the Dead is very instructive for our text. The passage (*Urk.* V, p. 176, Spruch 99) reads: " I bring to thee this serpent . . . I put him for thee in it (the barque), with his head in thy hand, (and) his tail in my hand," "that we may *gw*ꜣ him between us for ourselves." Here the meaning " pull him out straight " or " straighten him out " would fit the passage and furnish us with exactly the meaning we need for our passage. Other uses of the word must, however, be considered. Construed with the preposition before the object it means to " besiege " (a city, Piankhi Stela, ll. 5, 7, 9, 32, 91). It appears over people drawing in a full net, and explaining their action (Davies, *Deir el-Gebrawi*, I, Pl. IV). It occurs in three passages, unfortunately much too fragmentary to be understood, in the London Medical Papyrus, and it is found once indicating some obscure action of the heart in Pap. Ebers (101, 5). Finally the Coffin Texts employ it twice (*Recueil de trav.* 29, p. 157; and 29, p. 158). In reduplicated form it is also found in the Biography of Ahmose, l. 25 (*Urk.* IV, p. 7). The meaning most probably to be drawn from these passages is something like " hold firmly." Grammatically *gw*ꜣ is probably a passive participle of which "his nose" is the subject in a relative sentence: "held fast by which is his nose." The interpretation of the participle as a purposive gerund is justified by common usage in Egyptian.

The subsequent treatment with grease, honey, and lint has been discussed above, Case 1 (I 3).

The surgeon takes it for granted that the practitioner is acquainted with the method of making and using this device. In Case 12, an injury to the upper part of the nose, and in Case 34, dislocation of the clavicle, these " rolls " are " bound " on. In Case 23, a slit of the outer ear, the " rolls " are used for padding the " back of the auricula," presumably with a bandage to hold everything in place.

GLOSS A

V 14–15

Explaining: Column of his nose

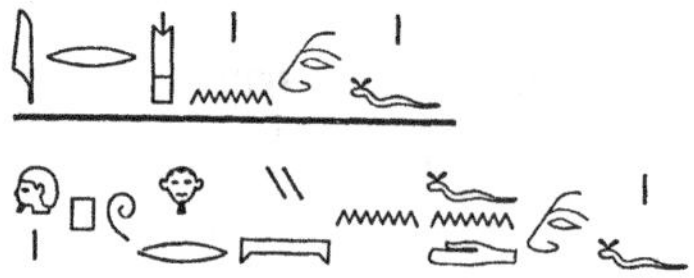

[a] This *ś* was omitted by the scribe in copying and was afterward inserted in the much too narrow space between *mś* and *d*.

Translation

As for: "The column of his nose," it means the outer edge of his nose as far as its side(s) on the top of his nose, being the inside of his nose in the middle of his two nostrils.

Commentary

fnd, "nose," is carefully spelled out by the commentator as *fnd*, and is evidently to be so read throughout our treatise wherever it means the nose as a whole, as distinguished from the nostrils. We find the writing twenty-one times in our treatise as against only two alphabetic spellings. One of the latter, however, is significant. It occurs in V 21 in a quotation from V 16, where, however, the scribe had written . This is a good demonstration that is everywhere to be read *fnd*. The dual found so frequently in our treatise is obviously a word for "nostrils" (*nares*), and is undoubtedly to be read *šr·ty* (see commentary on Case 13, VI 3). Anatomically *fnd* (originally *fnḏ*) means the entire nose, that is at least the *nasus externus*, which includes the *ossa nasalia*, and how far back into the *cavum nasi* our surgeon would have carried its limits is nowhere indicated.

. . . . . *tp* . . . *ḥry* interpreted by itself would be rendered "the upper head." *Tp* is used anatomically to designate the "heads," "tips," or "ends" of various bones (see commentary on in Case 1, p. 85), and this might lead us to conclude that our gloss intends to designate the *radix nasi* and the upper end of the *ossa nasalia*. Gloss A in Case 12, however, quite precisely defines the *šty·t* of the nose as "the middle of the nose, as far as the back, extending to the region between the eyebrows" (V 21). This is surely the *ossa nasalia*, leaving us only the lower and outer part of the nose as the part concerned in Case 11. These considerations lead us to conclude that *tp* . . . *ḥry*, if rendered the "upper tip" or "upper head" must refer exclusively to the soft or cartilaginous tissues of the flexible outer nose, where it articulates with the *ossa nasalia*.

should evidently be read *gś·wy-fy*, "its two sides." The scribe has certainly omitted the under , for the following context leaves no doubt that the two sides of the nose are included. "The two sides on the top of his nose" must designate the two lateral *cartilagines*. To these soft tissues of the nose the explanation now adds also the soft central portion of the interior, the *septum*.

m ḫnw fnd-f, "being the inside of his nose." With these words the commentator passes from his indication of the *external* limits of the " column of the nose " to define its *internal* situation and limits. It should be noted that *m ẖnw* might of course be understood here as the common preposition " in the inside of," without seriously altering the sense : but the interpretation of *m* as meaning " being," or " even," a very common use of it, makes the discussion much more clear.

 *ḥry-yb mśd·ty-fy,* " the middle of his two nostrils," is not clear without defining the meaning of *mśd·ty* " the two nostrils " beyond cavil. The word is rare, and sufficiently unfamiliar, even to the ancient reader, to require definition in the next gloss, q.v. The word *ḥry-yb,* " middle " is used anatomically by our treatise to indicate the " middle region," like the " middle of the crown " (of the head, IV 1) or the " middle of the palm " (IV 8) ; or a middle member of some kind like the " middle of the nose " (V 21) in the next case ; or, as an adjective, the " middle " vertebra of the neck (X 16). The last example resembles the use of the word in our passage, except that, having no single word for the body of tissue which he is here discussing (like " vertebra "), the surgeon simply calls it the " middle." Indeed the *m* here, in *m ḥry-yb,* might be considered as meaning, " even," "being," or "to wit,' giving us the rendering " being the middle," as in *m ẖnw* just discussed above. The tissue intended is of course the *septum nasi,* the wall between the two nostrils (*nares*).

Our ancient commentator does not define any of the tissue he is discussing as bone or cartilage, but it is highly probable that he is exclusively describing what a layman might call the soft nose, that is, all of the external nose except the *ossa nasalia.* If this conclusion is correct, then the " break " which Case 11 treats is a rupture between the nasal bones and the cartilage which impinges upon them—a very common type of broken nose at the present day. In that case the Egyptian surgeon intended only the cartilaginous portions of the nose to be designated by the term " column of the nose." Nevertheless, like our colloquial term " bridge of the nose," the designation " column of the nose " may have been sufficiently loose in its application to include enough of the nasal bone to enable the surgeon to speak of the injury as a " break *in* the column of the nose."

GLOSS B

V 15

Explaining : His two nostrils

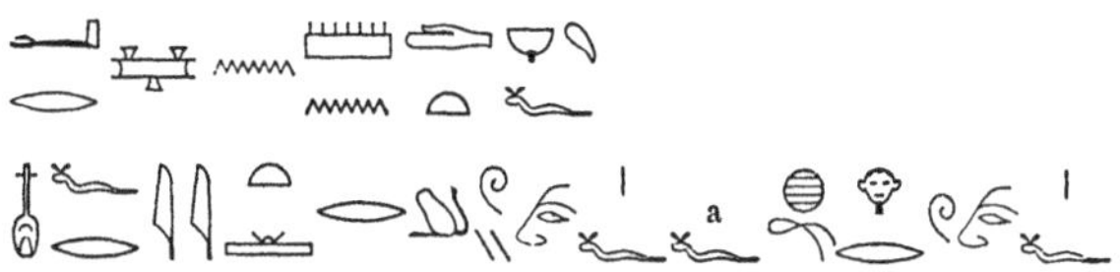

[a] This *f* is placed low in the line and there are above it and below it traces of erasures. As Smith himself noticed (Vol. II, p. ix, 2nd col.), the scribe originally wrote  and corrected it to *fḫ*. See commentary.

Translation

As for: " His two nostrils," [it means] the two sides of his nose extending to his [two] cheek[s], as far as the back of his nose; the top of his nose is loosened.

Commentary

 *mnd·t*[*y*]-*f*[*y*], " his two cheeks " should obviously be in the dual, as is shown by the dual of *ḏr·wy,* " the two sides." It is a word which has been little understood. In the first place it has been frequently confused with the common word  *mnḏ,* " breast " (*mamma*). It has also been confused with the eye, or some part of the eye; for it appears in lists of members of the body associated with the eyes, Book of the Dead, (Budge, 172, from Nebseni 32–33, 15 and 18). In the common phrase *ś-ḥb mnd·ty,* "to make festive (meaning "to paint") the two *mnd·t*" (Hymn to Amon 11, 2 and also of other divinities), it is obvious the reference must be to painting the eyes or the region of the eyes. It must be recalled, however, that eye-paint extends down upon the cheeks. The general situation of the *mnd·t* is indicated by the position it occupies in the list of cases in our treatise, which takes up injuries to the head in the following order: calvaria, forehead, eyebrows, nose, nostrils, *mnd·t* (three cases: 15, 16, and 17), temporal region, ear, mandible, lips, and chin. The *mnd·t,* therefore, is taken up between the nose and nostrils on the one hand, and the temporal region and ear on the other. In the transition from the nose and nostrils to the temporal region and the ear, we of course pass over the cheek, the *maxilla* and *zygoma*; and this is certainly the meaning of *mnd·t*. Moreover the injuries of the *mnd·t* (Cases 15, 16 and 17) are such as could not possibly occur to the eye or the nostril, both of which meanings have been wrongly assigned to *mnd·t*. These injuries are a " perforation " (*thm*), a " split " (*pšn*), and a " smash " (*śd*). The first two are never found in our treatise in anything but bone. While we may render *mnd·t* therefore " cheek," we must understand that it may also mean the *maxilla* and the adjoining portion of the *zygoma* as far back as the temporal bone. This accords with the passage in the Coffin Texts; " Re rises in the east of the sky, he shines thence 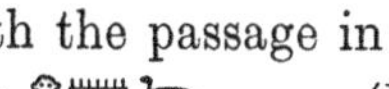 (*ḥr mnḏ·ty-ṯ*) upon thy two cheeks," meaning " thy face " (*Recueil de trav.* 27, p. 232). This must be the word which occurs in the singular as far back as the Old Kingdom in the mastabas, e. g.,  (Tomb of Mereruka A 3, East wall). See also *Mutter und Kind,* III 9.

fḫ, the well-known word "to loosen," is a scribal correction. There is evidently a statement here that it is the top of the nose which is broken, or *fḫ* "loosened;" and the traces of the erased signs support Smith's conclusion that the scribe originally wrote *wnḫ*, "dislocate," although this would of course be incorrect, for our surgeon carefully distinguishes between *ḥśb*, "break," and *wnḫ*, "dislocate."

We are now in a position to understand the ancient commentator's explanation of *mśd·ty*, "the two nostrils." The "two sides of his nose" may be understood as including the *alae nasi*, the cartilaginous wings of the nose, together with the adjoining lateral cartilage above. The remainder of the explanation would seem to indicate the other tissue surrounding and forming the *nares*, the limit on either side being the cheeks. These indications correspond with those which may be drawn from the scanty sources elsewhere. In Pap. Ebers (99, 5–6) the list of canals or vessels includes four in the *mśd·ty*, the "two *mśd·t*," two of which conduct an exudation and two blood. The exudation *nśw·t* is obviously the secretions of the nose. At Edfu the air and again the incense enters the (*mśd·t*) "nostrils" of the god (Rochem, *Edfou*, I, 569 and 571). See also Book of Breathings (British Mus. Pap. 9995, II 1 in Budge, *Book of the Dead*, Vol. III, p. 136). Finally it should be noted that our word seems to have nothing to do with "leg," or "thigh" or the like used both of men and of cattle in food lists, unless we consider the possibility that the *alae nasi* were conceivably regarded as the "thighs" of the nose.

CASE TWELVE

V 16–VI 3

A BREAK IN THE NASAL BONE

This injury, while confined to the external bone, is certainly higher up than the preceding case, and in contrast with it quite certainly affects the bone. Thus these two cases of nose injuries are arranged like the wounds of the head in our treatise, which discussed first the injuries which were confined to overlying fleshy tissue without affecting the bones, and thereafter proceeded to fractures and similar injuries of the bones themselves. The case is interesting in that it is the first one we have met which involves setting the bone. The term for "set" is literally "cause to fall," followed by the words "so that it is placed in its position," or, more freely, "lying in its place." Not until after the nose is set does the surgeon cleanse the nostrils of the coagulated blood, called "every worm of blood." After the insertion into the nostrils of tampons of linen saturated with grease, this internal packing is externally reinforced by two stiff splint-like rolls, literally "posts" or "spars" of linen, probably laid one on each side, and "bound on." The three glosses are very instructive, especially the quietly rational explanation of "every worm of blood" as the coagulated blood "likened to a worm which subsists in the water."

TITLE

V 16

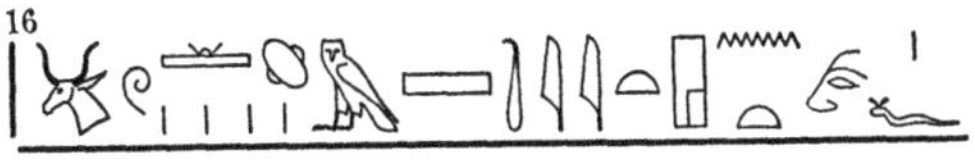

Translation

Instructions concerning a break in the chamber of his nose.

Commentary

As we shall see in the course of the treatment (V 17–20), our surgeon means the nasal bone by his curious designation " chamber."

EXAMINATION

V 16–17

Translation

If thou examinest a man having a break in the chamber of his nose, (and) thou findest his nose bent, while his face is disfigured, (and) the swelling which is over it is protruding, (conclusion in diagnosis).

Commentary

The terms are all discussed in the glosses, except the last remark, which has been explained in the commentary on Case 4, examination, II 3–5 (pp. 144–147).

DIAGNOSIS

V 17

Translation

Thou shouldst say concerning him : " One having a break in the chamber of his nose. An ailment which I will treat."

Commentary

The terms will be found discussed in the treatment and in Gloss A. The diagnosis is again a mere memorandum of a cue-word or two, as in the two preceding cases, to which the favourable verdict 1 is appended. See commentary in Case 1 (I 2) and discussion in the introduction (pp. 46 ff. and 73).

TREATMENT

V 17–20

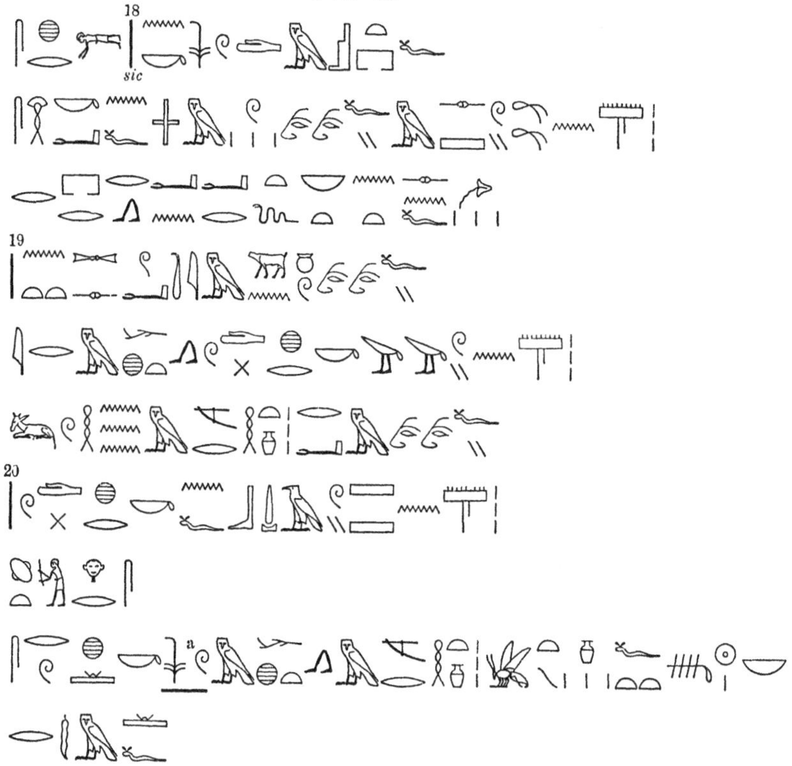

[a] This word was omitted by the scribe, but the omission was discovered and the word subsequently inserted in the space over *k*, in red ink.

Translation

Thou shouldst force it to fall in, so that it is lying in its place, (and) clean out for him the interior of both his nostrils with two swabs of linen until every worm of blood which coagulates in the inside of his two nostrils comes forth. Now afterward thou shouldst place two plugs of linen saturated with grease and put into his two nostrils. Thou shouldst place for him two stiff rolls of linen, bound on. Thou shouldst treat him afterward with grease, honey, (and) lint every day until he recovers.

Commentary

The surgeon is charged to set the fracture as the first step in the treatment. It is quite clear that he is dealing with a dislodged portion of bone which must be forced back into position. As the region where the break has occurred extends, according to Gloss A, as far up as the area between the eyebrows, it is obvious that the break is either in the nasal bone, or has ruptured the suture between the *os nasale* and the frontal bone. In view of this description of the setting of the fracture, we cannot doubt that the " chamber " (*šty·t*) of the nose is the nasal bone. See discussion of Gloss A.

ymyw, " interior," which occurs in only one other passage in our papyrus, will be found discussed in Case 22 (VIII 11).

sš·wy, " two swabs." The corresponding passage in Case 11 has . It might at first be concluded that the text in Case 12 should be accepted as the correct reading and that we should understand Case 12 as furnishing the alphabetic writing of . It should be recalled, however, that the word *sš* properly means " splint " and that there is no word *sš*, " swab," outside of Case 12, unless we except the incorrect *šwš* of Case 14. See full discussion in Case 7, Gloss C, III 18.

ʿnʿr·t, " worm," see Gloss C.

ṯs, " coagulate," is a derived meaning. The common meaning of the word is " to tie," " to knot." It is used physiologically to designate the growing together of the fontanel on the crown of an infant's head in Case 8 (IV 11), and its use in our case quite appropriately suggests the knotting together, as it were, of stringy coagulations, looking like worms.

šsm(?)·wy, " two swabs." See Case 11 (V 11–12) and Case 7, Gloss C (III 18).

bḏ'·wy, " two stiff rolls," see discussion in Case 11, V 13.

The final treatment with grease, honey, and lint has been discussed in Case 1, I 3.

GLOSS A

V 20–21

Explaining : Break in the chamber of his nose

Translation

As for: "A break in the chamber of his nose," it means the middle of his nose as far as the back, extending to the region between his two eyebrows.

Commentary

šty·t, "chamber." This is the word really explained in the gloss, which does not take up the word "break" at all. Throughout the literature of ancient Egypt *šty·t* is a religious word, and its appearance in our case is certainly its only medical or surgical use, if not its sole occurrence in a secular document. It is commonly employed to designate any sacred chamber. Hence we find it applied to the tomb (Pap. Boulaq 10, verso, 5, 10, 10–11, 13), or even to the world of the dead, as in the Book of the Gates; but it was especially a general term for any sacred room, chamber, or building. Thus the room for the mourning women at Dendera and at Edfu is called *šty·t*. Likewise the crypts in the temple of Dendera are so called, and similarly an outlying chapel by the temple of Ombos. It is incessantly applied to the dwellings of the gods, especially to that of Sokar, or of the mortuary gods like Osiris and Anubis, but also of Ptah. In the papyri of the Nineteenth and Twentieth Dynasties it is commonly written *št'y·t*, and was evidently connected by the scribes of that age with the word *št'*, "to be secret, inaccessible." It appeared, however, in the form *šṯ·t* as early as the Old Kingdom, and the *t* was certainly originally *ṯ*. Hence the connection with *št'*, "to be secret, inaccessible," which had *t*, is doubtful. Our surgeon writes the word in every case with the determinative of a house, and must be comparing the upper bony portion of the nose with a building, just as he designated the rest of it a "column." That he had any esoteric suggestion in mind is highly improbable. The less accessible portion of the external nose, the remotest from the entrance to the *nares*, suggests to the surgeon the barred and less accessible chamber of a sanctuary or temple. The term "chamber" at once raises the question whether the surgeon was not thinking of the frontal *sinus*, especially in view of the extension of the *šty·t* to "the region between his eyebrows." The instructions given the physician for setting the broken *šty·t*, however, show quite clearly that it was a bone which might be forced from its normal position, to which the surgeon must restore it, and if so it is difficult to see how it could include the chamber of the frontal *sinus*. See commentary on treatment (V 17–18).

pḥ·wy, "the back" or "end," has anatomical meanings which are not always clear in the case of a short organ like the nose. It is used repeatedly to designate the "end" of the ramus (Case 7, III 17; Case 22, VIII 10; VIII 14 twice; Case 25, IX 3), which is said to be the "end" (*pḥ·wy*) of the mandible. Three times it means the "end" of the mandible (*wgw·t*, Case 7, III 17; III 18; Case 18, VII 14; and *ʿr·t*, Case 22, VIII 14), and once it is used of the end of the phallus (Case 31, X 20).

We have already had the *pḥ·wy* of the nose in Case 11 (V 15), and in our Gloss A, although not followed by the words " of his nose " (as in V 15), *pḥ·wy* obviously designates a part of the nose. In these two passages where it refers to the nose, it can hardly refer to the outer end of the nose in Case 11, and certainly does not do so in Case 12. It seems required then to render the word in accordance with its original meaning " back," literally " buttocks." This rendering would indicate that the *pḥ·wy* of the nose extends at least somewhat toward the interior. It is conceivable, however, that the surgeon is thinking of an " end " of the nose toward the frontal bone, at the point where the nose does actually come to an end and the frontal bone begins. This view becomes more plausible if the phrase " extending etc." is regarded as modifying *pḥ·wy*, with some such meaning as " the end that extends to the middle of the eyebrows." There is nothing in the grammar to exclude this rendering. See the discussion of  *ᶜr*, " extend," " penetrate," etc. in Case 1, pp. 87–88.

GLOSS B

V 21–VI 1

Explaining: His nose bent, while his face is disfigured

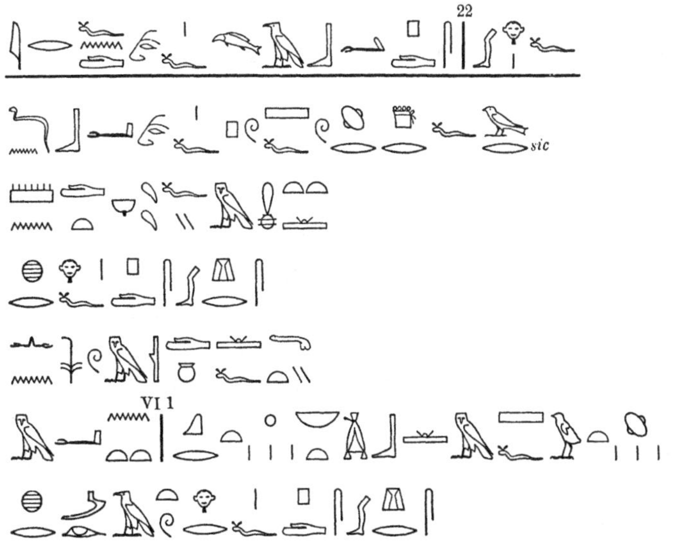

Translation

As for: "His nose bent, while his face is disfigured," it means his nose is crooked and greatly swollen throughout; his two cheeks likewise, so that his face is disfigured by it, not being in its customary form, because all the depressions are clothed with swellings, so that his face looks disfigured by it.

Commentary

ẖ'b, "bent." There is no such verb known outside of our treatise, but its meaning is determinable. The bent spiral wire on the crown of Lower Egypt is called *ẖ'b·t,* as is well known. There is a designation of a sickle with bent blade likewise *ẖ'b.* Cf. also *ẖ'bb* with determinative of two sickles in the Eloquent Peasant, 107 ; and *ḥb* with a bent arm in Pyr. 1041 d, which may be added to Sethe's discussion in *Zeitschrift,* 57 (1922), p. 17. Besides the above evidence we have now the indications of the gloss, which explains *ẖ'b* by the word *ḏnb,* "crooked." The few known examples of this word are fortunately sufficient to determine its meaning. A dwarf with feet turned inward is called *ḏnb* (Newberry, *Beni Hasan,* Vol. II, pl. XVI). Another with crooked feet has the same inscription (*ibid.,* pl. XXXII). On a Middle Kingdom stela in Leyden (V 89, Boeser, *Beschreibung der Aegyptischen Sammlung,* Vol. II, pl. XXVII) a man is named "crooked Kheti," that is , *ẖty ḏnb.* With these examples may be compared the Middle Kingdom passage : "who follows in the way without deflecting (*ḏnb,* British Mus. Stela No. 572, l. 13 in *Hieroglyphic Texts from Egyptian Stelae,* pt. II, pl. 22).

mnd·ty-fy, "his two cheeks." *Mnd·ty* has been discussed in Case 11, Gloss B, V 15.

pdś, "disfigured," is of course one of the well-known examples of a word built up by adding *ś* to the root, here the word *pd,* "foot." It means originally to "trample," "lay waste," especially of fields or landscape, as in Uni's wasting of the fields of the Asiatics (*Urk.* I, p. 103, l. 23). Cf. also the obscure incantation in Ebers 30, 7, in which *pdś* indicates the destruction of a city. With reference to the face or head the only other known passage describes a lion as *pdś tp,* "with head bruised" or "disfigured," Book of the Dead (Naville, 17, 100 and 106–107). This is exactly parallel with our *pdś ḥr-f,* "his face is disfigured." The writing = "his face" (instead of) is also found in III 20.

m ḳd-f mty, "in its customary form." In this phrase *m* is really equivalent to "possess" ("be *in* possession of"), to "have." See the bull "in" a certain color (Pap. D'Orbigny, XIV, 5), meaning that he "had" such and such a color.

ḳr·wt, "depressions," literally "holes," is a word otherwise entirely unknown. There can be no doubt, however, that it is a form related to the familiar word *ḳrr·t,* "hole."

ẖr can hardly be rendered otherwise than above ; but it is not the customary meaning. In the above two passages its syntax seems to be related to that of the *ẖr*-form in clauses of result, e. g., above, Case 7 (III 7–8).

GLOSS C

VI 1–3

Explaining: Every worm of blood which coagulates in the inside of his two nostrils

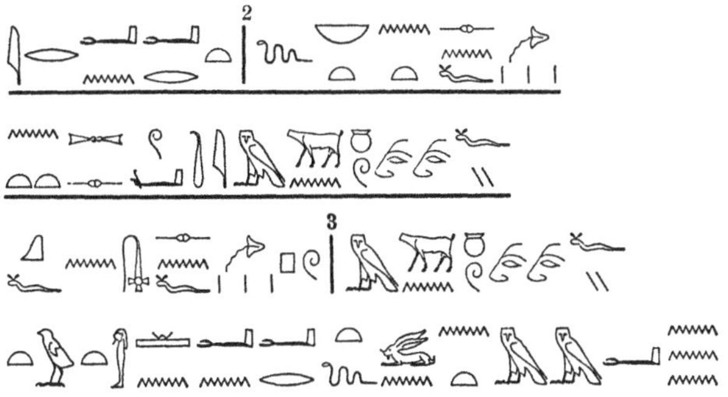

Translation

As for: "Every worm of blood which coagulates in the inside of his two nostrils," it means the clotting of blood in the inside of his two nostrils, likened to the ʿnʿr·t-worm, which subsists in the water.

Commentary

 *ḳfn*, "clotting," is doubtless some word for "thickening," but elsewhere usually meaning "to bake." Its meaning here can hardly be questioned. See also Kahun Papyri (7, 29), where it is once likewise connected with blood.

 *twt*, "likened," is more than the mere preposition *mj*, "like." See the same use in Case 45, XV 18; and the causative *ś-twt* in Case 7, IV 2.

 *ʿnʿr·t* is an unknown worm occurring elsewhere than in our treatise only once, as an ingredient of a prescription for exterminating the hair of a rival beauty, called the "hated one" (Pap. Ebers, 67, 3–4). It is evidently some slender and slimy worm thought to resemble the fibrous, stringy formations in coagulated blood. Some one familiar with the life in the pools of the Nile inundation might be able to identify it.

 *wnn·t*, "which subsists," is an interesting example of the verb *wnn* in its ancient meaning, that is, indicating far more than merely "to be," the meaning to which it finally weakened. Our example may be compared with the admonition in the Proverbs of Ptahhotep to cherish a wife as long as thou "livest" (*wnn·t-k*, Pap. Prisse, 10, 10).

CASE THIRTEEN

VI 3–7

COMPOUND COMMINUTED FRACTURE IN THE SIDE OF THE NOSE

In Cases 11 and 12 the injured part is " the middle of his nose " (Case 11, V 14–15 ; Case 12, V 21). Case 13 is followed by a case of injury affecting only *one* nostril (Case 14) and Case 15 shifts completely over to one cheek. In the diagnosis of Case 13 the injury is said to be " in his nostril ; " he bleeds from only one nostril and one ear ; and the bleeding is distinctly stated, in this connection (VI 5), to be " on the side of him having this smash." The injury is sufficiently far over on one side to affect the ear, and we must conclude from all these facts that the use of " nose " (*fnd*) in the title and its first occurrence in the examination (twice in all), is unquestionably in both cases an error for " nostril " (*šr·t*). While we render the Egyptian word *šr·t* as " nostril," it is obvious from such a case as this that it means far more than the orifice. It includes also the surrounding tissue extending far enough laterally to include some of the bony tissue on each side of the nose, the uppermost part of the maxilla, known as the " frontal process," which rises almost as high as the root or top of the *os nasale.* Along the sides of the latter this frontal process of the maxilla adjoining the nasal bone might very easily be included by our surgeon in his notion of the structure of the nose. This may explain why the injury in our case is regarded as hopeless, and the surgeon prescribes no treatment. The fracture has burst through into the *cavum nasi*, so that the surface over it yields or " breaks through " like an opening door, under the fingers of the surgeon, and he records the unfavorable verdict without suggesting any treatment. The injury must be very much like the compound comminuted fracture (*šd*) of the maxilla and zygoma in Case 17, to which the surgeon also appends the unfavorable verdict 3 (VII 5), although he does follow it with suggestions of rest and simple remedies in hope of possible survival.

TITLE

VI 3

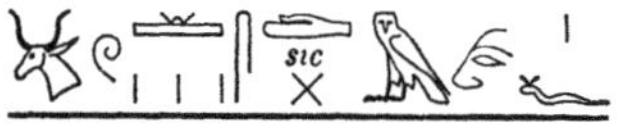

Translation

Instructions concerning a smash in his nostril.

Commentary

On the surgical meaning of " smash " (*šd*) as a compound comminuted fracture, see commentary on Case 5 (II 11).

šr·t-f, " his nostril." The demonstration that we are to read *šr·t*, " nostril," and not *fnd*, " nose," as written ( ) by the scribe, has already been given in the introduction to this case. It occurs four times in this case, and in only two out of the four has the scribe written the word correctly (VI 5 and 6). It is instructive to compare the next case (14), where the same word occurs five times, each time written correctly. This abbreviated writing is found outside our document only from the Eighteenth Dynasty on; hence its earliest appearance is here in this case. In all earlier texts the word is written alphabetically *šr·t*. Its anatomical meaning has been unavoidably touched upon in the introduction to this case. It should be further noted that the word is distinguished from *fnd*, " nose " in such passages as the following:

" The sweet North Wind for thy nose (*fnd*), the wind for thy nostril (*šr·t*)." (Tomb of Rekhmire, *Urk.* IV, p. 1166, l. 1; cf. Petrie, *Medum*, pl. XXIV; Book of the Dead, Naville, 172, 14 and 46). Nevertheless it is commonly used in the singular for " nose;" e.g., in the well-known list of parts of the body in Pap. Ebers 103, 17 (=Pap. Berlin 3038, 16, 4); but it should be noted that in this list all other double parts of the body are also in the singular, as also in Pap. Berlin 3038, 16, 2; and *Mutter und Kind* III 9. Very important for the anatomical meaning of the word is the phrase " the two sides of his nose " (Pap. Leyden 343, verso 5, 4–5, in Gardiner's copy for the *Wörterbuch*). It is quite clear here that the singular of the word must indicate the nose, while the meaning " nostrils " is equally evident for the dual in such a passage as " Give me this sweet breath that is in thy two nostrils " (Book of the Dead, Naville, 56, 3 Aa). We must conclude, therefore, that in the twelve passages in our papyrus stating that as a result of an injury in the head the patient is discharging blood , " from his two nostrils," we are to read *šr·ty*. There are seven more examples of the writing which we are to read *šr·ty* in Papyrus Smith, which furnish the best evidence on this point. They are as follows: Case 11 (V 12), Case 12 (V 18, 19 bis, VI 2, and VI 3), and Case 22 (VIII 11). To sum up: *šr·t* is used for " nose," or for " nostril," and anatomically, especially as shown by Pap. Smith, e.g., Case 14, it includes the tissue surrounding the nostril and adjacent to it as already shown in the introduction to Case 13.

This word *šr·t* is a good example of the difficulties experienced by our surgeon due to the complete lack of technically precise terms for designating organs and parts of the body. He is here, as quite commonly elsewhere, obliged to take over into his scientific workshop a term which formerly served only as a loose popular designation such as the modern surgeon has displaced by exact terms created by adaptation of Latin.

EXAMINATION

VI 4–6

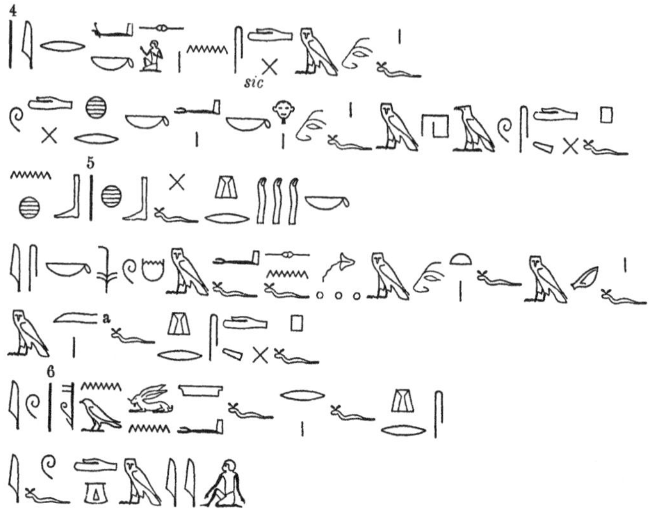

[a] The text has [hieroglyph], but the parallels elsewhere show clearly that the correct reading is [hieroglyph] as given above. See commentary below.

Translation

If thou examinest a man having a smash in his nostril, thou shouldst place thy hand upon his nose at the point of this smash. Should it crepitate under thy fingers, while at the same time he discharges blood from his nostril (and) from his ear, on the side of him having that smash; it is painful when he opens his mouth because of it; (and) he is speechless, (conclusion in diagnosis).

Commentary

 *šd m šr·t-f.* That we are to read *šr·t*, " nostril," in this phrase, and not *fnd*, " nose," has been demonstrated in the introduction to this case.

 *ḥr fnd-f*, " upon his nose," on the other hand, is not to be altered to *ḥr šr·t-f*; for the phrase which follows it, *m h'w šd pf*, " at the point of that smash," would in that case be superfluous. It is probably the correct use of the word *fnd*, " nose," in this passage which has misled the scribe to write " nose " twice incorrectly in the preceding context, that is, title and beginning of examination.

 *nḫbḫb*, " break through " or " crepitate." This rare word is not found in any of the medical documents outside of our treatise. It is an archaic word found otherwise only in religious texts of great age: three times in the Pyramid Texts and once at Abydos. It appears in the Pyramid Texts parallel with the word *wn*, " open," with reference to *bolts* (Pyr. 194 a), to *doors* (Pyr. 1361b), and to a *coffin* (Pyr. 2009 a).

At Abydos it is said of doors (Mariette, *Abydos*, I, 40 a, 11). It should be noted that the Pyramid passage applying *nẖbẖb* to the coffin has been restored with his customary sagacity by Sethe; and one cannot doubt the correctness of the restoration. This passage indicates that the word means somewhat more than "open," and suggests the idea of violent opening. It probably means something like "break open." In our papyrus we find it employed five times as a technical surgical term, applied in each case to a fracture and indicating some kind of movement of the fracture under the surgeon's fingers. The cases are as follows:

Case 13, a compound comminuted fracture at one side of the nose. "It *nẖbẖb* under thy fingers" (VI 4–5).

Case 17, a compound comminuted fracture in the maxilla. "It *nẖbẖb* under thy fingers" (VII 2).

Case 24, a break in the mandible. "It *nẖbẖb* under thy fingers" (VIII 23).

Case 37, a break in the arm. "It *nẖbẖb* under thy fingers" (XII 16).

Case 44, a "break in the ribs of his sternum." "They *nẖbẖb* under thy fingers" (XV 7–8).

With the above material before him the modern surgeon is better able to determine the meaning of *nẖbẖb* than the orientalist, and Dr. Luckhardt, after examination of the above evidence, confirms my conjecture, that it means "crepitate."

yśk św ḥm dy-f snf, "while at the same time he discharges blood." A first glance at this passage might lead one to conclude that we have here an unusual verb *ḥm-f*, "he discharges," as if it were a surgical specialization of the verb or , "to repel, turn back," or the like. The same text occurs again in Case 17 (VII 3). Nevertheless it would be an error to accept this verb. We have here undoubtedly the particle *ḥm*, written without determinative as frequently. The after it is not a determinative, but must be read , giving us the customary statement *dy-f snf*, "he discharges blood," as in the duplicate passage (VII 2–3) cited below (see also VIII 7). I am unable to cite another example of *yśk św ḥm* followed by a verb in the *śḏm-f* form, but essentially the same construction with *ḥm* is found in the Sinuhe passage: (Sinuhe R 15), which Gardiner renders "Even now he was returning" (see his *Notes on the Story of Sinuhe*, p. 168), the force of the *ty św ḥm* being very well brought out by "Even now," as I have tried to render our *yśk św ḥm* by "while at the same time." See also the following paragraph.

(corrected from), *m gś-f*, "on the side of him." The evidence for this correction is as follows. The phrase: *m gś-f ẖry śḳr pf*, "on the side of him having that injury," occurs six times in our treatise (twice with the variant *yh pn*, IV 15–16, for *śḳr pf*). Indeed one of these six passages is very similar to our passage in VI 5 (except for the omission of the particle *ḥm* and the parallel term *śḳr* " injury," in place of our *śd* " smash "). It reads :

(VII 2–3) and contains , where our text has . The source of the error is moreover evident. The combination occurs in the next line and without doubt the scribe's eye fell upon it in the original from which he was copying.

dgm-y, " he is speechless," is explained by our ancient author himself in Case 22, Gloss C.

Diagnosis

VI 6–7

Translation

Thou shouldst say concerning him : " One having a smash in his nostril. An ailment not to be treated."

Commentary

As in the preceding three cases we have the diagnosis again reduced to a mere catchword, probably serving only as a memorandum, or possibly a student's note, to which the essential item, verdict 3, has been appended. See commentary on Case 5 (II 15) and discussion in the Introduction (pp. 46–48 and 73). The injury is so serious that it is regarded as fatal and no treatment is added.

CASE FOURTEEN

VI 7–14

FLESH WOUND IN ONE SIDE OF THE NOSE PENETRATING TO THE NOSTRIL

As an examination of the introduction to Case 13 will show, Case 14 is the last of the cases discussing injuries to the nose. Like Case 13 it carries the place of the injury toward one side, that is away from the middle of the nose (Cases 11 and 12), so that in Case 15 we leave the nose entirely and deal with the maxillary region.

TITLE

VI 7

Translation

Instructions concerning a wound in his nostril.

EXAMINATION

VI 7–9

Translation

If thou examinest a man having a wound in his nostril, piercing through, shouldst thou find the two lips of that wound separated from each other, thou shouldst draw together for him that wound with stitching.

Commentary

This examination makes it clear that we are dealing with an injury which affects only the soft tissue. It has pierced from the outside into the interior of the nostril, a condition indicated by the rare word *yšdb,* which is explained by the surgeon in a gloss (VI 13–14). See Gloss A at end of case. The inclusion of the stitching in the examination is our surgeon's usual custom; see commentary on Case 10, V 6. Dr. Luckhardt remarks: "Again a good indication in favor of stitching, since such a wound is likely to lead to a retraction of the wound edges, because of severance of the underlying cutaneous muscles."

š'^t, "separated," is again a new word. It occurs four times in our papyrus, once with the determinative as above, twice with (XII 4; XII 10), and once followed by corrupt text which contains (XVI 18–19). It always occurs as predicate of a noun following *gmy* "find," and is obviously a form of the pseudo-participle. It has nothing to do with the noun *š'^t,* "filth," which appears from the Empire on, especially in the rituals. It may be identical with the verb *š'^t,* "to damage" or the like, which is found from the Book of the Dead onward, e.g., Naville, 125, Introduction, 9–10; 125, 42; 17, 80. It is always construed in our document with the preposition, a construction which I have not been able to find elsewhere. This may be due to its specialized surgical meaning, for it does not occur in any of the other medical papyri. The translation suggested above is based largely on our passage in Case 14, which states that " the two lips of that wound are *šʼt* from each other," whereupon the surgeon is charged to " draw together that wound with stitching." The implication is certainly strongly in favor of the meaning " separated " for *šʼt*. There is a similar implication in Case 47 regarding the gaping gash which is stated to be *šʼt*, and must then be drawn together with stitching (XVI 18–20). In Case 36, a broken arm, the surgeon finds the arm " hanging down and *šʼt-y* from its fellow " (XII 9–10). A similar statement is made in Case 35 in which the surgeon finds a broken clavicle " short and *šʼt* from its fellow " (XII 3–4). If " fellow " means the other arm and the other clavicle respectively in these last two cases, *šʼt* cannot of course mean " separated." But " fellow " in these two passages probably refers to the other piece of bone which has been separated by the fracture, and such an interpretation will permit us to render " separated " in all the cases employing *šʼt*.

šny, " each other," is a dual of the pronoun *šn*, " they, their," and literally means " they (or them) both." It is found also referring to two bandages in Case 35 (XII 7, corrupt) and Case 36 (XII 13, bis), where we have mention of " one of them both " (, slight correction) and " the other of them both " (). It is well known that this dual form of the pronoun disappeared at an early date, giving place to the plural form which supplanted it. Its appearance in our treatise is another evidence of its great age.

ydr, " stitching." See commentary on Case 10, V 6, pp. 227–231.

DIAGNOSIS

VI 9

Translation

Thou shouldst say concerning him : " One having a wound in his nostril, piercing through. An ailment which I will treat."

Commentary

The diagnosis is again merely a catchword as so often in the preceding cases. The commentary on " wound " will be found in Case 1, lost introductory column (pp. 82–84). On " nostril " see Case 13, VI 3.

yšdb, " piercing through " will be found discussed in Gloss A of this case.

On the concluding verdict 1, see commentary in Case 1 (I 2) and consult also the introduction (pp. 46 ff.).

Treatment

VI 9–12

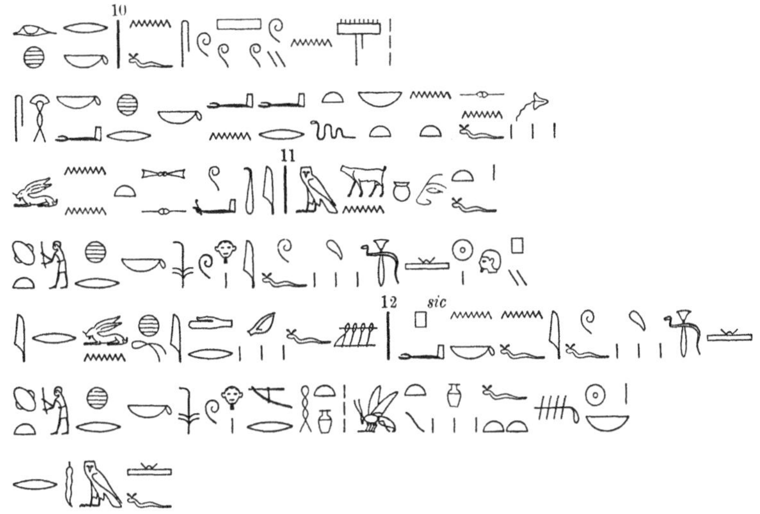

Translation

Thou shouldst make for him two swabs of linen, (and) thou shouldst clean out every worm of blood which has coagulated in the inside of his nostril. Thou shouldst bind it with fresh meat the first day. When its stitching loosens, thou shouldst take off for him the fresh meat, (and) thou shouldst bind it with grease, honey (and) lint every day until he recovers.

Commentary

šwš·wy is without doubt a scribal error for " two swabs." See the discussion of the parallel in Case 12 (V 18), and especially the full treatment in Case 7, Gloss C (III 18).

The interesting term " every worm of blood " has been treated in Case 12, Gloss C (VI 1–3), and the use of *ṯs*, literally " to knot," with the meaning " coagulate," is taken up in Case 12 (V 19).

On the use of " fresh meat " see Case 1 (I 2–3).

wnḫ, " loosens," is fully discussed in Case 10, V 6 under *ydr*. The query arises whether *wnḫ* in our passage may not refer to the expected and harmless absorption and loosening of gut stitching, for the reason that it is not followed by any further efforts to draw together the gash such as are made in Cases 10, 23, and 47. But such absorption could not occur within a day. See the discussion in Case 10.

is doubtless to be read *ydr* as elsewhere, not *yd·t*. See full discussion of the word, including our passage, in Case 10 (V 6).

is probably to be read *šsp-yn-k*, as a prescriptive form, but the dative after the imperative, especially with *šsp*, is of course common.

On the use of " grease, honey, and lint " see Case 1 (I 2–3).

Gloss A

VI 12–14

Explaining: A wound in his nostril piercing through

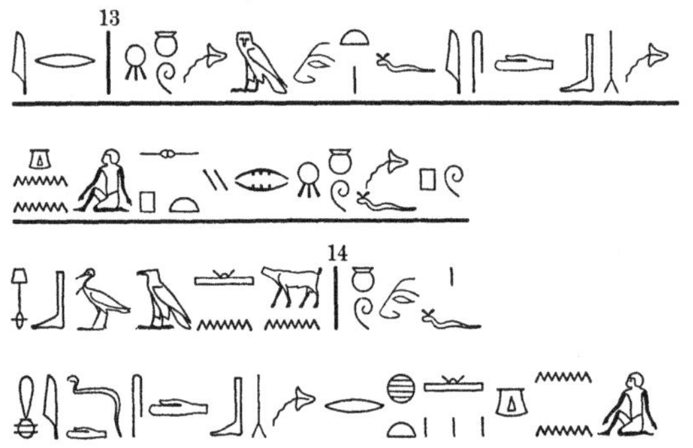

Translation

As for: " A wound in his nostril, piercing through," it means that the two lips of his wound are soft, opening to the inside of his nose, as one says: " Pierced through " concerning soft things.

Commentary

This explanation is curiously enough repeated in another case, Gloss A, Case 26, which contains some interesting variants noted below. The word which the commentator is specifically explaining is

yśdb, " piercing through." The explanation is not particularly successful in making clear the meaning of *yśdb*. Besides the four occurrences of the word in Case 14, it is further found nine times in our treatise, four of which are in Case 26. These passages are really more valuable in determining the meaning of the word than any other source, for the word is unknown outside of our document.[1] In Case 26,

[1] It is evidently not related to the well-known *śdb* of the Book of the Dead, which appears as in the Pyramid Texts (1340b, etc.) and means " damage " or the like. Nor has it any discernible connection with regularly occurring in the Pyramid Texts in parallelism with *ʿnḫ*, "life" (Pyr. 167 a; 168 a; 176–178). We cannot suppose that it is related to *śḏb*, " instruments," or the like, e. g., Naophoric Statue in the Vatican, 2. See *infra*, p. 18, 7th line from top.

a wound in the lip, the injury is described as " piercing through (*yśdb*) to the inside of his mouth " (IX 7 ; IX 9 ; IX 11–12). Similarly in Case 28 a wound in the throat is described as " piercing through (*yśdb*) to his gullet " (IX 19 ; IX 22). Helpful light on the meaning of this passage is thrown by a detailed comparison with Case 27, a " gaping wound in the chin." The parallel passages are as follows :

Case 27. " If thou examinest a man having a gaping wound in his chin," 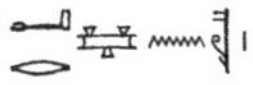.

Case 28. " If thou examinest a man having a gaping wound in his throat," 
.

Except for the two different parts of the body concerned, the two passages are identical until we reach the final descriptive phrase, where Case 27 has " penetrating to the bone," and Case 28 has " piercing through (*yśdb*) to his gullet." Thus it would seem highly probable that *yśdb* is nearly synonomous with 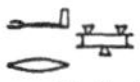 *ʿr*, " penetrate," the latter being here used where the penetration reaches a solid body, the former (*yśdb*) where it comes through into a void. In Case 34 the surgeon likewise describes a rupture of overlying soft tissue which he finds accompanying a dislocation of the clavicle, as " piercing through (*yśdb*) to the inside " (XI 21), meaning, of course, the interior of the trunk. In Case 37, a broken arm with a rupture of the overlying soft tissue, the meaning of *yśdb* is not so clear (XII 20; XII 21). The surgeon first describes a fracture " having a wound over it " and regards this injury as one with which he can deal (verdict 2). He then adds : " If, however, thou findest that wound which is over the fracture with blood issuing from it, piercing through (*yśdb*) to the interior of his injury, thou shouldst say '. . . A case not treatable' " (Verdict 3, XII 19–21). See commentary on Case 37.

The form of the verb is interesting. With one exception (our gloss above), the word is always written 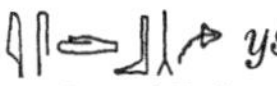 *yśdb*, with initial  in all the thirteen passages in which it occurs : and it should be noted with reference to the sole occurrence of  *śdb*, that the parallel text (IX 12) has *yśdb*. The context would indicate that we have in this word in every passage a participial form. In our Case 14 *yśdb* occurs three times in the phrase " a wound in his nostril, piercing through." In none of these three passages does *yśdb* take a feminine *t*, which would show agreement with *šr·t* (feminine), " nostril." It must qualify *wbnw*, " wound," which is masculine, and we must therefore regard *yśdb* as an *active* participle, describing the condition of the wound. It is evidently then an imperfect active participle, having the vowel after the second radical, and therefore taking a prosthetic  before the double consonance at the beginning of the word. Confirming this identification is the occurrence of the form  *yśdb·w* (XI 21), with the ending . See Erman, *Grammatik*[3], par. 390, p. 203. The form *śdb* in our gloss (VI 14), which seems to make a sentence by itself, might be a perfect passive participle, and has been so considered in the translation, notwithstanding the occurrence of *yšdb* in the parallel gloss (IX 12).

wb' n might possibly be considered as an *n*-form of the verb, with *ẖnw fnd-f* ("the inside of his nose") as the subject, giving us the sentence: "The inside of his nose has opened." The surgical and anatomical conditions in these cases, however, are not described by the use of the *n*-form (except with the negative, e. g., II 14). It seems to me certain that we have here the common phrase *n ẖnw*, "to the inside," found also in Case 5 (II 16; II 17) with *hrp*, "sink;" Case 6 (II 24) with *wb'* "open;" Case 26 (IX 9; IX 11) with *yšdb*, and (IX 12) with *wb'*, "open;" Case 32 (XI 8) with *hrp*, "sink" (*n* omitted by error of scribe); Case 34 (XI 21) with *yšdb*, "piercing through;" and Case 37 (XII 20), the same. We must regard *wb' n*, "opening to," as exactly parallel with *ʿr n*, "penetrating to," so common in the cranial cases in this treatise.

my ḏd, "as one says," perhaps literally a passive participle, "like what is said," or better an impersonal passive, "as is said," is represented by , literally "he says" in the repetition of this gloss in Case 26, Gloss A.

The plural of *yẖ·t*, "things," is treated as usual as a masculine, *gnn* following without any indication of agreement in gender. See Case 31, commentary on X 19.

CASE FIFTEEN

VI 14–17

PERFORATION OF THE BONE IN THE REGION OF THE MAXILLA AND THE ZYGOMA

With Case 15 we pass from injuries of the nose to those in the maxillary region, including likewise injuries to the zygoma in all probability. Injuries in this region are treated in the three cases 15, 16, and 17: Case 15 discussing a "perforation" (*thm*), Case 16 a "split" (*pšn*), and Case 17 a "smash" (*šd*) or compound comminuted fracture. The arrangement of these cases of injuries in the region mentioned is the same as that which we have found in the discussion of injuries of the skull: Case 3 treating a "perforation," Case 4 a "split," and Case 5 a "smash."

Our surgeon regards a perforation of the bone in this region as an injury which he can cure, notwithstanding the fact that there is possibly a diseased condition of the wound. The remedy which he applies, a mineral called *ymrw*, which cannot be identified, would be interesting if it were safe to conclude that it was a mineral poison acting as a disinfectant, but the reader should be warned that this is pure conjecture. Our inability to identify this mineral is another illustration of our lack of information regarding the terms belonging to the ancient Egyptian *materia medica*.

Title

VI 14

Translation

Instructions concerning a perforation in his cheek.

Commentary

 The reading *thm* is clear from the examination (VI 15). For full commentary see Case 3 (I 18).

 *mnd·t*, "cheek," is used here as a designation of the *maxilla* and the contiguous portions of the *zygoma*, even as far back as the temporal bone. See commentary in Case 11 (V 15).

Examination

VI 15–16

Translation

If thou examinest a man having a perforation in his cheek, shouldst thou find there is a swelling, protruding and black, (and) diseased tissue upon his cheek, (conclusion in diagnosis).

Commentary

On *thm m mnd·t-f*, "a perforation in his cheek," see title above. Commentary on *ṯḥb yšw-y*, "the swelling protruding," will be found in Case 4 (II 4).

 *km* may mean "black" here, although with this meaning it usually has the determinative 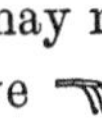, while its meaning with the determinative  is usually "to be complete." It should be noted, however, that in the following case (VI 18–19), the wording of the examination of which is exactly parallel to our passage, we find: "If thou examinest a man having a split (*pšn*) in his cheek, shouldst thou find there is a swelling, protruding and red, on the outside of that split, etc.;" that is, we have a color designation immediately following the observation regarding the swelling.

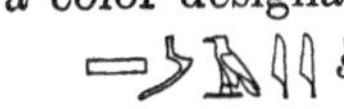 *šm'y*. This term is the same as  *šm'y* of Case 41, see Gloss A.

Diagnosis

VI 16

Translation

Thou shouldst say concerning him: "One having a perforation in his cheek. An ailment which I will treat."

Commentary

Again, as so often, the diagnosis is merely a hasty memorandum, omitting all that should follow the introductory catchwords. On the meaning of these see commentary on the title. On the significance of the concluding verdict, see commentary on Case 1 (I 2) and also the introduction (pp. 46 ff.).

Treatment

VI 16–17

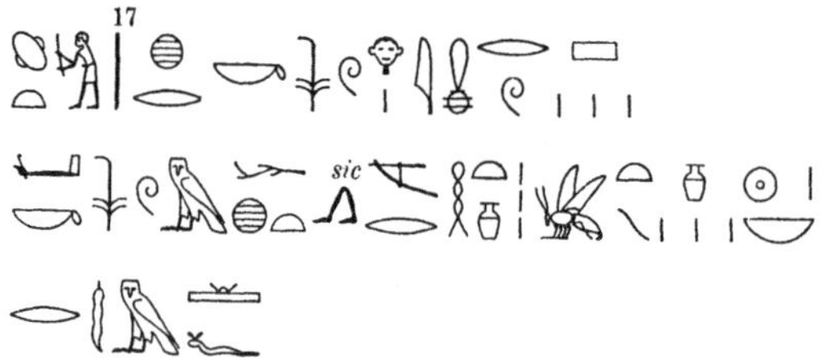

Translation

Thou shouldst bind it with *ymrw* and treat it afterward [with] grease (and) honey every day until he recovers.

Commentary

ymrw, which we may call *imru*, must be identical with *ymrw*, which occurs seven times in our treatise. The writing with = *mr*, which is found in two other passages (IX 6 and X 11), is further evidence of the archaic origin of our treatise, for it is known only in the Old Kingdom, or in religious texts retaining the old orthography. The determinative shows that it is a mineral, which, however, we are unable to identify, as it is entirely unknown outside of Pap. Smith. It can hardly be the same as the like-sounding *yśmry*, commonly guessed at as "emery," which appears for example in Asiatic tribute (Sethe, *Urk*. IV, p. 686). If we really have in our case here an example of gangrene, one would like to see in *imru* some poisonous mineral which would act as a disinfectant; though, if so, it is obvious that the nature of its effects would not have been understood by the ancient surgeon.

śrwḫ-k, "thou shouldst treat." Although the customary determinative of *śrwḫ* is the book roll, nevertheless we cannot doubt that we should read as *śrwḫ* in this passage, as a comparison of the corresponding passage in Case 16 immediately following will show.

The omission of *m* "with" before *mrḥ·t*, "grease," is frequent in Pap. Smith; but it is not due to the fact that *mrḥ·t* begins with *m*, for it is also often found omitted before *by·t*, "honey," and even *ydr*, "stitching" (Case 26, IX 8).

On the use of grease and honey see commentary on Case 1 (I 2–3).

CASE SIXTEEN

VI 17–21

SPLIT OF THE BONE IN THE REGION OF THE MAXILLA AND THE ZYGOMA

This case is the second of the group of three (Cases 15, 16, and 17) treating injuries of the maxillary region. See the introduction to Case 15. The case is regarded as one quite curable.

TITLE

VI 17–18

Translation

Instructions concerning a split in his cheek.

Commentary

On the surgical meaning of "split" (*pšn*). see commentary, Case 4 (II 2). See also preceding Case 15 (VI 14).

EXAMINATION

VI 18–19

Translation

If thou examinest a man having a split in his cheek, shouldst thou find that there is a swelling, protruding and red, on the outside of that split, (conclusion in diagnosis).

Commentary

" Shouldst thou find . . . that split " is found also in Case 8 (IV 6), referring to a fracture of the skull (except that our passage in Case 16 has inserted the additional detail " red "). Consult commentary on Case 8 (IV 6), and, on " swelling protruding," see also Case 4 (examination), II 4.

DIAGNOSIS

VI 19–20

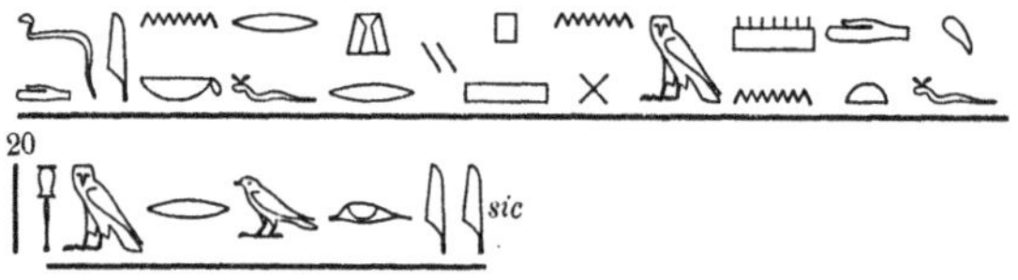

Translation

Thou shouldst say concerning him : " One having a split in his cheek. An ailment which [I] will treat."

Commentary

As in a number of the preceding cases the diagnosis contains only a memorandum repeating the title, the verdict at the end forming the important item. On this verdict consult commentary on Case 1 (I 2) and the introduction (pp. 46 ff.).

TREATMENT

VI 20–21

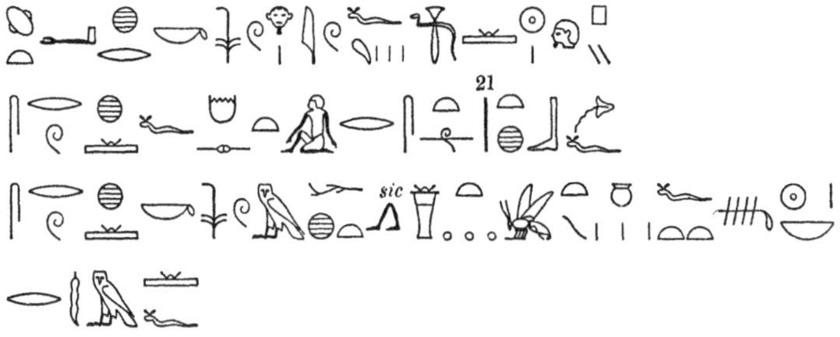

Translation

Thou shouldst bind it with fresh meat the first day. His treatment is sitting until its swelling is reduced (lit. drawn out). Thou shalt treat it afterward [with] grease, honey, (and) lint every day until he recovers.

Commentary

On the treatment with "fresh meat," see commentary on Case 1 (I 2–3); and on "grease, honey, and lint" see Case 1 (I 2–3). The term "swelling" (*tḫb*) is discussed in full in Case 4 (II 4). The chief item in the treatment is "sitting," that is quiet and rest; see Case 4 (II 7).

CASE SEVENTEEN

VII 1–7

COMPOUND COMMINUTED FRACTURE OF THE BONE IN THE REGION OF THE MAXILLA AND THE ZYGOMA

This is the third in the series of three progressively more serious injuries to the bone in the maxillary region, beginning with Case 15. As in the case of a similar injury to the skull (Case 5), to the nasal bone (Case 13), and to the temporal bone (Case 22) the surgeon appends the fatal verdict 3, "An ailment not to be treated." In view of these analogous cases just cited (5, 13, and 22), our verdict in Case 17 is probably correct, and the stereotyped words, following the conventional treatment with grease, honey, and lint, "until he recovers," are doubtless to be regarded as a scribal error. See discussion of these passages below, and see Pl. VII, Fig. 14.

TITLE

VII 1

Translation

Instructions concerning a smash in his cheek.

Commentary

On the surgical meaning of *šd* "smash," really a compound comminuted fracture, see commentary on Case 5 (II 11).

EXAMINATION

VII 1–4

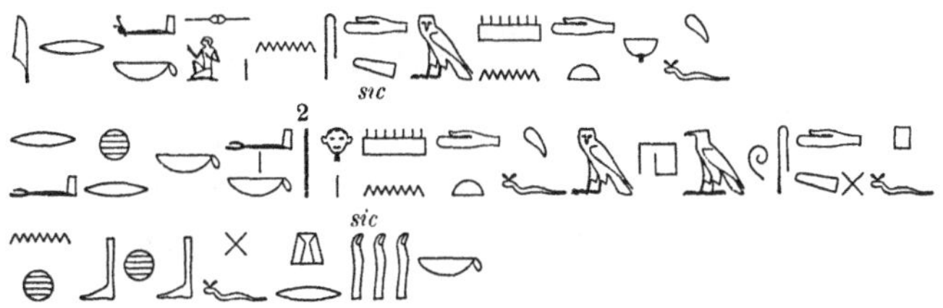

Translation

If thou examinest a man having a smash in his cheek, thou shouldst place thy hand on his cheek at the point of that smash. Should it crepitate under thy fingers, while he discharges blood from his nostril, (and) from his ear on the side of him having that injury; (and) at the same time he discharges blood from his mouth, while it is painful when he opens his mouth because of it, (conclusion in diagnosis).

Commentary

The parallel passage in Case 13 (VI 4–6) has interesting variants. The surgeon uses *wdy* "put, place" interchangeably with *rdy*, literally "give," when the object is the hand placed on the injury.

M h'w, which I have rendered "at the point of," probably suggests some local refinement which may not have been sufficiently suggested by this rendering. See parallel in Case 13.

On *nḫbḫb*, " crepitate," see commentary on Case 13 (VI 4–5).

On *yśk św* in l. 2 and *yśk św ḥm* in l. 3 see commentary on Case 13 (VI 5).

Both the nostril and the ear on the side which has suffered the injury are affected. The apparent writing *śḳn*, as in IV 15 (see also original, IV 7), is to be read *śḳr*.

The discharge of blood from the mouth, as well as from the nostril and the ear, shows that the wound has broken through and ruptured the tissue in the oral cavity. Naturally the facial muscles are effected, making it painful to open the mouth, just as in Case 13.

DIAGNOSIS

VII 4–5

[a] The scribe wrote by error immediately after. He then wrote over this and added at the end.

Translation

Thou shouldst say concerning him : "One having a smash in his cheek, while he discharges blood from his nostril, from his ear, (and) from his mouth, (and) he is speechless. An ailment not to be treated."

Commentary

The diagnosis is fuller than in the two preceding cases, in which it offers only a repetition of the title. It adds also the interesting circumstance that the patient is speechless. This word, *dgmy*, " he is speechless," is explained by the surgeon himself in Case 22, Gloss C, q. v. This remark regarding speechlessness is dropped in here as a single word in Egyptian, whereas in Case 13, where it has been properly inserted as part of the examination, the same Egyptian verb has been introduced by a preceding auxiliary verb , *yw-f*, "he is" (VI 6). See discussion of this diagnosis in the Introduction (p. 50).

This verdict, regularly used of fatal cases, will be found discussed in Case 5 (II 15). I formerly regarded it in our case as an obvious error of the scribe, in view of the phrase " until he recovers," at the end of the case. Indeed the scribe has made the same error and corrected it back to verdict 1, " a case which I will treat," in Case 35. An examination of Case 13, however, makes it quite possible that the verdict is correct and the *conclusion* (VII 7) an error. See Case 13, introduction.

TREATMENT

VII 5–7

Translation

Thou shouldst bind with fresh meat the first day. His ⸢relief⸣ is sitting until its swelling is reduced (lit. drawn out). Thou shalt treat it afterward [with] grease, honey (and) lint every day, until he recovers.

Commentary

This treatment is identical with that in the preceding case, but we cannot suppose that the scribe has absentmindedly raised his eyes to the treatment in the preceding case (immediately above our case in his original roll), and thus copied the wrong treatment; for he has written the extraordinary for *śrwḫ-f*, " his treatment " (VI 20), and he has written the variant for of VI 21, besides the cursive for the fuller *by·t*, "honey," of VI 21. As for the conclusion, " until he recovers," it is so frequent in our treatise after the treatment with "grease, honey and lint," that the scribe may have written it quite thoughtlessly, without having seen it in the original before him. It is quite possible therefore that this conclusion is an error and that the fatal verdict above is correct.

sry-f, " his ⌜relief⌝," is not an error, for it is found in two other passages in our treatise, three in all. In each case it is written exactly as above, without any determinative, in a verbless sentence with " sitting " as the predicate noun. In both the other cases it is followed by the copulative *pw* (Case 20, VIII 5 ; and Case 32, XI 6–7). In our Case 17 it may be used in connection with a fatal condition of the patient ; in Case 20 it is certainly so used ; but in Case 32 it is immediately followed by the clause " until he recovers." If the meaning above suggested is correct, it is applied both to relief in a favorable, as well as in a hopeless case, in which temporary alleviation is all that can be expected. The rendering hazarded is based on a very uncertain identification of our word with the causative *ś-rwy*, "to cause to flee," used of exorcising spirits, and as a legal term, of " transferring " a person or property levied for tax payments, a term which might possibly be applied by our surgeon to relief from physical suffering. In all three occurrences of the word we find *s* instead of the *ś* needed to justify the etymology suggested. In any case it should be noted that our puzzling word is found in all three cases in a context which elsewhere repeatedly has *śrwḫ-f*, " his treatment," in place of our *sry-f*—a fact which shows that *sry-f* must have some meaning which will make sense when substituted for *śrwḫ-f*, " his treatment."

CASE EIGHTEEN

VII 7–14

A WOUND IN THE SOFT TISSUE OF THE TEMPLE, THE BONE BEING UNINJURED

This case is the first of a group of five cases of injuries affecting the temporal region between the eye and the ear. The surgeon has thus been passing from the nose backward towards the ear, which follows this group of five cases. Like the first eight cases in the treatise, discussing injuries to the head, our group begins with a flesh wound affecting only the overlying soft tissue (Case 18) and passes then to deeper and more serious wounds affecting the bone: a perforation (*thm*, Cases 19 and 20), a split (*pšn*, Case 21), and a compound comminuted fracture (*śd*, Case 22).

The discussion includes two interesting glosses, the first explaining the size and nature of the flesh wound, the second defining the new term *gm'*, and showing that it was closely equivalent to our modern popular word "temple."

TITLE

VII 7

Translation

Instructions concerning a wound in his temple.

Commentary

The important new word *gm'*, "temple," or "temporal bone," is explained by the surgeon himself at the end of this case in Gloss B, q. v.

EXAMINATION

VII 7–9

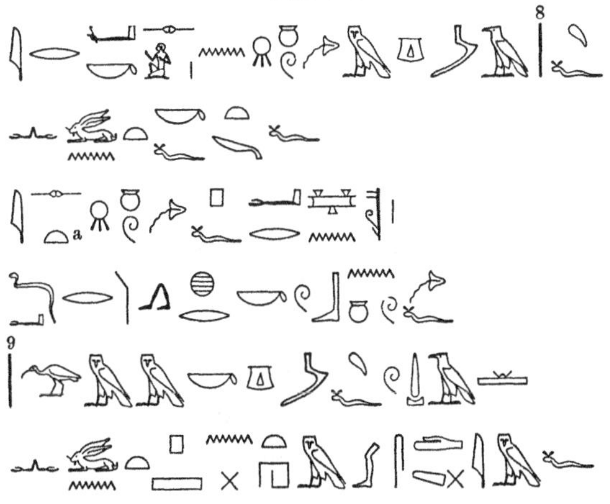

[a] The scribe has apparently written *r*, at least it is unusually large for *t*. Such a large *t* is however occasionally found, and the gloss in l. 12, quoting this passage, writes *t*.

Translation

If thou examinest a man having a wound in his temple, it not having a gash, while that wound penetrates to the bone, thou shouldst palpate his wound. Shouldst thou find his temporal bone uninjured, there being no split, (or) perforation, (or) smash in it, (conclusion in diagnosis).

Commentary

The parallel passage in Case 27 (IX 14–15) offers interesting and important variants. Grammatically it is interesting to find above *gmm-k,* " shouldst thou find," parallel with *yr gmy-k,* " If thou shouldst find " in Case 27. More important is the following variant :

Case 18 : 

" Shouldst thou find his *gm*ʾ uninjured."

Case 27 : 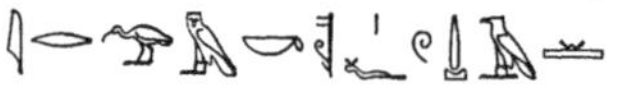

" If thou shouldst find his bone uninjured " (IX 14–15).

The full discussion of *gm*ʾ, " temple," will be found in Gloss B, in connection with the surgeon's own explanation of the word ; but the point to be made here is the evident application of the word both to a bone and to the soft tissue lying over it. We observe that the injury is assumed both by the title and the first clause of the examination to be in the patient's *gm*ʾ, whereas the latter part of the examination (beginning l. 9) states quite clearly that the *gm*ʾ is " uninjured " and has no " split, perforation, (or) smash in it." The specified injuries are those of the bone (*pšn* and *thm* are used exclusively of bone, *śd* primarily) and the parallel passage above cited, referring to the chin, actually employs the word " bone " where our case has *gm*ʾ. It is obvious therefore that our surgeon is describing an injury which has penetrated the soft tissue overlying the bone and exposing it, but without inflicting any injury upon it. We find, therefore, wide latitude in the anatomical meaning of *gm*ʾ, here rendered " temple " and " temporal bone," which will be found discussed in the commentary on Gloss B, where the Egyptian surgeon is noticeably vague in his definition of *gm*ʾ, and is probably intentionally so ; for he calls it " the region thereof between the corner of his eye and the ⌜orifice⌝ of his ear, at the end of his mandible " (p. 275). His terms leave it quite uncertain, therefore, whether the designation *gm*ʾ includes the bone or refers exclusively to the overlying soft tissue. The superficial area included is indicated with fair precision, but like our own word " temple ", the Egyptian *gm*ʾ does not suggest what is included below the surface (see pp. 275–277 and Pl. V, Fig. 11).

On the meaning of the term *kf·t,* " gash," see commentary on Case 1, pp. 90–92.

On " palpate " (*ḏʿr*) consult commentary on Case 1, pp. 92–93.

On " penetrates to the bone " (*ʿr n ḳś*) see Case 1, pp. 87–89.

Pšn, " split," confined to injuries of the bone, has been discussed in Case 4 (II 2).

Thm, " perforation," also confined to injuries of the bone, has been discussed in Case 3 (I 18).

Śd, " smash," primarily used of injuries to the bone, but sometimes of soft tissue, is discussed in Case 5 (II 11).

The order of the three injuries excluded from this case is different from that of the following four cases (19–22), in which they are taken up, viz., *thm, pšn, śd.*

DIAGNOSIS

VII 9–10

Translation

Thou shouldst say concerning him: "One having a wound in his temple. An ailment which I will treat."

Commentary

Considering the surgeon's vague use of *gmꜣ*, "temple," in this case (see commentary on examination), this memorandum serving in the place of the diagnosis is singularly insufficient. It merely repeats the title, as in the cases on the maxillary region (Cases 15–17). For the practical surgeon, however, the line of action he is to follow is introduced in the favorable verdict 1, which is explained in Case 1 (I 2) and discussed also in the introduction (pp. 46 ff.).

TREATMENT

VII 10–11

[a] Preposition *m*, "with" omitted as commonly.

Translation

Thou shouldst bind it with fresh meat the first day, (and) thou shouldst treat afterward [with] grease, (and) honey every day, until he recovers.

Commentary

On this frequent remedy, fresh meat followed by grease and honey, often with lint added, see Case 1, treatment (I 2–3). The case is evidently a simple one, and recovery is regarded as certain.

Gloss A

VII 11–13

Explaining: A wound, not having a gash, while it penetrates to the bone.

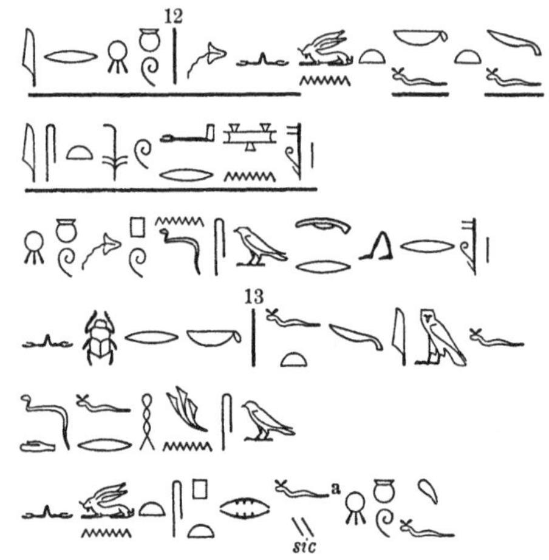

[a] The scribe at first wrote "its two lips," and then discovered that his original had "his wound" instead of the pronoun "its." He therefore canceled "its" ( ) with a vertical stroke of red ink over the black. *Wn·t* and *t* of *kf·t* (l. 12) are also corrections entered in black in the rubric.

Translation

As for: "A wound, not having a gash, while it penetrates to the bone," it means that the wound is contracted, reaching as far as the bone, (though) there is no gash in it. He speaks of (its) narrowness, his wound not having two lips.

Commentary

The scribe again demonstrates his carelessness in quoting an excerpt from the text of the case, which has "that wound" (VII 8) instead of "it" as quoted (VII 12).

This wound in the temple is of the same kind as that in the head, described in Case 1, where much the same terms are employed to indicate the character of the wound as a small rupture of the soft tissue, such as would be produced by falling and striking the head on a stone, or such as would result from the blow of a club. Compare Case 1, diagnosis (I 1–2) and Gloss B (I 9–10). This gloss explains the phrase in the text "while his wound does not have two lips" and states the meaning as: "his wound is narrow; without gaping of one (lip) from the other." Compare also Case 1, Gloss C. The gloss is of interest as showing the surgeon's intention to create precise terms for flesh wounds just as he does for injuries to the bone. This gloss, furthermore, correlates well with the term *gm'* as sometimes designating the soft tissue of the temple.

GLOSS B

VII 13–14

Explaining: His *gmꜣ*

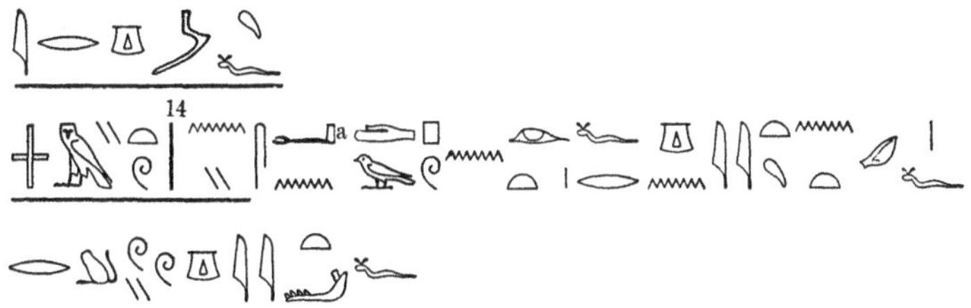

[a] The two signs have been canceled by two oblique strokes in red ink over the black.

Translation

As for: "His *gmꜣ*," it means the region thereof between the corner of his eye and the ⌜orifice⌝ of his ear, at the end of his mandible.

Commentary

ymytw (or *ymywty*) literally means "between." It is, however, twice used elsewhere in our document to designate the "region between" or the "tissue between," that is, it becomes a substantive meaning "what is between." The two examples are:

"It means what is between shell and shell of the skull," a description of the sutures (Case 7, III 16, Gloss A); and

"it means the middle of his nose . . . ., extending to the region between his two eyebrows" (Case 12, Gloss A, V 21). These two passages quite justify our rendering "region between" in Case 18.

ny. The force of the particle is not wholly clear here, although it can be understood as meaning "thereto" or "therefor," somewhat in the sense of "thereof." See commentary on verdict 3, Case 5 (II 15).

šꜥnd, corrected to *šd*. The two signs *ꜥn* have been canceled by the scribe with two oblique strokes of red ink over the black. Such a word as *šd*, with determinative of the evil bird, is however unknown; whereas the word *šꜥnd*, although corrected by the scribe, is a perfectly good word with the right meaning for this passage. The correction is therefore in all probability an error by the scribe.

Šꜥnd is employed as the opposite of *š-wsḫ*, "make broad" (Lepsius, *Denkmaeler*, III, 18, 7); as the opposite of *š-ꜥšꜣ*, "make numerous" (Pap. Leyden 347, 3, 3); and as the opposite of *š-ꜥꜣ*, "make great" (Tomb of Neferhotep, Duemichen, *Hist. Inschr.*

II 40a, 11). It is clear from these examples that *ś-ʿnd* means " to diminish " (transitive), or more specifically in the three cases cited, " to make narrow," " to make few," " to make small." Confirmatory examples will be found in Edfu (Rochem. I 294 ; I 429 = Piehl, *Inscr.* II 3 D*a*) ; Gardiner, *Admonitions*, p. 30 ; Dévaud, *Maximes de Ptahhotep*, p. 19 ; and Gunn, *Syntax*, p. 15, example 89. The meaning " to make narrow " fits our passage very well. It must indicate the narrow end of the eye, as distinguished from the broad end, a difference accentuated very strongly by Egyptian eye-paint. Our surgeon is designating the outside corner of the eye.

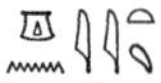 *gny·t* " ⌜orifice⌝ " is possibly to be transliterated  *gry·t*. It is a new and unknown anatomical term, not found in any other ancient document. As a part of the ear, it renders a little more definite one limit or boundary of the region which the surgeon is defining. Whether it designates a portion of the auricle or outer ear, or indicates the orifice itself, we cannot decide on the basis of this passage, the only occurrence of the word thus far known.

" At the end of his mandible." The preposition *r* is the usual one indicating proximity to a member of the body ; compare such well-known phrases as *r ḫḫ*, " at the throat " (used of a necklace) ; or *r fnd*, " at the nose " (used of a flower, or the symbol of life). It is grammatically possible, however, that *r*, the regular preposition introducing the other limit after the word " between," is to be so construed here. This would give us " the corner of his eye " as one limit, while the other limit would be double, " the ⌜orifice⌝ of his ear " and " the end of his mandible." An examination of the actual anatomy of the head, however, is conclusive in excluding this rendering. We must understand *r* as meaning " at."

 *gmꜣ-f*. The region connoted by this word, as defined in our gloss therefore, is that between the eye and the ear, at the end of the mandible, and this conclusion is clearly confirmed by the other evidence in our document. It is interesting to observe that the ancient surgeon finds it necessary to define the term *gmꜣ*, as if it were unfamiliar to his generation. It is certainly so to ours, for the word is entirely new to us, and is not found in any other document. Fortunately it occurs no less than twenty-two times in the Edwin Smith Papyrus. Of these, three passages are very helpful in determining its meaning. One of them is our Gloss B, just discussed. Before taking up the other two, we should note the position of our case with reference to what has preceded and what follows. After discussing wounds of the skull, including the frontal bone and eyebrows, the surgeon has proceeded to take up injuries to the bridge of the nose, to one nostril, to the cheek and maxillary region. He then takes up the *gmꜣ*, and follows it with a discussion of the ear. He thus proceeds from the nose, through the maxilla and the *gmꜣ* to the ear. The order and sequence of his discussion, therefore, would suggest that in taking up the *gmꜣ* he is proceeding through the temporal region to the ear. Gloss B has just confirmed this conclusion, and we may now

proceed to examine the other two instructive occurrences of the word *gmꜣ* in our papyrus.

We find symptoms arising from a gaping wound in the skull, partially described as follows: "Stiffening on the part of the ligaments at the end of his ramus,"

"which are fastened to his *gmꜣ*, that is at the end of his jaw, without moving to and fro, so that it is not easy for him to open his mouth because of his pain" (Case 7, Gloss B, III 17–18). The ligaments which operate the mandible are here said to be "fastened to his *gmꜣ*," making the identification of *gmꜣ* as "temporal bone" quite certain. The reference is of course to the temporal muscle, which is attached to the coronoid process and to the temporal bone.

The third instructive example is found in a discussion of the ramus, the inner or upper end of the mandible. It defines the ramus as follows:

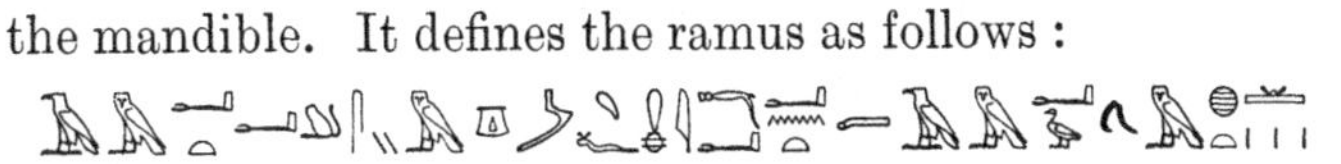

"as for the ramus, its end is in his *gmꜣ* as the claw of an *ꜣmʿ*-bird grasps an object" (Case 22, Gloss A, VIII 14–15 q. v.). We have here a very interesting description of the forked upper end of the ramus as engaging in the *gmꜣ*, just as the claw of an *ꜣmʿ*-bird (obviously some two-toed bird) clutches a thing. The reference is of course to the *fossa temporalis*, the depression in the lower part of the temporal bone, into which the condyle is articulated, while the coronoid process, together with the *incisura mandibulae* between it and the condyle, passes around to the inner side of the zygomatic process, which it clasps, as it were, like the claw of a two-toed bird. See Pl. V.

It is quite clear then, that the ancient term *gmꜣ* refers to the temporal bone, but certainly not to the whole of it. The limits defined in our Gloss B confine it to the region between the outer corner of the eye and the ear "at the end of his mandible." These limits would include only the outer and anterior portions of the temporal bone, especially the zygomatic process, and also the portion of the zygoma lying between the eye and the ear. It should be further noted that *gmꜣ* defines a *region*, and hence, as we have already seen in the examination, it may designate either the underlying bone or the soft tissue lying over it. It would seem therefore that our surgeon in developing his terminology for the parts of the human skull did not strictly follow the natural divisions suggested by the sutures, but was doubtless somewhat governed by the popular designations available, just as we employ a term "temple" to designate the flat area between the forehead and the ear, which does not at all correspond in extent to the temporal bone, and might include both the bone in this region and the overlying soft tissue. Our popular term "temple", therefore, is a very satisfactory modern equivalent of the ancient Egyptian *gmꜣ*.

CASE NINETEEN

VII 14–22

A PERFORATION IN THE TEMPLE

This case is the second in the group of five cases of wounds in the temple (Cases 18–22). It is also the first of two which deal with a " perforation," possibly of the bone in the first case, and certainly so in the second (Case 20). Full discussion of the term *thm,* " perforation," will be found in Case 3 (I 18). The difference between the two cases of " perforation " (19 and 20) is unmistakable as far as the patient's condition is concerned. Case 19 is curable by simple treatment ; Case 20 is incurable and only alleviatory measures are suggested. In Case 19 the patient's eye on the *injured* side is " blood-shot " and his neck is stiff ; in Case 20 *both* eyes are blood-shot and *both* are discharging, while blood also issues from both nostrils, and the patient is unable to speak. It is possible that in Case 20 the perforation has been so deep that the rupture of internal tissues has affected both the eye and the nostril on the opposite side from the wound, as well as the eye and the nostril on the injured side of the head. The weapon which presumably caused the injury has perhaps thrust more deeply in Case 20 than in Case 19, but the use of the dual " two eyes," " two nostrils " in Case 20 may be a scribal error in writing (see commentary).

Some further indication of this difference, included in the actual descriptions of the two wounds themselves, might therefore be expected, and it is possible that we have this indication suggested by the surgeon in the examination (VII 15) in Case 19 in the words, " a perforation in his temple, a wound being upon it ; " for it is conceivable that we should render " the wound being *over* it " (the temporal bone), and therefore perhaps confined to the overlying soft tissue. Indeed it is difficult to find any other satisfactory explanation of the little circumstantial verbless sentence, " a (or the) wound being upon it."

TITLE

VII 14–15

Translation

Instructions concerning a perforation in his temple.

Commentary

Full commentary on this injury, a " perforation " (*thm*) of the skull, will be found in Case 3 (I 18). On the term " temple " (*gmꜣ*) see the preceding case, Gloss B (VII 13–14).

EXAMINATION

VII 15–17

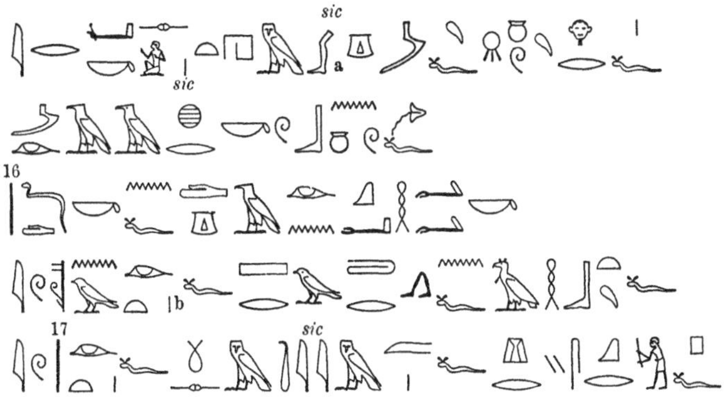

[a] The scribe has omitted the preposition " in " (*m*).

[b] The scribe has corrected out this stroke, canceling it with an oblique cross stroke in red ink over the black.

Translation

If thou examinest a man having a perforation (*thm*) [in] his temple, a wound being upon it, thou shouldst inspect his wound, saying to him : "Look at thy two shoulders." Should his doing so be painful (even though) his neck turns around (only) a little for him, while his eye on the side of him having that injury is blood-shot, (conclusion follows in diagnosis).

Commentary

This is one of the examinations in which a certain capability or function of a part of the body is tested by the physician by means of directions given to the patient.

 *šry*, " little," is in a position which makes it somewhat uncertain whether we should connect it with the preceding or the following context. Normally, as an adverb, it should follow the proposition to which it belongs, and we should render " should his doing so a little be painful ; " but this leaves the following proposition without much force, as a weak circumstantial clause, " when he has turned his neck around." In the above translation I have understood *šry* as a predicate adjective in a sentence of which the following proposition is the subject, thus : " even though little be that his neck turns for him." The proposition *pẖr n-f nḥb·t-f*, " his neck turns for him " (regarding *n-f* as a dative), may quite properly serve as the subject of *šry*, " little." To accept an *n*-form, unless it were nominal, as the subject of *šry*, would not be so easy.

 *šsm-ty*, " blood-shot," found only in the medical papyri, is fully explained by the surgeon in a gloss at the end of this case. The grammatical form with the double  for *y*, is of course wrong, but occurs several times in our treatise, see especially Case 31 (X 15).

šḳr, "injury," seemingly written *šḳn*, occurs so written in Case 8 (IV 15) and also in Case 17 (VII 3).

On the force of "a wound being upon it," see the introduction to this case.

DIAGNOSIS

VII 17–18

[a] The scribe made an erasure here while the ink was wet, and made a subsequent alteration now indistinct and uncertain. Below is evidently a *w*; but the traces above it show two indistinct oblique strokes over a horizontal stroke: hardly *pḥ*, which moreover makes no sense.

Translation

Thou shouldst say concerning him: "One having a perforation in his temple ⌜-⌝, while he suffers with stiffness in his neck. An ailment which I will treat."

Commentary

The symptom "he suffers with stiffness in his neck" occurs seventeen times in our papyrus, and never elsewhere with the introduction *yw-f*, "he is." Hence it is unlikely that the scribe intended to use this auxiliary verb here; nor do the visible traces in the lacuna favor such a reading. Hence the uncertain word must belong to the preceding *gmꜣ-f*. No probable restoration of the word suggests itself.

Full commentary on the phrase, "he suffers, etc." will be found in Case 3 (I 20). It is a symptom which the surgeon recognizes especially as accompanying injuries to the skull, and is therefore recorded in each of the group of six such cases (three to eight inclusive). It is interesting to notice that the surgeon established the presence of this symptom by experiment with the patient's ability to turn his neck and look at either shoulder. In Case 5, a very serious compound fracture of the skull, the surgeon *records* the symptom (II 13–14), but it is not stated that he directed the patient to make an effort to look at his shoulders. We have there the simple statement that he could not do so. The point here is that the stiffness was discovered by actual experiment in the examination, and then recorded in the diagnosis. Here then is a case of sound inductive reasoning after experiment—a method in no wise different from that of the modern surgeon, but appearing here for the first time in the history of science as known to us. (See introduction, pp. 48–51). On the favorable verdict 1, see Case 1 (I 2).

TREATMENT

VII 18–19

Translation

Thou shouldst put him at his mooring stakes until the period of his injury passes by, (and) thou shouldst treat with grease, honey, (and) lint every day until he recovers.

Commentary

On the extraordinary figure of speech, " put him at his mooring stakes," see Case 3 (I 22–23). The obscure phrase " until the period of his injury passes by " is discussed in Case 3 (I 23). The nominal form of the verb here (*śwʾ·t*) is unusual ; the other four cases containing this passage have *św'y*. On the familiar treatment, see Case 1 (I 3).

GLOSS A

VII 19–22

Explaining : His two eyes are blood-shot.

Translation

As for : " His two eyes are blood-shot," it means that the color of his two eyes is red like the color of *śʾś*-flowers. The " Treatise on What Pertains to the Embalmer " says concerning it : " His two eyes are red ⸢with⸣ disease like an eye at the end of its weakness."

Commentary

The inaccuracy of the scribe in quoting " his two eyes," whereas the text of the case (VII 17) has " his eye," and expressly stipulates that it is the eye *on the injured side* which is meant, is an outstanding example of the carelessness with which he has copied our treatise. In the explanation he continues the dual as is evident especially from the writing .

 must certainly be read *yr·ty-f(y)*, as shown by the following feminine verbal form *šsm-ty* ; for the other word for eye, of uncertain spelling, is masculine.

 šsm-ty, " is blood-shot " is really a color designation. As a verb it is found elsewhere only twice, where it is also applied to the color of the eyes : Pap. Ebers 38, 18 and 109, 20. As a substantive it occurs as a designation of bandages as far back as the Pyramid Texts (2114b) and of a kind of stone in the Annals of Thutmose III (Sethe, *Urk.* IV, p. 706, l. 12), and probably designated reddish or red-streaked objects. Perhaps with such a meaning as a *masculine* noun in Pap. Ebers 37, 7 ; 41, 3 ; 41, 16 ; 41, 2 ; it is evidently so in the case of the *feminine* noun *šsm·t* where it is used together with *dšr*, "red, inflamed" (Pap. Ebers, 62, 9). No other examples of the word are known.

Yrtyw as a color designation, especially as a word for " color," is discussed in Case 7 (III 21). At the same time, in our gloss it is possible that this puzzling word may have its older more original meaning " blue," and be intended to designate the white of the eye, which so often has a bluish cast, especially when an eye is blood-shot. The objection to this interpretation is the repetition of the word with the *šʾś*-blossoms, where it would seem to be superfluous if it designated some particular color of the blossoms. On the other hand the phrase " like the color of *šʾś*-blossoms " would be expected.

 šʾś, is a plant or blossom otherwise found only in the Berlin Medical Papyrus (3038), 9, 8. It is impossible to identify it here.

 Ṯʾw, " book," or " treatise " is discussed in Case 5 (II 17). It would seem that some current treatise on the practice of the embalmer is cited by the surgeon. The quotation from this book confirms the meaning of *šsm* as " red," or " blood-shot," but is otherwise obscure.

 Ḏʾw is a very general word for " ailing," or " affected," and is applied to diseased eyes in the case of a woman in the Kahun Medical Papyrus (3, 10), where it is written *ḏʾy*. In the Pyramid Texts (1658b) *ḏʾw* is contrasted with *mʾʿw*, " straight, right, correct." Dévaud suggests that (in *Mutter und Kind*) is the ancestor of the Coptic ϫⲟ (*κυρτός*), " crooked," or " hump-backed " and would make *ḏʾy·t* mean " something crooked " as opposed to *mʾʿ·t*, " something straight." The feminine *ḏʾ·t*, meaning " sickness, wretchedness," is very common. Compare both masc. and fem. in Pap. Ebers 1, 15. All this is of slight value in determining the specific force of *ḏʾw* in the quotation from the Treatise on What Pertains to the Embalmer.

The comparison " like an eye at the end of its weakness " eludes explanation. The verb *ʾhd*, meaning " to be weak " or the like is rare. It is found in Medinet

Habu referring to the limbs (de Rougé, *Inscr. hiér.* 145, 56) and also in the Book of the Sky Cow (29), where it is written . See an uncertain example in Pap. Ebers 102, 7. Consult commentary on Case 6 (II 21).

CASE TWENTY

VII 22-VIII 5

A WOUND IN THE TEMPLE PERFORATING THE BONE

This case is the third in the group of five cases of wounds in the temple (Cases 18–22). It is also the second of two which deal with a " perforation " of the temple (Cases 19 and 20), and as we have seen in the introduction of Case 19, is much the more serious of the two. Our case illustrates the progressively increasing seriousness of the cases in this group of five. The introductions to Cases 18 and 19 should be read before undertaking the study of this case. The reader will find it instructive also to examine Case 3 in the course of studying Cases 19 and 20.

The description of symptoms in Case 20 is among the most vivid and picturesque paragraphs in the entire papyrus.

TITLE

VII 22

Translation

Instructions concerning a wound in his temple, penetrating to the bone, (and) perforating his temporal bone.

Commentary

The discussion of *gmꜣ*, " temple," will be found in Case 18, Gloss B (VII 13–14). The injury, though consisting chiefly of a " perforation " (*thm*), is evidently much more serious than in Case 19, which also deals with a " perforation." This injury is discussed in Case 3 (I 18), where this abbreviated writing of the word,  *thm*, is also taken up.

EXAMINATION

VII 22–VIII 3

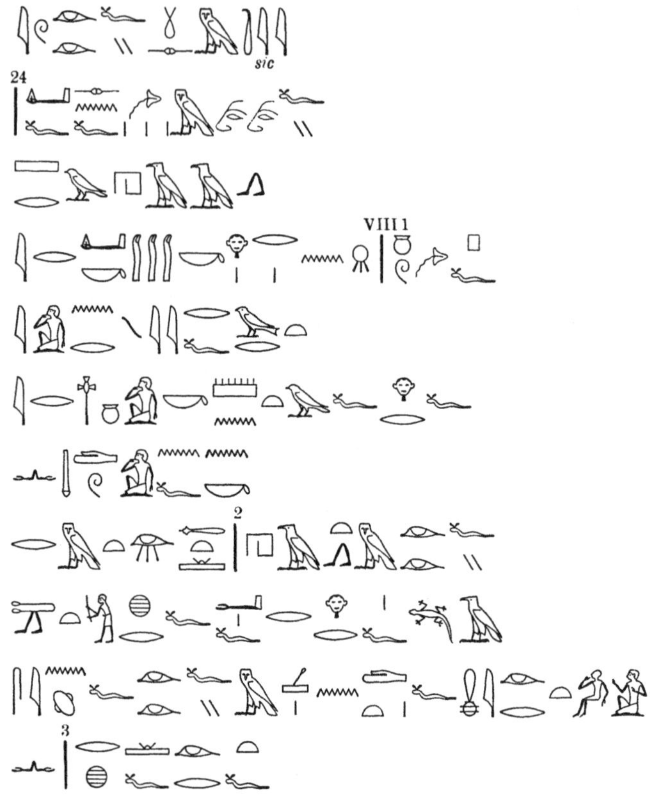

Translation

If thou examinest a man having a wound in his temple, penetrating to the bone, (and) perforating his temporal bone, while his two eyes are blood-shot, he discharges blood from both his nostrils, and a little drops; if thou puttest thy fingers on the mouth of that wound (and) he shudder exceedingly; if thou ask of him concerning his malady and he speak not to thee; while copious tears fall from both his eyes, so that he thrusts his hand often to his face that he may wipe both his eyes with the back of his hand as a child does, and knows not that he does so, (conclusion follows in diagnosis).

Commentary

The term " blood-shot " (*šsm-ty*) has been discussed in the preceding case.

 *šr hꜣꜣ*, "a little drops." Here we have the use of *hꜣy*, " to fall," in the very specific application to falling drops, as in this same examination, referring to falling tears (VIII 1–2). It occurs with the same meaning in our document in VIII 11 (of blood from the nostrils), X 22 (of urine from the male member), and XVI 6–7 (of water). A good parallel is found in Case 41:  " secretions drop therefrom " (XIII 22–XIV 1; same in Case 47, XVII 9–10).

These usages of the word, which have arisen directly from its meaning "to fall," have resulted in a further series of medical applications of it. It is applied to various discharges, excretions, outflows and the like in Papyrus Ebers (43, 1; 41, 4; 42, 15; 96, 17; 42, 16; 91, 16; 88, 19; 56, 9; 106, 14; 51, 18; 37, 4), in Papyrus Hearst (III 6), and the Kahun Medical Papyrus (2, 27; 2, 29; 2, 30). In a highly specialized application, the word designates a miscarriage (Turin, Papyri, ed. Pleyte et Rossi LV, 1), and in an interesting passage it is used in the phrase  meaning "death by miscarriage" (Magical Texts of the Empire, transcribed by Gardiner for the Berlin Dictionary, 121). In the well-known passages in Charms for Mother and Child (*Mutter und Kind*) it is applied to the expulsion of disease, and so in the idiom *rdy h'y*, "cause to go forth," it is applied to the effect of remedies on disease in the medical papyri (Pap. Ebers 39, 14–15; 51, 19; 94, 11; 73, 20–21; Hearst III 4 (corrupt, comp. Ebers 51, 19); Pap. Berlin 3038, 11, 7).

"If . . . . . . he shudder exceedingly" is a description of a symptom found six times in our papyrus. See full commentary in Case 4 (II 4).

If we accept the text as we find it, this examination reveals a more serious condition of the patient than in the preceding case, in which only the eye on the injured side of the head was blood-shot and there is no mention of a discharge of blood from the nose. In Case 20, however, *both* eyes are blood-shot and discharge, while blood issues from both nostrils. These symptoms would indicate rupture of internal tissue so deep as to affect even the eye and the nostril on the opposite side of the head from the injury. It should not be forgotten, however, that owing to the ease with which the words "his eye" may be transformed in Egyptian to "his two eyes" by the addition of two tiny strokes of the pen, our scribe has repeatedly written the dual out of habit, where only the singular was intended. Compare for example four occurrences of this error in Case 22. Admitting this possible correction however, the symptoms of speechlessness and the dazed, half unconscious manner in which the patient continually wipes the exudations from his eye, would suggest a more serious injury than in the preceding case.

DIAGNOSIS

VIII 3–4

Translation

Thou shouldst say concerning him : " One having a wound in his temple, penetrating to the bone, (and) perforating his temporal bone ; while he discharges blood from both his nostrils, he suffers with stiffness in his neck, (and) he is speechless. An ailment not to be treated."

Commentary

" Penetrating to the bone " (*ʿr n ḳs*) will be found discussed in Case 1 (I 2).

" Perforating " (*thm*), see Case 3 (I 18).

" Temple " and " temporal bone " (*gmꜣ*), see Case 18, Gloss B.

" Stiffness in his neck " (*ṯsw m nḥb·t-f*), see Case 3 (I 20).

" He is speechless " (*dgm-y*), see Case 22, Gloss C, where the surgeon himself explains the word.

The first half of the diagnosis was already contained in the title, the discharge of blood from the nostrils was observed in the examination, the stiffness of the neck new and is rather a symptom, as in the preceding case, than a particular in a diagnosis. Finally the surgeon repeats, seemingly by the use of a technical term (for he later thinks it necessary to explain it in a gloss, Case 22, Gloss C), the fact that the patient is speechless. On the hopeless verdict see Case 5 (II 15). This is another evidence of the very serious character of Case 20 as contrasted with Case 19.

See another example of 𓈖 for 𓂝 in Case 8 (IV 11).

TREATMENT

VIII 4–5

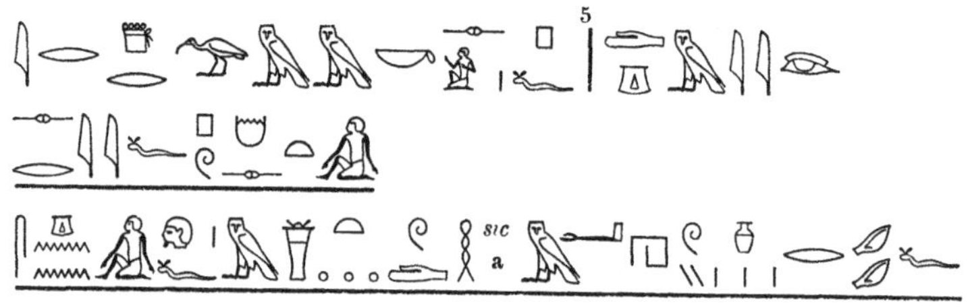

[a] The scribe has left an empty space here, as if he intended it for the determinative of *wdḥ*, "pour," which, however, he has failed to insert.

Translation

Now when thou findest that man speechless, his ⌜relief⌝ shall be sitting ; soften his head with grease, (and) pour ⌜milk⌝ into both his ears.

Commentary

 *yr ḏr* again introduces a reference to an observation already made in the examination and diagnosis, and *ḏr* must therefore have some such force here as " at the beginning," or " above," which is perhaps sufficiently suggested by simply rendering " Now when." Compare Case 4 (II 6) and Case 8 (IV 10).

On " his ⌜relief⌝ " (*sry-f*) see Case 17, VII 6.

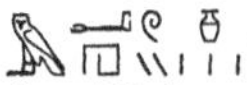 *mhwy*, "⌜milk⌝" is not the usual word. It occurs in the Middle Kingdom in the Kahun Medical Papyrus (2, 10) written  and in Papyrus Ebers essentially as here : 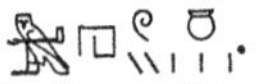. It is not a common term. As an ingredient in prescriptions it is found in Pap. Hearst IX 2 ; Pap. Ebers 33, 10 ; 33, 7 ; 49, 7 (emend) ; 82, 2–3. As produced by or made of fat, ointment, or grease, it occurs in the *mhwy n mrḥ·t* of Kahun Med. Pap. 2, 10 and Berlin Med. Pap. 3038, 16, 8 ; 18, 3 ; 18, 6 ; 19, 4. It is perhaps employed as a verb in the Kahun Med. Pap. (3, 4). It is possible that it means cream.

The omission of the frequent clause " until he recovers " after the treatment is noticeable. The treatment is evidently only alleviatory until the patient is released by death.

CASE TWENTY-ONE

VIII 6–9

A SPLIT IN THE TEMPORAL BONE

This case is the fourth in a series of five dealing with injuries to the temple (Cases 18–22). The surgeon's memoranda on the case are very brief, and he seems to regard it as an injury rather less serious than the " perforation " in Case 20. It will be found instructive to read at the same time Case 4 discussing a similar injury in the skull.

Title

VIII 6

6 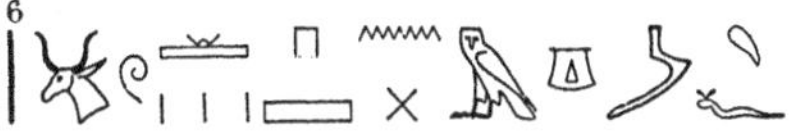

Translation

Instructions concerning a split in his temple.

Commentary

The nature of the injury which our surgeon calls a " split " (*pšn*) will be found discussed in Case 4 (II 2).

On the meaning of " temple " (*gmꜣ*) see Case 18, Gloss B.

EXAMINATION

VIII 6–8

Translation

If thou examinest a man having a split in his temple, shouldst thou find a swelling protruding on the outside of that split, while he discharges blood from his nostril and from his one ear having that split, (and) it is painful when he hears speech, because of it, (conclusion follows in diagnosis).

Commentary

" Swelling " (*t̲hb*) will be found discussed in Case 4 (II 4), which must be carefully studied in order to understand our case.

It is interesting to observe that the injury is so close to the neighboring ear that this " his one ear " is spoken of as " having that split ; " and the ear is furthermore so close to the wound that hearing sound is painful. We should perhaps render *md·t* as " sound " rather than as literally " speech."

DIAGNOSIS

VIII 8–9

Translation

Thou shouldst say concerning him : " One having a split in his temple, while he discharges blood from his nostril and his ear having that injury. An ailment with which I will contend."

Commentary

On *šḳr*, " injury," see Case 8 (IV 7). For the other terms see the references in the examination.

The diagnosis merely repeats the observations already noted in the examination and adds no new conclusions.

On the doubtful verdict 2, indicating a case too doubtful for prediction of the outcome, see Case 4 (II 6), and consult the introduction (pp. 45–47).

TREATMENT

VIII 9

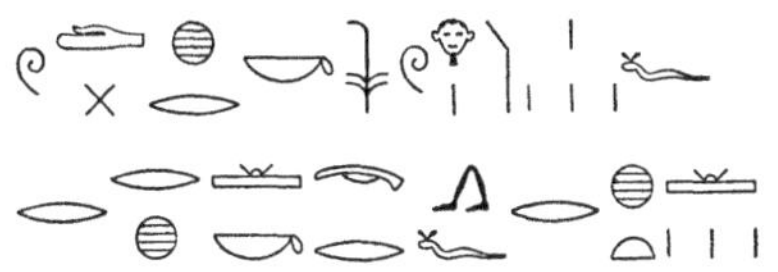

Translation

Thou shouldst put him at his mooring stakes, until thou knowest he has reached a decisive point.

Commentary

On the meaning of this extraordinary treatment, see Case 3, Gloss D (II 1–2), where the ancient commentator found it necessary to include an explanation.

The meaning of " reach a decisive point " is discussed in Case 4, Gloss C.

CASE TWENTY-TWO

VIII 9–17

COMPOUND COMMINUTED FRACTURE OF THE TEMPORAL BONE

This case is the last of five injuries of the temporal region and the temporal bone. The nature of the injury, which our surgeon calls *šd*, is discussed by him in Case 5 (II 11). It is the most serious case in the group, and includes the neighbouring ear in the area of the injury, so that in the course of his examination the surgeon is charged to probe the ear and seemingly to remove splinters of bone. The examination is followed by Verdict 3, the hopeless verdict, and no treatment is suggested.

Some interesting anatomy is included in the discussion. The word " chin " occurs for the first time in the medical papyri. The three explanatory glosses are instructive, especially Gloss A, where the word *ʾmʿ·t*, " ramus," thus far found only in our papyrus, is interestingly compared with the claw of a two-toed bird, which engages in the temporal bone as the bird's two-toed claw clutches an object. It is another striking example of our surgeon's ability to find familiar objects in the material world surrounding his readers by which to describe the shape of the organs or parts which he is explaining,—a method still practiced in all branches of natural science at the present day.

TITLE

VIII 9

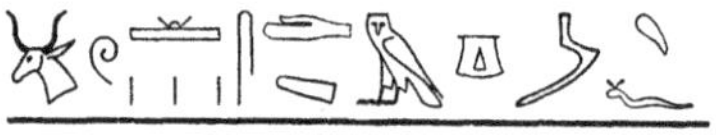

Translation

Instructions concerning a smash in his temple.

Commentary

The surgeon's understanding of a " smash " (*šd*) will be found discussed in Case 5 (II 11); and a gloss explaining *gmꜣ*, " temple," has been included by the ancient commentator in Case 18 (VII 13–14).

EXAMINATION

VIII 10–12

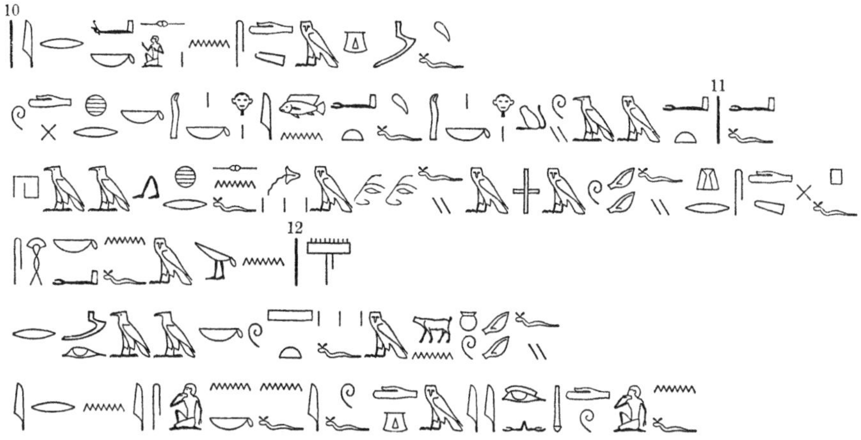

Translation

If thou examinest a man having a smash in his temple, thou shouldst place thy thumb upon his chin (and) thy finger upon the end of his ramus, so that the blood will flow from his two nostrils (and) from the interior of his ear having that smash. Cleanse (it) for him with a swab of linen until thou seest its fragments (of bone) in the interior of his ear. If thou callest to him (and) he is speechless (and) cannot speak, (conclusion follows in diagnosis).

Commentary

This interesting examination involves the surgeon in cleansing the nostrils and the ear on the injured side. The detailed instructions for placing the thumb and finger are presumably for applying pressure and inducing a flow of blood.

The question might arise whether we are to understand that the first [hieroglyphs] "thy finger" was intended to designate the *thumb*. The spreading and stretching of the other fingers from the chin to the head of the mandible would result in a rather ineffective and cramped position of the hand. In Case 25 (IX 4) the surgeon uses [hieroglyphs] *ʿn·t* "claw" for the entire group of four fingers, and then unmistakably designates the thumb by [hieroglyphs]. We are therefore entitled to conclude that he would employ *ḏbʿ* "finger" to mean thumb in Case 22.

[hieroglyphs] *ynʿ·t*, "chin," is a very rare word. Ember suggests a relationship with Hebrew לֹעַ (*Oriens*, No. 1, vol. I, Jan. 1926, p. 7, No. 10). The word is not found in any of the Egyptian medical papyri, and occurs outside of Papyrus Smith only in a masculine form employed once in the Pyramid Texts (1308a), where it is written [hieroglyphs]. The chin beard seems to be the significant thing about the determinative. In our papyrus it is employed five times, that is in four more examples besides Case 22. In Case 25, a dislocation of the mandible, the surgeon is to put his two "claws" (*ʿn·ty*, meaning two groups of four fingers each) "under the *ynʿ·t*" of the patient. The remaining three examples are all in Case 27. The position of this case in the treatise leaves little doubt as to the region designated by *ynʿ·t*. Case 23 carries us from the temple to the ear, Cases 24 and 25 are injuries of the mandible, Case 26 is a wound in the lip and the context shows that the *upper* lip is meant, while Case 27 deals with a wound in the *ynʿ·t*, which must be the lower part of the front of the face, having bone underlying the soft tissue. The meaning "chin" is obvious.

The anatomical term "end of his ramus" is interestingly explained in Gloss A (VIII 14–15).

The doubled form of the verb *h*ʾʾ in *h*ʾʾ-*ẖr* is also found in the Mathematical Papyrus. On the medical use of *h*ʾʾ see Case 20 (VII 24).

"His two nostrils." The scribe's unfortunate habit of writing any paired member or organ in the dual, even when it is obvious and important that only *one* should be designated, should be remembered here. It may be that he intended to write "his nostril." Compare the next paragraph.

[hieroglyphs] "his two ears" is of course an obvious error for *mśḏr-f*, "his ear," as the following phrase "having that smash" shows. The ear next to the injured temple is so close that it is referred to as "having" or "carrying," or "bearing" (*ẖr*) the injury, and this fact makes it certain that only one ear, the one on the injured side, is here designated. Compare the same mistake in the next sentence.

 *šk*, " cleanse," will be found explained in Case 11 (V 11), where the omission of the object " it " is also discussed. The " swab (or ' plug ') of linen " will also be found discussed in the commentary on Case 11 (V 11).

 *wš·t-f*, " his *wš·t*," is a difficult term which is explained in Gloss B at the end of our case (VIII 15–16).

 *ymyw*, " interior," literally " that which is in," probably designates here the inside of the ear, not the exudation which is to be cleaned out. In Case 12 (V 18) *ymyw* might designate the " content " of the nostrils, in view of the fact that it is the direct object of the verb *šk* " clean out." In both passages however it is more probably a variant of *ẖnw*, " interior."

The syntax of the conditional sentence at the end of the examination is unusual, beginning with the employment of the *n*-form after the conditional particle *yr*—a combination which is rare. The pseudo-participle (*dgm·y*) followed by a  + *n*-form for the imperfect is of course common (cf. Gunn, *Syntax*, Chap. XII) ; but the two clauses here belong to the protasis after *yr*, continuing the description of the symptoms on the basis of which the surgeon makes the diagnosis which is really the apodosis. It is also true that the two clauses, *yw-f dgm-y n mdw-n-f*, form an apodosis after " If thou callest to him," but the experimental calling and the observed result together form a composite protasis leading to the conclusion expressed in the diagnosis.

Diagnosis

VIII 13–14

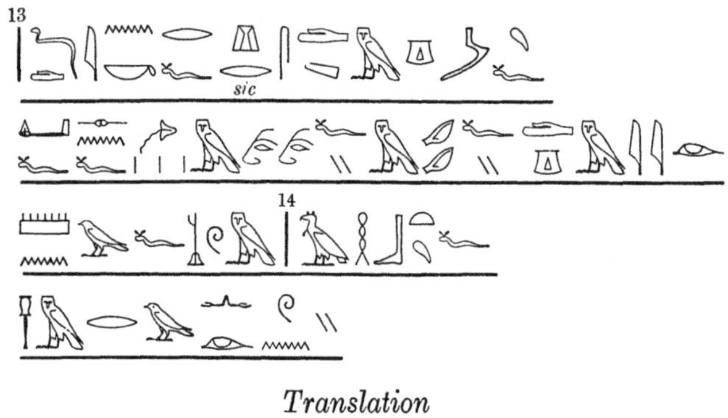

Translation

Thou shouldst say concerning him : " One having a smash in his temple ; he discharges blood from his two nostrils and from his ear ; he is speechless ; (and) he suffers with stiffness in his neck. An ailment not to be treated."

Commentary

All of the terms employed have already been discussed above. The dual " two ears " is undoubtedly an error as in two places in the examination. " He is speechless " (*dgm-y*) is explained by the surgeon at the end of the case in Gloss C (VIII 16–17), and the final item, stiffness in the neck, has been discussed in Case 3 (I 20). See the discussion of this diagnosis in the introduction (p. 51). The unfavorable verdict 3 has been explained in Case 5 (II 15) and also in the introduction (pp. 45–47). It is a case so serious that the surgeon cannot deal with it, and therefore follows the diagnosis by no suggested treatment.

GLOSS A

VIII 14–15

Explaining: The end of his ramus.

Translation

As for: "The end of his ramus," it means the end of his mandible. The ramus (*ʾmʿ·t*), the end of it is in his temple just as the claw of an *ʾamʿe*-bird (*ʾmʿ*) grasps an object.

Commentary

 *pḥ·wy*, "end," as an anatomical term is discussed in Case 7 (III 17) and Case 12 (V 21).

 *ʾmʿ·t*, "ramus," is evidently a technical anatomical term. Our papyrus contains the only known examples, of which there are eight. It is twice written with a *w*, as the fourth radical (III 17 and IX 3). It is likely to have been a word meaning "fork" or something similar, and this would explain its application (in the masculine *ʾmʿ*) to a two-toed bird. In Case 8 it is employed to describe a forked bone in the shoulder (IV 17–18), and that is obviously its application here. In our gloss we have the following parallelism:

"the end of his *ʾmʿ·t*."
"the end of his mandible."

The second phrase is used by the commentator as the equivalent of the first. This might lead us to the conclusion that the *ʾmʿ·t* is merely another term for mandible. This conclusion would be wrong however. In Case 25 (IX 3–4) we have the phrase:

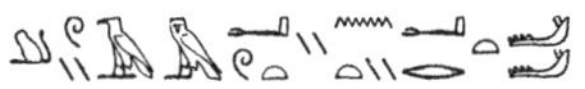

"the end of the two *ʾmʿw·t* of the two (sides of the) mandible." This not only shows that the *ʾmʿ·t* is part of the mandible, but also that there were two of them, one on each side of the mandible. The other indications of the position of the *ʾmʿ·t* in Papyrus Smith confirm and amplify what we have just learned. In Case 7 (III 17) the ligaments which operate the mandible are referred to as "the ligaments at the end of his *ʾmʿw·t*, which are fastened to his temporal bone, that is at the end of his jaw" (see commentary on III 17). In treating a case of dislocation of the mandible (Case 25), the surgeon is directed to place his thumbs "on the two *ʾmʿw·t* of the two (sides of) the mandible in the inside of his mouth" and his "two claws (= groups of fingers) under his chin." Finally our own gloss (VIII 14–15) states that the end of the *ʾmʿ·t* is "in his temple,"—a statement which can leave no doubt that *ʾmʿ·t* designates the ramus. The articulation of the ramus with the bones of the skull is then very interestingly compared with the grasp of a bird's claw. Before discussing the possible identity of this bird, we should note that the phrase  "claw of the *ʾamʿe*" is treated as a single word, to which is appended the determinative . This is obviously the claw of some two-toed bird, inserted here more or less as a drawing, or sketch of the bird's claw. It is of course an otherwise entirely unknown hieratic sign. To this two-toed bird's claw the ramus is appropriately compared, for its familiar forked head, terminating in the condyle and coronoid process, readily suggests such a forked or two-toed claw. See Pl. V, Fig. 11.

The identity of the *ʾamʿe*-bird is a difficult problem. He does not occur in any other scientific document of Ancient Egypt; but he is depicted once in a Twelfth Dynasty tomb at Benihasan[1] and both Rosellini and Champollion reproduce his colors. It should be borne in mind, however, that both in the colors themselves and in the distribution of the colors to form the markings distinguishing a given bird, the Egyptian painter allowed himself wide latitude. The old publications of nearly a century ago were likewise very inaccurate in such matters.

I have submitted these Benihasan paintings to the specialists at the Gizeh Zoological Gardens near Cairo and also to the eminent ornithologist Professor Dr. A. Koenig of Mecklenburg who has made a special study of African birds. Professor Koenig has kindly informed me that the only known two-toed bird is the ostrich, and has taken the trouble to study the paintings in detail. They are obviously not the ostrich, but the ancient painter's colors, if at all in harmony with those of the bird himself, do not, in Professor Koenig's opinion, permit identification with any African bird known at the present day. This was also the opinion of Major Borman, Director of the Gizeh Zoological Gardens.

[1] No. 15, Newberry, Vol. II, pl. IV = Lepsius, *Denkmaeler*, Text II, p. 98 = Rosellini, *Mon. civ.*, IX = Champollion, *Monuments* IV, pl. CCCL = Champollion, *Notices descr.*, II, p. 366.

Gloss B

VIII 15–16

Explaining: Thou seest his *wš·t* in the interior of his ear.

Translation

As for: "Thou seest its fragments (*wš·t*) in the interior of his ear," it means that some of the fragments (*wš·t*) of the bone come away to adhere to the swab which was introduced to cleanse the interior of his ear.

Commentary

wš·t, "fragments." The ancient commentator's practice of not infrequently including the word to be explained as an essential part of the explanation sometimes makes his commentary difficult to understand. We note in the first place that in the explanation the *wš·t* (plural) are said to be "of the bone," and that they can furthermore "come away" adhering to the cleaning swab introduced into the inner ear. If now we recall the nature of the injury as defined by the ancient surgeon himself, we find that a *šd*, "smash," is stated in Case 5 to be "a smash of his skull (such that) bones, getting into that smash, sink into the interior of his skull" (II 16). A similar injury of the skull in Case 4 results in carrying splinters of bone inward so that "fragments remain sticking in the flesh of his head and do not come away" (II 9). The word employed for fragments is *sp·w*. It is highly probable that our word *wš·t* is simply a synonym of *sp·w*, "fragments." The origin of this meaning for the otherwise entirely unknown word *wš·t* may possibly be the familiar word *wš*, "to be empty, to be bare, to be destroyed." The last meaning might conceivably be applied to fragments of shattered bone.[1]

The dual, "his two ears," is again twice written by the scribe incorrectly for the singular "his ear." *M ẖnw* after *šk*, "cleanse," may possibly be a noun formation with *m*, i. e. *mẖnw*, meaning "interior" rather than "in the interior," which leaves *šk* without an object. See another possible example in Case 26 (IX 7).

[1] The word (for), occurring twice in the Empire (Pap. Ebers 14, 11 and Pap. Leyden 345, verso 2, 9–10) is very unlikely to have any connection with our word *wš·t*.

Gloss C

VIII 16–17

Explaining: He is speechless.

[a] This is an error of the scribe which he has corrected by a cross inserted afterward in red ink over the black and intended to cancel the . The word is therefore to be read *ʿḳ·t*, not *ʿḳ·t-f*.

Translation

As for: " He is speechless," it means that he is silent in sadness, without speaking, like one suffering with ⌜feebleness⌝ (*dgy*) because of something that has entered from outside.

Commentary

The word *dgm-y* explained in this gloss is rare and difficult. Outside of our papyrus the word is known only twice: once applied to a sick ox in the Kahun Veterinary Papyrus (l. 59) and again in a very obscure passage in the Metternich Stela (l. 202). These throw no light on its meaning. It is used in five different cases in Papyrus Edwin Smith, where it occurs nine times as follows:

Case 13, Compound Comminuted Fracture in the Side of the Nose. The patient is unable to open his mouth except with much pain and he is *dgm*.

Case 17, Compound Comminuted Fracture of the Bone in the Region of the Maxilla and the Zygoma. The patient is unable to open his mouth except with much pain, and he is *dgm*.

Case 20, Wound in the Temple, the Bone Being Perforated. The patient is semiunconscious, makes no reply when questioned as to his condition, and is *dgm*.

Case 22, Compound Comminuted Fracture in the Temple. According to the examination (VIII 12), " if thou callest to him, he is *dgm*, and he cannot speak," while according to the above gloss, *dgm* means " his being silent in sadness, without speaking."

Case 33, Broken Neck, One Vertebra of the Neck Being Crushed into the Next. The patient's arms and legs are paralysed, he is *dgm* and unable to speak.

In view of this evidence it can hardly be doubted that *dgm* means " to be speechless," so widely interpreted, however, that it could also designate the inability of an ox to use his voice; that is, it had originally some such meaning as "to be voiceless." The root is doubtless triliteral, and the at the end is of course the ending of the third masculine singular of the pseudo-participle.

gmw is a rare word meaning "mourning, sadness" or "to mourn." During the Seven Years' Famine recounted in the Famine Stela (1–2), the king says, "I mourn () in the great seat in the palace." The noun *gmw*, "mourning, sadness," is found in the Tale of Sinuhe (R, l. 9). A feminine noun, seemingly with the same meaning, is found in the Book of the Dead (ed. Naville, 7, 3 Ca) and in the Book of Apophis (Brit. Mus. Pap. 10188, 26, 13).

dgy, ⌜"feebleness,"⌝ is not a rare word, but its medical or pathological significance is difficult to determine. It is obviously something undesirable, and may mean something like "be feeble" or "feebleness," "be paralysed" or "paralysis." In the description of the fleeing king of the Libyans on the Israel Stela it is said of him: "His two feet were *dgy*" (l. 6).

"Something that has entered from the outside" is our surgeon's designation of an external physical cause. See full commentary in Case 8, Glosses C and D.

CASE TWENTY-THREE

VIII 18–22

A SLIT IN THE OUTER EAR

This is the only case in our treatise which deals exclusively with the ear, although a number of injuries to the head have involved the ear. It is a very simple case of a wound by which the outer ear has been slit, and furnishes one of the clearest of this earliest known group of cases which obliged the surgeon to resort to sewing up the wound. According to his custom the ancient surgeon has here included the instructions to stitch up the wound in his paragraph on the examination, preceding the diagnosis. The treatment therefore begins with the wound already stitched, and concerns itself with what is to happen after that point has been reached, especially with the contingency that the wound does not heal and that the stitching loosens. The "lips of his wound" are then to be kept together with linen rolls placed as pads behind the auricle, until with the application of the inevitable "grease, honey (and) lint," the wound finally heals.

TITLE

VIII 18

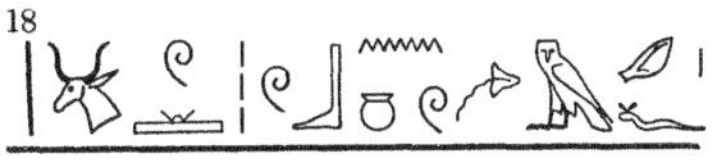

Translation

Instructions concerning a wound in his ear.

Commentary

The surgeon's understanding of the word *wbnw*, " wound," will be found discussed in Case 1 (pp. 81–84). "Ear" has been treated in Case 4 (II 4). It is to be read *mśḏr* here, and its anatomical meaning in this case will appear as the discussion proceeds.

EXAMINATION

VIII 18–19

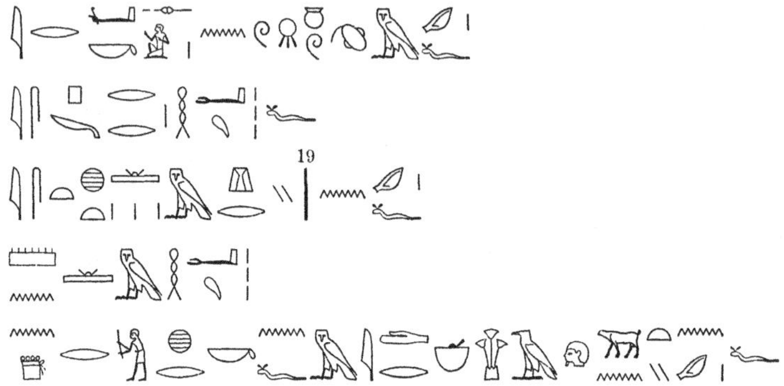

Translation

If thou examinest a man having a wound in his ear, cutting through its flesh, the injury being in the lower part of his ear, (and) confined to the flesh, thou shouldst draw (it) together for him with stitching behind the hollow of his ear.

Commentary

 *mśḏr*, " ear," has been discussed as to the reading in Case 4 (II 4). Anatomically its range of meaning in Egyptian is wide, as it is in English. It occurs twenty-five times in Papyrus Smith, and of these examples six are in our Case 23. Of the remaining nineteen examples, thirteen occur in the statement that the patient discharges blood from his ear, meaning of course the orifice of the ear. In Case 22 the ear is mentioned four times in the phrase " interior of his ear ; " in Case 20 a medicament is " poured into his two ears " (VIII 5). In all these cases the orifice or the *inner* ear is the meaning of *mśḏr*. The anatomical description in Case 18, locating the *gmꜣ* as between the corner of the eye and the 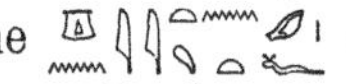 (VII 14), possibly " ⌈orifice⌉ of his ear," may be dealing with the outer or the inner ear, or both. In our Case 23, however, it is obvious that the surgeon is discussing an injury of the outer ear, the auricle.

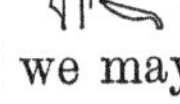 *yśp*, " cutting," is a new word, of which only one other occurrence is known, if we may accept its probable identity with the similar word found in a descriptive phrase inscribed over a man working with mallet and chisel in an Old Kingdom relief scene :  (Davies, *Deir el-Gebrâwi*, I, pl. XVI). Here *ysp* evidently designates

the act of chiseling or cutting, and its determinative of an axe is doubtless a variant of the knife appearing in the Smith Papyrus.

r-r', "through," literally "into the mouth of," is a compound preposition not very well understood. It is not certain that the rendering "through" adequately represents its meaning here. The prepositions in our papyrus are employed to designate positions, situations and local relations confined within such narrow local and physical limits, that the traditional renderings applying to more spacious situations are insufficient or even incorrect.

ḥʿ·w-f, "its flesh." It is obvious that the pronoun here does not refer to the patient ("his flesh"), but to the masculine "ear," that is, "its flesh," meaning of course the flesh or soft tissue of the outer ear.

yḫ·t, "injury" (literally "thing") will be found discussed in the commentary on Case 4; see II 3 (2 b).

mn m, "confined to," is a rather free rendering of one of the anatomical meanings of this phrase, when it may be rendered "attached to." See Case 4, Gloss A (II 9). Reverting to its original meaning "remaining in," we see that its significance here, "confined to," is not at all unnatural.

nḏry, "draw together," as employed surgically will be found discussed in Case 10 (V 6).

ydr, "stitching," one of the six earliest known examples of surgical stitching, has been fully treated in Case 10 (V 6). The modifications following "stitching" are not easy to understand. As rendered above they seem to be intended to indicate the side on which the surgeon will stitch the wound, suggesting that he will work on the convex side of the auricle, the side next to the head. We are again confronted by the difficulty in rendering our old and familiar prepositions when applied within very restricted local limits. *Ḥ'*, "behind," often means "around" or "beside." *H̱nty*, rendered "hollow" is otherwise unknown, and the meaning "hollow," which doubtless refers to the concave side of the auricle, is based on the common and related word *ẖnw*, "interior, inside." If now we accept the rendering "with stitching behind the hollow of his ear" as containing a correct interpretation of the local terms *ḥ'* and *ẖnty*, we have still to interpret these instructions in terms of the surgeon's actual manual and physical procedure. The wound has slit the auricle from front to back, and the surgeon might therefore pass the needle back and forth between back and front of the auricle. It would seem, however, that these directions are so phrased as to instruct the surgeon to work exclusively from the back of the auricle, that is, to keep his needle there, thrusting it both in and out again from the back of the auricle.

In this examination our surgeon has included the directions to stitch the wound together, in accordance with his custom of inserting instructions regarding purely physical manipulation in the examination rather than in the treatment.

DIAGNOSIS

VIII 19–20

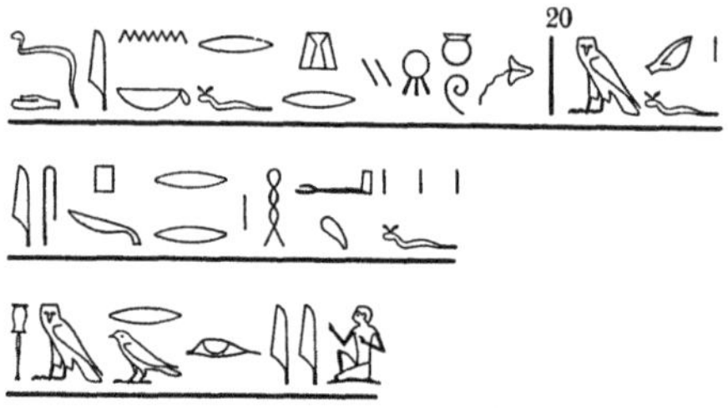

Translation

Thou shouldst say concerning him: "One having a wound in his ear, cutting through its flesh. An ailment which I will treat."

Commentary

These words are only a repetition of the beginning of the examination to which the favorable verdict has been appended. On this verdict see the commentary in Case 1 (I 2), and the discussion in the introduction (pp. 45 ff.).

TREATMENT

VIII 20–22

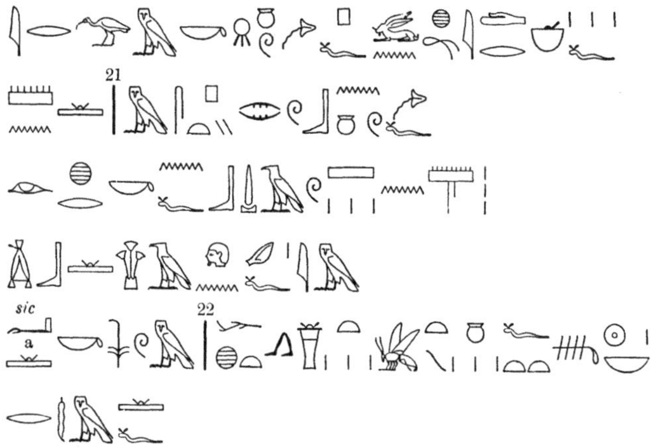

[a] The scribe has inserted a small globular object under the hand. See Vol. II, pl. VIII, l. 21.

Translation

If thou findest the stitching of that wound loose (and) sticking in the two lips of his wound, thou shouldst make for him stiff rolls of linen (and) pad the back of his ear therewith. Thou shouldst treat it afterward [with] grease, honey (and) lint every day until he recovers.

Commentary

The initial condition literally reads "If thou findest that wound, its stitching loosened,"—a common participial construction. Full commentary on *ydr*, "stitching," will be found in Case 10 (V 6), and *mn m*, "sticking in," has been treated in Case 4 (II 9). "Rolls" (*bdꜣ·w*) or "plugs" of linen have been taken up in Case 11 (V 13).

 *ḥꜣ* is not the preposition here. It is followed by the genitive *n*, which never appears with the preposition and hence must be a noun, here meaning "back." Grammatically it is probably the subject: "wherewith the back of his ear is to be padded." The question arises whether the loosening of the stitching is due to the absorption of surgical gut or the like, used in the stitching, a result desired and intended by the surgeon; or due to failure of the wound to heal, so that the rolls of linen placed behind the *auricula* are a substitute intended to accomplish the healing together, which the surgeon's stitching failed to do. An examination of the related material discloses four cases (10, 14, 23, and 47) in which the stitching is found loose. They have been discussed in Case 10 (V 6), and the loose stitching found to be due to failure to heal (see p. 230). On "grease, honey (and) lint," see Case 1 (I 3).

CASE TWENTY-FOUR

VIII 22–IX 2

A FRACTURE OF THE MANDIBLE

This case is the first of two concerning injuries to the mandible. Although the surgeon calls the injury *ḥśb*, not so serious a type of fracture as *śd*, a compound comminuted fracture, it is nevertheless a case which he regards as fatal, and he suggests no treatment.

Title

VIII 22

Translation

Instructions concerning a fracture in his mandible.

Commentary

 *ḥśb*, "fracture," has been fully treated in Case 11 (V 10).

Examination

VIII 22–23

[a] The demonstrative was at first omitted by the scribe and afterward inserted.

Translation

If thou examinest a man having a fracture in his mandible, thou shouldst place thy hand upon it. Shouldst thou find that fracture crepitating under thy fingers, (conclusion follows in diagnosis).

Commentary

The surgical meaning of *nḫbḫb*, "crepitate," lit. "break open," "break through" will be found discussed in Case 13 (VI 4–5).

Diagnosis

VIII 23-IX 2

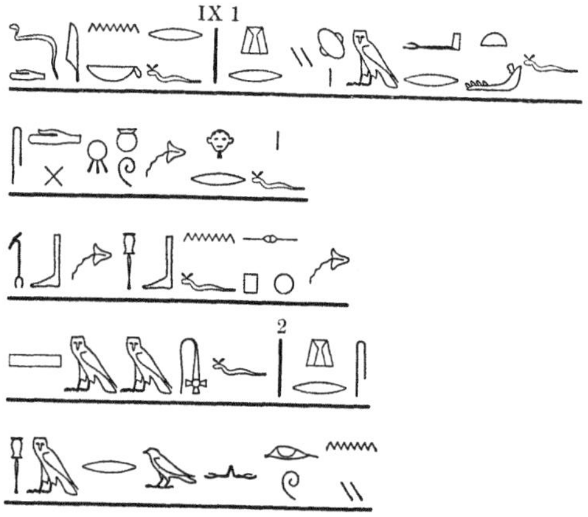

Translation

Thou shouldst say concerning him: "One having a fracture in his mandible, over which a wound has been inflicted, ⌈- - - -⌉ (and) he has fever from it. An ailment not to be treated."

Commentary

 *šd*, "inflicted," lit. "broken open," as used of soft tissue overlying an injured bone, is discussed in Case 5 (II 11).

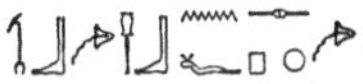 is totally unintelligible.

The injury is here shown to be a fracture of the mandible such that the soft tissue overlying the fracture has been ruptured. The three or four unintelligible words following this observation probably described further the injury to the soft tissue. The injury is serious enough to cause fever, and permit no hope of the patient's recovery. The unfavorable verdict is followed by no treatment. See the discussion of this verdict in Case 5 (II 15) and in the introduction (pp. 46–47). The diagnosis as a whole will be found discussed in the introduction (pp. 45–51).

CASE TWENTY-FIVE

IX 2–6

A DISLOCATION OF THE MANDIBLE

This case is of unusual interest. The surgeon's directions for the reduction of the dislocated mandible, with the "thumbs upon the ends of the two rami of the mandible in the inside of his mouth," while the fingers of both hands are clutching the mandible below, that is on the outside, are so detailed as to the position of the surgeon's hands that the manipulation can be compared with that shown in the drawing of the process by Apollonios of Kitium in his commentary on Hippocrates. See introduction above, pp. 16–17 and Pl. VI, Fig. 12. There can be no doubt but that the Hippocratic manipulation was identical with that of our treatise, and Dr. Luckhardt informs me that the modern manipulation is also still the same as described in our papyrus.

According to his custom our surgeon has included his instructions for the physical manipulation of the injury in the *examination*. The treatment which follows is evidently intended merely to soothe the strained muscles and irritated tissues after the surgeon has restored the dislocated mandible to its proper place.

TITLE

IX 2

Translation

Instructions concerning a dislocation in his mandible.

Commentary

Wnḫ, "dislocation," has been treated in Case 10 (under *ydr*, V 6). *ʿr·t*, "mandible," is fully discussed in Case 7 (III 16).

EXAMINATION

IX 2–5

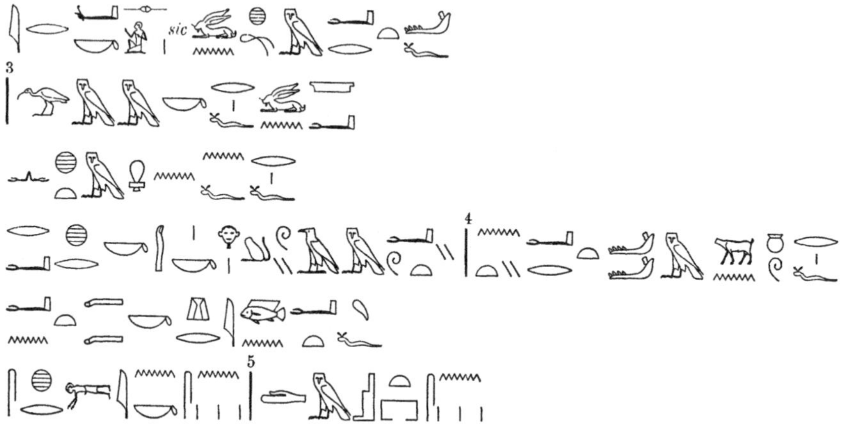

Translation

If thou examinest a man having a dislocation in his mandible, shouldst thou find his mouth open (and) his mouth cannot close for him, thou shouldst put thy thumb(s) upon the ends of the two rami of the mandible in the inside of his mouth, (and) thy two claws (meaning two groups of fingers) under his chin, (and) thou shouldst cause them to fall back so that they rest in their places.

Commentary

 *ʾmʿw·ty*, "the two rami," written in the dual, has been discussed in Case 22, Gloss A (VIII 14). The feminine dual of the following genitive 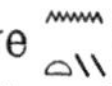 *n·ty* is an archaic survival almost unknown outside of Papyrus Edwin Smith, and an important evidence of the early date of the text.

In accordance with our ancient surgeon's custom we find the physical manipulation of the injury included in the examination and not in the treatment.

 *ʿn·ty*, literally "two claws," means of course the two groups of fingers of both hands exclusive of the thumbs. See discussion in Case 8, Gloss E.

 although written in the singular, must be dual, as the connection clearly shows; for the surgeon is to put his  on each of the two rami. The use of *ʿn·ty* for the fingers also shows that  must designate the thumb. It is also used for the thumb in Case 22, q.v.

d, " so that they rest " (from *wdy*), is of course a pseudo-participle of resulting condition, as long ago recognized by Erman (*Grammatik*³, § 332, p. 175). The subject of this verbal form is a pronoun, of which the antecedent is the same as that of *śn*. The latter must be either the two rami, or the mandible itself considered as a dual. *śn* is not written as a dual; another example perhaps in Case 11 (V 13). The disregard of the fact that the subject of *d* is a *feminine* noun in the dual is also to be expected after the pronoun .

DIAGNOSIS

IX 5

Translation

Thou shouldst say concerning him: " One having a dislocation in his mandible. An ailment which I will treat."

Commentary

The diagnosis is, as so frequently, merely a repetition of the title (q. v. for references to the commentary), to which the favorable verdict 1 has been appended. On this verdict see the commentary in Case 1 (I 2) and in the introduction (pp. 45 ff.).

TREATMENT

IX 5–6

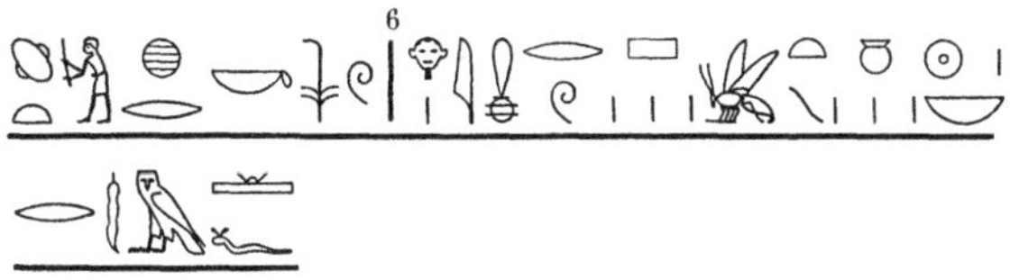

Translation

Thou shouldst bind it with *ymrw*, (and) honey every day until he recovers.

Commentary

On *ymrw* see Case 15 (VI 17) and for treatment with honey see Case 1 (I 3). The treatment is evidently intended merely to soothe the strained ligaments and tissues.

CASE TWENTY-SIX

IX 6–13

A WOUND IN THE UPPER LIP

This case is another convincing example of the ancient surgeon's employment of stitching to draw together a wound in the soft tissue. He does not state anywhere that the wound is in the *upper* lip, but the instructions are to probe " as far as the column of the nose," indicating clearly that the wound is in the upper lip. The discussion is accompanied by a single gloss, explaining the meaning of a rare word (*yśdb*) for " piercing through." This gloss furnishes an interesting example of the ancient commentator's carelessness in collecting his materials, for in inserting this gloss he forgot that he had already included it once in Case 14 (VI 12–14), in explaining the character of a wound in the nostril.

TITLE

IX 6

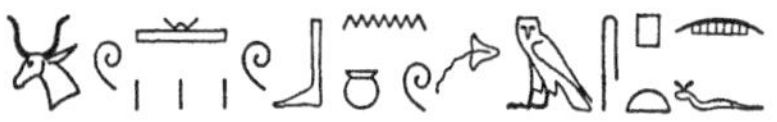

Translation

Instructions concerning a wound in his lip.

Commentary

Wbnw, " wound," will be found discussed in Case 1 (pp. 81–84).

EXAMINATION

IX 6–8

Translation

If thou examinest a man having a wound in his lip, piercing through to the inside of his mouth, thou shouldst examine his wound as far as the column of his nose. Thou shouldst draw together that wound [with] stitching.

Commentary

yśdb, "piercing through," has been treated in Case 14, Gloss A (VI 12–14).

mḫnw, " the inside," is a noun formation of *ḫnw* with *m*. Compare Case 22, Gloss B (VIII 16), which perhaps contains a similar example ; but it should be noted that the text of our case in the parallel passages in the diagnosis and in Gloss A writes *n ḫnw* not *n mḫnw*.

ywnw n fnd-f, " column of his nose," will be found discussed in Case 11 (V 14), Gloss A.

nḏry, " draw together," has been treated in Case 10 (V 6).

ydr, " stitching," is also discussed in the same connection. The omission of the preposition *m*, " with," is very common in our treatise, especially before the names of medicaments. This peculiarity suggests for the document the character of rapid memoranda. It may also raise the question whether these omissions are possibly survivals from an archaic stage which practiced the omission of prepositions, as for example on the Palermo Stone.

DIAGNOSIS

IX 8–9

[a] The scribe wrote and then covered one stroke of with the head of , leaving the other stroke visible.

Translation

Thou shouldst say concerning him : " One having a wound in his lip, piercing through to the inside of his mouth. An ailment which I will treat."

Commentary

See commentary on the examination, of which this diagnosis is a partial repetition, to which the favorable verdict 1 has been added. On this verdict see commentary on Case 1 (I 2) and the introduction (pp. 45 ff.).

This diagnosis is another good illustration of the fact that the diagnosis is often regarded as not necessarily containing any other conclusion than the statement of the practical course of procedure which the surgeon is to follow, that is, the verdict. See Introduction, p. 48.

TREATMENT

IX 9–11

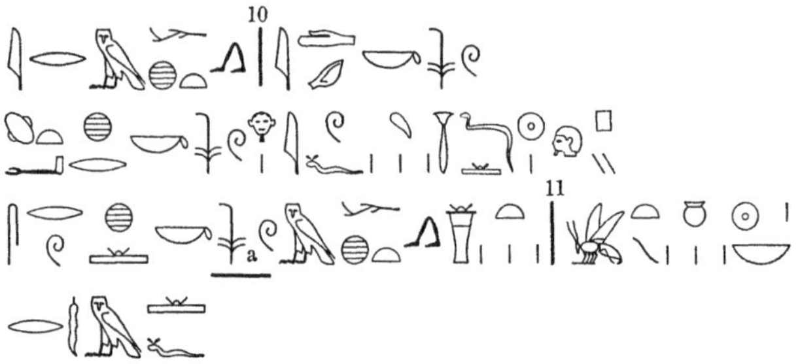

[a] This word was at first omitted by the scribe and afterward inserted in red ink in a passage written in black.

Translation

Now after thou hast stitched it thou shouldst bind it with fresh meat the first day. Thou shouldst treat it afterward [with] grease (and) honey every day until he recovers.

Commentary

 *ydr*, " stitch," is one of only *two* cases in our treatise, in which it is employed as a verb. See Case 10 (V 6) where it is fully discussed.

On the treatment with fresh meat, followed by grease and honey, see Case 1 (I 2–3).

We notice that as usual the surgeon places the stitching of the wound in the examination, and that the treatment is a matter of medicaments. His reversion to the stitching at the beginning of the treatment is not usual. It is found also in Case 10 (V 7). In Case 10, however, he provides for the possibility that the wound may not heal after stitching. In our case he does not apprehend any such contingency.

Dr. Luckhardt remarks : " Because of the high vascularity of the lips, wounds in them heal with great rapidity and by primary intention (*per primam intentionem*), i. e., without infection, in spite of the fact that neck wounds may be infected. But a stitch in the lip, especially if the cut is deep and at right angles to it, is important to prevent gaping and subsequent healing with a separation of the cut edges (because of the transection of the *m. orbicularis oris*)."

GLOSS A

IX 11–13

Explaining : A wound in his lip piercing through to the inside of his mouth.

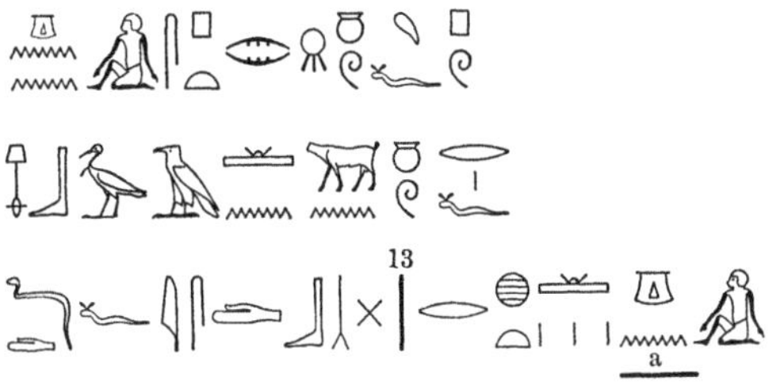

[a] The scribe at first incorrectly omitted the ~~~~, and afterward inserted it in red ink in a passage written in black.

Translation

As for : " A wound in his lip, piercing through to the inside of his mouth ;" it means that the two lips of his wound are soft, opening to the inside of his mouth. One says : " Pierced through " (*yśdb*) concerning soft things.

Commentary

This explanation of the meaning of *yśdb*, " piercing through," has already been given by the ancient commentator in discussing a wound in the nostril (Case 14, VI 12–14). The text in our gloss is a little fuller than in Case 14, and the variant " he says," where Case 14 has " as is said " or " as one says " is of slight consequence. By *gn*, " soft," the commentator doubtless means " permeable," or " penetrable." See commentary on Case 14, Gloss A.

CASE TWENTY-SEVEN

IX 13–18

A GAPING WOUND IN THE CHIN

This case is the last in the series discussing injuries to the head (*caput*). The preceding case dealt with a wound in the upper lip, and in Case 27 the discussion passes to the region below the mouth, which the surgeon calls 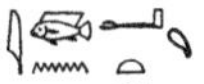 *ynꜥ·t*, " chin." It is interesting to observe that in Case 26, a wound in the upper lip, we are informed that the wound has " two lips " (IX 12), and that the surgeon is to close it with stitching ; whereas in Case 27, a similar wound as the description shows, he employs the " two strips," doubtless adhesive tape, to accomplish the same purpose, as will be seen by an examination of the discussion of " two strips " in Case 2 (I 15). The explanation is perhaps to be found in the different situation of the two wounds.

TITLE

IX 13

Translation

Instructions concerning a gaping wound in his chin.

Commentary

 *wbnw n kf·t*, "gaping wound," is fully discussed in Case 1 (examination), pp. 91–92.

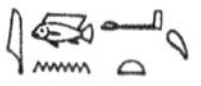 *ynʿ·t*, "chin" is treated in Case 22 (VIII 10).

EXAMINATION

IX 13–15

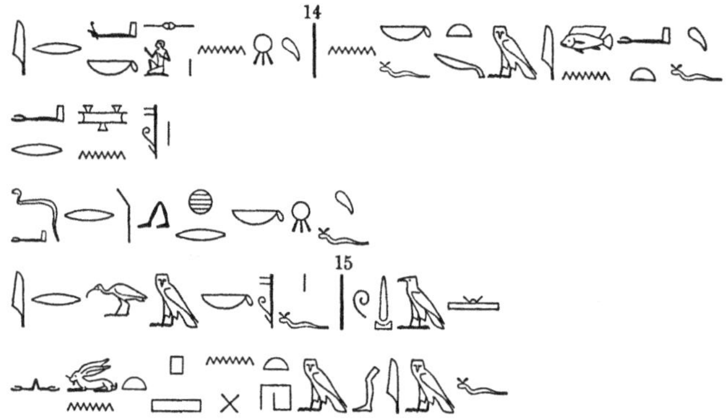

Translation

If thou examinest a man having a gaping wound in his chin, penetrating to the bone, thou shouldst palpate his wound. If thou shouldst find his bone uninjured, not having a split, (or) a perforation in it, (conclusion follows in diagnosis).

Commentary

"Penetrating to the bone" (*ʿr n ḳś*) has been discussed in Case 1, pp. 87–88.

Ḏʿr, "probe," or "palpate," see Case 1 (pp. 92–93) and Case 8 (IV 5).

On uninjured bone under the wounded tissue, and the list of possible injuries to the bone enumerated as not present, see Case 2 (I 13–14, and Gloss C, I 17) and especially Case 18 (VII 9), from which it will be seen that our text has omitted one (*šd*, "compound comminuted fracture") of the three injuries to the bone usually enumerated by our ancient author in such cases. Commentary on these injuries will be found in Case 4 (*pšn*, "split," II 2) and Case 3 (*thm*, "perforate," I 18). It is at this point, at the conclusion of the examination, that this treatise is inclined to insert instructions for the physical manipulation of the injury, which in this present case, however, are included in the treatment. See Introduction, p. 42.

DIAGNOSIS

IX 15–16

Translation

Thou shouldst say concerning him: "One having a gaping wound in his chin, penetrating to the bone. An ailment which I will treat."

Commentary

See examination above (IX 13–15), of which the diagnosis is a partial repetition, followed by the favorable verdict 1. See the discussion of this verdict in the commentary on Case 1 (I 2) and in the introduction (pp. 45 ff.).

TREATMENT

IX 16–18

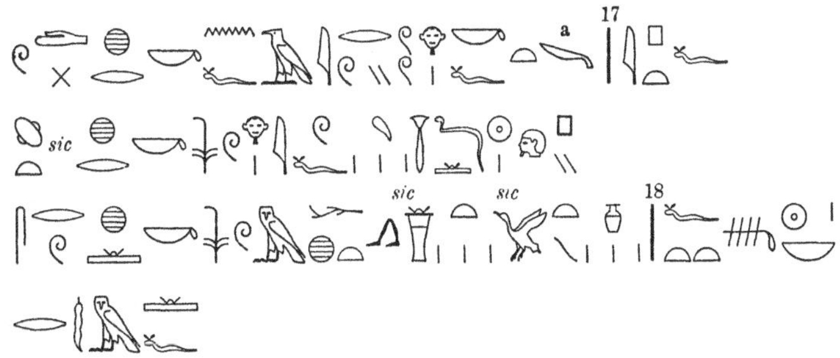

[a] The knife drips blood, but the character is not available in the fount.

Translation

Thou shouldst apply for him two strips on that gash. Thou shouldst bind it with fresh meat the first day, (and) thou shouldst treat it afterward [with] grease, honey (and) lint every day until he recovers.

Commentary

On the meaning of the "two strips," probably adhesive tape, see Case 2 (I 15). Our example is a significant indication of the function of the "two strips," for they are employed here on the chin for the same kind of injury, which in the preceding case, a wound in the upper lip, required surgical stitching.

On this difference in treatment between this and the preceding case Dr. Luckhardt remarks : " Wounds of the chin are likely to gape *less* than wounds of the lip, particularly if the wound of the chin is parallel with the course of the fibers of the *m. triangularis* and platysma. Hence we have stitching in the preceding case as against taping in Case 27."

The use of the plural of the word " gash " (*kf·t*), which cannot be brought out in the translation, is discussed in the commentary on *kf·t* in Case 1. On the treatment with fresh meat, followed by grease, honey, and lint, see also Case 1. The meaning of " until he recovers " is likewise discussed under Case 1.

CASE TWENTY-EIGHT

IX 18–X 3

A GAPING WOUND IN THE THROAT PENETRATING TO THE GULLET

After the discussion of twenty-seven miscellaneous injuries in various parts of the head, the surgeon now moves downward and in Case 28 takes up an injury in the throat. It is a gaping knife wound which penetrates to the gullet, so that if the injured man drinks water it issues from the mouth of the wound. Included in the examination is the stitching of the wound, a physical manipulation such as our surgeon customarily inserts in his examination, confining the treatment to the external application of medicaments. Such a classification of the surgical operation suggests that as a mechanical manipulation it was not regarded by ancient Egyptian medicine as properly belonging to the treatment, which was a matter of recipes and medicinal applications. We have here a suggestion of specialization. See Introduction, p. 42. If a second examination discloses that the fever persists, a second treatment is prescribed, and it is interesting to observe that in spite of the persistent fever, the patient is placed on his normal diet, or as the Egyptian surgeon phrases it, he is moored at his mooring stakes (compare Case 3, Gloss D).

The organization of the discussion is as follows :

I

Title (IX 18)
First examination and instructions to stitch (IX 18–21).
Diagnosis and verdict 2 (IX 21–22).
First treatment (X 1–2).

II

Second examination (X 2).
Second treatment (X 2–3).

TITLE

IX 18

Translation

Instructions concerning a wound in his throat.

Commentary

On "wound" see Case 1 (pp. 81–84). The anatomical meaning of *ḫꜥm*, "throat," will be found discussed immediately below.

EXAMINATION

IX 18–21

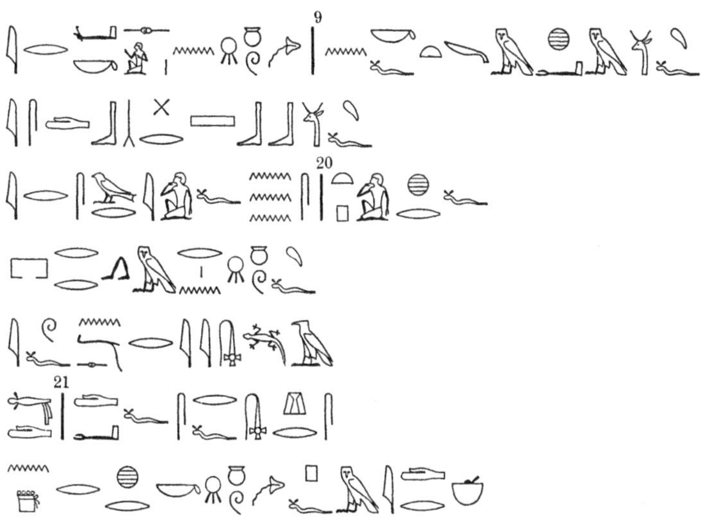

Translation

If thou examinest a man having a gaping wound in his throat, piercing through to his gullet; if he drinks water he ⸢chokes⸣ (and) it comes out of the mouth of his wound; it is greatly inflamed, so that he develops fever from it; thou shouldst draw together that wound with stitching.

Commentary

"Gaping wound" (*wbnw n kf·t*) has been fully discussed in Case 1 (pp. 90–92).

 *ḫꜥm*, or *ḫꜥmw*, "throat," is a rare word the anatomical meaning of which has never been studied or determined. In Papyrus Ebers there is a case of fatty swellings on the *ḫꜥm*, which require lancing, but the text does not contain any

intimation of the meaning of *ẖꜥm* (Pap. Ebers 105, 1–8). The only other case (Ebers 76, 8) in the medical papyri is likewise of no assistance. Outside of the medical papyri only two examples of the word are known (Petrie, *Dendereh*, pl. XXXVII G, l. 686 and Lacau, *Sarcophages*, Vol. I, p. 144 = Cairo 28052), both of which are in hopelessly obscure passages. We are therefore dependent on Papyrus Edwin Smith for the meaning of the word. It is not found in our document outside of Case 28, which, however, fairly well discloses its meaning. We are told in the above examination that the wound in the *ẖꜥm* penetrates to the gullet (*šbb*). *H̱ꜥm* therefore means "throat" rather than "neck," for which our surgeon regularly employs *nḥb·t*.

Yšdb, "piercing through," has been discussed in Case 14 (VI 14).

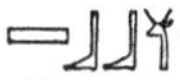 *šbb*, "gullet," is not a common word. The following parallel passages in the Book of the Dead, however, determine its meaning:

 Book of the Dead, ed. Naville, 172, 22 (Aa).

 *Ibid.*, 172, 19 (Aa).

It will be seen in these two passages that *šbb* is used as a variant of *ḥty·t*, a well-known word for "throat."

 *štp-ẖr-f* "he chokes," is really a guess. The *ẖr*-form of the verb indicates that it expresses the result which follows upon the act of drinking. We should possibly regard this choking or gasping as the cause for the issuance of the water from the mouth of the wound, and render, "so that it comes out, etc." *Stp* is seemingly a ἅπαξ λεγόμενον.

nsr-y, "it is inflamed," is explained in Case 41, Gloss A, q. v. The masculine pronoun might be taken here as designating the patient. A study of the parallel cases, however, shows that *nsr* is employed to describe the *local* inflammation; its subject is often the wound. The result for the patient is fever as here.

 *šrf*, "fever," will be found discussed in Case 41, Gloss B, where the ancient commentator has thrown some light on it.

On surgical stitching see *nḏry*, "draw together," and *ydr*, "stitching," in Case 10 (V 6).

DIAGNOSIS

IX 21–22

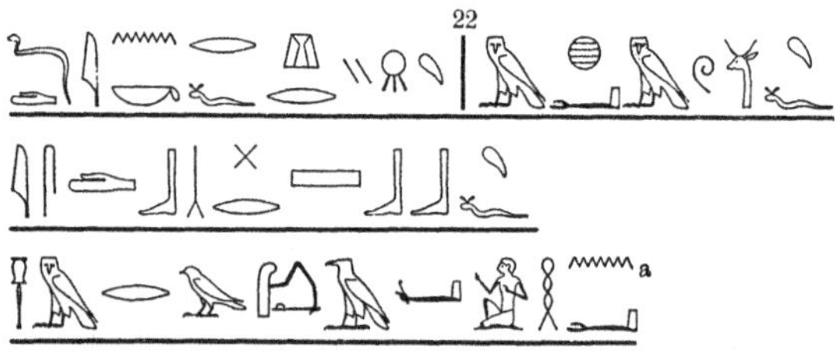

[a] Probable traces of the first word of the treatment, afterward smeared out.

Translation

Thou shouldst say concerning him: "One having a wound in his throat, piercing through to his gullet. An ailment with which I will contend."

Commentary

The terms will be found discussed in the preceding examination, of which the diagnosis is an incomplete repetition of the first part. The omission of "gaping" (*n kf·t*) is probably a scribal error. The doubtful verdict 2 will be found discussed in Case 4 (II 6). See also the introduction (pp. 45 ff.).

First Treatment

X 1–2

Translation

Thou shouldst bind it with fresh meat the first day. Thou shouldst treat it afterward [with] grease, honey (and) lint every day, until he recovers.

Commentary

On the treatment with fresh meat followed by grease, honey and lint, see Case 1 (I 2–3).

Second Examination

X 2

[a] This word *šw* was omitted by the scribe and was afterward inserted as a correction in red ink over black.

Translation

If, however, thou findest him continuing to have fever from that wound, (conclusion in following second treatment).

Commentary

In view of the fact that the first treatment deals with the fever arising from the inflammation in the wound, we expect some other symptom to be disclosed from the second examination, which necessitates additional treatment. We must conclude therefore that *šmm,* " to be hot, feverish " in the second examination, either means a greater degree of fever than *śrf,* the synonym employed in the first examination (IX 21) ; or the verbal form *šmm-f* in the second examination indicates continuance, perhaps persistent continuance of the fever. The latter is the more probable conclusion. In Case 47 the fourth examination employs *šmm-f* in precisely the same connection. On the other hand when a case has not yet disclosed any fever and it is discovered in a second examination, the surgeon says, " If, then, thou findest that man, his flesh having developed (*n*-form) fever," as we find it in Case 7, second examination (III 8–9). See also the discussion of the words for fever in our treatise, in Case 41, Gloss A.

SECOND TREATMENT

X 2–3

Translation

Thou shouldst apply for him dry lint in the mouth of his wound, (and) moor (him) at his mooring stakes until he recovers.

Commentary

Regarding the application of " dry lint," apparently without a bandage, Dr. Luckhardt remarks : " In a case of high fever because of infection, the dry lint was perhaps indicated to promote drainage in place of the usual grease and honey ointment. By capillary attraction it would hasten the absorption of the wound secretion and the pus."

The discussion of *ftt,* " lint," will be found in Case 1 (I 3).

The strange figure of speech " moor him at his mooring stakes " is explained in Case 3, Gloss D (II 1–2).

CASE TWENTY-NINE

X 3–8

A GAPING WOUND IN A CERVICAL VERTEBRA

The preceding case concerning an injury which must have been located somewhere in the general anterior portion of the neck involved only soft tissue. The surgeon now proceeds to the back of the neck and takes up five cases of injuries to the cervical vertebrae (Cases 29–33). In only one of these (Case 31, X 16) does he designate which of the cervical vertebrae he means. In Case 31 he refers to the possible extension of the injury further down to affect the spine, and also the peculiar character of the symptoms when the " middle " cervical vertebra is the one affected.

The injury in Case 29 is one most likely incurred in battle. It not only left a yawning gash in the overlying soft tissue but also " perforated " one of the cervical vertebrae. It caused stiffness of the neck, but was not deep enough to induce paralysis of any of the limbs, as we find happening in other cases of this group. The surgeon returns the doubtful verdict, and probably regards a cure as possible.

Title

X 3

Translation

Instructions concerning a gaping wound in a vertebra of his neck.

Commentary

On the terms employed see the examination below.

Examination

X 3–6

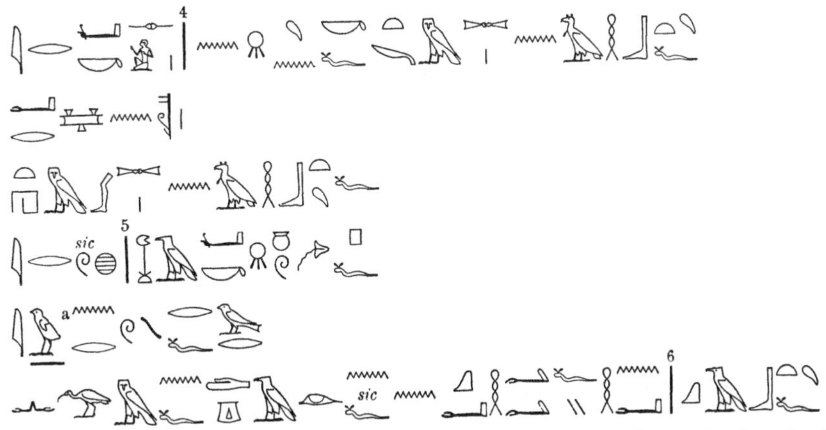

a In this space the scribe at first wrote *r* with black ink. He afterward came back and with red ink inserted the *w*-bird directly on the *r*. There is possibly an intimation here that *yw* and *yr* were almost identical in pronunciation, either being used as the prosthetic vowel.

Translation

If thou examinest a man having a gaping wound in a vertebra of his neck, penetrating to the bone, (and) perforating a vertebra of his neck; if thou examinest that wound, (and) he shudders exceedingly, (and) he is unable to look at his two shoulders and his breast, (conclusion follows in diagnosis).

Commentary

The discussion of " gaping wound " will be found in Case 1 (pp. 91–92).

ṯs, " vertebra " is treated under Case 31, Gloss A.

ṯhm, " perforating." See Case 3 (I 18), and consult p. 272.

wḫʾ is obviously an error for the usual *ḫʾy*, " examine." The corresponding context in Case 4 (examination, II 3–5) has *ḏʿr*, " probe," at this point.

ʾnrw rf, " he shudders," see Case 4 (II 4).

n gmy-n-f, " he is unable," has been explained in Case 3, examination (I 19–20) and Gloss B (I 25–26). *Dgʾ-n-f* is an error for *dgʾ-f*, see Case 3, *ibid.*

DIAGNOSIS

X 6–7

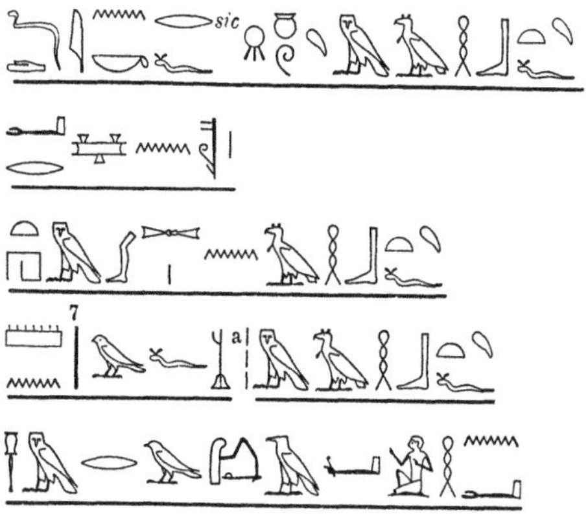

[a] The scribe at first wrote here, and no plural strokes. He afterward inserted the plural strokes in black ink over the *w* which was in red.

Translation

Thou shouldst say concerning him : " [One having] a wound in his neck, penetrating to the bone, perforating a vertebra of his neck, (and) he suffers with stiffness in his neck. An ailment with which I will contend."

Commentary

The word " gaping " (*n kf·t*) found even in the brief title has been omitted, doubtless by scribal error, in the diagnosis. It is noticeable also that the situation of the wound " in a vertebra " is likewise omitted in the diagnosis, though included in both title and examination. Except for the addition of the words " perforating a vertebra " we would not know from the diagnosis that a vertebra had been injured. This is perhaps the worst case of scribal carelessness in the whole document.

The last symptom, " stiffness in his neck," has been treated in Case 3 (I 20). On *mn*, " to suffer," see Case 3 (I 20). On the uncertain verdict 2 see Case 4 (II 6) and the introduction (pp. 45 ff.). This diagnosis is also discussed in the introduction (p. 51).

TREATMENT

X 7–8

Translation

Thou shouldst bind it with fresh meat the first day. Now afterward moor (him) at his mooring stakes until the period of his injury passes by.

Commentary

On the treatment with fresh meat see Case 1 (I 2–3).

The remainder of the treatment will be found discussed in the commentary on the treatment in Case 3 (I 21–23).

CASE THIRTY

X 8–12

SPRAIN IN A CERVICAL VERTEBRA

The term employed by the ancient surgeon to designate this injury (*nrw·t*) is unknown elsewhere, and indeed was not clear even to the *ancient* reader without explanation (Gloss A). It is from this explanation that the rendering " sprain " has been derived. There is no mention of any wound in the overlying tissue, and it was not regarded as serious ; the surgeon expected to effect a cure.

TITLE

X 8

Translation

Instructions concerning a sprain in a vertebra of his neck.

Commentary

The terms will be found discussed in the commentary below.

EXAMINATION

X 9–10

Translation

If thou examinest a man having a sprain in a vertebra of his neck, thou shouldst say to him: "Look at thy two shoulders and thy breast." When he does so, the seeing possible to him is painful.

Commentary

nrw·t, "sprain," is explained in Gloss A below.

On the surgeon's test of the patient's ability to twist his head to either side or to drop his face, see Case 3, examination (I 20).

yrr-f, "when he does so," is doubtless a conditional use of the so-called emphatic form, like *gmm-k*, "when thou findest," so common in this papyrus. The is written rather small; to read *t* is grammatically possible, but we find occasionally written as small as this, e.g., twice in this very case (ll. 11–12), in which is even smaller than in our *yrr-f*. See also *yr* as compared with *yst* (VIII 18).

ḫpr mꜥ-f, literally means "done by him." So we find *ḫpr mꜥ-y ḏs-y*, "done by me myself" (Shipwreck, 22–23). A similar example is in *Gespräch eines Lebensmüden*, p. 21; Semneh Stela of Sesostris III, l. 6; and finally in Papyrus Ebers (21, 14–15) we have the title of a remedy for expelling "ailments arising from the *pnd*-worm," more literally "done by" this worm. In this last example the feminine *t* shows that *ḫpr·t* is an attributive participle belonging to *mr·wt*, "ailments," the immediately preceding noun. This is likely to be the construction of *ḫpr mꜥ-f* (literally "done by him") in our passage. That is, *ḫpr* is an attributive modifier of the infinitive *mʾʾ*, "to see," so that we may render literally "the seeing done by him;" or including the potential element sometimes implied by the participle, we may render, "the seeing which may be done by him," or more freely "the seeing possible to him." It is, of course, obvious that it is not the "seeing" itself which is the source or cause of the pain, but rather the movement making the seeing possible. This movement, however, is sufficiently indicated by the preceding words "When he does so."

The reader will find the surgeon's methods of making his observations discussed on pp. 40–41, (*a*) to (*e*); see especially (*e*). The patient must have turned his face downward and then to right and left alternately, so that he looked obliquely downward, in a position somewhat cramped even for a sound neck, and sure to cause pain in a sprained one. We are not informed whether in our Case 30, the surgeon noted the patient's distress (resulting from the movement of his head) by ocular observation, or by further questioning of the patient.

DIAGNOSIS

X 10

Translation

Thou shouldst say concerning him: "One having a sprain in a vertebra of his neck. An ailment which I will treat."

Commentary

On *nrw·t*, "sprain," see commentary on Gloss A.

"Vertebra" will be found discussed in Case 31, Gloss A (p. 328). The diagnosis is again only a repetition of the title, to which the favorable verdict 1 has been appended. See Case 1 (I 2) and consult the introduction (pp. 45 ff.).

TREATMENT

X 10–12

Translation

Thou shouldst bind it with fresh meat the first day. Now afterward thou shouldst treat [with] *ymrw* (and) honey every day until he recovers.

Commentary

The second occurrence of *m ḫt*, "afterward" is an error due to the fact that the word is sometimes inserted at this point (after *śrwḫ-k*) e. g., VIII 21–22. On the treatment with fresh meat followed by *ymrw* see Case 1 (I 2–3) and Case 15 (VI 17).

GLOSS A

X 12

Explaining : A sprain.

Translation

As for : " A sprain," he is speaking of a rending of two members, (although) it (= each) is (still) in its place.

Commentary

ng·t, " break " or " rend apart," is discussed in Case 6 (II 19).

ʿ·ty, " two members," is a word applied to limbs, members, organs, etc., and designating almost any part of the body. It must here be employed by the surgeon with reference to two neighbouring vertebrae which have been forced apart. Grammatically *ʿ·ty* is the subject of the infinitive *ng·t*, and introduced by the particle *yn*. This construction will be found discussed in Case 5, Gloss A (II 16–17).

In the clause " it (each) is in its place," the antecedent of " it " (an Egyptian feminine) is evidently *ʿ·t*, " member," meaning one of the two separated vertebrae. The only other feminine noun in the passage, the infinitive *ng·t* " rending apart," is not likely to be the antecedent. It can hardly be said to have a " place." The meaning obviously is, that the two members are wrenched apart, although each (the text actually reads " it ") still remains " in its place." The remark is intended to indicate that no actual dislocation has taken place.

nrw·t, "sprain," occurs in the medical papyri only in our treatise, where it is found in three cases (30, 42 and 48). In Cases 30 and 48 it designates a trouble in a vertebra of the spinal column ; in Case 42 it affects the thoracic ribs. Judging from the above gloss, *nrw·t* concerns the articulation of one vertebra with another, or of the thoracic ribs with the sternum. This articulation has suffered sufficient strain so that a rending or wrenching (*ng·t*) has occurred ; but the vertebra or rib (referred to in the gloss above as " member," *ʿ·t*) is still " in its place." This is in accord with what we find in Case 42, where the thoracic ribs are affected by *nrw·t*, and it is distinctly stated that there is no " dislocation " (*wnḫ*), " nor is it broken " (*ḥśb*). An injury which has produced a rending of an articulation without a dislocation or an actual break is evidently what we would call a " sprain." It is difficult to trace the origin of the word to any known root. It is a feminine noun formed from a third weak root, for it is written three times in Case 48, or . It may have some connection with the verb *nry*, meaning " to shrink," " to shudder," or the like, as used in our document and discussed in Case 4 (II 4). It evidently has inclined in its semantic history in a different direction from the other feminine noun *nr·t*, " fright, terror " (Pyr. 1488 a ; Louvre C, 87, an Empire tomb stela), or still another feminine noun or *nr·t*, " neck " in the phrase *r nr·t-f*, " at his neck," said of a collar (*Tomb of Senebtisi*, p. 66).

CASE THIRTY-ONE

X 12–22

DISLOCATION OF A CERVICAL VERTEBRA

This is one of the most interesting cases in the papyrus, especially in the pathological details, but also in the knowledge of anatomy revealed. The surgeon has observed that the dislocation of a cervical vertebra causes paralysis of arms and legs, or as the Egyptian idiom expresses it, the patient "is unconscious of his two arms and his two legs." He has noted that the patient exhibits an erection of the phallus and has no control over the discharge of urine. He differentiates between a dislocation of a *lower* cervical vertebra near the backbone, which causes paralysis of the arms and legs, and dislocation of the *middle* cervical vertebra which causes an *emissio seminis*, a phenomenon observed in modern times in the case of a criminal whose neck has been broken by hanging. Dr. Luckhardt remarks : " Priapism is certainly a characteristic sign of cord involvement in the cervico-dorsal region. In this case the lesion must have been below the fourth cervical vertebra, since the patient was still breathing."

The examination (X 13–16) yields the surgeon an unusually long and interesting list of symptoms. The diagnosis, however, is scanty and merely lists the paralysis of arms and legs, and the escape of urine. The verdict is of course unfavorable. No treatment of any kind is suggested. It is evident that the case is one which excites the surgeon's interest,—an interest which we may properly term scientific. He records the phenomena observed with no hope of being able to treat or assist the injured man, but obviously solely from his interest in the facts observable.

The three glosses are important, and doubtless indicate that the words explained were already old and no longer fully understood. The explanation of *wnḫ*, " dislocation " is very valuable, because the ancient commentator uses two different words to elucidate the meaning of *wnḫ*, whereas he elsewhere often makes the word to be defined itself the chief defining term. The discussion of *mnš'*, "*emissio seminis* " and *nny*, " dribble " also enrich our knowledge of the Egyptian dictionary.

TITLE

X 12–13

Translation

Instructions concerning a dislocation in a vertebra of [his] neck.

Commentary

The terms will be found discussed below.

EXAMINATION

X 13–16

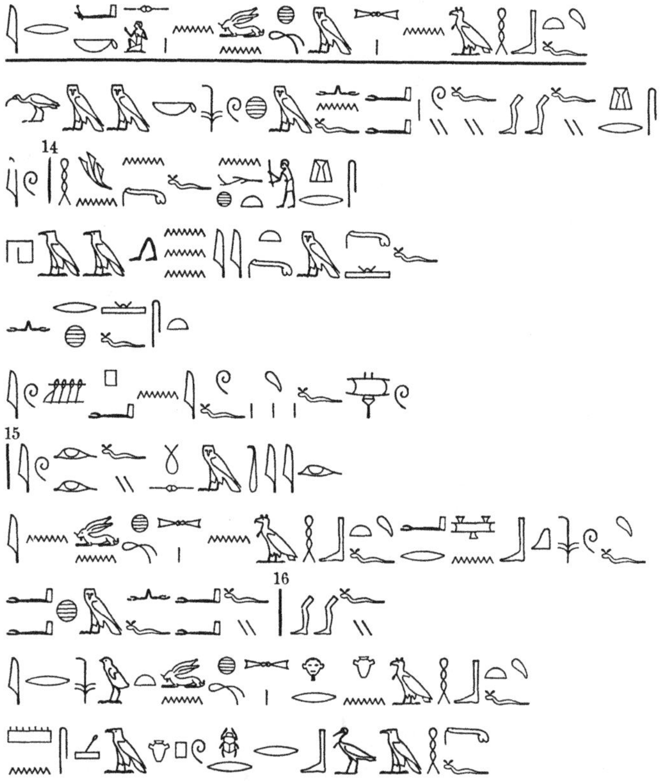

Translation

If thou examinest a man having a dislocation in a vertebra of his neck, shouldst thou find him unconscious of his two arms (and) his two legs on account of it, while his phallus is erected on account of it, (and) urine drops from his member without his knowing it; his flesh has received wind; his two eyes are blood-shot; it is a dislocation of a vertebra of his neck extending to his backbone which causes him to be unconscious of his two arms (and) his two legs. If, however, the middle vertebra of his neck is dislocated, it is an *emissio seminis* which befalls his phallus.

Commentary

"Dislocation" and "vertebra" will be found discussed in Gloss A.

ḫmy, "to be unconscious of," literally "not to know," occurs only in Cases 31 and 33 in a pathological sense. It evidently means "both to lose control of," and "to have no feeling in" either the arms or legs. A similar use of this verb applied to the entire person or the entire body, first understood by Gardiner, occurs in the Tale of Sinuhe where the hero says: "I became unconscious in his presence," literally, "I knew not myself etc." See Gardiner, *Notes on the Story of Sinuhe*, p. 96 (B. 253).

nḫt is already known with the pathological meaning, "to be stiff," e. g. Case 7 (III 17). It is here applied to an erection of the phallus.

*h*ʾʾ, "fall, drop, dribble" has been discussed in Case 20 (VII 24).

"member" is without doubt some special word for the phallus written here with the word-sign. The determinative is not wholly clear in l. 14, but there can be no doubt about it in l. 22, where it is obviously a papyrus roll. The question of the phonetic reading is difficult. The most probable reading is *bʾḥ*, as in the common preposition *m bʾḥ*. Written out *bʾḥ*, it occurs in Pap. Ebers 49, 14 and 93, 2; likewise in Naville, *La Litanie du Soleil*, pl. XIV, ll. 37–38 and spelled (where it is distinguished from *ḥnn*); and again Theban Table of Hours () II 16, 7, written "her phallus "(!), and showing that the word originally meant sexual organ without distinction of sex (see the variant in Tomb 6 which has though *rr·t* is the female hippo); *ibid.*, 17, 6; 18, 5; 20, 2, and written once (as if to be read *mt*?). Compare Champollion, *Monuments*, pl. 272. No example of a word *mt*, "phallus," has yet been found, but we may compare *mt*, "suppository" (Pap. Ebers 9, 8; 31, 11; 31, 13; 31, 15; 33, 3; 33, 16; 33, 19) and for the vulva also (*ibid.*, 94, 17; 94, 21). *Mt* meaning "man" is found only in the Pyramid Texts (510 c, 601 b). The evidence is therefore in favor of the reading *bʾḥ*.

literally "his flesh has received wind" or "breath." On this curious statement Dr. Luckhardt remarks: "One of the early signs of severe spinal cord involvement or actual transection is meteorism. The normal movements of the intestine are interfered with; gases develop in the bowel and are not discharged. As a result there is great distension of the abdomen." This observation by modern medical science seems to explain what our ancient surgeon had in mind in this case.

šsm-ty, "are blood-shot," has been discussed in Case 19 (VII 19–20),

Gloss A. The incorrect instead of might be regarded as an effort to write the dual, but we find the same writing with a singular subject, e.g., Case 19 (VII 17).

ʿr n, "extending to," in an anatomical sense, will be found discussed in Case 1 (title).

bkśw, "backbone," is an ancient word, found several times in the Pyramid Texts. Its meaning "backbone" is fairly evident. In the first place we find vertebra or vertebrae of the *bkśw* (e.g. Pyr. 229 b and 409 b). The determinative in the Pyramid Texts is several times written thus: , evidently three vertebrae seen from the front or back and showing the connections of the ribs; or , seen from above or below, and showing the articular surfaces and the round *foramina* of three of the twelve thoracic vertebrae. Finally the passage of Pap. Smith which we are discussing shows that the *bkśw* approaches near the cervical vertebrae, but does not include them. The chief occurrences of *bkśw,* which is probably a plural (see e.g., the plural genitive *nw* used with it in Pap. Ebers 65, 16) are the following: applied to animals (serpent, grasshopper (!), bird, etc.), Pyr. 1772 b; Great "Amduat," twelfth hour; Ebers 65, 10; 65, 16; a vertebra or vertebrae of *bkśw,* besides two Pyr. references above, Lacau, *Textes Religieux*, p. 78 (XXVII), l. 47 b; Book of the Dead, Naville, 31, 5; in list of parts of the body of a giant in Theban Table of Hours IX, Tomb 6, Tomb 9, etc. (written with eight times); miscellaneous, Naville, *La Litanie du Soleil*, pls. XIII, l. 26; XXXI, l. 25; XIV, l. 37, and XLVII, l. 47; Great "Amduat," tenth hour (Leyden, Turin, Seti II); same in seventh hour; Book of the Dead, Naville, 149, 5 (determinative of balances evidently wrong); *ibid.*, Chap, 133, 2; Pyr. 234 c.

While the title and the beginning of the examination do not localize the injury further than to place it somewhere in the cervical vertebrae, the conclusion of the examination proceeds to assume two different and more precise localizations of the dislocation: first one near or extending to the thoracic vertebrae, that is at the lower end of the cervical vertebrae; the other higher up and affecting only the "middle vertebra of his neck." The surgeon seems to indicate that in these two cases the symptoms vary: in the first case he finds paralysis of arms and legs; in the second there is loss of control of the sexual organ, and an *emissio seminis* results. The word for this phenomenon (*mnś*ʾ) is explained by the ancient commentator in Gloss B.

DIAGNOSIS

X 16–17

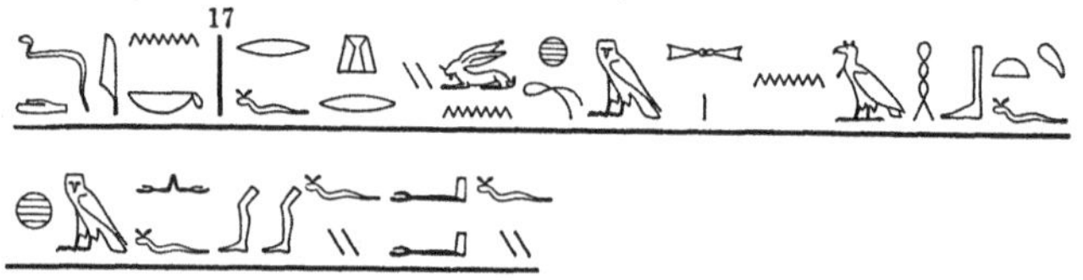

Translation

Thou shouldst say concerning him : " One having a dislocation in a vertebra of his neck while he is unconscious of his two legs and his two arms, and his urine dribbles. An ailment not to be treated."

Commentary

The last symptom is explained by the ancient commentator in Gloss C below. The other matters requiring comment have already been discussed. This diagnosis is interesting in its connection with the examination ; see introduction (p. 51). The unfavorable verdict 3 has been discussed fully in the commentary on Case 5 (II 15) ; see also the introduction (pp. 46–48). As usual when this verdict appears, the surgeon does not venture to suggest any treatment.

GLOSS A

X 17–19

Explaining : A dislocation in a vertebra of his neck.

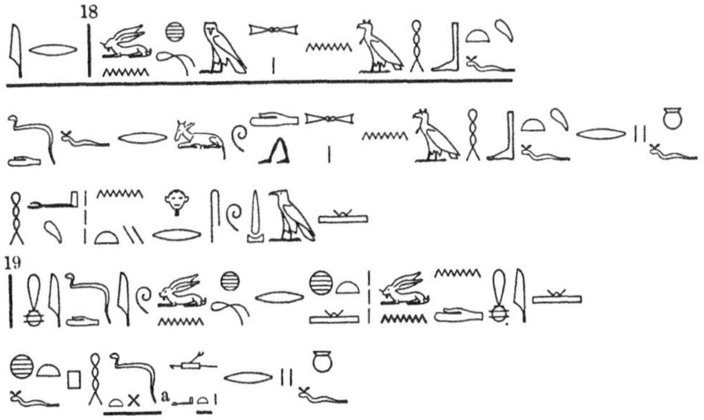

[a] In writing these two words *pḥḏ-t wꜥ·t*, the scribe made some error, which he erased by smearing it out while still wet, producing a smudge. He then inserted in red ink the following corrections : the last three signs of *pḥḏ-t*, and a ⌓ which he crowded in between the ⌐ and the stroke. Compare *wꜥ·t* in V 9 (bis).

Translation

As for : " A dislocation (*wnḫ*) in a vertebra of his neck," he is speaking of a separation of one vertebra of his neck from another, the flesh which is over it being uninjured ; as one says, " It is *wnḫ*," concerning things which had been joined together, when one has been severed from another.

Commentary

ṯs, "vertebra." The evidence in our papyrus, especially in this case, conclusively shows that "vertebra" is the correct rendering for this word. It is a rendering which has long been common, although anatomically it has not hitherto been wholly certain. The word occurs thirty-two times in our document. Of these, twenty-five are accompanied by the following genitive, "of his neck," and four by "of his backbone." Only thrice (XI 10, 11 and 15) does it occur in Payyrus Smith without one or the other of these modifiers. The examination (X 15–16) shows that there are *ṯs*, which are lower down in the neck near the "backbone," and that there is a "middle *ṯs* of his neck." It can hardly be doubted that *ṯs* is here the middle one of the seven cervical vertebrae. The recognition of a middle *ṯs* in the neck also shows that there is a series of *ṯs*. According to our Gloss A these *ṯs* are attached each to the next, and a forcible separation may take place in case of a dislocation (*wnḫ*). On the other hand, in Case 33 we learn that when a man falls head foremost and strikes violently on his head, it "causes that one *ṯs* (of the neck) crush into the next one" (XI 11). The correctness of "vertebra" as the meaning of *ṯs* is therefore evident.

dmy, "join," as the two lips of a wound are joined by healing (Case 10, V 9), is evidently here the word describing the relation of two *ṯs*, or "vertebrae" before they have been separated by the "dislocation" (*wnḫ*).

wnḫ, "dislocation," is the word which the commentator especially intends that this gloss shall explain. In this purpose he has been unusually successful. In the first place he does not, as so often in other glosses, employ the word he desires to explain as the most important designating term in the explanation itself. On the contrary he gives us two different words as suggesting the meaning of *wnḫ* : one being "separation" (*ywd*) and the other "severance, detachment" (*pḥḏ*) or the like. The first refers to a "separation" between two contiguous vertebrae, the second to the "severance" from each other of two things which had been joined together. It will be seen then that a *wnḫ* takes place between *two* things, each of which has an identity of its own. Although joined together they did not at first form *one* thing, like a single bone, which is broken into two pieces. An important differentiation between *wnḫ* and a "fracture" (*ḥšb*) is found in Case 42 (XIV 18), where an injury of the "ribs of his thorax" is said to be neither a *wnḫ* nor a "fracture" (*ḥšb*). *Wnḫ* therefore does not mean a fracture of any kind (*šd* or *ḥsb*) ; it quite evidently designates something that happens to the *articulation* between two bones, and must mean "dislocation." This meaning which emerges so clearly from the ancient commentator's explanation in Gloss A is interestingly confirmed by a study of the further use of the word in our document.

In Case 25 it designates a dislocation of the mandible, and the surgeon is directed how to apply his fingers so that the displaced mandible may fall back into its proper position. Similarly in Case 34 *wnḫ* is applied to a dislocation of the two clavicles or collar-bones, and in this case, too, the surgeon is charged to force them back into their places. A *wnḫ* " in the ribs of his breast " in Case 43 is described in Gloss A as a " displacement of the heads of the ribs of his breast " (XV 3–4). This word " displacement " (*nft*) is also applied to the *wnḫ* of the clavicles in Case 34.

The use of *wnḫ* to describe the condition of surgical stitching that has become " loose " is discussed in Case 10 (under *ydr* in V 6). The only other occurrence of *wnḫ* in the medical papyri is in Pap. Ebers (31, 20), where it designates an ailment or condition in the anus which is treated with ointment applied on lint. What this ailment called *wnḫ* may be is entirely problematical.

yḫ·t, " things," must be a plural here (possibly a dual), in view of the following phrase, " one . . . . from another." The lack of any feminine sign of agreement, as in the form of *wnn*, is common with the noun *yḫ·t* in our document, as indeed also elsewhere, especially when *yḫ·t* is in the plural. The following are the examples in Papyrus Smith : III 1 ; VI 14 ; IX 13 ; XII 5 and 11 ; XIII 10 and 11 ; XVI 1, 13 and 16 ; some of the preceding may be singular ; the following are certainly singular : II 3 and 20 ; IV 10.

Wnn is of course common with the force of a past tense ; its use here to throw the following participle *dmy* into a pluperfect is interesting.

pḥḏ-t(w), " has been severed," is a rare word which seems to be used only in the medical papyri. It is used of the dismembering and cutting up of animals for external medical application : of a bird (Pap. Ebers, 76, 9) ; of a lizard (Berlin Medical Pap., 3038, 3, 2). It is also employed of the cutting open of tissue with a lancet over a swelling or cist (Pap. Ebers 109, 6). Similarly it even appears as an intransitive verb to designate the rending or breaking of tissue over a pus cist (*ibid.*, 91, 13 ; 91, 18). In all these examples the word denotes the severance of animal tissue, but our gloss would indicate that it had a wider usage to indicate severance or detachment of any object from another to which it had been attached (*dmy*).

, *wʿ·t*, feminine, is of course out of agreement with the in *r šn-nw-f*. Compare the same incongruity in V 9 and conversely in I 10 and consult commentary, pp. 114 and 116.

GLOSS B

X 19–21

Explaining : It is an *emissio seminis* which befalls his phallus.

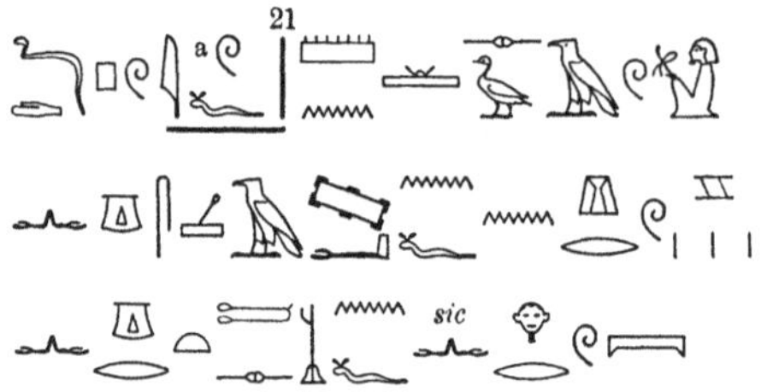

[a] This word *yw-f* was at first inadvertently omitted by the scribe, and was afterward inserted in red in the space at the end of line 20.

Translation

As for: "It is an *emissio seminis* which befalls his phallus," (it means) that his phallus is erected (and) has a discharge from the end of his phallus. It is said: "It remains stationary" (*mn s'w*), when it cannot sink downward (and) it cannot lift upward.

Commentary

mnś', "*emissio seminis,*" is a rare word which has been shown by Kees to mean onanism, self-pollution (*Zeitschr. für Aegypt. Sprache* 57, p. 110). The ancient commentator makes it clear that he is using the word for an involuntary emission. This meaning is even suggested in the text to be explained, by the use of *ḫpr r*, "happen to," which frequently is used in an unfavorable sense like our "befall." The determinative of a jar employed in the text (X 16) is due to the fact that there is a word *mnś'*, meaning "jar." Gloss B has the correct text with the determinative of a phallus.

nšw, "discharge," is fully explained in Case 41, Gloss E (XIV 15–16). The interpretation of *ẖr*, the preposition so often used by our surgeon to introduce the cause of a symptom, is difficult. It follows directly after "phallus" (*ḥnn*) in the examination (X 14), to introduce the cause, that is, the injury. It is possible that we should understand our gloss as meaning that the phallus is erected as a result of the emission. *H̱r* is, however, employed so often with the meaning "possess" that this meaning seems not improbable here.

Having quite adequately explained *mnś'*, the commentator proceeds with a *second* explanation, perhaps led to do so by an idiom or proverb, *yw-f mn s'w*, "It remains stationary," in which the occurrence of *mn* and *s'*, one following the other, have suggested to the commentator some connection with *mnś'*, "emissio." It would seem highly improbable that the two words *mn* "remain" and *s'w*, "protect" (rendered above "be stationary") should have any etymological connection with *mnś'*, "emissio." The commentator has either been misled by the simple paronomasia, or found it too attractive to be resisted.

In the translation of this idiom or proverb, the rendering of *s'w* as "be stationary " is based entirely upon the explanatory statements which follow, and which clearly indicate that the member is stationary. Whether we should understand *s'w* to be the common verb " protect " or the less common Empire word *s'w*, " break, fracture," or the like, applied to members of the body, may be left uncertain.

gś', " sink," is a relatively rare word, not otherwise found in the medical papyri. Its meaning is established by its use in the Eloquent Peasant where it occurs six times. Of these, five (77 (B 2) = 312 (B 1) ; 87 (B 2) = 322–323 (B 1) ; 96 ; 162 and 163) are employed to indicate the incorrect deflection of a pair of balances by which the peasant suggests divergence from justice, symbolized by the balances. In the sixth example (92) *gś'* designates the collapse of a timber or support and is parallel with *śbn*, which is the of the Pyramid Texts, used to designate the "fall" of a serpent. Any one who has seen an upreared cobra in Egypt will understand at once the meaning of *śbn*, employed so regularly in serpent charms in the Pyramid Texts, adjuring the serpent to " fall " or " sink down." In this passage then (Peasant 92), *gś'*, parallel with *śbn*, evidently means " to sink " or " to sink down." In Pap. Prisse it is used once figuratively to indicate the " yielding " of an opponent (13, 4).

An interesting parallel between our opposed *ṯsy n ḥrw*, " lift upward " and *gś' n ḫrw*, " sink downward " is furnished in a different pathological connection concerning an ailment of the heart in Pap. Ebers (101, 16–17) :

" It does not rise upward,
it does not fall downward."

The potential meaning of the negatived *n*-form is highly probable here. The use of the negative for the usual is made certain by the parallel in the preceding proposition. Compare Case 32 (XI 3).

GLOSS C

X 21–22

Explaining : While his urine dribbles.

Translation

As for: " While his urine dribbles," it means that urine drops from his phallus and cannot hold back for him.

Commentary

nny, rendered " dribble " above is a common word but is unknown as applied to human physiology outside of our treatise. Its commonest meaning is " to be weary." It is sometimes applied to the slow movement of the back-water of the inundation, e. g.,

sic

" Thou art the great flood, settling itself upon the fields " (Brugsch, *Reise nach der Grossen Oase*, Tafel XXVII, 40–41). This and other such examples indicate conclusively that a slow, sluggish movement of water is implied. The corresponding noun for sluggishness of food movement *nnw*, which is a word for "weariness, laziness " is twice employed in Pap. Ebers in a case of digestive trouble (36, 21; 37, 3). It is employed in Case 8 (IV 14) to describe the motion of half paralysed limbs. Our commentator explains *nny* in Gloss C by the word *h*'', which in its medical applications means "to fall, to drop," and is the verb employed when the quantity of fluid is small. See e.g., Case 20, VII 24, where *h*'' is discussed in the passage "a little (of the fluid) drops " (*h*''). " Dribble " is evidently, therefore, a fair rendering of our verb *nny*. In quoting from the text in X 17 the commentator has misspelled the word, using the noun form *nnw*. The text, though lacking a determinative, has the correct form *nny*.

, probably to be read *b'ḥ*, is discussed above, in the examination (X 14).

is obviously a scribal error for *š'ḳ*, "draw together, pull together, contract " and the like. In medical usage it is found with the direct object , " vulva " (Ebers 96, 9–10; 96, 6–7); and with the direct object "pupil of the eye" (Ebers 57, 2–3, see Loret, *Recueil de Trav.* 1, p. 132). In these passages it must mean " contract the vulva (or vagina)," or " contract the pupil of the eye." Besides such examples, with an organ of the body as the direct object, we find it also with " urine " as the direct object (Ebers 50, 13 = Hearst V 2), where its meaning is probably " restrain, withhold, control, hold back " or the like. The occurrence of this phrase *š'ḳ mwy·t*, " control (or hold back) the urine " (Ebers 50, 13), makes our restoration of the verb *š'ḳ* in Pap. Smith quite certain. It should be noted, however, that in our passage, *mwy·t*, " urine " is the *subject*, whereas in Pap. Ebers it is the object of *š'ḳ*, " restrain, hold back." The potential meaning of the negatived *n*-form is again quite probable.

CASE THIRTY-TWO

XI 1–9

DISPLACEMENT OF A CERVICAL VERTEBRA

This is the fourth of the group of five cases (29 to 33) treating injuries of the cervical vertebrae. In such groups the surgeon has usually proceeded from less to more serious cases. Case 32 however, which is regarded as an injury quite capable of successful treatment, has been placed after a dislocation of a cervical vertebra (Case 31). It deals with a displacement of one of the cervical vertebrae, an injury which we would be inclined to regard as serious but to which the ancient surgeon appends verdict 1. He also adds to the treatment of the patient the clause " until he recovers." The gloss at the end, explaining the term " displacement " (*nsw·t*), is one of the best and clearest in our papyrus.

It is in this case that the ancient scribe has made use of a scribal device of great interest. At the beginning of line four he unintentionally omitted the words " Thou shouldst say concerning him," the opening formula of the diagnosis. Having later noticed the omission, however, he inserted the lacking words at the top of the column (see Plate XI), and then called attention to the insertion by means of a red cross (see end of line three, Plate XI). This cross is the lineal ancestor of our asterisk.

Title

XI–1

Translation

Instructions concerning a displacement in a vertebra of his neck.

Commentary

The terms will be found discussed below, especially in the gloss.

Examination

XI 1–3

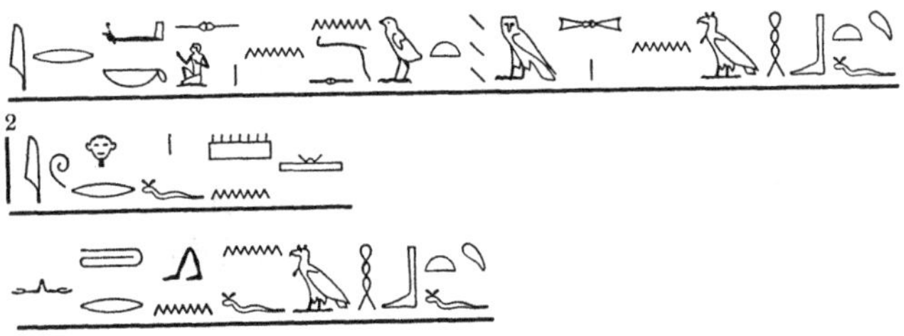

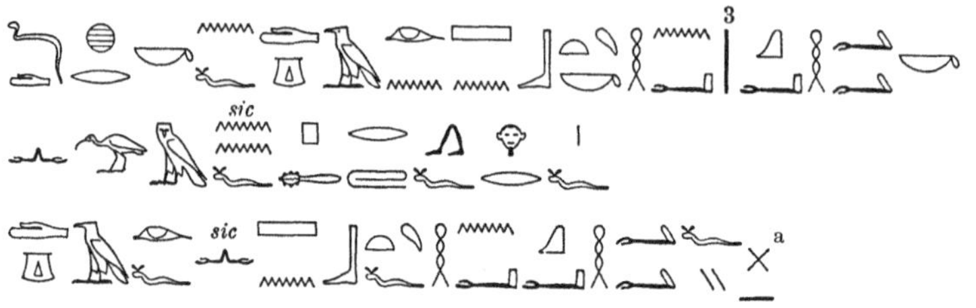

[a] This cross inserted in red is the ancient scribe's asterisk, explained in footnote [a] under diagnosis (XI 3–4, p. 335).

Translation

If thou examinest a man having a displacement in a vertebra of his neck, whose face is fixed, whose neck cannot turn for him, (and) thou shouldst say to him : " Look at thy breast (and) thy two shoulders," (and) he is unable to turn his face that he may look at his breast (and) his two shoulders, (conclusion follows in diagnosis).

Commentary

nsw·t, " displacement," is explained in Gloss A, q. v.

mn, " fixed," has a number of interesting anatomical uses in our document, which have been discussed in Case 4 (II 9). It is here used pathologically to indicate that owing to an injury of a cervical vertebra the neck cannot turn and the face remains " fixed " as it were, looking in one direction.

We have here another good case of the potential force of the negatived *n*-form.

šnb·t, " breast," is a word that has commonly been rendered " body, surface of the body, skin," etc. Its real meaning is, however, " breast." See for example the epithet meaning " big-breast " as a designation of a hawk or falcon in the Pyramid Texts (1048 c). The phrase *šnb·t*, " make festive (= adorn) the breast " in the Empire tomb scenes is another example in point. See Davies-Gardiner, *Tomb of Amenemhet*, pl. XXX, l. G, and p. 43, n. 13, where he also renders " breast." Our case above is a clear demonstration of this meaning, for a comparison with other cases shows that they employ the well-known word *ḳ'b·t*, " breast," where our case has *šnb·t*. For example, Case 30 (X 9) has

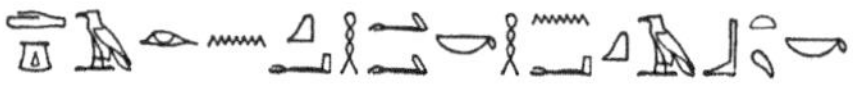

in the directions for testing the patient's ability to turn his neck, where Case 32 (XI 2–3) has

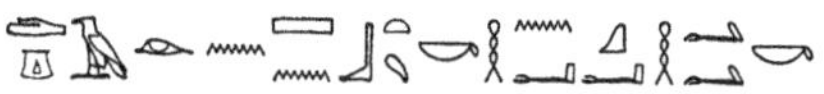

Case 30 puts " shoulders " first and " breast " second, while Case 32 reverses this order ; but otherwise the two texts are strictly parallel and the equivalence between *šnb·t* and *ḳ'b·t* is obvious. The anatomy of *ḳ'b·t* is explained by the ancient commentator in Case 40, Gloss A (XIII 17) and in Case 43, Gloss A (XV 3–4).

is obviously an error for
for the usual is found also in the preceding case (X 21).

DIAGNOSIS

XI 3–4

[a] These words *ḏd-yn-k r-f*, "Thou shouldst say concerning him," were unintentionally omitted by the scribe in the text at the beginning of l. 4. It was an omission too large to be inserted above the line in the text, as he sometimes did. He therefore wrote the missing words in red at the top of the column of text and called attention to the omission in the text at the proper point by a cross, likewise in red. He inserted the cross at the end of l. 3 however, not wishing to break the smooth right-hand edge of his column with anything added at the beginning of l. 4. This red cross is of course the ancestor of our asterisk.

Translation

Thou shouldst say concerning him: "One having a displacement in a vertebra of his neck. An ailment which I will treat."

Commentary

The diagnosis again consists only of the title with the favorable verdict 1 added, as noted in the introduction (pp. 48 ff.). On verdict 1 see Case 1 (I 2), and the introduction (pp. 46 ff.). The terms employed in the diagnosis will be found discussed below.

TREATMENT

XI 4–7

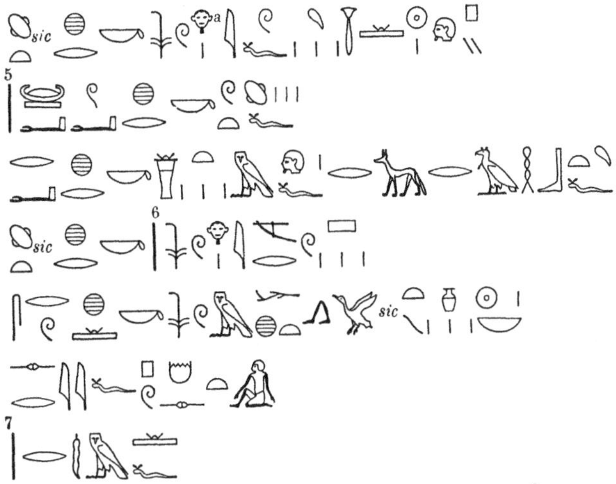

[a] It is possible that the scribe wrote

Translation

Thou shouldst bind it with fresh meat the first day. Thou shouldst loose his bandages and apply grease to his head ⌜as far as⌝ his neck, (and) thou shouldst bind it with *ymrw*. Thou shouldst treat it afterward [with] honey every day, (and) his ⌜relief⌝ is sitting until he recovers.

Commentary

On the treatment with fresh meat see the discussion in Case 1 (I 2–3).

is doubtless a sportive writing of the verb *s͗ʾby*, "to traverse," especially in the phrase "to traverse the marshes" in hunting. See Mariette, *Abydos* I 49 e; 49 f; Newberry, *El-Bersheh*, pt. I, XX. It perhaps originally meant "to jackal the marshes," ignoring the confusion between and . I do not know of any other example of our phrase here, *r sʾby r*, literally "to traverse as far as" which probably means simply "as far as." It would be analogous with *r mn m*, "to remain with," the well-known compound preposition for "as far as."

On bandaging with *ymrw* see Case 15 (VI 17).

The word *by·t*, "honey" written with a sign like the flying bird instead of the bee is common in our document, e. g., VII 6.

sry-f, "his ⌜relief⌝" is discussed in Case 17 (VII 6).

"Sitting" as used in treatment in Papyrus Smith will be found discussed in Case 4 (II 7).

GLOSS A

XI 7–9

Explaining: A displacement in a vertebra of his neck.

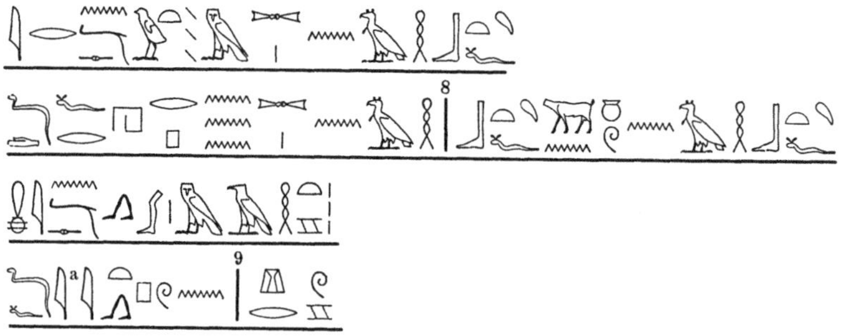

[a] The scribe at first wrote , and then corrected the to simply by drawing the oblique cross stroke in hieratic through the . It is practically certain that he intended to write *ḏfy·t*, not *ḏfty·t*.

Translation

As for: "A displacement in a vertebra of his neck," he is speaking concerning a sinking of a vertebra of his neck [to] the interior of his neck, as a foot settles into cultivated ground. It is a penetration downward.

Commentary

This gloss is one of the most successful discussions appended by the ancient commentator. He first explains the meaning of *nsw·t,* which we have rendered " displacement " by the use of the word *hrp,* " to sink " (see commentary on Case 5, II 13), before he employs the related verb *nsy,* " go, lead, introduce." His use of this related verb is wisely combined with the subject " foot " and the phrase " into (or ' in ') cultivated ground," so that there can be no doubt of its meaning. The picture is that of a foot sinking into soft, plowed ground.

The omission of the preposition before *ẖnw,* " interior " is probably a scribal error. We have the combination of *n ẖnw* with *hrp,* " sink," twice in Case 5.

nsy is a verb of going, otherwise known only in late texts like those of Edfu and Dendera. It is possible that the word is used here only with the meaning " go, walk " in soft soil, and that the added idea of sinking *into* the soft soil is contained solely in the verb *ḏfy·t* ; but it is more probable that the verb *nsy* means "to sink" or " to settle," and that our word *nsw·t* is derived from the verb *nsy.*

ḏfy·t, " penetration," is a rare word. The verb, with the obvious meaning " penetrate," is found in the following passage :

" O ye who pass by, if ye wish to live, etc.

so shall ye penetrate the stela of this tomb, and enter into the writings that are in it " (Theban tomb of , *Mission archéologique française,* Vol. V, Aba, pl. VI, left, ll. 9–10). Here *ḏfy,* rendered above " penetrate," is parallel with *ʿḳ m,* " enter into." This meaning fits our context in Gloss A perfectly.

In view of the ancient commentator's explanation therefore, it is clear that the injury assumed in Case 32 is a displacement of one of the cervical vertebrae, it being understood that the vertebra has been displaced directly toward the inside, that is toward the front of the injured man. It is a question for the pathologists to decide whether an injury of this kind would so easily respond to external treatment as our surgeon assumes, for in neither verdict nor treatment does the surgeon regard it as a serious case.

CASE THIRTY-THREE

XI 9–17

A CRUSHED CERVICAL VERTEBRA

This case is the last of the group of five treating injuries of the cervical vertebrae. It is the most serious probably in the entire group. The surgeon is at pains to explain just how the injury occurred, and this makes the case one of the most interesting in our treatise. Many of the injuries it discusses are such as could be expected only in war, or in a case of murderous assault. It is explained in Case 33, however, that the injured man has fallen headlong and has struck on his head, driving a vertebra of his neck with such violence into the next that the first vertebra is crushed into the other, the two remaining jammed thus together, and forming what modern surgeons call an "impacted fracture" as Dr. Luckhardt informs me. This is such an accident as might happen any day in civil life in ancient Egypt, especially among workmen who were employed in such great numbers on the vast buildings of the Pharaohs, like the pyramids and temples. The surgeon appends verdict 3, the fatal verdict, and makes no reference to any treatment.

It is quite clear that the presence of this case in our document is due to scientific interest in the symptoms displayed and the nature of the injury. The account contains some old terms which the commentator considers it wise to explain in two interesting glosses.

Title

XI 9

Translation

Instructions concerning a crushed vertebra in his neck.

Commentary

The title literally reads "a crush in a vertebra of his neck." The noun "crush" (*šḫm*) will be found discussed below in Gloss A, p. 340.

Examination

XI 9–12

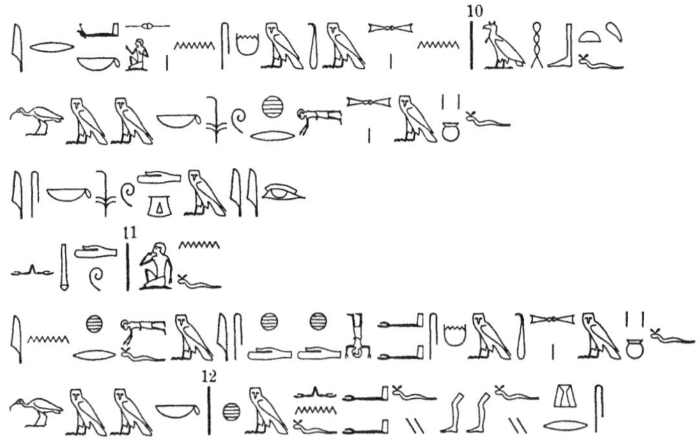

Translation

If thou examinest a man having a crushed vertebra in his neck (and) thou findest that one vertebra has fallen into the next one, while he is voiceless and cannot speak; his falling head downward has caused that one vertebra crush into the next one; (and) shouldst thou find that he is unconscious of his two arms and his two legs because of it, (conclusion follows in diagnosis).

Commentary

śḥm, " crush " is explained in Gloss A.

ḫr, "has fallen," is an unusual application of the common verb " fall," and is perhaps peculiar to surgery. The explanation in Gloss A shows that it means " penetrate," the force of the man's fall driving one vertebra into the next.

dgm-y, " speechless, voiceless," has been explained in Case 22, Gloss C (VIII 16–17).

yśḫdḫd, " be head downward," is discussed in Gloss B (XI 15–17).

ḫmy, " be unconscious," literally " not to know," employed to indicate paralysis of arms and legs, has been discussed in Case 31 (X 13).

DIAGNOSIS

XI 12–13

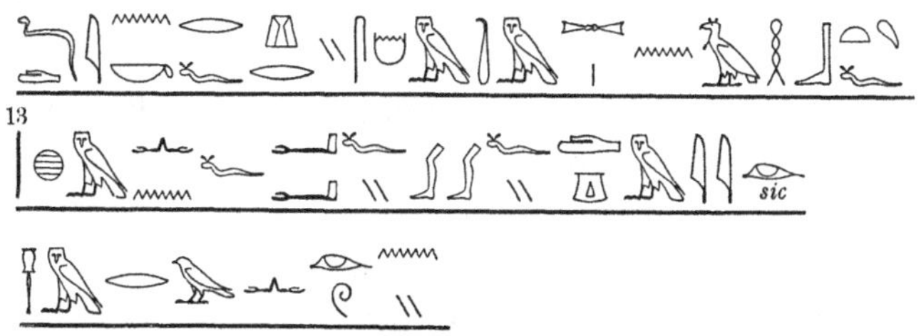

Translation

Thou shouldst say concerning him: "One having a crushed vertebra in his neck; he is unconscious of his two arms (and) his two legs, (and) he is speechless. An ailment not to be treated."

Commentary

The terms will all be found discussed above, except *śḥm*, which is treated in Gloss A. It is interesting, and grammatically important to notice that the *n*-form of the verb, *ḫmy-n-f*, is employed with a permansive meaning parallel with that of the following pseudo-participle (*dgm-y*).

Verdict 3 indicates that there is no hope of recovery. See Case 5 (II 15). It is therefore, as usual, followed by no directions for treatment.

GLOSS A

XI 13–15

Explaining : A crushed vertebra in his neck.

[a] This ⊂⊃ was at first omitted by the scribe and afterward inserted above the line in red.

Translation

As for : " A crushed vertebra in his neck," he is speaking of the fact that one vertebra of his neck has fallen into the next, one penetrating into the other, there being no movement to and fro.

Commentary

śḥm, "to crush," is a very old word appearing in the Pyramid Age written , though it is otherwise mostly written with . It means "to crush," especially with blows, as with a pestle. Two men pounding with large pestles are depicted in a tomb painting at Benihasan and the accompanying inscription calls their work *śḥm* (Tomb 15, Newberry, Vol. II, pl. VI). A small stela in the Cairo Museum has the word *śḥm* written with the determinative of a man pounding with a pestle in a mortar. This writing suggests that the determinative of *śḥm*, (XI 15) is intended to represent a pestle in a mortar. Indeed in Papyrus Hearst (X 6), in the next example quoted, the determinative of the word *šd*, "mortar" in hieratic is ᴗ, exactly like the curved line at the bottom of which is therefore probably a mortar. The ingredients of a prescription in Papyrus Hearst are "crushed (*śḥm-ty*) in a stone mortar" (Pap. Hearst X 5–6 ; compare Pap. Ebers 77, 3). In the model kitchens sometimes placed in tombs, grain is both crushed in a mortar and ground in a hand mill. These two processes applied to a jar of grain are designated in Pap. Ebers (75, 15) " crushed (*śḥm*) and ground." The trampling and crushing by oxen on a threshing floor is called *śḥm* in the tomb of Sennofer (Sethe's copy). In the medical papyri a noun *śḥm*, meaning " a trituration " is derived from the verb *śḥm*, " to crush." Thus in the Kahun Medical Papyrus (3, 7) we have *sic* " a trituration (*śḥm*) of natron;" and in Papyrus Ebers (86, 10) "trituration (*śḥm*) of *ḏ'r·t* " (some kind of fruit). Related to this noun, a crushed substance, a triturated drug, is our word *sḥm* in Case 33. Literally rendered the injury is " a crush in a vertebra of the neck ; " that is, the crushed vertebra is called " a crush." This is perhaps what is meant in Papyrus Ebers in a recipe intended to prevent "abrasions" (*śḥm·w*) occasioned by some ailment in the teeth (Pap. Ebers 72, 13).

Ḫr, " fall " in this unusual connection, is discussed above (l. 10).

The gloss indicates that one vertebra has been driven so firmly against and into the next that the two are adhering and preventing all independent motion of either.

GLOSS B

XI 15–17

Explaining : His falling head downward has caused that one vertebra crush into the next.

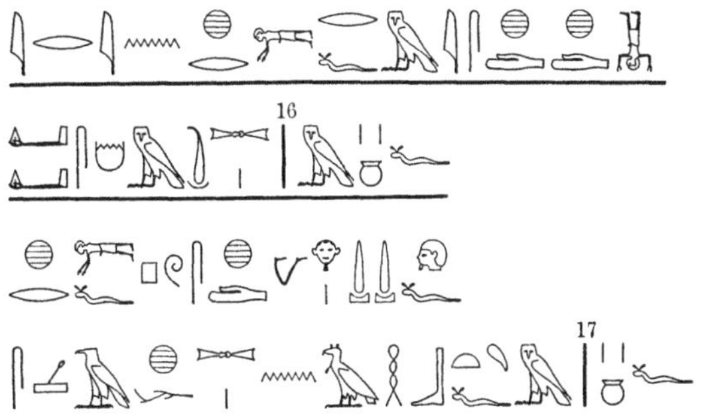

Translation

As for : " His falling head downward has caused that one vertebra crush into the next," it means that he has fallen head downward upon his head, driving one vertebra of his neck into the next.

Commentary

The repetition of *r* in *ḫrr-f*, after the determinative, is an obvious scribal error, suggestive of oral dictation. The text in XI 11, from which the scribe is quoting is correctly written *ḫr-f*.

śḫd, and the reduplicated *śḫdḫd*, are probably derived from the simplex *ḫdy*, " to stream, to flow," most familiar to us in the common verb *ḫdy*, " to float down stream." The causative *ś-ḫd* is used originally of clothing with the meaning "hang down." This is especially true when the hanging object is inverted, as when a goddess lets her breasts hang down. For this idea of hanging inverted, the Pyramid Texts employ the determinative (Pyr. 2171a). Similarly the stars hang from the sky (Pyr. 1516 b). See also Pyr. 2155 b. Finally the dead are said to walk *śḫdḫd* (see Lacau, *Textes relig.*, Chap. XXIII, A, p. 67 = *Recueil de trav.*, 29, p. 151, l. 59, compare determinative in B. Confer also *Zeitschrift*, 49 (1911), p. 58) and the determinative is that of a man with head down and feet up. The word is sufficiently old and unfamiliar to lead our commentator to explain it by the phrase *ḥr ḏ'ḏ'-f*, "upon his head."

 *š'ẖ*, "driving," is an otherwise unknown word, and the meaning given has been derived from the context in this case.

CASE THIRTY-FOUR

XI 17–XII 2

DISLOCATION OF THE TWO CLAVICLES

In this case we have two examinations, the first of which discloses only a dislocation without other injury; the second an injury of the overlying soft tissue, an injury which penetrates to the interior. These are conditions which the surgeon found in two different cases, as our text shows clearly enough. This conclusion is further corroborated by the fact that Case 36, a fracture of the humerus corresponding to our first examination in Case 34, is discussed by itself as a complete case, while the conditions corresponding to the second examination in Case 34 have become a new case (Case 37). Dr. Luckhardt here makes the important observation: "In the second case it is plain that the surgeon is discussing a backward dislocation, the first case being probably a forward dislocation of the collar-bone. In a so-called backward dislocation of the collar-bone the head of the bone lies behind the upper end of the sternum. This head presses on the trachea, esophagus, and larger vessels of the neck, causing difficulty in breathing and swallowing. Because of such pressure a semi-comatose condition may supervene. In modern surgery the head of the bone is excised if ordinary methods of reduction fail."

In the first case (34, first examination) the surgeon first prescribes the reduction of the dislocated bones to their sockets, together with proper adjustment of pads and bandages to hold them in place, and soothing applications. After the second case, however, the surgeon offers no diagnosis, and no treatment. The injury to the soft tissue is described in the same terms as in the alternative examination in Case 37 (XII 19–20), where verdict 3 follows, and there can be no doubt that the second examination in Case 34 is regarded as having disclosed a hopeless case, notwithstanding verdict 1, which follows it (see commentary below).

The case closes with an interesting explanation of the term "a dislocation in his two clavicles" by the ancient commentator, which demonstrates his knowledge of the bones of the thorax, contains an unusual excursion into the internal anatomy beneath this region, and furnishes us with a number of new anatomical terms.

The question arises whether the consistent writing of the dual "his two collar-bones" throughout this case is due to a common scribal habit in writing the dual when mentioning members which are in pairs, and therefore possibly an error for the singular. It is important to note that the treatment twice uses " it " (" bind it " and "treat it," XI 19–20) to designate the injury; while the second examination mentions finding a " rupture (of the soft tissue) over it " (the dislocation, XI 21). In this case only one collar-bone would be dislocated. In the first treatment (XI 19), however, the surgeon returns the dislocated bone(s ?) to "their" place; while in Gloss A the dislocation is described as affecting " the heads " (plural) of the bones concerned, and the articulation of " their heads " is further explained. The rendering " his two collar-bones " seems therefore to be justified.

TITLE

XI 17

Translation

Instructions concerning a dislocation in his two collar-bones.

Commentary

The terms are discussed below.

FIRST EXAMINATION

XI 17–18

Translation

If thou examinest a man having a dislocation in his two collar-bones, shouldst thou find his two shoulders turned over, (and) the head(s) of his two collar-bones turned toward his face, (conclusion follows in diagnosis).

Commentary

 gmm is an error for *gmm-k*. See the same context in Case 35, after *yr ḫ'y-k* (XII 3).

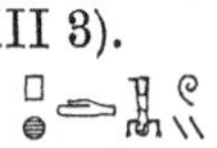 *pḫd-wy*, " turned over," is discussed in Case VIII (IV 14). The form is evidently a pseudo-participle, and as one of the rare duals of this verbal form another evidence of the early age of our document.

" The head(s) of his two collar-bones " is explained in Gloss A. The remark seems to indicate that the S-shaped clavicle, when dislocated, twists or turns somewhat, so that the "head," the end next the sternum, turns upward toward the patient's face.

First Diagnosis

XI 18–19

Translation

Thou shouldst say concerning him : " One having a dislocation in his two collar-bones. An ailment which I will treat."

Commentary

The terms will be found discussed below. The diagnosis again consists of the verdict appended to a repetition of the title of the case. This verdict is explained in Case 1 (I 2). See also the introduction (pp. 46 ff.).

First Treatment

XI 19–21

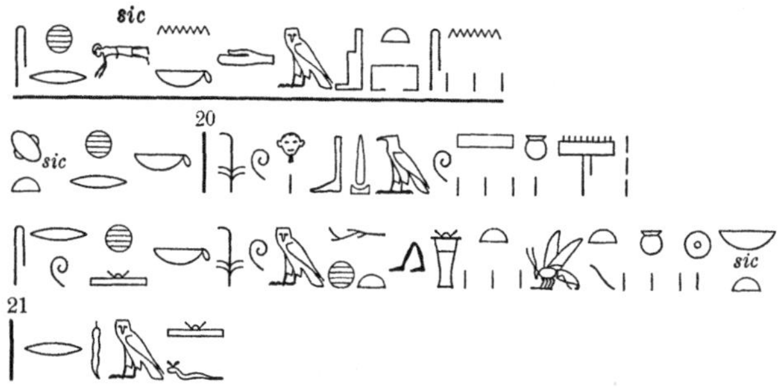

Translation

Thou shouldst cause (them) to fall back, so that they rest in their places. Thou shouldst bind it with stiff rolls of linen; thou shouldst treat it afterward [with] grease (and) honey every day, until he recovers.

Commentary

The surgeon has here placed the physical manipulation of the injury in the treatment, where it really belongs, and not in the examination, where he has customarily placed it (compare Case 25). The slight error in the writing of *š-ḫr-yn-k* may be corrected by comparison with the surgeon's account of a dislocated mandible, where he uses *verbatim* the same language (IX 4–5). The omission of all directions for manipulating the dislocation, such as we find so carefully given in Case 25 (IX 3–4), and such as he gives in the next case, a fracture of the clavicle, is noteworthy. It may well be due to inadvertent omission by our notoriously inaccurate scribe.

bḏ'·w, "stiff rolls," is explained in Case 11 (V 13).

On the use of grease and honey see Case 1 (I 3).

Second Examination

XI 21

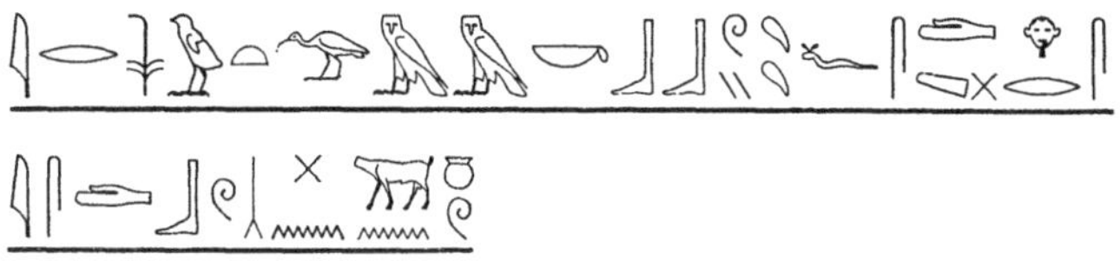

Translation

If, however, thou shouldst find his two collar-bones having a rupture (of the tissue) over it, penetrating to the interior, (conclusion in second diagnosis).

Commentary

šd, "rupture," will be found discussed in Case 5 (II 11). It refers here to a rupture of the soft tissue over the dislocation and penetrating the wall of the thorax to the interior. The first examination assumes that the overlying soft tissue is uninjured ; The second examination discloses an injury of this tissue, which constitutes a new case, to which a new verdict is appended. Dr. Luckhardt raises the question : "Does not the rupture here refer to most of the ligaments about the clavicular manubrium joints ? "

Second Diagnosis

XI 22

22

Translation

(Thou shouldst say) : " An ailment which I will treat."

Commentary

The diagnosis consists only of the favorable verdict (see Case 1, I 2), which after declaring " I will treat," is curiously enough followed by no treatment. There are thirty cases in our treatise containing this favorable verdict. In twenty-nine of these cases this verdict is immediately followed by a description of the treatment. The only exception is the above example in our present case (34). It should be noted furthermore that in all other cases prescribing no treatment, the verdict is regularly verdict 3 (e.g., Case 7, III 13 ; Case 8, IV 12 ; Case 37, XII 21). In this particular, Case 37 throws important light on Case 34. Turning to Case 37 we find that it falls into two parts exactly parallel with the two parts of our Case 34. The second part in both cases (37 and 34) is an alternative condition of the soft tissue overlying a dislocation or fracture, the soft tissue having suffered a dangerous rupture which pierces entirely through. Now in Case 37 the description of this injury to the soft tissue in the examination is followed by a diagnosis concluding with the unfavorable verdict 3. The parallel second examination in Case 34, describing the injury to the soft tissue in the same terms as in Case 37, should therefore likewise be followed by a diagnosis including verdict 3. This will be clear if we place the corresponding portions of the two cases parallel :

Case 34.  (XI 21).

,, 37.  . . . . (XII 19).

,, 34. 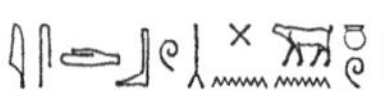 (XI 21).

,, 37. 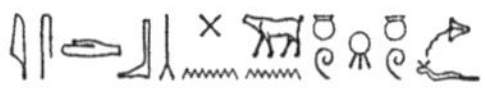 . . . . (XII 20).

,, 34.  (XI 22).

,, 37.  (XII 21).

In view of the above evidence we can hardly doubt that in Case 34, our second diagnosis (XI 22) should contain verdict 3 in place of verdict 1.

It may be objected that a scribal copyist would not copy so important a remark as the verdict incorrectly. In the very next case (35), however, it will be found that he has done this very thing. He at first wrote verdict 3, although his original from which he was copying undoubtedly contained verdict 1. To be sure he noticed his error before he finished and corrected it by inserting verdict 1 over verdict 3. In our case we must conclude that he not only made the error, but also that he failed to notice it. The probability is that the cases of dislocation of the clavicle known to our surgeon, in which there was also injury of the overlying soft tissue, had been fatal cases. It is perhaps significant that in the only gloss appended to our case, the commentator calls attention to the " two canals " underlying the region of the injury, canals which lead to the lungs. It may have been an injury in close proximity to these canals which the surgeon's experience had led him to think was too dangerous to be treated. The mere physical difficulties involved in reducing a backward dislocation were probably beyond the skill of the ancient surgeon. He had not yet learned to excise the head of the bone (see Dr. Luckhardt's remark, p. 342) ; he had no treatment for such dislocations and he probably lost most of them.

GLOSS A

XI 22–XII 2

Explaining: A dislocation in his two collar-bones.

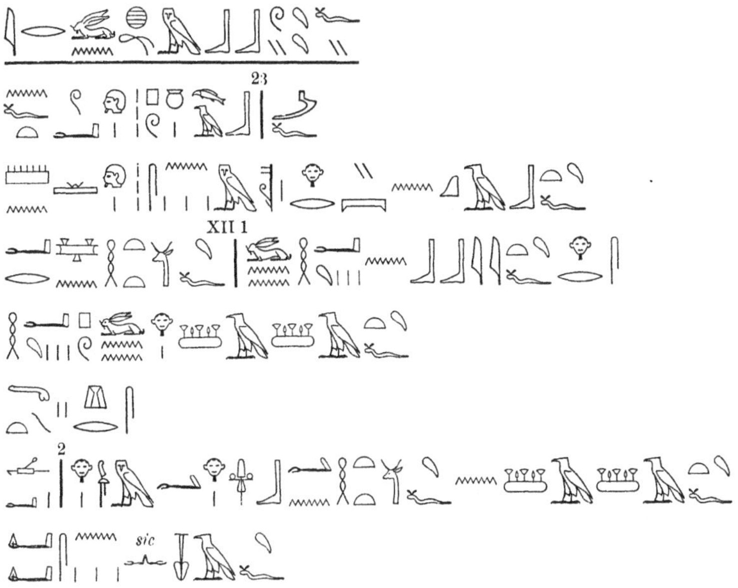

Translation

As for: "A dislocation in his two collar-bones," it means a displacement of the heads of his sickle-bone(s). Their heads are attached to the upper bone of his breast, extending to his throat, over which is the flesh of his gorget, that is the flesh that is over his bosom. Two canals are under it: one on the right and (one) on the left of his throat (and) of his bosom; they lead to his lungs.

Commentary

wnḫ, "dislocation" is discussed in Case 10 under *ydr* (V 6) and Case 14 (VI 11).

bb·wy-fy, "his two collar-bones" is a new word, the meaning of which is derived from this gloss. It is not found in any other Egyptian document now known to us. It is doubtless related to the rare word *bb*, "collar" (Piankhi Stela, l. 112), otherwise known only in Ptolemaic inscriptions. The word *bwbw*, the material for a chain or necklace (Pap. Harris 52 b, 2), is perhaps related. We learn from the ancient surgeon's interesting description in this gloss, that the heads of the two *bb·wy* are attached to, or articulated with the upper bone of the breast (*manubrium sterni*) "extending to his throat." There can be no doubt therefore that the two *bb·wy* are the collar-bones.

nft, "displacement," is a new word, at least in this form. We may compare the Coptic ⲛⲟⲩϥⲧ, "turn around, draw aside, to let out." See also ⲛⲟⲩⲧϥ in Spiegelberg, *Koptisches Handwörterbuch*, p. 81, and his . The determinative of a cord, and the use of *nft* to explain *wnḫ*, suggest that it means "detachment, loosening, displacement." The special application in this case to the displacement of the heads of the clavicles from their articulation with the *sternum* is paralleled by the use of the same word to describe the dislocation of the heads of the ribs which articulate with the *sternum* in Case 43 (XV 4).

ḫ'b, "sickle-bone," is a rare word not otherwise known in the medical papyri. It occurs once in the Book of the Gates and Coffin Texts (Grapow, *Urk.* V, p. 161) where it means simply "sickle." There is clear parallelism between *wnḫ*, "dislocation" with *nft*, "displacement," as one pair, and *bb·wy-fy*, "his two collar-bones" with *ḫ'b-f*, "his sickle-bone(s)" as the other pair. That is to say, *ḫ'b* is a word meaning "sickle," which is applied to the collar-bone, and is a more popular designation of that bone than *bb*, which needed explanation. The slightly S-shaped form of the clavicle probably gave rise to the suggestion that it resembled an Egyptian sickle, so that it was finally termed a sickle, just as the modern term clavicle is the old Latin word "a little key." Thence came the application of the word *ḫ'b*, "sickle" to the neck; see *ḫ'b*, "neck" in Kahun Medical Pap. 1, 19 as the opposite of *ḫpd·w*, "buttocks." It also appears as part of the body of the constellation, the Giant (), listed between *šw·ty*, "two sides" and *mnd·t*, "cheek," an order of parts which does not aid us much. In the Theban Table of Hours it appears with the Giant () in II, III, IV, and VI, with the writing (see Champollion, *Monuments*, pl. CCLXXII, 17). In our text *ḫ'b* should be plural, for the word "heads" immediately preceding is in the plural; and the words "their heads" in the next sentence must refer back to *ḫ'b* as a plural ("their"). See below.

. . . . . *mn* . . . . . . *m*, "attached to," meaning "articulated with" is discussed in Case 4 (II 9).

"Their heads" is probably intended to refer back to *ḫ'b*, "sickle-bone," which should be written in the plural (or dual). Otherwise the only other noun to which "their" can refer is *bb·wy-fy*, "his two collar-bones."

ḳs ḥry n ḳ'b·t-f, "upper bone of his breast," is quite clearly, as shown by this gloss, the topmost bone of the *sternum*, the *manubrium sterni*, the bone with which the heads or inner ends of the two clavicles are articulated.

ḳ'b·t, "breast," will be found discussed in Case 40, Gloss A (XIII 17).

ḥty·t, "throat," is a very old word, already found in the Pyramid Texts, which also employ a masculine (Pyr. 606 d). The general meaning "throat" is well established, e. g., as the seat of thirst in Sethe, *Urk.* IV, p. 482. As we have shown above, it occurs as the variant of *šbb*, "gullet" in the Book of the Dead

(Naville, 172, 19 Aa = 172, 22 Aa). See Case 28 (IX 19). Its mention here is useful as aiding to define the upper limit of the region concerned in the injury.

 *bby·t*, "gorget," is a very rare word. It is doubtless a derivative from  *bb*, "collar-bone," already discussed above. Gardiner tells me that it occurs in the unpublished Ramesseum Glossary papyrus, following *ḳ'b·t*, "breast." Unfortunately this list observes no orderly arrangement, and no safe conclusion can be drawn from the juxtaposition of *bby·t* and *ḳ'b·t*. In our gloss, however, the flesh of the *bby·t* is said to be "over it," that is over the throat (*ḥty·t*). The *bby·t* is therefore evidently the soft tissue covering the general region of the front of the throat extending downward toward the top of the *sternum* (*manubrium*), for this tissue is at once explained by the ancient commentator as that of the bosom also. No common English word for this region seems to exist, and the little current designation "gorget" may perhaps serve to suggest the meaning of the Egyptian word.

 *š'š'·t*, "bosom," is likewise a very rare word, and heretofore of quite uncertain meaning. It occurs twice as the seat of an uncertain disease, a swelling appearing on the *š'š'y·t* (Pap. Ebers 104, 14 and 104, 17). Neither these two nor the only other known example of the word (Mariette, *Dendérah*, I 73 a) throw any useful light on its meaning. Our passage shows clearly that it means the region of the lower throat extending downward to the upper part of the *sternum*. We can hardly doubt therefore that it is related to the word  *š'š'y·t*, "necklace," which hangs down from the neck over this region. The somewhat vague word "bosom" would seem to be a fair rendering.

The item with which the gloss closes is of unusual interest, for the surgeon here turns to the internal anatomy beneath the region he is discussing, and makes a remark possibly explaining why a rupture of the tissue in this region was so dangerous. When we recall that the surgeon suggests no treatment for the case disclosed in the second examination, we may raise the question whether he had not had experience with some case, in which a dislocation of the clavicle was accompanied by a rupture not only of the overlying soft tissue but also of one of the large blood-vessels beneath,—an injury from which the patient rapidly bled to death. The vessels of which the commentator is speaking he calls *mt*, and it should be remembered that this term *mt* means not only "canal," but also "ligament, tendon." See Case 1 (I 6) and Case 7 (III 17). Since writing the above I have received Dr. Luckhardt's important remark inserted in the introduction to this case, in view of which he adds the following observation: "There is therefore a direct relation between the description of the dislocated clavicle and the structure beneath the sternum. Of course the canals mentioned may be the bronchi (left and right) and not blood-vessels, particularly in view of the commentator's statement that they lead to the *lungs*." Dr. Luckhardt also mentions the fact that the branching of the trachea into the bronchi occurs at the level of the third and fourth ribs.

CASE THIRTY-FIVE

XII 3–8

A FRACTURE OF THE CLAVICLE

The surgical procedure prescribed in this case, having, even in the Seventeenth Century B.C., evidently developed from long experience, is very interesting. The patient is laid prostrate on his back, with some object placed under him between his shoulder blades, of such a height that the shoulders are somewhat raised from the bed or floor, permitting the surgeon to spread the shoulders, probably by pressing down, so that the fractured bone is longitudinally stretched, and the fractured ends can be fitted together. It is unfortunate that the two bandages which are then applied, presumably to prevent disturbance of the fracture, are so described that their position, as affecting the fractured clavicle, is not clear.

TITLE

XII 3

Translation

Instructions concerning a break in his collar-bone.

Commentary

 *ḥsb,* "break" or "fracture," is explained in Case 11 (V 10). It is quite clear that there is only one "break" discussed in this case. The scribe's writing of the dual *bb·wy,* "two collar-bones," is either an error from the habit of writing the word so often in the dual, or is a loose form of expression, employing "his two collar-bones" with the meaning "either one of the two."

EXAMINATION

XII 3–4

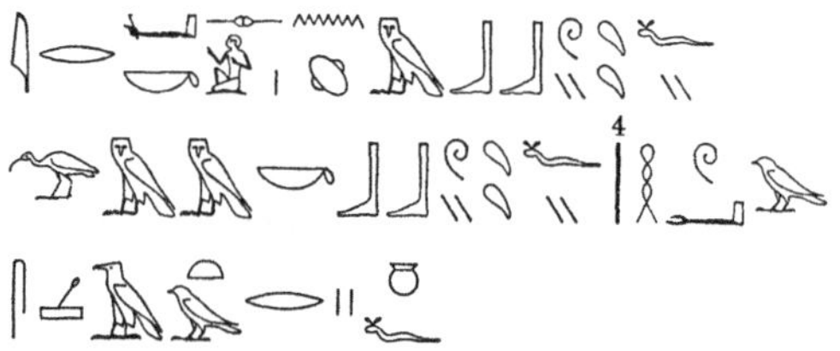

Translation

If thou examinest a man having a break in his collar-bone, (and) thou shouldst find his collar-bone short and separated from its fellow, (conclusion follows in diagnosis).

Commentary

On the nature of the injury see commentary under title.

ḥwʿ, "short." This meaning has been demonstrated by Gunn, *Recueil de trav.*, 39, p. 101. See especially *ḥwʿ*, "dwarf" (determinative inexact in type). It is here a verb in pseudo-participle.

šʾt, "separated" is discussed in Case 14 (VI 8). The physical situation here described is due to a single break in one clavicle; the other clavicle must not be considered as playing any part in the situation. In view of these facts we must conclude that the separation referred to is between the two pieces of the broken clavicle. As the text stands the description is obviously incomplete; before "separated" we expect the words "one piece," that is, "(one piece) separated from its fellow."

Diagnosis

XII 4

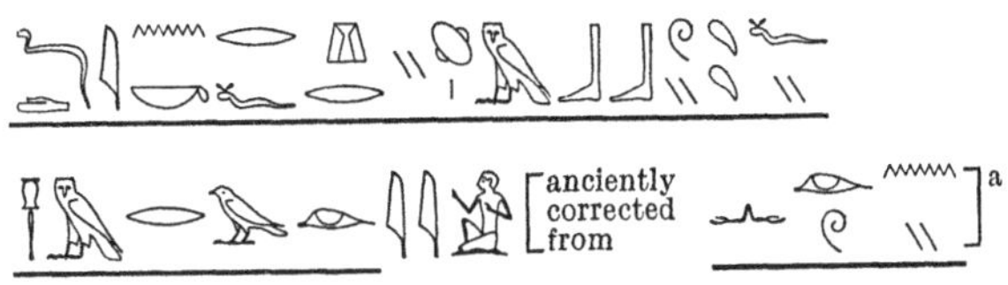

[a] The scribe at first wrote verdict 3, five signs all in red. He then corrected the error and converted the text into verdict 1. He canceled the red with a cross stroke in black, and the red in the same way. He inserted in black so that one was over and the other over . The insertion of at the end completed the reading of verdict 1. The was left in red unaltered. Cf. Vol. II, Pl. XII.

Translation

Thou shouldst say concerning him: "One having a break in his collar-bone. An ailment which I will treat."

Commentary

The diagnosis is again a repetition of the title, followed by the verdict (see introduction, pp. 48 ff.). On the favorable verdict 1 see commentary on Case 1 (I 2) and introduction (pp. 46 ff.).

Treatment

XII 4–8

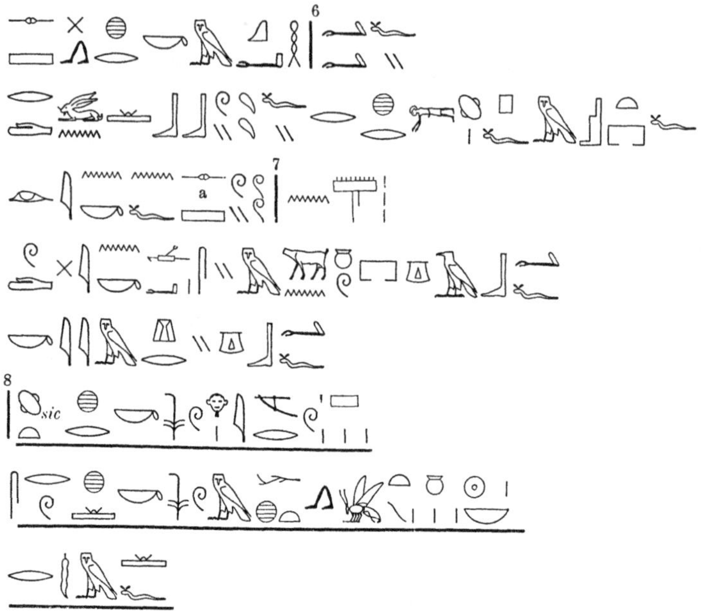

[a] The scribe has omitted the two cross-strokes on *s*.

Translation

Thou shouldst place him prostrate on his back, with something folded between his two shoulder-blades ; thou shouldst spread out with his two shoulders in order to stretch apart his collar-bone until that break falls into its place. Thou shouldst make for him two splints of linen, (and) thou shouldst apply one of them both on the inside of his upper arm and the other on the under side of his upper arm. Thou shouldst bind it with *ymrw*, (and) treat it afterward [with] honey every day, until he recovers.

Commentary

śṯsw, " prostrate on his back," is otherwise known in the medical papyri in Pap. Ebers (36, 7), in which a man suffering with digestive trouble is to be examined by the physician, *śṯsy*, " prostrate on his back." The determinative is a man lying prostrate with face up, and with both arms *down* toward the waist, not up, as in the only available type. It is important for our case to demonstrate that the word indicates this posture, particularly the detail, that the patient lies with face up. The evidence for this is conclusive. Fallen enemies are said to lie " *śṯsy*," and the determinative is that of a human figure prone, with face up (Annals of Thutmose III, *Urk.* IV, p. 659 ; see also *Recueil de trav.*, 2, p. 143). Swimmers in the celestial ocean are depicted in the water face up and are said to be *śṯsy·w* (Great " Amduat," 10th Hour, Seti II, Turin and Leiden). The dead, being embalmed and lying as a mummy does, face up, is called *śṯsy* (Ritual of Embalmment, Pap. Boulaq 3, I, 19), and the embalmed dead are referred to in the same way (*Buch vom Durchwandeln der Ewigkeit,* Berlin Pap. 3044, l. 23). The indications from sources outside of Papyrus Smith are quite conclusive on this point. In our document also, even in the hieratic, the determinative is clearly that of a prone human figure, lying face up, as shown by the feet in both cases, and in XII 11 also by the arms which are thrown upward. The root is probably IV-lit. with a fourth weak radical, and in our passage the form is a pseudo-participle, as likewise in Pyr. 685a (noted by Dévaud).

ḳ' b, "folded," which occurs only here and in the duplicate passage (XII 11) is in both cases left without a determinative. It may be that we should ignore this extraordinary lack of the determinative, and that we should accept the writing as it is, and understand the word *ḳ'b,* "to double, to fold over, be folded," meaning a piece of linen or the like folded to give it thickness and height, as required by this situation. It is conceivable also that the is possibly an error for and that we have here the well-known word *ḳ'y,* "high." It is evident that the object here designated is intended to be placed between the prostrate patient's shoulder blades, supporting him and lifting the shoulders from the bed or the floor. The lack of any sign of agreement in gender between *ḳ'b* and *yḫ·t,* "thing" is common in our document throughout.

mšʿḳ·ty-fy, "his two shoulder-blades," literally "his two razor-blades," is discussed in Case 47 (XVI 18).

sny (sš?), "spread out," evidently designates the act of spreading the shoulder apart. Compare the discussion of this procedure in the next case where it is repeated for a fractured *humerus.*

dwn, "stretch apart," is discussed in Case 7 (III 19–20).

"Until that break falls into its place" is an inexact expression doubtless meaning until the bones or pieces of bone on each side of the break fall into their places, so that the fractured ends fit together.

sš·wy, "two splints," has been discussed in Case 7, Gloss C (III 18).

. . . . should be read *wʿ-śny* . . . . . *kyy-śny,* in accordance with the repetition of these directions in the next case (XII 13), which has :

. . . . , "one of them both, ... the other of them both." The genitive *śny* after *kyy* shows clearly that we must also expect a genitive *śny* after *wʿ,* and the appearing after *wʿ* (before *śny*) is obviously a scribal error.

g'b, "arm" or "upper arm," see next case. An indication of what the Egyptian meant by the phrase "inside of the arm" is doubtless to be found in the expression , lit. "inside of the two arms," a term meaning "embrace." The application of the two splints is quite clear, and indeed this description of their application is the best evidence of the nature of the two as splints, which would not otherwise have been certain. One of them is applied to the anterior surface of the arm, which the papyrus calls the " inside of the arm," and the other to the opposite side, which, especially when the arm is crooked, is naturally described by the Egyptian as the " under side of the arm." The effect of this position on the fractured bone is not clear, but is clearer in the next case, a fracture of the humerus, in which the positions of the two splints are identical with those in Case 35.

Ymrw will be found discussed in Case 15 (VI 17). On the use of honey for wounds and injuries see Case 1 (I 3).

This process of setting and treating a fractured clavicle is repeated verbatim for a broken humerus in the next case, in which the physical relationships involved are somewhat clearer than in Case 35. The two cases should be studied together.

CASE THIRTY-SIX

XII 8–14

A FRACTURE OF THE HUMERUS

The ancient surgeon's discussion of this case closely resembles that of the fractured clavicle in Case 35. It is obvious from these two cases that a fracture of this nature, if free from complications, was regarded by the surgeon of the Third Millennium B. C. as an injury with which he was quite able to cope. He appends to both cases verdict 1, and proceeds to prescribe the treatment for both fractures in the same language.

We cannot doubt that our surgeon was acquainted with dislocation of the humerus, which is probably more common than dislocation of the ribs, discussed in this treatise (Case 43). His two cases of injury of the clavicles are: first a dislocation (Case 34) and second a fracture (Case 35). One would therefore expect that the first case of injury of the humerus would be a dislocation and the second a fracture, rather than two kinds of fracture. There is indication here that a case has been omitted at some time in course of copying. One's first thought is that Case 36 may be an error for a dislocation instead of a fracture; for the two subdivisions of Case 37 are exactly parallel with those of Case 35, and similarly we expect Case 36 to be parallel with 34, a dislocation, but the treatment in Case 36 is too closely parallel to the fracture treatment in Case 35 to be applied to a dislocation.

TITLE

XII 8–9

Translation

Instructions concerning a break in his upper arm.

Commentary

ḥsb, " break " or " fracture," is explained in Case 11 (V 10).

g'b, " upper arm," is discussed in Case 35 ; further discussion will be found in the treatment below (XII 12), showing that it means " upper arm," and here of course the bone (*humerus*) of the upper arm.

EXAMINATION

XII 9–10

Translation

If thou examinest a man having a break in his upper arm, (and) thou findest his upper arm hanging down, separated from its fellow, (conclusion follows in diagnosis).

Commentary

dḥ, "hang down," see Dévaud, *Zeitschrift*, 49 (1911), p. 132. It is not found elsewhere in the medical papyri. More literally it means simply to " be low, sink down," as shown for example in the following antithetic use with *ḳ'y*, " be high:" " Re is high, the enemies are low (*dḥ'*) " (Hymn to Re-Harmakhis, Berlin Pap. 3050, Col. 4, l. 4). It is also written where the determinative suggests a sinking of the arm. In our passage it evidently describes the helpless hanging of the broken arm.

š't-y, " separated," is discussed in Case 14 (VI 8). As only one arm is discussed here, it is clear that the separation mentioned is that between the two pieces of bone produced by the fracture. As in Case 35 (XII 4) the description is incomplete ; before " separated " we expect the words " one piece ; " that is " (one piece) separated from its fellow."

DIAGNOSIS

XII 10

Translation

Thou shouldst say concerning him: "One having a break in his upper arm. An ailment which I will treat."

Commentary

The terms have all been discussed above. The diagnosis, as so often in this treatise, is simply a memorandum,—nothing more indeed than the title itself, with the essential note, the favorable verdict 1 appended. See Case 1 (I 2) and introduction (pp. 48 ff.).

Verdict 1; see Case 1 (I 2).

TREATMENT

XII 10–14

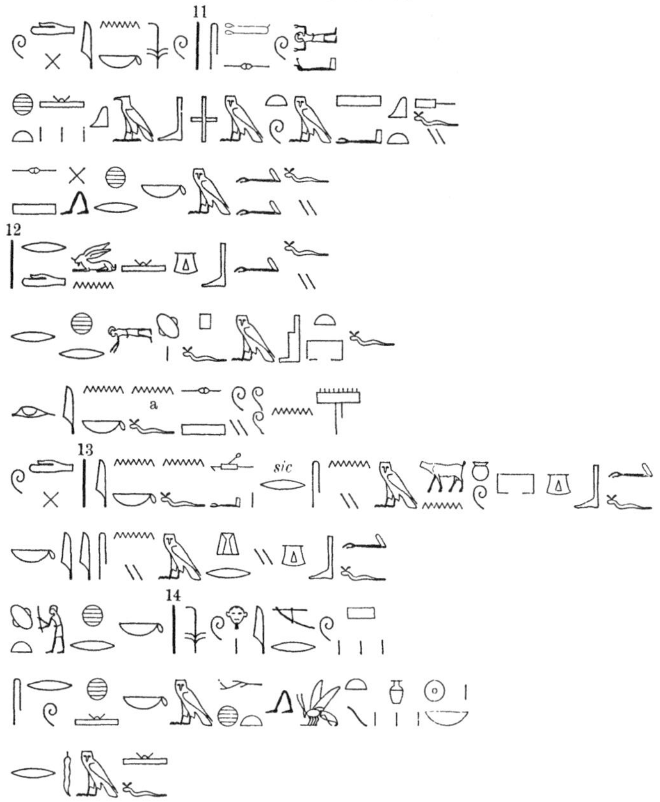

[a] The 𓈖 in 𓈖𓆑 looks like 𓂋, but is doubtless only an unusually thick 𓈖.

Translation

Thou shouldst place him prostrate on his back, with something folded between his two shoulder-blades; thou shouldst spread out with his two shoulders, in order to stretch apart his upper arm until that break falls into its place. Thou shouldst make for him two splints of linen, (and) thou shouldst apply for him one of them both on the inside of his arm, (and) the other of them both on the under side of his arm. Thou shouldst bind it with *ymrw*, (and) treat afterward [with] honey every day until he recovers.

Commentary

This treatment is verbatim a repetition of that in the preceding case, except that the stretching apart here affects the upper arm (*g'b*), whereas in Case 35 it affected the collar-bone (*bb*). The terms are all treated in the commentary on Case 35, but there are some variants in Case 36 which should be noticed. The use of *g'b*, " upper arm," just noted, is of value in explaining " spread out with his two shoulders." Such a procedure would have no effect upon the upper arm unless two persons on opposite sides of the patient should each grasp an arm and pull against each other, thus stretching the fractured arm, and permitting the surgeon to fit together the fractured ends of the *humerus*.

g'b, " upper arm," is commonly used as a loose designation of the arm, and its Coptic descendant **ϭⲃⲟⲓ̈** also seems to mean " arm," without suggesting upper arm or forearm. Nevertheless the physical situation above described makes it probable that *g'b* is used by our surgeon to designate the upper arm. If he is speaking of a break in the forearm, we miss any indication whether it is in the *ulna* or the *radius*. Moreover, he speaks of " that break," with the demonstrative in the singular, showing that he has but one fracture in mind. Still more important is the fact that to stretch the forearm it would not be necessary to involve both shoulders ; whereas the stretching of the *humerus* is much more naturally accomplished in the manner above described by pulling from both shoulders. The application of the bandages to the fractured *humerus* is prescribed in the same terms as for the fractured collar-bone in Case 35.

The correction of the superfluous 𓂋 in *wꜥ r śny*, has been explained above in Case 35.

CASE THIRTY-SEVEN

XII 14–21

A FRACTURE OF THE HUMERUS WITH RUPTURE OF OVERLYING SOFT TISSUE

The sole difference between this and the preceding case of fracture of the *humerus* lies in the injury to the overlying soft tissue. The surgeon has met two different cases of this kind. In the first the tissue is not deeply ruptured, and apparently does not bleed, at least not outwardly ; in the second the wound bleeds and the rupture of the tissue penetrates clear through to the fracture itself. The surgeon regards the first case as doubtful, and appends the verdict 2, followed by treatment ; but the second case is hopeless, and received verdict 3, followed by no treatment. It would seem then that the laceration of the soft tissue overlying a fracture of the *humerus* was regarded in ancient Egyptian surgery as a fatal injury.

TITLE

XII 14–15

Translation

Instructions concerning a break in his upper arm, with a wound over it.

Commentary

 *ḥsb*, "break," and  *g'b*, "upper arm," see Case 36. On "wound," see Case 1 (title).

FIRST EXAMINATION

XII 15–16

Translation

If thou examinest a man having a break in his upper arm, over which a wound has been inflicted, (and) thou findest that that break crepitates under thy fingers, (conclusion follows in diagnosis).

Commentary

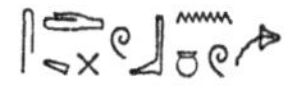 *šd wbnw*, "a wound has been inflicted," is an idiom more literally meaning "a wound has been smashed" over it (the fracture). See Case 1, discussion of *wbnw*, "wound," A 4.

 *nẖbẖb*, "crepitates," see Case 13 (VI 4–5).

FIRST DIAGNOSIS

XII 16–17

Translation

Thou shouldst say concerning him : " One having a break in his upper arm, over which a wound has been inflicted. An ailment with which I will contend."

Commentary

The terms have all been discussed above. The diagnosis consists only of the title, with the doubtful verdict 2 appended. See Case 4 (II 6), and introduction (pp. 46–48).

First Treatment

XII 17–19

Translation

Thou shouldst make for him two splints of linen ; thou shouldst bind it with *ymrw* ; (and) thou shouldst treat it afterward [with] grease, honey and lint every day until thou knowest that he has reached a decisive point.

Commentary

It is very extraordinary that we have here no instructions for setting the broken bone. In the preceding case the measures for bringing together again the two pieces of bone are carefully described, and only after this difficult operation are the two linen splints mentioned. The position of each is then carefully indicated. All this is taken for granted in Case 37, where the treatment consists chiefly of catch-words suggesting measures which are doubtless quite familiar to the surgeon. It is only on this supposition that we can understand the omission of all directions for the application of the "two bandages." The setting of the bone itself must be implied in the mere injunction to make the bandages.

 *sš·wy*, "two splints," will be found discussed in Case 7 (III 18) and Case 12 (V 18).

Binding with *ymrw* is discussed in Case 15 (VI 17).

Treatment with " grease, honey and lint " has been explained in Case 1 (I 3).

" Until thou knowest that he has reached a decisive point " has been treated in Case 4, Gloss C. Compare also Case 3 (I 23).

SECOND EXAMINATION

XII 19–20

Translation

If, however, thou findest that wound which is over the break, with blood issuing from it, and piercing through to the interior of his injury, (conclusion in second diagnosis).

Commentary

The second examination discloses two new particulars: the bleeding of the overlying wound; and the rupture of the tissue inward to what the surgeon calls "the interior of his injury (*wbnw*)" indicating that the wound is not merely an abrasion but a rupture of the tissue, presumably right down to the fracture itself. It is probable therefore that the meaning of wound in this last phrase is the "injury" as a whole, a meaning which the use of the term *wbnw*, "wound" in our document quite justifies our assuming in this case. See commentary on *wbnw* in Case 1.

 *yśdb*, "piercing through," is discussed in Case 14, Gloss A (VI 13–14), where this passage in Case 37 has received some attention. This example again illustrates the Egyptian surgeon's experience that a serious rupture of the soft tissue over a fracture creates a condition which he cannot hope to treat successfully.

SECOND DIAGNOSIS

XII 20–21

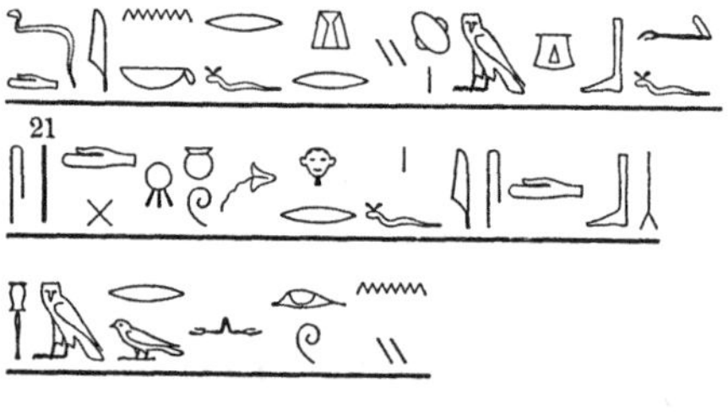

Translation

Thou shouldst say concerning him: "One having a break in his upper arm, over which a wound has been inflicted, piercing through. An ailment not to be treated."

Commentary

The terms have all been discussed above.

The conclusion is the unfavorable verdict 3 ; see commentary on Case 5 (II 15), and especially the introduction (pp. 46–48). This verdict is, as usual, not followed by any treatment. The difference between this fracture and that of the preceding case (36) consists solely in the existence of a penetrating wound in the overlying soft tissue in the latter case, which is regarded by the surgeon as a situation too serious to be treated.

CASE THIRTY-EIGHT

XII 21–XIII 2

A SPLIT IN THE HUMERUS

This is the last of the three cases concerned with injuries of the humerus. Contrary to the custom of the ancient author he has placed at the end of the group a case which he regards as relatively simple and to which he appends verdict 1. It is the shortest case in the entire treatise, occupying only a scant four lines.

The seriousness of a "split" (*pšn*) depends upon its situation. If it is in the skull (*calvaria*), it may be a serious and doubtful case (see Case 4). The same is true if it is in the temple (Case 21) ; but if it is in the maxillary region (Case 16), or in the humerus as in our case, it is not a serious injury. See the discussion in Case 4 (II 2, and Gloss A, II 8–9).

TITLE

XII 21

Translation

Instructions concerning a split in his upper arm.

Commentary

 *pšn*, "split," has been discussed in Case 4 (II 2). It is an injury occurring only in bones, and hence *g'b* must here designate the *humerus* itself.

EXAMINATION

XII 22–XIII 1

Translation

If thou examinest a man having a split in his upper arm, (and) thou shouldst find the swelling protruding, on the outside of that split, which is in his upper arm, (conclusion follows in diagnosis).

Commentary

 *ṯḫb*, " swelling," has been fully discussed in Case 4 (II 4).

 *yšww*, " protruding," is explained *ibid.*

 *ḥr š'*, " on the outside of," see Case 8 (IV 6).

DIAGNOSIS

XIII 1

Translation

Thou shouldst say concerning him : " One having a split in his upper arm. An ailment which I will treat."

Commentary

The terms have all been discussed above. As so frequently before, the diagnosis consists merely of the subject followed by the verdict, in this case favorable. See Case 1 (I 2) and introduction (pp. 46 ff.).

TREATMENT

XIII 2

Translation

Thou shouldst bind it with *ymrw* ; thou shouldst treat it afterward [with] honey every day until he recovers.

Commentary

On binding with *ymrw* see the discussion of Case 15 (VI 17). The treatment with honey is discussed in Case 1 (I 3).

CASE THIRTY-NINE

XIII 3–12

TUMORS OR ULCERS IN THE BREAST PERHAPS RESULTING FROM INJURY

This case is the first of a series of eight (39 to 46) concerned with ailments of the breast, by which is meant both the sternum and the soft tissue overlying it (see Case 40, Gloss A). The nature of the ailment (called *bn·wt*) is not wholly clear, but the available evidence adduced below would indicate some kind of tumors, or possible ulcers. The occurrence of such a case of disease after a series of thirty-eight cases of *injuries* requiring surgical treatment raises the question whether it is introduced into this treatise because it required cauterization, essentially a minor surgical operation ; or because the *bn·wt* were superinduced by some antecedent injury. There is perhaps some reference to this injury in the phrase *mꜣ yh-f*, "because of his *yh*," in which *yh* may mean "injury," and probably does so in our case (see Case 3, I 23). It should be noticed also that the text refers to a *wbnw*, possibly "wound," as designating one of the *bn·wt* (XIII 9). The only other case of *bn·wt* in our papyrus, however, contains no such hints of any connected injury or wound (Case 45).

The treatment by cauterization is the oldest known reference to this practice.

Title

XIII 3

Translation

Instructions concerning tumors with prominent head in his breast.

Commentary

Discussion of all terms will be found below.

Examination

XIII 3–5

Translation

If thou examinest a man having tumors with prominent head in his breast, (and) thou findest that the swellings have spread with pus over his breast, (and) have produced redness, while it is very hot therein, when thy hand touches him, (conclusion follows in diagnosis).

Commentary

On "tumors with prominent head" see Gloss A.

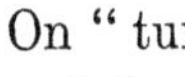 *tw*ꜣ·*w*, "swellings," is a rare word. It is not found again in our treatise, and is otherwise known only in four passages in Pap. Ebers. In the treatment of some uncertain kind of tumor or pustule (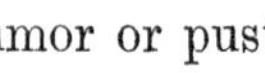 *ḥnḥn·t*), the physician is enjoined as follows:

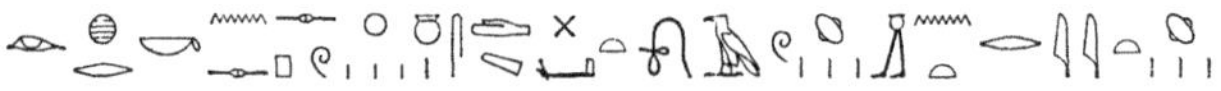

"Thou shouldst make for her applications for breaking open the swellings (*tw*ꜣ·*w*) and drawing off the pus" (Pap. Ebers 104, 10–11).

B. Ebbell has recently suggested with much probability that *ḥnḥn·t* in Pap. Ebers and also in *Mutter und Kind* means "Lymphdrüsenschwellung" or swelling of the lymphatic glands (*Zeitschrift für aegyptische Sprache* 63 (1927), pp. 73 f.). See also Pap. Ebers 105, 5, a case in which the "swellings" (*tw*ꜣ·*w*) in the fat of the throat are to be "broken open" (*šd*) by applications. Again in the same ailment the physician shall "make for it applications for drawing off the swellings (*tw*ꜣ·*w*) in his throat" (Pap. Ebers 105, 13). The fourth example (Pap. Ebers 105, 18) is not so clear. In our case (Smith XIII, 4), the *tw*ꜣ·*w* are likewise clearly accompanied by pus. The word may possibly be connected in origin with  *tw*ꜣ, "lift."

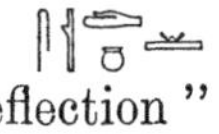 *šḳd*, "spread," may perhaps be cognate with 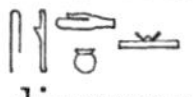 *šḳd*, "slope, deflection" (of a pyramid), with a meaning verging toward "divergence, spread;" but no other occurrence of the word in the medical papyri is known.

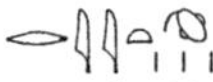 *ry·t*, "pus," often read *ty·t*; but see Case 6 (III 1).

 *tmš·w*, "redness." It is well known that ancient color designations are loose, indefinite, and greatly lacking in precision; but the root *tmš* is known to designate red in general. The form *tmš·w* is doubtless a formation like *nfr·w*, "beauty." On the color *tmš*, see Case 7, Gloss F (III 20–21).

DIAGNOSIS

XIII 5–6

a The scribe at first wrote the plural form *yry-n-śn*, all in red like the rest of the context. He afterward canceled the *śn* with an oblique stroke through the *ś* and a vertical stroke through the *n* and plural strokes, and inserted *f* before the *śn*. All these alterations were inserted in black on the red.

Translation

Thou shouldst say concerning him : " One having tumors with prominent head in his breast, (and) they produce ⸢cists⸣ of pus. An ailment which I will treat with the fire-drill."

Commentary

" Tumors with prominent head " will be found discussed in the gloss. There can be no doubt that *bn·wt*, " tumors " is in the plural, for it is followed by the plural demonstrative in XIII 7. Hence the ancient scribe's correction from *yry-n-śn*, " they produce " to *yry-f*, " it produces," or " he produces " is probably wrong. If the antecedent is *bn·wt*, the correction is obviously wrong, and to understand *f*, " he " as referring to the patient is hardly permissible.

On *ry·t*, " pus " see Case 6 (III 1).

On the favorable verdict 1, see commentary on Case 1 (I 2), and introduction (pp. 45–47).

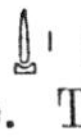 *ḏ'*, " fire-stick " or " fire-drill " is the well-known Egyptian device for kindling fire. The hieroglyph is a good representation of the implement. It doubtless furnished the surgeon with the most convenient means of procuring a hot point for application to the tumors. The pointed top of the stick was whirled between the palms, while the thicker lower end revolved in a hollow in a block of wood. The friction quickly produced fire, and when the end of the fire-stick was glowing, the surgeon could apply it to the tumor. There is a reference to a " hot lancet " in Pap. Ebers 108, 8. It is not usual to connect the verdict directly with the device to be employed ; but it occurs again in Case 46 (XVI 3) and five times in Pap. Ebers (Wreszinski's 860, 866, 869, and 870 " with lancet " ; and 200 " with applications "). See further discussion below.

TREATMENT

XIII 6–9

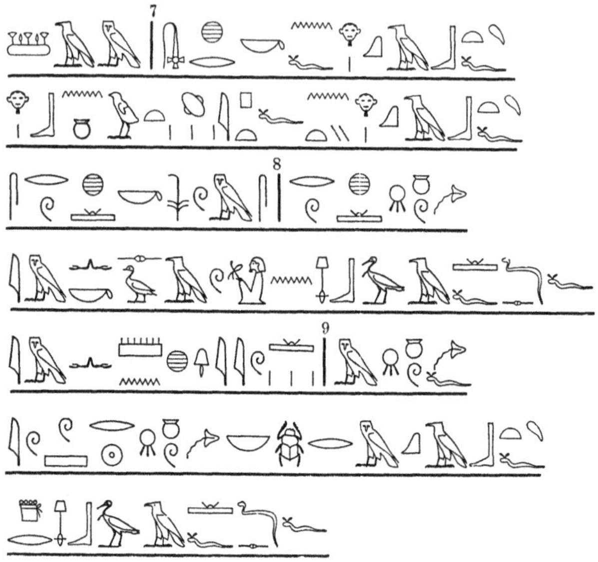

Translation

Thou shouldst burn for him over his breast (and) over those tumors which are on his breast. Thou shouldst treat him with wound treatment. Thou shouldst not prevent its opening of itself, that there may be no *mnḫy·w* in his wound (sore?). Every wound (sore?) that arises in his breast dries up as soon as it opens of itself.

Commentary

*š*ꜣ*m*, "burn," is a rare word, of which there is only one other medical example known, viz., Pap. Ebers (109, 15): "Thou shouldst burn it over fire." In this passage *š*ꜣ*m*, "burn" has heretofore been read *š*ꜣ*w*, with final *w*. In our text a careful examination of the word leaves no doubt that it is written *š*ꜣ*m*. When the scribe makes the uppermost hook of the hieratic *m* hastily it sometimes almost disappears, leaving a sign that can with difficulty be distinguished from *w*; e. g. in the word *ṯrm* (IV 3, end of line), the *m* is scarcely distinguishable from *w*. In view of *š*ꜣ*m* in XIII 6–7, we can hardly doubt that we are to read *š*ꜣ*m* also in Pap. Ebers 109, 15. See also the incorrect for (XIV 15). Dévaud notes *š*ꜣ*m* in *hieroglyphic* (Quibell-Lacau, *Saqqara* (1906–07), p. 58), parallel with .

The use of cauterization, for which the glowing tip of a fire-drill seems to have been employed, is interesting. In Pap. Ebers (109, 15) there may be some question whether the burning applies to the reed knife or lancet, which the surgeon is to harden by heating; or to the cauterization of the lanced cist. Cf. Ebers 108, 8.

śrwḫ wbnw, "treatment of a wound" or "wound treatment," is rendered according to the prevailing meaning of *wbnw* in our treatise; but it should be recalled that the term *wbnw* is sometimes loosely applied to a sore, as indeed it seems to be in the immediately following context in this treatment (XIII 9). The term "wound treatment" is employed in only one other passage in our treatise, where it designates an externally applied remedy for allaying inflammation. See Case 46, XVI 7–8.

The *n* preceding the subjunctive verb after *sʾw*, "prevent," is unusual and superfluous, and must be regarded as a scribal error.

mnḫy·w is otherwise unknown and its meaning cannot be established.

GLOSS A

XIII 9–12

Explaining: Tumors with prominent head in his breast.

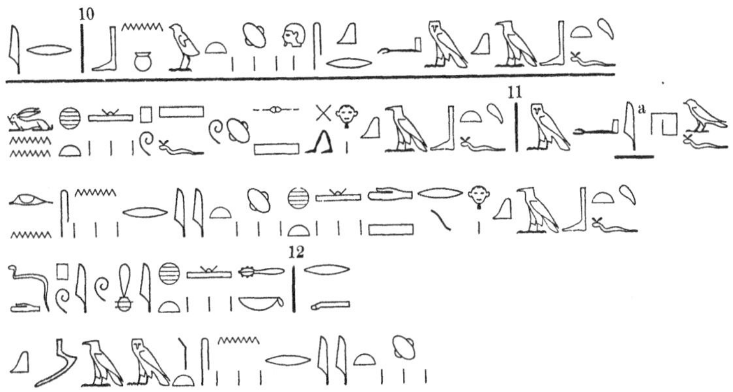

a The scribe omitted by mistake and afterward inserted it in red ink.

Translation

As for: "Tumors with prominent head in his breast," it means that there are swellings spreading over his breast because of his injury; they produce pus and redness on his breast; (as) it is said: "It is like ⌜parti-colored⌝ things," whose product is pus.

Commentary

bn·wt, "tumors," is a difficult word, of which the suggested rendering is doubtless only a very rough approximation. We learn at once that the *bn·wt* have *tp śkr*, which as we shall indicate below means "a prominent head." The examination (XIII 4) informs us that the physician finds "swellings" (*twʾ·w*), which spread over the breast, accompanied by pus, redness, and a very fevered surface (XIII 5). These observations are confirmed by our gloss, which explains that *bn·wt tp śkr* means swellings spreading over his breast, producing redness and pus. The allusion at the end of the gloss is, as we shall see, unfortunately not clear. The rendering " tumors " is further confirmed by Case 45, in which another variety of *bn·wt* are treated. In the examination (XV, 9–14) they are said to be cool, without fever, with no granulation or fluid (*mw,* literally " water "). In Gloss A Case 45 further explains that this second type of *bn·wt* is swellings spreading on the breast, having a touch or surface like that of a kind of ball, and they are likened to an unripe *ḥmꜣy·t*-fruit, which is described as hard and cool to the touch (XV 18–19). *Bn·wt* may occur, according to Case 45 (XV 15) " in every member " (*m ꜥ·t nb·t*), and this remark is confirmed by Papyrus Ebers, which states that *bn·wt* may be found 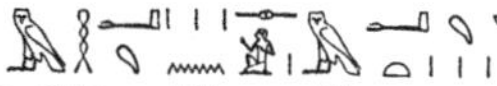 " in the flesh of a man in any member " (Pap. Ebers 72, 10–11). The other examples in Papyrus Ebers are important. In one case the *bn·wt* are *ḥr ḳꜣb·t,* " on the breast " (Pap. Ebers 71, 2). Again we find the case of a woman suffering from a " devouring (*wnm·t,* " cancer "?) in the vulva, producing *bn·wt* in her vagina " (Pap. Ebers 95, 17), or from " *ḳmy·t* (leucorrhea ?) in the vulva, producing *bn·wt* in her vagina " (Pap. Ebers 96, 2–3). In three cases we find *bn·wt* in the teeth, which must of course mean in the contiguous gums. The physician has a recipe for " preventing crumbling (*śḫm*) arising from *bn·wt* in the teeth " (Pap. Ebers 72, 13), and also for " preventing *bn·wt* in the teeth and restoring the gums " (*ḥꜥ·w,* literally " flesh," Pap. Ebers 72, 14–15, repeated in 89, 10). Twice in Pap. Ebers the *bn·wt* are said to be in a *wbnw* (Ebers 70, 24–71, 1), as above in Pap. Smith (XIII 9), raising the question of rendering " sore " or " wound." The above examples comprise all the occurrences of the word in the medical papyri. Elsewhere it is known only once, in the Book of the Dead, in a passage where the deceased says : " When I am led to the fields where the gods cut their food, then may the horns of Khepri be turned aside, and may *bn·wt* arise in the eye of Atum " (Naville, 93, ll. 5–6). Summarizing this material it may be said that the hard *bn·wt* of Case 45 may have been boils, while their occurrence in the teeth in Papyrus Ebers suggests ulcers. The rendering " tumors " may serve at least as approximating the ancient meaning of the word.

Since writing the above comments and since they have been in proof, I find that B. Ebbell has recently discussed the nature of these *bn·wt* (*Zeitschrift für aegyptische Sprache,* 63 (1927), pp. 71–73). He concludes that the word designates a " gangränöses Geschwür," that is a gangrenous ulcer or sore. He regards the masculine word *bnw* (*Mutter und Kind,* III 4), which I had relegated to a footnote, as identical with our *bn·wt,* and quotes the instructive charm addressed to it as an exorcism :

" Thou *bnw,* brother of blood,
Friend of pus,
Father of *ḥnḫn·t,*
Jackal of Upper Egypt,"

which associates the *bnw* with blood, pus, swellings of the lymphatic glands (according to Ebbell), and the evil odor of the Upper Egyptian jackal.[1]

tp šḳr, " prominent head " refers to the point at which, as we also say, the tumor " comes to a head." The word *tp,* " head," used in this sense is found in Papyrus Ebers in the description of a suppurating tumor, of which it is said :

" Thou findest its head (*tp*) sharp and elevated like a breast " (*mamma* ; Pap. Ebers 104, 15–16). On the further anatomical or medical use of *tp,* "head" see Case 1 (title), and Case 10 (V 5). *šḳr* "prominent, elevated " is a rare and unusual term, which seems to have no connection with the well-known word *šḳr,* " strike." The rendering suggested is supported by the fact that in Case 46 the Gloss writes *tp šḳr,* while the text of the case writes and (XV 20 and XVI 2). See Case 46. Dr. Ware has suggested to me the well-known parallel use of *šḳr* meaning " to raise, lift, set up " as of a ladder in the Pyramid Texts (e. g. Pyr., 1431c).

yḫ·t, with modifiers, consult Case 4 (II 3), p. 142. It is probably plural here, though singular in Case 46 (XVI 13).

mʿ yh-f, "because of his injury." It is not quite certain that *yh* always means an " injury," as contrasted with a disease ; otherwise we might conclude that the *bn·wt* in this case were due to an injury, and the reference to a *wbnw* (XIII 9) would indicate a wound.

ry·t, " pus," see Case 6 (III 1).

yḫ·t ẖkr, " ⌜parti-colored⌝ ", literally " adorned," if this *ẖkr,* with the determinative is to be identified with the common *ẖkr,* " adorn." The *ẖkr*-ornament is sometimes gayly colored. The text refers to matters for comparison, which elude the present editor.

CASE FORTY

XIII 12–17

A WOUND IN THE BREAST

This is the second of the group of eight cases discussing ailments of the breast. The wound is one which penetrates the soft tissue and perforates the upper part of the *sternum* (*ḳ'b·t*), which the surgeon calls *ḥnt'*, meaning the *manubrium*, as he explains in a gloss at the end. Ancient methods of warfare made wounds of this kind common ; a wound " perforating the manubrium " is likely to have been inflicted by a spear. Presumably none of the underlying organs was injured, for the treatise appends the hopeful verdict and prescribes simple external applications, leading to recovery.

[1] *Bnw* was discussed many years ago by Oefele, *Zeitschrift für aegyptische Sprache,* 39 (1901), p. 149.

The gloss at the end is another illustration of the origin of anatomical terms in natural objects, and combined with the other references to *ḳ'b·t* in our papyrus makes it possible to determine the Egyptian names both for the *sternum* and the *manubrium*.

TITLE

XIII 12

Translation

Instructions concerning a wound in his breast.

Commentary

"Wound" will be found discussed in Case 1 (title), "breast" is explained in Gloss A at the end of our case.

EXAMINATION

XIII 12–14

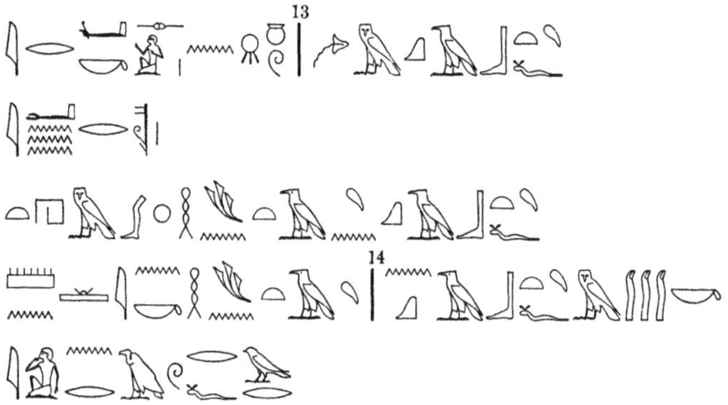

Translation

If thou examinest a man having a wound in his breast, penetrating to the bone, perforating the *manubrium* of his *sternum*, thou shouldst press the *manubrium* of his *sternum* with thy fingers, (although) he shudders exceedingly, (conclusion follows in diagnosis).

Commentary

 *yʿ*, "penetrating," is the same as 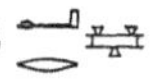 *ʿr*, "penetrating," discussed in Case 1 (title), q. v.

 *thm*, "perforating," is discussed in Case 1 (under *wbnw*) and Case 3 (I 18).

 *ḥnt'*, "manubrium," is explained in Gloss A at the end of this case.

mn, "press," is doubtless a transitive or *piʿel* form of the common verb *mn*, "abide, endure, be firm, etc.," with a causative meaning, "to make firm, to press." As the second main verb after the conditional particle *yr*, it is parallel with the common *gmm-k*, which we have found so often as the second conditional verb.

ynrw r-f, "he shudders," is explained in Case 4 (II 4).

DIAGNOSIS

XIII 14–15

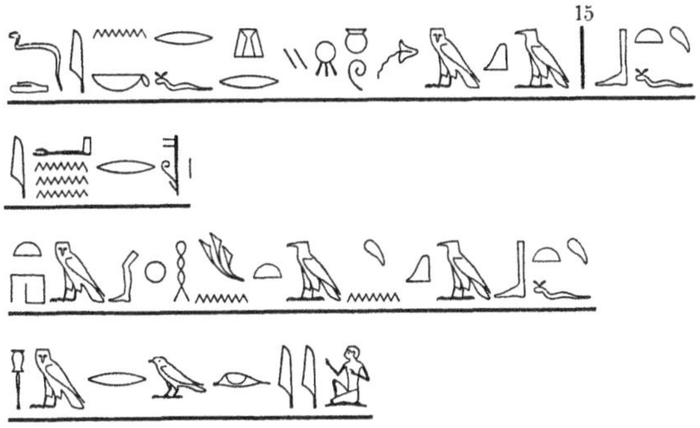

Translation

Thou shouldst say concerning him: "One having a wound in his breast, penetrating to the bone, perforating the *manubrium* of his *sternum*. An ailment which I will treat."

Commentary

The diagnosis repeats only the terms of the examination, where the discussion will be found. The favorable verdict 1 forming the conclusion will be found discussed in the commentary on Case 1 (I 2); see also introduction (pp. 45–47).

TREATMENT

XIII 15–16

Translation

Thou shouldst bind it with fresh meat the first day; thou shouldst treat it afterward [with] grease, honey, and lint every day, until he recovers.

Commentary

Treatment with fresh meat followed by the application of grease, honey and lint, will be found discussed in Case 1 (I 2–3). See the commentary on " until he recovers " in the same connection.

GLOSS A

XIII 17

Explaining : The manubrium of his sternum.

Translation

As for : "The *manubrium* of his *sternum*," (it means) the upper head of his *sternum*; it is like as it were a porcupine.

Commentary

We have in this gloss another explanation of the designation of a bone of the human skeleton which is drawn from its resemblance to some animal or part of an animal, like the *ʾmʿ·t*, " ramus," so called because of its resemblance to the two-toed claw of the *ʾmʿ*-bird (pp. 215, 293–294). The animal in our case is called *ḥntʾ*, and very little is known about him. A recipe for a hair tonic in Papyrus Ebers has as its chief ingredient the hair of *ḥntʾ* (Pap. Ebers 66, 12), from which it is obvious that the animal must have vigorous and robust hair. Another recipe prescribes *śr·t n·t ḥnty*, " the spine of a *ḥnty* " (Pap. Ebers 92, 7), which is doubtless the same animal as the *ḥntʾ*, and seems probably to be a hedgehog or porcupine. The latter animal is depicted on the ancient Egyptian monuments. No other evidence for the identity of the *ḥntʾ* is available. The appearance of the thorax seen from in front, especially the *sternum* with the spreading ribs which diverge from it like the legs of an insect, strongly suggests an animal, and the comparison with a porcupine is quite possible. The difficulty lies in the further limitation of the *ḥntʾ* by our surgeon as being the " upper head " of the breast (*sternum*), as we shall see below. If we limit *ḥntʾ* to the *manubrium*, as our gloss clearly does, the resemblance to a porcupine is far from obvious, though it might still suggest an animal.

ḳʾb·t, " breast," is a word of which the meaning has been commonly misunderstood as the " nipple " of the *mamma*. It occurs sixty-five times in Pap. Smith in sufficiently varied use to indicate its meaning with some precision. In eight passages, where the surgeon desires to ascertain the patient's ability to use the muscles and vertebrae of the neck, he directs the patient to look " at his two shoulders and his breast (*ḳʾb·t*)." See Cases 3, 4, 5, 7, 29 and 30. In these cases *ḳʾb·t* obviously means the breast in general. It is used in thirty-four passages to locate swellings, tumors, or abscesses, some of which secrete pus and have to be drained (Cases 39 and 46) or are so described as to show that they are in the soft tissue (Case 45) ; and wounds in the soft tissue (Case 41), which may penetrate to and include the bone (Case 40). The remaining twenty-three passages containing the word use it in a more limited sense, designating bone. They are very instructive. In Case 34, a dislocation of the clavicles, these bones are described as follows :

" Their heads are attached to (articulated in) the upper bone of his *ḳʾb·t* " (XI 23). Here *ḳʾb·t* is clearly the *sternum*, and its " upper bone " is of course the *manubrium sterni*. The explanation of the *ḫntʾ* in our Gloss A as " the upper head of his *ḳʾb·t*," is obviously a variant of the term " upper bone of his *ḳʾb·t* " in Case 34. The use of *ḳʾb·t* to designate the *sternum* is corroborated by Gloss A in Case 43, which refers to the thoracic ribs as

" the ribs of his *ḳʾb·t*, which are attached to (articulated in) his *ḳʾb·t* " (XV 4). In the same case the patient suffers with pains in his sides, which the surgeon explains in Gloss B as follows :

"It means: he suffers in the articulations thereof (viz., of his two sides, including their ribs) in his *ḳʾb·t* " (XV 5). In accordance with this evidence there are fourteen passages mentioning the true ribs (*costae verae*) as " the ribs of his *ḳʾb·t*" in Cases 42, 43 and 44.

Summarizing the evidence for the meaning of *ḳʾb·t* in our papyrus, we find it used as a designation for the breast in general, for the soft tissue overlying the bony structure, and finally quite specifically for the *sternum*. It nowhere means the *mamma* in particular or any part of it, and the Coptic **ⲉⲕⲓⲃ̅ⲉ**, *mamma* is evidently a later and secondary development.

tp ḥry, " upper head," employing " head " in an anatomical sense to designate the end of a bone, will be found discussed in Case 1 (title).

my ḫpr·t m, literally " like what happens (or what has happened) in," or " like what is " (with porcupine as predicate introduced by *m*), which occurs also in Case 42 (XIV 21), is perhaps only a circumlocution for " as it were," meaning simply " like."

CASE FORTY-ONE

XIII 18–XIV 16

AN INFECTED OR POSSIBLY NECROTIC WOUND IN THE BREAST

This is one of the most completely discussed cases in the papyrus. It is the third in the group of eight cases concerned with the breast. The examination is one of the most detailed presentations of the pathological conditions which we find in our treatise, and the interesting glosses add much to this description. Gloss A especially explains the sluggish character of the wound, its refusal to heal, and quotes from the venerable " Treatise on What Pertains to a Wound," which we find quoted also in Case 5, Gloss A. The data seem hardly sufficient, however, to determine whether the wound is infected or in a necrotic condition.

The treatment is medicinally very elaborate. It consists of external local applications, which are systematically arranged in a succession of three stages :

1. Cooling applications for drawing out the inflammation :
   a. Various leaves, etc., bandaged on.
   b. The same.
2. Astringent applications for drying up the wound :
   a. Ointment of mineral salts bandaged on.
   b. The same.
3. Poultices :
   a. Various herbs bandaged on.

Unfortunately the drugs employed cannot be identified in more than a few cases. It is of interest to note that in the first recipe for allaying the inflammation (1, *a* and *b*) there seems to be salicin or salicylic acid, in the form of willow (*salix*) leaves, although in modern times before its synthetic production, salicin was obtained from willow *bark* rather than the leaves. The astringent applications (2, *a* and *b*) contain copper and sodium salts; the only constituent of the poultices which can be identified is sycamore leaves. The surgeon was evidently accustomed to find these agencies effective, for he gives the case the hopeful verdict, and adds to the treatment the injunction to treat the same trouble in any part of the body in the same way.

At the end the commentator has added five important explanations of terms not otherwise clear, including an already ancient color designation (*tmś*), which he had once before explained in Case 7, Gloss F (III 20–21). In the other four glosses the commentator is especially interested in the discussion of the feverish and inflamed condition of the wound and in explaining the terms involved. In so doing he quotes from the already ancient and now lost " Treatise on What Pertains to a Wound."

TITLE

XIII 18

Translation

Instructions concerning a diseased wound in his breast.

Commentary

The terms will be found discussed below.

EXAMINATION

XIII 18–XIV 1

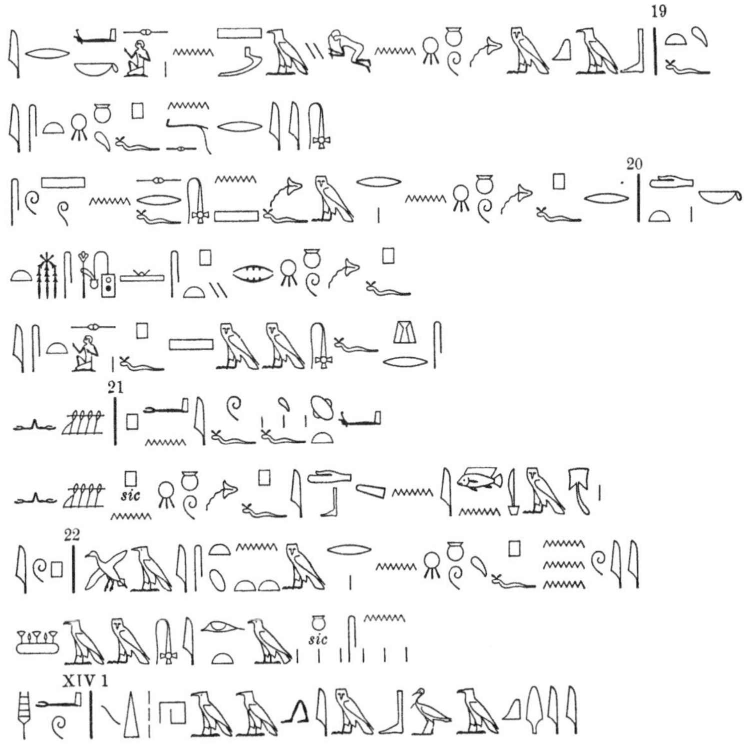

Translation

If thou examinest a man having a diseased wound in his breast, while that wound is inflamed and a whirl of inflammation continually issues from the mouth of that wound at thy touch; the two lips of that wound are ruddy, while that man continues to be feverish from it; his flesh cannot receive a bandage, that wound cannot take a margin of skin; the ⌜granulation⌝ which is in the mouth of that wound is watery, their surface is hot and secretions drop therefrom in an oily state, (conclusion follows in diagnosis).

Commentary

 *šm'y*, "diseased," see Gloss A.

 *k'b·t*, "breast," see above, Case 40, Gloss A (XIII 17).

 *nsr-y*, "inflamed," see Gloss A (XIV 8).

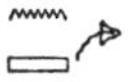 *nšw*, "issue," see below, Gloss E.

 *tmś*, "ruddy," see below, Gloss C.

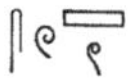 *śwš*, "whirl," see below, Gloss B.

 *srf*, "heat, inflammation," see below, Gloss B.

 *ydb*, "margin," is really a topographical term meaning "shore." Its medical or surgical use here is quite parallel with 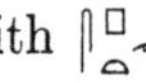 *śpt* "lip," which is also a word for "shore." The reference is to the contracting margin of newly forming skin around a healing wound.

 *p'ys·t*, ⌜"granulation"⌝, is an otherwise entirely unknown word. The translation is a suggestion by Dr. Luckhardt. The word lacks any indication of the plural, but it is resumed by a plural pronoun in the next clause.

 *mwy*, "be watery," is a rare verb, of course cognate with the noun  *mw*, "water." It occurs in the same connection in Papyrus Ebers (91, 8); 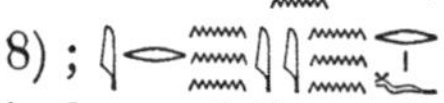 "if its (the ear's) mouth is watery." There seems to be a non-medical use of the verb in the obscure passage 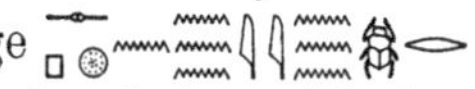 (Eloquent Peasant B 1, 258).

 *š'm*, rendered above "be hot," is a transitive verb in Case 39 (XIII 6–7). The meaning is obviously that of an intransitive verb here. The reading *š'm*, rather than *š'w*, is here quite certain.

 *yrty·w*, "surface," see Case 7 (III 20).

 *ʿḥʿ·w*, "secretions," is the word originally meaning a "pile" of grain or goods, then a "measure" or a "quantity," as in mathematics. Its medical application is known chiefly from our papyrus, where it occurs three times as follows:  "Secretions (*ʿḥʿ·w*) drop therefrom in an oily state (Case 41, XIII 22–XIV 1).  "Secretions (*ʿḥʿ·w*) dropping therefrom are cool (Case 47, XVII 9–10).  "They generate no secretions of fluid" (Case 45, XV 13). With this we may compare  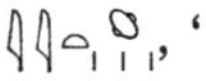, "It forms secretions of pus" (Pap. Ebers 105, 19).

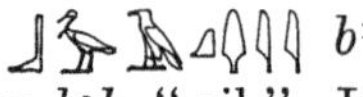 *b'ḳ-y*, "in an oily state," is doubtless a verb derived from the noun *b'ḳ*, "oil." It may be compared with the verb *mwy*, "be watery" used immediately above (XIII 22). Grammatically it is parallel in construction with 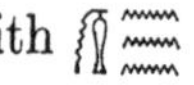 *ḳbb*,

"be cool," occupying an analogous position in the example quoted above from Case 47 (XVII 9–10). It may of course be derived from the verb  *b'ḳ*, "to be clear," and the only other example of our word in the medical literature would at first sight seem to support this meaning. In Case 46 we find  "*b'ḳ* like fluid under thy hand" (XV 21–XVI 1). The reference is to a "swelling (*ṯḥb*) very large, protruding on his breast." We have only to understand "protruding" (*yšw-y*) as meaning "discharging" and we obtain an excellent rendering for *b'ḳ* etc., namely "clear like water under thy hand." Against this interpretation, however, there are conclusive objections. In the first place the touch of the hand is obviously not the means for observing clearness, a quality appreciable only by the eyes. The very fact that the quality here observed is one appreciable by the touch of the hand shows that it must belong to the order of physical qualities like hot or cold, hard or soft and the like. Furthermore a study of all the cases in which the above "swelling" (*ṯḥb*) and "protrude" (*yšw*) occur, makes it highly improbable that a fluid exudation is here meant. The reference is to a protruding swelling which is here discerned by the fingers to be soft or "oily like fluid under thy hand." See the commentary on *ṯḥb* and *yšw* in Case 4 (II 4).

Diagnosis

XIV 1–2

Translation

Thou shouldst say concerning him: "One having a diseased wound in [his] breast, it being inflamed, (and) he continues to have fever from it. An ailment which I will treat."

Commentary

The terms have all been discussed in the preceding commentary on this case, or in the glosses which follow. On the favorable verdict 1 see Case 1 (I 2) and the introduction (pp. 45–47). Since rendering *šmm-f*, "he continues to have fever," I note that Gardiner in his new *Grammar* (pp. 352 f.) especially emphasizes "*repetition* or *continuity*" as implied in the geminated form. This is good Semitic as well as Egyptian usage, as noted above, *supra*, pp. 315–316.

TREATMENT

XIV 2–8

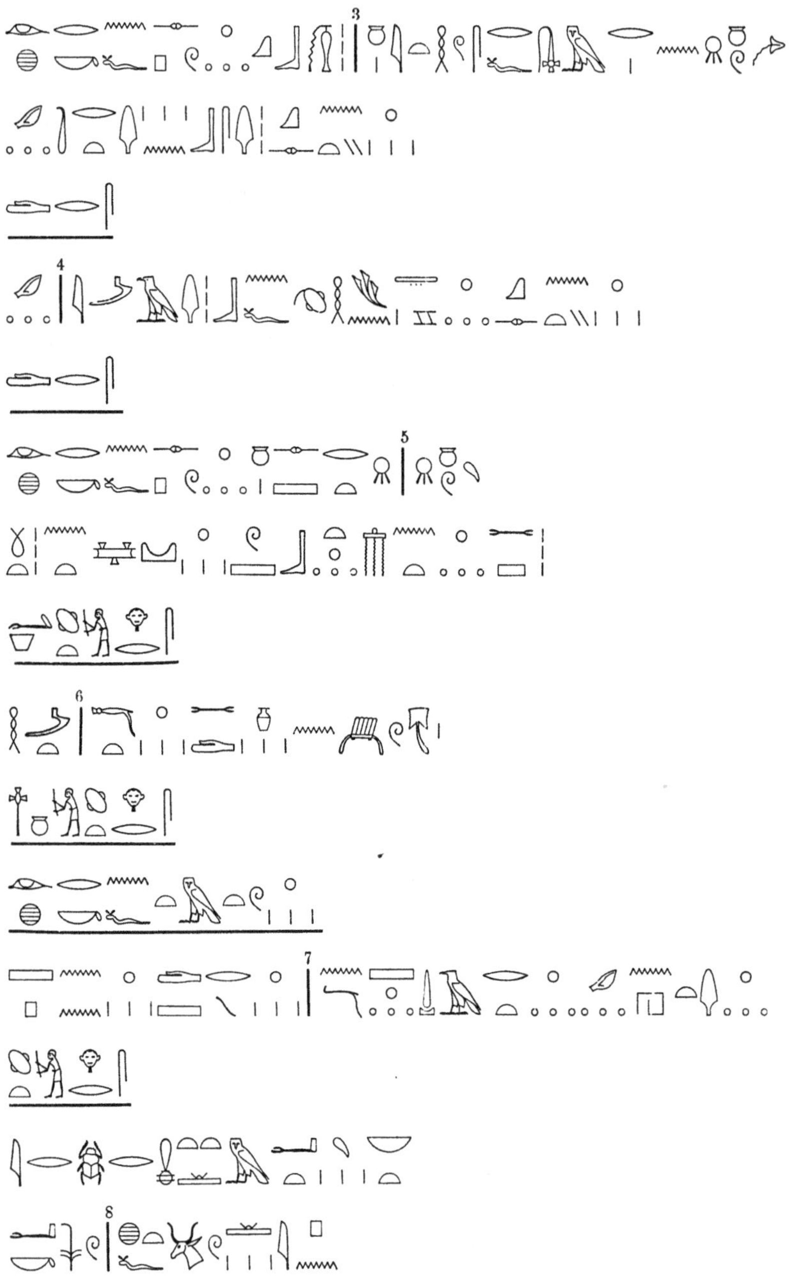

Translation

Thou shalt make for him cool applications for drawing out the inflammation from the mouth of the wound :

a. Leaves of willow,
nbś-tree,
ḳsnty.
Apply to it.

b. Leaves of *ymꜣ*-tree,
dung,
ḥny-tꜣ,
ḳsnty.
Apply to it.

Thou shalt make for him applications for drying up the wound :

a. ⌜Powder⌝ of green pigment
wšb·t,
ṯḥn·t
grease.
Triturate ; bind upon it.

b. Northern salt,
ibex grease.
Triturate ; bind upon it.

Thou shalt make for him poultices :

Red *špnn,*
garden tongue,
ḏꜣr·t,
sycamore leaves.
Bind upon it.

If the like befalls in any member, thou shalt treat him according to these instructions.

Commentary

The following notes contain the little that is known regarding the character and identity of the herbs, minerals, and other constituents of the five recipes above prescribed, and the form in which they are employed.

 *sp·w,* "applications," is a word of varied meanings. The meaning "fragments" has been discussed in Case 4 (II 9). Its more common meaning is "remedy" in a very general sense. It is usually used in the plural as in our text, though referring to a single recipe, e.g., Pap. Ebers 40, 7 ; 40, 21 ; 39, 10 ; and is quite commonly

introduced by the injunction "Thou shalt make for him remedies," followed by the genitive *nw* with the effect of the remedy, the name of the ailment or the ailing organ, or by the content of the prescription, e.g., Pap. Hearst III 17; IV 9 = Ebers 2, 7 b; Hearst IV 14 = Ebers 50, 6–9; Hearst I 1 = Ebers 11, 3; Ebers 73, 13; etc. Very much less commonly it occurs in the singular, e.g., Ebers 39, 17; 7, 11; Kahun Medical Pap. 3, 19; 3, 15; 3, 17; 3, 20; Ebers 39, 17, 19; 42, 11; 36, 9. Cooling applications as in our case are found also in Pap. Ebers: (Ebers 43, 1) and (Ebers 91, 5–6). It may finally be noted that while *sp* almost invariably designates a *medicinal* remedy, it may, though very rarely, also indicate a *magical* remedy, e.g. Kahun Medical Pap. 3, 23; *Mutter und Kind*, VIII 3–4.

yṯḥ, "draw out," is a verb primarily designating the application of physical power in drawing a heavy object like a monument, and hence the determinative of a coil of rope. Its use in the medical papyri elsewhere is limited to three examples in Pap. Ebers, in which the remedy acts to "draw out" (*yṯḥ*) "blood" (Ebers 70, 4–5; and 96, 13) or a "swelling" (*tw᾽·w*) (Ebers 105, 13), meaning in the latter case doubtless the content of the swelling, so that in these cases the object of the verb is material substance. In the two cases employing this word in Pap. Edwin Smith however, the object of the verb is the word *śrf*, "heat, inflammation" (Pap. Smith XIV 3; XVI 8), an intangible thing, which could be allayed to be sure, but only figuratively "drawn off," although even among us the phrase "draw out inflammation" is not unusual.

ḏrḏ, "leaves," is a difficult word. It is universally written with the ear, and the reading *ḏrḏ* is known only from a single passage where it is written out in the Berlin Medical Papyrus 3038 (Verso 3, 7). It is a part of various trees (Hearst XV, 4; XVI, 3) of which the following are known:

and once "divine *ḏrḏ*," which are explained as (Berlin Med. Pap. 3038, 10, 5). The rendering "leaves" is not wholly certain; the word might possibly mean "bark" (*cortex*), and indeed in the case of willow, the bark is medicinally more efficacious than the leaves.

nbś, a tree mentioned as far back as the Old Kingdom, and occurring in Greek as -νουψ, but not yet identified with certainty. The word *ḏrḏ*, ("leaves," or "bark") may possibly be understood also with *nbś*.

ḳsnty, occurring at the conclusion of each of the first two recipes, may possibly refer to some form of preparing the preceding ingredients. It is more probably, however, an additional ingredient, an herb which is written 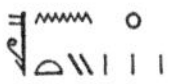 *ksnty* (Pap. Ebers 45, 4) and  in the corresponding passage in Hearst (VII 2). This is probably the same as  (Ebers 46, 18 and 73, 2 ; see variants in Hearst X 1 and V 8). It has not yet been identified.

 *ymꜣ* is an unidentified fruit tree.

 *bnf*, as used in the medical papyri, is, with the exception of one passage, always followed by the name of some animal. We have the *bnf* of cattle (Ebers 87, 10 ; 104, 5 ; Berlin Med. Pap. 3038, verso, 2, 8) ; of an ox (Ebers 22, 7) ; of a fish (Ebers 62, 6 ; 65, 6). It appears outside the medical papyri probably as early as the Pyramid Texts (1464 b, doubtful). In our papyrus, where it is used twice, the other passage has "the *bnf* of an ox" or "bull" (XVI 9). Judging from this passage our recipe in Case 41 has probably omitted the word ox by error. One might be tempted to read *bnf ḥny-tꜣ*, and interpret *ḥny-tꜣ* as the animal *ḥntꜣ*, "porcupine," which we met in Case 40. This supposition is rendered improbable by the fact that we find *ḥny-tꜣ*, written 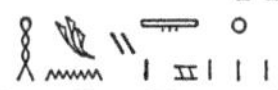 occurring twice in Pap. Ebers (79, 21 ; and 96, 1) as an ingredient by itself. In Pap. Smith (XVI 9), furthermore, the word is written 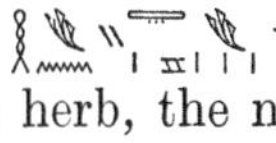 with the determinative of a plant. We must conclude then that it is an herb, the name of which terminates in  *tꜣ*, "earth, ground." Compare the plant name "ground-hair" written also with 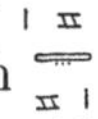 in Pap. Ebers (43, 16). It cannot be identified with any known plant. These considerations make it highly probable that our scribe has unintentionally omitted the word ox after *bnf*. The determinative in the Pyramid Texts suggests that *bnf* means "excrement" or "dung."

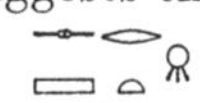 *s-šr·t*, "drying up," is evidently derived from the verb  *s-wšr*, occurring so written only once (Pap. Ebers 40, 4). Otherwise, without the *w*, it occurs seven times in Pap. Ebers (62, 21 ; 65, 15 ; 82, 21 ; 95, 3 ; 95, 15 ; 92, 5 and 70, 13). Of these passages five are pharmaceutical and refer to the drying of drugs (62, 21 ; 65, 15 ; 82, 21 ; 95, 3 ; 95, 15). The other two refer to treatment : one to the drying up of a running ear (92, 5, read *s-šr·t* as in Smith XIV 4) and the other to the drying up of a wound (70, 13) as in our Case 41. A case quite parallel to ours is found in Pap. Ebers (91, 5 ff.) prescribing the treatment of an ear. After the use of cooling applications to reduce the inflammation, combined with absorbents, the text prescribes :  "If its (the ear's) mouth is watery, thou shouldst make for him poultices for drying a wound" (Ebers 91, 8–9).

In our case the process of drying up the wound is accomplished by two prescriptions, both of which are ointments. The basis of the first is merely called "fat" or "grease" (*ʿdy*), while the second prescribes "ibex grease." The remedies carried by these bases are the following minerals, two of which cannot be identified :

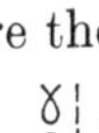 *šš·t*, is a difficult word, which probably indicates the form in which the mineral

is used, like powder, crystals, or the like ; but its occurrence in a single passage as an ingredient of a prescription (Ebers 56, 12) without the name of a mineral following would indicate that it must be used exclusively in connection with one mineral, the name of which might therefore on occasion be omitted. The only other known occurrences of the word (see next paragraph) combine it with *w'ḏw*, " green pigment " as in our case.

w'ḏw, " green pigment," is given an eccentric writing, which is doubtless archaic. The sign *ḏw*, is found at the end of the word in the Pyramid Texts (1681 a), but outside of our papyrus no other example is known with the sign *w'*. There can be no doubt about the reading *w'ḏw*, however, for the combination *šsy·t n·t w'ḏw*, " powder of green pigment " is found in Pap. Ebers (78, 5–6), and again with exactly the same writing as in Ebers in Pap. Hearst (XII 1). The word *w'ḏw*, really meaning simply " green " is applied especially to the green pigment used as a cosmetic for painting the eyes ; but also designates a green pigment employed by Egyptian artists in painting. It consisted of copper salts (chiefly basic carbonate according to Lucas), which the physicians had discovered were astringent. It is employed for drying a wound in the same way in Case 46 (XVI 10), written .

wšb·t is an entirely unidentifiable mineral, known elsewhere in the Egyptian documents only in two passages, both in Pap. Ebers. The first is a recipe for softening hard or stiffened tissues (Ebers 80, 9–10) and the other is a recipe for the treatment of a *wbnw* (" wound " or " sore ") in the breast, which is evidently a case like ours. In this recipe (Ebers 70, 1–3) *wšb·t* is employed along with " northern salt " just as in the two astringent recipes of Pap. Smith (XIV 4–6), and applied in the form of an ointment. As a medicinal agent it was also doubtless an astringent.

ṯḥn·t is another unknown mineral, which is not unlikely some form of mineral glass, in view of the word *ṯḥn* employed by the Egyptians both for glaze or glazed ware, and glass. It is not elsewhere found in our papyrus, and is known otherwise only in four passages in Pap. Ebers (49, 21 ; 80, 6 ; 105, 15 ; 108, 16), where the usual reading is an error for (see Moeller, *Palaeogr.* I, No. 504, where the hieratic sign for No. 417 has been mistaken for). It is employed once internally for urinary troubles, but otherwise in an ointment externally for softening hard or stiffened tissues or for drawing off the content of a swelling ; and once in a magical charm (Ebers 108, 16).

has been given the determinative of a stone by our scribe, but the prescription is obviously an ointment like the next one and we must conclude that the scribe has written in error for *'dy* " fat, grease."

nḏ, " triturate," has been graphically abbreviated by our scribe who has drawn a hand and arm over a mortar. A comparison with the directions following the next prescription shows that this abbreviation stands for *nḏ*, " triturate."

*ḥm*ꜣ*·t mḥ·t*, "northern salt" is evidently one of the salt minerals from the northern desert along the west side of the Delta, chiefly chloride of sodium. It is commonly used in Pap. Ebers in recipes for the same purpose.

is a defective writing for *ny*ꜣ*w*, also written *nr*ꜣ*w* (XVI 11) the name of *Ibex Nubiana*. See Gaillard, *Revue d'Ethnogr. et de Sociol.*, 1912, p. 338.

tmt·w, "poultices," is fully discussed in Case 9 (IV 21).

špnn is an unidentified drug, presumably an herb. It is once called *špnn·w nw špn* "*špnn* (pl.) of *špn* " (Pap. Ebers 93, 3), indicating that *špn* is an herb, as shown by its determinative, of which the *špnn* (pl.) are parts, like blossoms, leaves, petals or the like. On the other hand *špnn* has identity of its own to stand alone in all other known examples, namely three passages in Pap. Ebers (64, 17 ; 64, 21 ; 65, 1) and one more in our papyrus (XVI 12). It is employed internally to quiet a crying child (Ebers 93, 3), and in ointments and poultices for scalp troubles (Ebers 64, 17 ; 64, 21 ; and 65, 1). Whether *dšr*, "red" is a designation of some drug, or merely a modifier of *špnn*, is not wholly certain.

*ns-š*ꜣ, "garden tongue," is evidently the same botanical term as found in Pap. Ebers (31, 12), in which the determinatives of *ns* and *š*ꜣ show that we are dealing with the words "tongue" and "garden." It is an unidentified plant employed in Pap. Ebers in a recipe for allaying inflammation in the anus. It occurs twice also in the London Medical Papyrus (6, 3 and 6, 6) where it is written , and seems to be employed in external applications for allaying inflammation.

*ḏ*ꜣ*r·t* is a fruit occurring very commonly in the medical papyri, which nevertheless cannot be conclusively identified. It is very common without any preceding or following modifiers in the following papyri : Ebers, Hearst, London, and Berlin 3038. It occurs also with various modifiers, as follows :

*Ḏ*ꜣ*r·t* . . . *ḏ*ꜣ*r·t n·t wḥ*ꜣ*·t*, " *ḏ*ꜣ*r·t* of the oasis " (Ebers 43, 16).

*Ḏ*ꜣ*r·t* "fresh (or "green") *ḏ*ꜣ*r·t* " (Ebers 14, 12 ; 53, 1 ; 54, 17 ; 65, 7).

*ḏ*ꜣ*r·t*, "inside of *ḏ*ꜣ*r·t*-fruit" (Ebers 47, 10, etc., Pap. Berlin 3038, 19, 11, etc.).

*ḏ*ꜣ*r·t*, "fruit of the *ḏ*ꜣ*r·t* " (Ebers *passim*, Hearst XVI, 11 ; also Pap. Berlin 3038).

*ḏ*ꜣ*r·t*, "fruit of the *ḏ*ꜣ*r·t* " (Hearst XIII 7).

*ḏ*ꜣ*r·t*, "⌜fiber⌝ (or something similar) of the *ḏ*ꜣ*r·t* " (Ebers 69, 8–9).

"juice of the *ḏ*ꜣ*r·t*" (Ebers 62, 1, etc.; Pap. Berlin 3038, 4, 4 ; etc.)

*ḏ*ꜣ*r·t*, "⌜tops⌝ of the *ḏ*ꜥ*r·t* " (Hearst IX 2). Munier, Deux recettes médicales coptes (in *Annales*, XVIII, 285–286) identifies our *ḏ*ꜣ*r·t* with the Coptic **ϫⲓⲉⲓⲣⲉ**, which he believes is the " *caroube*."

GLOSS A

XIV 8–11

Explaining : A diseased wound in his breast, inflamed.

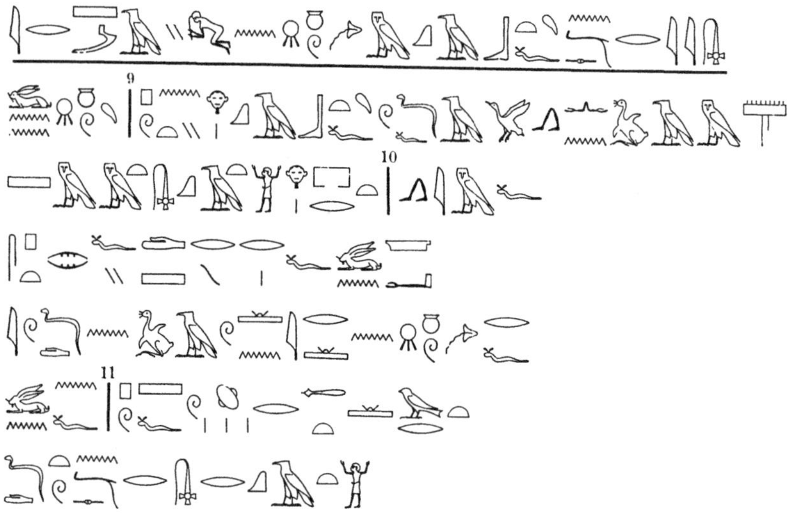

Translation

As for : " A diseased wound in his breast, inflamed," it means that the wound which is in his breast is sluggish, without closing up ; high fever comes forth from it, its two lips are red, (and) its mouth is open. The " Treatise on What Pertains to a Wound " says concerning it : " It means that there is very great swelling ; (and) ' inflamed ' is said concerning the height " (of the fever).

Commentary

šm'y, "diseased," is a word not otherwise known in the medical papyri. It is probably a different word from , an epithet applied to the Asiatics in the Eighteenth Dynasty (*Urk.* IV 390 and 740). It seems to be found elsewhere only in the following late texts of Ptolemaic date. In the Edfu temple we find the words : "protecting thy body against *šm'y* " (Ptolemy IV, Rochemonteix, *Edfou*, I, 237) ; and again "They (the gods) protect thee against *šm'y* " (*Ibid.*, 278). At Philae the goddess Wosret is called " Wosret, mistress of *šm'y* " (Philae, Berlin Dictionary photograph No. 505, reign of Neos Dionysos). At Kom Ombo the temple inscriptions have "Exorcising (*ś-ḫr*) the *šm'y* " (De Morgan, *Ombos* I, pp. 44, 45, 8–9). From these examples we would conclude that *šm'y* must mean some form of disease or decay, and in the last example the demons of disease. It is therefore probably some general word for disease. Applied to a wound which refuses to heal, as in the present case, it would be difficult to decide whether the ancient surgeon means some form of infection, or a gangrenous condition of the tissue—necrosis. The grammatical construction in which the term is here used literally "disease (decay?) of a wound," is that "wound" really has the force of an adjective, "wound disease," like "house of stone," meaning "stone house." What is intended is doubtless the disease or decay that arises in a wound. In Case 15 the noun *šm'y* seems to be used for "diseased tissue." It was not considered dangerous, for Case 15, the only other case in which it is known, a perforation of the bone in the region of the maxilla and zygoma, also receives the favorable verdict and the patient recovers (Case 15, VI 15–16). The curious writing of the last radical, with \\, seemingly after the determinative, occurs four times in Case 41, but in Case 15 the last radical is written , and there is no determinative. In all probability the \\ should be written *above* the determinative in a hieroglyphic transliteration. We should without doubt recognize *š'mw* (Pap. Edwin Smith XX 1; XX 9), meaning "demons of disease," as another form of our word *šm'y*.

nsr-y," inflamed," is of course derived from the common verb *nsr*, "to burn," with its nouns *nsr* and *nsr·t*, "flame." It is not common in a pathological sense, for it is not otherwise found with the above meaning "inflamed" in the medical papyri. It occurs in an Empire magical text with this meaning:

"Another spell (*šn·t*) for inflammation arising on the ⌜leg⌝" (Leyden Pap. 345, Leemans, *Monuments égyptiens*, pl. CXXXI, I, II, l. ⌜12⌝). In our papyrus, however, it is employed eight times in a pathological sense. These passages are important for determining whether the word means local inflammation, or designates a general condition of fever, affecting the patient's whole body. As we have just seen in the examination in Case 41 (XIII 19), the wound itself is *nsr-y*: "while that wound is *nsr-y*" (XIII 19). The same description is repeated verbatim in Case 47 (XVII 8) and again in the same case, with a slight variant (XVII 12). In view of these examples it is obvious in Case 28 that , following as it does directly upon the words "his wound," (*wbnw-f*), must be rendered "it (the wound) is inflamed," and not "he (the patient) has fever." This conclusion harmonizes perfectly with the fact that when the *wound* is *nsr-y*, the *patient* develops fever; so in Case 28: "it (the wound) is greatly inflamed (*nsr-y*), so that he (the patient) develops fever from it" (IX 20–21). This is paralleled by a variant, and hence strongly confirmatory, description of the same phenomenon in Case 41: "...... a diseased wound in his breast, "inflamed, (and) he continues to have fever (*šmm-f*) from it " (XIV 2). This wording is repeated verbatim in Case 47 (XVII 11). The same case describes this situation further on in very explicit terms which cannot be mistaken :

" If, then, thou findest that man continuing to have fever (*šmm-f*), while that wound is inflamed (*nsr-y*) " (XVII 12).

It is obvious, therefore, that the verb *nsr* is employed to describe local inflammation, rather than a general condition of fever involving the whole system.

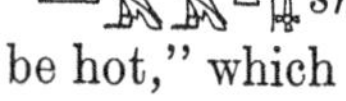

šmm·t, "fever," is derived from an old intransitive verb,  *šmm*, " be hot," which was later used transitively, but was originally intransitive as the old causative cognate form *s-ḫmm* and *s-šmm*, " to heat" shows. The verb is employed pathologically six times in our treatise. In two of these passages the *patient* is unmistakably the subject:  "while that man continues to be feverish from it " (Case 41, XIII 20). The second case has just been quoted above (Case 47, XVII 12). In the other four cases (Case 24, IX 1; Case 28, X 2; Case 41, XIV 2; Case 47, XVII 11, repetition of XIV 2) the subject is the pronoun and might refer either to the wound or the patient, but the context is decisive in indicating the patient. We may therefore conclude that in our papyrus the *verb* always indicates general fever of the patient and not local inflammation. The *noun, šmm·t,* however, is not so decisive. In our gloss above (XIV 9) *šmm·t* is said to come forth from it (the wound). This must refer to local inflammation. The adjective "high" applied to it is interesting, and seemingly exactly parallel with our use of " high " in the common phrase " high fever." It is superfluous to state that it obviously does not refer to the thermometer, an instrument unknown to the ancient world. Even our own use of "high" to describe a fever is probably far older than the introduction of the bedside thermometer. Literally rendered the Egyptian *šmm·t ḳ꜠·t* means " high heat," which is said to come forth from it (the wound). The reference is to the physical sensation of heat affecting the hand when it is laid on the wound, as the explanation in Gloss E discloses. The Egyptian thinks of such heat as streaming from a wound. In this case the heat is extreme, and " high " used thus to describe it is doubtless equivalent to " exceedingly," or "extremely." As we shall see in Gloss D *šmm·t* is probably used there also to designate local inflammation. In the third and last passage employing the *noun* (Case 47, XVII 13–14) it probably means " fever," describing the patient's general condition. Summarizing the evidence in our papyrus we may say that the verb *šmm* regularly means " to be feverish," but this precise use of the verb is probably an accident in view of the employment of the cognate noun *šmm·t* to designate either " fever " or " inflammation " of a local character. It should be noted that the verb *šmm* in Case 28 (X 2) is introduced in a second treatment after *šrf* has been employed to describe the patient's condition in the examination. It may be therefore that *šmm* indicates a greater degree of fever than *śrf*. In that case the three words for an abnormal degree of heat in a patient would be distinguished as follows. *Nsr* is employed exclusively to designate local inflammation as just demonstrated above ; *šmm* perhaps implies an extreme degree of fever but may also (at least in the noun form) describe local inflammation ; while *śrf* possibly indicates a milder degree of fever but usually designates local inflammation. On *śrf* see Gloss B (XIV 11–12).

The venerable book on wounds, here called " Treatise on What Pertains to a Wound," from which our ancient commentator quotes, is cited also in Case 5, Gloss A (II 16–17). See commentary *ibid.*

Gloss B

XIV 11–12

Explaining : A whirl of inflammation in his wound.

Translation

As for : " A whirl of inflammation in his wound," it means a whirl of inflammation which circulates through the interior of his entire wound.

Commentary

śwš, " whirl," is derived from the verb *śwš*, meaning " to twist cord " or similar (see Great " Amduat," 10th Hour) and it occurs in connection with spinning in *Mutter und Kind* (verso), 11, 1. The noun used in a pathological sense is confined to Case 41. With the meaning " coil, bandage, wrapping," the noun is used once in Papyrus Ebers (95, 11), and this meaning in our treatise is discussed in Case 7 (III 18) and Case 11 (V 11). Its pathological meaning is obscure. In Papyrus Ebers we find a recipe for treating a *śwš n t'w*, " *śwš* of heat " in the heart (Pap. Ebers 44, 8). Among the glosses in the papyrus we find explained " the fall of a *śwš* on his heart," which is defined by the gloss in the following words : " It means the fall of a *śwš* of heat upon his heart " (Pap. Ebers 102, 6–7). Among recipes for the eyes is one for the treatment of " a *śwš* of heat in the two eyes " (Pap. Ebers 57, 13). These are the only pathological examples known in the medical papyri besides its occurrence above in Case 41. It can hardly be doubted that the " *śwš* of heat (*t'w*) " occurring three times in Papyrus Ebers is parallel with our " *śwš* of inflammation (*śrf*) " in Case 41.

In our gloss the *św‘* is explained as one which " circulates " throughout the entire interior of the wound, and the meaning of going around, whirling, twisting is evidently inherent in the verb, employed as it is to designate the twisting of cord. The thought suggested by *św‘* seems to be a twisting, whirling circulation of the heat. This is no more remarkable than our use of the Greek word *paroxysm,* derived from a verb meaning " to sharpen " (ὀξύνω).

śrf, "inflammation," is not common as a pathological term in the medical papyri. It is more usually employed of artificial heat. In the preparation of prescriptions and of *kyphi*-incense we find it in Berlin Papyrus 3038 (7, 12) and Papyrus Ebers (76, 14). Prescriptions are brought to the warmth (*śrf*) of the finger (Ebers 76, 1; 8, 2; 9, 14; 10, 6; 4, 10; 89, 17; 54, 16–17; 94, 13–14; 69, 21; 81, 6; and confer 66, 5); to an agreeable warmth (Ebers 23, 19; 53, 9; 24, 3; 71, 12–13); between two warmths (tepid ?, Ebers 46, 10; 24, 6; Berlin 3038, 12, 12); or merely warmed up (only medical, Ebers 12, 3; 35, 20). Outside of our treatise the use of the noun " fever, feverish heat " is not frequent (Berlin 3038, 8, 7; Hieratic Writing Tablet, Brit. Museum 5645, verso, l. 9, see Gardiner, *Admonitions of an Egyptian Sage,* p. 100). It is employed 14 times in Papyrus Edwin Smith if we include XIV 16 where the writing is without doubt to be read *śrf.* In all of these cases it is possible to render " inflammation ; " of these it *must* mean local inflammation in ten passages (Case 41, XIII 19, XIV 3, 11, 12, 15, 16; Case 45, XV 12; Case 46, XVI 8; Case 47, XVII 9, and 14). This meaning is also quite probable in Case 39, XIII 5. Nevertheless, being a word originally meaning " to heat," or " heat," *śrf* may mean " fever." It is quite clear that it means " fever " in the three following interesting cases (7, 28, 47) in which it indicates the first appearance of fever (A) disclosed by examination, as contrasted with a second examination revealing persistence of fever (B) already noted in the first examination :

(A) " If then, thou findest that the flesh of that man has developed fever from that wound " (Case 7, III 8–9) employs *śrf,* "fever ;" while (B), " If, however, thou findest him continuing to have fever " (Case 28, X 2) uses the verb *šmm,* " to be hot, have fever." See also Case 28 (IX 21) and Case 47 (XVII 6–7).

m wbnw-f, " in his wound," are words which have been inserted in the quotation and are not to be found in the text, where they would be quite superfluous in view of the following phrase " from the mouth of that wound."

GLOSS C

XIV 12–13

Explaining: Its two lips are ruddy

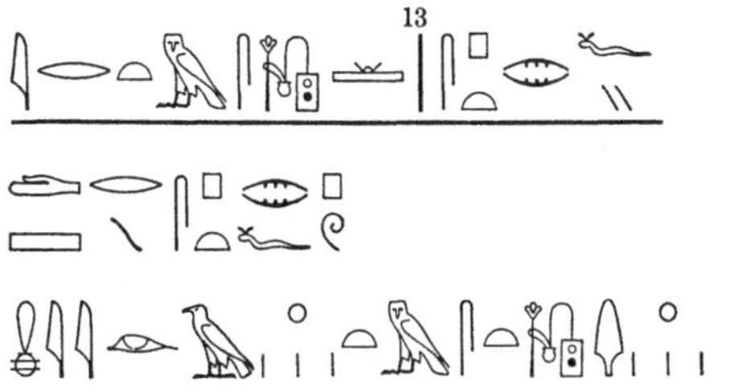

Translation

As for: "Its two lips are ruddy," it means that its two lips are red like the color of the *tmś·t*-tree.

Commentary

 *tmś*, "ruddy," is evidently an archaic color designation which had become more or less unfamiliar to the reader of the Seventeenth Century B.C.; for after applying the term to a patient's face in Case 7, our treatise appended an explanation, using the same term *dšr*, "red" to describe the hue indicated by *tmś*. See Case 7, Gloss F (III 20–21) where full discussion will be found. The surgeon then repeated this explanation in our Case 41, Gloss C.

GLOSS D

XIV 13–15

Explaining: His flesh cannot receive a bandage.

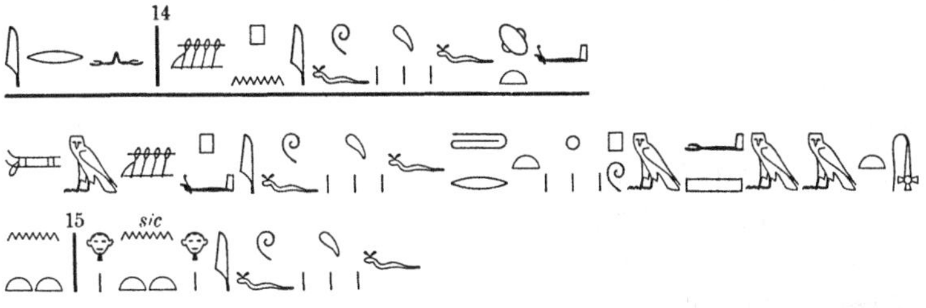

Translation

As for: "His flesh cannot receive a bandage," it means that his flesh will not receive the remedies because of the inflammation which is in his flesh.

Commentary

The surgeon identifies " bandage " with the remedies bandaged on, and explains that the inflammation (*šmm·t*, possibly " fever "), prevents the patient's flesh from absorbing these remedies. The repetition of *ntt ḥr* is obviously a scribal error.

GLOSS E

XIV 15–16

Explaining: While heat continually issues from the mouth of his wound at thy touch.

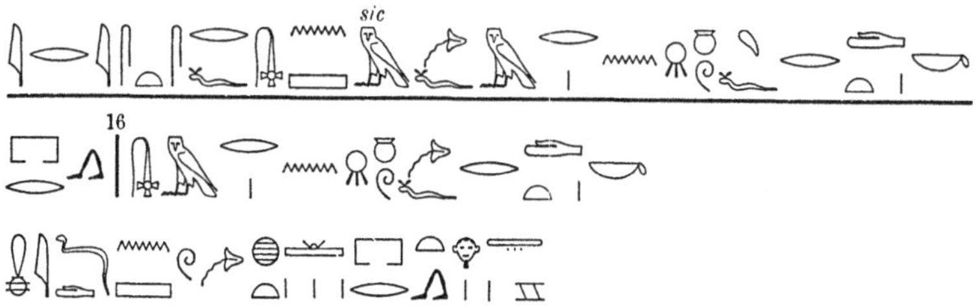

Translation

As for : " While heat continually issues (*nšw*) from the mouth of his wound at thy touch," (it means) that heat comes forth from the mouth of his wound at thy touch; as it is said that a thing which has come forth entirely, has issued (*nšw*)."

Commentary

This gloss covers some material already explained in Gloss B ; that is they both include the word *šrf*. Hence the quotation from the text of the case has, probably intentionally, omitted everything between *yšt* and *šrf* (XIII 19), which would have included *šwš n* (before *srf*) already explained in Gloss B.

is obviously an error by the scribe who has mistaken the *w* in *nšw* for *m* and read *nšm* instead of *nšw*. This is an error sometimes made by modern scholars in reading hieratic. See for example the word *š'm*, usually misread *š'w* in Pap. Ebers (109, 15). Cf. commentary on Case 39 (XIII 6–7). The scribe has written the word correctly in l. 16. *nšw*, " issue " is a rare word derived from the uncommon verb *nš*, " drive out." This *transitive* verb is found as far back as the Old Kingdom ; compare "I drove out (, *nš-n-y*) the domain officials who were there" (Uni, l. 9, *Urk.* I, p. 100). In the Pyramid Texts we find *nẖy*, designating the treatment of a new-born child (Pyr. 1965 a, infinitive *nẖw·t, ibid.*). This *nẖy* must be a variant form of *nšw*. The explanation in Gloss E above shows that *nšw* is equivalent in meaning to *pry*, " go forth." We have here therefore an *intransitive* verb *nšw* meaning " to issue," the use of which is confined to our treatise where it occurs four times, three times in Case 41 and once in Case 47. The curious writing in Case 47

(XVII 9) is of course an abbreviation, writing the word with the determinative, or word-sign already found in the Old Kingdom in the form (see Uni above). The word has been discussed by Sethe in *Zeitschrift*, 57 (1922), p. 21 (*Gött. Totenbuchstudien*). We have already met the noun *nšw*, " issue, discharge " in Case 31 (X 20). It must be related to the word [1] (Pyr. 199 a) and [1] (Pyr. 1270 b), which must mean something like " emanation." Compare also " water " (Pyr. 25 c) in the term *nš-rnpw*, " fresh water." In the Middle Kingdom the noun *nšw* is used as a designation of an uncertain disease (*Mutter und Kind*, 1, 2 ; 3, 1 *et passim*).[2] See Case 6, Gloss A (II 24–25). Cf. an exudation of the nose (Pap. Ebers 99, 6).

is evidently an abbreviated writing of , *śrf*, discussed above under Gloss B.

ḥr tꜣ, literally " upon the ground ; " see Case 4 (II 9), p. 154.

CASE FORTY-TWO

XIV 16–22

A SPRAIN OF THE STERNO-COSTAL ARTICULATIONS

This case is the fourth in the group of eight cases concerning the breast, and the first in a smaller group of three dealing with the ribs. These three cases are as follows :

Case 42, sprain of the sterno-costal articulations.
,, 43, dislocation of the true ribs.
,, 44, break in the true ribs.

We meet with the Egyptian word *ḫn·w*, " ribs " for the first time in these three cases, and it does not occur in any other oriental document of this remote age. In the above cases the word is always followed by the qualification *nw ḳꜣb·t*, " of the *sternum* " in a total of fourteen passages. Our surgeon's term for the true ribs (*costae verae*) is therefore evidently *ḫn·w nw ḳꜣb·t*, " ribs of the *sternum* ; " but the designation was not sufficiently clear to the reader of the Seventeenth Century B. C. and the commentator has added a gloss to explain it.

TITLE

XIV 16–17

[1] There are no exact hieroglyphic types for these highly specialized determinatives.

[2] This word has been discussed from the medical point of view by Oefele, who suggests that it means *Pemphigus* (*Zeitschrift*, 39 (1901), pp. 149 f.).

Translation

Instructions concerning a sprain in the ribs of his breast.

Commentary

Full discussion of the terms will be found below.

EXAMINATION

XIV 17–18

18

Translation

If thou examinest [a man having a sprain in the ribs of his breast], (and) he suffers in the ribs of his breast, not having a dislocation, (and) it is not broken, while that man continues to suffer with it and shudders exceedingly, (conclusion follows in diagnosis).

Commentary

The usual form of the examination runs : " If thou examinest a man having," followed by the name of the trouble or ailment already mentioned in the title. It is clear therefore that our scribe has here omitted the words which are inserted within brackets in the above translation.

The exclusion of a dislocation and a broken bone by means of the negative *n wnt* is customarily indicated in our document by the mere enumeration of the injuries not found, which follow the negative *n wnt* as nouns ; e. g.:

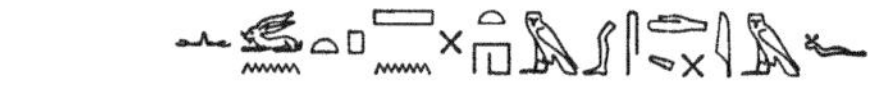

" Not having a split, a perforation (or) a smash in it " (Case 18, VII 9). *N ḥśb-f* therefore, following *n wnt wnḫ*, is unusual, and the question might arise whether in *n ḥśb-f* is not possibly the preposition , giving us the rendering " because of his break " or the like. This possibility is, however, excluded by the fact that the next case (43) is a " dislocation " (*wnḫ*) and the next (44) is a " break " (*ḥśb*). It is clear that we have a group of three cases of injuries to the ribs, the first being a " sprain," without a dislocation or a fracture ; the second being a dislocation (*wnḫ*) ; and the third a break or fracture (*ḥśb*). The three cases are arranged in a succession of increasing seriousness, like the first five cases in the treatise.

n ḥśb-f, " it is not broken," is perhaps to be understood as a predicative negative $n+$ infinitive with suffix, where we more commonly have *nn*. See Gunn, *Syntax*, Chaps. XXV and XVII. The identification of the antecedent of the pronoun is important. The meaning of the verb is such that the pronoun must refer to a bone, and the only masculine noun preceding is either the patient or one of the ribs (*ḥn*). It is obvious therefore that the surgeon desires to state that the rib is not broken, although the wrench or sprain is exceedingly painful.

 *mn*, " suffer," see the discussion in Case 1 (I 9) and Case 3 (I 20).

 *ʾnr*, " shudder " or the like ; see Case 4 (II 4).

DIAGNOSIS

XIV 19

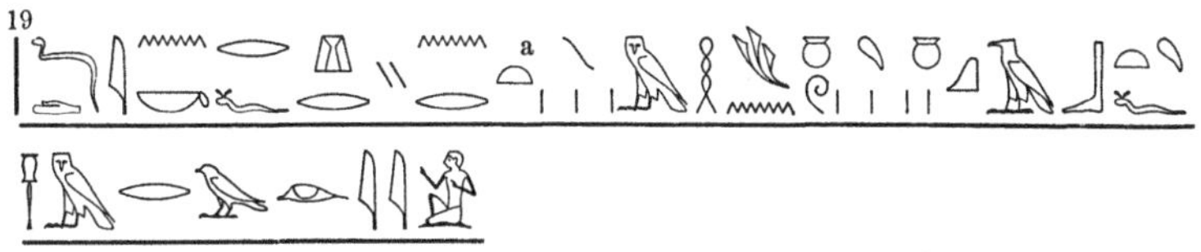

[a] The scribe intended to write *nrw·t*, with written, as he has done throughout Case 48 ; but he changed his mind at once and having written he inserted over the , both being in red ink. Both signs are still legible.

Translation

Thou shouldst say concerning him : " One having a sprain in the ribs of his breast. An ailment which I will treat."

Commentary

 *nrw·t*, "sprain," is explained in Case 30. On the remaining terms, see below. On Verdict 1, the favorable verdict, see Case 1 (I 2).

The diagnosis is again a repetition of the title followed by the verdict. See introduction (pp. 48 ff.).

TREATMENT

XIV 19–20

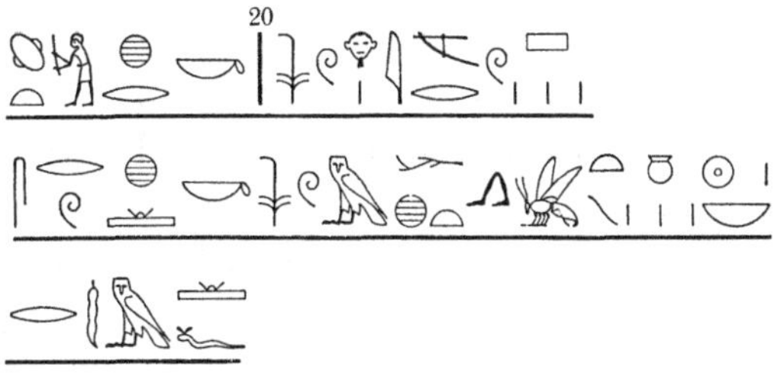

Translation

Thou shouldst bind it with *ymrw* ; thou shouldst treat it afterward [with] honey every day until he recovers.

Commentary

On treatment with *ymrw*, see Case 15 (VI 17); and with honey, Case 1 (I 3).

GLOSS A

XIV 20–22

Explaining: Ribs of his breast.

Translation

As for: "Ribs of his breast," it means the bones of his *sternum*; being spine(s) like as it were a spine-roast.

Commentary

ḥn·w, "ribs," is a word which we meet in this case for the first time; for it is unknown outside of Papyrus Edwin Smith. In this gloss the ancient commentator has given a colloquial explanation, drawn from the daily familiarity of his readers with meats served as household food. It is not as good an explanation as we find in the next case (43, Gloss A), where a dislocation of the *ḥn·w* is explained as "a displacement of the heads of the *ḥn·w* of his breast, which are fastened to (articulated in) his *sternum* (*ḳꜣb·t-f*)." It is clear then that the *ḥn·w*, on the basis of Case 43 (Gloss A) alone, are the seven (sometimes eight) true ribs which are articulated in the *sternum* on each side (fourteen in all), and our case is therefore a sprain or wrenching of the sterno-costal articulations, while Case 43 is that of an actual rending of these articulations, producing a dislocation. Our gloss is evidently using the word "breast" with the meaning "sternum" (see Case 40, Gloss A, XIII 17). The commentator does not mean, however, that "the bones of his *sternum*" are the parts of the *sternum* itself, like the *manubrium*; he means the bones attached to the *sternum*, as is shown by Gloss A in Case 43, that is, the true ribs.

śr·t, "spine" or "thorn." The hieratic writing is misleading, and seems at first sight to be almost certainly *św·t*, which is the more tempting in view of *św·t*, "grain" or *śwy·t* "bead" (Berlin, *Mittheilungen aus den Or. Samml.*, VIII, p. 29). Compare Lacau, *Sarcophages*, vol. 2, p. 22 (Cairo, 28089). This last word, *św·t*, is used to designate a pill, bolus, or suppository in Pap. Ebers (14, 9; 4, 20; 22, 4; 31, 20; 34, 2). In all likelihood, however, we should not read in this gloss any of the words just cited. We recall that in Case 40 the *manubrium* is called *ḫnt'*, and in the accompanying explanation (Case 40, Gloss A, XIII 17), this word is identified with *ḫnt'*, "porcupine." Now in Pap. Ebers we find that the "spine of a porcupine" is called *śr·t n·t ḫnty* (Ebers 92, 7). The *sternum*, with the ribs diverging from it, was therefore thought to look roughly like a porcupine with his bristling spines. It is highly probable, therefore, that in our gloss above the commentator is talking about the diverging ribs as "spines." The hieratic ligatures *wt* and *rt* are often practically identical. Compare the ligature *wt* (Moeller, *Palaeogr.* I, p. 68, IV, Sinuhe, 37) and *rt* (*ibid.*, p. 71, XXIX, Sinuhe h, 182). Notwithstanding the high top of our ligature (XIV 21 and 22), so characteristic of the ligature *wt* (see *bn·wt*, XV 10), it seems much more probable that we should read *rt*, and translate "spine." *Any* explanation of the word requires that it should be in the plural. Such abrupt changes from plural to singular are not rare in oriental documents ; compare Case 30, Gloss A (last clause, X 12). It has therefore been rendered "spines" in the translation.

my ḫpr·t m has already been discussed in Case 40, Gloss A, where it cannot mean "like what is in," as it might very well be rendered here. In view of the unlikelihood of this meaning in Case 40, it has not been employed here in Case 42.

ḥwn, "roast" or the like, is a meat dish ready for the table. A picture of it, lying in a bowl, is often shown as the determinative of the word *ḥwn* in the food lists displayed on tomb chapel walls, at the end of the series of *meat* dishes, e. g., Newberry, *Beni Hasan*, Vol. I, Tomb 2, Pl. XVIII ; Cairo, Tomb-stela 20057 ; Mariette, *Abydos*, I, 33, 29. The earliest examples are from the Middle Kingdom. It is evidently a cut of meat containing ribs, which seems to have been colloquially called a "spine cut," or a "spine roast," from the ribs still in it, as our housekeepers say, "a rib-roast." Other orientalists may be able to offer some other explanation of this gloss, but it is very improbable that any intelligible explanation can be derived from the reading *św·t*.

CASE FORTY-THREE

XIV 22–XV 6

A DISLOCATION IN THE STERNO-COSTAL ARTICULATIONS

This case is the fifth in the group of eight cases concerning the breast and the second in the smaller series of three having to do with the ribs. The cause of the dislocation is not stated but the surgeon finds redness over the "heads" of the ribs and there is pain in the sides, where swellings appear.

The discussion says nothing of any surgical effort to reduce the dislocated bones, but proceeds at once to alleviatory remedies externally applied, and the patient is expected to recover. The case is followed by three instructive glosses giving us valuable surgical and anatomical data.

TITLE

XIV 22

Translation

Instructions concerning a dislocation of the ribs of his breast.

Commentary

The terms will be found discussed below. The genitive nw between *wnḫ* and *ḥn·w* is a scribal error; see examination and diagnosis.

EXAMINATION

XIV 22–XV 1

Translation

If thou examinest a man having a dislocation of the ribs of his breast, (and) thou findest that the ribs of his breast are ⸢projecting⸣, and their heads are ruddy, while that man suffers continually with swellings in his two sides, (conclusion follows in diagnosis).

Commentary

wnḫ, "dislocation," has been discussed in Case 10 (V 6 under *ydr*); also in Case 14 (VI 11), and especially in Case 31 (X 17–19).

ḥn·w, "ribs," has been discussed under Gloss A of the preceding case.

ḳ'b·t, "breast," is here a designation of the *sternum*. It has been discussed in Case 40 (XIII 17).

ḫ'ś, "⸢projecting⸣," is a new word unknown anywhere else in Egyptian documents. A word written *ḫ'ś*, occurring in the Amon Ritual (Berlin Pap. 3055, 34, 1–2) designates some action connected with the face, but is otherwise entirely obscure. It may have some connection with our word, which has the determinative of face. The meaning "to project" is a conjecture, suggested by the following statement, "their heads are ruddy." The dislocation is of course due to an injury; but the surgeon does not state that the overlying tissue covering the dislocation has been ruptured. In stating that the heads of the ribs are ruddy, he can hardly mean that they are projecting through the overlying soft tissue, and are visible. What he probably means is that the soft tissue over the dislocation is bruised and congested, while the heads of the ribs in a *forward* dislocation, though invisible, are projecting.

št·wt, "swellings," is without doubt the familiar word *št·t*, "swelling," though written without , for the phrase , a repetition of our passage, except for , is known (Pap. Berlin 3038, 4, 9).

šw·ty, "two sides," is discussed in Gloss C (p. 400).

DIAGNOSIS

XV 1–2

Translation

Thou shouldst say concerning him: "One having a dislocation in the ribs of his breast. An ailment which I will treat."

Commentary

The terms will be found discussed above, and in the glosses. The insertion of *m*, "in," is a variant not found in the preceding text. We again find the diagnosis consisting of a repetition of the title with the verdict added. See introduction (pp. 48 ff.). On the favorable verdict 1 see Case 1 (I 2) and introduction (pp. 46 ff.).

TREATMENT

XV 2–3

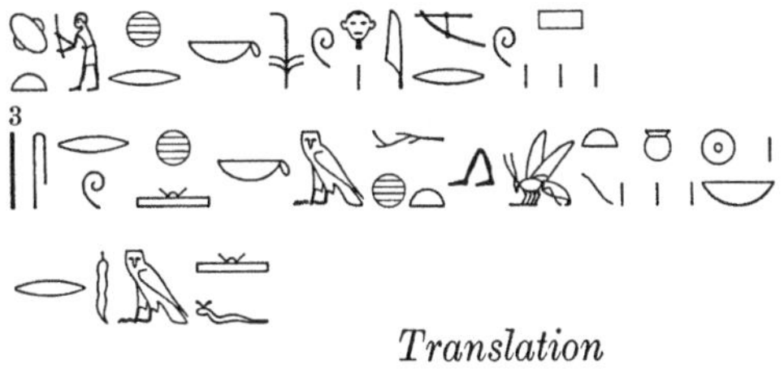

Translation

Thou shouldst bind it with *ymrw*; thou shouldst treat afterward [with] honey every day, until he recovers.

Commentary

Treatment with *ymrw* has been discussed in Case 15 (VI 17), and the use of honey has been taken up in Case 1 (I 3).

GLOSS A

XV 3–4

Explaining: A dislocation in the ribs of his breast.

Translation

As for: "A dislocation in the ribs of his breast," it means a displacement of the heads of the ribs of his breast (*sternum*), which are fastened to his breast (*sternum*).

Commentary

 *nft*, "displacement," is discussed in Case 34, Gloss A (XI 22), where it is applied to the heads of the dislocated clavicles, as here to the heads of the dislocated ribs.

 *tp·w*, "heads," applied to the sterno-costal tips of the ribs by the ancient surgeon is interesting, in view of the fact that modern anatomy designates these tips as "capitulae," or "little heads." It is applied by our surgeon also to the heads of the clavicles in Case 34. See the discussion of  as an anatomical term in our document in Case 1 (pp. 84–87) and Case 10 (V 5).

 *mn m*, "fastened to," literally "being fast in," meaning "articulated in," as an anatomical term has been discussed in Case 4 (II 9).

 *ḳ'b·t*, "breast," is obviously used here to designate the *sternum*; see the discussion in Case 40, Gloss A (XIII 17).

GLOSS B

XV 4–5

Explaining: He suffers with swellings in his two sides.

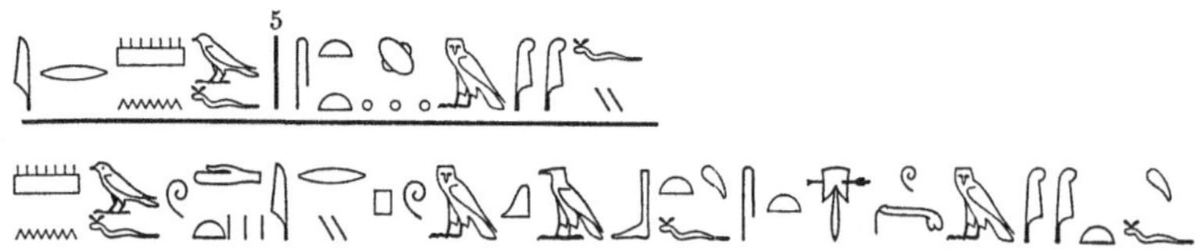

Translation

As for : " He suffers with swellings in his two sides," it means that he suffers in the articulations thereof in his breast (*sternum*) ⌜spreading⌝ in his two sides.

Commentary

šw·ty, " two sides," is discussed in the next gloss.

wd·t, " articulations," is a new word, not found elsewhere in our document, nor indeed in any other Egyptian document. The meaning above suggested is derived from the technical and surgical use of the verb *wdy,* " put, place," to designate the return of a dislocated bone to its socket, e.g., a dislocated mandible in Case 25 (IX 5), or dislocated clavicles in Case 34 (XI 19). The feminine noun *wd·t,* in the plural, might therefore mean " puttings," or " placings," and designate the point where one bone is put or placed into another, that is, the articulation.

śtw, " spreading," is a very uncertain guess based on the use of the verb *śty,* to describe the scattering of inflammation or fever in Case 47 (XVII 14). We have here in our case, however, an unusual writing, and one gains the impression that the text is not correct. The determinative suggests that it may be connected with the verb used in Pap. Ebers (91, 12) to describe the discharge of secretion in the ear. It is not at all impossible that the scribe was intending to write *śt·wt,* " swellings," in which case it would be construed as parallel with " articulations," giving us the rendering : " he suffers in the articulations thereof in his breast, and (in) the swellings in his two sides."

GLOSS C

XV 5–6

Explaining : His two sides.

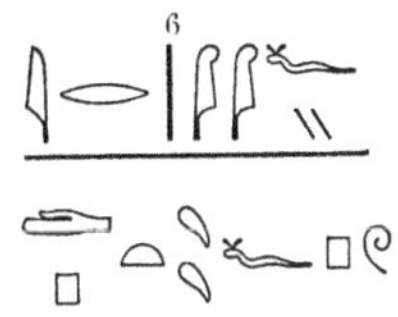

Translation

As for : " His two sides," it means his two flanks.

Commentary

dp·ty, " two flanks," is a rare word, of which the exact anatomical application is still to be better determined. It seems to be the ancestor of the Coptic ϯⲡⲉ " groin," used in the Coptic version of the Old Testament to render the Greek ὀσφύς, " hip " and Hebrew חֲלָצַיִם, (dual) " two loins," " two hips." It has been treated by Dévaud (*Étymologie Copte,* pp. 18–20). His oldest example (Middle Kingdom

Glossary from the Ramesseum) lists three different internal parts possessing a *dp·t*. The first two are anatomically unidentified; the third is called "*dp·t* of the anus." In its earlier history the word evidently was very general, requiring some identifying modifier. It had therefore some range of application, like *ʿr·ty*, meaning "buttocks" or "two sides of the mandible" (see pp. 187 f.), and was probably an unprecise designation like our "flanks" for sides. In the Golénischeff Glossary (7, 10, continuation of Pap. Hood) there is a list of parts of the body which has: "back, ribs, loins, buttocks" and then *dp* and *ḳnḳn·t*. A list of members of the body in a papyrus in Turin (ed. Pleyte-Rossi, 125, 8; magical texts of the Empire copied by Gardiner) contains (*sic*) "the *dp·t* of his back," and Pap. Ebers (40, 20) mentions *dp* in connection with an ailment in the right side. In our case the swelling evidently extended beyond the area over the dislocated ribs and over the patient's sides.

šw·ty, "two sides," is hardly a specific anatomical term, for it may mean "side" with reference even to the head; e.g., "He placed (his) eye(s) in their sides," viz. one on each side of the head (Rochem, *Edfou*, I, 417=Piehl, *Inscr.* II, 20 g). In the lists of the parts of the body in the Tables of Hours we find occurring after "cheek" (*mnd·t*) and tongue, and again on both sides of (in I); the same order is found in II, III (before neck), IV, V, VI, examples which indicate that the two sides of the head are meant. Again (in III) *šw·ty* is found after "buttocks" (*ḫpd*) and *mnd·t*, an order indicating great confusion. The Berlin Medical Papyrus 3038 (4, 8–9) contains a prescription for removing "swellings in his two sides," presumably the two sides of the body. In a case of heart trouble of some kind Pap. Ebers states "he suffers continually in his two sides" (Pap. Ebers 41, 14), a statement which must refer to the two sides of the body. In Leyden papyrus 348 (verso 5, 7) *šw·ty* is listed between the arm and fingers and the back, a placing which is evidently significant.[1] The word is usually in the dual, but among the eight examples of it in our treatise there are four in the plural in Case 47. One of these possibly refers to the "sides" of a wound, a use of the word which is parallel with the "side of a ligament" (Pap. Ebers 82, 16). The only other example of the singular of *šw·t* is in the case of a patient with heart trouble, who suffers some displacement of the heart due to fatty growths "in his left side (*šw·t*)" (Pap. Ebers 101, 14). In this case *šw·t* obviously designates the left side of the body in the general region overlying the heart. This passage in Papyrus Ebers illustrates a use of the word closely analogous to our case where the swellings in question occupy the region over the kidneys.

[1] Incidentally it may be mentioned that this passage compares the word *šw·ty* with the two feathers of Min, and thus determines the correctness of the reading *šw·ty*. I owe this remark to Gardiner.

CASE FORTY-FOUR

XV 6–9

FRACTURED RIBS

This case is the sixth in the group of eight cases concerning the breast, and the third of the smaller series of three dealing with the ribs. The examination shows that the injury is more than a fracture of the true ribs (" ribs of his breast "), for the soft tissue overlying the fractured ribs has been ruptured, and the shattered ribs give way under the pressure of the surgeon's fingers. The fatal verdict 3 is appended, and is followed by no treatment, showing that the surgeon had no expectation of the patient's recovery. We cannot but wonder whether the surgeon had never met a case of fracture of the ribs without a serious rupture of the overlying soft tissue, as in Case 36, a fractured humerus, which the surgeon is able to cure ; whereas in Case 37 when he finds a serious flesh wound overlying the fracture, he regards it as a fatal case just like our Case 44. We would like to know whether our surgeon had never successfully treated a case of fractured ribs. It is possible that we have a scribal omission here, and that an entire case has fallen out by carelessness of the scribe.

TITLE

XV 6

Translation

Instructions concerning a break in the ribs of his breast.

Commentary

 *ḥśb,* " break," has been discussed in Case 11 (V 10). On *ḥn·w,* " ribs " see Case 42 (XIV 20–21) ; *ḳ'b·t,* " breast " has been explained in Case 40 (XIII 17).

EXAMINATION

XV 6–8

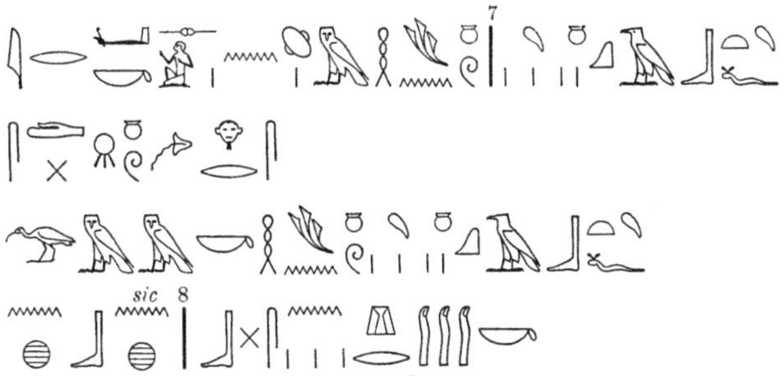

D d

Translation

If thou examinest a man having a break in the ribs of his breast, over which a wound has been inflicted; (and) thou findest that the ribs of his breast crepitate under thy fingers, (conclusion follows in diagnosis).

Commentary

The word *ḥśb,* "break," is in the singular, but it is stated to be "in the ribs," suggesting that the expression "break in the ribs" indicates that several ribs are broken. This indication is rendered certain by the fact that the surgeon's fingers find the "ribs" (plural) yielding to pressure and giving way, so that "they crepitate" (lit. "break through"). In addition to this situation, the soft tissue overlying the fractures has been ruptured forming an open wound.

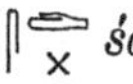 *śd,* "inflicted," will be found discussed in Case 5 (II 11). Compare Case 37 for a similar wound over a fractured bone.

 *wbnw,* "wound," has been discussed in Case 1 (pp. 81–84).

 *nḫbnḫb* is an error for  *nḫbḫb,* "crepitate," which will be found discussed in Case 13 (VI 4–5).

DIAGNOSIS

XV 8–9

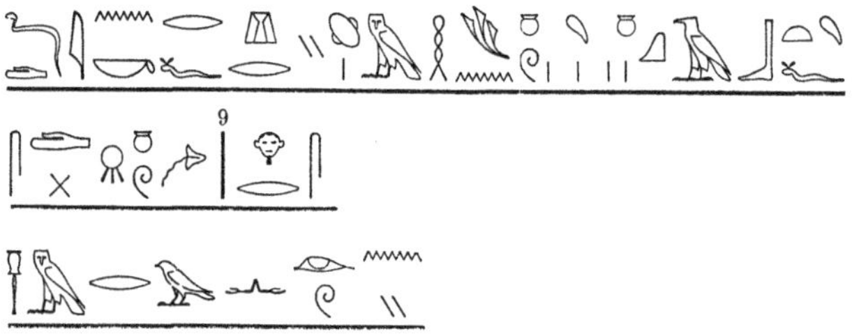

Translation

Thou shouldst say concerning him: "One having a break in the ribs of his breast, over which a wound has been inflicted. An ailment not to be treated."

Commentary

The terms have all been discussed above, especially under the examination.

On the unfavorable verdict 3 see Case 5 (II 15) and also the introduction (pp. 46 ff.). In view of this verdict the surgeon considers the case hopeless and hence adds no treatment.

CASE FORTY-FIVE

XV 9–19

BULGING TUMORS ON THE BREAST

This case is the seventh in a group of eight concerning ailments of the breast. The tumors described differ essentially from those treated in Case 39. It is clear furthermore that these bulging tumors result from a disease and not from an injury which may be the source of the tumors of Case 39. There seems to have been no treatment known to the physician, either for these tumors or for the same trouble appearing anywhere on the body. It is possible that the detailed description devoted to them both in the text and in the interesting gloss at the end of the case may enable the modern pathologist to determine the nature of the disease described.

TITLE

XV 9

Translation

Instructions concerning bulging tumors on his breast.

Commentary

bn·wt, "tumors," is discussed in Case 39, Gloss A (XIII 9–12). On "bulging" see the explanation in the gloss on this case (45).

ḳ'b·t, "breast" is treated in Case 40 (XIII 17).

EXAMINATION

XV 9–14

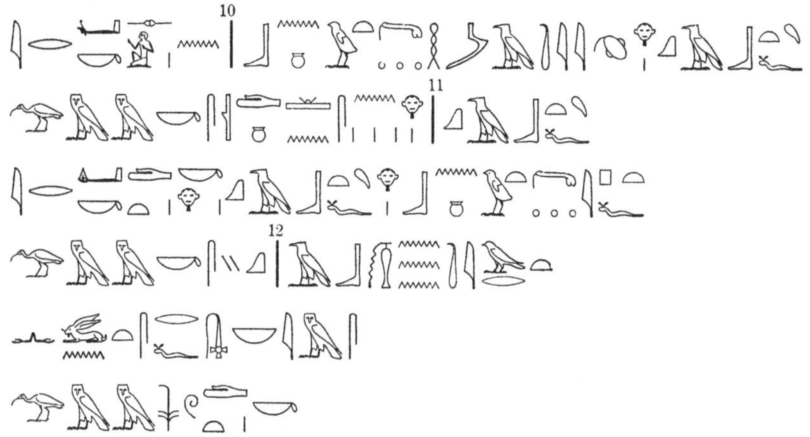

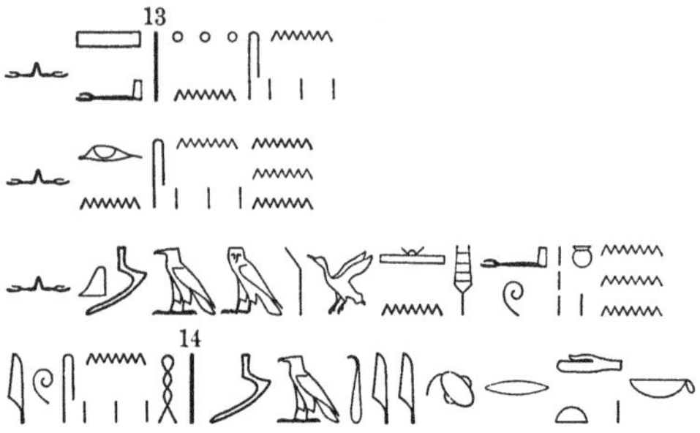

Translation

If thou examinest a man having bulging tumors on his breast, (and) thou findest that [swellings] have spread over his breast ; if thou puttest thy hand upon his breast upon these tumors, (and) thou findest them very cool, there being no fever at all therein when thy hand touches him ; they have no granulation, they form no fluid, they do not generate secretions of fluid, and they are bulging to thy hand, (conclusion follows in diagnosis).

Commentary

The description of these tumors on the breast has some resemblances in form to the description of a different variety of tumor in Case 39. We find there, however, that the subject of the verb " they have spread " is the noun *tw**·w*, " swellings " (XIII 4). It is obvious that the scribe has omitted the word in Case 45 (XV 10, between *gmm-k* and *šḳd-n-šn*) by error.

bn·wt, " tumors," is discussed in Case 39, Gloss A (XIII 9–12), where a totally different variety of *bn·wt* is described.

*ḥm**ty* is discussed in the gloss at the end of the case.

The three negative statements all seem to be in the same form, raising the question whether *šʿ*, " sand," known hitherto only as a noun, may not here be used as a verb, meaning " to be sandy," that is " to be granulated," just as the noun *mw*, " water " is used by our surgeon as a verb meaning " to be watery " (Case 41, XIII 22).

ʿḥʿ·w, " secretions," is discussed in Case 41 (XIII 22–XIV 1).

mw, " fluid," literally " water " is an elastic word widely applied in medicine and botany to the juices of fruits and plants, or the secretion of a sore, ulcer or wound.

DIAGNOSIS

XV 14–15

Translation

Thou shouldst say concerning him: "One having bulging tumors. An ailment with which I will contend."

Commentary

The terms are all discussed above or in the gloss at the end of the case.

Verdict 2, the doubtful verdict, has been discussed in Case 4 (II 6).

TREATMENT

XV 15–16

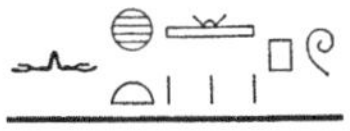

Translation

There is no ⌜treatment⌝. If thou findest bulging tumors in any member of a man, thou shalt treat him according to these directions.

Commentary

 *n yḫ·t pw*, "there is no ⌜treatment⌝," literally means "there is nothing." It stands immediately after the verdict, that is, in the position usually occupied by the treatment. In view of the fact that all treatment is lacking, the terse statement "there is nothing" probably means "there is no treatment." On the highly varied use of  *yḫ·t*, "thing," see Case 4 (II 3). The curious injunction "thou shalt treat him," when no treatment is offered in the discussion, must mean that the treatment is omission of treatment.

GLOSS A

XV 16–19

Explaining: Bulging tumours on his breast.

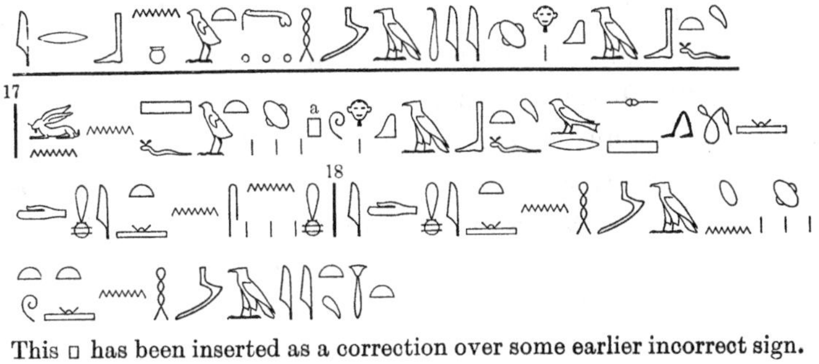

[a] This □ has been inserted as a correction over some earlier incorrect sign.

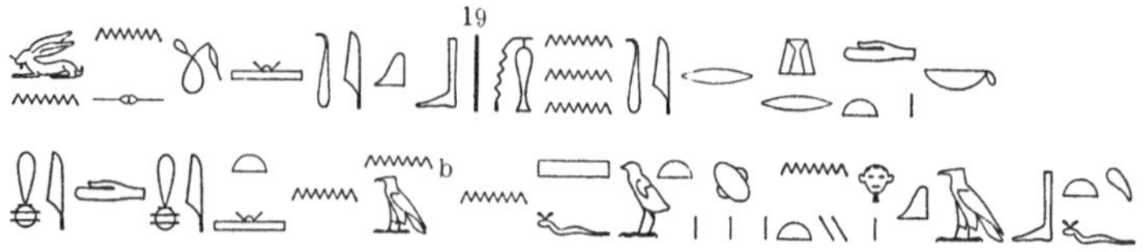

[b] This [hieroglyph] was at first omitted by error of the scribe and he afterward inserted it in red ink.

Translation

As for "Bulging tumors on his breast," it means the existence of swellings on his breast, large, spreading and hard; touching them is like touching a ball of wrappings; the comparison is to a green *hemat*-fruit, which is hard and cool under thy hand, like touching those swellings which are on his breast.

Commentary

[hieroglyphs] *bn·wt*, "tumors," a variety quite different from those treated in Case 39, Gloss A (XIII 9–12).

[hieroglyphs] *ḥm'ty*, "bulging," is without doubt connected with [hieroglyphs] *ḥm'y·t*, a fruit of unknown identity occurring only in our treatise. From l. 18 of this gloss we learn that when this fruit is green it is hard and cool to the touch. In the magical treatise on the verso of our papyrus the preparation of this fruit for use in a recipe required that it be bruised, dried, husked, winnowed, and the "fruit" (*pr·t*) sifted (XXI 9–13). In this recipe the determinative is [hieroglyph] not [hieroglyph] as in our gloss. This is the common writing of *ḥm'y·t*, "salt" from the XVIIIth Dynasty on; but the description of the preparation of the *ḥm'y·t*-fruit leaves no doubt whatever that it is to be distinguished from salt, and regarded as a vegetable product. It may have been a rotund fruit, much like a ball, and hence possibly given a name derived from [hieroglyphs] *ḥm'*, "ball' (l. 18). It is possible that [hieroglyphs] *ḥm'* means "to be round, rotund," from which we have the masculine noun *ḥm'*, "ball," the feminine noun *ḥm'y·t*, "rotund," meaning the fruit; while the form following *bn·wt*, "tumors," might be a pseudo-participle modifying *bn·wt*, and meaning "swelling like a ball," rendered above "bulging."

[hieroglyphs] *dmy* is a familiar verb meaning "to reach, touch, arrive at, adhere, join, attach" and the like; e. g., to touch the ground in obeisance in Shipwreck, ll. 137–138 and Sinuhe, B 200–201. It is not common in medical or surgical use and is known in the medical papyri elsewhere only in Pap. Ebers where it occurs twice in rather obscure connections (Pap. Ebers 91, 14–15 and 109, 9–10). In our papyrus it is used of the adhesion of one lip of a wound to the other in healing (Case 10, V 9), of the adhesion of a fragment of bone to a cleansing swab of linen (Case 22, VIII 16), of the cohesion of two parts of a thing afterward separated by breakage (Case 31, X 19), and finally of the touching of the tumor or the fruit by the surgeon's fingers in our gloss.

CASE FORTY-SIX

XV 20–XVI 16

AN ABSCESS WITH PROMINENT HEAD ON THE BREAST

This case is the last in a group of eight concerning ailments in the breast. The abscess which it discusses is not very definitely defined beyond the facts that it is soft and secretes pus, that it protrudes, has a prominent head, is cool or clammy and without redness. It is several times called a *wbnw*, " wound " or " sore," and once a *yh*, " injury," or " ailment," leaving open the possibility that a wound or injury may have been the origin of it, just as in Case 39. Dr. Luckhardt remarks : " I wonder if he is treating a so-called ' cold abscess.' It would certainly fit the description. An abscess which is cold to the touch and not ruddy or inflamed is of a tuberculous nature."

The treatment resembles that in Case 41, but is slightly more elaborate, containing four stages, whereas Case 41 contains but three. These four stages are :

1. Cool applications, which seem incompatible with the symptom of a cool or clammy surface of the abscess. One of these two applications contains mason's mortar, the only ingredient besides water, identifiable.

2. " Wound-treatment," which is to be employed only if the preceding treatment has failed. It consists of an application containing acacia and sycamore leaves, ox dung, and two more unidentified ingredients, and was intended to allay inflammation, which we must conclude has succeeded the " clamminess of surface " observable before treatment began.

3. An astringent application including the copper salts employed for the same purpose in Case 41, and the other ingredients included there.

4. Poultices also like those which concluded the treatment in Case 41.

Three glosses at the end discuss the terms needing explanation.

TITLE

XV 20

20

Translation

Instructions concerning an abscess with prominent head in his breast.

Commentary

All the terms will be found discussed below, especially in connection with the three glosses at the end (pp. 413–415).

EXAMINATION

XV 20–XVI 2

Translation

If thou examinest a man having an abscess with prominent head in his breast, (and) thou findest a very large swelling protruding on his breast, oily, like fluid under thy hand, while they produce some clamminess of the surface, (and) their faces have no ruddiness, (conclusion follows in diagnosis).

Commentary

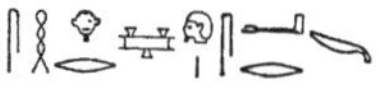 *śḥr tp śʿr* (var. *śḳr*), see Gloss A.

 *ṯhb*, "swelling," see Case 4 (II 4).

 *yšwy*, "protruding," see Case 4 (II 4).

 *ḳʾb·t*, "breast," see Case 40 (XIII 17).

 *bʾḳ*, "oily," see Case 41 (XIV 1).

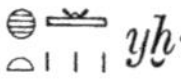 *yẖ·t* (lit. "thing"), see Case 4 (II 3).

 *nʿbʾ*, "pallor," see Gloss B.

 *tmś*, "ruddiness," see Gloss C.

It is important to note that while the title and the examination seem to refer to a single "abscess" (*śḥr*), the description suggests that there is a group of abscesses. "They" (XVI 1) and "their faces" (XVI 2) can refer to nothing other than *śḥr*, "abscess," which is treated as in the plural. On the other hand the occurrence of *m rʾ n wbnw m ḳʾb·t-f*, "from the mouth of the wound (sore ?) in his breast" (XVI 8) again indicates that the trouble is a single abscess, although the text further on (XVI 15) again employs the plural pronoun, "their" (in "their skin") in referring to the ailment. The question arises whether *n tmś n* may not be regarded as a negative followed by the *n*-form of a verb *tmś*, "to be red," the subject being "their faces," giving us the meaning, "their faces are not red." See further discussion of Gloss C below.

DIAGNOSIS

XVI 2–4

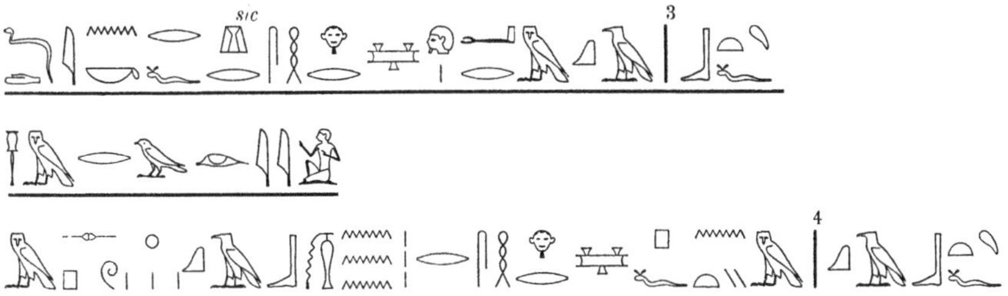

Translation

Thou shouldst say concerning him: "One having an abscess with prominent head in his breast. An ailment which I will treat with cold applications to that abscess which is in his breast."

Commentary

See commentary below, especially Gloss A. In this diagnosis the verdict concluding it at the same time connects with the treatment as in Case 39, q. v. and it is at this point difficult to make any separation between diagnosis and treatment. See introduction (p. 46).

TREATMENT

XVI 4–12

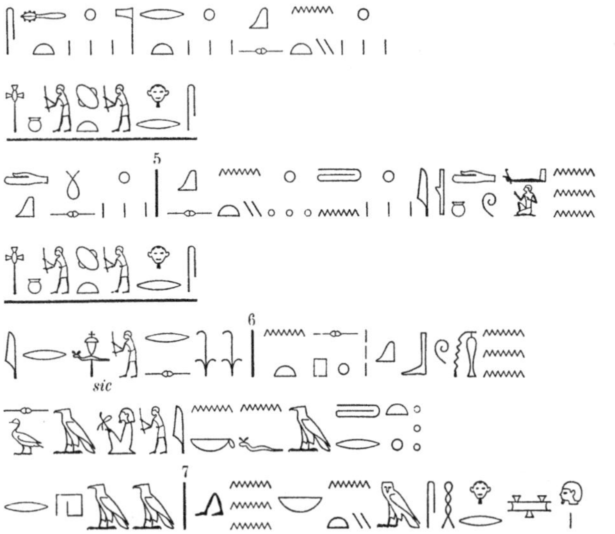

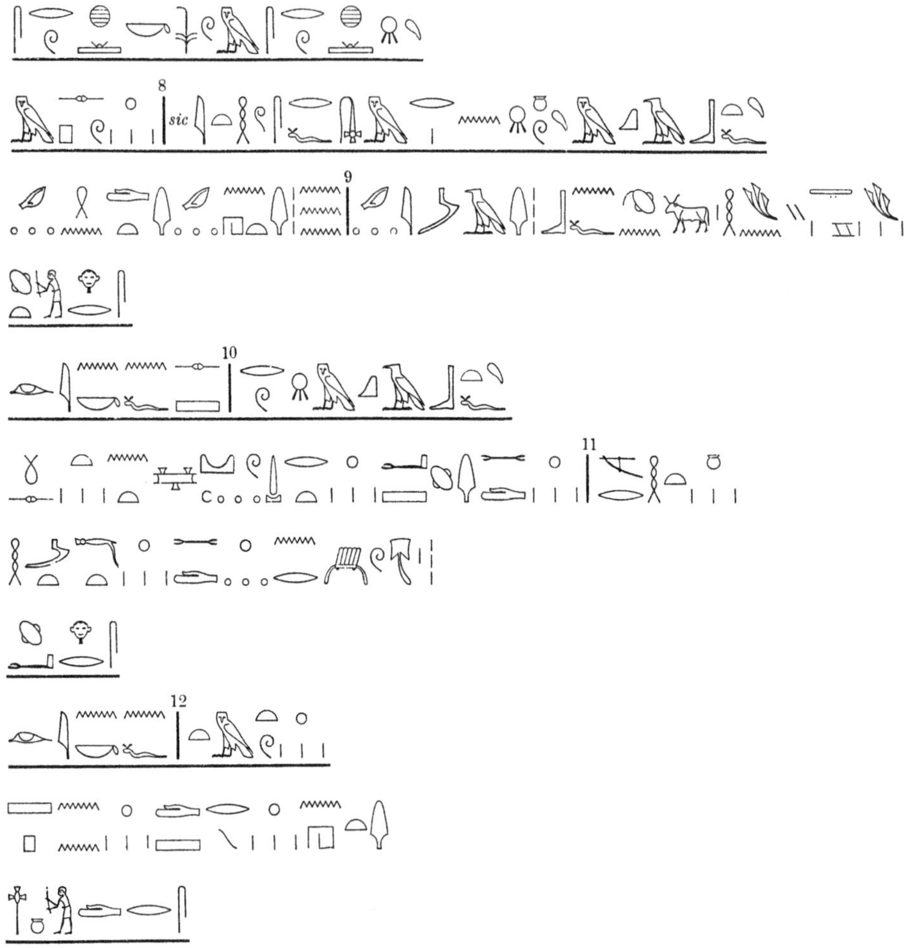

Translation

a. *Śẖ·t*-fruit,
ntr·t,
ḳsnty,
Triturate, bind upon it.

b. Fruit of *šs*,
ḳsnty,
mason's mortar,
water,
Triturate, bind upon it.

If there is resistance to these cooling applications, thou shouldst avoid those remedies until all fluid which is in the abscess with a head exudes.

Thou shouldst treat him with wound-treatment, with applications for drawing out the inflammation from the mouth of the wound (sore ?) in his breast :

Leaves of acacia,
sycamore,
juice of *ym*ʾ-leaves,
ox dung,
*ḥny-t*ʾ,
Bind upon it.

Thou shouldst make for him astringents, in his breast :

a. ⌜Powder⌝ of green pigment,
*ḏ*ʾ*r·t* of cedar,
ointment fat,
northern salt,
ibex grease,
Bind upon it.

Thou shouldst make for him poultices :

Red *špnn*,
sycamore,
Triturate, apply to it.

Commentary

The verdict is immediately connected with the treatment, an arrangement found also in Papyrus Ebers in several cases (see p. 365).

sp·w, " applications," see Case 41 (XIV 2), where the purpose of the " cool applications " is stated to be " drawing out the inflammation from the mouth of the wound " (XIV 2–3). In our Case 46 we have the same statement of the purpose of a certain " treatment," called " wound-treatment " (XVI 7–8), which is, however, the second stage of the entire treatment (see introduction to Case 46). The word " applications " (*sp·w*) seems to be sufficiently verbal in force to take the preposition *r*, literally "at the abscess," like *r fnḏ*, "at the nose" or *r ḫḫ*, "at the throat," well-known uses of the preposition *r* with parts of the body.

šḫ·t is a frequently recurring fruit, from the Old Kingdom on. The Pyramids write (or), and the Old Kingdom . It was gained by a process of pounding, doubtless to free it from husks (see Newberry, *El Bersheh*, pt. 1, pl. XXXI) and was obtained in two varieties and , that is " white " and " green." It is common in the offering lists beginning as far back as the Pyramid Texts (108 b and c, 96 b) ; see also Mariette, *Mastabas*, D 16, p. 215 and D 38, p. 269. It was so plentiful that it was kept in granaries, e.g., Tomb of Kagemni (Sixth Dynasty). It continued in very common use, appearing regularly in the offering lists, e.g., in the great Medinet Habu calendar, down to Saitic times. In medicine its use has hitherto been known only in Pap. Ebers and Pap. Hearst; see Ebers 10, 21; 37, 14 = duplicate 38, 14); 41, 4; 43, 5 (twice); 82, 21 (= Hearst VIII 17); 89, 20–21 (Hearst XIII 12); 90, 9 and 10 (twice). A drink known only in Pap. Ebers (90, 6) called  *šḫ·t*, was probably prepared from this fruit. Its use in our Case 46 as an externally applied, local febrifuge is an added datum to be noted in identifying this drug, but no satisfactory identification has yet been offered.

 *ntr·t* is an unidentified drug, otherwise known only in Pap. Ebers (48, 16; 48, 18; 79, 1), in prescriptions which do not enable us to identify it. It is possibly a preparation of natron, the native sesquicarbonate of sodium, found in great quantities in the Egyptian deserts, especially on the west side of the Nile valley, and known to the Egyptians at a very early date under the name  *nṯry*, a designation from which our word *nitre* has descended through Greek *νίτρον* and our word *natron* likewise through Arabic نطرون "*natrun*," which reached us through the Spanish and French.

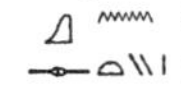 *ḳsnty*, see Case 41 (XIV 3).

The first "application," consisting of the above three drugs, is dry; the second "application" was mixed with water and must have been a soft paste.

 *dḳ(r)*, "fruit," has been hastily written by the scribe, or was perhaps an intentional abbreviation. The lack of the determinative is noticeable, but the spelling with omission of the *r* is common. Compare the frequent form ; or the late form  as in Pap. Harris frequently.

 *šs* is an unknown plant or tree, not occurring elsewhere as a botanical name, and hardly to be connected with the Empire word  *šs*, "grain."

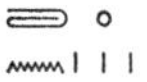 *dbn*, "mortar," is not a common medicament. It is otherwise known only in two cases in Pap. Ebers where it appears as an ingredient in an externally applied remedy for a pus-secreting sore (75, 1). In this recipe it is triturated with a juice (as in our Case 46 with water) and the word  stands alone without the mason. In Ebers 48, 17, however, we find 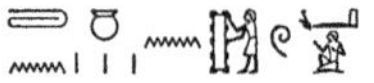 *dbn n yḳdw*, with genitive *n* connecting the two words. (Cf. Pap. Hearst XIV 17). In this second recipe the mortar, together with the other remedies, is triturated with water, just as in our Case 46, and is externally applied "for cooling a head, when it is ailing," perhaps headache.

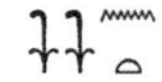 is of course a scribal error for 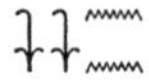 *nn*, "these."

"These cooling applications" (XVI 5–6) of course refers back to the two preceding prescriptions. If they are ineffective the physician is to resort to "wound-treatment," for allaying the inflammation, a treatment here consisting of a long prescription containing much the same ingredients which we find employed for the same purpose in Case 41 (XIV 2–4), where the discussion of these drugs will be found. The term " wound treatment " is otherwise found in our treatise only in Case 39, where it is employed after cauterization. See Case 39, XIII 7–8.

The third stage of treatment consists of an astringent prescription for drying up the abscess (or abscesses ?) of much the same content as we found employed for the same purpose in Case 41 (XIV 4–6).

The fourth stage repeats the poultices found in Case 41 (XIV 6–7), though with two ingredients omitted.

GLOSS A

XVI 12–14

Explaining : An abscess with prominent head in his breast.

Translation

As for : " An abscess with prominent head in his breast," it means that there is a large swelling due to the injury which is in his breast, soft like a fluid under the hand.

Commentary

šḥr, " abscess," is an entirely new word, unknown in any other Egyptian document. We learn from this gloss that it is a soft swelling, and the treatment (XVI 6–7) states that it contains pus. On these two data rest the justification for translating the term " abscess."

tp šḳr, " prominent head," is written in the title (XV 20) and in the examination (see also *tp ʿr* in XVI 2). We can hardly assume that the occurrence of *ʿr* twice and *šʿr* once, is due to incorrect writing by the scribe. It seems probable that we have here the familiar verb *ʿr*, " rise, ascend," suggesting the idea of a " rising," that is a " prominent head." See commentary on the same term applied to a tumor in Case 39 (XIII 10).

yḫ·t, " thing," is seemingly rather superfluous here. See discussion, p. 142.

ḥr yh, " due to the injury," literally " on account of the injury." One is tempted to see a *local* meaning in the preposition, and to render " over the injury," meaning on the spot or place of the injury. This rendering is unlikely in view of the variant text in Case 39 which reads : 

"It means that there are swellings spreading over his breast because of his injury" (XIII 10–11). *Yh* may, as in Case 39, designate *disease*, rather than *injury*, and there is no way of settling this uncertain point.

gn, "soft," of course refers back to the swelling.

GLOSS B

XVI 14–15

Explaining: Clamminess of their surface.

Translation

As for: "Clamminess of their surface," it means their skin is not hot.

Commentary

nʿbꜣ, "clamminess," is a word entirely unknown outside of this Case (46). It is here parallel with *nbybyw*, "be hot," preceded by a negative, and must therefore contain the idea of being cool.

yrtyw, "surface," is discussed in Case 7 (III 20). It is here parallel with *ynm*, "skin," which also has the well-established meaning "surface."

nbybyw, "be hot," is derived from the simplex *nby*, a well-known verb meaning "to burn, be hot." No other example of the reduplicated verb is known.

It may be noted that the quotation of the text of the case in the gloss is inaccurate; before *nʿbꜣ* has been omitted and the suffix *sn*, "their" is not in the original text of the case (XVI 1).

GLOSS C

XVI 15–16

Explaining: There is no ruddiness upon it.

Translation

As for: "There is no ruddiness upon it," it means that there is no redness upon it.

Commentary

The quotation varies essentially from the original text of the case (XVI 2), which has : "their faces have no ruddiness," or more literally "there is no ruddiness to their faces," in which the phrase "to their faces" has become "upon it" (singular), giving us an interesting suggestion of the meaning of the words "to their faces."

 *tmś*, "ruddiness," must be an archaic word which aroused special apprehension that it would not be understood, for this is the third time that the commentator has explained it as "redness." See commentary on Case 7 (III 20, Gloss F).

 *yḫ·t*, literally "thing," employed as here with a following adjective, is discussed in Case 4 (II 3), p. 142.

CASE FORTY-SEVEN

XVI 16–XVII 15

A GAPING WOUND IN THE SHOULDER

This case deals with the soft tissue enveloping the articulation of the shoulder. Although not as long as Case 7, the discussion of Case 47 is very intelligently and systematically organized, and is more complicated indeed than that of Case 7. It first follows the case through two stages of progress toward recovery. It then takes up an alternative second stage (third examination) which is unfavorable. It is attended with inflammation of the wound and with fever, which the modern surgeon would presumably consider due to infection. The patient's condition is declared critical (verdict 2). Two different developments may follow this stage : one unfavorable with continuance of the fever (fourth examination) ; the other with abatement of the fever (fifth examination) and presumable recovery.

These five examinations are introduced as follows :

First Examination

With the customary formula, "If thou examinest a man having etc."

Second Examination

, "If thou findest that wound etc." (XVII 3).

Third Examination

, "If, however, thou findest that wound etc." (XVII 6–7).

Fourth Examination

, "If, then, thou findest that man continuing to have fever" (XVII 12).

Fifth Examination

 "If, however, his fever abates, etc." (XVII 13–14).

On the correlation of the last two examinations by means of the introductory 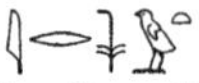 "If however," compare the same correlation of two alternative examinations in Case 7, introduction to case (p. 175).

The organization of the discussion may be outlined as follows :

I. Normally Favorable Development :

1. First Stage :

First Examination, stitching of wound, verdict 1, simple first treatment.

2. Second Stage :

Second Examination, stitching loose (possibly absorbed), open wound drawn together with plaster, simple treatment and recovery.

II. Doubtful Development :

1. Alternative Second Stage :

Third Examination, inflammation of wound, stitching loose (possibly absorbed), wound open and suppurating, fever, patient's condition critical, verdict 2. Leading either to :

2. Final unfavorable condition :

Fourth Examination, disclosing inflammation and continued fever, no applications, normal diet, no medicine ; outcome uncertain.

Or to :

3. Final favorable condition :

Fifth Examination, fever abates, inflammation disappears, simple treatment, patient recovers.

A point concerning which there is some doubt is the interpretation of the statement that the surgeon finds the wound with "its stitching loose." This question has been discussed in Case 10 (V 6). While the indications are that the wound has failed to close wholly by healing, and has still to be drawn together by plaster, the fact that it at once enters the second stage and heals, would indicate the possibility that the loose stitching had simply been absorbed. If not, however, then we must consider that the stitching proved insufficient, obliging the surgeon to resort to plaster for drawing the gash together.

TITLE

XVI 16

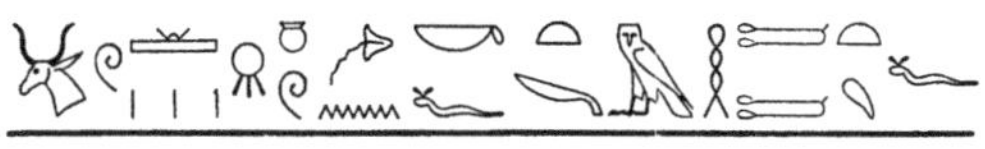

Translation

Instructions concerning a gaping wound in his shoulder.

Commentary

The terms are all discussed in the examination below.

First Examination

XVI 16–20

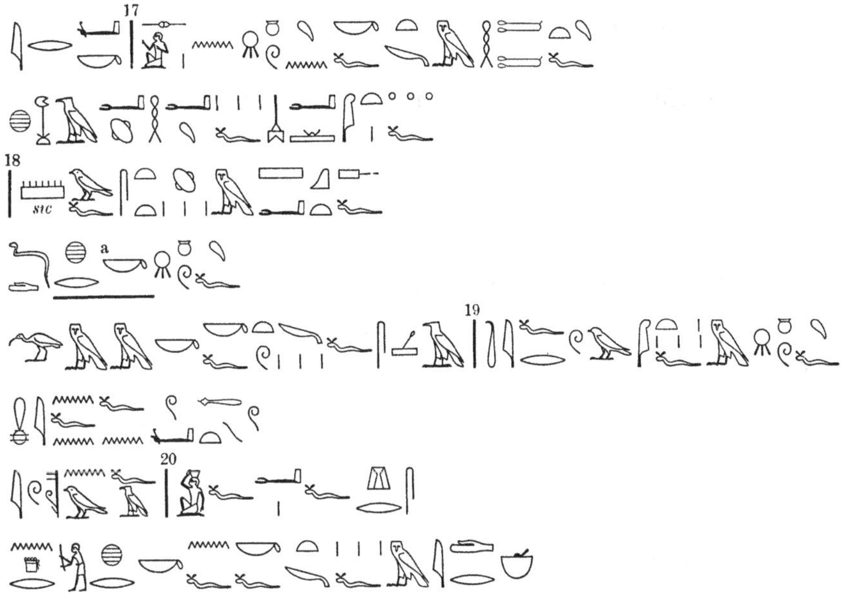

[a] The scribe wrote *ḏd wbnw-f*, which is nonsense. He then inserted in red ink, in the insufficient space between *ḏd* and *wbnw-f*, the three letters, *ḫr-k*, making *ḏd-ḫr-k*. On the meaning see commentary.

Translation

If thou examinest a man having a gaping wound in his shoulder, its flesh being laid back and its sides separated, while he suffers with swelling (in) his shoulder blade, thou shouldst palpate his wound. Shouldst thou find its gash separated from ⌜-⌝ its sides in his wound, as a roll of linen is unrolled, (and) it is painful when he raises his arm on account of it, thou shouldst draw together for him his gash with stitching.

Commentary

 *wbnw n kf·t*, "gaping wound," is an injury treated in Cases 2 to 7, as found in the head. On *kf·t* see Case 1, pp. 90–92.

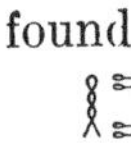 *ḫtt·t*, "shoulder," a meaning long ago demonstrated by Dévaud. It is not a common word, see Pap. Ebers 110, 2 and confer the verb 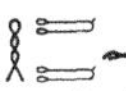 *ḫtt*, "to carry on the shoulder" (Pyr. 2171 b; determinative in type inexact) or as in English "to shoulder."

ḫꜣꜥ, "laid back." Dévaud calls my attention to an example of *ḫꜣꜥ* with , as a variant of *ḫꜣꜥ* with , in Lacau, *Textes religieux*, p. 49. A parallel passage in Pap. Ebers (64, 12) shows that we have here the familiar verb ; compare :

In this passage the variant *ywf*, " flesh " for is very instructive.

wdꜥ, "separate," is not a word with an established surgical or anatomical meaning. It is in this passage however, as in the parallel from Pap. Ebers just cited above, intended to be understood in its original meaning, " separate," from which its more common meaning, " distinguish," " judge " is derived.

šw·t-f, "its sides," while written with the plural strokes is obviously a dual in sense, and is written in the dual in the Ebers parallel. The pronoun, both here and with " flesh," may of course be rendered " his " and might be referred to the patient. A comparison of the parallel in XVII 5–6 in our Case 47, however, shows that it must refer to the wound and not to the patient.

št·wt, " swelling " or " swellings," has been discussed in Case 43, XV 1.

mšꜥḳ·t, "shoulder-blade," is a feminine noun derived from the rare word *mẖꜥḳ* (*mšꜥḳ*), " razor," known from the following three examples :

mẖꜥḳ (*British Museum Inscr. in the Hieratic Character*, pl. XVI, 5633 verso, left l. 5, in a list).

mẖꜥḳ·w (Merneptah Libyan War, Mariette, *Karnak*, 55, 61, in list of spoil).

sic *mẖꜥḳ* (Sign Papyrus X, l. 5, explaining).

These examples are all sufficiently late to contain only *ẖ*, and include no writing with *š*, so commonly alternating with *ẖ* in the Pyramid Texts. In Papyrus Edwin Smith, however, all four occurrences of the word have *š* (Case 35, XII 5 ; Case 36, XII 11 ; Case 47, XVI 18, XVII 2), furnishing another indication of the great age of our document, for this interchange of *ẖ* and *š* had ceased by the end of the Old Kingdom, let us say about 2500 B.C. The shape of the shoulder-blade suggested to the Egyptian surgeon the bronze razor, of which the hieratic determinative furnishes one form, and the first example above discloses another. It is a curious coincidence that the phonetic history of the Germanic " Schulterblatt " (literally " shoulder-leaf ") has resulted in the English " shoulder-blade," so closely parallel to the ancient Egyptian " razor-blade " for the same bone. The term is otherwise unknown in the medical papyri, or in any early Egyptian document before the Ptolemaic Age, when it is found in five passages in the Dendera temple, in a list of the parts of the body of Osiris (Mariette, *Dendérah*, IV 42 =Dümichen, *Geographische Inschr.* I 82; III 1; III 43, three times). In all these passages it is written with *ẖ*, with one exception which has *ḫ*.

ḏd-ḥr-k is obviously an error for *ḏʿr-ḥr-k*, "thou shouldst palpate;" compare Case 4, II 3, where we have *ḏʿr-ḥr-k* in the same context.

evidently contains a corruption of the text after *šꜣty*. The discussion of *šꜣty* in Case 14 (VI 8) shows that it means "separated," especially if followed by *r*. It is obvious that we should read the *r* in the text immediately after *šꜣty*, leaving the enigmatic before *šw·t-f*. The phrase "in his wound," directly following, introduces a reference to the patient, and it may be that we should understand the immediately preceding *f*, in *šw·t-f*, as referring to the patient, not to the wound, and thus giving us "*his* side" not "*its* side." If we disregard the plural strokes, so often superfluous, we then have a reference here to the side of the patient. If the wound were not on the top of the shoulder, the surgeon might mean that a portion of the severed tissue was thrown back like a flap, and separated from the side of the patient. This leaves unexplained the enigmatic , for the text really reads "separated from the of his side." This explanation is in close agreement with the probable meaning of the following comparison, "as a roll of linen is unrolled." The inner face of the flap of severed tissue would then be designated by *kf·wt-f*, lit. "its gashes," as demonstrated in the commentary on Case 1, examination (pp. 90–91), where the "two lips" of the wound are exactly parallel with the plural *kf·wt*, literally "gashes," not meaning more than one gash, but designating the two surfaces of severed tissue which are to be drawn together by the surgical stitching.

nfnfn, "unrolled," is a new word, unknown outside of this passage. The meaning proposed above is a guess, suggested by the context, and in harmony with the determinative, a coil.

ʿw·t, "roll of linen," is a very ancient word, found for example in the reliefs of Hesire, and occurring also in the tomb lists.

nḏry, "draw together," will be found discussed in Case 10 (V 6).

ydr, "stitching," see commentary *ibid.*

FIRST DIAGNOSIS

XVI 20–XVII 2

Translation

Thou shouldst say concerning him: " One having a gaping wound in his shoulder, its flesh being laid back and its sides separated, while he suffers with swelling (in) his shoulder blade. An ailment which I will treat."

Commentary

All the terms have been discussed above in the commentary on the examination. The favorable verdict at the end is explained in Case 1 (I 2); see also introduction (pp. 46 ff.).

First Treatment

XVII 2–3

Translation

Thou shouldst bind it with fresh meat the first day.

Commentary

On the treatment with fresh meat see Case 1 (I 2–3).

This treatment is assumed by the surgeon to be successful and leads to a second examination disclosing normal progress of the patient toward a second favorable stage which, in the judgement of the surgeon, does not require a second diagnosis. The following account of the new conditions therefore passes naturally over any diagnosis directly to the concluding treatment as the patient advances to complete recovery.

Second Examination and Treatment

XVII 3–6

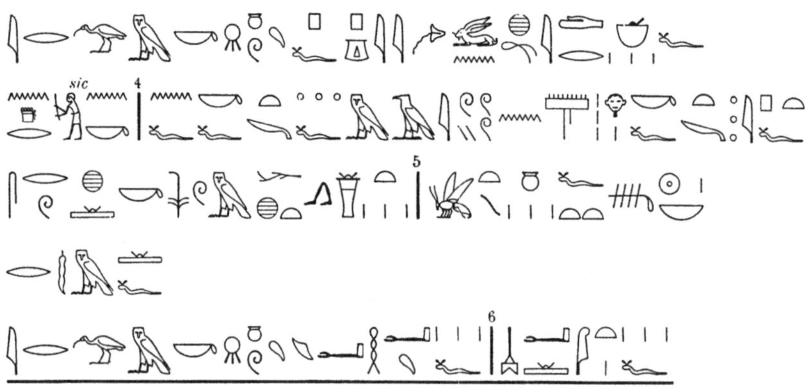

Translation

If thou findest that wound open and its stitching loose, thou shouldst draw together for him its gash with two strips of linen over that gash ; thou shouldst treat it afterward [with] grease, honey, (and) lint every day until he recovers.

If thou findest a wound, its flesh laid back, its sides separated, in any member of a man, thou shouldst treat it according to these directions.

Commentary

pgy, "open," is without doubt a form of the verb *pg'* "to spread out, to open." The determinative is employed to indicate its surgical use, just as we find in our treatise, which a parallel passage in Pap. Ebers shows is the common verb (see above commentary on XVI 17). A suggestive derivative from our verb *pg'* is the noun *pg*, " bowl," or flat open vessel, spreading and opening as a wound might do. The verbal form *pgy* is probably a pseudo-participle.

On the loosening of the stitching, see Case 10 (V 6).

'y·wy, " two strips," doubtless adhesive tape, see Case 2 (I 15) and Case 10 (V 9). It is important to note that " gash " is here in the plural, designating the two faces of the gash, which are to be drawn together by the plaster. See commentary, *ibid.*

On treatment with grease, honey, and lint see Case 1 (I 3).

Third Examination

XVII 6–10

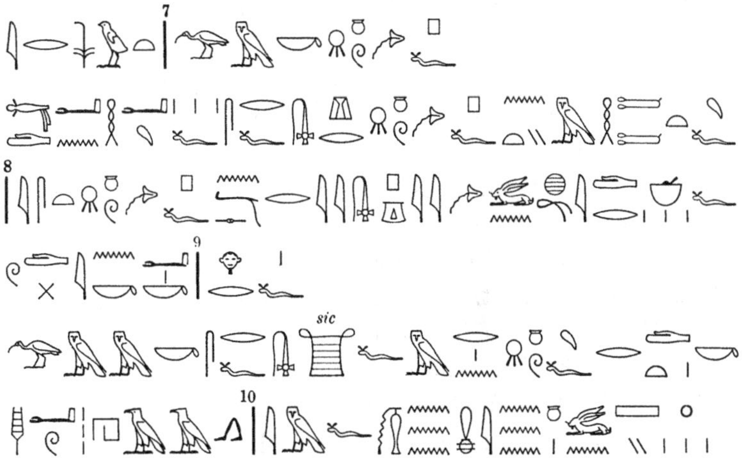

Translation

If, however, thou findest that his flesh has developed inflammation from that wound which is in his shoulder, while that wound is inflamed, open, and its stitching loose, thou shouldst lay thy hand upon it. Shouldst thou find inflammation issuing from the mouth of his wound at thy touch, and secretions discharging therefrom are cool like *wenesh*-juice, (conclusion follows in second diagnosis).

Commentary

While the second stage of the treatment led to uninterrupted recovery, an alternative development of the case disclosed in this third examination shows the presence of infection and the discharge of pus. The contrast is marked. The surgeon's observation that he finds "that wound open and its stitching loose," already contained in the *second* examination (pp. 420–421), was not followed by unfavorable results (see Case 10, p. 230). Here in our *third* examination however, the "open" wound, with "its stitching loose," is found to be "inflamed" and discharging "secretions." While the second examination, omitting any diagnosis, proceeds directly to treatment with favorable result, this third examination discloses a condition so questionable that the surgeon appends the uncertain verdict 2 (p. 243).

The beginning of the third examination really reads, more literally rendered: "If, however, thou findest that wound, his flesh has developed inflammation from that wound which is in his shoulder," in which the first "that wound" would have been resumed by a pronoun, except for the fact that a relative clause ("which is in his shoulder") followed, and it could not be appended to a pronoun.

śrf, "inflammation," has been discussed in Case 41 (XIV 12).

nsr-y, "inflamed," is taken up in Case 41 (XIV 8).

On the loosening of the stitching see Case 10 (V 6 under *ydr*).

nšw, "issue," is of course an abbreviated writing of *nšw*, discussed in Case 41 (XIV 15).

ꜥḥꜥ·w, "secretions," will be found discussed in Case 41 (XIII 22–XIV 1, p. 376). The question may arise whether secretion discharging from a feverish and inflamed wound would be cool.

wnšy, "*wenesh*-juice," is a substance not yet satisfactorily identified. The plant is referred to as far back as the Old Kingdom; see *wnš* in Berlin 13466. See also Griffith, *Hieratic Papyri from Kahun and Gurob*, pl. XXVII, l. 21, which mentions *wnš*-fruit. It occurs frequently in Pap. Ebers and also Berlin 3038. In later times it occurs in the Dendera temple (Mariette, *Dendérah*, I 17), where it is *parallel* with wine; and three times in the same temple, *for* wine (*ibid.* II 76; III 16 c, and III 19 p). Loret has suggested that it is to be identified with coriander (see *Recueil de trav.* 15, p. 105); but this identification seems uncertain.

DIAGNOSIS FOLLOWING THIRD EXAMINATION

XVII 10–11

Translation

Thou shouldst say concerning him : " One having a gaping wound in his shoulder, it being inflamed, and he continues to have fever from it. An ailment with which I will contend."

Commentary

Although this diagnosis follows the third examination it is not the third diagnosis, for the second examination revealed normal progress toward recovery and was therefore followed by no diagnosis. The insertion of a diagnosis with a different verdict after the third examination shows that we have disclosed by it an alternative second stage of the case.

The terms have all been discussed above. It is important to note that *nsr-y*, " it being inflamed," refers to the wound ; while *šmm-f*, " he has fever," refers to the patient. See the discussion in Case 41 (XIV 8–9). The doubtful verdict 2 has been discussed in Case 4 (II 6). See also introduction (pp. 46 ff.).

FOURTH EXAMINATION

XVII 12

Translation

If, then, thou findest that man continuing to have fever, while that wound is inflamed, (conclusion in following treatment).

Commentary

On the distinction between "fever" and "inflammation" see Case 41 (XIV 8–9). No treatment follows the above diagnosis because the surgeon evidently desires first to introduce one of the two alternative stages which he knows will follow the condition revealed by the third examination. He therefore passes at once to the unfavorable persistence of the inflammation and fever, for which the following treatment can do nothing. Like English "as," which may mean either "while" or "because," *yšk* here has much of the force of "because." This is demonstrated by the parallel passage in Case 28 (X 2), which in place of this *yšk* clause has *ẖr wbnw pf*, "on account of (or, because of) that wound."

TREATMENT FOLLOWING FOURTH EXAMINATION

XVII 12–13

Translation

Thou shalt not bind it; thou shalt moor (him) at his mooring stakes, until the period of his injury passes by.

Commentary

On the meaning of the extraordinary injunction, "moor (him) at his mooring stakes," see Case 3 (I 22–23) and *ibid.*, Gloss D (II 1–2). It is obvious that the surgeon can do nothing but await the course of nature, meantime feeding the patient a normal diet. Discussion of the concluding temporal clause and the unusual determinative of *yh*, "injury," will be found on p. 135.

FIFTH EXAMINATION

XVII 13–14

Translation

If, however, his fever abates and the inflammation in the mouth of his wound dissipates entirely, (conclusion in following treatment).

Commentary

We have here disclosed a final favorable outcome, which, as after the second examination, is followed by no diagnosis.

On  *y't*, "abates," more literally "is diverted" or "turned aside," see commentary on Case 7 (IV 3).

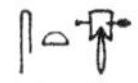 *šty*, "dissipates," means more literally "scatters," as for example in the scattering of seed-grain.

 *r tʾ*, "entirely," literally "to the ground," is discussed in Case 4, Gloss A (II 9).

TREATMENT FOLLOWING FIFTH EXAMINATION

XVII 14–15

Translation

Thou shouldst treat him afterward [with] grease, honey, (and) lint every day, until he recovers.

Commentary

We find here the final favorable outcome possible after the disclosure of the unfavorable conditions listed in the third examination. On the simple treatment with grease, honey, and lint, see Case 1 (I 3).

CASE FORTY-EIGHT

XVII 15–19

A SPRAIN IN A SPINAL VERTEBRA (INCOMPLETE)

This, the last case in our treatise, is the first of what was doubtless a series of discussions of injuries to the spine, beginning with the less serious, an arrangement which we have found was likewise that of similar groups of cases, like the series of five cases of injuries to the temple (Cases 18 to 22). The case is a simple one, unfortunately incomplete, breaking off abruptly at the beginning of an interesting treatment by manipulation. Inspection of the original or the facsimile of Plate XVII discloses the fact that the scribe stopped in the middle of a line, in the middle of a sentence; in the middle of a case. With his pen full of ink and with space on the papyrus sheet before him for several columns more, he laid down his pen and never copied any more of the remarkable surgical treatise we have been studying. See Introduction, Vol. II, p. xii.

TITLE

XVII 15

Translation

Instructions concerning a sprain [in] a vertebra of his spinal column.

Commentary

The terms will be found discussed below. It is obvious that our scribe has omitted the preposition " in ". See commentary below.

EXAMINATION

XVII 15–18

Translation

If thou examinest [a man having] a sprain in a vertebra of his spinal column, thou shouldst say to him : " Extend now thy two legs (and) contract them both (again)." When he extends them both he contracts them both immediately because of the pain he causes in the vertebra of his spinal column in which he suffers.

Commentary

The form of the examination is always : " If thou examinest *a man having* ; " hence it is clear that the scribe has omitted by error the words " a man having."

 *nrw·t*, " sprain," is discussed in Case 30, Gloss A (X 12). It is regularly followed by the preposition  *m*, " in," as here, and hence it is clear that this  has been omitted by scribal error in the title.

 *ṯs*, " vertebra," has been discussed in Case 31, Gloss A (X 18).

 *psd*, originally *pšḏ*, has long been known to mean " back," but primarily " spine " or " spinal column."

 *m'ʿ*, " extend," is evidently an anatomical or physiological use of the verb *m'ʿ*, " send, dispatch, lead." A very apt illustration of its meaning in our passage is found in the Great " Amduat " 10th Hour, where Horus says to *swimmers* :  " Stroke (or paddle) the Celestial Ocean with your feet " (Leyden, Turin and Seti, II 19). This is exactly the motion which is

required of our patient with the injured spine. Dr. Grapow calls my attention to a similar use of the word in the Book of the Dead (ed. Budge, Chap. 11, 3, cf. Pap. of not in Naville): " I extended my arm as lord of the *wrr·t*-crown."

mʿ, " now," presumably the rather rare particle ; it is written with a ligature which might possibly be read *rd*, the phonetic writing of " foot " before the determinatives . Compare the similar writing of the ligature in XIII 11.

ḳrf, " contract " or " draw in," is a rare verb, and, with one exception, unknown in the medical papyri. Its meaning however can be determined from two passages in the Book of the Dead. We find the deceased saying : " Geb. . . . . has opened my two jaws, he opens my blind eyes, and he stretches out my two contracted legs " (ed. Naville, 26, 7, Pb). Again the deceased is addressed as follows :

" Geb opens for thee thy two blind eyes ; he stretches out thy two contracted legs " (ed. Budge, 169, 2–3). In this example it is important to note that Geb's action in the first line is one which reverses and overcomes blindness ; that is, the condition indicated by the word after " eyes " is more or less the opposite of that resulting from the god's action. In the second line therefore the word after legs must denote a condition rather the opposite of that produced by the god when he " stretches out " the legs of the deceased. They are therefore in a condition of contraction or constriction. These examples enable us also to understand a passage in an obscure case in the Berlin Medical Papyrus (3038, verso I 11): " Thou shalt contract her arm." An example in *Mutter und Kind* (3, 7) is not clear. On the other hand, in connection with cases of stiffness and rheumatoid troubles, Papyrus Ebers contains the following instructive example of the *noun* derived from our verb, in the title of a recipe for "stretching out the contractions (*ḳrf·wt*) and softening the stiffness" (Pap. Ebers 85, 5–6). Here again the noun *ḳrf·wt*, "contractions" is opposed to the verb *dwn*, " stretch out," as is the verb *ḳrf*, "contract" in the two examples from the Book of the Dead. In our treatise the verb *ḳrf* occurs only in the above examination, where it twice appears opposed to the verb *mʾʿ*, " extend." The meaning " contract " or " constrict " would seem to be established.

yrr-f, " (which) he causes," literally " he makes," may also be rendered " when he does (so)," as a parenthesis, before " in the vertebra."

mn·y-f, " in which he suffers," literally, " his made-to-suffer," seemingly a passive participle ; for *mn*, " to suffer " is a transitive verb in Egyptian. See discussion in Case 3 (I 20).

DIAGNOSIS

XVII 18

Translation

Thou shouldst say concerning him: "One having a sprain in a vertebra of his spinal column. An ailment which I will treat."

Commentary

The terms have all been discussed above. This diagnosis, as so commonly, consists only of the title, followed by the verdict. On this verdict see Case 1 (I 2) and the introduction (pp. 46 ff.).

TREATMENT

XVII 18–19

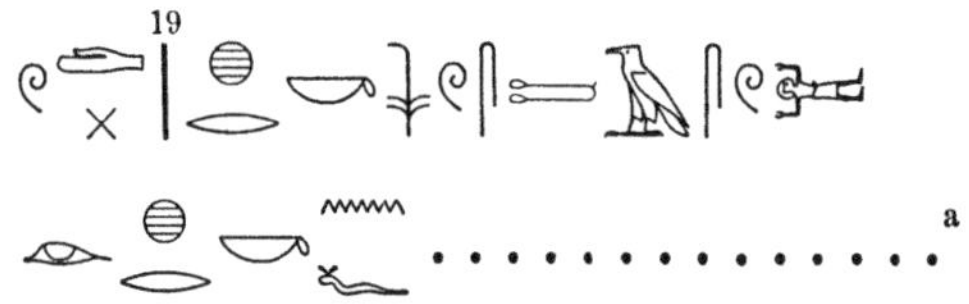

[a] The scribe wrote the preceding diagnosis in red ink. On resuming the black ink pen he filled it very full and when he stopped as indicated above in the middle of l. 19, his pen was still flooded with ink producing broad and intensely black lines. The interruption, whatever it may have been, therefore appears to have been a sudden one, unexpected by the scribe. See Vol. I, p. xv; Vol. II, p. xii.

Translation

Thou shouldst place him prostrate on his back; thou shouldst make for him . . . .

Commentary

šṯ'św, "prostrate on his back," is usually written *šṯs(y)*, without the appearing here. See discussion in Case 35 (XII 5).

The last sentence has been left incomplete by the scribe, and the discussion of the case remained unfinished. See full discussion in the introduction to Volume II, p. xii.

CONSECUTIVE TRANSLATION OF THE SURGICAL TREATISE

NOTES FOR THE GUIDANCE OF THE READER

The reader should note that the introduction to this treatise has been lost, and hence the abruptness of the beginning. Furthermore, no modern reader will be able to understand this ancient surgical treatise as presented in the following consecutive translation unless he consults the introductory material at the beginning of this volume. In order to gain a general knowledge of the background necessary to an understanding of the document, pages 1 to 25 of the General Introduction should be carefully read. Equally or even more indispensable is an acquaintance with pages 33 to 73 of the Special Introduction.

In the long section called Translation and Commentary, which begins on page 78, and forms the bulk of the volume, the discussion of each separate case is introduced by explanatory material. In attempting to read any particular case in the following consecutive translation, therefore, the reader should turn back to the case in question in the Translation and Commentary, which he will find it very easy to do because the case numbers are inserted as running heads at the top of the page. He should then read the introduction to each case before attempting to read the translation in the following consecutive rendering. The introduction to Case 1 will be found on page 78; the introduction to Case 2 will be found on page 118; Case 3 on page 125, etc.

Some few technical terms, names of medicaments, etc., of which we do not know the meaning, have been carried over in the form of transliterations in italics, even in this consecutive translation. They will be found explained in the Commentary.

It should be noted that the case numbers and the titles of the case subdivisions are insertions of the modern editor.

CASE ONE

Bottom lines of lost column to I 12

A WOUND IN THE HEAD PENETRATING TO THE BONE

Title

[Instructions concerning a wound in his head, penetrating to the bone of his skull.]

Examination

[If thou examinest a man having a wound in his head, penetrating to the bone of his skull, (but) not having a gash, thou shouldst palpate his wound (or, thou shouldst lay thy hand upon it); shouldst thou find his skull uninjured, not having a perforation, a split, or a smash in it,] (conclusion in diagnosis).

Diagnosis

[Thou shouldst say regarding him: "One having a woun]d in his head, while his wound does [not] have two lips, - - -, nor a gash, although [it penetrates to the bone of] his head. An ailment which I will treat."

Treatment

Thou shouldst bind it with [fresh] meat [the first day] (and) treat afterward with grease, [honey] (and) lint every day until he recovers.

Gloss A

As for: "Thou examinest a man," [it means] counting any one - - [⌜like cou]nting⌝ things with a bushel. (For) examining (*ḫ'·t*, literally "measuring") is [⌜like⌝] one's [⌜counting⌝] a certain quantity with a bushel, (or) counting something with the fingers, in order to [know] - - -. It is measuring (*ḫ'·t*) things with a bushel which - - - one in whom an ailment is [cou]nted, like measuring (*ḫ'·t*) the ailment of a man; [in order to know the action] of the heart. There are canals (or vessels, *mt*) in it (the heart) to [every] member. Now if the priests of Sekhmet or any physician put his hands (or) his fingers [upon the head, upon the back of the] head, upon the two hands, upon the pulse, upon the two feet, [he] measures (*ḫ'y*) [to] the heart, because its vessels are in the back of the head and in the pulse; and because its [pulsation is in] every vessel of every member. He says "measure" (*ḫ'·t*) regarding his [⌜wound⌝] because of the vessels (*mt·w*) to his head and to the back of his head and to his two feet - - - - his heart in order to recognize the indications which have arisen therein; meaning [⌜to meas]ure it⌝ in order to know what is befalling therein.

Gloss B

As for: "While his [wou]nd does not have [two lips]," it means his wound is narrow, [not wide]; without gaping of one (lip) from the other.

Gloss C

As for: "Penetrating to [the bone of his skull, (but) not having a gash]," it means that there is a gaping of the flesh, although ⌜-⌝ - - - - ⌜-⌝ over the bone of his skull, without gaping [of one (lip) from the other], being narrow, not wide.

CASE TWO

I 12–18

A GAPING WOUND IN THE HEAD PENETRATING TO THE BONE

Title

Instructions concerning a [gaping] wound [in his head], penetrating to the bone.

EXAMINATION

If thou examinest a man having a [gaping] wound [in] his [head], penetrating to the bone, thou shouldst lay thy hand upon it (and) [thou shouldst] pal[pate hi]s [wound]. If thou findest his skull [uninjured, not hav]ing a perforation in it, (conclusion in diagnosis).

DIAGNOSIS

Thou shouldst say regarding [him]: " One hav[ing a gaping wou]nd in his head. An ailment which I will treat."

TREATMENT

[Thou] shouldst bind [fresh meat upon it the first day ; thou shouldst apply for him two strips of linen, and treat afterward with grease, honey, (and) lin]t every day until he recovers.

GLOSS A

As for: " A [gaping] wound [in his head penetrating to the bone," it means] - - - - - - - - his wound.

GLOSS B

As for: " Two strips of linen," [it means] two bands [of linen which one applies upon the two lips of the gaping wound in order to cause that one join] to the other.

GLOSS C

As for: " Not having a split, a perforation, (or) [a smash in it," it means] - - - - .

CASE THREE

I 18–II 2

A GAPING WOUND IN THE HEAD PENETRATING TO THE BONE AND PERFORATING THE SKULL

TITLE

[Instructions concerning] a gaping [wo]und in his head, penetrating to the bone (and) perforating his [skull].

EXAMINATION

[If thou examinest a man having a gaping wound in] his [head], penetrating to the bone, (and) perforating his skull; thou shouldst palpate his wound; [shouldst thou find him unable to look at his two shoulders] and his [br]east, (and) suffering with stiffness in his neck, (conclusion in diagnosis).

DIAGNOSIS

Thou shouldst say [regarding] him: "One having [a gaping wound in his head, penetrating to the bone, (and) per]forating his skull, while he suffers with stiffness in his neck. An ailment which I will treat."

TREATMENT

Now [after thou has stitched it, thou shouldst lay] fresh [meat] upon his wound the first day. Thou shouldst not bind it. Moor (him) [at his mooring stakes until the period of his injury passes by]. Thou shouldst [tre]at it afterward with grease, honey, and lint every day, until he recovers.

GLOSS A

[As for: "Perforating his skull," it means] - - - - his skull, a contracted smash, through his incurring a break like a puncture of a (pottery) jar, - - - - - - - - - which he incurred.

GLOSS B

As for: "Unable to look at his two shoulders and [his] bre[ast," it means it is not easy for him to look at] his two shoulders (and) it is not easy for him to look at his breast.

GLOSS C

As for: "Suffering with stiffness in his neck," it means a lifting up (resulting) from his having incurred this injury, which has shifted into his neck, so that his neck (also) suffers with it.

GLOSS D

As for: "Moor (him) at his mooring stakes," it means putting him on his customary diet, without administering to him a prescription.

CASE FOUR

II 2–11

A GAPING WOUND IN THE HEAD PENETRATING TO THE BONE AND SPLITTING THE SKULL

TITLE

Instructions concerning a gaping wound in his head, penetrating to the bone, (and) splitting his skull.

EXAMINATION

If thou examinest a man having a gaping wound in his head, penetrating to the bone, (and) splitting his skull, thou shouldst palpate his wound. Shouldst thou find something disturbing therein under thy fingers, (and) he shudders exceedingly, while the swelling which is over it protrudes, he discharges blood from both his nostrils (and) from both his ears, he suffers with stiffness in his neck, so that he is unable to look at his two shoulders and his breast, (conclusion in diagnosis).

DIAGNOSIS

Thou shouldst say regarding him: "One having a gaping wound in his head, penetrating to the bone, (and) splitting his skull; while he discharges blood from both his nostrils (and) from both his ears, (and) he suffers with stiffness in his neck. An ailment with which I will contend."

TREATMENT

Now when thou findest that the skull of that man is split, thou shouldst not bind him, (but) moor (him) at his mooring stakes until the period of his injury passes by. His treatment is sitting. Make for him two supports of brick, until thou knowest he has reached a decisive point. Thou shouldst apply grease to his head, (and) soften his neck therewith and both his shoulders. Thou shouldst do likewise for every man whom thou findest having a split skull.

GLOSS A

As for: "Splitting his skull," it means separating shell from shell of his skull, while fragments remain sticking in the flesh of his head, and do not come away.

GLOSS B

As for: "The swelling (*tḫb*) which is over it protrudes," it means that the swelling (*šfw·t*) which is over this split is large, rising upward.

GLOSS C

As for: "(Until) thou knowest he has reached a decisive point," it means (until) thou knowest whether he will die or he will live; for he is (a case of) "an ailment with which I will contend."

CASE FIVE

II 11–17

A GAPING WOUND IN THE HEAD WITH COMPOUND COMMINUTED FRACTURE OF THE SKULL

TITLE

Instructions concerning a gaping wound in his head, smashing his skull.

EXAMINATION

If thou examinest a man having a gaping wound in his head, penetrating to the bone, (and) smashing his skull; thou shouldst palpate his wound. Shouldst thou find that smash which is in his skull deep (and) sunken under thy fingers, while the swelling which is over it protrudes, he discharges blood from both his nostrils (and) both his ears, (and) he suffers with stiffness in his neck, so that he is unable to look at his two shoulders and his breast, (conclusion in diagnosis).

Diagnosis

Thou shouldst say regarding him: " One having a gaping wound in his head, penetrating to the bone, (and) smashing his skull, while he suffers with stiffness in his neck. An ailment not to be treated."

Treatment

Thou shalt not bind him, (but) moor (him) at his mooring stakes, until the period of his injury passes by.

Gloss A

As for: " Smashing his skull," it means a smash of his skull (such that) bones, getting into that smash, sink into the interior of his skull. The " Treatise on What Pertains to His Wounds " states: " It means a smash of his skull into numerous fragments, which sink into the interior of his skull."

CASE SIX

II 17–III 1

A GAPING WOUND IN THE HEAD WITH COMPOUND COMMINUTED FRACTURE OF THE SKULL AND RUPTURE OF THE MENINGEAL MEMBRANES

Title

Instructions concerning a gaping wound in his head, penetrating to the bone, smashing his skull, (and) rending open the brain of his skull.

Examination

If thou examinest a man having a gaping wound in his head, penetrating to the bone, smashing his skull, (and) rending open the brain of his skull, thou shouldst palpate his wound. Shouldst thou find that smash which is in his skull [like] those corrugations which form in molten copper, (and) something therein throbbing (and) fluttering under thy fingers, like the weak place of an infant's crown before it becomes whole—when it has happened there is no throbbing (and) fluttering under thy fingers until the brain of his (the patient's) skull is rent open—(and) he discharges blood from both his nostrils, (and) he suffers with stiffness in his neck, (conclusion in diagnosis).

Diagnosis

[Thou shouldst say concerning him]: " An ailment not to be treated."

TREATMENT

Thou shouldst anoint that wound with grease. Thou shalt not bind it; thou shalt not apply two strips upon it: until thou knowest that he has reached a decisive point.

GLOSS A

As for: "Smashing his skull, (and) rending open the brain of his skull," (it means) the smash is large, opening to the interior of his skull, (to) the membrane enveloping his brain, so that it breaks open his fluid in the interior of his head.

GLOSS B

As for: "Those corrugations which form on molten copper," it means copper which the coppersmith pours off (rejects) before it is ⌜forced⌝ into the ⌜mould⌝, because of something foreign upon it like ⌜wrinkles⌝. It is said: "It is like ripples of pus."

CASE SEVEN

III 2–IV 4

A GAPING WOUND IN THE HEAD PENETRATING TO THE BONE AND PERFORATING THE SUTURES

TITLE

Instructions concerning a gaping wound in his head, penetrating to the bone, (and) perforating the sutures of his skull.

EXAMINATION

[If thou examinest a man having a gaping wound in his head, penetrating to the bone, (and) perforating the sutures of his skull], thou shouldst palpate his wound, (although) he shudders exceedingly. Thou shouldst cause him to lift his face; if it is painful for him to open his mouth, (and) his heart beats feebly; if thou observe his spittle hanging at his two lips and not falling off, while he discharges blood from both his nostrils (and) from both his ears; he suffers with stiffness in his neck, (and) is unable to look at his two shoulders and his breast, (conclusion in diagnosis).

FIRST DIAGNOSIS

Thou shouldst say regarding him: "One having a gaping wound in his head, penetrating to the bone, (and) perforating the sutures of his skull; the cord of his mandible is contracted; he discharges blood from both his nostrils (and) from both his ears, while he suffers with stiffness in his neck. An ailment with which I will contend."

FIRST TREATMENT

Now as soon as thou findest that the cord of that man's mandible, his jaw, is contracted, thou shouldst have made for him something hot, until he is comfortable, so that his mouth opens. Thou shouldst bind it with grease, honey, (and) lint, until thou knowest that he has reached a decisive point.

SECOND EXAMINATION

If, then, thou findest that the flesh of that man has developed fever from that wound which is in the sutures of his skull, while that man has developed *ty*ʾ from that wound, thou shouldst lay thy hand upon him. Shouldst thou find his countenance is clammy with sweat, the ligaments of his neck are tense, his face is ruddy, his teeth and his back [-], the odor of the chest of his head is like the *bkn* (urine) of sheep, his mouth is bound, (and) both his eyebrows are drawn, while his face is as if he wept, (conclusion in diagnosis).

SECOND DIAGNOSIS

Thou shouldst say regarding him: "One having a gaping wound in his head, penetrating to the bone, perforating the sutures of his skull; he has developed *ty*ʾ, his mouth is bound, (and) he suffers with stiffness in his neck. An ailment not to be treated."

THIRD EXAMINATION

If, however, thou findest that that man has become pale and has already ⌜shown exhaustion⌝.

THIRD TREATMENT

Thou shouldst have made for him a wooden brace padded with linen and put into his mouth. Thou shouldst have made for him a draught of *wʿḥ*-fruit. His treatment is sitting, placed between two supports of brick, until thou knowest he has reached a decisive point.

GLOSS A

As for: "Perforating the sutures of [his skull]," it means what is between shell and shell of his skull; and that the sutures are (composed) of hide.

GLOSS B

As for: "The cord of his mandible is contracted," it means a stiffening on the part of the ligaments at the end of his ramus, which are fastened to his temporal bone, that is at the end of his jaw, without moving to and fro, so that it is not easy for him to open his mouth because of his pain.

GLOSS C

As for: "The cord of his mandible," it means the ligaments which bind the end of his jaw, as one says, "the cord" of a thing in (or as) a splint.

GLOSS D

As for: "His countenance clammy with sweat," it means that his head is a little sweaty, as (we say), "A thing is clammy."

Gloss E

As for: "The ligaments of his neck are tense," it means that the ligaments of his neck are stretched stiff by reason of his injury.

Gloss F

As for: "His face is ruddy" (*tmś*), it means that the color of his face is red, like the color of *tmś·t*-pigment.

Gloss G

As for: "The odor of the chest of his head is like the *bkn* of sheep," it means that the odor of his crown is like the urine of sheep.

Gloss H

As for: "The chest of his head," it means the middle of his crown next to his brain. The likening of it is to a chest.

Gloss I

As for: "His mouth is bound, (and) both his eyebrows are drawn, while his face is as if he wept," it means that he does not open his mouth that he may speak, both his eyebrows are distorted, one drawing upward, the other drooping downward, like one who winks while his face weeps.

Gloss J

As for: "He has become pale and has already ⌜shown exhaustion⌝," it means becoming pale, because he is (a case of) "Undertake [⌜him⌝], do not desert [⌜him⌝]," in view of the exhaustion.

CASE EIGHT

IV 5–18

COMPOUND COMMINUTED FRACTURE OF THE SKULL DISPLAYING NO VISIBLE EXTERNAL INJURY

Title

Instructions concerning a smash in his skull under the skin of his head.

Examination

If thou examinest a man having a smash of his skull, under the skin of his head, while there is nothing at all upon it, thou shouldst palpate his wound. Shouldst thou find that there is a swelling protruding on the outside of that smash which is in his skull, while his eye is askew because of it, on the side of him having that injury which is in his skull; (and) he walks shuffling with his sole, on the side of him having that injury which is in his skull, (conclusion in diagnosis).

DIAGNOSIS

Thou shouldst account him one whom something entering from outside has smitten, as one who does not release the head of his shoulder-fork, and one who does not fall with his nails in the middle of his palm; while he discharges blood from both his nostrils (and) from both his ears, (and) he suffers with stiffness in his neck. An ailment not to be treated.

TREATMENT

His treatment is sitting, until he ⌜gains color⌝, (and) until thou knowest he has reached the decisive point.

SECOND EXAMINATION

Now as soon as thou findest that smash which is in his skull like those corrugations which form on molten copper, (and) something therein throbbing and fluttering under thy fingers like the weak place of an infant's crown before it knits together—when it has happened there is no throbbing and fluttering under thy fingers, until the brain of his (the patient's) skull is rent open—(and) he discharges blood from both his nostrils and both his ears, (and) he suffers with stiffness in his neck, (conclusion in second diagnosis).

SECOND DIAGNOSIS

[Thou shouldst say concerning him]: "An ailment not to be treated."

GLOSS A

As for: "A smash in his skull under the skin of his head, there being no wound at all upon it," it means a smash of the shell of his skull, the flesh of his head being uninjured.

GLOSS B

As for: "He walks shuffling with his sole," he (the surgeon) is speaking about his walking with his sole dragging, so that it is not easy for him to walk, when it (the sole) is feeble and turned over, while the tips of his toes are contracted to the ball of his sole, and they (the toes) walk fumbling the ground. He (the surgeon) says: "He shuffles," concerning it.

GLOSS C

As for: "One whom something entering from outside has smitten" on the side of him having this injury, it means one whom something entering from outside presses, on the side of him having this injury.

GLOSS D

As for: "Something entering from outside," it means the breath of an outside god or death; not the intrusion of something which his flesh engenders.

GLOSS E

As for: "One who does not release the head of his shoulder-fork, and who does not fall with his nails in the middle of his palm," it means that he says: "One to whom the head of his shoulder-fork is not given, and one who does not fall with his nails in the middle of his palm."

CASE NINE

IV 19–V 5

WOUND IN THE FOREHEAD PRODUCING A COMPOUND COMMINUTED FRACTURE OF THE SKULL

TITLE

Instructions concerning a wound in his forehead, smashing the shell of his skull.

EXAMINATION

If thou examinest a man having a wound in his forehead, smashing the shell of his head, (conclusion in treatment).

TREATMENT

Thou shouldst prepare for him the egg of an ostrich, triturated with grease (and) placed in the mouth of his wound. Now afterward thou shouldst prepare for him the egg of an ostrich, triturated and made into poultices for drying up that wound. Thou shouldst apply to it for him a covering for physician's use; thou shouldst uncover it the third day, (and) find it knitting together the shell, the color being like the egg of an ostrich.

That which is to be said as a charm over this recipe:

Repelled is the enemy that is in the wound!
Cast out is the ⌜evil⌝ that is in the blood,
The adversary of Horus, ⌜on every⌝ side of the mouth of Isis.
This temple does not fall down;
There is no enemy of the vessel therein.
I am under the protection of Isis;
My rescue is the son of Osiris.

Now afterward thou shouldst cool [it] for him [with] a compress of figs, grease, and honey, cooked, cooled, and applied to it.

GLOSS A

As for: "A covering for physician's use," it is a bandage which is in the hand of the embalmer, and which he (the physician) applies to this remedy which is on this wound which is in his forehead.

CASE TEN

V 5–9

A GAPING WOUND AT THE TOP OF THE EYEBROW, PENETRATING TO THE BONE

TITLE

Instructions concerning a wound in the top of his eyebrow.

EXAMINATION

If thou examinest a man having a wound in the top of his eyebrow, penetrating to the bone, thou shouldst palpate his wound, (and) draw together for him his gash with stitching.

DIAGNOSIS

Thou shouldst say concerning him: "[One having] a wound in his eyebrow. An ailment which I will treat."

TREATMENT

Now after thou hast stitched it, [thou shouldst bind] fresh meat upon [it] the first day. If thou findest that the stitching of this wound is loose, thou shouldst draw (it) together for him with two strips (of plaster), and thou shouldst treat it with grease and honey every day until he recovers.

GLOSS A

As for: "Two strips of linen," it means two bands of linen, which one applies upon the two lips of the gaping wound, in order to cause that one (lip) join to the other.

CASE ELEVEN

V 10–15

A BROKEN NOSE

TITLE

Instructions concerning a break in the column of his nose.

EXAMINATION

If thou examinest a man having a break in the column of his nose, his nose being disfigured, and a ⌜depression⌝ being in it, while the swelling that is on it protrudes, (and) he has discharged blood from both his nostrils, (conclusion in diagnosis).

DIAGNOSIS

Thou shouldst say concerning him: "One having a break in the column of his nose. An ailment which I will treat."

TREATMENT

Thou shouldst cleanse (it) for him [with] two plugs of linen. Thou shouldst place two (other) plugs of linen saturated with grease in the inside of his two nostrils. Thou shouldst put [him] at his mooring stakes until the swelling is reduced (lit. drawn out). Thou shouldst apply for him stiff rolls of linen by which his nose is held fast. Thou shouldst treat him afterward [with] grease, honey, (and) lint, every day until he recovers.

GLOSS A

As for : " The column of his nose," it means the outer edge of his nose as far as its side(s) on the top of his nose, being the inside of his nose in the middle of his two nostrils.

GLOSS B

As for : " His two nostrils," [it means] the two sides of his nose extending to his [two] cheek[s], as far as the back of his nose ; the top of his nose is loosened.

CASE TWELVE

V 16–VI 3

A BREAK IN THE NASAL BONE

TITLE

Instructions concerning a break in the chamber of his nose.

EXAMINATION

If thou examinest a man having a break in the chamber of his nose, (and) thou findest his nose bent, while his face is disfigured, (and) the swelling which is over it is protruding, (conclusion in diagnosis).

DIAGNOSIS

Thou shouldst say concerning him : " One having a break in the chamber of his nose. An ailment which I will treat."

TREATMENT

Thou shouldst force it to fall in, so that it is lying in its place, (and) clean out for him the interior of both his nostrils with two swabs of linen until every worm of blood which coagulates in the inside of his two nostrils comes forth. Now afterward thou shouldst place two plugs of linen saturated with grease and put into his two nostrils. Thou shouldst place for him two stiff rolls of linen, bound on. Thou shouldst treat him afterward with grease, honey, (and) lint every day until he recovers.

Gloss A

As for: " A break in the chamber of his nose," it means the middle of his nose as far as the back, extending to the region between his two eyebrows.

Gloss B

As for: " His nose bent, while his face is disfigured," it means his nose is crooked and greatly swollen throughout; his two cheeks likewise, so that his face is disfigured by it, not being in its customary form, because all the depressions are clothed with swellings, so that his face looks disfigured by it.

Gloss C

As for: " Every worm of blood which coagulates in the inside of his two nostrils," it means the clotting of blood in the inside of his two nostrils, likened to the *ʿnʿr·t*-worm, which subsists in the water.

CASE THIRTEEN

VI 3–7

COMPOUND COMMINUTED FRACTURE IN THE SIDE OF THE NOSE

Title

Instructions concerning a smash in his nostril.

Examination

If thou examinest a man having a smash in his nostril, thou shouldst place thy hand upon his nose at the point of this smash. Should it crepitate under thy fingers, while at the same time he discharges blood from his nostril (and) from his ear, on the side of him having that smash; it is painful when he opens his mouth because of it; (and) he is speechless, (conclusion in diagnosis).

Diagnosis

Thou shouldst say concerning him: " One having a smash in his nostril. An ailment not to be treated."

CASE FOURTEEN

VI 7–14

FLESH WOUND IN ONE SIDE OF THE NOSE PENETRATING TO THE NOSTRIL

Title

Instructions concerning a wound in his nostril.

EXAMINATION

If thou examinest a man having a wound in his nostril, piercing through, shouldst thou find the two lips of that wound separated from each other, thou shouldst draw together for him that wound with stitching.

DIAGNOSIS

Thou shouldst say concerning him : " One having a wound in his nostril, piercing through. An ailment which I will treat."

TREATMENT

Thou shouldst make for him two swabs of linen, (and) thou shouldst clean out every worm of blood which has coagulated in the inside of his nostril. Thou shouldst bind (it) with fresh meat the first day. When its stitching loosens, thou shouldst take off for him the fresh meat, (and) thou shouldst bind it with grease, honey (and) lint every day until he recovers.

GLOSS A

As for : " A wound in his nostril, piercing through," it means that the two lips of his wound are soft, opening to the inside of his nose, as one says : " Pierced through " concerning soft things.

CASE FIFTEEN

VI 14–17

PERFORATION OF THE BONE IN THE REGION OF THE MAXILLA AND THE ZYGOMA

TITLE

Instructions concerning a perforation in his cheek.

EXAMINATION

If thou examinest a man having a perforation in his cheek, shouldst thou find there is a swelling, protruding and black, (and) diseased tissue upon his cheek, (conclusion in diagnosis).

DIAGNOSIS

Thou shouldst say concerning him : " One having a perforation in his cheek. An ailment which I will treat."

TREATMENT

Thou shouldst bind it with *ymrw* and treat it afterward [with] grease (and) honey every day until he recovers.

CASE SIXTEEN

VI 17–21

SPLIT OF THE BONE IN THE REGION OF THE MAXILLA AND THE ZYGOMA

Title

Instructions concerning a split in his cheek.

Examination

If thou examinest a man having a split in his cheek, shouldst thou find that there is a swelling, protruding and red, on the outside of that split, (conclusion in diagnosis).

Diagnosis

Thou shouldst say concerning him: "One having a split in his cheek. An ailment which [I] will treat."

Treatment

Thou shouldst bind it with fresh meat the first day. His treatment is sitting until its swelling is reduced (lit. drawn out). Thou shalt treat it afterward [with] grease, honey, (and) lint every day until he recovers.

CASE SEVENTEEN

VII 1–7

COMPOUND COMMINUTED FRACTURE OF THE BONE IN THE REGION OF THE MAXILLA AND THE ZYGOMA

Title

Instructions concerning a smash in his cheek.

Examination

If thou examinest a man having a smash in his cheek, thou shouldst place thy hand on his cheek at the point of that smash. Should it crepitate under thy fingers, while he discharges blood from his nostril, (and) from his ear on the side of him having that injury; (and) at the same time he discharges blood from his mouth, while it is painful when he opens his mouth because of it, (conclusion in diagnosis).

Diagnosis

Thou shouldst say concerning him: "One having a smash in his cheek, while he discharges blood from his nostril, from his ear, (and) from his mouth, (and) he is speechless. An ailment not to be treated."

TREATMENT

Thou shouldst bind with fresh meat the first day. His ⌜relief⌝ is sitting until its swelling is reduced (lit. drawn out). Thou shalt treat it afterward [with] grease, honey, (and) lint every day until he recovers.

CASE EIGHTEEN

VII 7–14

A WOUND IN THE SOFT TISSUE OF THE TEMPLE, THE BONE BEING UNINJURED

TITLE

Instructions concerning a wound in his temple.

EXAMINATION

If thou examinest a man having a wound in his temple, it not having a gash, while that wound penetrates to the bone, thou shouldst palpate his wound. Shouldst thou find his temporal bone uninjured, there being no split, (or) perforation, (or) smash in it, (conclusion in diagnosis).

DIAGNOSIS

Thou shouldst say concerning him: "One having a wound in his temple. An ailment which I will treat."

TREATMENT

Thou shouldst bind it with fresh meat the first day, (and) thou shouldst treat afterward [with] grease, (and) honey every day until he recovers.

GLOSS A

As for: "A wound, not having a gash, while it penetrates to the bone," it means that the wound is contracted, reaching as far as the bone, (though) there is no gash in it. He speaks of (its) narrowness, his wound not having two lips.

GLOSS B

As for: "His *gmꜣ* (temple)," it means the region thereof between the corner of his eye and the ⌜orifice⌝ of his ear, at the end of his mandible.

CASE NINETEEN

VII 14–22

A PERFORATION IN THE TEMPLE

TITLE

Instructions concerning a perforation in his temple.

EXAMINATION

If thou examinest a man having a perforation (*thm*) [in] his temple, a wound being upon it, thou shouldst inspect his wound, saying to him : " Look at thy two shoulders." Should his doing so be painful (even though) his neck turns around (only) a little for him, while his eye on the side of him having that injury is blood-shot, (conclusion follows in diagnosis).

DIAGNOSIS

Thou shouldst say concerning him : " One having a perforation in his temple ⌜-⌝, while he suffers with stiffness in his neck. An ailment which I will treat."

TREATMENT

Thou shouldst put him at his mooring stakes until the period of his injury passes by, (and) thou shouldst treat with grease, honey, (and) lint every day until he recovers.

GLOSS A

As for : " His two eyes are blood-shot," it means that the color of his two eyes is red like the color of *š̌ʾś*-flowers. The " Treatise on What Pertains to the Embalmer " says concerning it : " His two eyes are red ⌜with⌝ disease like an eye at the end of its weakness."

CASE TWENTY

VII 22–VIII 5

A WOUND IN THE TEMPLE PERFORATING THE BONE

TITLE

Instructions concerning a wound in his temple, penetrating to the bone, (and) perforating his temporal bone.

EXAMINATION

If thou examinest a man having a wound in his temple, penetrating to the bone, (and) perforating his temporal bone, while his two eyes are blood-shot, he discharges blood from both his nostrils, and a little drops ; if thou puttest thy fingers on the mouth of that wound (and) he shudder exceedingly ; if thou ask of him concerning his malady and he speak not to thee ; while copious tears fall from both his eyes, so that he thrusts his hand often to his face that he may wipe both his eyes with the back of his hand as a child does, and knows not that he does so, (conclusion follows in diagnosis).

DIAGNOSIS

Thou shouldst say concerning him : " One having a wound in his temple, penetrating to the bone, (and) perforating his temporal bone ; while he discharges blood from both his nostrils, he suffers with stiffness in his neck, (and) he is speechless. An ailment not to be treated."

Treatment

Now when thou findest that man speechless, his ⌜relief⌝ shall be sitting; soften his head with grease, (and) pour ⌜milk⌝ into both his ears.

CASE TWENTY-ONE

VIII 6–9

A SPLIT IN THE TEMPORAL BONE

Title

Instructions concerning a split in his temple.

Examination

If thou examinest a man having a split in his temple, shouldst thou find a swelling protruding on the outside of that split, while he discharges blood from his nostril and from his one ear having that split, (and) it is painful when he hears speech, because of it, (conclusion follows in diagnosis).

Diagnosis

Thou shouldst say concerning him: " One having a split in his temple, while he discharges blood from his nostril and his ear having that injury. An ailment with which I will contend."

Treatment

Thou shouldst put him at his mooring stakes, until thou knowest he has reached a decisive point.

CASE TWENTY-TWO

VIII 9–17

COMPOUND COMMINUTED FRACTURE OF THE TEMPORAL BONE

Title

Instructions concerning a smash in his temple.

Examination

If thou examinest a man having a smash in his temple, thou shouldst place thy thumb upon his chin (and) thy finger upon the end of his ramus, so that the blood will flow from his two nostrils (and) from the interior of his ear having that smash. Cleanse (it) for him with a swab of linen until thou seest its fragments (of bone) in the interior of his ear. If thou callest to him (and) he is speechless (and) cannot speak, (conclusion follows in diagnosis).

Diagnosis

Thou shouldst say concerning him: "One having a smash in his temple; he discharges blood from his two nostrils and from his ear; he is speechless; (and) he suffers with stiffness in his neck. An ailment not to be treated."

Gloss A

As for: "The end of his ramus," it means the end of his mandible. The ramus (*ʾmʿ·t*), the end of it is in his temple just as the claw of an *ʾamʿe*-bird (*ʾmʿ*) grasps an object.

Gloss B

As for: "Thou seest its fragments (*wš·t*) in the interior of his ear," it means that some of the fragments (*wš·t*) of the bone come away to adhere to the swab which was introduced to cleanse the interior of his ear.

Gloss C

As for: "He is speechless," it means that he is silent in sadness, without speaking, like one suffering with ⌜feebleness⌝ (*dgy*) because of something that has entered from outside.

CASE TWENTY-THREE

VIII 18–22

A SLIT IN THE OUTER EAR

Title

Instructions concerning a wound in his ear.

Examination

If thou examinest a man having a wound in his ear, cutting through its flesh, the injury being in the lower part of his ear, (and) confined to the flesh, thou shouldst draw (it) together for him with stitching behind the hollow of his ear.

Diagnosis

Thou shouldst say concerning him: "One having a wound in his ear, cutting through its flesh. An ailment which I will treat."

Treatment

If thou findest the stitching of that wound loose (and) sticking in the two lips of his wound, thou shouldst make for him stiff rolls of linen (and) pad the back of his ear therewith. Thou shouldst treat it afterward [with] grease, honey, (and) lint every day until he recovers.

CASE TWENTY-FOUR

VIII 22–IX 2

A FRACTURE OF THE MANDIBLE

Title

Instructions concerning a fracture in his mandible.

Examination

If thou examinest a man having a fracture in his mandible, thou shouldst place thy hand upon it. Shouldst thou find that fracture crepitating under thy fingers, (conclusion follows in diagnosis).

Diagnosis

Thou shouldst say concerning him: "One having a fracture in his mandible, over which a wound has been inflicted, ⌜- - - -⌝ (and) he has fever from it. An ailment not to be treated."

CASE TWENTY-FIVE

IX 2–6

A DISLOCATION OF THE MANDIBLE

Title

Instructions concerning a dislocation in his mandible.

Examination

If thou examinest a man having a dislocation in his mandible, shouldst thou find his mouth open (and) his mouth cannot close for him, thou shouldst put thy thumb(s) upon the ends of the two rami of the mandible in the inside of his mouth, (and) thy two claws (meaning two groups of fingers) under his chin, (and) thou shouldst cause them to fall back so that they rest in their places.

Diagnosis

Thou shouldst say concerning him: "One having a dislocation in his mandible. An ailment which I will treat."

Treatment

Thou shouldst bind it with *ymrw*, (and) honey every day until he recovers.

CASE TWENTY-SIX

IX 6–13

A WOUND IN THE UPPER LIP

Title

Instructions concerning a wound in his lip.

Examination

If thou examinest a man having a wound in his lip, piercing through to the inside of his mouth, thou shouldst examine his wound as far as the column of his nose. Thou shouldst draw together that wound [with] stitching.

Diagnosis

Thou shouldst say concerning him: "One having a wound in his lip, piercing through to the inside of his mouth. An ailment which I will treat."

Treatment

Now after thou hast stitched it thou shouldst bind it with fresh meat the first day. Thou shouldst treat it afterward [with] grease (and) honey every day until he recovers.

Gloss A

As for: "A wound in his lip, piercing through to the inside of his mouth," it means that the two lips of his wound are soft, opening to the inside of his mouth. One says: "Pierced through" (*yśdb*) concerning soft things.

CASE TWENTY-SEVEN

IX 13–18

A GAPING WOUND IN THE CHIN

Title

Instructions concerning a gaping wound in his chin.

Examination

If thou examinest a man having a gaping wound in his chin, penetrating to the bone, thou shouldst palpate his wound. If thou shouldst find his bone uninjured, not having a split, (or) a perforation in it, (conclusion follows in diagnosis).

Diagnosis

Thou shouldst say concerning him: "One having a gaping wound in his chin, penetrating to the bone. An ailment which I will treat."

Treatment

Thou shouldst apply for him two strips on that gash. Thou shouldst bind it with fresh meat the first day, (and) thou shouldst treat it afterward [with] grease, honey (and) lint every day until he recovers.

CASE TWENTY-EIGHT

IX 18–X 3

A GAPING WOUND IN THE THROAT PENETRATING TO THE GULLET

TITLE

Instructions concerning a wound in his throat.

EXAMINATION

If thou examinest a man having a gaping wound in his throat, piercing through to his gullet; if he drinks water he ⌜chokes⌝ (and) it comes out of the mouth of his wound; it is greatly inflamed, so that he develops fever from it; thou shouldst draw together that wound with stitching.

DIAGNOSIS

Thou shouldst say concerning him: "One having a wound in his throat, piercing through to his gullet. An ailment with which I will contend."

FIRST TREATMENT

Thou shouldst bind it with fresh meat the first day. Thou shouldst treat it afterward [with] grease, honey, (and) lint every day, until he recovers.

SECOND EXAMINATION

If, however, thou findest him continuing to have fever from that wound, (conclusion in following second treatment).

SECOND TREATMENT

Thou shouldst apply for him dry lint in the mouth of his wound, (and) moor (him) at his mooring stakes until he recovers.

CASE TWENTY-NINE

X 3–8

A GAPING WOUND IN A CERVICAL VERTEBRA

TITLE

Instructions concerning a gaping wound in a vertebra of his neck.

EXAMINATION

If thou examinest a man having a gaping wound in a vertebra of his neck, penetrating to the bone, (and) perforating a vertebra of his neck; if thou examinest that wound, (and) he shudders exceedingly, (and) he is unable to look at his two shoulders and his breast, (conclusion follows in diagnosis).

DIAGNOSIS

Thou shouldst say concerning him : " [One having] a wound in his neck, penetrating to the bone, perforating a vertebra of his neck, (and) he suffers with stiffness in his neck. An ailment with which I will contend."

TREATMENT

Thou shouldst bind it with fresh meat the first day. Now afterward moor (him) at his mooring stakes until the period of his injury passes by.

CASE THIRTY

X 8–12

SPRAIN IN A CERVICAL VERTEBRA

TITLE

Instructions concerning a sprain in a vertebra of his neck.

EXAMINATION

If thou examinest a man having a sprain in a vertebra of his neck, thou shouldst say to him : " Look at thy two shoulders and thy breast." When he does so, the seeing possible to him is painful.

DIAGNOSIS

Thou shouldst say concerning him : " One having a sprain in a vertebra of his neck. An ailment which I will treat."

TREATMENT

Thou shouldst bind it with fresh meat the first day. Now afterward thou shouldst treat [with] *ymrw* (and) honey every day until he recovers.

GLOSS A

As for : " A sprain," he is speaking of a rending of two members, (although) it (=each) is (still) in its place.

CASE THIRTY-ONE

X 12–22

DISLOCATION OF A CERVICAL VERTEBRA

TITLE

Instructions concerning a dislocation in a vertebra of [his] neck.

EXAMINATION

If thou examinest a man having a dislocation in a vertebra of his neck, shouldst thou find him unconscious of his two arms (and) his two legs on account of it, while his phallus is erected on account of it, (and) urine drops from his member without his knowing it ; his flesh has received wind ; his two eyes are blood-shot ; it is a dislocation of a vertebra of his neck extending to his backbone which causes him to be unconscious of his two arms (and) his two legs. If, however, the middle vertebra of his neck is dislocated, it is an *emissio seminis* which befalls his phallus.

DIAGNOSIS

Thou shouldst say concerning him : " One having a dislocation in a vertebra of his neck, while he is unconscious of his two legs and his two arms, and his urine dribbles. An ailment not to be treated."

GLOSS A

As for : "A dislocation (*wnḫ*) in a vertebra of his neck," he is speaking of a separation of one vertebra of his neck from another, the flesh which is over it being uninjured ; as one says, " It is *wnḫ*," concerning things which had been joined together, when one has been severed from another.

GLOSS B

As for : " It is an *emissio seminis* which befalls his phallus," (it means) that his phallus is erected (and) has a discharge from the end of his phallus. It is said : " It remains stationary " (*mn sꜣw*), when it cannot sink downward (and) it cannot lift upward.

GLOSS C

As for : " While his urine dribbles," it means that urine drops from his phallus and cannot hold back for him.

CASE THIRTY TWO

XI 1–9

DISPLACEMENT OF A CERVICAL VERTEBRA

TITLE

Instructions concerning a displacement in a vertebra of his neck.

EXAMINATION

If thou examinest a man having a displacement in a vertebra of his neck, whose face is fixed, whose neck cannot turn for him, (and) thou shouldst say to him : " Look at thy breast (and) thy two shoulders," (and) he is unable to turn his face that he may look at his breast (and) his two shoulders, (conclusion follows in diagnosis).

DIAGNOSIS

Thou shouldst say concerning him : " One having a displacement in a vertebra of his neck. An ailment which I will treat."

Treatment

Thou shouldst bind it with fresh meat the first day. Thou shouldst loose his bandages and apply grease to his head ⌜as far as⌝ his neck, (and) thou shouldst bind it with *ymrw*. Thou shouldst treat it afterward [with] honey every day, (and) his ⌜relief⌝ is sitting until he recovers.

Gloss A

As for: "A displacement in a vertebra of his neck," he is speaking concerning a sinking of a vertebra of his neck [to] the interior of his neck, as a foot settles into cultivated ground. It is a penetration downward.

CASE THIRTY-THREE

XI 9–17

A CRUSHED CERVICAL VERTEBRA

Title

Instructions concerning a crushed vertebra in his neck.

Examination

If thou examinest a man having a crushed vertebra in his neck (and) thou findest that one vertebra has fallen into the next one, while he is voiceless and cannot speak; his falling head downward has caused that one vertebra crush into the next one; (and) shouldst thou find that he is unconscious of his two arms and his two legs because of it, (conclusion follows in diagnosis).

Diagnosis

Thou shouldst say concerning him: "One having a crushed vertebra in his neck; he is unconscious of his two arms (and) his two legs, (and) he is speechless. An ailment not to be treated."

Gloss A

As for: "A crushed vertebra in his neck," he is speaking of the fact that one vertebra of his neck has fallen into the next, one penetrating into the other, there being no movement to and fro.

Gloss B

As for: "His falling head downward has caused that one vertebra crush into the next," it means that he has fallen head downward upon his head, driving one vertebra of his neck into the next.

CASE THIRTY-FOUR

XI 17–XII 2

DISLOCATION OF THE TWO CLAVICLES

TITLE

Instructions concerning a dislocation in his two collar-bones.

FIRST EXAMINATION

If thou examinest a man having a dislocation in his two collar-bones, shouldst thou find his two shoulders turned over, (and) the head(s) of his two collar-bones turned toward his face, (conclusion follows in diagnosis).

FIRST DIAGNOSIS

Thou shouldst say concerning him: " One having a dislocation in his two collar-bones. An ailment which I will treat."

FIRST TREATMENT

Thou shouldst cause (them) to fall back, so that they rest in their places. Thou shouldst bind it with stiff rolls of linen; thou shouldst treat it afterward [with] grease (and) honey every day, until he recovers.

SECOND EXAMINATION

If, however, thou shouldst find his two collar-bones having a rupture (of the tissue) over it, penetrating to the interior, (conclusion in second diagnosis).

SECOND DIAGNOSIS

[Thou shouldst say concerning him]: " An ailment which I will treat." (Scribal error, cf. pp. 345 f.)

GLOSS A

As for: " A dislocation in his two collar-bones," it means a displacement of the heads of his sickle-bone(s). Their heads are attached to the upper bone of his breast, extending to his throat, over which is the flesh of his gorget, that is the flesh that is over his bosom. Two canals are under it: one on the right and (one) on the left of his throat (and) of his bosom; they lead to his lungs.

CASE THIRTY-FIVE

XII 3–8

A FRACTURE OF THE CLAVICLE

TITLE

Instructions concerning a break in his collar-bone.

EXAMINATION

If thou examinest a man having a break in his collar-bone, (and) thou shouldst find his collar-bone short and separated from its fellow, (conclusion follows in diagnosis).

DIAGNOSIS

Thou shouldst say concerning him: "One having a break in his collar-bone. An ailment which I will treat."

TREATMENT

Thou shouldst place him prostrate on his back, with something folded between his two shoulder-blades; thou shouldst spread out with his two shoulders in order to stretch apart his collar-bone until that break falls into its place. Thou shouldst make for him two splints of linen, (and) thou shouldst apply one of them both on the inside of his upper arm and the other on the under side of his upper arm. Thou shouldst bind it with *ymrw*, (and) treat it afterward with honey every day, until he recovers.

CASE THIRTY-SIX

XII 8–14

A FRACTURE OF THE HUMERUS

TITLE

Instructions concerning a break in his upper arm.

EXAMINATION

If thou examinest a man having a break in his upper arm, (and) thou findest his upper arm hanging down, separated from its fellow, (conclusion follows in diagnosis).

DIAGNOSIS

Thou shouldst say concerning him: "One having a break in his upper arm. An ailment which I will treat."

TREATMENT

Thou shouldst place him prostrate on his back, with something folded between his two shoulder-blades; thou shouldst spread out with his two shoulders, in order to stretch apart his upper arm until that break falls into its place. Thou shouldst make for him two splints of linen, (and) thou shouldst apply for him one of them both on the inside of his arm, (and) the other of them both on the under side of his arm. Thou shouldst bind it with *ymrw*, (and) treat afterward [with] honey every day until he recovers.

CASE THIRTY-SEVEN

XII 14–21

A FRACTURE OF THE HUMERUS WITH RUPTURE OF OVERLYING SOFT TISSUE

TITLE

Instructions concerning a break in his upper arm, with a wound over it.

FIRST EXAMINATION

If thou examinest a man having a break in his upper arm, over which a wound has been inflicted, (and) thou findest that that break crepitates under thy fingers, (conclusion follows in diagnosis).

FIRST DIAGNOSIS

Thou shouldst say concerning him : " One having a break in his upper arm, over which a wound has been inflicted. An ailment with which I will contend."

FIRST TREATMENT

Thou shouldst make for him two splints of linen ; thou shouldst bind it with *ymrw* ; (and) thou shouldst treat it afterward [with] grease, honey, (and) lint every day until thou knowest that he has reached a decisive point.

SECOND EXAMINATION

If, however, thou findest that wound which is over the break, with blood issuing from it, and piercing through to the interior of his injury, (conclusion in second diagnosis).

SECOND DIAGNOSIS

Thou shouldst say concerning him : " One having a break in his upper arm, over which a wound has been inflicted, piercing through. An ailment not to be treated."

CASE THIRTY-EIGHT

XII 21–XIII 2

A SPLIT IN THE HUMERUS

TITLE

Instructions concerning a split in his upper arm.

EXAMINATION

If thou examinest a man having a split in his upper arm, (and) thou shouldst find the swelling protruding, on the outside of that split, which is in his upper arm, (conclusion follows in diagnosis).

Diagnosis

Thou shouldst say concerning him: "One having a split in his upper arm. An ailment which I will treat."

Treatment

Thou shouldst bind it with *ymrw*; thou shouldst treat it afterward [with] honey every day until he recovers.

CASE THIRTY-NINE

XIII 3–12

TUMORS OR ULCERS IN THE BREAST PERHAPS RESULTING FROM INJURY

Title

Instructions concerning tumors with prominent head in his breast.

Examination

If thou examinest a man having tumors with prominent head in his breast, (and) thou findest that the swellings have spread with pus over his breast, (and) have produced redness, while it is very hot therein, when thy hand touches him, (conclusion follows in diagnosis).

Diagnosis

Thou shouldst say concerning him: "One having tumors with prominent head in his breast, (and) they produce ⌜cists⌝ of pus. An ailment which I will treat with the fire-drill."

Treatment

Thou shouldst burn for him over his breast (and) over those tumors which are on his breast. Thou shouldst treat him with wound treatment. Thou shouldst not prevent its opening of itself, that there may be no *mnḫy·w* in his wound (sore?). Every wound (sore?) that arises in his breast dries up as soon as it opens of itself.

Gloss A

As for: "Tumors with prominent head in his breast," it means that there are swellings spreading over his breast because of his injury; they produce pus and redness on his breast; (as) it is said: "It is like ⌜parti-colored⌝ things," whose product is pus.

CASE FORTY

XIII 12–17

A WOUND IN THE BREAST

Title

Instructions concerning a wound in his breast.

EXAMINATION

If thou examinest a man having a wound in his breast, penetrating to the bone, perforating the *manubrium* of his *sternum*, thou shouldst press the *manubrium* of his *sternum* with thy fingers, (although) he shudders exceedingly, (conclusion follows in diagnosis).

DIAGNOSIS

Thou shouldst say concerning him: "One having a wound in his breast, penetrating to the bone, perforating the *manubrium* of his *sternum*. An ailment which I will treat."

TREATMENT

Thou shouldst bind it with fresh meat the first day; thou shouldst treat it afterward [with] grease, honey, (and) lint every day, until he recovers.

GLOSS A

As for: "The *manubrium* of his *sternum*," (it means) the upper head of his *sternum*; it is like as it were a porcupine.

CASE FORTY-ONE

XIII 18–XIV 16

AN INFECTED OR POSSIBLY NECROTIC WOUND IN THE BREAST

TITLE

Instructions concerning a diseased wound in his breast.

EXAMINATION

If thou examinest a man having a diseased wound in his breast, while that wound is inflamed and a whirl of inflammation continually issues from the mouth of that wound at thy touch; the two lips of that wound are ruddy, while that man continues to be feverish from it; his flesh cannot receive a bandage, that wound cannot take a margin of skin; the ⌜granulation⌝ which is in the mouth of that wound is watery, their surface is hot and secretions drop therefrom in an oily state, (conclusion follows in diagnosis).

DIAGNOSIS

Thou shouldst say concerning him: "One having a diseased wound in [his] breast, it being inflamed, (and) he continues to have fever from it. An ailment which I will treat."

TREATMENT

Thou shalt make for him cool applications for drawing out the inflammation from the mouth of the wound :

a. Leaves of willow,
nbś-tree
ḳsnty.
Apply to it.

b. Leaves of *ymꜣ*-tree,
dung,
ḥny-tꜣ,
ḳsnty.
Apply to it.

Thou shalt make for him applications for drying up the wound :

a. ⌜Powder⌝ of green pigment
wšb·t,
ṯḥn·t
grease.
Triturate ; bind upon it.

b. Northern salt,
ibex grease.
Triturate ; bind upon it.

Thou shalt make for him poultices :

Red *špnn*,
garden tongue,
ḏꜣr·t,
sycamore leaves.
Bind upon it.

If the like befalls in any member, thou shalt treat him according to these instructions.

GLOSS A

As for : " A diseased wound in his breast, inflamed," it means that the wound which is in his breast is sluggish, without closing up ; high fever comes forth from it, its two lips are red, (and) its mouth is open. The " Treatise on What Pertains to a Wound " says concerning it : " It means that there is very great swelling ; (and) ' inflamed ' is said concerning the height " (of the fever).

GLOSS B

As for: " A whirl of inflammation in his wound," it means a whirl of inflammation which circulates through the interior of his entire wound.

GLOSS C

As for: " Its two lips are ruddy," it means that its two lips are red like the color of the *tmś·t*-tree.

GLOSS D

As for: " His flesh cannot receive a bandage," it means that his flesh will not receive the remedies because of the inflammation which is in his flesh.

GLOSS E

As for: " While heat continually issues (*nšw*) from the mouth of his wound at thy touch," (it means) that heat comes forth from his wound at thy touch; as it is said that a thing which has come forth entirely, has issued (*nšw*)."

CASE FORTY-TWO

XIV 16–22

A SPRAIN OF THE STERNO-COSTAL ARTICULATIONS

TITLE

Instructions concerning a sprain in the ribs of his breast.

EXAMINATION

If thou examinest [a man having a sprain in the ribs of his breast], (and) he suffers in the ribs of his breast, not having a dislocation, (and) it is not broken, while that man continues to suffer with it and shudders exceedingly, (conclusion follows in diagnosis).

DIAGNOSIS

Thou shouldst say concerning him: " One having a sprain in the ribs of his breast. An ailment which I will treat."

TREATMENT

Thou shouldst bind it with *ymrw*; thou shouldst treat it afterward [with] honey every day until he recovers.

GLOSS A

As for: " Ribs of his breast," it means the bones of his sternum; being spine(s) like as it were a spine-roast.

CASE FORTY-THREE

XIV 22–XV 6

A DISLOCATION IN THE STERNO-COSTAL ARTICULATIONS

TITLE

Instructions concerning a dislocation of the ribs of his breast.

Examination

If thou examinest a man having a dislocation of the ribs of his breast, (and) thou findest that the ribs of his breast are ⸢projecting⸣, and their heads are ruddy, while that man suffers continually with swellings in his two sides, (conclusion follows in diagnosis).

Diagnosis

Thou shouldst say concerning him: " One having a dislocation in the ribs of his breast. An ailment which I will treat."

Treatment

Thou shouldst bind it with *ymrw*; thou shouldst treat afterward [with] honey every day, until he recovers.

Gloss A

As for: " A dislocation in the ribs of his breast," it means a displacement of the heads of the ribs of his breast (*sternum*), which are fastened to his breast (*sternum*).

Gloss B

As for: " He suffers with swellings in his two sides," it means that he suffers in the articulations thereof in his breast (*sternum*) ⸢spreading⸣ in his two sides.

Gloss C

As for: " His two sides," it means his two flanks.

CASE FORTY-FOUR

XV 6–9

FRACTURED RIBS

Title

Instructions concerning a break in the ribs of his breast.

Examination

If thou examinest a man having a break in the ribs of his breast, over which a wound has been inflicted; (and) thou findest that the ribs of his breast crepitate under thy fingers, (conclusion follows in diagnosis).

Diagnosis

Thou shouldst say concerning him: " One having a break in the ribs of his breast, over which a wound has been inflicted. An ailment not to be treated."

CASE FORTY-FIVE

XV 9–19

BULGING TUMORS ON THE BREAST

TITLE

Instructions concerning bulging tumors on his breast.

EXAMINATION

If thou examinest a man having bulging tumors on his breast, (and) thou findest that [swellings] have spread over his breast; if thou puttest thy hand upon his breast upon these tumors, (and) thou findest them very cool, there being no fever at all therein when thy hand touches him; they have no granulation, they form no fluid, they do not generate secretions of fluid, and they are bulging to thy hand, (conclusion follows in diagnosis).

DIAGNOSIS

Thou shouldst say concerning him: "One having bulging tumors. An ailment with which I will contend."

TREATMENT

There is no ⌈treatment⌉. If thou findest bulging tumors in any member of a man, thou shalt treat him according to these directions.

GLOSS A

As for: "Bulging tumors on his breast," it means the existence of swellings on his breast, large, spreading and hard; touching them is like touching a ball of wrappings; the comparison is to a green *hemat*-fruit, which is hard and cool under thy hand, like touching those swellings which are on his breast.

CASE FORTY-SIX

XV 20–XVI 16

AN ABSCESS WITH PROMINENT HEAD ON THE BREAST

TITLE

Instructions concerning an abscess with prominent head in his breast.

EXAMINATION

If thou examinest a man having an abscess with prominent head in his breast, (and) thou findest a very large swelling protruding on his breast, oily, like fluid under thy hand, while they produce some clamminess of the surface, (and) their faces have no ruddiness, (conclusion follows in diagnosis).

DIAGNOSIS

Thou shouldst say concerning him: "One having an abscess with prominent head in his breast. An ailment which I will treat with cold applications to that abscess which is in his breast."

TREATMENT

a. *Šḫ·t*-fruit,
ntr·t,
ḳsnty,
Triturate, bind upon it.

b. Fruit of *šs*,
ḳsnty,
mason's mortar,
water,
Triturate, bind upon it.

If there is resistance to these cooling applications, thou shouldst avoid those remedies until all fluid which is in the abscess with a head exudes.

Thou shouldst treat him with wound-treatment, with applications for drawing out the inflammation from the mouth of the wound (sore ?) in his breast:

Leaves of acacia,
sycamore,
juice of *ym*ʾ-leaves,
ox dung,
*ḥny-t*ʾ,
Bind upon it.

Thou shouldst make for him astringents, in his breast:

a. ⌈Powder⌉ of green pigment,
*ḏ*ʾ*r·t* of cedar,
ointment fat,
northern salt,
ibex grease.
Bind upon it.

Thou shouldst make for him poultices:

Red *špnn*,
sycamore.
Triturate, apply to it.

Gloss A

As for: "An abscess with prominent head in his breast," it means that there is a large swelling due to the injury which is in his breast, soft like a fluid under the hand.

Gloss B

As for: "Clamminess of their surface," it means their skin is not hot.

Gloss C

As for: "There is no ruddiness upon it," it means that there is no redness upon it.

CASE FORTY-SEVEN

XVI 16–XVII 15

A GAPING WOUND IN THE SHOULDER

Title

Instructions concerning a gaping wound in his shoulder.

First Examination

If thou examinest a man having a gaping wound in his shoulder, its flesh being laid back and its sides separated, while he suffers with swelling (in) his shoulder blade, thou shouldst palpate his wound. Shouldst thou find its gash separated from ⌜-⌝ its sides in his wound, as a roll of linen is unrolled, (and) it is painful when he raises his arm on account of it, thou shouldst draw together for him his gash with stitching.

First Diagnosis

Thou shouldst say concerning him: "One having a gaping wound in his shoulder, its flesh being laid back and its sides separated, while he suffers with swelling in his shoulder blade. An ailment which I will treat."

First Treatment

Thou shouldst bind it with fresh meat the first day.

Second Examination and Treatment

If thou findest that wound open and its stitching loose, thou shouldst draw together for him its gash with two strips of linen over that gash; thou shouldst treat it afterward [with] grease, honey, (and) lint every day until he recovers.

If thou findest a wound, its flesh laid back, its sides separated, in any member of a man, thou shouldst treat it according to these directions.

Third Examination

If, however, thou findest that his flesh has developed inflammation from that wound which is in his shoulder, while that wound is inflamed, open, and its stitching loose, thou shouldst lay thy hand upon it. Shouldst thou find inflammation issuing from the mouth of his wound at thy touch, and secretions discharging therefrom are cool like *wenesh*-juice, (conclusion follows in second diagnosis).

DIAGNOSIS FOLLOWING THIRD EXAMINATION

Thou shouldst say concerning him: "One having a gaping wound in his shoulder, it being inflamed, and he continues to have fever from it. An ailment with which I will contend."

FOURTH EXAMINATION

If then, thou findest that man continuing to have fever, while that wound is inflamed, (conclusion in following treatment).

TREATMENT FOLLOWING FOURTH EXAMINATION

Thou shalt not bind it; thou shalt moor (him) at his mooring stakes, until the period of his injury passes by.

FIFTH EXAMINATION

If, however, his fever abates and the inflammation in the mouth of his wound dissipates entirely, (conclusion in following treatment).

TREATMENT FOLLOWING FIFTH EXAMINATION

Thou shouldst treat him afterward [with] grease, honey, (and) lint every day, until he recovers.

CASE FORTY-EIGHT

XVII 15–19

A SPRAIN IN A SPINAL VERTEBRA (INCOMPLETE)

TITLE

Instructions concerning a sprain of a vertebra [in] his spinal column.

EXAMINATION

If thou examinest [a man having] a sprain in a vertebra of his spinal column, thou shouldst say to him: "Extend now thy two legs (and) contract them both (again)." When he extends them both he contracts them both immediately because of the pain he causes in the vertebra of his spinal column in which he suffers.

DIAGNOSIS

Thou shouldst say concerning him: "One having a sprain in a vertebra of his spinal column. An ailment which I will treat."

TREATMENT

Thou shouldst place him prostrate on his back; thou shouldst make for him . . . .

PART II

THE INCANTATIONS AND RECIPES

(THE VERSO)

THE INCANTATIONS AND RECIPES

(The Verso)

SPECIAL INTRODUCTION

The group of texts to which we have prefixed the title: "The Incantations and Recipes" has no internal connection whatever with the Surgical Treatise. These texts are like stray and disconnected memoranda which a modern reader might write on the fly-leaf of a book. In the first place they are physically separated from the Surgical Treatise by two things: (1) a blank space at the end of Case 48, with which the Surgical Treatise stops; (2) by the fact that they occupy four and a half columns *on the back* of the papyrus which bears the Surgical Treatise *on the front.* Furthermore, they are in subject-matter a totally different body of writings as a glance at the table of contents will demonstrate. Their method, their purpose, and their conception of disease are identical with those of the well-known recipe papyri like Papyrus Ebers or Hearst, and in sharp contrast with that of the Surgical Treatise. They form a magical hodge-podge, without plan or arrangement, and we must regard these incantations and recipes on the verso of the Edwin Smith Papyrus as in no conceivable respect a continuation of the Surgical Treatise. This obvious fact is emphasized here, even at the risk of being repetitious, because some readers of the present writer's preliminary reports on the new papyrus seem to have gained the impression that the group of magical texts on the back form part of the Surgical Treatise.

As already remarked in the general introduction, the same scribe who wrote the seventeen columns of the Surgical Treatise on the front of the papyrus abruptly abandoned the copying of that important document in the middle of a case, and, much to our regret, never completed the copy. Presumably at a later date, he turned over the roll, then not less than sixteen feet long, and leaving a blank and unwritten space at the end of the front, and a second such space at the beginning of the back, he began to write on the back the miscellaneous group of incantations and recipes, a list of which is as follows:

Eight Incantations against Pest:

This list at once discloses the fact that these writings on the back do not form an organized or coherent treatise like that on the front. A more grotesquely incoherent hodge-podge could hardly be conceived. Of the four and a half columns, nearly three are devoted to incantations exorcising some form of annual epidemic or pest, and to these the copyist appends a column and a half containing five recipes: one for female troubles, three for improving the complexion, and the fifth for some ailment of the anus.

The animistic conception of disease is interestingly illustrated. The bearers of the pest are not only malignant divinities, genii, and demons of disease, but also the disembodied dead, male and female, both human and animal. It is of interest, and possibly of scientific importance to note that the pest might be borne by other agencies, notably the wind. We have here doubtless the earliest occurrence of the belief in pest-laden winds. Again we find an entire incantation devoted to the unfortunate who has accidently swallowed a fly.

In view of modern knowledge of the fly as a carrier of diseases like dysentery, this early example of similar experience is notable. Similarly we observe that the pest must be exorcised from food, bedding, and household articles. The process is so strikingly suggestive of the modern practice of disinfection, that the reader should be warned against any such conc usion. It is barely possible that the ancient Egyptian physicians had noticed that this unidentified disease had been communicated through bedding or food, but the method of rendering these things innocuous, as prescribed on the back of our papyrus, is magical incantation pure and simple, and has not the remotest resemblance to the modern processes of disinfection. Microscopic life was entirely unknown to medical practice throughout the ancient world, and must have remained unknown until the introduction of lenses and the microscope in the Seventeenth Century of our era.

It is unnecessary to devote further space to the discussion of the five recipes occupying the last two columns of the verso. The " Recipe for Transforming an Old Man into a Youth " (XXI 9–XXII 10) is a very interesting example of the apothecary's art, furnishing, as it does, full directions how to make an aqueous solid extract; but as a remedy it proves to be nothing more than a face paste believed to be efficacious in removing wrinkles and other facial evidences of old age.

These last two recipes, copied by a different scribe from the one who copied the Surgical Papyrus and all the preceding material on the verso, bear on the question of the date of our copy. The writing of this latter scribe is small, crabbed, and ungraceful. It makes the impression of being later than the time of the first scribe. It is possible that our roll, bearing all that the first scribe had written (I 1–XXI 8) was in use for a generation before the second scribe added the last two recipes (XXI 9–XXII 14). The final owner or user, for whom the second scribe copied the last two recipes, may have been contemporary with the scribe of Papyrus Ebers. He may indeed have been the owner both of our document and Papyrus Ebers, thus making it quite possible that the two papyri were found together by the modern natives, and brought to Edwin Smith together.

Regarding the age of these incantations and recipes on the verso, there is little to establish a precise date. The section XVIII 1 to XXI 8 shows some indications of an earlier date than our copy, but the last two recipes, written by the second scribe, are probably not equally old.

TRANSLATION AND COMMENTARY

EIGHT INCANTATIONS AGAINST PEST

XVIII 1–XX 12

THESE interesting exorcisms are directed against some form of annually recurring disease called " the pest of the year " or even merely " this year," an epidemic which cannot be identified. Various divinities and disease demons are regarded as bearing this pest,—and the charms are accordingly addressed to these maligant beings. The most prominent among these is Sekhmet, a goddess often associated with war and destruction. In one charm the hostile beings are enumerated as men, gods, spirits, and the dead (XVIII 18). Again they are summarized as " every male spirit, every female spirit, every male dead, every female dead, the form of every animal, the one (fem.) which the crocodile has taken, the one which the serpent has stung, the one which has perished by the knife, (or) the one who has died in his bed." It will be seen that the dead, both of men and animals, occupy a prominent place among malignant beings who afflict the living. The charms operate not merely to banish the hostile powers, but also to call in beneficient divinities and spirits to aid in the protection of the patient. All these divinities, spirits, genii, or demons are introduced with allusions, usually very obscure, to incidents in the sacred myths now largely lost, producing a magical hocus-pocus difficult to understand at best, and sometimes quite unintelligible.

The manner of uttering these charms is carefully prescribed and was evidently considered important, for five of the incantations are followed by full directions for pronouncing them in connection with certain acts and equipment. Thus the man to be protected by the first incantation must wear two vulture feathers while the charm is pronounced over him ; the beneficiary of the second incantation must pronounce it himself while carrying a piece of *des*-wood around the outside of his house ; again everything in a man's house may be protected from pest if he says the seventh incantation, while he has before him a *nefret*-flower, bound with a strip of linen to a piece of *des*-wood, which he passes over the food, the bed, and other objects in the house.

The bearers of the pest are any of the malicious beings listed above, as those against which the exorcisms are employed ; but there may also be some other sources. It is interesting to note that the bearer of the pest may be the wind (XVIII 8–9 ; and 12–13). It enters at the mouth and throat, and to prevent this a man should wear about his neck a band of linen bearing written upon it the words of the fifth incantation. Even asses, " the *besbes*-goose," and " the green-breasted goose " may enter his throat unless prevented by this charm (XIX 12). Again the bearer of the pest is a fly which a man may accidentally swallow, and the sixth incantation is entirely devoted to such a case. It raises an interesting question of possible knowledge of the fact that the fly is a bearer of disease. In this connection it is important to observe that the seventh charm is directed against the possible lurking of the pest in food, bedding, or any of the articles in the house.

Title of the First Incantation

XVIII 1

XVIII 1

Translation

Incantation for exorcising the wind of the pest of the year.

Commentary

" The pest of the year " presumably designates an annual epidemic of some kind. There is no indication of the character of the disease anywhere in the following text. It is characteristic of these magical exorcisms, which are both exorcisms and recipes, that there should be no proper examination, and no conclusions regarding the seat and the nature of the disease. The word  *y'd·t*, rendered above as " pest," has been touched upon by Gardiner in his *Admonitions of an Egyptian Sage* (p. 25), where the common application of the word as a term of opprobrium is mentioned, and especially the frequent occurrence of the term " *y'd·t* of the year " in magical texts. The medical significance of *y'd·t* still remains to be cleared up. The genitive *rnp·t* " year," apparently adjectival, would be more in accordance with common usage if joined by the genitive *n·t* "of;" but the direct genitive does not preclude understanding *rnp·t* as adjectival in force, and equivalent to " annual."

First Incantation

XVIII 1–8

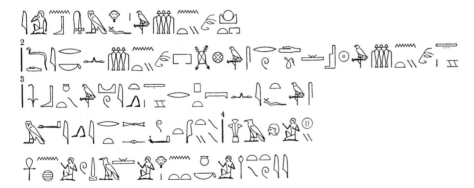

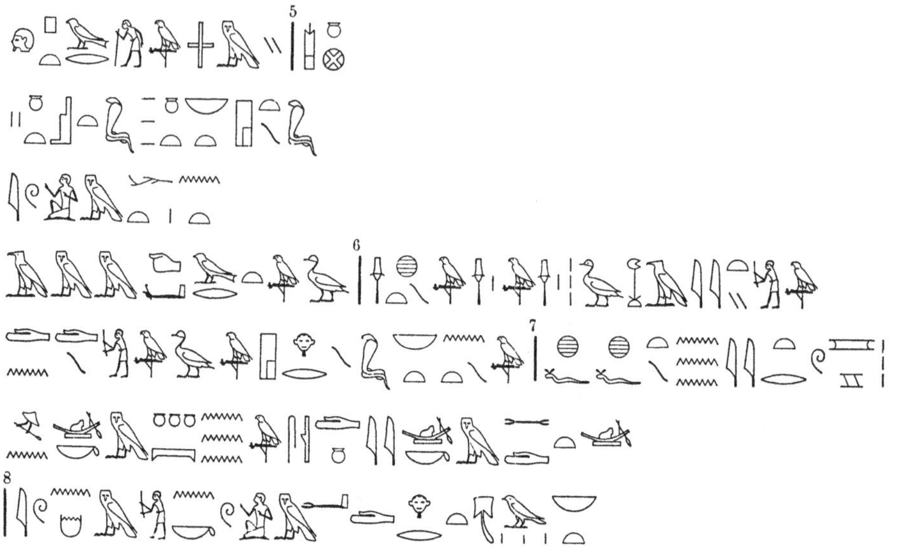

Translation

O Flame-in-His-Face! Presider over the horizon, speak thou to the chief of the Hemesut-house, who makes Osiris, first of the land, to flourish. O Nekhbet, lifting the earth to the sky for her father, come thou, bind the two feathers around me, around me, that I may live and flourish because I possess this White One. The first is the Great One dwelling in Heliopolis; the second is Isis; the third is Nephthys; while I am subject to thee (fem.).

O Seizer-of-the-Great-One, son of Sekhmet, mightiest of the mighty, son of the Disease-Demon, Dened, son of Hathor, mistress of the crown (*nt*), and flooder of the streams; when thou voyagest in the Celestial Ocean, when thou sailest in the morning barque, thou hast saved me from every sickness.

Commentary

The incantation consists of adjurations addressed to hostile demons, as well as to protecting divinities, and filled with obscure epithets and allusions.

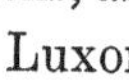 *Ḥmś·wt* are personifications of graces and good qualities who appear at royal births, as in the birth scenes of Hatshepsut at Deir el-Bahari, and of Amenhotep III at Luxor. Isis and Nephthys are familiar as beneficent goddesses, but Sekhmet is a goddess of terror and destruction, and throughout these incantations is closely connected with the pest.

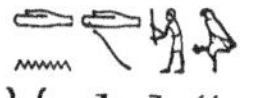 *Dnd* is the name of a demon doubtless derived from the old word  *ḏnd*, "anger, wrath" (Pyr. 63 b and 2072 d). Compare also *ḏnḏn* and *dndn*; likewise the barque called *Ḏnd-ḏndrw*. 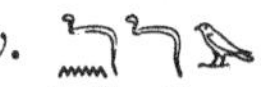 *dnḏ* is an ailment in Pap. Ebers 102, 7 (compare also *ibid.* 102, 10). As a god *Dnd* appears as one of the four ram-headed

divinities in the Book of the Portals, 12th hour, upper row (Ramses VI, Tausert, Ramses III, but not Seti II). Written *Dndn* this god appears as early as the Pyramid Texts (200 d), and as *Dndnw*, Pyr. 1254 b. In late times he still survives as [hieroglyphs] or [hieroglyphs] *Dndn* in Edfu and Dendera (Rochem. I, p. 525 and II, p. 25 ; Mariette, *Dendérah*, I 28).

[hieroglyphs] *ḫ'y·ty*, "Disease-Demon," is evidently a derivative from [hieroglyphs] *ḫ'y·t*, "disease," but seems to be a rather rare word. It appears in the plural in the Book of the Dead, Chapter CXLIX (ed. Budge, 1898, Text, p. 372), as a designation of malignant demons.

[hieroglyphs] *ḫfḫf·t*, "flooder," or "flooding" (fem.) is rare. See Pyr. 295 c where it is parallel with [hieroglyphs]. Compare also Pyr. 298 a.

[hieroglyphs] *dḫr·t*, "sickness," is common in the medical papyri. See Pap. Hearst IX 10; Pap. Ebers 41, 20; 52, 20; 89, 16; 89, 18; 101, 1–2 (twice); 100, 18–20 where it is explained in a gloss. A charm against snake-poison adjures the vessels of the body not to take up (*šsp*) [hieroglyphs] "the excretion of sickness" (Pap. Turin, ed. Pleyte-Rossi, 131, l. 11, magical text of the Empire, copied by Gardiner, ll. 10–11).

Conclusion of the First Incantation

XVIII 8–9

Translation

Incantation against this year, with the breath of every evil wind.
Horus, Horus, healthy despite Sekhmet, is around all my flesh for life.

Commentary

The point of this conclusion is of course a mythological reference to the success of the youthful Horus against his enemies. The flesh of the speaker of the charm is perhaps parallel with the flesh of Osiris, the father of Horus, who shielded his father's body. The same charm is found again in XIX 9 and XX 11.

This final charm introduced at the end is preceded by what appears to be a concluding title, such as are so commonly found at the end of a charm in the Coffin Texts. The determinative of *nf·t* "breath," is incorrectly written, by habit of the scribe, with following *w*, as in the common word *ṯ'w* "wind," always written with the sail and *w*. See following context.

Directions for Pronouncing the First Incantation

XVIII 9–11

Translation

Speak the words over two vulture feathers, with which a man has covered himself, placed as his protection in every place where he goes. It is a protection against the year, expelling sickness in the year of pest.

Commentary

The two feathers here used in pronouncing the spell are of course applied to the man to be protected, while uttering the passage (XVIII 3–4) of the spell referring to the two feathers. It would seem that any person not yet suffering from disease, who assumes the two feathers, and pronounces the incantation, is assured of protection against the pest.

Title of the Second Incantation

XVIII 11–12

Translation

Another (incantation) for exorcising the plague-bearing wind, the demons of disease, the malignant spirits, messengers of Sekhmet.

Commentary

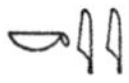 *ky*, "another," is a common introduction in the medical papyri for a new recipe for the same purpose as the last. It passed on into Greek treatises as ἄλλως

or ἄλλο. See Wessely's publication of the Greek magical Papyri in Paris and London in *Denkschriften der Wiener Akademie*, 1888. We have in this fact a clear indication of the use of the old Egyptian papyri in Greek times.

nḏs·tyw, "malignant spirits," is a rare word of vague meaning not closely determined. I find no other example of its appearance outside of our papyrus, except in a copy of a Karnak inscription made by Sethe for the Berlin *Wörterbuch*, in a text of Graeco-Roman age, which suggests that *nḏs·tyw* are genii or semi-divine beings of some kind (*Wörterbuch* copies by Sethe, 4, 44).

Second Incantation

XVIII 13–15

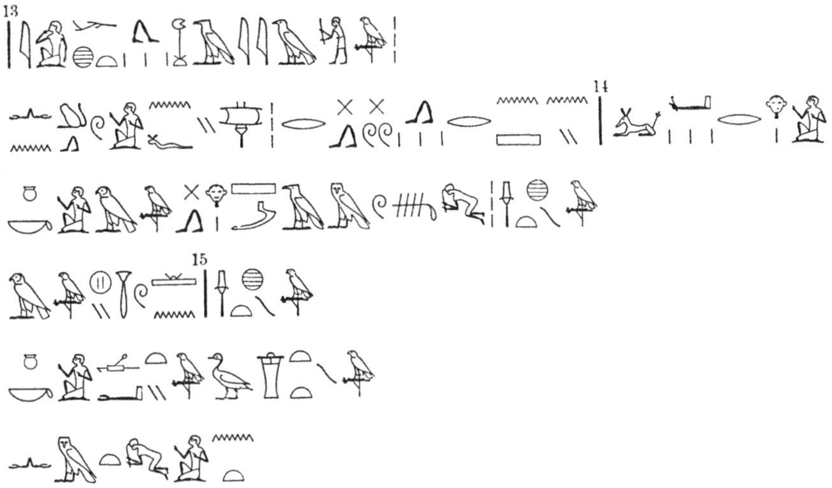

Translation

Withdraw, ye disease demons. The wind shall not reach me, that those who pass by may pass by to work disaster against me. I am Horus who passes by the diseased ones of Sekhmet, (even) Horus, Horus, healthy despite Sekhmet. I am the unique one, son of Bastet. I die not through thee (fem.)

Commentary

In these incantations, " those who pass by " is a designation of all the hostile, disease-bearing demons or beings against whom the charms are directed. The picture seems to be that these malignant spirits pass by on the wind, as if borne by it. We notice that this incantation is to be uttered while the man pronouncing it goes around the *outside* of " his house," thus evidently preventing the dangerous winds from entering the house. We have here doubtless the earliest occurrence of the notion of pestilential or disease-bearing winds.

Directions for Pronouncing the Second Incantation

XVIII 15–16

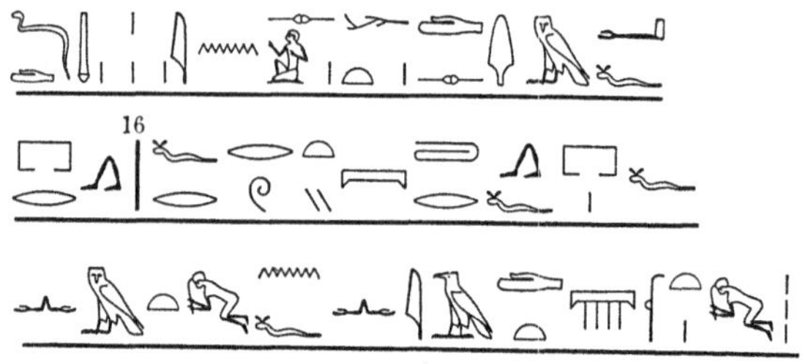

Translation

Let the words be spoken by a man having a stick of *des*-wood in his hand, while he comes forth into the open and goes around his house. He cannot die by the pest of the year.

Commentary

The alleged power of the incantation is doubtless due to the unidentifiable wood which the man pronouncing the charm carries in his hand as he makes the circuit of his house, walking around the *outside,* and thus preventing the winds from entering.

Title of the Third Incantation

XVIII 17

Translation

Another protection against the pest of the year.

Third Incantation

XVIII 17–19

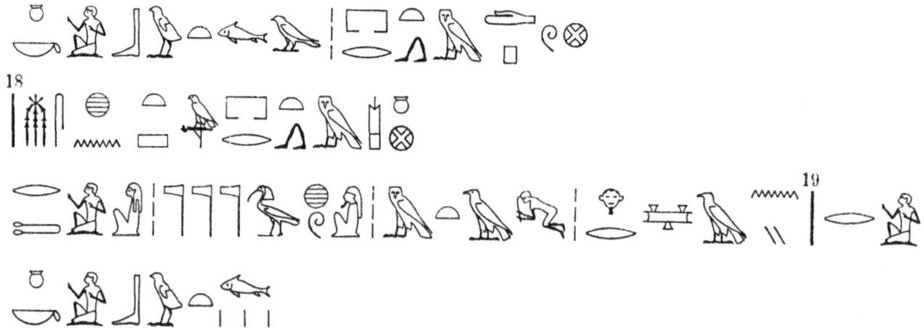

Translation

I am the abomination that came forth out of Buto. O Meskhenet, that came forth out of Heliopolis; O men, O gods, O spirits, O dead, be ye far from me. I am the abomination.

Commentary

The protection consists in becoming something abhorred which the spirits dare not approach. The form *ḥr-tywny*, a plural pseudo-participle, is found again in the singular with the same meaning in the next charm (XIX 2). Its optative force is unusual. Gardiner calls my attention to its similar use in *Mutter und Kind* (8, 6–8, several times).

Fourth Incantation

XVIII 19–XIX 2

Translation

Another (incantation). I am the healthy one in the way of the passer by. Shall I be smitten, while I am healthy? I have seen the great disaster. O this fever, do not assail me, (for) I am the one who has come forth out of the disaster. Be thou far from me.

Commentary

A charm the effectiveness of which consists in its asseverations of safety and escape, a common device in Egyptian magic.

Fifth Incantation

XIX 2–9

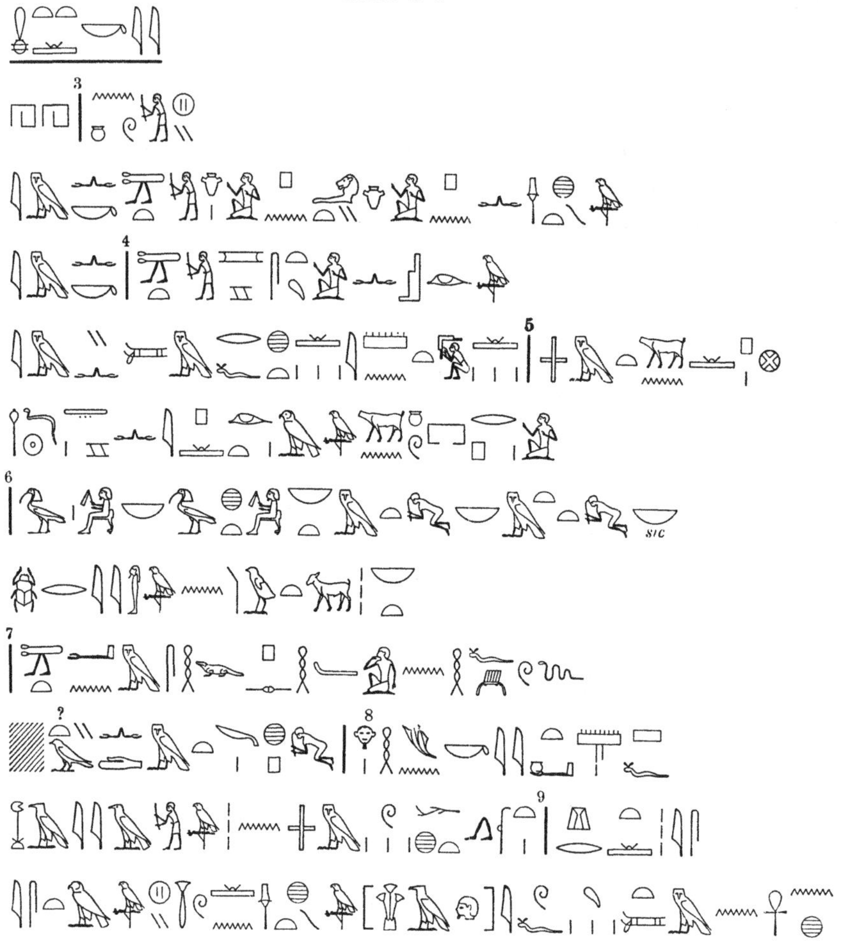

Translation

Copy of another (incantation). O Jubilation, Jubilation, take not this my heart, nor this my breast for Sekhmet. Take not my liver for Osiris, in order that the hidden things that are in Buto may not, shall not enter into my seat on the morning of counting the Horus-eye, even every male spirit, every female spirit, every male dead, every female dead, the form of every animal, the one (fem.) which the crocodile has taken, the one (masc.) which the serpent has stung, the one which has ⌜perished⌝ by the knife, (or) the one who has died in his bed. Ye demons of disease, of the followers of the year and its yield, lo, Horus, even Horus, healthy despite Sekhmet, is [around] all my flesh for life.

Commentary

The force of the charm seems to be exerted against a group of the dead, both men and animals residing in Buto, and who are first called, therefore, " the hidden things that are in Buto," as a kind of group designation followed by a list of the members of the group. They belong in the innermost center of Buto, for the unusual phrase , literally " dwelling in the inside of," must have some special significance here.

The two negatives together, , are probably a double negative for the sake of emphasis ; the verb to which they most probably belong is , where we would expect *ḫn*, "approach." literally means "my mat," here used for " my seat." The verb before " knife " has been smeared by the scribe's finger and is illegible ; but the context and parallelism show clearly that it must mean something like " perish." Presumably the slaughter of an animal with the knife is the form of death here intended. *ḫp*, rendered above " die," is doubtless connected with the verb *ḫpy*, " to go " or " depart." The final statement of the charm is found also in XVIII 9 and XX 11, and from these parallels we are able to supply the word *ḥ᾽*, " around," omitted by error of the scribe.

Directions for Pronouncing the Fifth Incantation

XIX 9–14

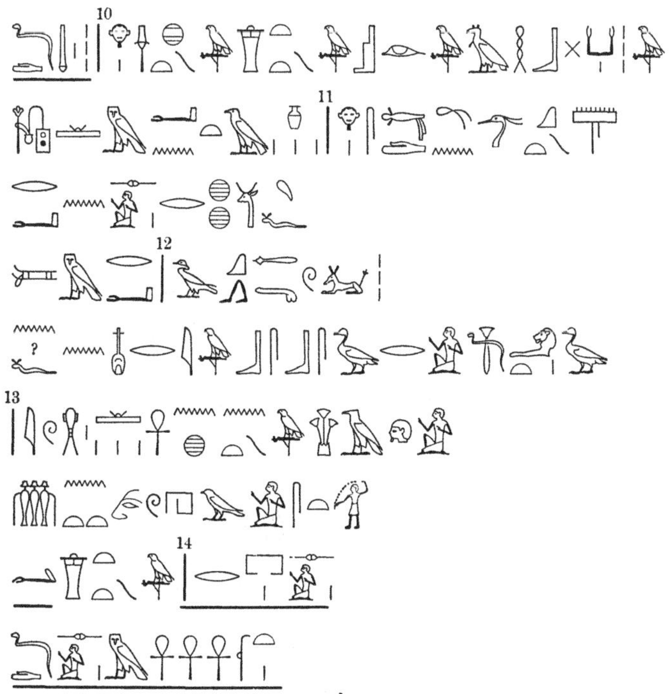

Translation

Speak the words over (images of) Sekhmet, Bastet, Osiris, and Neheb-kau, written with frankincense on a band of fine linen and attached to a man at his throat. It will prevent asses from entering, - - the *besbes*-goose to me, and the green-breasted goose. The protection of the life of Neit is around me, (even of) her who is over the escaped of the sower. Bastet is repelled from the house of a man. A man shall say (it) at the life of the year.

Commentary

The mention of the asses and the geese is of course in harmony with the inclusion of the animals in the charm in l. 6. There is apparently corruption of the text in the passage  which remains unintelligible. The *besbes*-goose is rare and found only in the mastaba tomb of Manofer (Sakkara Tomb 17, Lepsius, *Denkmäler,* II 70 = Berlin 1108). It is evidently an old word. The "green-breast" is better known and occurs in the Middle Kingdom a number of times, and once in the Empire. Neither variety can be identified with exactness. The obscure epithet after Neit (or should we render "crown" as in XVIII 6?) is quite unintelligible. Bastet as an unfriendly goddess is also found in XIX 20. The "life of the year" perhaps means the "yield of the year," that is, at harvest time; but this is uncertain.

Title of the Sixth Incantation

XIX 14

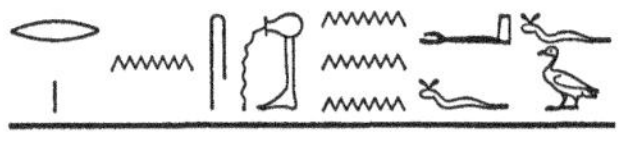

Translation

Incantation for cleansing a fly.

Commentary

Although not clear in this title, the case is one of a man who accidentally swallowed a fly, thought to be a bearer of disease, here presumably the pest.

Sixth Incantation

XIX 14–18

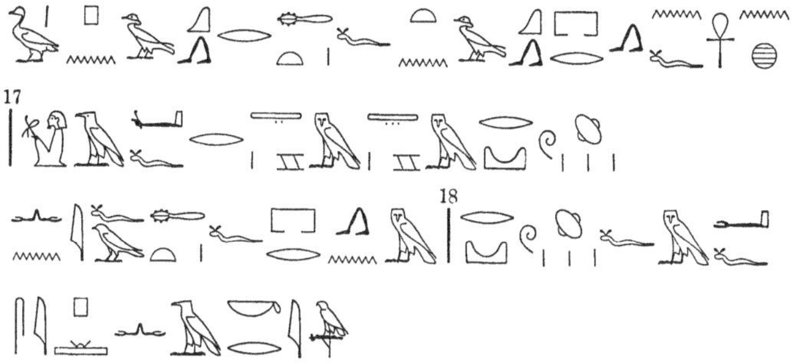

Translation

The mouth of this man who is under my fingers, and so forth, is the mouth of a ⌈hungry⌉ calf, when he comes forth from his mother's womb. This insect which has entered into this his belly, (although) he has entered, shall come forth alive, issuing to the ground as earth or as excrement, without injuring his belly, (but) coming forth as his excrement from him, having been assigned to Akeru.

Commentary

As literally stated in the title the charm is for cleansing the fly, not for cleansing the man of the fly. Nevertheless the first statement of the incantation is that the mouth of the man who has swallowed the fly is as the mouth of a new-born calf, that is, entirely clean. It is evidently considered highly important that the stomach and intestines should be relieved of the fly.

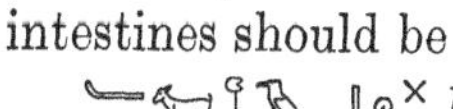 *bḥs ḥ'bw,* rendered above "⌈hungry⌉ calf" is a rare term of great age. It is known elsewhere only in the Pyramid Texts (225 b). The difficulty is the word *ḥ'bw,* which is of uncertain meaning. Important for our passage is a similar statement in the Pyramid Texts. The dead king is purified, and one says to him:  "Thy mouth is the mouth of a milk-calf on the day on which he is born" (Pyr. 27 d). The parallelism would suggest that *ḥ'bw* might possibly mean "sucking" or the like. "Akeru" is an earth-god, to whom the excrement is here consigned.

Title of the Seventh Incantation

XIX 18–19

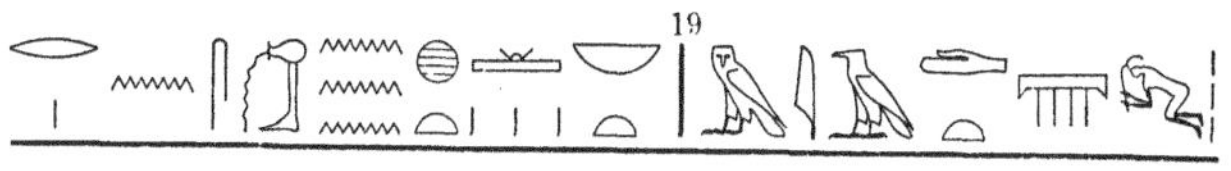

Translation

Incantation for cleansing everything from pest.

Seventh Incantation

XIX 19–XX 5

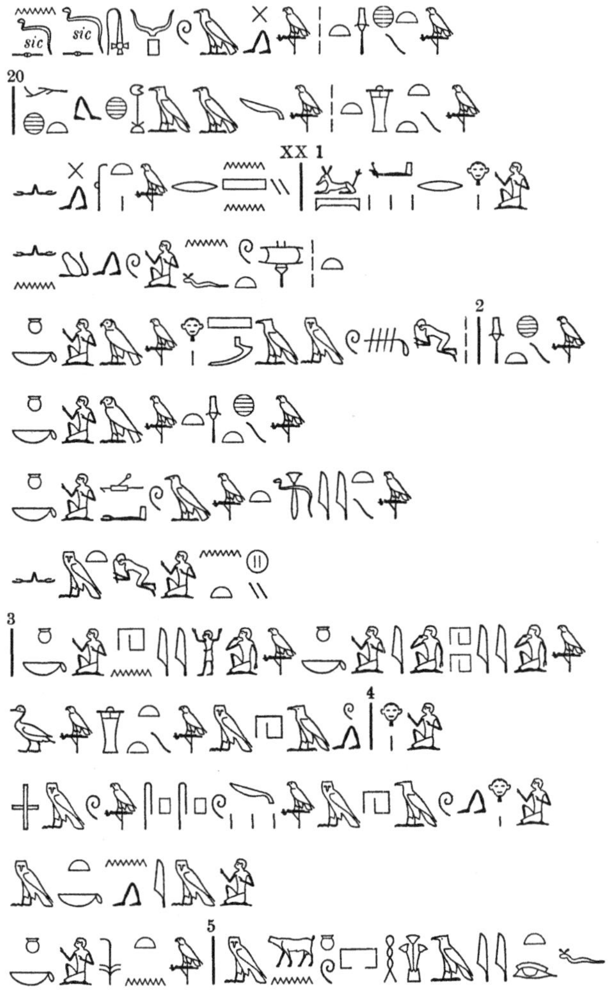

Translation

Thy messengers are consumed, O Sekhmet; thy demons of disease retreat, O Bastet. The Year does not pass by to work disaster against me. Thy breath does not reach me. I am Horus over the diseased ones of Sekhmet, I am thy Horus, O Sekhmet; I am thy unique one, O Buto. I die not by thee; I die not by thee. I am the rejoicing one, I am the jubilating one. O son of Bastet, descend not upon me; O Dweller in the *Sepsepu*, approach me not, draw not near me. I am the king in the midst of his ⌜shelter⌝.

Commentary

The charm is full of obscure allusions. *nḏsḏs*, probably meaning to "burn, consume," is a rare word occurring elsewhere seemingly only in the Book of the Dead, ed. Naville, 78, 32. The obscure "*sepsepu*" may possibly be connected with the Ptolemaic word *spsp*, "to rob" or similar. The older word *špšp*, "to tousle, disarrange, pull, drag" (Carter-Newberry, *Tomb of Thoutmôsis*, IV, 46042) makes little or no sense here. The last word, *ḥ'y·t*, rendered with uncertainty "⌜shelter⌝," is unknown elsewhere.

Directions for Pronouncing the Seventh Incantation

XX 5–8

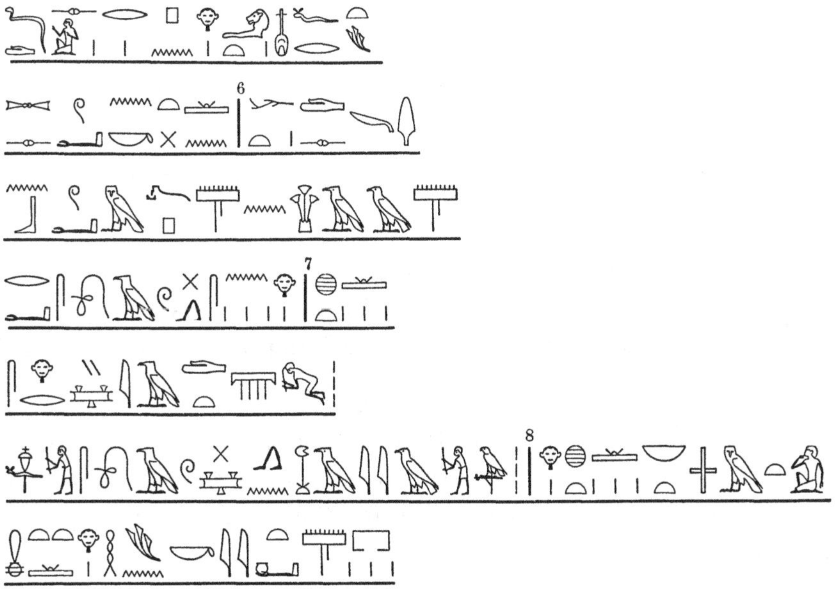

Translation

Let a man say this incantation before a *nefret*-flower, bound to a piece of *des*-wood, and tied with a strip of linen. Let them be passed over the things; the pest will be exorcised, (and) the passage of the disease-demons by everything that is eaten, likewise by the beds, will be prevented.

Commentary

nfr·t is a still unidentified flower, and *des*-wood is likewise uncertain. The latter was used against the pest in the Second Incantation (XVIII 15). *ḥ'·tyw* is commonly considered to mean "clothing," as in the Pyramid Texts (737 b) or later, Gayet, *Le Temple de Louxor*, pl. 12, 4 (Eighteenth Dynasty) and Dümichen, *Historische Inschriften*, II 36 d (Medinet Habu, Eighteenth Dynasty); but it seems obvious that we must render linen in our incantation.

Eighth Incantation

XX 8–11

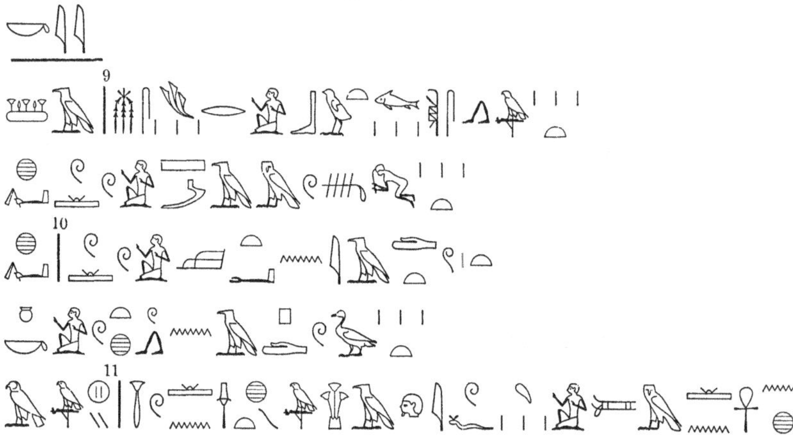

Translation

Another (incantation). A *shames*-flower is on me, the abomination of thy followers. Thy diseased ones avoid me, the stretching of thy snare avoids me; I am the escaped one of thy birds. Horus, Horus, healthy despite Sekhmet, is around all my flesh for life.

Commentary

The identity of the  *š'mś* or "*shames*-flower" is unknown. It is evidently some flower supposed to be effective in warding off pest, and may have been some marsh flower growing like a thicket and thus furnishing a refuge for birds in escaping the snare of the fowler.

Directions for Pronouncing the Eighth Incantation

XX 11–12

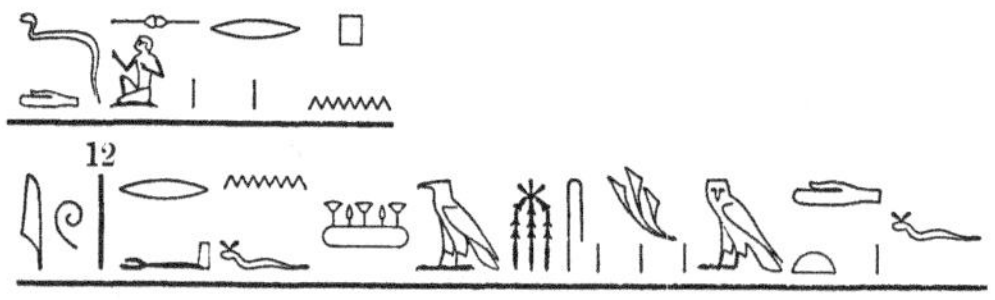

Translation

Let a man say this incantation when a *shames*-flower has been given to him in his hand.

Commentary

This is in accordance with the statement in the charm, "A *shames*-flower is on me." This eighth incantation concludes the series employed in exorcising the pest. The following recipe is for a female trouble and has no connection with the pest series.

RECIPE FOR FEMALE TROUBLES

XX 13–XXI 3

This case, like those in the latter part of Papyrus Ebers, begins with an examination. No title is prefixed. The diagnosis clearly indicates suspension or interruption of the menses. The treatment consists of three recipes: one internal and two external. The composition of the internal remedy is too uncertain to permit any opinion regarding its efficacy; while the ointments applied externally were quite obviously of no value. The final fumigation was rather a matter of toilet than of medical treatment.

EXAMINATION

XX 13–14

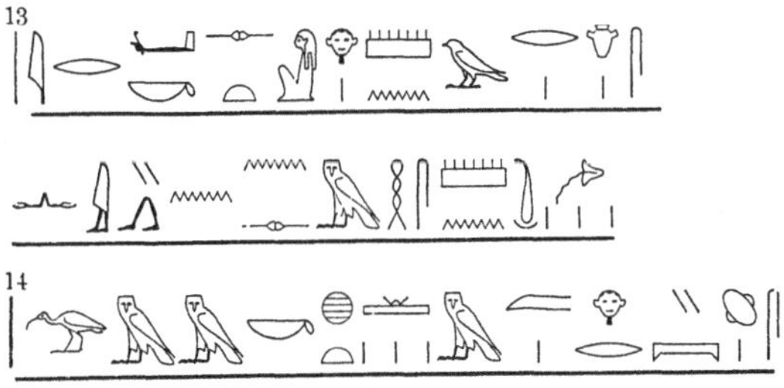

Translation

If thou examinest a woman suffering in her abdomen, so that the menstrual discharge cannot come away for her; and thou findest trouble in the upper part of her vulva, (conclusion follows in diagnosis).

Commentary

It is obvious that in this recipe the word *r'-yb*, commonly meaning "stomach," is applied here to the female organs, especially the uterus, and as doubtless loosely used to designate this region, perhaps best rendered by "abdomen," as above. The most common term, usually employed by the Egyptians for this region, is the more general designation *ẖ·t*, "belly, womb." See XIX 15, 16, and 17.

The word rendered "vulva" is written with the determinative only, and should perhaps be otherwise interpreted. See the word vulva in the diagnosis.

Diagnosis

XX 14–15

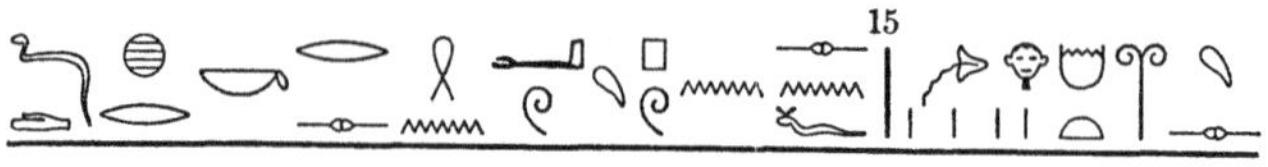

Translation

Thou shouldst say concerning her: " It is obstruction of the blood in her vulva."

First Treatment, Internal and External

XX 15–17

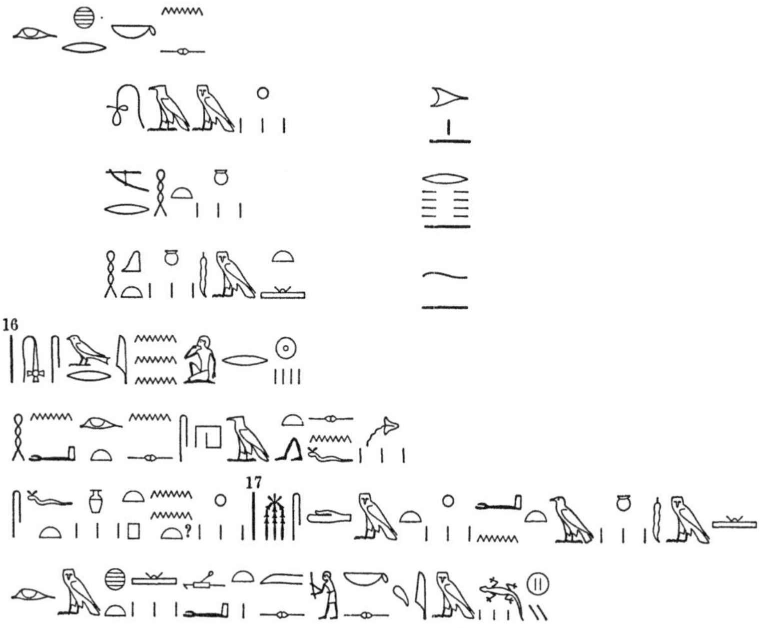

Translation

Thou shouldst prepare for her:

Wam,	$\frac{1}{16}$
Grease,	$\frac{1}{8}$
Sweet beer	$\frac{1}{8}$

Cooked and drunk for four days.

Besides preparing for her (the prescription called) " Discharge of the blood " (as follows): Oil, *tepnenet*, eye-paint, sweet frankincense. Mix, (and) anoint the organ therewith very frequently.

Commentary

The first drug in the internal prescription, which was to be carried by the beer as a solvent, is unfortunately entirely unknown and cannot be identified. A plant of this name occurs twice in Pap. Ebers (92, 17 and 69, 11), and once in the Berlin Medical Papyrus (3038, 5, 12); and the fruit of this plant is employed in recipes in Hearst (VIII 6; IX 6–7; V 3 and duplicates in Ebers). See also Ebers 18, 8; 21, 22; 22, 3; 22, 5; 5, 1; 50, 15; 18, 14; and Pap. Berlin (3038, 1, 2). Presumably it is this unidentified fruit which is employed here.

As commonly in the Egyptian medical papyri, the solids are enumerated first and the solvent which is to carry them is placed at the end. The measures of parts seem to be in two different series. Wam is measured by the *heket*, a common grain measure containing almost 300 cubic inches. Our common bushel contains about 7½ *heket*. Roughly a *heket* was a little more than half a peck, that is a little more than four quarts, and a sixteenth of a *heket* would therefore have been a trifle over half a pint of the *wam* fruit, of which the patient is to take a decoction. The grease is followed by the fraction ⅛ which does not imply any unit of measure; but the sign after the sweet beer indicates ⅛ of a heket which would be a little over a pint.

The external remedy also begins with an unknown drug. The eye-paint was black antimony. Its Egyptian name  *mśdm·t* has been corrupted into Coptic ⲥⲧⲏⲙ Greek *στίμμι*, and finally Latin *stibium*. Whether the ingredients when mixed formed a powder or an ointment is uncertain without knowing more about *tepnenet*, but the verb " anoint " suggests ointment.

The word employed for the female organ here,  *ks*, is not known elsewhere.

Alternative External Treatment

XX 18–XXI 3

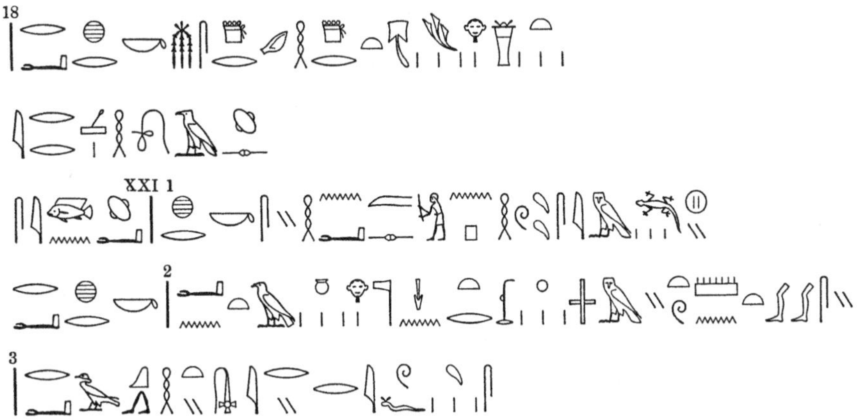

Translation

Thou shouldst put *hezret*-ears into ointment. If afterward she has an evil odor, wipe her off and anoint her two labia therewith very frequently. Thou shouldst apply frankincense and incense between her two loins, (and) cause the smoke thereof to enter her flesh.

Commentary

The active agency in the ointment prescribed is a plant evidently having leaves which resemble the ears of an animal. This animal, *ḥḏr·t*, is known from a list of villages in an Old Kingdom mastaba (No. 45, Lepsius, *Denkmäler*, II 29), in which the determinative looks something like a hyena. See also Cairo 20066 and 20055, both from the Middle Kingdom. In the storming of Dapur (Lepsius, *ibid.* III 166), Sethe, collating the original, suggests a *Springmaus* or some similar creature. It must have been some animal not distasteful to the Egyptians, for the word occurs as the name of both men and women.

npḥ·wy (dual) is anatomically uncertain, but occurs with meanings which must be connected with the lower part of the trunk; hence the rendering above, which may be too much localized. The purpose of the incense burning is of course obvious.

TWO RECIPES FOR THE COMPLEXION

XXI 3–8

These are obviously toilet preparations having no place among medical recipes, although a number of recipes for such preparations are included in the Papyrus Ebers. The ingredients are again of too uncertain identity for us to say much regarding the virtue of these two preparations for the complexion.

I. Recipe for Transforming the Skin

XXI 3–6

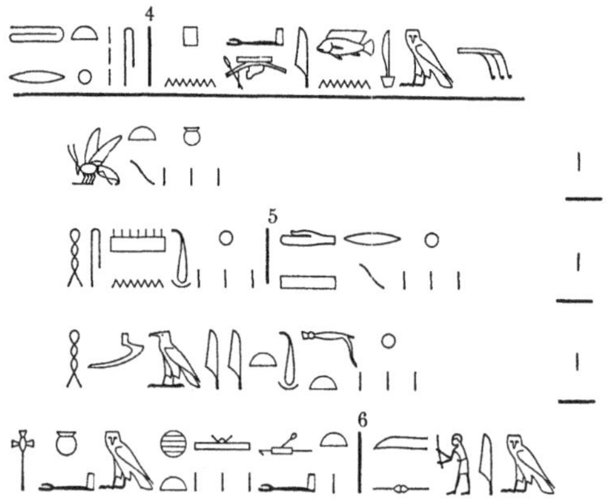

Translation

A recipe for transforming the skin :

Honey,	1
Red natron,	1
Northern salt,	1

Triturate together (and) anoint therewith.

Commentary

If the natron here called *ḥśmn* is the same as the other variety *nṯry*, discussed above in Case 46, its chief ingredient was a sesquicarbonate of sodium. See commentary on XVI 4. " Northern salt " will be found discussed in Case 41 (XIV 5–6) and was chiefly chloride of sodium.

II. Recipe for Beautifying the Face

XXI 6–8

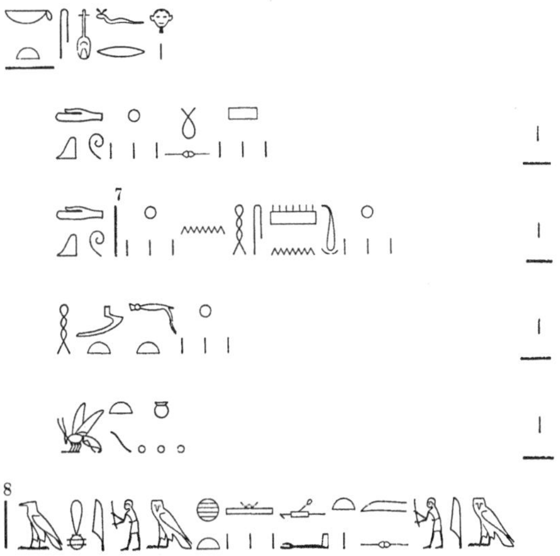

Translation

Another (recipe) for beautifying the face :

Alabaster ⌜kernels⌝,	1
Natron ⌜kernels⌝,	1
Northern salt,	1
Honey,	1

Mix together, (and) anoint therewith.

Commentary

The uncertain word *dḳw*, rendered "⌜kernels⌝," is elsewhere a designation for a preparation of grain. It may here possibly designate the physical form in which the alabaster and the natron were employed.

RECIPE FOR TRANSFORMING AN OLD MAN INTO A YOUTH

XXI 9–XXII 10

Thus far the writing of the Papyrus Edwin Smith was the work of a single scribal hand, which copied all the material on the recto (seventeen columns) and three columns and eight lines on the verso. The last twenty-six lines (XXI 9–XXII 14) were added by a different hand at some later date. The two recipes added by this second scribe have no relation to each other whatsoever ; but it is obvious that the first of the two, which we are now taking up, was suggested by the preceding recipes for the complexion ; this recipe for transforming an old man into a youth being simply another face ointment designed to banish the traces of age from the face.

As an illustration of the apothecary's art in the Sixteenth Century B.C., this recipe is of unusual interest. It describes in great detail the preparation of an aqueous solid extract of an unidentified fruit, and the successive stages of the process are fully explained. The resulting paste or ointment is externally applied, and the directions for use assure us that the result is complete removal of all signs of age. It will be seen then that what we have in this early oriental predecessor of the elixir of life is simply a face paste which will remove wrinkles. It seems to have claimed no effect upon the waning vitality of an old man. It is of interest to note that like the later elixir of life it was to be kept in a precious vase or flask of semi-precious stone.

Title

XXI 9

9 

Translation

Beginning of the Book of Transforming an Old Man into a Youth.

Commentary

While the meaning of this title is perfectly clear, a slight verbal modification of the rendering proposed is possible. The idiom . . . . . . *yr·t* . . . . . . *m*, meaning "to transform . . . . into," literally to "make . . . . . into" is well known. In oriental hyperbole, when a boastful official digs a well in the desert he says : "I made the highlands a river, and the upper valleys a water way" (see Lepsius, *Denkmäler*, II 149, e, ll. 10–11, and the author's *Ancient Records*, I, paragr. 447). My friend Professor Golénischeff suggests that we should find here two other idiomatic uses of *yr·t*, "to make," which are also well established, viz. "to pass" (time), or again "to make" an official, meaning "to be" such an official. He quotes the well-known passage from Papyrus Prisse (5, 2):

and renders, "To be an old man is evil for people in every respect" (or "to pass old age is evil etc."). While we may object to render the form as an infinitive in Papyrus Prisse, Professor Golénischeff's suggestion seems to be perfectly possible in our passage. It would not essentially alter the meaning of the title, which in either case signifies much the same thing, whether we render as above or call it with Professor Golénischeff "the Book of Passing Old Age as a Youth."

Directions for Making the Recipe

XXI 9–XXII 7

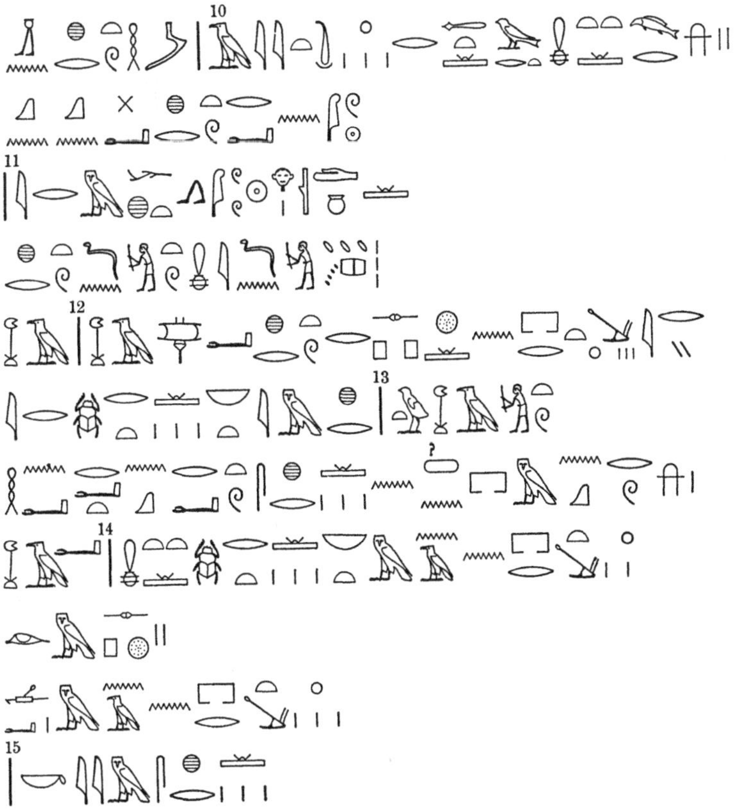

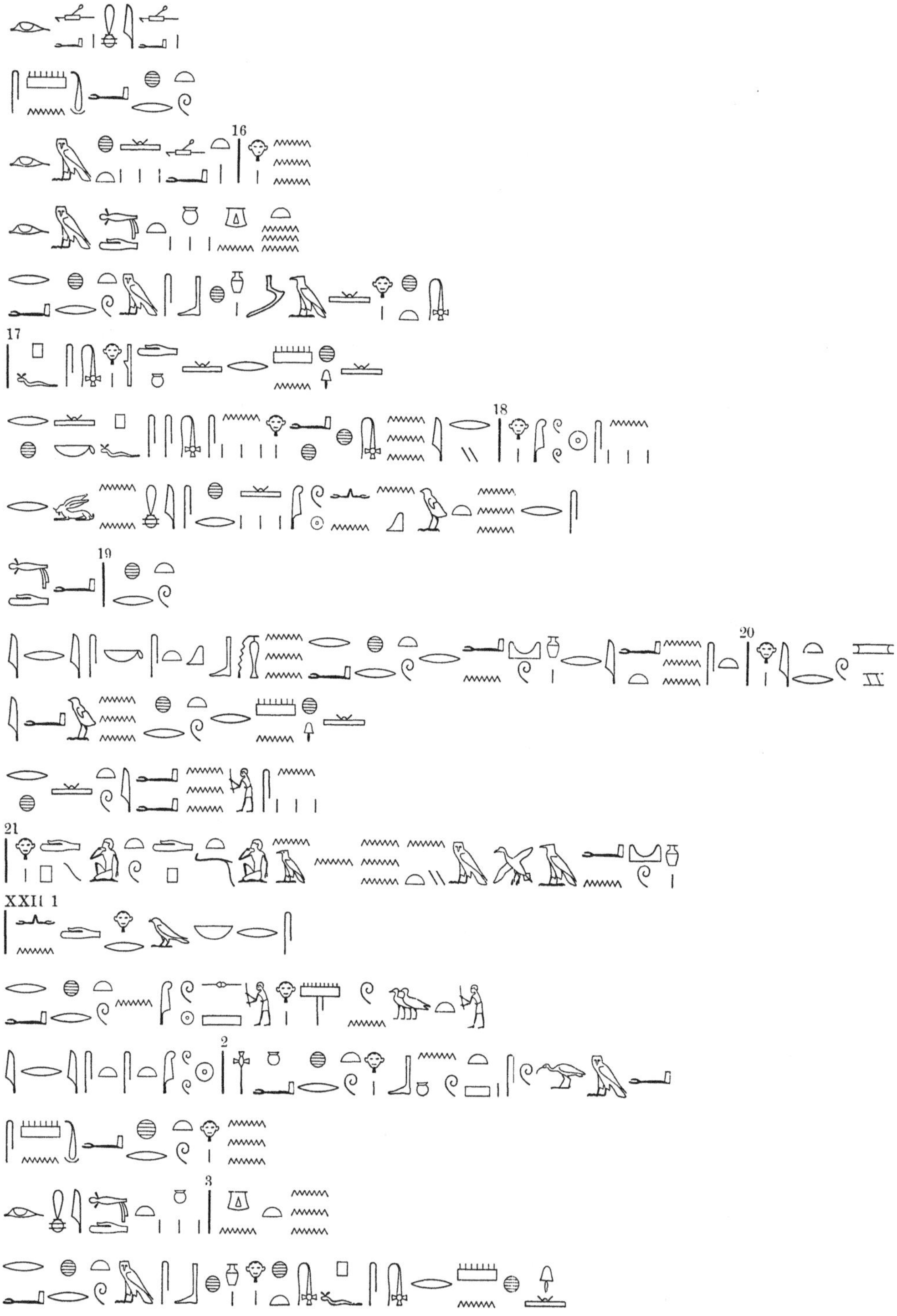
16
17
18
19
20
21
XXII 1
2
3

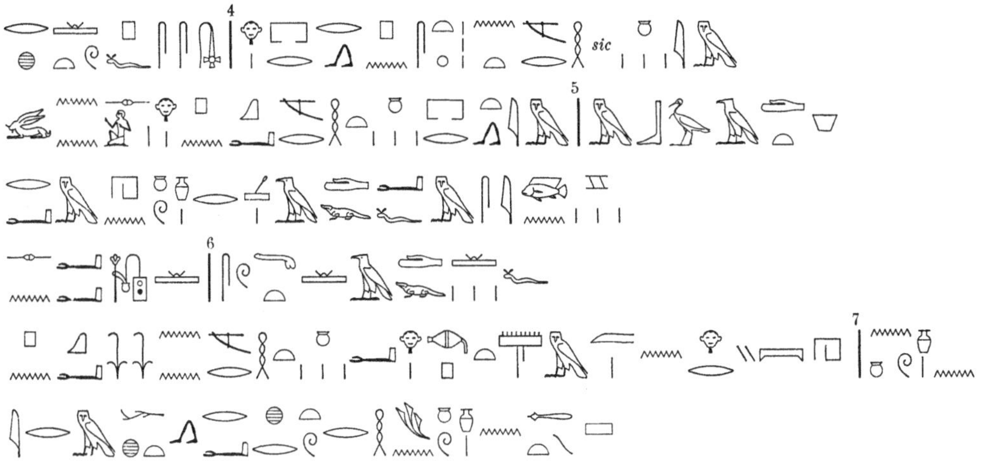

Translation

Let there be brought a large quantity of *hemayet*-fruit, about two khar. It should be bruised and placed in the sun. Then when it is entirely dry let it be ⌜husked⌝ as grain is ⌜husked⌝, and it should be winnowed until (only) the fruit thereof remains. Everything that comes therefrom shall be measured, (and) let it be sifted after the manner of the ⌜threshing floor⌝ with the sieve. Measure likewise everything that comes from these fruits and make them into two portions: one consisting of these fruits and the other even so. Treat one like the other.

(First Process)

Let it be set aside, mixed with water. Make into a soft mass and let it be placed in a new jar over the fire (and) cooked very thoroughly, making sure that they boil, evaporating the juice thereof and drying them, until it is like dry, without moisture therein. Let it be dug out (of the jar). Now when it is cool, let it be put into (another) jar in order to wash it in the river. Let it be washed thoroughly, making sure that they are washed by tasting the taste of this water that is in the jar (until) there is no bitterness at all therein. It should be placed in the sun, spread out on launderer's linen. Now when it is dry, it should be ground upon a grinding mill-stone.

(Second Process)

Let it be set aside in water. Make like a soft mass and let it be placed in a jar over the fire and cooked thoroughly, making sure that it boils, that the fluids of the mass may go forth therefrom. A man shall dip out the mass that has come of it with a dipper. Put into a *hin*-jar after it is ⌜of the consistency⌝ of clay. Rub and make thick its ⌜consistency⌝. Dip out this mass and put upon a linen cover on the top of this *hin*-jar. Now afterward it should be put into a vase of costly stone.

Commentary

There is much that is not clear in this interesting account of the processes for making an aqueous extract. In the first place the fruit from which it is made cannot be identified. It will be found discussed in Case 45 (XV 15). It evidently had a hard husk or shell, which suggests that it might even have been a variety of nut.

ḫ'r must be a loose use of the term here as " measure." It can hardly be 2½ bushels, making a total of 5 bushels, as computed by Griffith in his excellent article (*Proceedings of the Socy. of Biblical Archaeol.*, 14 (1892), p. 421).

ḏn, " thresh," or possibly ⸢*nḏ*⸣, perhaps meaning " to husk," is slightly uncertain in the reading. The is thrown back under the , so that one is uncertain whether the *n* or the *ḏ* is to be read first. It may possibly be an alphabetic writing of *nḏ*, " grind," although if so, it would be the only example of this writing in our papyrus.

In favor of the reading *ḏn*, Dévaud recalls (Sall. I 4, 12 and Amenemope 19, 9), probably meaning " threshing floor " ; compare S. **ϫⲛⲟⲟⲩ :** B. **ϭⲛⲱⲟⲩ.** This etymology would indicate the meaning " thresh " for our verb *ḏn*.

The meaning of " everything that comes therefrom " is not wholly clear. It might mean exclusively the kernel or meat extracted from the husk ; it might also include the husk which in the immediately following instructions might form the second portion.

is a word of uncertain reading, and the meaning furthermore is also unsettled. It might also be read .

Very important for an understanding of these directions is the meaning of the " two portions." As noted just above, it might at first be supposed to mean the husks as one portion and the fruits or kernels as the other. This would seem to be involved in the phrase " one consisting of these fruits ; " but the other portion is not sufficiently described in the following directions to make its character unequivocal. In any case we must conclude that the " two portions " are both subjected to the same two processes for making an aqueous extract. These two processes are identical in the beginning stages. They both begin as follows :

First Process: (XXI 15–16) ;
Second Process: (XXII 2–3),

the second being somewhat shortened. They then proceed with the steps for producing a thick decoction by boiling and evaporation. The language of the two shows interesting variants, important for our knowledge of the Egyptian dictionary. The first process concludes with the production of a dry powder, while the second results in a mass obviously of thick consistency, which is kept in a vase.

The relation of the two processes is obscure. There is no explicit indication in the text where the directions for the second process begin. Furthermore the product resulting from the first process is never mentioned again. Indeed the directions for using the preparation (XXII 7) clearly show that the finished preparation is a soft mass with which the user can " anoint " himself. These facts seem to show that the dry powder produced by the first process (and otherwise dropped in XXII 2, without further reference being made to it) is again placed to soak in water (XXII 2) just as at first (XXI 15–16), and is then boiled and evaporated a second time, to form at last a thick paste. In that case we must suppose that the directions to make two portions simply indicate that the quantity of the fruit taken was too large to be made up in one lot, and that the apothecary is therefore to divide it up into two lots merely for making.

šd·t, meaning "mass" or similar, I was at first inclined to read *ʿd·t* " fat," used like *mrḥ·t*, " grease," in this passage for designating a soft mass; but Dévaud calls my attention to the Coptic ⲁⲩⲱ ⲛ̄ⲥⲉⲧⲙ̄ϯϩⲁϩ ⲙ̄ⲙⲟⲟⲩ ⲉⲣⲟⲥ ⲉⲧⲣⲉⲡϣⲱⲧⲉ ϭⲛⲟⲛ (Zoega, *Cat.*, p. 562, 14), which makes the reading *šd·t* perfectly certain. For the *šd*-sign see also XXI 18.

śbḫ, " jar," is a new word, seemingly unknown elsewhere.

nḳw·t, " moisture," is also an unknown word, but the context here renders this translation fairly certain. See Coptic etymologies, pp. 595 f.

The curious use of before finite forms of the verb in l. 17 and again in l. 21 raises a question of syntax. Sethe suggests that it simply means " and " as sometimes between two nouns.

ʿḫḫ, " evaporate," is not known elsewhere with this meaning. In the examples known (Daressy, *Recueil de trav.* 16, 125 and Dümichen, *Geogr. Inschr.*, IV, 113) it means " consume."

śwgm, "grinding," is not otherwise known with the causative *ś* with the following preserved. The simplex occurs in an interesting Old Kingdom relief scene showing two women grinding. One says: " Grind thoroughly," and the other replies: " I am grinding as hard as I can " (Erman, *Reden*, pp. 18–19, from Cairo 1534). The causative with loss of the is found in Pap. Ebers (21, 12), where a recipe is to be triturated in " in a stone mortar " " until you pulverize it." *wgm* as a kind of grain, evidently from the root " to grind," occurs in the Ramesseum List Papyrus 261, and again *Urk.* IV 687.

pnś·t is otherwise unknown except in two passages in Pap. Ebers, which do not aid us as to the meaning. An examination of the parallel passage in the first process (XXI 17) shows that our *pnś·t* is parallel with " the juice thereof." *Pnś·t* must therefore mean something like " fluids."

ʾd (possibly to be read:) is an entirely unknown word. The rendering above is a guess. Just what happens to the mass placed in the *hin*-jar is not at all clear. At the end of the *hin*-jar stage the soft mass is spread on a piece of linen stretched over the top of the jar, seemingly as old-fashioned cottage cheese is so placed in order to drain it, the fluid draining back into the jar. It was at this stage still fluid enough to be " dipped."

At the close of the second process the resulting paste is ready for use, and is therefore placed in a toilet vase of some costly stone like lapis lazuli, jasper, or possibly alabaster or aragonite.

Directions for Use

XXII 7–10

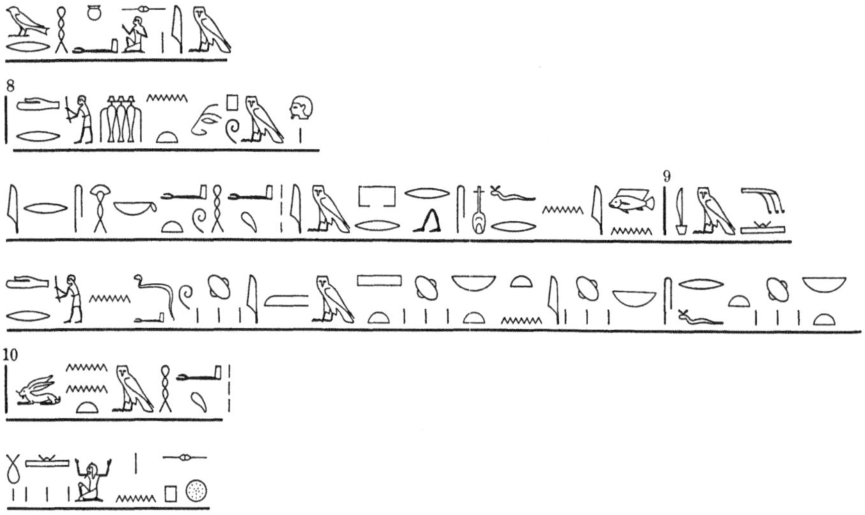

Translation

Anoint a man therewith. It is a remover of ⌜wrinkles⌝ from the head. When the flesh is smeared therewith, it becomes a beautifier of the skin, a remover of ⌜blemishes⌝, of all ⌜disfigurements⌝, of all signs of age, of all ⌜weaknesses⌝ which are in the flesh. Found effective myriads of times.

Commentary

The passage contains a series of uncertain words which are not found elsewhere. These are all enclosed in half-brackets. The word *tny* is evidently a derivative of the familiar word *tny* " grow old," and must mean something like " signs of old age." The other words undoubtedly list some of the unsightly external indications of advanced age, but it is impossible to determine their specific meanings.

RECIPE FOR SOME AILMENT OF THE ANUS AND VICINITY

XXII 11–14

The examination, introduced by the verb "inspect" (*m''*) in place of the usual "examine" (*ḫ'y*), is hardly worthy of the name, and recalls the lack of a full examination so usual in the recipe papyri. As there is no diagnosis, the recipe follows directly upon the brief examination, the whole case occupying only a little over three lines.

Examination

XXII 11–12

Translation

If thou inspectest a man ailing in his anus, (and) whether standing or sitting, suffering very greatly with seizures in both his legs, (conclusion in treatment).

Commentary

 *nḏr·wt*, "seizures," is a word not found elsewhere in Egyptian documents. It may possibly be derived from the well-known word 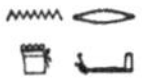 *nḏry*, "to seize," and hence the rendering above.

Treatment

XXII 12–14

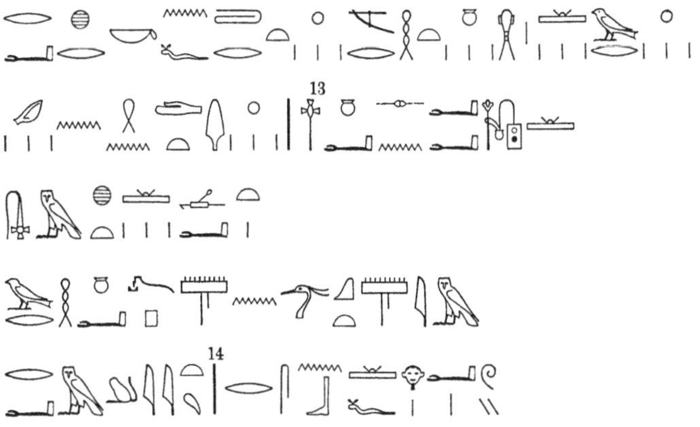

Translation

Thou shouldst give to him a recipe, an ointment of great protection (as follows): Acacia leaves, ground, triturated and cooked together. Smear a strip of fine linen therewith and place in the anus, that he may recover immediately.

Commentary

śtp, "strip," is not a common word. It is found made of "fine linen" (*pḳ·t*) as here, in Turin Papyri, ed. Pleyte and Rossi, 31, 3 and 77, 17; and in Pap. Leyden I 346, 2, 3. Gardiner calls my attention to it also in his transcription of Pap. Leyden 947, 12, 9. As a magical bandage it is also mentioned in *Mutter und Kind* VIII 3; the London Medical Papyrus 14, 8–9. Made of *ḥ'ty* it appears in the Kahun Medical Papyrus 2, 8 and in Pap. Hearst I 16; and without indication of the material it appears again in Pap. Hearst X 8–9.

CONSECUTIVE TRANSLATION OF THE INCANTATIONS AND RECIPES

N.B. The sub-titles have all been inserted by the modern editor and are not found in the original text. Each of the ancient titles has likewise been introduced by a title inserted by the present editor.

EIGHT INCANTATIONS AGAINST PEST

Title of the First Incantation

XVIII 1

Incantation for exorcising the wind of the pest of the year.

First Incantation

XVIII 1–8

O Flame-in-His-Face! Presider over the horizon, speak thou to the chief of the Hemesut-house, who makes Osiris, first of the land, to flourish. O Nekhbet, lifting the earth to the sky for her father, come thou, bind the two feathers around me, around me, that I may live and flourish because I possess this White One. The first is the Great One dwelling in Heliopolis; the second is Isis; the third is Nephthys; while I am subject to thee (fem.).

O Seizer-of-the-Great-One, son of Sekhmet, mightiest of the mighty, son of the Disease-Demon, Dened, son of Hathor, mistress of the crown (*nt*), and flooder of the streams; when thou voyagest in the Celestial Ocean, when thou sailest in the morning barque, thou hast saved me from every sickness.

Conclusion of the First Incantation

XVIII 8–9

Incantation against this year, with the breath of every evil wind.

Horus, Horus, healthy despite Sekhmet, is around all my flesh for life.

Directions for Pronouncing the First Incantation

XVIII 9–11

Speak the words over two vulture feathers, with which a man has covered himself, placed as his protection in every place where he goes. It is a protection against the year, expelling sickness in the year of pest.

Title of the Second Incantation

XVIII 11–12

Another (incantation) for exorcising the plague-bearing wind, the demons of disease, the malignant spirits, messengers of Sekhmet.

Second Incantation

XVIII 13–15

Withdraw, ye disease demons. The wind shall not reach me, that those who pass by may pass by to work disaster against me. I am Horus who passes by the diseased ones of Sekhmet, (even) Horus, Horus, healthy despite Sekhmet. I am the unique one, son of Bastet. I die not through thee (fem.).

Directions for Pronouncing the Second Incantation

XVIII 15–16

Let the words be spoken by a man having a stick of *des*-wood in his hand, while he comes forth into the open and goes around his house. He cannot die by the pest of the year.

Title of the Third Incantation

XVIII 17

Another protection against the pest of the year.

Third Incantation

XVIII 17–19

I am the abomination that came forth out of Buto. O Meskhenet, that came forth out of Heliopolis ; O men, O gods, O spirits, O dead, be ye far from me. I am the abomination.

Fourth Incantation

XVIII 19–XIX 2

Another (incantation). I am the healthy one in the way of the passer by. Shall I be smitten, while I am healthy ? I have seen the great disaster. O this fever, do not assail me, (for) I am the one who has come forth out of the disaster. Be thou far from me.

Fifth Incantation

XIX 2–9

Copy of another (incantation). O Jubilation, Jubilation, take not this my heart, nor this my breast for Sekhmet. Take not my liver for Osiris, in order that the hidden things that are in Buto may not, shall not enter into my seat on the morning of counting the Horus-eye, even every male spirit, every female spirit, every male dead, every female dead, the form of every animal, the one (fem.) which the crocodile has taken, the one (masc.) which the serpent has stung, the one which has ⸢perished⸣ by the knife, (or) the one who has died in his bed. Ye demons of disease, of the followers of the year and its yield, lo, Horus, even Horus, healthy despite Sekhmet, is [around] all my flesh for life.

Directions for Pronouncing the Fifth Incantation

XIX 9–14

Speak the words over (images of) Sekhmet, Bastet, Osiris, and Neheb-kau, written with frankincense on a band of fine linen and attached to a man at his throat. It will prevent asses from entering, - - the *besbes*-goose to me, and the green-breasted goose. The protection of the life of Neit is around me, (even of) her who is over the escaped of the sower. Bastet is repelled from the house of a man. A man shall say (it) at the life of the year.

Title of the Sixth Incantation

XIX 14

Incantation for cleansing a fly.

Sixth Incantation

XIX 14–18

The mouth of this man who is under my fingers, and so forth, is the mouth of a ⸢hungry⸣ calf, when he comes forth from his mother's womb. This insect which has entered into this his belly, (although) he has entered, shall come forth alive, issuing to the ground as earth or as excrement, without injuring his belly, (but) coming forth as his excrement from him, having been assigned to Akeru.

Title of the Seventh Incantation

XIX 18–19

Incantation for cleansing everything from pest.

Seventh Incantation

XIX 19–XX 5

Thy messengers are consumed, O Sekhmet; thy demons of disease retreat, O Bastet. The Year does not pass by to work disaster against me. Thy breath does not reach me. I am Horus over the diseased ones of Sekhmet, I am thy Horus,

O Sekhmet; I am thy unique one, O Buto. I die not by thee; I die not by thee. I am the rejoicing one, I am the jubilating one. O son of Bastet, descend not upon me; O Dweller in the *Sepsepu*, approach me not, draw not near me. I am the king in the midst of his ⌜shelter⌝.

Directions for Pronouncing the Seventh Incantation

XX 5–8

Let a man say this incantation before a *nefret*-flower, bound to a piece of *des*-wood, and tied with a strip of linen. Let them be passed over the things; the pest will be exorcised, (and) the passage of the disease-demons by everything that is eaten, likewise by the beds, will be prevented.

Eighth Incantation

XX 8–11

Another (incantation). A *shames*-flower is on me, the abomination of thy followers. Thy diseased ones avoid me, the stretching of thy snare avoids me; I am the escaped one of thy birds. Horus, Horus, healthy despite Sekhmet, is around all my flesh for life.

Directions for Pronouncing the Eighth Incantation

XX 11–12

Let a man say this incantation when a *shames*-flower has been given to him in his hand.

RECIPE FOR FEMALE TROUBLES

XX 13–XXI 3

Examination

XX 13–14

If thou examinest a woman suffering in her abdomen, so that the menstrual discharge cannot come away for her; and thou findest trouble in the upper part of her vulva, (conclusion follows in diagnosis).

Diagnosis

XX 14–15

Thou shouldst say concerning her: "It is obstruction of the blood in her vulva."

First Treatment, Internal and External

XX 15–17

Thou shouldst prepare for her :

Wam,	$\frac{1}{16}$
Grease,	$\frac{1}{8}$
Sweet beer,	$\frac{1}{8}$

Cooked and drunk for four days.

Besides preparing for her (the prescription called) " Discharge of the blood " (as follows) : Oil, *tepnenet*, eye-paint, sweet frankincense. Mix, (and) anoint the organ therewith very frequently.

Alternative External Treatment

XX 18–XXI 3

Thou shouldst put *hezret*-ears into ointment. If afterward she has an evil odor, wipe her off and anoint her two labia therewith very frequently. Thou shouldst apply frankincense and incense between her two loins, (and) cause the smoke thereof to enter her flesh.

TWO RECIPES FOR THE COMPLEXION

XXI 3–8

I. Recipe for Transforming the Skin

XXI 3–6

A recipe for transforming the skin :

Honey,	1
Red natron,	1
Northern salt,	1

Triturate together (and) anoint therewith.

II. Recipe for Beautifying the Face

XXI 6–8

Another (recipe) for beautifying the face :

Alabaster ⌜kernels⌝,	1
Natron ⌜kernels⌝,	1
Northern salt,	1
Honey,	1

Mix together, (and) anoint therewith.

RECIPE FOR TRANSFORMING AN OLD MAN INTO A YOUTH

XXI 9–XXII 10

Title

XXI 9

Beginning of the Book of Transforming an Old Man into a Youth.

Directions for Making the Recipe

XXI 9–XXII 7

Let there be brought a large quantity of *hemayet*-fruit, about two khar. It should be bruised and placed in the sun. Then when it is entirely dry let it be ⌜husked⌝ as grain is ⌜husked⌝, and it should be winnowed until (only) the fruit thereof remains. Everything that comes therefrom shall be measured, (and) let it be sifted after the manner of the ⌜threshing floor⌝ with the sieve. Measure likewise everything that comes from these fruits and make them into two portions: one consisting of these fruits and the other even so. Treat one like the other.

(First Process)

Let it be set aside, mixed with water. Make into a soft mass and let it be placed in a new jar over the fire (and) cooked very thoroughly, making sure that they boil, evaporating the juice thereof and drying them, until it is like dry, without moisture therein. Let it be dug out (of the jar). Now when it is cool, let it be put into (another) jar in order to wash it in the river. Let it be washed thoroughly, making sure that they are washed by tasting the taste of this water that is in the jar (until) there is no bitterness at all therein. It should be placed in the sun, spread out on launderer's linen. Now when it is dry, it should be ground upon a grinding mill-stone.

(Second Process)

Let it be set aside in water. Make like a soft mass and let it be placed in a jar over the fire and cooked thoroughly, making sure that it boils, that the fluids of the mass may go forth therefrom. A man shall dip out the mass that has come of it with a dipper. Put into a *hin*-jar after it is ⌜of the consistency⌝ of clay. Rub and make thick its ⌜consistency⌝. Dip out this mass and put upon a linen cover on the top of this *hin*-jar. Now afterward it should be put into a vase of costly stone.

Directions for Use

XXII 7–10

Anoint a man therewith. It is a remover of ⌜wrinkles⌝ from the head. When the flesh is smeared therewith, it becomes a beautifier of the skin, a remover of ⌜blemishes⌝, of all ⌜disfigurements⌝, of all signs of age, of all ⌜weaknesses⌝ which are in the flesh. Found effective myriads of times.

RECIPE FOR SOME AILMENT OF THE ANUS AND VICINITY

XXII 11–14

Examination

XXII 11–12

If thou inspectest a man ailing in his anus, (and) whether standing or sitting, suffering very greatly with seizures in both his legs, (conclusion in treatment).

Treatment

XXII 12–14

Thou shouldst give to him a recipe, an ointment of great protection (as follows): Acacia leaves, ground, triturated and cooked together. Smear a strip of fine linen therewith and place in the anus, that he may recover immediately.

PART III

THE INDICES

EGYPTIAN GLOSSARY

EXPLANATIONS AND ABBREVIATIONS

References to Part I, the Surgical Treatise on the recto, are all double, that is, first by case and second by column and line. Thus, C. = " Case ", that is, one of the forty-eight cases of the Surgical Treatise; the number is that of the case; thus " C. 25 " = Case 25. In the second reference the Roman numerals designate the *columns* of the original manuscript; while the following Arabic numerals designate the *lines* of the original manuscript. The numbering of the lines is not consecutive throughout the document, but begins anew with each column.

References to Part II, the Incantations and Recipes, the magical material on the verso (which has nothing to do with the Surgical Treatise), are, in the case of an incantation, double; that is, first by incantation, and second by column and line. Thus "I. 4" = Incantation No. 4.

A reference in black letter thus: **C. 18, VII 13,** indicates the particular passage in the commentary where full discussion of a word or passage will be found. Occasionally more than one such black letter reference indicates that the discussion was necessarily divided. All other references indicate merely the occurrence of the word.

The half-brackets (⌜——⌝) indicate that the word so enclosed is of uncertain meaning. If they enclose hieroglyphs or a transliteration, the half-brackets indicate an uncertain reading or uncertain restoration.

" g." after a proper name = god or goddess.

A brief explanation of the transliteration of hieroglyphic into Roman letters will be found on pp. xxi and xxii, and should be consulted by non-Egyptologists.

ꜣ		O!: I. 1, XVIII 1.
ꜣ.T		period: **C. 3, I 23** restored; C. 4, II 7; C. 5, II 16; C. 19, VII 18; C. 29, X 8; C. 47, XVII 13.
ꜣYŚ		brain; also with plural strokes: **C. 6, II 18**, 19, 22, 23–24, 24; C. 7, IV 1; C. 8, IV 12.
ꜣB		of uncertain meaning: C. 24, IX 1.
ꜣPD		bird: I. 8, XX 10.
ꜣMY		mix: XXI 8.
ꜣMꜥ		an unidentified two-toed bird, **C. 22, VIII 15.**

ʾMʿ·T (ʾMʿW·T) — fork, ramus, or with det. , or ; also (once only III 17), (once only IX 3), (once only IV 8): C. 7, III 17; **C. 8, IV** 8, **17,** 18; **C. 22, VIII** 10–11, **14 bis;** C. 25, IX 3.

ʾMM-WR·T — Seizer-of-the-Great-One (a hostile demon): I. 1, XVIII 5.

ʾNRY — shudder; also (III 3), (VIII 1), (X 5), (XIII 14), (XIV 18): **C. 4, II 4;** C. 7, III 3; C. 20, VIII 1; C. 29, X 5; C. 40, XIII 14; C. 42, XIV 18.

ʾ[R]·WY or YR·WY — two strips; also (once only XVII 4), (once only II 23), (once only IX 16), (once only I 16); **C. 2, I 15**, restored, 16; C. 6, II 23; **C. 10, V** 8, **9;** C. 27, IX 16; C. 47, XVII 4.

ʾHT — weakness, exhaustion, weak place: **C. 6, II 21; C. 7, IV 4 bis.** See also NHD and HD.

ʾHḌ — be weak: **C. 19, VII 21–22.**

ʾḤ·T — cultivated ground: C. 32, XI 8.

ʾH̱W — spirit, also (XIX 6): I. 3, XVIII 18; I. 5, XIX 6. ʾH̱·T (), female "spirit": I. 5, XIX 6.

ʾH̱·T — horizon: I. 1, XVIII 1.

ʾH̱·T — Isis: C. 9, V 2, 3.

ʾKR — Akeru: **I. 6, XIX 18.**

ʾD — ⌜to be of the consistency⌝: XXII 5.

⌜consistency⌝: **XXII 6.**

YʾBY — left: C. 34, XII 2.

YʾW — old man: XXI 9.

YʾT — distort, turn aside: **C. 7, IV 3;** C. 47, XVII 13.

YʾD·T — snare: I. 8, XX 10.

YʾD·T — pest; also with det. : I. 1, XVIII 11; I. 7, XIX 19, XX 7.

YʾD·T-RNP·T — pest of the year; also (XVIII 1): **I. 1, XVIII 1;** I. 2, XVIII 16; I. 3, XVIII 17.

YY — come away; also (XX 13): C. 22, VIII 16; XX 13.

Yʿ — see ʿR.

YʿY — wash, or with further det. ; also (XXI 20): XXI 19, 20 bis.

YW — Used as main verb:

YW+subject+prepositional phrase: C. 1, I 6; C. 7, III 11; C. 9, V 3; C. 30, X 12; C. 31, X 19; I. 1, XVIII 5; I. 5, XIX 13.

YW without subject+prepositional phrase: C. 6, III 1; C. 39, XIII 11.

YW+subject+predicate noun: C. 9, V 3.

YW+predicate adjective+subject: C. 7, III 3; C. 13, VI 5; C. 17, VII 3; C. 19, VII 16; C. 21, VIII 7; C. 47, XVI 19.

Used as auxiliary verb:

YW+main verb in n-form: C. 5, II 16; C. 19, VII 20; C. 31, X 14; C. 41, XIV 10; I. 1, XVIII 8; I. 4, XIX 1.

YW+main verb in simple form: C. 39, XIII 9; I. 8, XX 11.

YW+subject+qualitative: C. 7, III 20; C. 8, IV 6; C. 11, V 10; C. 13, VI 6; C. 19, VII 16; C. 20, VII 23; C. 22, VIII 12, 16; C. 28, IX 20; C. 31, X 13, 15, 20; C. 32, XI 2; C. 41, XIII 21; C. 45, XV 13.

⌜YW᾿⌝ — ox: C. 46, XVI 9.

YWF — flesh, meat:

YWF of the patient: C. 31, X 14; C. 41, XIII 21, XIV 14 bis, 15; XXI 3.

YWF as a medicament:

WT-ḪR-K ŚW ḤR YWF W᾿Ḏ the first day, followed immediately by use of grease, honey and sometimes lint: **C. 1, I 2;** C. 2, I 14 restored; C. 18, VII 10; C. 26, IX 10; C. 27, IX 17; C. 28, X 1; C. 40, XIII 16.

WT-ḪR-K ŚW ḤR YWF W᾿Ḏ the first day, followed by ŚRWḪ-F ḤMS(Y)·T R ŚT᾿ TḪB-F and then use of grease, honey and lint: C. 16, VI 20; C. 17, VII 5.

WT-ḪR-K ŚW ḤR YWF W᾿Ḏ the first day; intervening attention to bandages and removal of meat, then use of grease, honey and lint: C. 14, VI 11, 12.

WT-ḪR-K (restored in C. 10) ŚW ḤR YWF W᾿Ḏ the first day, followed by attention to bandages, then use of grease and honey with sometimes lint (C. 47) or YMRW (C. 32): C. 10, V 7; C. 32, XI 4; C. 47, XVII 2.

YWF (*cont.*)

WT-Ḫ̱R-K ŚW ḤR YWF W'Ḏ the first day, followed immediately by YMRW and honey: C. 30, X 11.

WT-Ḫ̱R-K ŚW ḤR YWF W'Ḏ the first day with no additional medicaments: C. 29, X 7.

WD-Ḫ̱R-K YWF . . . ḤR WBNW: C. 3, I 22 restored.

YWF in incantations: I. 1, XVIII 9; I. 5, XIX 9; I. 8, XX 11.

YWNW — column: **C. 11, V** 10 bis, 11, **14;** C. 26, IX 8.

YWNW — Heliopolis: I. 1, XVIII 5; I. 3, XVIII 18.

YWḤ — saturate: C. 11, V 12; C. 12, V 19.

YWTY — one who does not; also (IV 8): C. 8, IV 8, 17 bis.

See also NTY, C. 8, IV 8.

YWD — separate: C. 4, II 9; C. 31, X 18.

YB — heart: C. 7, III 3; I. 5, XIX 3.

Ś·T YB, "pulse": **C. 1, I 7** bis.

YP — to count: **C. 1, I** 3, **4 ter (twice restored)**, 5; I. 5, XIX 5.

YP·T — bushel: C. 1, I 4 bis, 5.

YPW — those: C. 6, II 25.

YPN — these, those: C. 6, II 20; C. 8, IV 10; C. 41, XIV 8; C. 45, XV 16; C. 47, XVII 6.

YPTF — those: **C. 27, IX 17**; C. 39, XIII 7; C. 45, XV 11; C. 47, XVII 4.

YF — injuring: I. 6, XIX 17.

YM — there: I. 1, XVIII 11.

therein: C. 1, I 5, 9 bis; C. 4, II 3; C. 6, II 20; C. 8, IV 10; C. 9, V 3; C. 39, XIII 5.

therewith: C. 4, II 8; C. 23, VIII 21; I. 1, XVIII 10; XX 17, XXI 1; XXI 6; XXI 8; XXII 7, 8, 13.

therefrom: C. 41, XIV 1; XXI 12, XXII 4 bis.

YMY — that is in: C. 9, V 2 bis.

(fem.) YMY·T ḪNW: **I. 5, XIX 5.**

one dwelling in: I. 1, XVIII 4. Dweller in (): I. 7, XX 4.

YMY·W ḪT, "followers": I. 5, XIX 8.

YMYW — that which is in (the "interior"), or without plural strokes: C. 12, V 18; **C. 22, VIII 11.**

YMYTW — between; also (once only XII 11): C. 7, III 15; C. 35, XII 5; C. 36, XII 11; XXI 2.

the region between (lit. " what is between "); also (twice III 16, V 21): C. 7, III 16; C. 12, V 21; **C. 18, VII 13.**

YMY — Verb of negation.

Negative commands: C. 3, I 22; C. 4, II 6; C. 5, II 15; C. 6, II 23 bis; C. 39, XIII 8; C. 47, XVII 12; I. 5, XIX 3 bis.

Negative purpose clause: C. 39, XIII 8; I. 5, XIX 4.

YMꜣ — an unidentified fruit tree: **C. 41, XIV 4;** C. 46, XVI 9.

YMN·WT — the hidden things: I. 5, XIX 4.

YMRW — unidentified mineral; also (three times only VI 17, IX 6, X 11).

YMRW used alone: **C. 15, VI 17**; C. 32, XI 6; C. 35, XII 8; C. 36, XII 14; C. 37, XII 17–18; C. 38, XIII 2; C. 42, XIV 20; C. 43, XV 2.

YMRW with honey: C. 25, IX 6; C. 30, X 11.

YMŠ·WT — ⌜disfigurements⌝: XXII 9.

YN — by: C. 8, IV 18; I. 2, XVIII 15.

YN at head of sentence, introducing subject: C. 1, I 5; C. 31, X 15; C. 33, XI 11, 15.

YN after infinitive, introducing so-called " logical subject ": C. 1, I 10, 11 bis; **C. 5, II 17;** C. 7, III 17; C. 30, X 12.

YN — negative: **C. 8, IV 17.**

YNY — bring, carry to: C. 33, XI 15; XXI 9.

" moving to and fro " (**C. 7, III 17**).

YNꜥ·T — chin: **C. 22, VIII 10;** C. 25, IX 4; C. 27, IX 13, 14, 16.

YNM — skin, or with det. , , or ; also (once only IV 5): C. 8, IV 5 bis, 12–13; C. 41, XIII 21; C. 46, XVI 15; XXI 4; XXII 8–9.

YNḤ — eyebrow, or with det. : C. 7, III 11, IV 2, 3; C. 10, V 6 bis, 7; C. 12, V 21.

YNK — first person pronoun " I ", emphatic: I. 2, XVIII 14, 15; I. 3, XVIII 17, 19; I. 4, XVIII 19, XIX 2; I. 7, XX 1, 2 bis, 3 bis, 4; I. 8, XX 10.

mine, belonging to me: I. 1, XVIII 4.

YR 𓇋𓂋 if, as for:

YR ḪꜣY-K: C. 1, lost column restored; C. 2, I 12; C. 3, I 19 restored; C. 4, II 3, C. 5, II 12; C. 6, II 18; C. 7, III 3; C. 8, IV 5; C. 9, IV 19; C. 10, V 6; C. 11, V 10; C. 12, V 16; C. 13, VI 4; C. 14, VI 7; C. 15, VI 15; C. 16, VI 18; C. 17, VII 1; C. 18, VII 7; C. 19, VII 15; C. 20, VII 22; C. 21, VIII 6; C. 22, VIII 10; C. 23, VIII 18; C. 24, VIII 22; C. 25, IX 2; C. 26, IX 6; C. 27, IX 13; C. 28, IX 18; C. 29, X 3; C. 30, X 9; C. 31, X 13; C. 32, XI 1; C. 33, XI 9; C. 34, XI 17; C. 35, XII 3; C. 36, XII 9; C. 37, XII 15; C. 38, XII 22; C. 39, XIII 3; C. 40, XIII 12; C. 41, XIII 18; C. 42, XIV 17; C. 43, XIV 22; C. 44, XV 6; C. 45, XV 9; C. 46, XV 20; C. 47, XVI 16; C. 48, XVII 15; XX 13.

YR introducing miscellaneous verbs: C. 2, I 13; C. 10, V 7; C. 14, VI 11; C. 20, VII 24, VIII 1; **C. 22, VIII 12**; C. 23, VIII 20; C. 27, IX 14; C. 28, IX 19; C. 29, X 4; C. 41, XIV 7; C. 45, XV 11, 15; C. 46, XVI 5; C. 47, XVII 3, 5; XXII 8; XXII 11.

YR ŚWT followed by verb: C. 7, III 8, 13; C. 28, X 2; C. 31, X 16; C. 34, XI 21; C. 37, XII 19; C. 47, XVII 6, 12, 13.

YR Ḏ R followed by GMM-K: C. 4, II 6; C. 7, III 7; C. 8, IV 10; C. 20, VIII 4.

YR NW: C. 1, I 6 restored.

YR YSK or YST: XXI 19, XXII 1.

YR M ḪT: C. 3, I 21; C. 9, IV 20, V 3; C. 10, V 7; C. 12, V 19; C. 26, IX 9; C. 29, X 7; C. 30, X 11; XXI 11, XXII 7.

YR R Śꜣ: XX 18.

YR introducing glosses: **C. 1, I 3,** 9, 10; C. 2, I 15, 16, 17; C. 3, I 24 restored, 25, 26, II 1; C. 4, II 8, 10 bis; C. 5, II 16; C. 6, II 23, 25; C. 7, III 15, 16, 18 bis, 19, 20, 21, IV 1, 2, 4; C. 8, IV 12, 13, 15, 16, 17; C. 9, V 4; C. 10, V 9; C. 11, V 14, 15; C. 12, V 20, 21, VI 1; C. 14, VI 12; C. 18, VII 11, 13; C. 19, VII 19; C. 22, VIII 14, 15, 16; C. 26, IX 11; C. 30, X 12; C. 31, X 17, 19, 21; C. 32, XI 7; C. 33, XI 13, 15; C. 34, XI 22; C. 39, XIII 9; C. 40, XIII 17; C. 41, XIV 8,

YR (*cont.*) 11, 12, 13, 15; C. 42, XIV 20; C. 43, XV 3, 4, 5; C. 45, XV 16; C. 46, XVI 12, 14, 15.

YR miscellaneous: C. 1, I 2; XXI 12.

YRY thereof: C. 43, XV 5; XXI 3; XXI 12, 17.

YR what pertains to: **C. 5, II 17**; C. 19, VII 21; C. 41, XIV 10.

YR·T eye; also (dual), (dual VII 19): C. 8, IV 6; C. 18, VII 14; C. 19, VII 17, 19, 20, 21 bis; C. 20, VII 23, VIII 2 bis; C. 31, X 15; I. 5, XIX 5.

YRY to make.

Used in prescriptions with the meaning "prepare": C. 4, II 7; C. 7, III 7, 14 bis; C. 9, IV 20 bis, 21; C. 14, VI 9; C. 23, VIII 21; C. 35, XII 6; C. 36, XII 12; C. 37, XII 17; C. 41, XIV 2, 4, 6; C. 46, XVI 9, 11; C. 48, XVII 19; XX 15, 16; XXI 14, 15, 16, XXII 2.

Used in descriptions of symptoms with the meaning "produce": **C. 7, IV 3;** C. 39, XIII 5, 6, 11; C. 45, XV 13; C. 46, XVI 1; C. 48, XVII 17.

to do: C. 4, II 8; C. 19, VII 16; C. 20, VIII 2, 3; **C. 30, X 10.**

to treat, as used in verdicts: **C. 1, I 2;** C. 2, I 14; C. 3, I 21; C. 5, II 15; C. 6, II 22; C. 7, III 13; C. 8, IV 9, 12; C. 10, V 7; C. 11, V 11; C. 12, V 17; C. 13, VI 7; C. 14, VI 9; C. 15, VI 16; C. 16, VI 20; C. 17, VII 5; C. 18, VII 10; C. 19, VII 18; C. 20, VIII 4; C. 22, VIII 14; C. 23, VIII 20; C. 24, IX 2; C. 25, IX 5; C. 26, IX 9; C. 27, IX 16; C. 30, X 10; C. 31, X 17; C. 32, XI 4; C. 33, XI 13; C. 34, XI 19, 22; C. 35, XII 4; C. 36, XII 10; C. 37, XII 21; C. 38, XIII 1; C. 39, XIII 6; C. 40, XIII 15; C. 41, XIV 2; C. 42, XIV 19; C. 43, XV 2; C. 44, XV 9; C. 46, XVI 3; C. 47, XVII 2; C. 48, XVII 18.

to administer: **C. 3, II 2.**

YRY M, "to transform into": XXI 9.

YRY M YḪ·T Wᶜ·T, "to mix": XX 17; XXI 15.

YRTYW color; also : **C. 7, III 20,** 21; C. 9, V 1; C. 19, VII 20 bis; C. 41, XIV 13.

surface (of a wound), or with det. ○: C. 41, XIII 22; C. 46, XVI 1, 14.

YH — injury, pain, or with det. (XVII 13).

YH to designate a specific wound or injury under discussion: C. 8, IV 15–16, 16; **C. 46, XVI 13.**

YH as source of symptoms: C. 3, II 1; C. 7, III 18, 20; C. 39, XIII 11.

R ŚWꜣY ꜣ·T YH-F: **C. 3, I 23 restored;** C. 4, II 7; C. 5, II 16; C. 19, VII 19; C. 29, X 8; C. 47, XVII 13.

YHHY — the jubilating one: I. 7, XX 3.

YḪ·T — thing

YḪ·T used without a qualitative modifier:

Designating some material object: C. 1, I 4 bis, 5; C. 7, III 18, 19; C. 22, VIII 15; I. 7, XIX 18, XX 7, 8.

Indicating something immaterial but neutral: C. 45, XV 15.

ŚPR-F R YḪ·T: C. 4, II 8, 10; C. 6, II 23; C. 7, III 8, 15; C. 8, IV 9; C. 21, VIII 9; C. 37, XII 19.

Indicating something immaterial and unfavorable as shown by further definition meaning "injury", "disease", etc.: C. 8, IV 5; C. 23, VIII 18; XX 14.

YḪ·T with a following modifier:

With adjective: **C. 7, III 7;** C. 14, VI 14; C. 26, IX 13; C. 39, XIII 11; C. 46, XVI 16.

With adverb YM, or adverbial phrase, followed by noun or participle: **C. 4, II 3;** C. 6, II 20, III 1; C. 8, IV 10.

With participle: C. 31, X 19; C. 35, XII 5; C. 36, XII 11; **C. 39, XIII** 10, **11;** C. 41, XIV 16; C. 46, XVI 13; I. 5, XIX 4.

With noun: C. 46, XVI 1.

MY YḪ·T: C. 7, III 12, IV 2.

YRY M YḪ·T Wꜥ·T, "to mix": XX 17; XXI 15.

M YḪ·T Wꜥ·T, "together": XXI 5; XXI, 8; XXII 13.

YŚ — I. 5, XIX 9.

YŚP — to cut: **C. 23, VIII 18,** 20.

YŚK — also (once only III 9).

Introducing circumstantial clause; "while": C. 7, III 9;

YŚK (*cont.*) C. 17, VII 2; C. 21, VIII 7; C. 33, XI 10; C. 39, XIII 5; C. 42, XIV 18; C. 43, XV 1; C. 47, XVII 12.

YŚK ŚW ḤM, "while at the same time": **C. 13, VI 5;** C. 17, VII 3.

YR YŚK, "now when": XXI 19.

YŚT also (once only VII 8).

Introducing circumstantial clauses; "while": C. 1, I, 9; C. 18, VII 8, 12; C. 23, VIII 18; C. 41, XIII 19, 20, XIV 15; C. 47, XVII 8.

Introducing a parenthetical clause; "although": C. 1, I 11.

YŚT YR, "although": C. 1, I 2.

YR YST, "now when": XXII 1.

YŚT miscellaneous: I. 5, XIX 9.

YŠ[W] spittle: C. 7, **III 3–4.**

YŠW·W protrude; or with det.; also (once only II 10), (twice only V 17; VI 19), (once only VI 15), (twice only VIII 6; XV 21), (once only XII 22): **C. 4, II 4,** 10; C. 5, II 13; C. 8, IV 6; C. 11, V 10; C. 12, V 17; C. 15, VI 15; C. 16, VI 19; C. 21, VIII 6; C. 38, XII 22; C. 46, XV 21.

YḲDW a mason: C. 46, XVI 5.

YT grain: XXI 11.

YTF father: I. 1, XVIII 3.

YTRW river: XXI 20.

streams: I. 1, XVIII 7.

YTḤ draw out; **C. 41, XIV 3**; C. 46, XVI 8.

YṮY take, take away; also (twice only III 17; XIX 7): C. 20, VIII 2; C. 33, XI 15; I. 5, XIX 3, 4, 7.

"moving to and fro" (**C. 7, III 17**).

YDB margin: **C. 41, XIII 21.**

YDR stitching (noun, surgical suture); or with det.; also, (once only VI 11), (once only V 8): **C. 10, V. 6,** 8; C. 14, VI 9, 11; C. 23, VIII 19, 20; C. 26, IX 8; C. 28, IX 21; C. 47, XVI 20; XVII 3, 8.

to stitch: C. 3, I 22 restored; C. 10, V 7; C. 26, IX 10.

ʿ — arm: C. 47, XVI 20.
  Patient unconscious of his ʿ·WY: C. 31, X 13, 15, 17; C. 33, XI 12, 13.
hand: C. 9, V 5; C. 20, VIII 2; I. 2, XVIII 15.
  ʿ of surgeon used in examination: C. 1, lost column restored; C. 2, I 13; C. 7, III 10; C. 13, VI 4; C. 17, VII 1; C. 24, VIII 23; C. 47, XVII 8.
  ḤR ʿ·WY, "immediately": C. 48, XVII 17; XXII 14.

ʿ·T — member: C. 1, I 6, 8; **C. 30, X 12;** C. 41, XIV 7; C. 45, XV 15; C. 47, XVII 6.

ʿʾ — many, great, greatly; also (once only XXII 12): C. 20, VIII 1; C. 46, XV 21; I. 4, XIX 1; XXII 12.

ʿʾ·T — greatness.
  R ʿʾ·T WR·T: C. 41, XIV 11; XXI 10.

ʿʾ — ass: I. 5, XIX 12.

ʿʾ·T — costly stone: XXII 7.

ʿʾ·T — ⌜mould⌝: **C. 6, III 1.**

ʿʾ·T — roll of linen: **C. 47, XVI 19.**

ʿW·T — sheep: **C. 7, III** 11, **21, IV 1.**
animal: I. 5, XIX 6.

ʿW[ʾ]TYW — adversary: C. 9, V 2.

ʿPR — incur (lit. "acquire"): **C. 3, I 24,** ⌜25⌝.

ʿFF — a fly; also (XIX 16): I. 6, XIX 14, 16.

ʿMʿ·T — see ʾMʿ·T.

ʿN·T — claw, finger-nails: C. 8, IV 8, 18 bis; dual = "two claws," indicating the two groups of four fingers of the surgeon's two hands, in setting dislocated mandible, **C. 25, IX 4.**
  ʿN·T-ʾMʿ, "claw of the *ʾamʿe*-bird": **C. 22, VIII 15.**

ʿNʿR·T — a kind of worm: **C. 12,** V 18, **VI** 1–2, **3;** C. 14, VI 10.

ʿNḪ — live: C. 4, II 11; I. 1, XVIII 4; I. 6, XIX 16.
life; also (once only XIX 14): I. 1, XVIII 9; I. 5, XIX 9, 13, 14; I. 8, XX 11.

ʿNTYW — frankincense, or with det. : I. 5, XIX 10; XX 17, XXI 2.

ʿNḎW — jar: XXI 19, 21.

ʿR
Yʿ[R] (older form) — to extend, to penetrate; also (C. 40, XIII 13, 15).

ʿR (*cont.*) — ʿR N, employed with other things than the term "bone": C. 11, V 15; C. 12, V 21; C. 31, X 15; C. 34, XI 23.
ʿR N ḲŚ: **C. 1, lost column** bis restored, I 2 restored, 10; C. 2, I 12, 13, 16 restored; C. 4, II 2, 3, 5; C. 5, II 12, 14; C. 6, II 18, 19; C. 7, III 2, 5, 12; C. 10, V 6; C. 18, VII 8, 12; C. 20, VII 22, 23, VIII 3; C. 27, IX 14, 16; C. 29, X 4, 6.
ʿR R ḲŚ: C. 3, I 18, 19, 21 restored.
Yʿ[R] R ḲŚ: C. 40, XIII 13, 15.

ʿR — elevated, prominent: C. 46, XV 20, XVI 2.
See also ŚʿR and ŚḲR.

ʿR·T — mandible, or with det.; also (once only IX 2): **C. 7, III** 6, 7, **16,** 18; C. 22, VIII 14; C. 24, VIII 22, 23, IX 1; C. 25, IX 2 bis, 4, 5.

ʿRF — to envelope: C. 6, II 24.

ʿḤʾ — contend, or with det. or: **C. 4, II 6,** 11; C. 7, III 6; C. 21, VIII 9; C. 28, IX 22; C. 29, X 7; C. 37, XII 17; C. 45, XV 14–15; C. 47, XVII 11.

ʿḤʿ — to stand: XXII 11.

ʿḤʿ·W — secretions, or without det.: **C. 41, XIII 22—XIV 1;** C. 45, XV 13; C. 47, XVII 9.

ʿḪḪ — evaporate: **XXI 17.**

ʿŠ — cedar, or the like: C. 46, XVI 10.

ʿŠʾ — numerous (adjective): C. 5, II 17.
often, greatly (adverbs); written , : C. 20, VIII 2; C. 28, IX 20; XX 17, XXI 1.

ʿḲ — enter; also : **C. 8, IV** 8, 15, **16 bis;** C. 22, VIII 17; C. 33, XI 14; I. 5, XIX 12; I. 6, XIX 16 bis; XXI 3.
Idiomatic with possible meaning of "undertake": **C. 7, IV 4.**

ʿD — to be whole: **C. 6, II 21.**

ʿD — grease, fat, or with det. ∘, also (once only XIV 5): **C. 41, XIV 5,** 6; C. 46, XVI 10, 11.

ʿḎN·T — ⌜crucible⌝: **C. 6, II 20,** 25; C. 8, IV 10.

Wʾ·T — cord; also (once only III 16): **C. 7, III** 6, 7, 16, **18 bis.**

Wʾ·T — way: I. 4, XVIII 19.

Wʾ·T — evil: **C. 9, V 2.**

WʾBW — of uncertain meaning: C. 24, IX 1.

WʾM — an unidentified drug: **XX 15.**

WʾḤ — apply: C. 28, X 2.

WʾḎ — fresh; also , , (once only X 1).

WT-ḪR-K ŚW ḤR YWF WʾḎ HRW TPY (YDR instead of WT by ancient error of omission V 7): **C. 1, I 3 restored;** C. 2, I 14 restored; C. 10, V. 7; C. 14, VI 11, 12; C. 16, VI 20; C. 17, VII 5; C. 18, VII 10; C. 26, IX 10; C. 27, IX 17; C. 28, X 1; C. 29, X 7; C. 30, X 11; C. 32, XI 4; C. 40, XIII 16; C. 47, XVII 2.

[YWF] WʾḎ HRW TPY ḤR WBNW-F: C. 3, I 22.

green; (once only XV 18).

WʾḎ·T: C. 45, XV 18.

WʾḎ — to be healthy: I. 1, XVIII 9; I. 2, XVIII 14; I. 5, XIX 9; I. 8, XX 11.

WʾḎW — green pigment; also : **C. 41, XIV 5;** C. 46, XVI 10.

WʾḎY·T — Buto: I. 7, XX 2.

WʾḎ-Ḥʾ·T — "green-breasted" (goose): I. 5, XIX 12.

WY — (dependent pronoun, first person, common, singular): I. 1, XVIII 8; I. 2, XVIII 13; I. 7, XX 1; I. 8, XX 10.

Wʿ — one: **C. 1, I 10,** 12 restored; C. 21, VIII 7; C. 31, X 19; C. 34, XII 1; XX 17; XXI 5; XXI 8; XXI 14, 15; XXII 13.

Wʿ, numeral, written I: XXI 4, 5 bis; XXI 6, 7 ter.

Wʿ . . . . Wʿ (also the fem.), "one . . . the other": C. 2, I 17 bis (once restored); C. 10, V 9 bis; C. 33, XI 14 bis; XXI 15 bis.

Wʿ-ŚNY, "one of them both": **C. 35, XII 7;** C. 36, XII 13.

Wʿ·TY — the unique one; also (XX 2): I. 2, XVIII 15; I. 7, XX 2.

WʿB — priests: C. 1, I 6.

WʿF — to contract: C. 8, IV 15.

WʿḤ — an unidentified fruit or grain: **C. 7, III 15.**

WBʾ — to open: C. 6, II 24; **C. 14, VI 13;** C. 26, IX 12; C. 39, XIII 8, 9.

WBNW — wound, or with det. , or (once only VIII 18); also , , , , , , , (twice only X 3, XII 17).

General: C. 1, I 8 restored; C. 2, I 13 restored, 16; C. 3, I 22; C. 9, V 2; C. 10, V 5, 7; C. 14, VI 7; C. 18, VII 7, 10; C. 23, VIII 18; C. 26, IX 6; C. 28, IX 18; C. 40, XIII 12.

WBNW N KF·T, "gaping wound": C. 2, I 12 bis, 14 restored, 15, 17 restored; C. 3, I 18 partly restored, 19 restored, 20–21 partly restored; C. 4, II 2, 3, 5; C. 5, II 11, 12, 14; C. 6, II 18, 18–19; C. 7, III 2, 5, 12; C. 10, V 9; C. 27, IX 13 bis, 15; C. 28, IX 18; C. 29, X 3, 4; C. 47, XVI 16, 17, XVII 10.

WBNW said to be without KF·T ("a gash"): C. 1, I 10; C. 18, VII 7, 11, 12.

WBNW N KF·T ...... Ḫ'ᶜ Ḥᶜ-F, WḎᶜ ŠW·WT-F: C. 47, XVII 1, 5.

Also ŠW·WT-F M WBNW-F: C. 47, XVI 19.

Miscellaneous characteristics:

Perforating, piercing (): C. 14, VI 7, 9, 13; C. 26, IX 7, 9, 11; C. 28, IX 21.

Penetrating (), without KF·T or without mention of KF·T: **C. 1, lost column bis** restored, I 1 restored; C. 10, V 6; C. 18, VII 8; C. 20, VII 22, 23, VIII 3; C. 29, X 6; C. 40, XIII 12–13, 14.

Cutting (): C. 23, VIII 18, 19.

Smashing (): C. 9, IV 19 bis.

ŚPT·WY WBNW-F, "two lips of his wound": C. 1, I 1, 10 restored; C. 14, VI 8, 13; C. 18, VII 13; C. 23, VIII 21; C 26, IX 12; C. 41, XIII 20; see also C. 10, V 9.

R' N WBNW-F, "mouth of his wound": C. 9, IV 20; C. 20, VII 24–VIII 1; C. 28, IX 20, X 3; C. 41, XIII 19, 22, XIV 3, 15, 16; C. 46, XVI 8; C. 47, XVII 9, 14.

ḪNW WBNW-F: C. 37, XII 20; C. 41, XIV 12.

WBNW PG[']-Y: C. 47, XVII 3.

WBNW ḤR-F (or -Ś): C. 8, IV 13; C. 19, VII 15; C. 24, IX 1; C. 37, XII 15 bis, 17, 21; C. 44, XV 7, 8.

WBNW PF NTY ḤR: C. 37, XII 19.

WBNW, symptoms resulting from: C. 7, III 9 bis;

WBNW (*cont.*) C. 28, X 2; C. 41, XIII 19, XIV 12; C. 47, XVII 7 bis, 8, 12; see also ṮŚW, "stiffness," etc.

WBNW, surgical and medical treatment of:

Palpation ( ): C. 1, lost column restored; C. 2, I 13; C. 3, I 19; C. 4, II 3; C. 5, II 12; C. 6, II 19; C. 7, III 2; C. 8, IV 6; C. 10, V 6; C. 18, VII 8; C. 27, IX 14; C. 47, XVI 18 (by error).

Inspecting ( ): C. 19, VII 15.

Examining ( ): C. 26, IX 7; C. 29, X 5.

Healing or drying: C. 9, IV 21; C. 39, XIII 9; C. 41, XIII 21, XIV 5, 8.

Miscellaneous treatment: C. 6, II 22; C. 9, V 5; C. 10, V 8, 9; C. 14, VI 8; C. 23, VIII 20; C. 26, IX 8; C. 28, IX 21; C. 39, XIII 8; C. 46, XVI 7.

WBNW obscure: C. 5, II 17; C. 39, XIII 9; C. 41, XIII 18 bis, XIV 1, 8, 10.

WP·T — crown (of the head): **C. 7, IV 1 bis.**

WPY — to account: C. 8, IV 7.

WPW·TYW — messengers; also (XIX 19): I. 2, XVIII 12; I. 7, XIX 19.

WNN — subsist: **C. 12, VI 3.**

to be; also (XVI 16): C. 7, III 16, 21; C. 9, V 5; C. 34, XII 1 bis; C. 40, XIII 17; C. 42, XIV 21; C. 45, XV 17; C. 46, XVI 13, 16; XXI 18, XXII 10.

WNN+qualitative: C. 7, III 19, 20; C. 14, VI 10; C. 19, VII 21; C. 22, VIII 17; C. 31, X 19, 20; C. 39, XIII 10; C. 41, XIV 8, 10; C. 43, XV 4; C. 45, XV 18.

WNN+ḤR with infinitive: C. 22, VIII 15; XXII 4.

WNT — only with negative N WNT: C. 1, I 1 restored, I 2; C. 2, I 14, 17; C. 8, IV 5, 13; C. 18, VII 8, 9, 12, 13; C. 27, IX 15; C. 42, XIV 18; C. 45, XV 12.

WN — open: C. 7, III 3, 7, 17, IV 2; C. 13, VI 6; C. 17, VII 4; C. 25, IX 3; C. 41, XIV 10.

WNM·T — diet: C. 3, II 2.

WNMY — right: C. 34, XII 2.

WNḪ — dislocation: C. 25, IX 2 bis, 5; **C. 31, X** 12, 13, 15, 16, 17, **18,** 19; C. 34, XI 17 bis, 19, 22; C. 42, XIV 18; C. 43, XIV 22 bis, XV 2, 3.
loosen, be loose (of surgical stitching): C. 10, V 8; **C. 14, VI 11;** C. 23, VIII 20; C. 47, XVII 3, 8. See also V 15.

WNŠY — "*wenesh*-juice": **C. 47, XVII 10.**

WR — large, great, greatly, very; also (once only XXII 12), (thrice only XV 12, XXI 10, XXII 12): C. 4, II 10; C. 6, II 24; C. 12, V 22; C. 39, XIII 5; C. 41, XIV 11; C. 45, XV 12, 17; C. 46, XV 21, XVI 13; XXI 10; XXII 12 bis.
WR·T (or WR) with the meaning "exceedingly" in the phrase "he shudders exceedingly": **C. 4, II 4;** C. 7, III 3; C. 20, VIII 1; C. 29, X 5; C. 40, XIII 14; C. 42, XIV 18.

WR — the great one: I. 1, XVIII 4.

WRM·W — corrugations, ripples: **C. 6, II 20,** 25, III 1; C. 8, IV 10.

WRḤ — anoint, smear: XXII 7; XXII 13.

WRD — to be feeble: **C. 7, III 3.**

WHY — to escape: I. 5, XIX 13.

WHNN — crown of the head; or with determinative : **C. 6, II 21;** C. 8, IV 11.

WḤʿ — to loose: C. 32, XI 5.

WSŠ·T — urine: C. 7, IV 1.

WŚYR — Osiris; also (once only XVIII 2): C. 9, V 3; I. 1, XVIII 2; I. 5, XIX 4, 10.

WŚḪ — wide: **C. 1, I 10** restored, 12.

WŠ·T — fragments; **C. 22, VIII** 12, 15, **16.**

WŠʿḲ·T — scribal error for *mšʿḳ·t,* q. v.

WŠB·T — an unidentified mineral: **C. 41, XIV 5.**

WŠR — to dry up: C. 39, XIII 9.

WGW·T — jaw; also (in dual, once only III 7), (once only VII 14): **C. 7, III** 7, **17,** 18; C. 18, VII 14.

WT — to bind; also , (three times only I 14, XVI 11, XVII 2), (two times only VI 20; IX 10).
WT in applying a medicament:
WT fresh meat: **C. 1, I 2;** C. 2, I 14; [C. 10, V 7 restored]; C. 14, VI 11; C. 16, VI 20; C. 17, VII 5; C. 18, VII 10;

WT (*cont.*) C. 26, IX 10; C. 27, IX 17; C. 28, X 1; C. 29, X 7; C. 30, X 10–11; C. 32, XI 4; C. 40, XIII 15; C. 47, XVII 2.

WT grease, honey and lint: C. 7, III 8; C. 14, VI 12.

WT YMRW (or YMRW and honey): C. 15, VI 16–17; C. 25, IX 5; C. 32, XI 5; C. 35, XII 8; C. 36, XII 13; C. 37, XII 17; C. 38, XIII 2; C. 42, XIV 19; C. 43, XV 2.

After a recipe, WT ḤR-S: C. 41, XIV 5, 6, 7; C. 46, XVI 4, 5, 9, 11.

WT in applying a surgical bandage for purely mechanical purposes, such as support, compression, etc.: C. 12, V 20; C. 34, XI 19.

Do not WT: C. 3, I 22; C. 4, II 6; C. 5, II 15; C. 6, II 23; C. 47, XVII 13.

WT bandage; also (once only XI 5): C. 32, XI 5; C. 41, XIII 21, XIV 14.

WT·W ( ), " wrappings ": C. 45, XV 18.

WT embalmer, professional bandager, or with det. : C. 9, V 5; C. 19, VII 21.

WTḪ to escape: I. 8, XX 10.

WDY put; also , (three times only II 7, 15; X 3), (once only II 1).

WDY the surgeon's hand or finger: C. 1, lost column restored; C. 2, I 13; C. 7, III 9; C. 13, VI 4; C. 22, VIII 10; C. 24, VIII 23; C. 47, XVII 8.

WDY a bandage, a surgical device or a medicament:

WDY with meaning " apply " used with bandage or other surgical device: C. 2, I 15 restored; **C. 11, V 11–12**; C. 12, V 20.

WDY . . . . M ḪNW: C. 35, XII 7; C. 36, XII 12–13.

WDY . . . RDY M: C. 12, V 19.

WDY with meaning " apply " used with the remedy: C. 41, XIV 3, 4; C. 46, XVI 12.

WDY, " apply " with ḤR, " upon," " to ": C. 3, I 22 restored; C. 6, II 23; C. 27, IX 16.

WDY, " place," to indicate the position of patient during examination or treatment: C. 7, III 15; C. 35, XII 4–5; C. 36, XII 10; C. 48, XVII 18–19.

WDY (*cont.*) WDY, " put " a fractured or dislocated bone " into its place ": C. 12, V 18; C. 25, IX 5; C. 34, XI 19.

WDY .... ḤR MNY·WT-F in diet directions: **C. 3, I 22,** II 1; C. 4, II 7; C. 5, II 15; **C. 11, V 12;** C. 19, VII 18; C. 21, VIII 9; C. 28, X 3; C. 29, X 8; C. 47, XVII 13.

WDY miscellaneous:

WD·T NHD and WD·T ʾHT meaning to ⸢show exhaustion⸣: C. 7, III 14, IV 4.

WD·T, " articulations," lit. " puttings ": **C. 43, XV 5.**

WDY M, " assail ": I. 4, XIX 1–2.

WDḤ — pour, pour off, **C. 6, II 25;** C. 20, VIII 5 (with gap where determinative should be).

WḎʾ — to be whole, uninjured: C. 1, lost column restored; C. 2, I 13–14 restored; **C. 8, IV 13;** C. 18, VII 9; C. 27, IX 15; C. 31, X 18.

to be healthy, to flourish: I. 1, XVIII 4; I. 4, XVIII 19, XVIII 19–XIX 1.

WḎʿ — separate: **C. 47, XVI 17,** XVII 1, 6.

WḎʿW — cists: C. 39, XIII 6.

WḎF — to be sluggish: C. 41, XIV 9.

BʾY — clammy; also (once only III 19), (once only III 19): **C. 7, III 10, 19 bis.**

BʾḤ — phallus, member; also (twice only X 14, 22): **C. 31, X 14,** 16, 20, 22.

BʾŚT·T — Bastet: I. 2, XVIII 15; I. 5, XIX 10, 13; I. 7, XIX 20, XX 3.

BʾḲ — to be in an oily condition; also (XIV 1): **C. 41, XIV 1;** C. 46, XV 21–XVI 1.

BʾD·T — dipper: XXII 5.

BY·T — honey; or with det. ○, also seemingly (although seeming may be cursive form of).

BY·T used alone: C. 32, XI 6; C. 35, XII 8; C. 36, XII 14; C. 38, XIII 2; C. 42, XIV 20; C. 43, XV 3; XXI 4; XXI 7.

Grease and BY·T: C. 9, V 4; C. 10, V 8; C. 15, VI 17; C. 18, VII 11; C. 26, IX 11; C. 34, XI 20.

Grease, BY·T and lint: **C. 1, I 3 restored;** C. 2, I 15 restored; C. 3, I 23; C. 7, III 8; C. 11, V 13; C. 12, V 20; C. 14, VI 12; C. 16, VI 21; C. 17, VII 6; C. 19, VII 19; C. 23,

BY·T (*cont.*)	VIII 22; C. 27, IX 17; C. 28, X 1; C. 37, XII 18; C. 40, XIII 16; C. 47, XVII 5, 15. YMRW and BY·T: C. 25, IX 6; C. 30, X 11.
BW	place: I. 1, XVIII 10.
BW·T	abomination; also (once only XVIII 17): I. 3, XVIII 17, 19; I. 8, XX 9.
BB·WY	collar-bones; also : **C. 34, XI** 17 bis, 18, 19, 21, **22**; C. 35, XII 3 ter, 4, 6.
BBY·T	gorget: C. 34, XII 1.
BN·WT	tumors, or with det. ; also (once only XIII 5–6), (once only XIII 3), (once only XV 9), (once only XIII 3): **C. 39, XIII** 3 bis, 5–6, 7, **10**; C. 45, XV 9, 10, 11, 14, 15, 16.
BNW·T	mill-stone: XXII 2.
BNF	excrement, dung: **C. 41, XIV 4;** C. 46, XVI 9.
BḤS	calf: I. 6, XIX 15.
BŚBŚ	a species of goose: I. 5, XIX 12.
BḲŚW	backbone: **C. 31, X 15.**
BKN	urine; also (III 21): **C. 7, III** 11, **21.**
BṮW	desert; forsake: **C. 7, IV 4.**
BḎ᾿·W	stiff rolls; also (V 20): **C. 11, V 13;** C. 12, V 20; C. 23, VIII 21; C. 34, XI 20.
P	mat, seat: **I. 5, XIX 5.**
P	Buto: I. 5, XIX 5.
P᾿	this, the; also (once only II 10): C. 1, I 11 (partly restored); C. 4, II 10; C. 9, V 5 bis; XXI 21.
P᾿W	to have done, ⌜to have incurred⌝; also (once only III 13): **C. 3, II 1;** C. 7, III 13, IV 4.
P᾿YŚ·T	⌜scabs⌝: **C. 41, XIII 21–22.**
P᾿ẖD	to turn over; also (once only XI 18): **C. 8, IV 14; C. 34, XI 18.**
P᾿Ḳ·T	fine linen; or without : I. 5, XIX 11; XXII 13.
P᾿Ḳ·T	shell (or squama of the skull); also (once only IV 19–20), (once only V 1), (once only IV 13): **C. 4, II 9 bis; C. 7, III 16 bis;** C. 8, IV 13; **C. 9, IV 19,** 19–20, **V 1.**

PY·W — ⌜wrinkles⌝: **C. 6, III 1.**

PW — also □ (once only IV 18).

Demonstrative adjective with meaning "this": **C. 9, IV 21.**

Used in nominal sentences as subject or copula: C. 1, I 11; C. 4, II 7; C. 5, II 17; C. 6, III 1; C. 7, III 15, 17, IV 2; C. 20, VIII 5; C. 31, X 16, 20 bis; C. 32, XI 6, 8; C. 34, XII 1; C. 39, XIII 11; C. 41, XIV 11; C. 45, XV 15; I. 1, XVIII 11 bis; XX 14; XXII 8.

Subject of apodosis in a gloss with the sense of "it means": **C. 1, I 4** restored, **10,** 11; C. 2, I 16 restored; C. 3, I 24 restored, 26 restored, II 1, 2; C. 4, II 9, 10, 11; C. 5, II 16; C. 6, II 25; C. 7, III 16, 17, 18, 19, 20, 21, IV 1 bis, 3, 4; C. 8, IV 13, 16 bis, 18; C. 9, V 5; C. 10, V 9; C. 11, V 14; C. 12, V 21, 22, VI 2; C. 14, VI 13; C. 18, VII 12, 14; C. 19, VII 20; C. 22, VIII 14, 16, 17; C. 26, IX 12; C. 31, X 22; C. 33, XI 16; C. 34, XI 22; C. 39, XIII 10; C. 41, XIV 9, 12, 13, 14; C. 42, XIV 21; C. 43, XV 4, 5, 6; C. 45, XV 17; C. 46, XVI 13, 15, 16.

R› PW, "or": C. 8, IV 16.

NT[T] PW, "because": C 1, I 7 bis.

PF — that: C. 4, II 6; C. 5, II 12, 16; C. 6, II 20, 23; C. 7, III 7, 8, 9 ter, 13; C. 8, IV 6, 7 bis, 10; C. 13, VI 4, 5; C. 14, VI 8 bis; C. 16, VI 19; C. 17, VII 2, 3; C. 18, VII 8; C. 19, VII 17; C. 20, VIII 1, 4; C. 21, VIII 7 bis, 8; C. 22, VIII 11; C. 23, VIII 20; C. 24, VIII 23; C. 26, IX 8; C. 28, IX 21, X 2; C. 29, X 5; C. 35, XII 6; C. 36, XII 12; C. 37, XII 16, 19; C. 38, XIII 1; C. 41, XIII 19 bis, 20 bis, 21, 22; C. 42, XIV 18; C. 43, XV 1; C. 46, XVI 3; C. 47, XVII 3, 7 bis, 8, 12 bis.

PN — this: C. 8, IV 16 bis; C. 9, V 3; C. 10, V 8; I. 5, XIX 3 bis, I. 6, XIX 14, 16; I. 7, XX 5; I. 8, XX 11; XXII 7.

PNŚ·T — fluids: XXII 4.

PNḲ — dip out: XXII 4, 6.

PR — house: I. 2, XVIII 16; I. 5, XIX 14. PR-ḤMŚ·WT, XVIII 2.

PRY — come forth: C. 12, V 18; C. 28, IX 20; C. 37, XII 19; C. 41,

PRY (*cont.*) — XIV 9–10, 15, 16; I. 2, XVIII 15; I. 3, XVIII 17, 18; I. 4, XIX 2; I. 6, XIX 15, 16, 17; XXII 4 bis.
become: XXII 8.

PR·T — fruit: XXI 12, 14 bis; , III 21, see p. 196.

PḤ — reach: I. 2, XVIII 13; I. 7, XX 1.

PḤ·WY — end, back.
PḤ·WY of the ramus: **C. 7, III 17;** C. 22, VIII 10, 14 bis; C. 25, IX 3.
PḤ·WY of the mandible: C. 7, III 17, 18; C. 18, VII 14; C. 22, VIII 14.
PḤ·WY of the nose: C. 11, V 15; **C. 12, V 21.**
PḤ·WY of miscellaneous: C. 19, VII 21; C. 31, X 20.
anus; written : XXII 11.

PḤWY·T — anus: XXII 13.

PḤḎ — detach, sever: **C. 31, X 19.**

PẖR — turn, turn around, circulate; also (once only XI 3): C. 19, VII 16; C. 32, XI 2, 3; C. 41, XIV 12; I. 2, XVIII 16.

PẖR·T — prescription, recipe, remedy: **C. 3, II 2;** C. 9, V 2, 5; C. 41, XIV 14; C. 46, XVI 6; XXI 3; XXII 12.

PSḤ — sting: I. 5, XIX 7.

PSD — spinal column, back; or without : C. 7, III 11; C. 48, XVII 15, 16, 17, 18.

PŚY — to cook; also (three times V 4; XX 16; XXII 13): C. 9, V 4; XX 16; XXI 17 bis, XXII 3 bis; XXII 13.

PŠN — split.
PŠN of the skull: C. 1, I 1 restored; C. 2, I 17; **C. 4, II 2,** 3, 5, 6, 8 bis, 10.
PŠN in maxilla: C. 16, VI 18 bis, 19 bis.
PŠN in the temple: C. 18, VII 9; C. 21, VIII 6 bis, 7 bis, 8.
PŠN in the chin: C. 27, IX 15.
PŠN in the arm: C. 38, XII 21, 22, XIII 1 bis.

PG [ʾ]·Y — open: **C. 47, XVII 3,** 8.

PDS — some process in metal working: **C. 6, III 1.**

PDŚ — disfigured, bruised: C. 11, V 10; **C. 12, V** 17, 21–22, **22,** VI 1.

FʾY — to rise, lift; also (III 3, with across): C. 4, II 10; C. 7, III 3; C. 47, XVI 19–20.

⌜FW⌝ — of unknown meaning: **C. 47 XVI 19.**

FND — nose; also (twice only V 14, 21): **C. 11, V** 10 ter, 11, 13, **14 quater,** 15 ter; C. 12, V 16 ter, 17, 21 ter, 22; C. 13, VI 4; C. 14, VI 14; C. 26, IX 8.

FḪ — to loosen: **C. 11, V 15.**

FTT — lint.

Dry FTT alone: C. 28, X 2.

Oil, honey, and FTT: **C. 1, I 3;** C. 2, I 15; C. 3, I 23; C. 7, III 8; C. 11, V 13; C. 12, V 20; C. 14, VI 12; C. 16, VI 21; C. 17, VII 7; C. 19, VII 19; C. 23, VIII 22; C. 27, IX 18; C. 28, X 1; C. 37, XII 18; C. 40, XIII 16; C. 47, XVII 5, 15.

FD — to sweat: C. 7, III 19.

FD·T — sweat: C. 7, III 10, 19.

FDW — four: XX 16.

M — in, on, to, etc. (indicating place where); also before suffix pronouns: C. 1, lost column bis restored, I 1 bis (once restored), 6, 7; C. 2, I 12 restored, 13 restored, 14 bis, 15 restored, 17 restored; C. 3, I 18, 19 restored, 20, 21 bis (once restored), II 1; C. 4, II 2, 3, 4, 5, 6, 8, 9; C. 5, II 11, 12, 13 bis, 14, 15; C. 6, II 18, 19, 20 bis, 22, 25; C. 7, III 2, 4, 5, 6, 9, 12, 13, 17, 18; C. 8, IV 5, 6 bis, 7 ter, 8, 9, 10, 12 bis, 15, 16, 18 bis; C. 9, IV 19 bis, 20, V 3, 5; C. 10, V 5, 6, 7; C. 11, V 10 bis, 11, 12, 14; C. 12, V 16 bis, 17, 18, 19 bis, 21, VI 2, 3 bis; C. 13, VI 3, 4 bis, 5, 6; C. 14, VI 7 bis, 9, 11, 13; C. 15, VI 14, 15, 16; C. 16, VI 18 bis, 19; C. 17, VII 1 bis, 2, 3, 4; C. 18, VII 7 bis, 9, 10, 13; C. 19, VII 15, 17 bis, 18; C. 20, VII 22, 23, VIII 3, 4; C. 21, VIII 6 bis, 8; C. 22, VIII 9, 10, 12, 13 bis, 14, 15; C. 23, VIII 18 ter, 19, 20, 21; C. 24, VIII 22, 23, IX 1; C. 25, IX 2 bis, 4, 5 bis; C. 26, IX 6, 7, 9. 11; C. 27, IX 13, 14, 15, 16; C. 28, IX 18, 19, 22, X 2; C. 29, X 3, 4, 6, 7; C. 30, X 8, 9, 10, 12; C. 31, X 12, 13, 17, 18; C. 32, XI 1 bis, 4, 5, 7; C. 33, XI 9 bis, 12, 13; C. 34, XI 17 bis, 19 bis, 22, 23; C. 35, XII 3 bis, 4, 6, 7 bis; C. 36, XII 9 bis, 10, 12, 13 bis; C. 37, XII 15 bis, 16, 20; C. 38, XII 21, 22, XIII 1 bis; C. 39, XIII 3, 4, 6, 9 bis, 10; C. 40, XIII 12, 13, 14; C. 41, XIII 18 bis, 22, XIV 1, 7, 8, 12; C. 42,

M (*cont.*) 𓅓

XIV 17, 19; C. 43, XV 1, 2, 3, 4, 5 ter; C. 44, XV 6 bis, 8; C. 45, XV 12, 15; C. 46, XV 20, 21, XVI 2, 3, 7, 8, 10, 13 bis; C. 47, XVI 16, 17, 19, XVII 1, 6, 7, 11, 14; C. 48, XVII 16, 17, 18; I. 1, XVIII 7; I. 2, XVIII 15; I. 4, XVIII 19; I. 7, XX 5; I. 8, XX 12; XX 14; XXI 9, 16, 21, XXII 3, 5, 6, 10; XXII 11, 13.

M, "in," introducing state or condition: **C. 12, V 22;** C. 22, VIII 17; C. 41, XIV 1.

M, "into," introducing limit of motion: C. 3, II 1; C. 5, II 16; C. 6, III 1; C. 32, XI 8; C. 33, XI 10, 11, 14 bis, 16 bis.

M, "into," introducing a change of state or condition: C. 5, II 17; C. 9, IV 21; XX 17; XXI 5; XXI 8; XXI 9, 14, 15, 16; XXII 13.

M, "from," indicating source: C. 4, II 4 bis, 6 bis; C. 5, II 13 bis; C. 6, II 22; C. 7, III 4 bis, 6 bis; C. 8, IV 8, 9 bis, 12 bis, 15, 16 bis; C. 11, V 11; C. 13, VI 5 bis; C. 17, VII 3 ter, 4, 5 bis; C. 20, VII 24, VIII 2, 4; C. 21, VIII 7 bis, 8 bis; C. 22, VIII 11 bis, 13 bis, 17; C. 28, IX 20; C. 31, X 14, 20, 22; C. 37, XII 19; C. 41, XIII 19, XIV 3, 10, 15, 16; C. 46, XVI 8; C. 47, XVII 9, 10; I. 3, XVIII 17, 18; I. 4, XIX 2; I. 6, XIX 15; XXI 14.

M, "from," indicating separation: I. 7, XIX 19; XXII 8.

M, "resulting from": C. 3, II 1.

M, "with," indicating means: C. 1, I 3, 4 ter, 5; C. 3, I 23; C. 6, II 23; C. 7, III 14; C. 8, IV 7, 13; C. 10, V 6, 8 bis; C. 11, V 12; C. 12, V 18, 19, 20, VI 1; C. 14, VI 9; C. 19, VII 19; C. 20, VIII 2, 5; C. 22, VIII 11; C. 23, VIII 19; C. 28, IX 21; C. 35, XII 5; C. 36, XII 11; C. 39, XIII 6, 7; C. 40, XIII 14; C. 46, XVI 3, 7 bis; C. 47, XVI 20, XVII 4; I. 5, XIX 10; I. 7, XX 6; XXI 13, XXII 5.

M, "with," introducing the cause of state or condition: C. 7, III 10, 19.

M, "with," giving further description: C. 33, XI 11, 15; C. 39, XIII 4; I. 1, XVIII 8.

M, "as," indicating purpose: C. 9, V 1; I. 1, XVIII 10.

M, "as," meaning "in form of": I. 6, XIX 17 ter.

WPY . . . . M: C. 8, IV 8.

M (*cont.*) 𓅓

M, indicating time when: I. 1, XVIII 11; I. 5, XIX 14.

M, " consisting of ": XXI 14, XXII 5.

M with copulative force: C. 4, II 11; C. 7, IV 4; C. 11, V 14.

M ḪT, " after," " afterward," " when ": C. 1, I 3; C. 2, I 15 restored; C. 3, I 22 restored, 23; C. 9, IV 20, V 3; C. 10, V 7; C. 11, V 13; C. 12, V 19, 20; C. 15, VI 17; C. 16, VI 21; C. 17, VII 6; C. 18, VII 11; C. 23, VIII 21; C. 26, IX 9, 10; C. 27, IX 17; C. 28, X 1; C. 29, X 8; C. 30, X 11 bis; C. 32, XI 6; C. 34, XI 20; C. 35, XII 8; C. 36, XII 14; C. 37, XII 18; C. 38, XIII 2; C. 40, XIII 16; C. 42, XIV 20; C. 43, XV 3; C. 47, XVII 4, 14; XXI 11, XXII 7.

M, idiomatic:

MY ḪPR·T M, " like as it were ": **C. 40, XIII 17;** C. 42, XIV 21.

MḤ M, " grasp ": C. 22, VIII 15.

WDY M, " assail ": I. 4, XIX 2.

TKN M, " draw near to ": I. 7, XX 4.

M ḪT N, " subject to ": I. 1, XVIII 5.

M ŚḪR, " even so ": XXI 15.

R MN M, " as far as ": C. 26, IX 8.

M MYT·T, " likewise ": C. 12, V 22.

M, partitive: XX 13.

M, used erroneously for NT: C. 8, IV 8.

M, scribal error: C. 8, IV 17; C. 39, XIII 3.

M 𓅓 ancient verb used to negative a command: C. 7, IV 4; I. 4, XIX 1; I. 7, XX 3, 4 bis.

M’’ 𓌳𓅓𓅓 to see, inspect, look (with meaning " appear "); also 𓌳𓅓 (twice only VI 1, XIX 1): C. 12, VI 1; C. 19, VII 15; C. 22, VIII 12, 15; C. 30, X 10; I. 4, XIX 1; XXII 11.

M’ʿ 𓌳𓂝𓂻 to extend: **C. 48, XVII 16, 17.**

M’ʿ 𓌳𓂝 temple (of the head): C. 9, V 3.

M’[W] 𓌳𓅓 new: XXI 16.

MY 𓅓𓂝𓇋𓂻 come (imperative): I. 1, XVIII 3.

MY 𓅓𓂝𓈗 water: C. 12, VI 3.

MY 𓐝𓇋 like, as: C. 1, I 4 bis restored: C. 3, I 24; [C. 6, II 20 restored],

MY (*cont.*) 21, III 1 bis; C. 7, III 11, 18, 19, 21 bis, IV 1, 3; C. 8, IV 10, 11; C. 9, V 1; C. 14, VI 14; C. 19, VII 20, 21; C. 20, VIII 2; C. 22, VIII 15, 17; C. 31, X 19; C. 32, XI 8; C. 39, XIII 11; **C. 40, XIII 17;** C. 41, XIV 13, 16; **C. 42, XIV 21;** C. 45, XV 17–18, 19; C. 46, XVI 1, 14; C. 47, XVI 19, XVII 10; XXI 11, 15; XXII 2.

MY ŚẖR, "like": XXI 18.

MY Yẖ·T, "as if": C. 7, III 12, IV 2.

likewise: C. 4, II 8.

MYT·T — the like, a copy: C. 41, XIV 7; I. 5, XIX 2.

MYT·T, "about": XXI 10.

M MYT·T, "likewise": C. 12, V 22.

MYT·T, "like," "likewise": C. 1, I 5; I. 7, XX 8; XXI 14.

MYŚ·T — liver: I. 5, XIX 4.

Mʿ — because of: C. 7, III 18, 20; C. 39, XIII 11; C. 41, XIV 14.

Mʿ NTT: C. 12, V 22.

from, indicating place: I. 6, XIX 18.

ẖPR Mʿ, "done by": **C. 30, X 10.**

NḤM Mʿ, 'save from": I. 1, XVIII 8.

now: **C. 48, XVII 16.**

[M]ʿND·T — morning barque: I. 1, XVIII 7.

MW — water, fluid (secretion), juice: C. 28, IX 19; **C. 45, XV 13** bis; C. 46, XVI 1, 5, 7, 8, 14; C. 47, XVII 10; XXI 16, 17, 21, XXII 2.

MWY — be watery: **C. 41, XIII 22.**

MWY·T — urine: C. 31, X 14, 17, 22 bis.

MW·T — mother: I. 6, XIX 16.

MWT — to die, death: C. 4, II 11; C. 8, IV 16; I. 2, XVIII 15, 16; I. 7, XX 2.

MWT — a dead person, or with ⌓ in fem.; also (XVIII 18): I. 3, XVIII 18; I. 5, XIX 6 bis.

MN — MN M, "fixed in," "attached to" (used anatomically): C. 7, III 17; C. 34, XI 23; C. 43, XV 4.

MN M, "confined to": **C. 23, VIII 19.**

MN M, "sticking in" (used of a foreign substance sticking in a wound): **C. 4, II 9;** C. 23, VIII 20.

MN (*cont.*) — fixed, rigid, stiff (as a symptom): **C. 32, XI 2.**
to press firmly (in feeling an injury): **C. 40, XIII 13.**
MN S'W: **C. 31, X 21.**
R MN M: C. 26, IX 8.

MN — someone: C. 1, I 3.

MN·T — something: C. 1, I 4 bis.

MN — to be sick, to suffer with; also [hieroglyph] (once only XVI 18).
MN ṮSW: **C. 3, I 20**, 21, 26; C. 4, II 4, 6; C. 5, II 13, 15; C. 6, II 22; C. 7, III 4, 6, 13; C. 8, IV 9, 12; C. 19, VII 18; C. 20, VIII 4; C. 22, VIII 13; C. 29, X 6–7.
MN miscellaneous: C. 3, II 1; C. 42, XIV 17, 18; C. 43, XV 1, 4, 5; C. 47, XVI 18, XVII 1; C. 48, XVII 18; XX 13; XXII 11 bis.
MN by error: **C. 1, I 9.**

MN·T — ailment: C. 1, I 5 bis; C. 20, VIII 1.

MN·TY — the two loins: XXI 2.

MNY·WT — mooring stakes: also [hieroglyph] (once only X 8).
WDY (or RDY) R T' ḤR MNY·WT-F: **C. 3, I 23** restored, II 2; C. 4, II 7; C. 5, II 15; C. 28, X 3; C. 29, X 8; C. 47, XVII 13.
WDY-Ḫ̆R-K ŚW ḤR MNY·WT-F: C. 19, VII 18; C. 21, VIII 9.
WDY-Ḫ̆R-K ḤR MNY·WT-F: C. 11, V 12.

MNḪ̆ — R MNḪ̆, "thoroughly": XXI 17, 20, XXII 3.

MNḪ̆Y·W — of unknown meaning: C. 39, XIII 8.

MNŚ' — *emissio seminis*; or with det. [hieroglyph]: **C. 31, X** 16, **19.**

MND·T — cheek; or without [hieroglyph]: **C. 11, V 15;** C. 12, V 22; C. 15, VI 14, 15, 16 bis; C. 16, VI 18 bis, 19; C. 17, VII 1 bis, 2, 4.

MR — ailment, hurt, once without det. (III 13).
MR in verdict 1: **C. 1, I 2;** C. 2, I 14; C. 3, I 21; C. 10, V 7; C. 11, V 11; C. 12, V 17; C. 14, VI 9; C. 15, VI 16; C. 16, VI 20; C. 18, VII 10; C. 19, VII 18; C. 23, VIII 20; C. 25, IX 5; C. 26, IX 9; C. 27, IX 16; C. 30, X 10; C. 32, XI 4; C. 34, XI 19, 22; C. 35, XII 4; C. 36, XII 10; C. 38, XIII 1; C. 39, XIII 6; C. 40, XIII 15; C. 41, XIV 2; C. 42,

MR (*cont.*) XIV 19; C. 43, XV 2; C. 46, XVI 3; C. 47, XVII 2; C. 48, XVII 18.

MR in verdict 2: **C. 4, II 6,** 11; C. 7, III 6; C. 21, VIII 8–9; C. 28, IX 22; C. 29, X 7; C. 37, XII 17; C. 45, XV 14; C. 47, XVII 11.

MR in verdict 3: **C. 5, II 15;** C. 6, II 22; C. 7, III 13; C. 8, IV 9, 12; C. 13, VI 6–7; C. 17, VII 5; C. 20, VIII 4; C. 22, VIII 14; C. 24, IX 2; C. 31, X 17; C. 33, XI 13; C. 37, XII 21; C. 44, XV 9.

MR — bind; also (once only III 18): C. 7, III 11, 13, 18, IV 2.

MRḤ·T — grease; also , or with , or , (once only I 23), (once only VII 6), (once only II 8).

MRḤ·T used alone: C. 4, II 8; C. 6, II 23; C. 11, V 12; C. 12, V 19; C. 20, VIII 5; C. 32, XI 5.

MRḤ·T and honey: C. 9, V 4; C. 10, V 8; C. 15, VI 17; C. 18, VII 11; C. 26, IX 10; C. 34, XI 20.

MRḤ·T with honey and lint: **C. 1, I 3;** C. 2, I 15 restored; C. 3, I 23; C. 7, III 8; C. 11, V 13; C. 12, V 20; C. 14, VI 12; C. 16, VI 21; C. 17, VII 6; C. 19, VII 19; C. 23, VIII 22; C. 27, IX 17; C. 28, X 1; C. 37, XII 18; C. 40, XIII 16; C. 47, XVII 4, 14.

MRḤ·T in prescription: C. 9, IV 20; C. 46, XVI 11; XX 15.

ointment: XX 18; XXII 12.

mass: **XXII 4** bis, 6.

MHWY — ⌜milk⌝: **C. 20, VIII 5.**

MḤ — to grasp: C. 22, VIII 15.

MḤ·T — see ḤM'·T MḤ·T.

MẖNT — countenance; also (III 18–19): **C. 7, III** 10, **18–19.**

MẖNW — interior: C. 22, VIII 16; **C. 26, IX 7.**

MŚḤ — crocodile: I. 5, XIX 7.

MŚẖN·T — Meskhenet, g.: I. 3, XVIII 18.

MŚD·TY — two nostrils: **C. 11, V 14-15,** 15.

MŚDM·T — eye paint: **XX 17.**

MŚḎR — ear: C. 13, VI 5; C. 17, VII 3, 5; C. 18, VII 14; C. 21, VIII 7, 8; **C. 23, VIII 18** bis, 19 bis, 20, 21.

MŚḎR (*cont.*) — MŚḎR·WY (): **C. 4, II 4,** 6; C. 5, II 13; C. 7, III 4, 6; C. 8, IV 9, 12; C. 20, VIII 5; C. 22, VIII 11, 12, 13, 15, 16.

MŚḎR·W-ḤḎR·T — " *Hezret*-ears " (leaves of some plant); or with det. : **XX 18.**

MŠꜥḲ·T — shoulder-blade; also (once only XII 5, scribal error of hieratic *w* for *m*; cf. *šꜣm* in XIII 6 where *w* has been corrected to *m*): C. 35, XII 5; C. 36, XII 11; **C. 47, XVI 18,** XVII 2.

MK·T — protection: C. 9, V 3.

MKꜣ — ⌜depression⌝: **C. 11, V 10.**

MKꜣ·TY — two supports; also (III 15): **C. 4, II 7;** C. 7, III 15.

M[K]Ḥꜣ — back of the head: **C. 1, I 7** bis (once restored), 8.

MT — vessel, canal: **C. 1, I 6, 7, 8 bis;** C. 9, V 3; C. 34, XII 1.
muscle, ligament, without det. : **C. 7, III** 10, 17, **18,** 19, 20.

MTR — customary; also (V 22): **C. 3, II 2;** C. 12, V 22.

MDW — speak: C. 7, IV 3; C. 20, VIII 1; C. 22, VIII 12, 17; C. 33, XI 10–11.
MDW as designation of " beating " of heart: **C. 1, I 8** restored; **C. 7, III 3.**

MDW — word: I. 1, XVIII 9; I. 2, XVIII 15; I. 5, XIX 9.

MD·T — speech: C. 21, VIII 8.

MḎ — deep: **C. 5, II 13.**

MḎ·T — compress: **C. 9, V 4.**

MḎꜣ·T — brace: **C. 7, III 14.**

MḎꜣ·T — book: XXI 9.

MḎD — to press: **C. 8, IV 16.**

N — also (ten times X 21; XI 3; XII 2; XVIII 2, 3, 9, 16; XIX 3, 4, 18).
N, " to," " for," dative of reference or indirect object: C. 2, I 15 restored; C. 3, I 26 bis (once restored), II 2; C. 4, II 7, 8; C. 5, II 17; C. 7, III 7, 14 bis, 17; C. 8, IV 14, 18; C. 9, IV 20 bis, 21, V 4; C. 10, V 6, 8; C. 11, V 11, 13; C. 12, V 18, 20; C. 14, VI 8, 10, 12; C. 19, VII 16 bis, 21; C. 20, VIII 1; C. 22, VIII 11, 12; C. 23, VIII 19, 21; C. 25, IX 3; C. 27, IX 16; C. 28, X 2; C. 30, X 9; C. 31, X 22; C. 32, XI 2 bis; C. 35, XII 6; C. 36, XII 12, 13; C. 37, XII 17;

N (*cont.*) C. 39, XIII 7; C. 41, XIV 2, 4, 6, 10; C. 46, XVI 9, 11; C. 47, XVI 20, XVII 4; C. 48, XVII 16, 19; I. 1, XVIII 2, 3; I. 5, XIX 3, 4; I. 6, XIX 18; I. 8, XX 12; XX 13, 15, 16; XXII 12.

N, "to," indicating place to which: C. 1, lost column bis restored, I 2 restored, 6, 7 restored, 8 ter, 10; C. 2, I 12, 13, 16 restored; C. 4, II 2, 3, 5; C. 5, II 12, 14, 15 (dittography), 16, 17; C. 6, II 18, 19, 24; C. 7, III 2, 5, 12; C. 8, IV 15; C. 10, V 6; C. 11, V 15; C. 12, V 21; **C. 14, VI 13;** C. 18, VII 8, 12; C. 20, VII 22, 23, VIII 3; C. 26, IX 7, 9, 11, 12; C. 27, IX 14, 16; C. 29, X 4, 6; C. 31, X 15; C. 34, XI 21, 23, XII 2; C. 37, XII 20.

N, "for," indicating duration of time: I. 1, XVIII 9; I. 5, XIX 9; I. 8, XX 11.

N, "despite": I. 1, XVIII 9; I. 2, XVIII 14; I. 5, XIX 9; I. 8, XX 11.

DG' N, "look at": C. 3, I 20 restored, 25, 26 bis (once restored); C. 4, II 5; C. 5, II 14; C. 7, III 5; C. 19, VII 16; C. 29, X 5; C. 30, X 9; **C. 32, XI** 2, **3.**

N, indicating possession: C. 46, XVI 2.

N miscellaneous:

RDY N, "apply to": C. 9, V 4; "attach to": I. 5, XIX 11; "put in": XXI 10, XXII 1.

DMY N, "touch," C. 45, XV 17, 18.

TWT N, "liken to": C. 7, IV 2; C. 12, VI 3; C. 45, XV 18.

N ḤRW, "upward": C. 7, IV 3; **C. 31, X 21.**

N H̱RW, "downward": C. 7, IV 3; C. 31, X 21; C. 32, XI 8.

GŚ N ḤRY, "top": XXII 6.

M H̱T N, "subject to": I. 1, XVIII 5.

N, scribal error: C. 39, XIII 8.

N, used for negative particle: **C. 6, II 21; C. 8, IV 11** bis; C. 20, VIII 4.

because of: C. 3, I 24; C. 22, VIII 17; C. 48, XVII 17; I. 2, XVIII 15, 16; I. 7, XX 2.

N[Y] (feminine) genitival adjective; also once (XIX 5), (IV 13): C. 1, lost column ter restored, I 2 restored, 8, 10 restored, 11; C. 2,

N[Y] (*cont.*) (feminine dual) I 12 ter (once restored), 14 restored, 15 bis (once restored), 16 bis (once restored), 17 restored; C. 3, I 18, 19 bis restored, 21 restored; C. 4, II 2, 3 bis, 5, 7, 9 bis; C. 5, II 11, 12 bis, 14, 17; C. 6, II 18 ter, 19 bis, 20, 21, 22, 24, 25, III 1; C. 7, III 2 bis, 5, 6 bis, 7, 9, 10, 11 bis, 12 bis, 14, 15 bis, 16 quater, 18, 19, 20, 21 bis, IV 1 ter, 3 bis; C. 8, IV 5 quater, 6, 8 ter, 10, 12, 13 ter, 15, 16 bis, 17 ter, 18 ter; C. 9, IV 19 bis, 20 ter, 21 bis, V 1, 2 bis, 4 bis; C. 10, V 5, 6 bis, 9 ter; C. 11, V 10 ter, 11 bis, 12, 13, 14 bis, 15; C. 12, V 16 ter, 17, 18 bis, 19, 20, 21 bis, VI 2; C. 13, VI 4; C. 14, VI 7, 10 bis; C. 15, VI 15; C. 16, VI 18, 19; C. 17, VII 1; C. 18, VII 7, 14 bis; C. 19, VII 21; C. 20, VII 23, 24, VIII 2; C. 21, VIII 6, 7; C. 22, VIII 10, 11, 16 bis; C. 23, VIII 18, 19 bis, 21 bis; C. 24, VIII 22; C. 25, IX 4; C. 26, IX 6, 8; C. 27, IX 13 bis, 14, 15; C. 28, IX 18, 19, 20, X 2; C. 29, X 3 bis, 4 quater, 6; C. 30, X 8, 9 bis, 10; C. 31, X 12, 13 bis, 15, 16, 17, 18 bis; C. 32, XI 1 ter, 4, 7 bis, 8; C. 33, XI 9 ter, 12, 13, 14, 16; C. 34, XI 17, 18, 20, 22, 23, XII 1, 2 bis; C. 35, XII 3, 7; C. 36, XII 9, 12; C. 37, XII 15, 17; C. 38, XII 22 bis; C. 39, XIII 3; C. 40, XIII 12, 13, 14, 15, 17 bis; C. 41, XIII 18 ter, 19 bis, 21, 22, XIV 1, 3 bis, 4, 5, 8, 10, 11, 15, 16; C. 42, XIV 17 bis, 19, 21 ter; C. 43, XIV 22 bis, 23 bis, XV 2, 3, 4 bis; C. 43, XIV 22 (*nw*, scribal error); C. 44, XV 6 bis, 7 bis, 8; C. 45, XV 9, 13, 15, 18, 19; C. 46, XV 20, XVI 8, 9, 10, 14; C. 47, XVI 16, 17 bis, XVII 1, 4, 6, 9, 10 bis, 14; C. 48, XVII 15, 16, 17, 18; I. 1, XVIII 1 bis, 8 bis, 10; I. 2, XVIII 11, 12; I. 3, XVIII 17; I. 5, XIX 5, 6, 8; I. 6, XIX 14 bis, 15 bis; I. 7, XIX 18, XX 5, 6, 7; I. 8, XX 10 bis; XX 14; XXI 7; XXI 9, 13, 14 bis, 21, XXII 1, 4, 7, 8, 9, 10; XXII 12, 13.

(plural)

N·T crown (of Lower Egypt): I. 1, XVIII 6.

N·T ⌜Neit⌝ g.: I. 5, XIX 13.

Nʾ these: C. 45, XV 19; XXI 14 bis, 21.

NY for which, or, for whom.

NY in verdict 3: **C. 5, II 15;** C. 6, II 22; C. 7, III 13; C. 8, IV 9, 12; C. 13, VI 7; C. 17, VII 5; C. 20, VIII 4;

NY (*cont.*) C. 22, VIII 14; C. 24, IX 2; C. 31, X 17; C. 33, XI 13; C. 37, XII 21; C. 44, XV 9.

NY with obscure meaning: C. 7, III 17; **C. 18, VII 14.**

NY-ŚWT king: I. 7, XX 4.

NYʾW ibex; also (XVI 11): **C. 41, XIV 6;** C. 46, XVI 11.

NYW ostrich: C. 9, IV 20, 21, V. 1.

NYŚ to call: C. 22, VIII 12.

Nʿʿ ⌜to gain color⌝: **C. 8, IV 9.**

NʿBʾ clamminess; also (XVI 1): **C. 46,** XVI 1, **XVI 14.**

NʿŠ puncture: **C. 3, I 24.**

⌜NWNW⌝ the Celestial Ocean: I. 1, XVIII 7.

NW this: C. 3, II 1.

NW weak particle in YR NW, "now if": C. 1, I 6.

NB every, all, any: C. 1, I 3, 6 bis (once restored), 8 bis; C. 2, I 15; C. 3, I 23; C. 4, II 8; C. 8, IV 5, 13; C. 9, V 2; C. 10, V 8; C. 11, V 13; C. 12, V 18, 20, VI 1, 2; C. 14, VI 10, 12; C. 15, VI 17; C. 16, VI 21; C. 17, VII 7; C. 18, VII 11; C. 19, VII 19; C. 23, VIII 22; C. 25, IX 6; C. 26, IX 11; C. 27, IX 18; C. 28, X 1; C. 30, X 11; C. 32, XI 6; C. 34, XI 20; C. 35, XII 8; C. 36, XII 14; C. 37, XII 18; C. 38, XIII 2; C. 39, XIII 9; C. 40, XIII 16; C. 41, XIV 7; C. 42, XIV 20; C. 43, XV 3; C. 45, XV 12, 15; C. 46, XVI 7; C. 47, XVII 5, 6, 15; I. 1 XVIII 8 bis, 10; I. 5, XIX 6 quinquies; I. 7, XIX 18, XX 8; XXI 12, 14, XXII 1, 9 ter.

NB·T mistress: I. 1, XVIII 6.

NB·T-Ḥ·T Nephthys, g.: I. 1, XVIII 5.

NB tie: I. 7, XX 6.

NBY-M-ḤR-F Flame-in-His-Face (a hostile demon): I. 1, XVIII 1.

NBYBYW be hot: **C. 46, XVI 15.**

NBŚ a kind of tree: **C. 41, XIV 3.**

NPʾPʾ to flutter: **C. 6, II 20,** 21; C. 8, IV 10–11, 11.

NPW enemy: **C. 9, V 3.**

NPḤ·WY two labia: **XXI 1.**

NF·T *sic* breath, wind; also (XVIII 13), (XX 1): I. 1, XVIII 8; I. 2, XVIII 13; I. 7, XX 1.

NFꜣ those: C. 46, XVI 6.

NFNFN unroll: **C. 47, XVI 19.**

N⌜F⌝NFRY of unknown meaning: **I. 5, XIX 12.**

NFR·T unidentified flower: **I. 7, XX 5.**

NFRY·T R as far as: C. 11, V 14, 15; C. 12, V 21.

NFT displacement: **C. 34, XI 22;** C. 43, XV 4.

NN, N negative particle; also (II 21; IV 11 bis; VIII 4).

: C. 1, I 1 restored, 2; C. 2, I 14 restored, 17; C. 8, IV 5, 13; C. 18, VII 8, 9, 12, 13; C. 27, IX 15; C. 42, XIV 18; C. 45, XV 12.

: **C. 5, II 15;** C. 6, II 22; C. 7, III 13; C. 8, IV 9, 12; C. 13, VI 7; C. 17, VII 5; C. 20, VIII 4; C. 22, VIII 14; C. 24, IX 2; C. 31, X 17; C. 33, XI 13; C. 37, XII 21; C. 44, XV 9.

With infinitive: **C. 1, I 10,** 11; C. 3, II 2; C. 7, III 17; C. 22, VIII 17; C. 33, XI 15; C. 41, XIV 9; **C. 42, XIV 18;** I. 6, XIX 17.

With *śdm-f* form: C. 6, II 21, III 1; C. 8, IV 11 bis; C. 9, V 3; C. 18, VII 12; C. 20, VIII 2; C. 31, X 14; I. 2, XVIII 13, 15; I. 7, XIX 20, XX 1, 2.

With N-form: **C. 3, I 20** restored, 25, 26 bis (once restored); C. 4, II 4, 9; C. 5, II 14; C. 6, II 21; C. 7, III 4 bis, 17; C. 8, IV 14; C. 20, VIII 1; C. 22, VIII 12; C. 25, IX 3; C. 29, X 5; C. 31, X 21 bis, 22; C. 32, XI 2, 3; C. 33, XI 10 C. 41, XIII 20, 21, XIV 13; C. 45, XV 12, 13 bis; I. 2, XVIII 16; XX 13.

With noun: C. 1, lost column restored, I 1 ⌜restored⌝, 11 restored; C. 9, V 3; C. 45, XV 15; C. 46, XVI 15; XXI 18; XXII 1.

With pronoun: C. 12, V 22.

With adjectival predicates: **C. 1, I 10** restored, 12.

Used for dative N or genitival adjective N[Y]: **C. 31, X 21;** C. 32, XI 3; C. 34, XII 2; I. 1, XVIII 2, 3, 9; I. 2, XVIII 16; I. 5, XIX 3, 4, 5, 7; I. 6, XIX 18.

NN — these, this; also (XXII 6): **C. 46, XVI 5–6;** XXII 6.

NNY — to move feebly, drag: **C. 8, IV 14.**
to dribble; also (X 22), (X 17): **C. 31, X 17, 22.**

NNM — to wander: **C. 3, II 1.**

NR'W — See NY'W.

NR·T — vulture: I. 1, XVIII 10.

NRW·T — sprain; or with det. ; also (twice only XVII 15, 16), or with det. (once only XVII 18): **C. 30, X** 8, 9, 10, **12;** C. 42, XIV 17, 19; C. 48, XVII 15, 16, 18.

NH·T — sycamore: C. 46, XVI 12.
ḎRḎ NH·T (, XIV 7; or without), "sycamore leaves": C. 41, XIV 7; C. 46, XVI 8.

NHD — exhaustion: C. 7, III 14.
See also 'HT and HD.

NHDHD — to throb: **C. 6, II 20,** 21; C. 8, IV 10, 11.

NḤ' — disturbing, foreign; or with det. : **C. 4, II 3-4;** C. 6, III 1.

NḤB·[T]-K'W — Neheb-kau, g.: I. 5, XIX 10.

NḤB·T — neck: C. 3, I 20, 21; II 1 ter; C. 4, II 4, 6, 8; C. 5, II 14, 15; C. 6, II 22; C. 7, III 4, 6, 10, 13, 19, 20; C. 8, IV 9, 12; C. 19, VII 16, 18; C. 20, VIII 4; C. 22, VIII 14; C. 29, X 3, 4 bis, 6 bis, 7; C. 30, X 8, 9, 10; C. 31, X 12–13, 13, 15, 16, 17, 18 bis; C. 32, XI 1 bis, 2, 4, 5, 7, 7–8, 8; C. 33, XI 9, 10, 12, 14 bis, 16.

NḤM — to save: I. 1, XVIII 8.

NḤM·T — rescue (noun): C. 9, V 3.

NḤḎ·WT — teeth: C. 7, III 10–11.

NḪB·T — Nekhbet, g.: I. 1, XVIII 3.

NḪBḪB — to break through, crepitate; also (once only XV 7–8): **C. 13, VI 4-5;** C. 17, VII 2; C. 24, VIII 23; C. 37, XII 16; C. 44, XV 7–8.

NḪT — to be stiff, or with det. (twice III 17, 20): C. 7, III 17, 20.
ḤNN NḪT (applied to erection of phallus): **C. 31, X 14,** 20.

Nẖ — fluid: **C. 6, II 24–25.**
See also NŠW.

NSY — to settle: **C. 32, XI 8.**

NSW·T — displacement: **C. 32, XI** 1 bis, 4, **7.**

NS-Š' — "garden tongue," a plant: **C. 41, XIV 7.**

NSR — to burn, to be inflamed: C. 28, IX 20; **C. 41,** XIII 19, **XIV 2, 8,** 11; C. 47, XVII 8, 11 12.

NSR·T — fever: I. 4, XIX 1.

NSR — anoint: **C. 6, II 22.**

NŠW — issue (verb); also (once only XIII 19), (once only XVII 9), (scribal error, once only XIV 15): **C. 41,** XIII 19, **XIV 15,** 16; C. 47, XVII 9.

issue, discharge (noun): **C. 31, X 20.**

See also NH̱.

NŠNY — disaster, to work disaster; or with det.: I. 2, XVIII 13–14; I. 4, XIX 1, 2; I. 7, XIX 20–XX 1.

NḲW·T — moisture: **XXI 18.**

NḲR — to sift: XXI 13.

NḲRW — sieve: XXI 13.

NKT·W — some, also , a piece (XX 5): C. 22, VIII 15; I. 7, XX 5.

NG'Y — to rend open: also (once only II 23), (once only X 12), (twice only II 22, IV 11): **C. 6, II** 18, **19,** 22, 23; C. 8, IV 11; C. 30, X 12.

NTY — (feminine) — which, also (twice only I 7 bis): C. 1, I 7 bis; C. 4, II 4, 10 bis; C. 5, II 13 bis; C. 6, II 20; C. 7, III 9; C. 8, IV 6, 7 bis, 10; C. 9, V 5 bis; C. 11, V 10; C. 12, V 17, 19, VI 2; C. 31, X 18; C. 37, XII 19; C. 38, XIII 1; C. 39, XIII 7; C. 41, XIII 22, XIV 9, 14, 15 (dittography); C. 45, XV 19; C. 46, XVI 3, 7, 13; C. 47, XVII 7; XXI 21.

one who: C. 7, IV 3.

NTT introducing proposition after particles meaning "because": **C. 7, IV 4.**

ḎR NTT: C. 4, II 11.

Mʿ NTT: C. 12, V 22.

ḤR NTT: I. 1, XVIII 4.

NTY used erroneously for YWTY: C. 8, IV 8.

NTY used for N[Y]: C. 8, IV 13.

NTNT — membrane; **C. 6, II 24.**

NṮR — god: C. 8, IV 16; I. 3, XVIII 18.

NT̲R·T — an unidentified drug: **C. 46, XVI 4.**

⌜ND̲⌝ — ⌜to husk⌝: **XXI 11** bis; more probably to be read , q. v.

ND̲ — to ask: C. 20, VIII 1.

ND̲ — triturate, grind; or with det. ; also (once only XIV 5): C. 9, IV 20, 21; **C. 41, XIV 5,** 6; C. 46, XVI 4, 5, 12; XXI 5; XXII 2; XXII 13.

ND̲M — to be easy, comfortable; also (I 26, twice, once restored; III 17; IV 14): C. 3, I 26 bis (once restored); C. 7, III 7, 17; C. 8, IV 14.

to recover.

R ND̲M-F ("until he recovers"): C. 1, I 3; C. 2, I 15; C. 3, I 23; C. 10, V 8; C. 11, V 14; C. 12, V 20; C. 14, VI 12; C. 15, VI 17; C. 16, VI 21; C. 17, VII 7; C. 18, VII 11; C. 19, VII 19; C. 23, VIII 22; C. 25, IX 6; C. 26, IX 11; C. 27, IX 18; C. 28, X 2, 3; C. 30, X 12; C. 32, XI 7; C. 34, XI 21; C. 35, XII 8; C. 36, XII 14; C. 38, XIII 2; C. 40, XIII 16; C. 42, XIV 20; C. 43, XV 3; C. 47, XVII 5, 15.

sweet: XX 15, 17.

ND̲RY — to draw together, or with det. ; also (twice only VI 8, IX 21): **C. 10, V 6,** 8; C. 14, VI 8; C. 23, VIII 19; C. 26, IX 8; C. 28, IX 21; C. 47, XVI 20, XVII 3.

ND̲R·WT — seizures: **XXII 11.**

ND̲S — little, contracted, narrow; also (once only VII 12): C. 1, I 10, 12; **C. 3, I 24;** C. 7, III 19; C. 18, VII 12.

ND̲S·TYW — malignant spirits: **I. 2, XVIII 12.**

ND̲SD̲S — consume: **I. 7, XIX 19.**

R — or before suffix pronouns.

R, "to," showing direction of motion: C. 2, I 17; C. 4, II 10; C. 10, V 9; C. 20, VIII 2, 5; C. 34, XI 18; I. 1, XVIII 3; I. 2, XVIII 16; ⌜I. 5, XIX 12⌝; I. 6, XIX 17.

R, "to," with meaning "as far as": C. 3, I 18, 19, 21 restored; C. 12, V 22; C. 18, VII 12, 14; C. 28, IX 19, 22; C. 40, XIII 13, 15; C. 41, XIV 11, 12; XXI 10.

ŚPR R YH̲·T, "to reach a decisive point": **C. 4, II** 8, **10;** C. 6, II 23; C. 7, III 8, 15; C. 8, IV 9; C. 21, VIII 9; C. 37, XII 19.

R (*cont.*) ⊂⊃

R, "to," used of application of medicaments: C. 41, XIV 3, 4; C. 46, XVI 3, 12.

R, "to," dative of reference: C. 7, III 3; C. 31, X 16, 20; C. 41, XIII 19, XIV 15, 16; C. 45, XV 14, 19; C. 46, XVI 5; C. 47, XVII 9.

R, indicating place into which: I. 5, XIX 5; I. 6, XIX 16; XXI 3; XXI 19, XXII 7.

R, indicating place at which (especially of parts of the body): **C. 6, II 25;** C. 7, III 4; C. 8, IV 10; **C. 18, VII 14;** C. 22, VIII 16; I. 1, XVIII 10; I. 5, XIX 11; I. 8, XX 9.

R, "concerning": C. 1, I 1 restored, 8; C. 2, I 14; C. 3, I 20 restored; C. 4, II 5; C. 5, II 14; C. 7, III 5, 12; C. 8, IV 14, 15; C. 10, V 7; C. 11, V 11; C. 12, V 17; C. 13, VI 6; C. 14, VI 9, 14; C. 15, VI 16; C. 16, VI 19; C. 17, VII 4; C. 18, VII 10, 13; C. 19, VII 17, 21; C. 20, VIII 3; C. 21, VIII 8; C. 22, VIII 13; C. 23, VIII 19; C. 24, VIII 23; C. 25, IX 5; C. 26, IX 8, 13; C. 27, IX 15; C. 28, IX 21; C. 29, X 6; C. 30, X 10, 12; C. 31, X 17, 18, 19; C. 32, XI 3, 7; C. 33, XI 12, 14; C. 34, XI 18; C. 35, XII 4; C. 36, XII 10; C. 37, XII 16, 20; C. 38, XIII 1; C. 39, XIII 5; C. 40, XIII 14; C. 41, XIV 1, 10, 11; C. 42, XIV 19; C. 43, XV 1; C. 44, XV 8; C. 45, XV 14; C. 46, XVI 2; C. 47, XVI 20, XVII 10; C. 48, XVII 18; XX 14.

R, "to," before infinitives: C. 7, III 3; C. 8, IV 14; C. 22, VIII 16.

R, "until": C. 4, II 7; C. 6, II 23; C. 7, III 8, 15; C. 8, IV 9 bis; C. 11, V 12; C. 12, V 18; C. 16, VI 20; C. 17, VII 6; C. 21, VIII 9; C. 22, VIII 12; C. 35, XII 6; C. 36, XII 12; C. 37, XII 18; C. 46, XVI 6; XXI 12, 18.

R NḎM-F: C. 1, I 3; C. 2, I 15; C. 3, I 23; C. 7, III 7; C. 10, V 8; C. 11, V 14; C. 12, V 20; C. 14, VI 12; C. 15, VI 17; C. 16, VI 21; C. 17, VII 7; C. 18, VII 11; C. 19, VII 19; C. 23, VIII 22; C. 25, IX 6; C. 26, IX 11; C. 27, IX 18; C. 28, X 2, 3; C. 30, X 12; C. 32, XI 7; C. 34, XI 21; C. 35, XII 8; C. 36, XII 14; C. 38, XIII 2; C. 40, XIII 16; C. 42, XIV 20; C. 43, XV 3; C. 47, XVII 5, 15.

R ŚW>Y >·T YH-F: C. 3, I 23 restored; C. 4, II 7; C. 5, II 15; C. 19, VII 18; C. 29, X 8; C. 47, XVII 13.

R (*cont.*) 𓂋

R, " in order to ": C. 1, I 4, 5, 9 bis; C. 2, I 17 restored; C. 10, V 9; C. 22, VIII 16; C. 35, XII 6; C. 36, XII 12; I. 2, XVIII 13; I. 7, XIX 20; XXI 19.

R, " in order that ": I. 2, XVIII 13; XXII 14.

R, " from," expressing separation: C. 1, I 10, 12 restored; C. 4, II 9; C. 7, III 16; C. 31, X 18, 19; I. 3, XVIII 19; I. 4, XIX 2; I. 5, XIX 14.

Ś’T R: **C. 14, VI 8;** C. 35, XII 4; C. 36, XII 10; C. 47, XVI 19.

R, with suffix pronoun, as emphatic or impersonal reflexive: C. 36, XII 9; I. 1, XVIII 2, 3; I. 4, XVIII 19; I. 5 XIX 4.

’NRY R-F: **C. 4, II 4;** C. 7, III 3; C. 20, VIII 1 C. 29, X 5; C. 40, XIII 14; C. 42, XIV 18.

R miscellaneous:

R, " as ": C. 8, IV 7.

R, " because of ": C. 6, III 1.

R, " or ": C. 4, II 11.

R, " for " (duration of time): XX 16.

R-Ś, " therein ": XXI 18, XXII 1.

R idiomatic:

WDY R T’, " moor ": C. 3, I 22, II 1; C. 4, II 7 C. 5, II 15; C. 28, X 3; C. 29, X 8; C. 47, XVII 13.

R T’, " off," " away," " entirely ": **C. 4, II 9;** C. 7 III 4; C. 47, XVII 14.

R H’W, " next to ": C. 7, IV 1.

R Ś’, " afterward," " after ": XX 18; XXII 5.

R MNḪ, " thoroughly ": XXI 17, 20, XXII 3.

R ḤR, " against ": I. 2, XVIII 14; I. 7, XX 1.

R R’, " through ": **C. 23, VIII 18,** 20.

R MN M, " as far as ": C. 26, IX 7.

R S’BY R, ⌜" as far as "⌝: **C. 32, XI 5.**

NFRY·T R, " as far as ": C. II, V 14, 15; C. 12, V 21

R, scribal errors: C. 33, XI 15; C. 36, XII 13.

R’ 𓂋𓏤 the mouth: C. 9, V 2; I. 6, XIX 14, 15.

R’ of the patient: C. 7, III 3, 8, 11, 13, 14, 18, IV 2, 3 C. 13, VI 6; C. 17, VII 3, 4, 5; C. 25, IX 3 bis, 4; C. 2 IX 7, 9, 12 bis.

R' (*cont.*) — R' of the wound: C. 9, IV 20; C. 20, VII 24; C. 28, IX 20, X 2; C. 41, XIII 19, 22, XIV 3, 10, 15, 16; C. 46, XVI 8; C. 47, XVII 9, 14.
incantation: I. 1, XVIII 1; I. 6, XIX 14; I. 7, XIX 18, XX 5; I. 8, XX 11.
R' PW, "or": C. 8, IV 16.
R R', "through": **C. 23, VIII 18,** 20.
R' used erroneously for GŚ: **C. 13, VI 5.**
See also ḤMW·T-R'.

R'-YB — abdomen: **XX 13.**

R'-ḪMN(W) — ⅛: XX 15.

RY·T — pus, or with det.: **C. 6, III 1;** C. 39, XIII 4, 6, 11, 12. Formerly read TY·T.

RW·T (RY·T) — pigment, color, is possible in **C. 7, III 21,** see p. 196.

RWTY — outside: **C. 8, IV** 8, 15, **16** ter; C. 22, VIII 17.
the open: I. 2, XVIII 16.

RWḎ — hard: C. 45, XV 17, 18.

RMY — to weep: C. 7, III 12, IV 2, 4.

RMY·T — tears: C. 20, VIII 1.

RMṮ·T — men: I. 3, XVIII 18.

RNP·T — year; or with det.: I. 1, XVIII 8, 11 bis; I. 5, XIX 8, 14; I 7, XIX 20.

RNPY — a youth: XXI 9.

RḪ — to know, recognize: C. 1, I 5 restored, 6 restored, 9 bis; C. 4, II 7, 10, 11; C. 6, II 23; C. 7, III 8, 15; C. 8, IV 9; C. 20, VIII 3; C. 21, VIII 9; C. 31, X 14; C. 37, XII 18; XXI 17, 20, XXII 3.

RḪTY — launderer: XXII 1.

RD — foot, leg; also (as dual, once only I 8): C. 1, I 7, 8; C. 31, X 13, 16, 17; C. 32, XI 8; C. 33, XI 12, 13; C. 48, XVII 16; XXII 11.

RDY — give: C. 8, IV 18; I. 8, XX 12; XXII 12.
cause that; also: C. 2, I 17 restored; C. 7, III 3, 7, 14 bis; C. 10, V 9; C. 22, VIII 16; C. 31, X 15; C. 33, XI 11, 15; I. 7, XX 6; XXI 3; XXI 13.
TM RDY, "prevent"; I. 5, XIX 11.

RDY (*cont.*) — discharge; written , also , DY: C. 4, II 4, 5; C. 5, II 13; C. 6, II 22; C. 7, III 4, 6; C. 8, IV 8, 12; C. 11, V 11; C. 13, VI 5; C. 17, VII 2, 3, 4; C. 20, VII 24, VIII 3; C. 21, VIII 7, 8; C. 22, VIII 13.

put (patient on normal diet): C. 3, II 2.

apply; also , :

RDY the hand or finger: C. 1, I 6; C. 17, VII 1; C. 20, VII 24; C. 25, IX 3; C. 45, XV 11.

RDY the remedy: C. 4, II 8; C. 9, IV 20, V 4; C. 32, XI 5; XXI 1.

RDY a bandage or similar: C. 2, I 17 restored; C. 7, III 14; C. 9, IV 21, V 5; C. 10, V 9; C. 12, V 19.

lead; written : C. 34, XII 2.

put, place; also (XXII 6): I. 1, XVIII 10; XX 18; XXI 10, 16, 19, XXII 1, 3, 5, 6, 7; XXII 13.

RDY N, "attach to": I. 5, XIX 11.

RḎW — excrement: I. 6, XIX 17, 18.

H'Y — enter, descend: C. 22, VIII 16; I. 7, XX 3, 4.

fall, drop, exude, discharge; also (once only VIII 2): **C. 20, VII 24,** VIII 2; **C. 22, VIII 11;** C. 31, X 14, 22; C. 41, XIV 1; C. 46, XVI 6–7; C. 47, XVII 9.

H'W — vicinity, neighbourhood, or with det. .

R H'W, "next to": C. 7, IV 1.

M H'W, "at the point of": C. 13, VI 4; **C. 17, VII 2.**

HN — chest: **C. 7,** III 11, 21, **IV 1,** 2.

HNY — the rejoicing one: I. 7, XX 3.

HNW — *hin*-jar: XXII 5, 6–7.

HRW — day; also : C. 1, I 3 bis (once restored); C. 2, I 14 restored, 15; C. 3, I 22, 23; C. 9, V 1; C. 10, V 7, 8; C. 11, V 13; C. 12, V 20; C. 14, VI 11, 12; C. 15, VI 17; C. 16, VI 20, 21; C. 17, VII 5, 7; C. 18, VII 11 bis; C. 19, VII 19; C. 23, VIII 22; C. 25, IX 6; C. 26, IX 10, 11; C. 27, IX 17, 18; C. 28, X 1 bis; C. 29, X 7; C. 30, X 11 bis; C. 32, XI 4, 6; C. 34, XI 20; C. 35, XII 8; C. 36, XII 14; C. 37, XII 18; C. 38, XIII 2; C. 40, XIII 16 bis; C. 42, XIV 20; C. 43, XV 3; C. 47, XVII 2, 5, 15; XX 16.

HRP	to sink: **C. 5, II 13,** 16, 17; C. 32, XI 7.
HHNW	jubilation: I. 5, XIX 2–3.
HD	weak place: C. 8, IV 11. See also ʾHT and NHD.
Ḥ·T-ḤR	Hathor, g.: I. 1, XVIII 6.
Ḥʾ	behind: **C. 23, VIII 19.** around: I. 1, XVIII 4, 9; I. 5, XIX 13; I. 8, XX 11.
Ḥʾ	back (noun): **C. 23, VIII 21.**
Ḥʾ·TYW	linen: **I. 7, XX 6.**
ḤʾY·T	covering: **C. 9, IV 21,** V 4.
ḤʾY·T	⌜shelter⌝: **I. 7, XX 5.**
Ḥʾ·T	the front: Ḥʾ·T ḤR, " forehead ": C. 9, IV 19 bis, V 5. ḤR Ḥʾ·T, " before ": I. 7, XX 5.
ḤʾTY-ʿ	beginning: XXI 9.
ḤʾTY	heart; also (once only I 9): C. 1, I 6, 7, 9. breast: I. 5, XIX 3.
ḤʾḤʾ	fumble: **C. 8, IV 15.**
Ḥʿ·W	flesh (plural): C. 1, I 11; C. 4, II 9; C. 7, III 8; C. 8, IV 13, 17; C. 23, VIII 18, 19, 20; C. 31, X 18; C. 34, XII 1 bis; C. 47, XVI 17, XVII 1, 5, 7; XXII 8, 10.
ḤWY	to smite: I. 4, XVIII 19.
ḤWʾ	to have an evil odor: XX 18.
ḤWʿ	short: **C. 35, XII 4.**
ḤWN	roast: **C. 42, XIV 21.**
ḤBŠ	linen; or without plural strokes. Used in surgical dressings: Strips of linen: C. 2, I 15 restored, 16; C. 10, V 9; C. 47, XVII 4. Bands of linen: C. 2, I 17 restored; C. 10, V 9. Swabs, plugs, or tampons of linen: C. 11, V 11, 12; C. 12, V 18, 19; C. 14, VI 10. Stiff rolls of linen: C. 11, V 13; C. 12, V 20; C. 23, VIII 21; C. 34, XI 20.

ḤBŚ (*cont.*) Splints of linen: C. 35, XII 7; C. 36, XII 12; C. 37, XII 17.

Padded with linen: C. 7, III 14.

ḤFʾW serpent: I. 5, XIX 7.

ḤM·T vulva; also (XX 14): **XX 14,** 15.

ḤM weak temporal particle.

YŚK ŚW ḤM, " while at the same time ": **C. 13, VI 5;** C. 17, VII 3.

ḤMW·T-Rʾ incantation: I. 1, XVIII 8.

and so forth: I. 6, XIX 15.

ḤMʾ ball: **C. 45, XV 18.**

ḤMʾ·T-MḤ·T northern salt; also (XXI 5): **C. 41, XIV 5-6;** C. 46, XVI 11; XXI 5; XXI 7.

ḤMʾY·T an unidentified fruit; or with dets.: **C. 45, XV 18;** XXI 9–10.

ḤMʾTY bulging; or with plural strokes: **C. 45, XV** 9, 10, 13–14, 14, 15, **16.**

ḤMSY to sit; or with det.: **C. 4, II 7;** C. 7, III 15; C. 8, IV 9; C. 16, VI 20; C. 17, VII 6; C. 20, VIII 5; C. 32, XI 6; XXII 11.

ḤMT copper: C. 6, II 20, 25 bis; C. 8, IV 10.

ḤMT·Y coppersmith: C. 6, II 25.

ḤN·W ribs: **C. 42, XIV** 17 bis, 19, **20–21;** C. 43, XIV 22, 22–23, 23, XV 2, 3, 4; C. 44, XV 6, 6–7, 7, 8.

ḤNY-Tʾ a kind of herb; also: **C. 41, XIV 4;** C. 46, XVI 9.

ḤNW jar, vase: C. 3, I 24; XXII 7.

ḤNʿ and, with: C. 3, I 20 restored, 25; C. 4, II 5, 8; C. 5, II 14; C. 7, III 5; C. 8, IV 8, 17, 18; C. 29, X 5; C. 30, X 9; C. 32, XI 2, 3; XXI 1; XXI 13.

ʿḤʾ ḤNʿ, " contend with ": C. 4, II 6, 11; C. 7, III 6; C. 21, VIII 9; C. 28, IX 22; C. 29, X 7; C. 37, XII 17; C. 45, XV 15; C. 47, XVII 11.

ḤNʿ, " besides ": XX 16.

ḤNN phallus: C. 31, X 14, 20 bis.

ḤNŚ narrowness: C. 18, VII 13.

HNKY·T bed; or with plural strokes: I. 5, XIX 8; I. 7, XX 8.

ḤNT'  porcupine: **C. 40, XIII 17.**

ḤNT'  manubrium: **C. 40, XIII** 13 bis, 15, **17.**

ḤR  Horus, g.: C. 9, V 2; I. 1, XVIII 9; I. 2, XVIII 14 bis; I. 5, XIX 5, 9; I. 7, XX 1, 2; I. 8, XX 10.

ḤR  face: C. 7, III 3, 10, 12, 20, 21, IV 2, 3; C. 12, V 17, 22 bis, VI 1; C. 20, VIII 2; C. 32, XI 2, 3; C. 34, XI 18; C. 46, XVI 2; XXI 6.

Ḥ'·T ḤR, "forehead": C. 9, IV 19 bis, V 5.

R ḤR, "against": I. 2, XVIII 14; I. 7, XX 1.

See also ḪFT-ḤR.

ḤR  upon, on, in, into, etc. (indicating place where or place to which); also : C. 1, lost column restored, I 7 quinquiens (twice restored); C. 2, I 13, 15 restored, 17 restored; C. 3, I 22; C. 6, II 23, III 1; C. 7, III 10; C. 8, IV 5, 13; C. 9, IV 21, V 5 bis; C. 10, V 9; C. 11, V 10 bis, 14; C. 12, V 20; C. 13, VI 4; C. 15, VI 16; C. 17, VII 2; C. 19, VII 15, 21; C. 20, VII 24; C. 22, VIII 10 bis; C. 24, VIII 23; C. 25, IX 3; C. 27, IX 16; C. 33, XI 16; C. 39, XIII 4, 7 ter, 10, 11; C. 41, XIV 5, 6, 7, 9, 15 bis (dittography); C. 45, XV 9, 10 bis, 11 bis, 16, 17, 19; C. 46, XV 21, XVI 4, 5, 9, 11, 15, 16; C. 47, XVII 4, 9; I. 5, XIX 8, 11; I. 7, XX 4 bis; XX 15, 18; XXI 20, XXII 1, 2 bis, 6.

ḤR Š' N: **C. 8, IV 6;** C. 16, VI 19; C. 21, VIII 6; C. 38, XII 22.

ḤR Y'BY: C. 34, XII 2.

ḤR WNMY: C. 34, XII 2.

ḤR, "on" (figurative): C. 3, II 2.

ḤR, "over" meaning "above": C. 1, I 11; C. 4, II 4, 10 bis; C. 5, II 13; C. 11, V 10; C. 12, V 17; C. 24, IX 1; C. 31, X 18; C. 34, XI 21, XII 1 bis; C. 37, XII 15 bis, 17, 19, 21; C. 44, XV 7, 9; XXI 16, XXII 3.

ḤR, "over" in the expression "to say a charm over": C. 9, V 2; I. 1, XVIII 9; I. 5, XIX 10.

ḤR, "over" ("in charge of"): I. 7, XX 1.

ḤR in the phrase ḤR MNY·WT-F, "at his mooring stakes": C. 3, I 23 restored II 2; C. 4, II 7; C. 5, II 15;

ḤR (*cont.*) — C. 11, V 12; C. 19, VII 18; C. 21, VIII 9; C. 28, X 3; C. 29, X 8; C. 47, XVII 13.

ḤR in WT ḤR, "to bind with": C. 1, I 2; C. 2, I 14 restored; C. 7, III 8; C. 10, V 7; C. 14, VI 11, 12; C. 15, VI 17; C. 16, VI 20; C. 17, VII 5; C. 18, VII 10; C. 25, IX 6; C. 26, IX 10; C. 27, IX 17; C. 28, X 1; C. 29, X 7; C. 30, X 11; C. 32, XI 4, 6; C. 34, XI 20; C. 35, XII 8; C. 36, XII 14; C. 37, XII 17; C. 38, XIII 2; C. 40, XIII 15; C. 42, XIV 20; C. 43, XV 2; C. 47, XVII 2.

ḤR, "with," used in "to mix or triturate with": C. 9, IV 20; XXI 16.

ḤR, "because of": C. 1, I 8; **C. 46, XVI 13.**

ḤR NTT: I. 1, XVIII 4.

ḤR, "in act of," "by" before infinitives: C. 7, IV 3; C. 8, IV 15; C. 22, VIII 16; C. 41, XIV 9; XX 13; XXI 17, 18, 21, XXII 4; XXII 11 bis.

ḤR miscellaneous: XXI 2; XXII 4.

ŚW>Y ḤR: I. 7, XX 6, 8 bis.

ḤR idiomatic:

ND̲ ḤR-F, "ask him": C. 20, VIII 1.

ḤR ‹·WY, "immediately": C. 48, XVII 17; XXII 14.

ḤR T>, "entirely": **C. 41, XIV 16.**

ḤR ḲD, "entirely": XXI 11, 17.

ḤR Ḥ>·T, "before": I. 7, XX 5.

ḤRY — upper: C. 34, XI 23; C. 40, XIII 17; XX 14.

TP . . . . ḤRY, "outer edge" (lit. the "upper tip"): **C. 11, V 14.**

M GŚ N ḤRY, "on the top": XXII 6.

ḤRW — top: C. 11, V 14, 15.

ḤRW — up; or without plural strokes; also (XVIII 3).

R ḤRW, "upward," "on high": C. 4, II 10; I. 1, XVIII 3.

N ḤRW, "upward": C. 7, IV 3; C. 31, X 21.

ḤRY-YB — middle; also .

Used as noun: C. 7, IV 1; C. 8, IV 8, 18 bis; **C. 11, V 14** C. 12, V 21.

Used as adjective: C. 31, X 16.

ḤRY — be far away: ḤR-TY (2nd pers. sing., XIX 2); ḤR-TYWNY (2nd pers. pl., XVIII 18); I. 3, XVIII 18; I. 4, XIX 2.

ḤḤ — myriad: XXII 10.

ḤŚB — a break, fracture (noun); also , (once only V 11): **C. 11, V 10** bis, 11; C. 12, V 16 bis, 17, 20; C. 24, VIII 22 bis, 23, IX 1; C. 35, XII 3 bis, 4, 6; C. 36, XII 9 bis, 10, 12; C. 37, XII 14, 15, 16 bis, 19, 20; C. 44, XV 6 bis, 8.

to break (verb); : C. 42, XIV 18.

ḤŚMN — natron: XXI 4; XXI 7.

ḤŚMN — menstrual discharge: XX 13.

ḤḲ·T — beer: XX 15.

ḤḲꜣ·T — grain measure.

$\frac{1}{8}$ heket (a little over one pint): **XX 15.**

$\frac{1}{16}$ heket (a little over $\frac{1}{2}$ pint): **XX 15.**

ḤKꜣ·W — charm, incantation: C. 9, V 1.

ḤTY — smoke: XXI 3.

ḤTY·T — throat: **C. 34, XI 23,** XII 2.

ḤTR — to be contracted: **C. 7, III** 6, 7, **16.**

ḤṮṮ·T — shoulder: **C. 47, XVI** 16, **17,** XVII 1, 7, 11.

ḤḎ — become light, bright.

ḤḎ Tꜣ, "the morning": I. 5, XIX 5.

ḤḎ·T — White One (name of goddess): I. 1, XVIII 4.

Ḫ·T — fire: XXI 16, XXII 3.

ḪꜣY — measure, examine, treat; also , (once only IX 7), , or with det. , (I 4; var. , I 9), (once only **X 4-5**, error), (once only XXI 13).

ḪꜣY in the formula YR ḪꜣY-K (): **C. 1**, lost column restored, **I 3;** C. 2, I 12; C. 3, I 19 restored; C. 4, II 3; C. 5, II 12; C. 6, II 18; C. 7, III 3; C. 8, IV 5; C. 9, IV 19; C. 10, V 6; C. 11, V 10; C. 12, V 16; C. 13, VI 4; C. 14, VI 7; C. 15, VI 15; C. 16, VI 18; C. 17, VII 1; C. 18, VII 7; C. 19, VII 15; C. 20, VII 22; C. 21, VIII 6; C. 22, VIII 10; C. 23, VIII 18; C. 24, VIII 22; C. 25, IX 2; C. 26, IX 6; C. 27, IX 13; C. 28, IX 18; C. 29, X 3; C. 30, X 9; C. 31, X 13;

Ḫ'Y (*cont.*) — C. 32, XI 1; C. 33, XI 9; C. 34, XI 17; C. 35, XII 3; C. 36, XII 9; C. 37, XII 15; C. 38, XII 22; C. 39, XIII 3; C. 40, XIII 12; C. 41, XIII 18; C. 42, XIV 17; C. 43, XIV 22; C. 44, XV 6; C. 45, XV 9; C. 46, XV 20; C. 47, XVI 16; C. 48, XVII 16; XX 13.

Ḫ'Y miscellaneous: **C. 1, I 4, 5 bis, 7, 8, 9;** C. 26, IX 7; C. 29, X 4–5; C. 47, XVII 6; XXI 13 bis.

Ḫ'Y·TY — Disease-Demon; also (plural XIX 20): **I. 1, XVIII 6;** I. 2, XVIII 12, 13; I. 5, XIX 8; I. 7, XIX 20, XX 7.

Ḫ'ʿ — to lay back; also (once only XVII 5): **C. 47, XVI 17,** XVII 1, 5.

Ḫ'BW — ⌜hungry⌝: **I. 6, XIX 15.**

Ḫ'Ḫ' — winnow: XXI 11–12.

Ḫ'Š — to ⌜project⌝: **C. 43, XIV 23.**

ḪʿM — throat; also (once only IX 22): **C. 28, IX** 18, **19,** 22.

ḪWY — avoid: I. 8, XX 9, 9–10.

ḪP — to die: **I. 5, XIX 7.**

ḪPR — arise, originate: C 1, I 9; C. 5, II 16; **C. 6, II** 20, **21,** 25; C. 8, IV 10, 11; XXI 12, 14.

befall (in unfavorable sense): **C. 1, I 9;** C. 18, VII 12; C. 31, X 16, 20; C. 39, XIII 9; C. 41, XIV 7.

exist (as in MY ḪPR·T = "what is"): **C. 40, XIII 17;** C. 42, XIV 21.

ḪPR participle with meaning "done": **C. 30, X 10.**

ḪPRW — form: I. 5, XIX 6.

ḪFḪF·T — the flooder: **I. 1, XVIII 7.**

ḪFT — according to: C. 41, XIV 8; C. 45, XV 16; C. 47, XVII 6.

when: C. 31, X 19.

ḪFT-ḤR — in view of: C. 7, IV 4.

ḪFTY — enemy: C. 9, V 2.

ḪMY — to be unconscious of: **C. 31, X 13,** 15, 17; C. 33, XI 12, 13.

ḪMT-NW — (fem.) third: C. 9, V 1; I. 1, XVIII 5.

ḪNT — in: **C. 1, I 8 restored.**

ḪNT — ⌜wrinkles⌝: XXII 8.

ḪNT — see MḪNT.

ḪNTY — one who is over, the first: I. 1, XVIII 1, 2; I. 5, XIX 13.

chief of the Hemesut-house: **I. 1, XVIII 2.**

ḪR — fall (literal): C. 8, IV 8, 17, 18; C. 33, XI 11, 15, 16.

ḪR indicating physiological or anatomical shift or movement: **C. 33, XI 10,** 14; C. 35, XII 6; C. 36, XII 12.

ḪR R Tʾ ("come off," "come away" and similar): **C. 4, II 9;** C. 7, III 4.

ḪR — so that: **C. 12, V 22,** VI 1.

ḪḪ — throat: I. 5, XIX 11.

ḪŚF — prevent, exorcise: I. 1, XVIII 1; I. 2, XVIII 11; I. 7, XX 7.

ḪŚF — resistance: C. 46, XVI 5.

ḪŚFY — ḪŚFY R, "to turn toward": C. 34, XI 18.

ḪT — wood: C. 7, III 14; I. 2, XVIII 15; I. 7, XX 6.

ḪT — after, afterward.

ŚRWḪ-K (ŚW) M ḪT: C. 1, I 3; C. 2, I 15 restored; C. 3, I 23; C. 11, V 13; C. 12, V 20; C. 15, VI 17; C. 16, VI 21; C. 17, VII 6; C. 18, VII 11; C. 23, VIII 22; C. 26, IX 10; C. 27, IX 17; C. 28, X 1; C. 30, X 11; C. 32, XI 6; C. 34, XI 20; C. 35, XII 8; C. 36, XII 14; C. 37, XII 18; C. 38, XIII 2; C. 40, XIII 16; C. 42, XIV 20; C. 43, XV 3; C. 47, XVII 4, 14.

YR M ḪT: C. 3, I 22 restored; C. 9, IV 20, V 3; C. 10, V 7; C. 12, V 19; C. 26, IX 9; C. 29, X 8; C. 30, X 11; XXI 11, XXII 7.

M ḪT N, "subject to": I. 1, XVIII 5.

YMY·W ḪT, "followers": I. 5, XIX 8.

ḪTY — retreat; also (imperative XVIII 13): I. 2, XVIII 13; I. 7, XIX 20.

ḪTM — to close: C. 25, IX 3.

H̱·T — ball (of the foot): **C. 8, IV 15.**

belly, womb: I. 6, XIX 15, 16, 17.

H̱ʾB — to bend: **C. 12, V** 16, **21.**

H̱ʾB — sickle-bone: **C. 34, XI 22-23.**

H̱ʾR — khar (unit of measure): XXI 10.

H̱N — use (noun): **C. 9, IV 21,** V 4.

H̱NW  interior, inside; also  (twice only V 12, VI 11); usually without 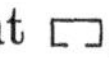, but see 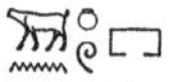 (twice only XII 7, 13).

H̱NW as noun: **C. 5, II 16**, 17; C. 6, II 24; C. 11, V 14; C. 14, VI 13–14; C. 26, IX 9, 11, 12; C. 32, XI 8; C. 34, XI 21; C. 37, XII 20; C. 41, XIV 12.

M H̱NW (): C. 6, II 25; **C. 11, V 12;** C. 12, V 19, VI 2, 3; C. 14, VI 11; C. 22, VIII 12, 15; C. 25, IX 4.

M H̱NW () before G·B ("arm"): **C. 35, XII 7;** C. 36, XII 13.

M H̱NW: I. 7, XX 5.

YMY·T H̱NW: **I. 5, XIX 5.**

See also MH̱NW.

H̱NW 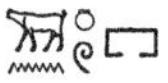 enter: **I. 5, XIX 5.**

H̱NY  to voyage: I. 1, XVIII 7.

H̱NTY  ⌜hollow⌝ (of the ear): **C. 23, VIII 19.**

H̱R  under: C. 4, II 4; C. 5, II 13; C. 6, II 21 bis; C. 8, IV 5 bis, 11 bis, 12; C. 9, V 5; C. 13, VI 5; C. 17, VII 2; C. 24, VIII 23; C. 25, IX 4; C. 34, XII 1; C. 37, XII 16; C. 44, XV 8; C. 46, XVI 1, 14.

H̱R, "because of" or "from" (source): C. 3, II 1; C. 7, III 9 bis; C. 8, IV 6; C. 12, V 22, VI 1; C. 13, VI 6; C. 17, VII 4; C. 21, VIII 8; C. 24, IX 2; C. 28, IX 21, X 2; C. 31, X 13, 14; C. 33, XI 12; C. 41, XIII 20, XIV 2; C. 47, XVI 20, XVII 7, 11.

H̱R with meaning "possess": C. 21, VIII 7, 8; C. 22, VIII 11; C. 31, X 20.

H̱R erroneously used for H̱RY: C. 7, III 5, 12; C. 13, VI 5, 6; C. 14, VI 9; C. 22, VIII 13; C. 46, XVI 2.

H̱R scribal error: C. 45, XV 19.

H̱RY  one having, one who has; also  (seven times only, III 5, 12; VI 5, 6, 9; VIII 13; XVI 2): C. 1, I 1 restored; C. 2, I 14; C. 3, I 20; C. 4, II 5; C. 5, II 14; C. 7, III 5, 12; C. 8, IV 6, 7, 15, 16; C. 11, V 11; C. 12, V 17; C. 13, VI 5, 6; C. 14, VI 9; C. 15, VI 16; C. 16, VI 19; C. 17, VII 3, 4; C. 18, VII 10; C. 19, VII 17 bis; C. 20, VIII 3; C. 21, VIII 8; C. 22, VIII 13, 17; C. 23, VIII 19; C. 24, IX 1; C. 25, IX 5; C. 26, IX 8; C. 27, IX 15; C. 28, IX 21; C. 30, X 10;

H̱RY (*cont.*) C. 31, X 17; C. 32, XI 4; C. 33, XI 12; C. 34, XI 19; C. 35, XII 4; C. 36, XII 10; C. 37, XII 16, 20; C. 38, XIII 1; C. 39, XIII 5; C. 40, XIII 14; C. 41, XIV 1; C. 42, XIV 19; C. 43, XV 2; C. 44, XV 8; C. 45, XV 14; C. 46, XVI 2; C. 47, XVII 1, 10; C. 48, XVII 18.

one who is under: I. 6, XIX 15.

H̱RY — lower part (of the ear): C. 23, VIII 18.

under side (of the arm): C. 35, XII 7; C. 36, XII 13.

H̱RW — or with det.

N H̱RW, "downward": C. 7, IV 3; C. 31, X 21; C. 32, XI 9.

H̱R·T — yield, production: I. 5, XIX 9.

H̱KR — ⌜parti-colored⌝: **C. 39, XIII 11-12.**

H̱RD — child, infant: C. 6, II 21; C. 8, IV 11; C. 20, VIII 2.

S — man: C. 1, lost column restored, I 3 restored, 5; C. 2, I 12; C. 3, I 19 restored; C. 4, II 3, 6, 8; C. 5, II 12; C. 6, II 18; C. 7, III 7, 8, 9, 13; C. 8, IV 5; C. 9, IV 19; C. 10, V 6; C. 11, V 10; C. 12, V 16; C. 13, VI 4; C. 14, VI 7; C. 15, VI 15; C. 16, VI 18; C. 17, VII 1; C. 18, VII 7; C. 19, VII 15; C. 20, VII 22, VIII 4; C. 21, VIII 6; C. 22, VIII 10; C. 23, VIII 18; C. 24, VIII 22; C. 25, IX 2; C. 26, IX 6; C. 27, IX 13; C. 28, IX 18; C. 29, X 3; C. 30, X 9; C. 31, X 13; C. 32, XI 1; C. 33, XI 9; C. 34, XI 17; C. 35, XII 3; C. 36, XII 9; C. 37, XII 15; C. 38, XII 22; C. 39, XIII 3; C. 40, XIII 12; C. 41, XIII 18, 20; C. 42, XIV 18; C. 43, XIV 22, XV 1; C. 44, XV 6; C. 45, XV 9, 16; C. 46, XV 20; C. 47, XVI 17, XVII 6, 12; I. 1, XVIII 10; I. 2, XVIII 15; I. 5, XIX 11, 14 bis; I. 6, XIX 14; I. 7, XX 5; I. 8, XX 11; XXII 4, 7, 11.

S·T — woman: XX 13.

Sꜣ — son; also , or without det.: C. 9, V 3; I. 1, XVIII 5, 6 bis; I. 2, XVIII 15; I. 7, XX 3.

SꜣBY — R SꜣBY R, ⌜"as far as"⌝: **C. 32, XI 5.**

Sꜣ — protection: I. 1, XVIII 10, 11; I. 3, XVIII 17; I. 5, XIX 13; XXII 12.

SꜣW — prevent: C. 39, XIII 8.

avoid; written : C. 46, XVI 6.

S’W — to issue: I. 6, XIX 17.

S’W — to be stationary: **C. 31, X 21.**

S’TW — ground: C. 8, IV 15.

SWNW — physician; also (once only I 6): C. 1, I 6; C. 9, IV 21, V 4.

SP — time, instance; **C. 7, IV 3 bis;** XXII 10.
SP ŚN-WY: I. 1, XVIII 4, 9; I. 2, XVIII 14; I. 5, XIX 3, 9; I. 7, XX 2; I. 8, XX 10; XX 17, XXI 1.

SPY — remain: XXI 12.

SP — portion: XXI 14.

SP·W — fragments: **C. 4, II 9;** C. 5, II 17.
applications; or without : **C. 41, XIV 2, 4;** C. 46, XVI 3, 6, 7.

SP — meaning uncertain: C. 24, IX 1.

SM’ — lungs: C. 34, XII 2.

SNY — spread, spread out; also (once only XV 17), or with det. (XXII 1): C. 35, XII 5; C. 36, XII 11; C. 39, XIII 10; C. 45, XV 17; XXII 1.

SNʿʿ — rub, triturate: XXII 5; XXII 13.

SNF — blood: C. 4, II 4, 5; C. 5, II 13; C. 6, II 22; C. 7, III 4, 6; C. 8, IV 8, 12; C. 9, V 2; C. 11, V 11; C. 12, V 18, VI 2 bis; C. 13, VI 5; C. 14, VI 10; C. 17, VII 2, 3, 4; C. 20, VII 24, VIII 3; C. 21, VIII 7, 8; C. 22, VIII 11, 13; C. 37, XII 19; XX 14–15, 16.

SRY — ⌜relief⌝: **C. 17, VII 6;** C. 20, VIII 5; C. 32, XI 6.

SŠ — splint, or with det. (once only V 18); also (once only VI 10).
SŠ and SŠ·WY (two splints): **C. 7, III 18;** C. 35, XII 6; C. 36, XII 12; C. 37, XII 17.
SŠ·WY probably error for ŚŠM·WY: **C. 12, V 18;** C. 14, VI 10.

SŠ — write: I. 5, XIX 10.

SŠR·T — drying up; also (XVI 9–10), (IV 21): **C. 9, IV 21; C. 41, XIV 4;** C. 46, XVI 9–10.

Ś·T — place: C. 12, V 18; C. 25, IX 5; C. 30, X 12; C. 34, XI 19; C. 35, XII 6; C. 36, XII 12.
Ś·T YB, “ pulse ”: **C. 1, I 7** bis.

Ś·T — Isis: I. 1, XVIII 5.

Ś› — back.
ḤR Ś› N, " on outside of ": **C. 8, IV 6;** C. 16, VI 19; C. 21, VIII 6–7; C. 38, XII 22.
M Ś› N, " with the back of ": C. 20, VIII 2.
R Ś›, " after," " afterward ": XX 18; XXII 5.

Ś›Ḥ·W — toes: C. 8, IV 14–15.

Ś›Ḫ — to drive (meaning to " force "): **C. 33, XI 16.**

Ś›[Ḳ] — to hold back: **C. 31, X 22.**

Ś›T — ⌜separate⌝, or with det. (XII 4); also (XVI 18–19), or with det. (XII 10): **C. 14, VI 8;** C. 35, XII 4; C. 36, XII 10; C. 47, XVI 18–19.

ŚY — (dependent pronoun, third person, feminine, singular; also used impersonally): C. 45, XV 11; C. 48, XVII 16, 17 bis; XXI 1.

ŚY — to shuffle: **C. 8, IV** 7, **13,** 15.

ŚYP — assign: I. 6, XIX 18.

ŚYN — wipe, wipe off; also (XX 18): C. 20, VIII 2; XX 18.

ŚYN — clay: XXII 5.

ŚʿND — corner: **C. 18, VII 14.**

ŚʿR — elevated, prominent: C. 46, XV 20.
See also ʿR and ŚḲR.

ŚʿḲ — to bring in, intrude: **C. 8, IV 17.**

ŚW — (dependent pronoun, third person, masculine, singular).
As object of verb: C. 1, I 2; C. 2, I 14 restored; C. 3, I 20 restored, 22 bis (once restored), 23; C. 4, II 7; C. 5, II 15; C. 6, II 23; C. 7, III 8; C. 8, IV 7; C. 9, V 1; C. 10, V 7 bis (once restored), 8; C. 11, V 13; C. 12, V 18, 20; C. 14, VI 11, 12; C. 15, VI 17 bis; C. 16, VI 20, 21; C. 17, VII 6; C. 18, VII 10; C. 19, VII 18; C. 21, VIII 9; C. 23, VIII 21; C. 25, IX 5; C. 26, IX 10 ter; C. 27, IX 17 bis; C. 28, X 1 bis, 2; C. 29, X 7; C. 30, X 11; C. 31, X 13; C. 32, XI 4, 6 bis; C. 33, XI 10; C. 34, XI 20 bis; C. 35, XII 5, 8 bis; C. 36, XII 10, 14; C. 37, XII 17, 18; C. 38, XIII 2 bis; C. 39, XIII 5, 7; C. 40, XIII 15, 16; C. 41, XIV 7; C. 42,

ŚW (*cont.*) — XIV 18, 20 bis; C. 43, XV 2; C. 45, XV 12, 16; C. 46, XVI 7; C. 47, XVII 2, 4, 6, 13, 14; C. 48, XVII 19.

YŚK ŚW: C. 17, VII 2; C. 21, VIII 7; C. 33, XI 10.

YŚK ŚW ḤM, "while at the same time": **C. 13, VI 5;** C. 17, VII 3.

YŚT ŚW: C. 18, VII 12.

YŚT YR ŚW: C. 1, I 2 restored.

NN ŚW M: C. 12, V 22.

ḎR NTT ŚW M: C. 4, II 11.

NTT ŚW . . . M: C. 7, IV 4.

ŚWꜣY — to pass by; also … (once only XX 7), … (once only XX 6): **C. 3, I 23** restored; C. 4, II 7; C. 5, II 15; C. 19, VII 18; C. 29, X 8; C. 47, XVII 13; I. 2, XVIII 13 bis, 14; I. 7, XIX 20, XX 6, 7.

the passer by: I. 4, XVIII 19.

ŚWꜥB — cleanse: I. 6, XIX 14; I. 7, XIX 18.

ŚWMT — to make thick: XXII 6.

ŚWR — to drink; or with det. …: C. 28, IX 19; XX 16.

ŚWḤ·T — egg: C. 9, IV 20, 21, V. 1.

ŚWŠ — a whirl: **C. 41,** XIII 19, **XIV 11,** 12.

ŚWGM — to grind: **XXII 2.**

ŚWT — weak adversative particle.

YR ŚWT, "if then" or "if however": C. 7, III 8, 13; C. 28, X 2; C. 31, X 16; C. 34, XI 21; C. 37, XII 19; C. 47, XVII 6, 12, 13.

ŚBN — to fall down: **C. 9, V 3.**

ŚBH̲ — jar: **XXI 16,** XXII 3.

ŚPNꜥ — transform: XXI 3–4.

ŚPR — reach; also …, … (once only II 7), … (once only II 10): C. 18, VII 12.

ŚPR R YH̲·T ("reach decisive point"): **C. 4, II 7, 10;** C. 6, II 23; C. 7, III 8, 15; C. 8, IV 9; C. 21, VIII 9; C. 37, XII 19.

ŚPŚPW — of uncertain meaning, probably disease-demons: **I. 7, XX 4.**

ŚPT — lip; also … (twice only V 9, VI 13).

ŚPT of the human mouth: C. 7, III 4; C. 26, IX 6, 7, 9, 11.

ŚPT (*cont.*) — ŚPT·WY (" two lips ") of a wound: **C. 1,** I 1, **10 restored;** C. 2, I 17 restored; C. 10, V 9; C. 14, VI 8, 13; C. 18, VII 13; C. 23, VIII 21; C. 26, IX 12; C. 41, XIII 20, XIV 10, 13 bis.

ŚFH̱Y — to release: **C. 8, IV** 8, **17.**

ŚFR·T — drawing or similar (of movement of an eyebrow): **C. 7, IV 3.**

ŚFT — oil: XX 16.

ŚMN — to set aside: XXI 15, XXII 2.

ŚN — (dependent pronoun, third person, common, plural): XXI 18.

ŚNW(Y) — two: C. 34, XII 1; XXI 10.

ŚN-NW — (fem.) — the second, the other: **C. 1, I 10,** 12 restored; C. 31, X 18, 19; C. 33, XI 10, 11, 14, 16, 17; C. 35, XII 4; C. 36, XII 10; I. 1, XVIII 5.

ŚNY — them both (dependent pronoun, third person common, dual); also by error (once only XII 7): **C. 14, VI 8; C. 35, XII 7;** C. 36, XII 13 bis.

⌜ŚNWR⌝ — ⌜cast out⌝: **C. 9, V 2.**

ŚNB — recover: XXII 14.

ŚNFR — beautify: XXI 6; XXII 8.

ŚNṮR — incense: XXI 2.

ŚR·T — spine, thorn: **C. 42, XIV 21, 22.**

ŚRWH̱ — treat, or with det. (once only II 7); also (twice only VI 17, XV 16), (once only VIII 21), (once only XIV 7).

ŚRWH̱ as a noun: **C. 39, XIII 7-8;** C. 46, XVI 7; see also ŚRWH̱-F PW H̱MS(Y)·T.

ŚRWH̱ with medicaments:

ŚRWH̱ with grease, honey and lint, with M: **C. 1, I 3;** C. 3, I 23; C. 10, V 8 (without lint); C. 12, V 20; C. 19, VII 19.

ŚRWH̱ with grease, honey and sometimes lint, without M: C. 2, I 15 restored; C. 11, V 13; **C. 15, VI 17;** C. 16, VI 21; C. 17, VII 6; C. 18, VII 11; C. 23, VIII 21; C. 26, IX 10; C. 27, IX 17; C. 28, X 1; C. 34, XI 20; C. 37, XII 18; C. 40, XIII 16; C. 47, XVII 4, 14.

ŚRWH̱ with honey, without M: C. 32, XI 6; C. 35,

ŚRWH̱ (*cont.*) XII 8; C. 36, XII 14; C. 38, XIII 2; C. 42, XIV 20; C. 43, XV 3.

ŚRWH̱ with YMRW and honey without M: C. 30, X 11.

ŚRWH̱, manner of:

ŚRWH̱ "according to these ŠŚ›W": C. 41, XIV 7; C. 45, XV 16.

ŚRWH̱ with ŚRWH̱ WBNW: C. 39, XIII 7; C. 46, XVI 7.

ŚRWH̱-F . . . . . . ḤMS(Y)·T: C. 4, II 7; C. 7, III 15; C. 8, IV 9; C. 16, VI 20.

ŚRWD to make flourish: I. 1, XVIII 2.

ŚRF inflammation, fever; also (once only XIII 19), (once only XIV 16): C. 7, III 9; C. 28, IX 21; C. 39, XIII 5; **C. 41,** XIII 19, **XIV** 3, **11–12, 12,** 15, 16; C. 45, XV 12; C. 46, XVI 8; C. 47, XVII 7, 9, 14.

ŚRF·WT ⌜weaknesses⌝: XXII 9.

ŚH›·T discharge: XX 16.

ŚḤM to crush; also (once only XI 15): **C. 33, XI** 9 bis, 11, 12, **13,** 15.

ŚḤR abscess; also (once only XV 20): **C. 46,** XV 20 bis, **XVI** 2, 3, 7, **12.**

ŚḤRY exorcise: I. 7, XX 7 (causative of ḤRY "be far away").

ŚḤḎ to become pale: **C. 7,** III 13, **IV 4** bis.

ŚH̱M mighty one; or with det.: I. 1, XVIII 6 bis.

ŚH̱M·T Sekhmet, g.; or with det.: C. 1, I 6; I. 1, XVIII 6, 9; I. 2, XVIII 12, 14, 15; I. 5, XIX 3, 9, 10; I. 7, XIX 19, XX 2 bis; I. 8, XX 11.

ŚH̱R

ŚH̱R N, "after the manner of": XXI 13.

MY ŚH̱R, "like": XXI 18.

M ŚH̱R, "even so": XXI 15.

ŚH̱R force to fall in, cause to fall back: C. 12, V 17; C. 25, IX 4; C. 34, XI 19.

ŚH̱T to stretch: I. 8, XX 10.

ŚH̱D to be head downward: **C. 33, XI 16.**

ŚḪDḪD — to be head downward:
M ŚḪDḪD, "head downward": **C. 33, XI** 11, **15.**

ŚḪ·T — an unidentified fruit: **C. 46, XVI 4.**

ŚḪBW — draught, a drink: **C. 7, III 14.**

ŚḪR — to cover: I. 1, XVIII 10.

⌜ŚŠM⌝ — swab, tampon, plug; also (VIII 16): **C. 11, V 11,** 12; C. 12, V 19; C. 22, VIII 11, 16.

ŚŠD — band, bandage; or without stroke, also (I 16): C. 2, I 16; **C. 9, V 5;** C. 10, V 9; I. 5, XIX 11.

ŚḲBB — to cause to be cool; also by error: **C. 9, V 4** bis.

ŚḲR — prominent, elevated; or with det. , or : **C. 39, XIII** 3 bis, 6, **10; C. 46, XVI 13.**
See also ŚʿR and ʿR.

ŚḲR — to smite, injury, or with det. : **C. 8, IV 7 ter,** 15; C. 17, VII 3; C. 19, VII 17; C. 21, VIII 8.

ŚḲD — to spread: **C. 39, XIII 4;** C. 45, XV 10.

ŚḲDY — sail: I. 1, XVIII 7.

ŚK — to cleanse, or with det. : **C. 11, V 11;** C. 12, V 18; C. 14, VI 10; C. 22, VIII 11, 16.
to smear: XXII 8.

ŚGNN — to soften: C. 4, II 8; C. 20, VIII 5.

ŚT — (dependent pronoun, third person, feminine, singular): C. 31, X 14; XXI 19 bis; XXII 1.

ŚTY — dissipate, scatter: **C. 47, XVII 14.**

ŚTW — ⌜spreading⌝: **C. 43, XV 5.**

ŚT[W] — sower: I. 5, XIX 13.

ŚT·WT — swellings: **C. 43, XV 1,** 5; C. 47, XVI 18, XVII 2.

ŚTY — odor: C. 7, III 11, 21, IV 1.

ŚTWT — see TWT.

ŚTP — to ⌜choke⌝: **C. 28, IX 19-20.**

ŚTP — strip: I. 7, XX 6; **XXII 13.**

ŚṮꜢ — reduce (lit. draw out); also (once only V 12): C. 11, V 12; C. 16, VI 20; C. 17, VII 6.

ŚṮSW — be prostrate on the back; also (once only XVII 19): **C. 35, XII 5;** C. 36, XII 11; C. 48, XVII 19.

ŚD — fracture, rupture, break open, inflict: also , .
ŚD of the bone (compound comminuted fracture):
ŚD of the skull: C. 1, I 1 restored; C. 2, I 17 restored; C. 3, I 24 bis; **C. 5, II 11,** 12 bis, 15, 16 ter, 17; C. 6, II 18, 19, 20, 23, 24; C. 8, IV 5 bis, 6, 10, 12, 13; C. 9, IV 19 bis.
ŚD in his nostril: C. 13, VI 3, 4 bis, 5, 6.
ŚD in his maxilla (MND·T-F): C. 17, VII 1 bis, 2, 4.
ŚD in his temple (GMʾ-F): C. 18, VII 9; C. 22, VIII 9, 10, 11, 13.
ŚD in the flesh (rupture):
ŚD of the meninges of the brain: C. 6, II 24.
ŚD of fleshy tissue overlying a fracture of the bone: C. 24, IX 1; C. 34, XI 21; C. 37, XII 15, 16, 20–21; C. 44, XV 7, 8.

ŚDY — distorted, drawn, or with det. : **C. 7,** III 11, **IV 2.**

ŚDB — to pierce through, without det. or with det. ×; the participle with prosthetic Y occurs 12 times: **C. 14, VI** 7–8, 9, 13, **14;** C. 26, IX 7, 9, 11, 12; C. 28, IX 19, 22; C. 34, XI 21; C. 37, XII 20, 21.

ŚḎM — to hear: C. 21, VIII 7.

ŠʾM — to burn: **C. 39, XIII 6-7** (where *m* is corrected from *w*; cf. MŠʿḲ·T s.v.).
to be hot: **C. 41, XIII 22.**

ŠʾMŚ — an unidentified flower: **I. 8, XX 8-9,** 12.

ŠʾŚ — an unidentified flower: **C. 19, VII 20.**

ŠʾŠʾ·T — bosom: **C. 34, XII 1, 2.**

ŠʿY — to be sandy, to be granulated: **C. 45, XV 12-13.**

ŠW — sun: XXI 10, XXII 1.

ŠWY — dry, be dry: C. 28, X 2; XXI 11, 18 bis, XXII 1.

ŠW·TY — two feathers: I. 1, XVIII 3, 10.

ŠW·TY — two sides, usually dual, but also (quater); (once only XV 5): **C. 43, XV** 1, 5 bis, **6; C. 47, XVI 17,** 19, XVII 1, 6.

ŠW — see YŠW·W

ŠBB — gullet; also (IX 22): **C. 28, IX 19,** 22.

ŠPNN — an unidentified drug: **C. 41, XIV 6**; C. 46, XVI 12.

ŠFW — to swell; also (XIV 11): C. 12, V 22; C. 39, XIII 10; C. 41, XIV 11; C. 46, XVI 13.

ŠFW·T — swelling: C. 4, II 10; C. 12, VI 1; C. 45, XV 17, 19.

ŠM — to walk, to go; or without det.: C. 8, IV 7, 13, 14 bis, 15; I. 1, XVIII 10.

ŠM·T, " action " (of the heart): C. 1, I 6 restored.

ŠM — hot (adjective): **C. 7, III 7.**

ŠMM — to have fever: C. 24, IX 1; **C. 28, X 2;** C. 41, XIII 20, XIV 2; C. 47, XVII 11, 12.

ŠMM·T — heat, inflammation, fever; or with plural strokes (I I I): **C. 41, XIV 9,** 14; C. 47, XVII 13–14.

ŠMꜣY — disease; also: C. 15, VI 15–16; **C. 41,** XIII 18 bis, **XIV** 1, **8.**

ŠMꜣ·W — diseased ones: I. 2, XVIII 14; I. 7, XX 1; I. 8, XX 9.

ŠMŚW — followers: I. 8, XX 9.

ŠNꜥW — obstruction: XX 14.

ŠNB·T — breast: **C. 32, XI 2,** 3.

ŠND·T — acacia:

ḎRḎ of ŠND·T, "acacia leaves;" also with det. (XXII 12): C. 46, XVI 8; XXII 12.

ŠR·T — nostril; also (twice only VI 3, 4).

ŠR·T used in the singular: **C. 13, VI 3,** 4, 5, 6; C. 14, VI 7 bis, 9, 11, 13; C. 17, VII 3, 4; C. 21, VIII 7, 8.

DY-F SNF M ŠR·TY-FY (his two nostrils): **C. 4, II 4,** 6; C. 5, II 13; C. 6, II 22; C. 7, III 4, 6; C. 8, IV 9, 12; C. 11, V 11; C. 20, VII 24, VIII 4; C. 22, VIII 13.

Proof passages that the writing (ŠR·TY) designates the nostrils: C. 11, V 12; C. 12, V 18, 19 bis, VI 2, 3; C. 22, VIII 11.

ŠRY — to be little: **C. 19, VII 16.**

a little: C. 20, VII 24.

ŠSP — receive, take; or without det.: **C. 31, X 14;** C. 41, XIII 20–21, 21, XIV 14 bis.

take off, remove: C. 14, VI 11–12.

ŠŚ — found effective: XXII 10.

ŠŚ — alabaster: XXI 6.

ŠŚ — an unidentified plant or tree: **C. 46, XVI 4.**

ŠŚ·T — ⌜powder⌝; also (XIV 5): **C. 41, XIV 5;** C. 46, XVI 10.

ŠŚ˒W — instructions; also , and (once only I 12).

ŠŚ˒W in titles of cases: **C. 1, lost column restored;** C. 2, I 12; C. 3, I 18 restored; C. 4, II 2; C. 5, II 11; C. 6, II 17–18; C. 7, III 2; C. 8, IV 5; C. 9, IV 19; C. 10, V 5; C. II, V 10; C. 12, V 16; C. 13, VI 3; C. 14, VI 7; C. 15, VI 14; C. 16, VI 17; C. 17, VII 1; C. 18, VII 7; C. 19, VII 14; C. 20, VII 22; C. 21, VIII 6; C. 22, VIII 9; C. 23, VIII 18; C. 24, VIII 22; C. 25, IX 2; C. 26, IX 6; C. 27, IX 13; C. 28, IX 18; C. 29, X 3; C. 30, X 8; C. 31, X 12; C. 32, XI 1; C. 33, XI 9; C. 34, XI 17; C. 35, XII 3; C. 36, XII 8; C. 37, XII 14; C. 38, XII 21; C. 39, XIII 3; C. 40, XIII 12; C. 41, XIII 18; C. 42, XIV 16; C. 43, XIV 22; C. 44, XV 6; C. 45, XV 9; C. 46, XV 20; C. 47, XVI 16; C. 48, XVII 15.

ŠŚ˒W with plural demonstrative: C. 41, XIV 8; C. 45, XV 16; C. 47, XVII 6.

indications: C. 1, I 9.

ŠŚM — to be bloodshot; or with det. : **C. 19, VII** 17, **19-20;** C. 20, VII 23; C. 31, X 15.

ŠTY·T — chamber; also (V 16 bis): **C. 12, V** 16 bis, 17, **21.**

ŠDY — develop, or with det. : C. 7, III 8, 9, 13; C. 28, IX 20–21; C. 47, XVII 7; dig out: XXI 18.

ŠD·T — mass: XXI 16; XXII 2.

Ḳ˒Y — high: C. 41, XIV 9.

Ḳ˒·T, height (noun): C. 41, XIV 11.

Ḳ˒B — to be folded: **C. 35, XII 5;** C. 36, XII 11.

Ḳ˒B·T — breast.

Ḳ˒B·T as designation for the breast in general, shown in the test of ability of patient to turn the face downward: C. 3, I 20, 25–26, 26; C. 4, II 5; C. 5, II 14; C. 7, III 5; C. 29, X 6; C. 30, X 9.

Ḳ˒B·T as designation for the soft tissue overlying the bony structure of the breast:

Swellings, tumors or abscesses in or on Ḳ˒B·T: C. 39, XIII 3, 4 bis, 6, 7 bis, 9, 10 bis, 11; C. 45, XV 9, 10, 11 bis, 16, 17, 19; C. 46, XV 20, 21 bis, XVI 2–3, 4, 8, 10, 13, 14.

Ḳ›B·T (*cont.*)

WBNW M Ḳ›B·T: C. 40, XIII 12, 13, 14–15; C. 41, XIII 18, 18–19, XIV 2, 8, 9.

Ḳ›B·T as designation for the sternum:

The manubrium of the Ḳ›B·T:

ḲŚ ḤRY N Ḳ›B·T-F: **C. 34, XI 23.**

TP ḤRY N Ḳ›B·T-F: **C. 40, XIII 17.**

ḤNT› N Ḳ›B·T-F: **C. 40, XIII** 13, 14, 15, **17.**

Articulations in the Ḳ›B·T:

MN M Ḳ›B·T-F: C. 43, XV 4.

WḌ·T M Ḳ›B·T-F: C. 43, XV 5.

ḤN·W (ribs) NW Ḳ›B·T-F: C. 42, XIV 17 bis, 19, 21 bis; C. 43, XIV 22, 23 bis, XV 2, 3, 4; C. 44, XV 6, 7 bis, 8.

ḲʿḤ — shoulder; also dual (five times I 20 restored, 25, 26, II 5, XII 11): C. 3, I 20 restored, 25, 26; C. 4, II 5, 8; C. 5, II 14; C. 7, III 5; C. 8, IV 8, 17, 18; C. 19, VII 16; C. 29, X 5; C. 30, X 9; C. 32, XI 3 bis; C. 34, XI 18; C. 35, XII 5–6; C. 36, XII 11.

ḲBB — to cool, to be cool, cool; cold; also (XIV 2), (twice XV 11–12, XVI 3), (XVII 10): C. 41, XIV 2; C. 45, XV 11–12, 18–19; C. 46, XVI 3, 6; C. 47, XVII 10; XXI 19.

See also SḲBB.

ḲFN — to clot: **C. 12, VI 2.**

ḲM› — to engender, produce, generate; also (once only XIII 12): C. 8, IV 17; C. 39, XIII 12; C. 45, XV 13.

ḲNḲN — bruise: XXI 10.

ḲR·WT — depressions: **C. 12, VI 1.**

ḲRF — contract: **C. 48, XVII 16,** 17.

ḲSNTY — possibly an unidentified herb: **C. 41, XIV 3,** 4; C. 46, XVI 4, 5.

ḲŚ — bone.

ʿR N ḲŚ: C. 1, lost column bis, restored, I 2 restored, 10 restored; C. 2, I 12, 13, 16 restored; C. 4, II 2, 3, 5; C. 5, II 12, 15; C. 6, II 18, 19; C. 7, III 2, 5, 12; C. 10, V 6; C. 18, VII 8, 12; C. 20, VII 22, 23, VIII 3; C. 27, IX 14, 16; C. 29, X 4, 6.

ḲŚ (*cont.*)

⌜R (or Y⌜[R]) R ḲŚ: C. 3, I 18, 19, 21 restored; C. 40, XIII 13, 15.

ŚPR R ḲŚ: C. 18, VII 12.

Miscellaneous uses of ḲŚ: C. 1, I 11; C. 5, II 16; C. 22, VIII 16; C. 27, IX 14; C. 34, XI 23; C. 42, XIV 21.

ḲŚN — to be painful, painful: C. 7, III 3; C. 13, VI 6; C. 17, VII 3; C. 19, VII 16; C. 21, VIII 7; C. 30, X 10; C. 47, XVI 19; C. 48, XVII 17.

ḲD — form: C. 12, V 22.

ḤR ḲD, entirely: XXI 11, 17.

K›P — droop: **C. 7, IV 3.**

K›P·T — linen cover: XXII 6.

KYY — the other, another: **C. 35, XII 7;** I. 2, XVIII 11; I. 3, XVIII 17; (fem.) I. 4, XVIII 19; I. 5, XIX 2; I. 8, XX 8; XXI 6; XXI 15.

KYY-ŚNY: C. 36, XII 13.

KFY — uncover: C. 9, V 1.

KF·T — gash, cut, to gape; or without det., also (once only I 11).

WBNW N KF·T: C. 2, I 12 restored, 13 restored, 14 restored, 15 restored, 17 restored; C. 3, I 18, 19 restored, 21 restored; C. 4, II 2, 3, 5; C. 5, II 11, 12, 14; C. 6, II 18, 19; C. 7, III 2, 5, 12; C. 10, V 9; C. 27, IX 13, 14, 15; C. 28, IX 19; C. 29, X 3, 4; C. 47, XVI 16, 17; XVII 1, 10.

KF·T with negative: **C. 1, lost column** restored, I 2, 10, 11 bis (once restored); C. 18, VII 8, 12, 12–13.

Drawing together the KF·WT with bandages or thread: C. 10, V 6; C. 27, IX 16; C. 47, XVI 20, XVII 4 bis.

Uncertain uses: C. 1, I 11; C. 47, XVI 18.

KM — black: **C. 15, VI 15.**

KS — the female organ: **XX 17.**

G›B — arm, upper arm; also (once only XII 7): **C. 35, XII 7 bis; C. 36, XII** 9 ter, 10, **12,** 13 bis; C. 37, XII 15 bis, 16, 20; C. 38, XII 21, 22, XIII 1 bis.

GW› — to hold firmly: **C. 11, V 13.**

GWŠ — to be askew: **C. 8, IV 6.**

GM› — temple (of human head); also .

GM' (*cont.*) 

Proof passages of the meaning of GM': C. 7, III 17; **C. 18, VII 9, 13;** C. 22, VIII 15.

General: C. 18, VII 7, 7–8, 10.

Cases involving THM, PŠN or ŚD M GM': C. 19, VII 15 bis, 17; C. 20, VII 22 bis, 23 bis, VIII 3 bis; C. 21, VIII 6 bis, 8; C. 22, VIII 9, 10, 13.

GMY 

find.

GMM-K, conditional:

After WD-ḪR-K (or WD-YN-K) ʿ-K: C. 1, lost column restored; C. 7, III 10; C. 24, VIII 23; C. 47, XVII 9.

After YR Ḥ'Y-K (sometimes with intervening conditions): C. 12, V 16; C. 14, VI 8; C. 15, VI 15; C. 16, VI 18; C. 21, VIII 6; C. 25, IX 3; C. 31, X 13; C. 33, XI 10, 11; C. 34, XI 17–18; C. 35, XII 3; C. 36, XII 9; C. 37, XII 16; C. 38, XII 22; C. 39, XIII 4, 5; C. 43, XIV 23; C. 44, XV 7; C. 45, XV 10, 11; C. 46, XV 21; XX 14.

After ḎʿR-ḪR-K: C. 3, I 19–20 restored; C. 4, II 3; C. 5, II 12; C. 6, II 19; C. 8, IV 6; C. 18, VII 9; C. 47, XVI 18.

YR GMY-K: C. 2, I 13; C. 10, V 7; C. 23, VIII 20; C. 27, IX 14; C. 45, XV 15; C. 47, XVII 3, 5.

YR ŚWT GMM-K: C. 34, XI 21; C. 37, XII 19.

YR ŚWT GMY-K: C. 7, III 8, 13; C. 28, X 2; C. 47, XVII 7, 12.

YR ḎR GMM-K: C. 4, II 6; C. 7, III 7; C. 8, IV 10; C. 20, VIII 4.

N GMY-N-F ("he is not able"): **C. 3, I 20** restored, 25; C. 4, II 4–5; C. 5, II 14; C. 7, III 4; C. 29, X 5; C. 32, XI 3.

GMM-[W]-K, relative form: **C. 4, II 8.**

GMM-K continuing treatment: C. 9, V 1.

GMW  sadness: **C. 22, VIII 17.**

GN  soft; also : **C. 26, IX 13;** C. 46, XVI 14; XXI 16; XXII 3.

GNY·T 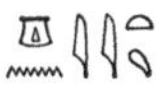 ⌜orifice⌝: **C. 18, VII 14.**

GNN  to be feeble: C. 8, IV 14.
to be soft: C. 14, VI 13, 14; C. 26, IX 12.

GR  to be silent: C. 22, VIII 17.

GRT — weak particle.
N GRT: C. 31, X 21.

GŚ — side.
M GŚ-F H̱RY followed by ŚD, ŚḲR or YH; C. 8, IV 6, 7, 15, 16; C. 17, VII 3; C. 19, VII 17.
GŚ miscellaneous: C. 9, V 2; C. 11, V 14; XX 14; XXII 6.

GŚ — anoint: XX 17; XXI 1; XXI 6; XXI 8.

GŚʾ — to sink: **C. 31, X 21.**

Tʾ — this: C. 9, V 5.

Tʾ — land, earth: I. 1, XVIII 2, 3; I. 6, XIX 17 bis.
R Tʾ and ḤR Tʾ, "away" or "off," with meaning of "entirely," "completely":
After H̱R ("fall"): **C. 4, II 9;** C, 7, III 4.
After PRY ("issue"): **C. 41, XIV 16.**
After ŚTY ("scatter"): **C. 47, XVII 14.**
WDY R Tʾ meaning "to moor" or "to land" (figurative): **C. 3, I 22,** II 1; C. 4, II 7; C. 5, II 15; C. 28, X 3; C. 29, X 8; C. 47, XVII 13.
ḤḎ Tʾ: I. 5, XIX 5.

TY·T — see RY·T.

TYʾ — of unknown meaning: **C. 7, III 9,** 13.

TWY — this: I. 1, XVIII 4; I. 4, XIX 1.

TWʾ·W — swellings: **C. 39, XIII 4.**

TWT — liken; also (XV 18): **C. 12, VI 3;** C. 45, XV 18.
ŚTWT (): C. 7, IV 2.

TB·T — sole; also (IV 14), (IV 15): C. 8, IV 7, 14 bis, 15.

⌜TP⌝ — head; also (three times only II 3, 25, IV 17).
Proof passages that (⌜TP⌝) means more than the calvaria:
"Skin" of TP-F: C. 8, IV 5 bis, 13.
"Flesh" of TP-F: C. 4, II 9.
"Chest" of TP-F: C. 7, III 11, 21, IV 1.
"Interior" of TP-F: C. 6, II 25.
TP used in gloss relating to [M]H̱NT ("countenance"): C. 7, III 19.
NḤB-T (neck) as part of TP: C. 32, XI 5.

⌜TP⌝ (*cont.*) — TP meaning *caput* in general: **C. 1, lost column** bis restored, I 1, 2, 7 restored, 8; C. 2, I 12 restored, 13 restored, 14, 15 restored; C. 3, I 18, 19 restored, 21 restored; C. 4, II 2, 3, 5, 8; C. 5, II 11, 12, 14; C. 6, II 18, 19; C. 7, III 2, 5, 12; C. 20, VIII 5; XXII 8.

TP, " head " of organs or parts of body:

TP as head or end of bone: C. 8, IV 8, 17, 18; C. 34, XI 18, 22, 23; C. 40, XIII 17; C. 43, XV 1, 4.

TP meaning " tip " of the toes: C. 8, IV 14.

TP meaning " top " of the eyebrow: C. 10, V 5, 6.

TP . . . ḤRY N[Y] FND: **C. 11, V 14.**

TP, " head " of tumors or abscesses: **C. 39, XIII** 3 bis, 6, **10; C. 46**, XV 20 bis, **XVI** 2, 7 **12.**

TP — used as preposition: **C. 7, III 14.**

TPY (fem.) — first (adjective): C. 1, I 3 restored; C 2, I 14 restored; C. 3, I 22; C. 10, V 7; C. 14, VI 11; C. 16, VI 20; C. 17, VII 6; C. 18, VII 11; C. 26, IX 10; C. 27, IX 17; C. 28, X 1; C. 29, X 7; C. 30, X 11; C. 32, XI 4; C. 40, XIII 16; C. 47, XVII 3.

the first (pronoun): I. 1, XVIII 4.

TPʾ·W — sutures: **C. 7, III** 2, 5, 9, 12, **15-16,** 16.

TPNN·T — an unidentified drug: XX 16.

TM·W — all; also : I. 1, XVIII 9; I. 5, XIX 9; I. 8, XX 11.

TM — negative verb; also (once only XIV 14): C. 7, IV 2; C. 8, IV 18 bis; C. 41, XIV 14; C. 46, XVI 15, 15–16; I. 5, XIX 4, 11.

TMŚ — ruddy; also (once only III 10), (once only XIII 20).

TMŚ referring to inflamed or feverish condition of parts of body: **C. 7, III** 10, **20;** C. 16, VI 19; C. 41, XIII 20, XIV 12; C. 43, XIV 23–XV 1.

redness, ruddiness (noun); also (XIII 5): C. 39, XIII 5; C. 46, XVI 2.

Proof passages of meaning of TMŚ:

Defining TMŚ as DŠR: **C. 46, XVI 15.**

Red like the color of TMŚ·T-fruit: **C. 7, III 21.**

Red like the color of the TMŚ·T-tree: **C. 41, XIV 13.**

TMT·W  poultices; also  (once only IV 21): **C. 9, IV 21;** C. 41, XIV 6; C. 46, XVI 12.

TN  this: C. 9, V 2; I. 1, XVIII 8; I. 6, XIX 16.

TNY 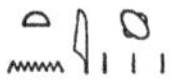 signs of old age: **XXII 9.**

TR·T  willow; C. 41, XIV 3.

THM  to perforate, perforation; also  (three times only VIII 3, XIII 13, 15),  (once only VI 14),  (once only VII 22).

THM in the skull: C. 1, I 1 restored; C. 2, I 14, 17; **C. 3, I 18,** 19, 21, 24 restored; C. 7, III 2, 5, 12, 15.

THM in the maxilla: C. 15, VI 14, 15, 16.

THM in the temporal bone: C. 18, VII 9; C. 19, VII 14–15, 15, 17; C. 20, VII 22, 23, VIII 3.

THM in the chin: C. 27, IX 15.

THM in cervical vertebra: C. 29, X 4, 6.

THM in the ḤNT› (manubrium) of the sternum: C. 40, XIII 13, 15.

TḪB  swelling, or with det. ,  (twice only II 10, 13), × (once only II 4): **C. 4, II 4,** 10; C. 5, II 13; C. 8, IV 6; C. 11, V 10, 12; C. 12, V 17; C. 15, VI 15; C. 16, VI 18, 21; C. 17, VII 6; C. 21, VIII 6; C. 38, XII 22; C. 46, XV 21.

TKN 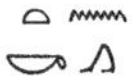 draw near: I. 7, XX 4.

Ṯ›W  treatise: **C. 5, II 17;** C. 19, VII 20–21; C. 41, XIV 10.

Ṯ›W  breath, wind: C. 8, IV 16; **C. 31, X 14;** I. 1, XVIII 1, 8; I. 2, XVIII 12.

Ṯ›M  to close up: C. 41, XIV 9.

ṮRM  to wink: **C. 7, IV 3.**

ṮḤN·T  kind of mineral: **C. 41, XIV 5.**

ṮS 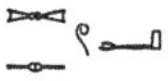 to knot, knit, join, to coagulate, or with det. : **C. 8, IV 11;** C. 9, V 1; **C. 12, V 19,** VI 2; C. 14, VI 10.

to bind; or with det. : I. 1, XVIII 3; I. 7, XX 5.

ṮS  vertebra.

ṮS N NḤB·T-F (vertebra of his neck): C. 29, X 3, 4 bis, 6; C. 30, X 8, 9, 10; **C. 31, X** 12, 13, 15, 16, 17, **18 bis;** C. 32, XI 1 bis, 4, 7 bis; C. 33, XI 9 bis, 12, 13, 14, 16.

T̠S (*cont.*)	T̠S N PSD-F (vertebra of his spinal column): C. 48, XVII 15, 16, 17, 18. T̠S without modifier but referring to T̠S N NḤB·T-F: C. 33, XI 10, 11, 15.
T̠SY	to lift, to hold up, or with det. : C. 3, II 1; C. 31, X 21.
T̠SW	stiffness, also , (twice only III 13, X 7): **C. 3, I 20,** 21, I 26–II 1; C. 4, II 4, 6; C. 5, II 13, 15; C. 6, II 22; C. 7, III 4, 6, 13; C. 8, IV 9, 12; C. 19, VII 18; C. 20, VIII 4; C. 22, VIII 13; C. 29, X 7.
D[ʾ]B·W	figs: C. 9, V 4.
DWN	to stretch, stretch apart, be tense; or with dets. or : **C. 7, III** 10, 19–20, **20;** C. 35, XII 6; C. 36, XII 12.
DBN	mortar: **C. 46, XVI 5.**
DP	to taste: XXI 21.
DP·T	taste (noun): XXI 21.
DP	Buto: I. 3, XVIII 17.
DP·TY	two flanks: **C. 43, XV 6.**
DM·T	knife: I. 5, XIX 7.
DMY	to touch, join: **C. 2, I 17 restored;** C. 10, V 9; **C. 31, X 19;** C. 45, XV 17, 18, 19. DMY R, "adhere to," with det. : C. 22, VIII 16.
DND	the name of a demon: **I. 1, XVIII 6.**
DR	repel, expel; also (XIX 13): C. 9, V 2; I. 1, XVIII 11; I. 5, XIX 13. remove; with det. : XXII 8, 9.
DḤ	hang down: **C. 36, XII 9.**
DḤR	skin: **C. 7, III 16.**
DḤR	bitterness: XXII 1.
DḤR·T	sickness, plague; or without det. : **I. 1, XVIII 8,** 11; I. 2, XVIII 12.
DS	an unidentified wood; also (XX 6): I. 2, XVIII 15; I. 7, XX 6.
DŠR	red; or with det. (VII 21), (XIV 6; XVI 12; XXI 5): C. 7, III 20; C. 19, VII 20, 21; C. 39, XIII 11; C. 41, XIV 6, 10, 13; C. 46, XVI 12, 16; XXI 5.

DḲW		⌜kernels⌝: **XXI 6,** 6–7.
DḲ[R]		fruit: **C. 46, XVI 4.**
DGʾ		to look at (with preposition N): C. 3, I 20 restored, 25, 26 bis (once restored); C. 4, II 5; C. 5, II 14; C. 7, III 5; C. 19, VII 16; C. 29, X 5; C. 30, X 9; C. 32, XI 2, 3.
DGY		⌜feebleness⌝: **C. 22, VIII 17.**
DGM		be speechless; or with dets., or without det.: C. 13, VI 6; C. 17, VII 5; C. 20, VIII 4, 5; **C. 22, VIII** 12, 13, **17;** C. 33, XI 10, 13.
Ḏʾ		fire-drill: C. 39, XIII 6.
ḎʾW		disease: **C. 19, VII 21.**
ḎʾR·T		an unidentified fruit: **C. 41, XIV 7.**
		ḎʾR·T ʿŠ: C. 46, XVI 10.
ḎʾḎʾ		head: C. 8, IV 13; C. 9, IV 20; C. 33, XI 16.
Ḏʿ·W		⌜blemishes⌝: XXII 9.
ḎʿR		probe, palpate; also (IV 5), (I 19), scribal error (XVI 18): **C. 1, lost column restored;** C. 2, I 13 restored; C. 3, I 19; C. 4, II 3; C. 5, II 12; C. 6, II 19; C. 7, III 2; **C. 8, IV 5–6;** C. 10, V 6; C. 18, VII 8; C. 27, IX 14; C. 47, XVI 18.
ḎW		evil: I. 1, XVIII 9.
ḎWY		lift: I. 1, XVIII 3.
ḎB·T		brick: **C. 4, II 7;** C. 7, III 15.
ḎBʾ		to clothe, pad: C. 7, III 14; C. 12, VI 1; C. 23, VIII 21.
ḎBʿ		finger, thumb: C. 1, I 4, 6; C. 4, II 4; C. 5, II 13; C. 6, II 21 bis; C. 8, IV 11 bis; C. 13, VI 5; C. 17, VII 2; C. 20, VII 24; C. 22, VIII 10 bis; C. 24, VIII 23; C. 25, IX 3; C. 37, XII 16; C. 40, XIII 14; C. 44, XV 8; I. 6, XIX 15.
ḎFY·T		penetration: **C. 32, XI 8.**
ḎN		to thresh: **XXI 11** bis.
ḎNB		crooked: **C. 12, V 22.**
ḎNN·T		skull (meaning the *calvaria*); also with stroke (II 12, 17, 24): **C. 1, lost column ter, restored,** 1, 11 bis (once restored); C. 2, I 13; C. 3, I 18 restored, 19, 21, 24 bis (once restored); C. 4, II 2, 3, 5, 6, 8, 9 bis; C. 5, II 11, 12, 13, 15, 16 ter, 17 bis;

ḎNN·T (*cont.*) C. 6, II 18 bis, 19 bis, 20, 22, 23, 24 bis; C. 7, III 2, 6, 9, 12–13, 16 bis (once restored); C. 8, IV 5 bis, 6, 7 bis, 10, 12 bis, 13; C. 9, IV 19.

ḎR R ḎR-F, "entire," "throughout" (literally "to its limit"): C. 12, V 22; C. 41, XIV 12.

ḎR·WY two sides: C. 11, V 15.

ḎR until: **C. 6, II 21;** C. 8, IV 11.

as soon as: C. 39, XIII 9.

YR ḎR, "now when," "now as soon as": **C. 4, II 6;** C. 7, III 7; C. 8, IV 10; **C. 20, VIII 4.**

ḎR NTT, "because," "for": C. 4, II 11.

ḎR·T hand, touch; also dual (twice only I 6, 7): C. 1, I 6, 7; C. 8, IV 8, 18 bis; C. 20, VIII 2; C. 39, XIII 5; C. 41, XIII 20, XIV 15, 16; C. 45, XV 11, 12, 14, 19; C. 46, XVI 1, 14; C. 47, XVII 9; I. 8, XX 12.

ḎRḎ·W leaves: C. 41, XIV 3 bis, 7; C. 46, XVI 8 bis, 9; XXII 12.

ḎS- self: C. 39, XIII 8, 9.

ḎD say, speak.

ḎD-YN-K in diagnosis: C. 1, I 1 restored; C. 2, I 14; C. 3, I 20; C. 4, II 5; C. 5, II 14; C. 7, III 5, 12; C. 10, V 7; C. 11, V 11; C. 12, V 17; C. 13, VI 6; C. 14, VI 9; C. 15, VI 16; C. 16, VI 19; C. 17, VII 4; C. 18, VII 9; C. 19, VII 17; C. 20, VIII 3; C. 21, VIII 8; C. 22, VIII 13; C. 23, VIII 19; C. 24, VIII 23; C. 25, IX 5; C. 26, IX 8; C. 27, IX 15; C. 28, IX 21; C. 29, X 6; C. 30, X 10; C. 31, X 16; C. 32, XI 3; C. 33, XI 12; C. 34, XI 18; C. 35, XII 4; C. 36, XII 10; C. 37, XII 16, 20; C. 38, XIII 1; C. 39, XIII 5; C. 40, XIII 14; C. 41, XIV 1; C. 42, XIV 19; C. 43, XV 1; C. 44, XV 8; C. 45, XV 14; C. 46, XVI 2; C. 47, XVI 20, XVII 10; C. 48, XVII 18.

ḎD-H̱R-K in diagnosis: XX 14.

YW ḎD-N, quoting a book: C. 5, II 17; C. 19, VII 20; C. 41, XIV 10.

MY ḎD in explanation in gloss: C. 7, III 18; C. 14, VI 14; C. 31, X 19; C. 41, XIV 16.

ḎD-F, introducing explanation in ancient gloss or citation in gloss from surgical treatise: C. 1, I 8; C. 8, IV 14, 15, 18;

ḎD (*cont.*)  C. 18, VII 13; C. 26, IX 12; C. 30, X 12; C. 31, X 18; C. 32, XI 7; C. 33, XI 14.

ḎD PW in glosses: **C. 1, I 10,** 11; C. 4, II 11; C. 6, III 1; C. 31, X 20; C. 39, XIII 11.

ḎD introducing surgeon's directions to patients in examination: C. 19, VII 16; C. 30, X 9; C. 32, XI 2; C. 48, XVII 16.

ḎD in directions for saying a charm or incantation: C. 9, V 1; I. 5, XIX 14; I. 7, XX 5; I. 8, XX 11.

ḎD MDW: I. 1, XVIII 9; I. 2, XVIII 15; I. 5, XIX 9.

ḎD miscellaneous: C. 1, I 9; C. 41, XIV 11; I. 1, XVIII 2.

ḎD used erroneously for ḎʿR: **C. 47, XVI 18.**

Words of Uncertain Phonetic Reading

 threshing-floor: XXI 13.

 linen: XXII 1.

—TY  ⌜perish⌝: **I. 5, XIX 7.**

GENERAL INDEX

P p

Medical literature (*cont.*)
  Egyptian, 3, 4
  divine origin, 5
  Greek, 7, 12
  "Secret Book of the Physician," possibly name of Edwin Smith Surgical Papyrus, 9–10
  Two early medical books quoted in Smith Papyrus:
  "Treatise on What Pertains to his Wounds," 162 f.; with variant title, "Treatise on What Pertains to a Wound," 384, 387
  "Treatise on What Pertains to the Embalmer" (or Bandager), 281 f.
Medical papyri, 4, 79, 86–87, 95, 98–99, 112, 129, 135, 146, 148, 169, 285, 287, 329, 332, 340, 368, 380, 381, 383, 387, 388, 412, 427, 475, 489
  See also Smith Papyrus, Ebers Papyrus, Hearst Papyrus, Berlin Medical Papyrus, London Medical Papyrus, Kahun Papyri
Medical terms, 10, 61–71, 88–89
  See also Surgical terms
Medicaments, 9, 54, 55–61, 97, 133, 374, 379–383
Medicine,
  ancient, 1
  Babylonian, 1, 2
  Assyrian, 1–2
  legal regulations of, 1
  god of, 3
  Egyptian, 3, 4
    relation to Greek, 16, 17
  European, 7
  distinction between surgery and, 7, 9, 18, 42–43, 57, 97
  Greek, 3, 5, 7, 9, 12, 13, 14, 15–17, 64, 105
  demoniacal, 15
  oldest science, 15
  schools of, 17–18, 72
Medicine (medicaments), 139
  external, 55–61, 97, 374, 379–383, 410–412, 488, 500
  internal, 99, 184–185, 488–489
"Medicine men," 15
Meissner, B., 1, 16
Membranes
  meningeal, 12, 60, 65, 70, 130, 157, 160, 164, 171, 172
Meningeal involvement, 130
Meningeal membranes, 164, 172
  rupture of, 12, 60, 65, 70, 130, 157, 160, 171
Meningitis, 130
Menses,
  suspension of, 487
Menstrual discharge, 487
Merneptah, 106
Meskhenet, 479
Messengers of Sekhmet, 476, 484
Meteorism, 325
Meyer-Steineg, 53, 64
Microscope, 471
Milk, as medicament, 286, 287
Mill-stone, 495
Mineral salts, 374, 379, 382
Mineral, as disinfectant, 57, 262, 264–265
Miscarriage, 285
"Mistress of the crown," 474
"Mix" (prescriptions), 488, 491, 495
Moeller, G., 28
Moharb Todrous, 24
"Mooring stakes," 10, 69, 132, 134–135, 139, 150, 161, 237, 239, 281, 289, 316, 319, 424
Morning barque, 474
Mortar,
  mason's, 60, 407, 410, 412
Motor cortex, 216
Mouth,
  painful to open, 177, 180, 184, 187, 254, 268
  bound, 181, 198
  wound penetrating to, 227, 228
  discharge from, 268
  clean (exorcism), 483
Mouth of wound, 219, 284, 313, 316, 375, 376, 379, 384, 390, 411, 422, 424
Movements of body,
  source of control of, 12
Mummy, 8
Muscles, 13, 67, 112, 113, 268, 303
  temporal, 65, 67, 188, 189, 191, 277
  rigid, 180
  cutaneous, 257
M. orbicularis oris, 308
M. triangularis, 312
Muscular articulation, 187
Musculature,
  of neck, 130
Musculus temporalis, 188
Mustapha Aga, 22, 75, 76

Naburianos, 16
Nabu-rimannu, *see* Naburianos
Nares, 244, 248
Nasal bone, 241, 242
  fracture of, 52, 56, 58, 146, 157, 160, 234, 235
  reduction of, 239, 244, 246–247
Nasus externus, 241
Natron, 412, 491
Natural science,
  earliest recorded observations in, 12, 15, 18
Naville, E., 23
Neck, 110
  injuries to, 12, 34, 36
  stiffness in, 50, 51, 127, 129–131, 137, 138, 141, 158, 166, 178, 206, 208, 279, 280, 286, 292, 317, 318
  softening applications on, 151
  ligaments of, 181, 192

LIST OF ABBREVIATED BOOK TITLES

Dümichen. *Geogr. Inschr.*	*Geographische Inschriften altägyptischer Denkmäler.*
Dümichen. *Hist. Inschr.*	*Historische Inschriften altägyptischer Denkmäler.*
Erman. *Reden.*	*Reden, Rufe und Lieder auf Gräberbildern des alten Reiches.* (Akad. d. Wiss., Berlin. Phil.-hist. Klasse. Abhandlungen. 1918, no. 15.)
Gauthier. *Inscr. dédicatoire.*	*La grande inscription dédicatoire d'Abydos.*
Leemans. *Mon. fun.*	*Monumens égyptiens du Musée d'antiquités des Pays-Bas à Leide.* III. *Monumens funéraires.*
Mitth. Orient. Samml.	Berlin, Staatliche Museen. *Mittheilungen aus den orientalischen Sammlungen.* IX. Steindorff. *Grabfunde des Mittleren Reichs.* II. Der Sarg des Sebk-o.
Pap. Anast. III and IV.	Papyrus Anastasi III and IV. *Select papyri in the hieratic character from the collections of the British Museum.* [Part 1, No. 2] 1842.
Pap. judic. de Turin.	Devéria, Théodule. *Le papyrus judiciaire de Turin.* (Extrait de la Bibliothèque égyptologique, t. V.)
Piehl. *Inscr.*	*Inscriptions hiéroglyphiques recueillies en Europe et en Égypte.*
Pyr.	Sethe, K. H. *Die altägyptischen Pyramidentexte.*
Recueil de trav.	*Recueil de travaux relatifs à la philologie et à l'archéologie égyptiennes et assyriennes.*
Rochem. *Edfou.*	Rochemonteix, M. de. *Le temple d'Edfou.* (Mémoires publiés par les membres de la Mission archéologique française au Caire, t. 10–11.)
Rosellini. *Mon. civ.*	*I monumenti dell' Egitto e della Nubia*, t. 2: *Monumenti civili.*
de Rougé. *Inscr. hiér.*	*Inscriptions hiéroglyphiques copiées en Égypte.*
Urk.	*Urkunden des ägyptischen Altertums*, hrsg. von Georg Steindorff. I. Sethe, K. H. "Urkunden des alten Reichs." III. Schäfer, H. "Urkunden der älteren Äthiopenkönige." IV. Sethe, K. H. "Urkunden der 18. Dynastie." V. Grapow, H. "Religiöse Urkunden."
Zeitschrift.	*Zeitschrift für ägyptische Sprache und Altertumskunde.*

ADDENDA

1. *The Date of the Edwin Smith Surgical Papyrus.*

After the discussion of the date of this surgical treatise was in print (pp. 28–29), my friend Professor Dévaud has recalled my attention to the question of the date of this papyrus as a manuscript, especially in view of the orthographic criteria which he published in his recent valuable treatise[1] on the dating of Egyptian papyri, and which had unfortunately escaped my notice. The orthography of Late Egyptian writing has long been used as a basis for recognizing the late date of Nineteenth- and Twentieth-Dynasty papyri. In this useful essay of Professor Dévaud he has carried the study of such orthographic indications back through the Eighteenth to the Twelfth Dynasty. By a careful examination of the writing of fifty-six selected words in thirty papyri, forming a chronological sequence from the Twelfth to the Eighteenth Dynasty, he has furnished new criteria for dating hieratic documents belonging to this general period—the period of our papyrus.

It is interesting to notice that these new orthographic criteria at once place our papyrus in the same general period indicated by the *palaeographic* evidence, as already discussed above (pp. 25–29),—that is, in the Westcar-Ebers-Hearst group of papyri. For the assignment of the Edwin Smith Papyrus to this general group, the palaeographic and orthographic evidence are therefore in complete agreement. The question at once arises, however, whether the new orthographic criteria will enable us to determine the date of the Edwin Smith Papyrus within narrower limits and to place it with certainty before or after the Papyrus Ebers. The evidence follows.

Of Professor Dévaud's fifty-six test words only a little over one-fourth are found in the Edwin Smith Papyrus, and unfortunately only a small proportion of these furnish any indications regarding the narrower limits just mentioned. These words are:

No. 50,[2] is a dual writing occurring only subsequent to Papyrus Ebers. It occurs but once in the Smith Papyrus (X 13). Of the other six occurrences of this dual, two are written (XVII 17; XXII 14) in the adverb *ḥr ʿwy*, which Dévaud writes me is not to be included in these dating criteria. The remaining four have , which is an archaic writing not included in Dévaud's list. Against four archaic writings the sole occurrence of one post-Ebers writing has little weight.

No. 51,[3] , so written very often in Papyrus Smith. In Ebers and earlier it is usually written without \. This might indicate that our papyrus follows Ebers, were

[1] Eugène Dévaud: *L'âge des papyri égyptiens hiératiques.* Paris, 1924.

[2] The numbers are those of Dévaud's publication.

[3] The use of a hieratic sign resembling for the bee in *by·t* "honey" is common in both Ebers and Smith, and has no bearing on the date. This bird-like sign may be another hieratic form for ; but for the sake of distinction it has been transliterated as in these volumes.

it not for the fact that \ in this word does occur also *before* Ebers, as cited by Dévaud from the Carnarvon Tablet (o. c., p. 8*).

No. 52, , occurs once in Papyrus Smith. The use of  in this word is not habitual until post-Ebers documents; but it is found as early as the Middle Kingdom in one document, viz., the Shipwreck (see Dévaud, o. c., p. 8*).

No. 54, , with the determinative  is unknown before Papyrus Hearst. It is significant that its sole occurrence in Papyrus Smith (XXI 20) is not in the Surgical Treatise but in the recipes on the verso, in the appendix by a second scribe, presumably later. Otherwise Papyrus Smith employs 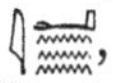, the form appearing in Papyrus Ebers and earlier, or the exceptional form  (once).

The above four writings comprise all the orthographic evidence pointing towards a post-Ebers date. We must place with the above evidence the following counter-indications.

No. 5, , found once in Papyrus Smith (XVIII 4), occurs only in the Twelfth Dynasty or earlier. Otherwise, in Papyrus Prisse and later, the phonetic elements before  are not employed, and had begun to disappear as early as Ptahhotep, L 1 (see Dévaud, o. c., pp. 7–8 and 1*). Ebers uses  without the phonetic elements preceding.

No. 15,  (also with ), appearing twice in Papyrus Smith, is an early form, like No. 5 just cited, written with phonetic elements first. This form is found only in Papyrus Prisse and earlier. After Prisse, beginning with the Thirteenth Dynasty (Kahun Papyri), the word is written  with the ideogram first and the phonetic elements following. Ebers has this form, and the earlier form in Papyrus Smith (as also in the case of No. 5 above) indicates that Smith is earlier than Ebers.

No. 33, , is a form occurring once in Papyrus Smith (IX 19), and again written with  (XX 16). The form without  is the invariable writing in the Thirteenth Dynasty Kahun Papyri and earlier. In Papyrus Westcar and later it is habitually written 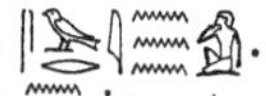. This is also the usual writing in Papyrus Ebers, although the form without  is not entirely unknown in Ebers.

Summing up the orthographic evidence, we find seven out of Dévaud's convenient list of words which have some significance for the date of our papyrus. Turning first to the possible indications of post-Ebers date, we find that two of the seven words listed above exhibit writings which are *usually* post-Ebers (Nos. 51 and 52); but occurrences of both of these forms are found earlier, as shown in Dévaud's table (o. c., p. 8*). They are therefore not unequivocally post-Ebers forms. Two more of the above list of seven are actually found *only* in post-Ebers manuscripts: one occurrence of the determinative 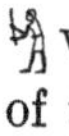 with  (XXI 20) and one occurrence of the dual writing 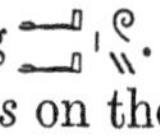. The single occurrence of the former is in the (presumably later) magical *mélanges* on the verso, and the latter is one writing among seven occurrences of the word, the remaining six being either as in Ebers or archaic and older than Ebers.

Over against this equivocal orthographic evidence for a post-Ebers date, we find three writings of words in the above list of seven (Nos. 5, once; 15, twice; and 33, once), two of which are not only older than Ebers, but are not found later than the Middle Kingdom. The scantiness of this orthographic evidence as a whole weakens its force, but if it is of any weight at all it points rather towards a pre-Ebers date and two of the last three writings would even fit a pre-Westcar date. In any case these slight orthographic data do not weaken the palaeographic evidence discussed above (pp. 25–29) that the Edwin Smith Papyrus was written somewhat earlier than the Papyrus Ebers, and possibly earlier than the Papyrus Westcar.

2. *Additional Textual Notes.*

I 9,  *ḥ'ty* (p. 103). This writing with  instead of  is of course not customary in hieratic, but a comparison of the first preserved sign in l. 9 (Vol. II, Pl. I) with the *ḥ'*-sign as found close by in l. 7 and (directly under this example) again in l. 8, shows clearly that we cannot regard the first preserved sign in l. 9 as . The top of *ḥ'* in ll. 7 and 8 is totally different from that of the sign in l. 9. On the other hand this first preserved sign in l. 9 has the exact form of , for example in  in II 11 (see Vol. II, Pl. II, l. 11). The evidence for the reading , therefore, seems to be good. On the reading *ḥ'ty* for  see Sethe, *Zeitschrift,* 39 (1901), p. 135; and Dévaud (*Sphinx,* XIII, pp. 98–100).

The following notes and references are due to Dévaud:

II 22, 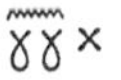 (pp. 165 and 166). On the reading, Dévaud calls attention to the proper name written  (Eleventh Dynasty Stela in the British Museum, *Am. Journal of Semitic Lang.,* XXXII, 17) and also  (Middle Kingdom Stela, Mus. Guimet C 6).

III 16,  *ʿr·t* (pp. 186, 187 f.). An interesting new example of the meaning "anus" is found in a Middle Kingdom Assiut text: "I eat with my mouth, I defecate with my *ʿr·t*" (Chassinat-Palanque, *Fouilles d'Assiout,* p. 100). It is important to note that *ʿr·t* is here written 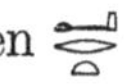 with animal buttocks as determinative.

III 17,  (p. 189). Dévaud states that he has a number of examples of this idiom in which it often seems to mean "change, modify, alter." These references are: de Morgan, *Catalogue des Monuments,* III, 245 (Ombos); *ibid.,* III, 19 (Ombos); Rochem., *Edfou,* II, 260, 11; Lepsius, *Denkmäler,* Text IV, p. 113; Mariette, *Dendérah,* II, 25; Ny Carlsberg E 70; Amélineau, *Nouvelles fouilles,* pp. 161 and 292; Berlin 6910 (*Zeitschrift,* II, 68, 27). The references have not been verified.

IV 2, 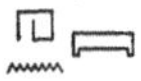 (p. 197). Compare the French "*boîte du crâne,*" and possibly Coptic **ⲁⲛ** in **ⲁⲛⲧⲏⲗⲙ** "skull," e. g., Judges, 9, 53.

VIII 10 (p. 291). Compare also the obviously related noun  (Zaubersprüche 4, 1; Pap. Mag. Vatican 4, 7; Pap. Leide 348, v°. 2, 4; 11, 10) and [hieroglyphs] (Pap. Boulaq 7, 2, 2; cf. Maspero, Pap. Louvre, p. 60), which also means "chin".

XI 22 and XV 4, [hieroglyphs] (p. 348). Compare also (Sinuhe, B. 274), presumably the same as the later *ntf* of Israel Stela 6; Pap. Anast. I, 24, 5; Magical Pap. Harris, verso, A, 6; etc. Important is Dévaud's observation, that in Proverbs 6, 35, **ⲟⲩⲇⲉ ⲛ̄ⲛⲉϥⲛⲟⲩⲧϥ** is parallel with **ⲟⲩⲇⲉ ϥⲛⲁⲃⲱⲗⲁⲛ** in the liturgic text. **ⲛⲟⲩⲧϥ** is thus identical with **ⲃⲱⲗ** "loosen," exactly the meaning also disclosed in Pap. Smith.

XXI 18 [hieroglyphs] (p. 497). Note also the contrast between "moist grapes", (B) **ⲟⲩⲁⲗⲟⲗⲓ ⲛ̀ϩⲏ ⲛ̀ⲗⲱⲕ**, and "dried grapes", **ⲟⲩⲁⲗϣⲱⲟⲩ**, in Numbers 6, 3; and likewise between "the green (juicy, moist) tree" **ⲡⲓϣⲉ ⲉⲧⲗⲏⲕ**, and "the dried" **ⲡⲉⲧϣⲟⲩⲱⲟⲩ**, in Luke 23, 31. In these two passages **ⲗⲱⲕ** and **ⲗⲏⲕ** evidently represent the same root as our *nḳ·wt*, "moisture", and Horner renders **ⲉⲧⲗⲏⲕ**, "lit. moist". The Old Egyptian verb corresponding to our noun *nḳ·wt* seems to have been lost, or has escaped notice.

3. *Discovery of a Single Example of Ancient Egyptian Trepanning.*

The statement (p. 56) that no Egyptian bodies thus far exhumed show any traces of the practice of trepanning must now be modified. Dr. Aleš Hrdlička of the United States National Museum, in a letter dated May 22nd, 1929, has kindly reported to me the discovery of a trepanned skull taken from one of the "deep pits at Lisht". He further states that it "belonged undoubtedly to one of the nobler families of the XIIth Dynasty". I am greatly indebted to the kindness of Dr. Hrdlička for a photograph of this unique specimen. It would seem, therefore, that trepanning was known to the ancient Egyptians, but was apparently very rarely practised, if we may judge by the rarity of surviving examples.

CORRIGENDA

P. 76, last paragraph, l. 1. For "Plate I A", read "Plate I".
P. 77, third paragraph, l. 3. For "Plate I A", read "Plate II".
P. 78, first paragraph, line 5. For "56 cm.", read "43 to 45 cm."
P. 78, first paragraph, line 6. For "Vol. II, 1 b", read "Vol. I̦I, pp. xi f."
P. 81, third paragraph, head of fourth line, insert alphabetic *n* in *wbnw* (VIII 18).
P. 131 (I 21), in the verdict. Enclose the first [hieroglyphs] in brackets.
P. 132, (I 23), in *mẖt*, enclose *m* in brackets.
P. 158 (II 13). For [hieroglyphs] read [hieroglyphs].
P. 162 (II 17). In *ḏnn·t* (first time), insert stroke after [hieroglyphs] and before [hieroglyphs].

ADDITIONAL CORRIGENDA

May 25, 1930

P. 11, for "Pl. I," read "Vol. I, Pl. II."

P. 475, in hieroglyphic text of XVIII 9, in "*ᶜnḫ*," delete second "*n*."

P. 493, in hieroglyphic text XXI 14, in "*pr·t*," third plural stroke, broken off in press, should be inserted.

Fig. 1. Egyptian Mandible of the Old Kingdom (about 3000–2500 B.C.)
In addition to the *mental foramen* are two borings which were made by the Egyptian surgeon to drain an abscess below the first molar. (Photograph by the kindness of Dr. E. A. Hooton, *Oral Surgery in Egypt during the Old Empire* (Harvard African Studies I), pl. I). Compare *infra*, p. 33.

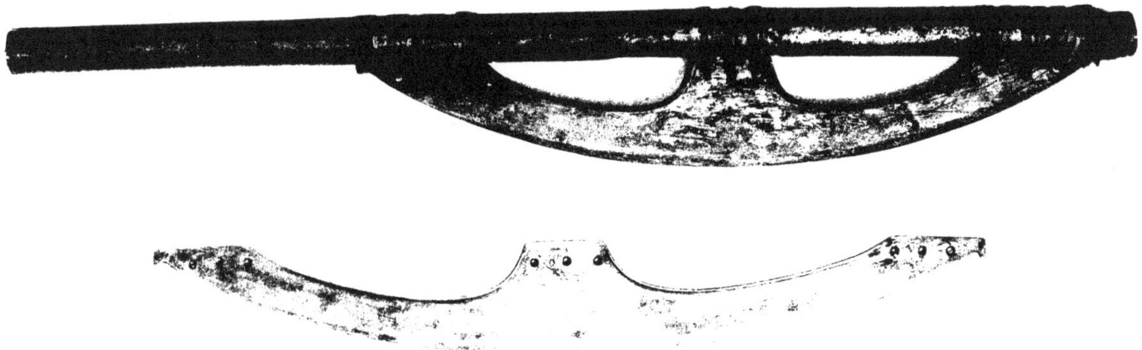

Fig. 2. Middle Kingdom Egyptian Battle Axes (about 2000 B.C.)
The hafting thongs are modern. The longer blade is 16½ inches long, and well able to produce the head wounds described in the Edwin Smith Papyrus. Compare Commentary on Case 4 and see Fig. 3, next plate.

Figs. 3 and 4. Sword cuts in Egyptian Skulls of a century or two before the Christian Era
ig. 3 (left) the cut and the resulting fractures caused death; in Fig. 4 (right) the art of the surgeon healed the wound and the man survived.
m G. Elliot Smith and F. Wood Jones, *The Archaeological Survey of Nubia.* (Report for 1907–1908.) Vol. II. *The Human Remains*, pl. XLI, Fig. 3, and pl. XLIII, Fig. 2.) Compare Commentary on Case 4.

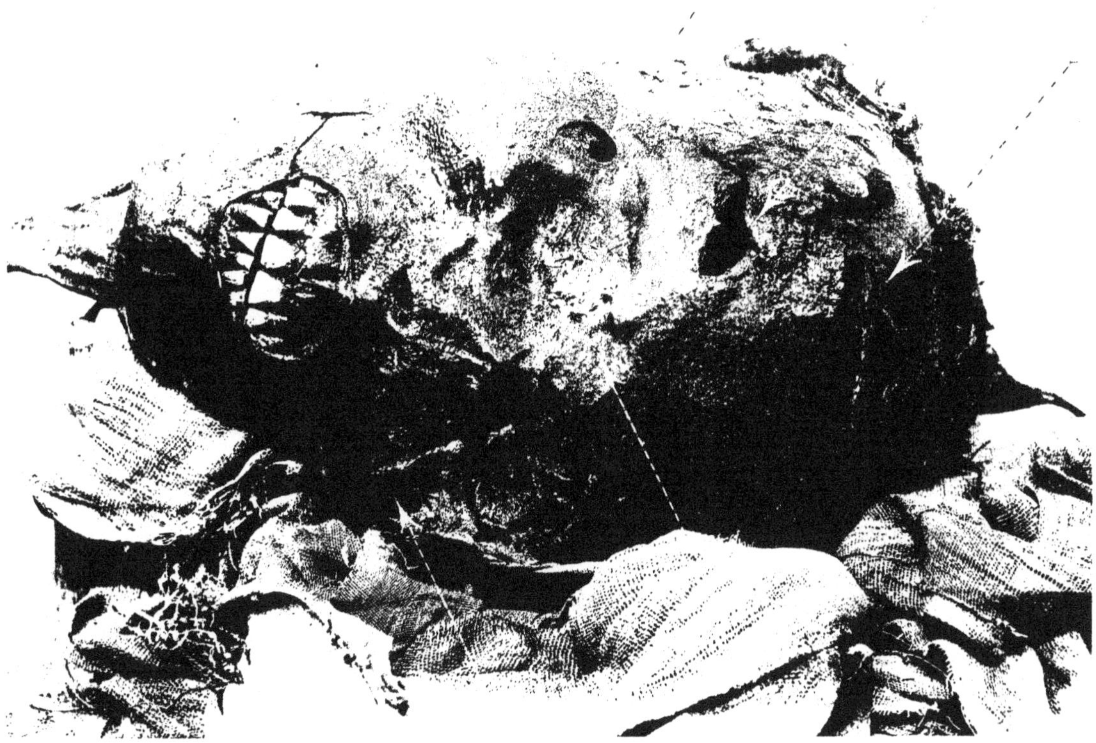

Fig. 5. Wounded Skull of the Pharaoh Sekenenre. (Early 16th century B.C.)
The arrows indicate the five terrible wounds in the head which caused the king's death. He was one of the opponents of the Hyksos and may, therefore, have received these wounds in battle. Several of these wounds are exactly those for which surgical treatment or operation is prescribed in the Edwin Smith Papyrus. (From G. Elliot Smith, *The Royal Mummies*, Cairo, 1912, pl. II.) Compare *infra*, p. 126.

Figs. 6 and 7. Elaborate Mummy Bandages of Roman Age

Compare Case 9. (From W. M. Flinders Petrie, *Roman Portraits and Memphis* (IV), London, 1911, pl. XI).

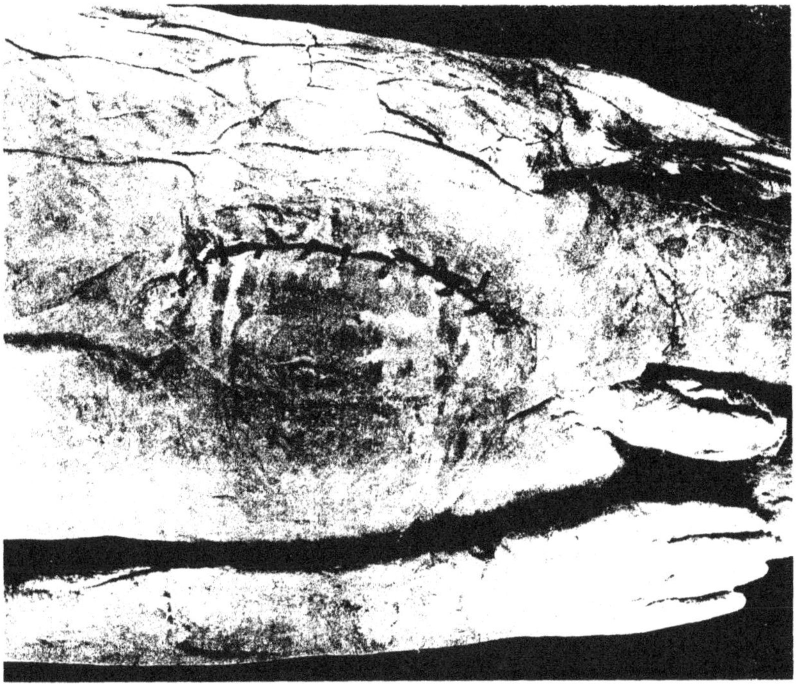

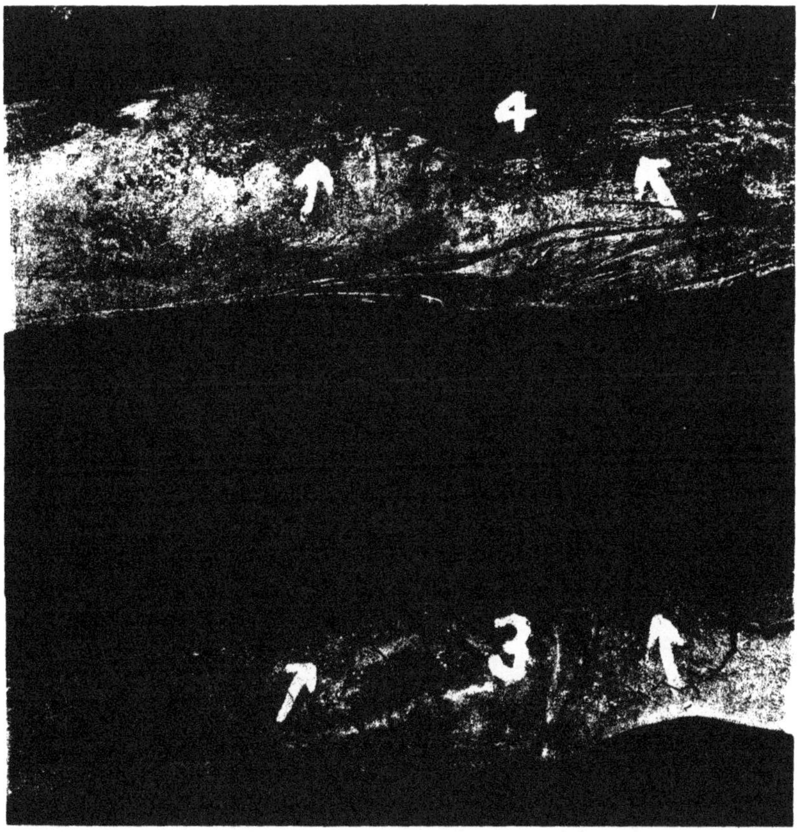

Figs. 8, 9, and 10. EMBALMING WOUNDS OF TWENTY-FIRST DYNASTY MUMMIES SEWN UP WITH STRING (Eleventh Century B.C.)

Photographs furnished by kindness of Dr. G. Elliot Smith. Fig. 8 is a wound in the abdomen, Fig. 9 (4) in the knee, and Fig. 10 (3) in the elbow. The extent of the wounds in Figs. 9 and 10 is marked by arrows. Compare Commentary on Case 10.

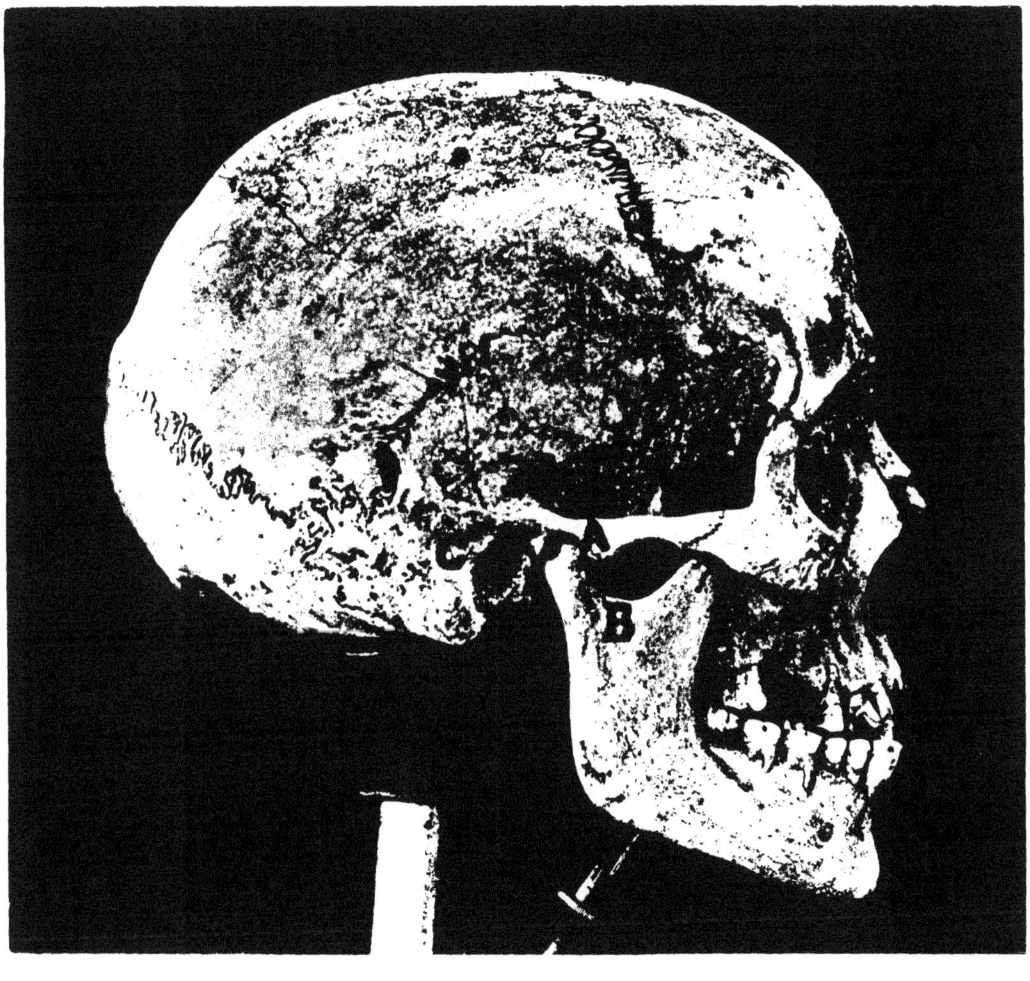

Fig. 11. Ancient Egyptian Skull probably of the Middle Kingdom (about 2000 B.C.)

A is the temporal bone called -*gema*ʾ (*gm*ʾ) in the Smith Papyrus; B is the *ramus,* with its claw-like fork at the top called in the Smith Papyrus ʾ*am*ʿ*et* (ʾ*m*ʿ·*t*), after the two-toed claw of the ʾ*am*ʿ*e*-bird; C is the orifice of the right ear. (From H. Stahr, *Die Rassenfrage im antiken Aegypten*, Berlin, 1907. Pl. III, Fig. 12). Compare *infra*, Cases 18–22.

Fig. 12. Reduction of a Dislocated Mandible by a Greek Surgeon as shown in an illustrated Commentary on Hippocrates

This commentary with illustrations was the work of Apollonius of Kitium (First Century B.C.) now surviving in a Florentine manuscript of the ninth century A. D. See H. Schoene, *Apollonius von Kitium*, Leipzig, 1896, Pl. XIV. Compare *infra*. pp. 16–17, and Case 25.

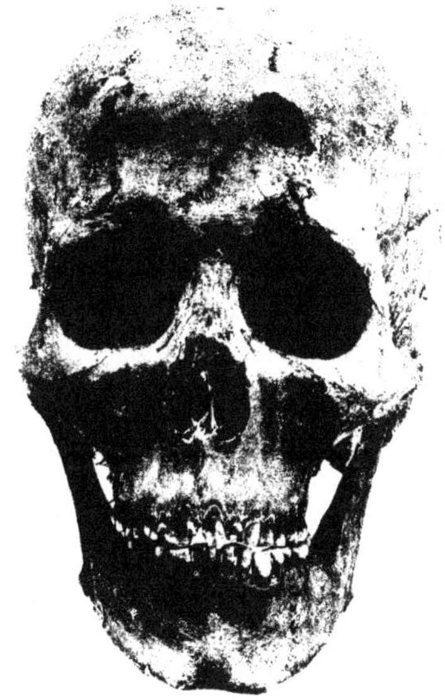

Figs. 13 and 14. Mace Wounds in Ancient Egyptian Skulls

Fig. 13 (left), skull of Harsiese, High Priest of Amon at Thebes (Ninth Century B.C.), discovered 1927 by the Oriental Institute, University of Chicago. It shows fatal wound in frontal bone with indications that death was not immediate. Fig. 14 (right), skull of Eleventh Dynasty soldier (Twenty-first Century B.C.), showing similar wound in frontal bone, also on right of nose. Discovered by Metropolitan Museum Expedition (*Bulletin*, Section II, Feb., 1928, p. 15). Photograph by kindness of Mr. A. M. Lythgoe.

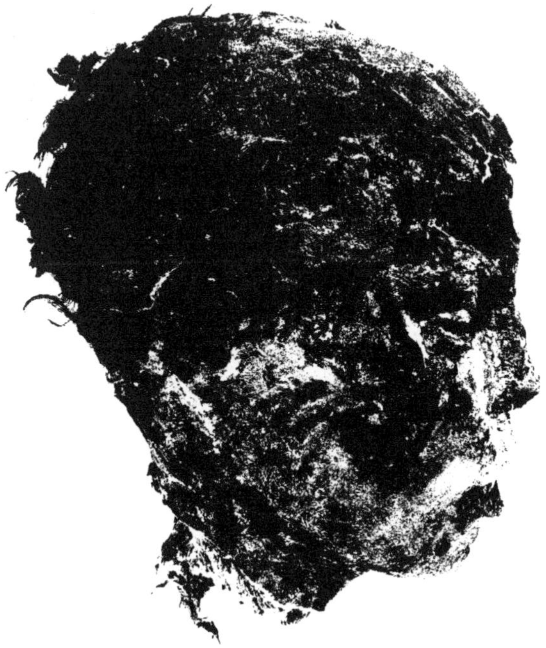

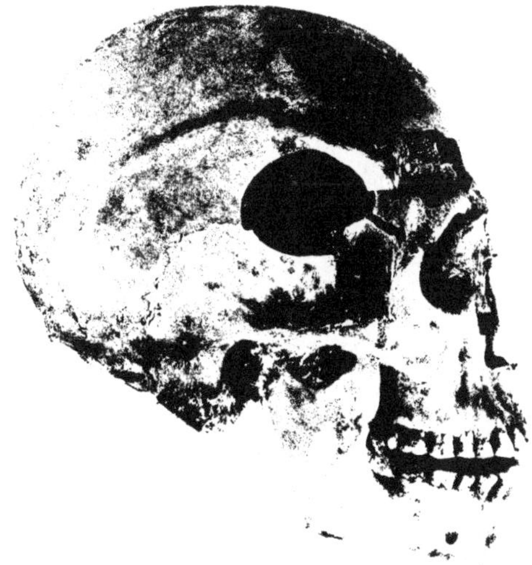

Figs. 15 and 16. Skull Wounds of Eleventh Dynasty Soldiers, Twenty-first Century B.C.

Both men received two wounds, one on the crown, the other over the right eye. Death was immediate as in the case of their comrade (Fig. 14). Discovered by Metropolitan Museum Expedition (*Bulletin, ibid.*, p. 17). Photographs by kindness of Mr. A. M. Lythgoe.

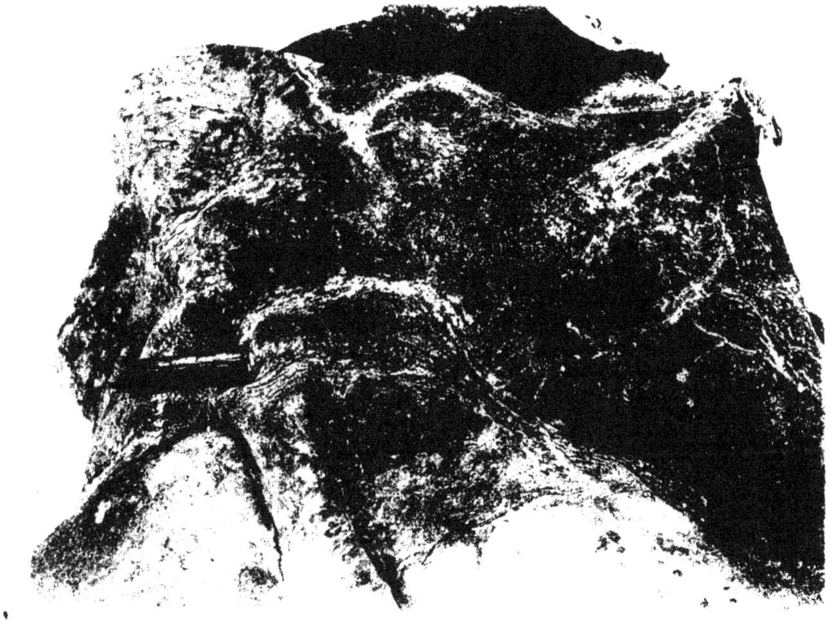

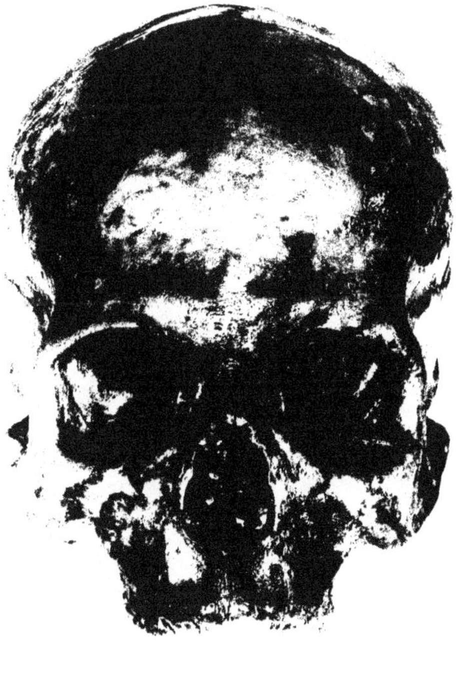

Figs. 17 and 18. Arrow Wounds of Eleventh Dynasty Soldiers (Twenty-first Century B.C.) with the Arrows still Sticking in the Wounds

Fig. 17 (upper) shows the arrow in the victim's shoulder; in Fig. 18 (lower) the arrow has penetrated the left eye and is visible in the photograph. Discovered by the Metropolitan Museum Expedition (*Bulletin*, *ibid.*, pp. 16–17). Photographs by kindness of Mr. A. M. Lythgoe.

9 781425 42914

CPSIA information can be obtained
at www.ICGtesting.com
Printed in the USA
BVHW011423220520
580024BV00008B/263

9 781162 92433